THE BLOOMSBURY HANDBOOK TO TONI MORRISON

THE BLOOMSBURY HANDBOOK TO TONI MORRISON

Edited by Kelly L. Reames and Linda Wagner-Martin

BLOOMSBURY ACADEMIC
LONDON • NEW YORK • OXFORD • NEW DELHI • SYDNEY

BLOOMSBURY ACADEMIC
Bloomsbury Publishing Plc
50 Bedford Square, London, WC1B 3DP, UK
1385 Broadway, New York, NY 10018, USA
29 Earlsfort Terrace, Dublin 2, Ireland

BLOOMSBURY, BLOOMSBURY ACADEMIC and the Diana logo
are trademarks of Bloomsbury Publishing Plc

First published in Great Britain 2023
Paperback edition published 2024

Copyright © Kelly L. Reames, Linda Wagner-Martin and contributors, 2023

The editors and contributors have asserted their right under the Copyright,
Designs and Patents Act, 1988, to be identified as Authors of this work.

For legal purposes the Acknowledgements on p. xvi constitute
an extension of this copyright page.

Cover image © Nobel laureate Toni Morrison photographed in Manhattan on
October 13, 2003 © Bruce Gilbert/Newsday RM via Getty Images

All rights reserved. No part of this publication may be reproduced or
transmitted in any form or by any means, electronic or mechanical,
including photocopying, recording, or any information storage or retrieval
system, without prior permission in writing from the publishers.

Bloomsbury Publishing Plc does not have any control over, or responsibility for,
any third-party websites referred to or in this book. All internet addresses given
in this book were correct at the time of going to press. The author and publisher
regret any inconvenience caused if addresses have changed or sites have
ceased to exist, but can accept no responsibility for any such changes.

A catalogue record for this book is available from the British Library.

Library of Congress Cataloging-in-Publication Data
Names: Reames, Kelly Lynch, editor. | Wagner-Martin, Linda, editor.
Title: The Bloomsbury handbook to Toni Morrison / edited by Kelly L. Reames and Linda Wagner-Martin.
Description: London ; New York : Bloomsbury Academic, 2023. | Series: Bloomsbury handbooks |
Includes bibliographical references and index. | Summary: "The first major collection of critical essays
to appear since Morrison's death in mid-2019, this book contains peviously unpublished essays which both
acknowledge the universal significance of her writing even as they map new directions. Essayists include pre-eminent
Morrison scholars, as well as scholars who work in cultural criticism, African American letters, American modernism,
and women's writing. The book includes work on Morrison as a public intellectual; work which places Morrison's writing
within today's currents of contemporary fiction; work which draws together Morrison's "trilogy" of Beloved, Jazz,
and Paradise alongside Dos Passos' USA trilogy; work which links Morrison to such Black Atlantic artists as Lubaina Himid
and others as well as work which offers a reading of "influence" that goes both directions between Morrison and Faulkner.
Another cluster of essays treats seldom-discussed works by Morrison, including an essay on Morrison as writer of
children's books and as speaker for children's education. In addition, a "Teaching Morrison" section is designed to help
teachers and critics who teach Morrison in undergraduate classes. The Bloomsbury Handbook to Toni Morrison will be
wide-ranging, provocative, and satisfying; a fitting tribute to one of the greatest American novelists"– Provided by publisher.
Identifiers: LCCN 2022031229 | ISBN 9781350239920 (hardback) | ISBN 9781350504905 (paperback) |
ISBN 9781350239937 (ebook) | ISBN 9781350239944 (epub) | ISBN 9781350239951 Subjects: LCSH: Morrison,
Toni–Criticism and interpretation. Classification: LCC PS3563.O8749 Z566 2023 | DDC 813/.6–dc23
LC record available at https://lccn.loc.gov/2022031229

ISBN: HB: 978-1-3502-3992-0
PB: 978-1-3505-0490-5
ePDF: 978-1-3502-3993-7
eBook: 978-1-3502-3994-4

Series: Bloomsbury Handbooks

Typeset by Newgen KnowledgeWorks Pvt. Ltd., Chennai, India

To find out more about our authors and books visit www.bloomsbury.com
and sign up for our newsletters.

*Dedicated to the Memory of
James W. Coleman*

CONTENTS

LIST OF ILLUSTRATIONS	x
FOREWORD—TONI MORRISON: A FRIEND OF MY MIND *Deborah E. McDowell*	xi
ACKNOWLEDGMENTS	xvi
Introduction *Kelly L. Reames and Linda Wagner-Martin*	1

Part One   Morrison's Novels

1 The Sight and Sound of Intersectionality in *The Bluest Eye* *Corinne Bancroft*	15
2 Re-Visiting the Unspeakable: Can Soaphead Church Be Redeemed? *Trudier Harris*	31
3 Do You Believe in Magic? #BlackGirlMagic in *The Bluest Eye* and *Beloved* *James A. Crank*	47
4 "Is? My Baby? Burning?": Segregation, Soldiers, and Civil Rights in Toni Morrison's *Sula* *Thomas Fahy*	59
5 Toni Morrison's Female Epistemology: Post-Nationalism, Diaspora, and Postcolonial Futures in *Tar Baby*, *Mouth Full of Blood*, and *Paradise* *Justine Baillie*	75
6 "How Can I Say Things that Are Pictures?": Foregrounding in *Beloved* *Jennifer Larson*	91
7 Rootlessness: Afro-Pessimism as Foundation in *Paradise* *Keith Clark*	101
8 *Love*: Toni Morrison's African American Gothic *Jameela F. Dallis*	123

9 "A Home for the Heart": Rootlessness, Richard Wright, and Toni Morrison's *Home* 141
Leslie Elaine Frost

10 The Ancestor, Passing, and Imagination in Toni Morrison's *God Help the Child* (2015) 155
Janine Bradbury

11 Arcs of Transcendence: The Religious Imagination of Toni Morrison 167
Gurleen Grewal

Part Two Morrison and the Contemporary World

12 "Unforgetting": Toni Morrison's *Beloved* and the National Memorial for Peace and Justice 183
Kristina K. Groover

13 Blues Lives Matter: Reading *Jazz* in the Era of George Floyd 197
Andrew Scheiber

14 Margaret Garner in History, Opera, and as Inspiration for *Beloved* 213
Kristine Yohe

15 Faulkner after Morrison 227
David H. Krause

16 Prospects for the Public Uses of "Toni Morrison" 245
Kirk Curnutt

17 Going to Ground in *Home*: Morrison's Mid-Century Political Modernism 261
Thadious M. Davis

18 "Only White Folks Got the Freedom to Hate Home": Strategic Empathy and Expanded Intersectionality since Morrison's *Home* 277
Marijana Mikić and Derek C. Maus

Part Three Morrison Teaching, Teaching Morrison

19 Toni Morrison and the Politics of Literary Generosity 295
Michael Nowlin

20 Soldiers, Identity, and Trauma: Teaching *Home* in a War Literature Course 307
Jennifer Haytock

21 Cotton Mather's Witches and Toni Morrison's *Paradise* 319
Janie Hinds

22 "What Are You without Racism?": Toni Morrison on Perfectionism and White Supremacy 331
Christopher S. Lewis

23 Teaching Toni Morrison's *Sula* in a "Post-Racial" Moment 343
   Marc K. Dudley

24 "Understand[ing] All Too Well What Is Meant": Teaching Toni Morrison's "Recitatif" 351
   Catherine Seltzer

25 Toni Morrison's *Home*: One Scene, Four Takes 363
   Trudier Harris

BIBLIOGRAPHY 381

CONTRIBUTORS 405

INDEX 409

ILLUSTRATIONS

12.1	National Memorial for Peace and Justice, Montgomery, Alabama, 2020	194
12.2	National Memorial for Peace and Justice, Montgomery, Alabama, 2020	194

FOREWORD
TONI MORRISON: A FRIEND OF MY MIND

DEBORAH E. MCDOWELL

I

I was vacationing at Myrtle Beach in South Carolina when my niece tapped me gently on the shoulder, waking me from a nap to whisper, "Auntie, I think your friend died. It's on CNN." What friend? Where? Still in the fog of sleep, I wondered if I actually had a friend whose passing would be covered on a cable news network. Rubbing sleep from my eyes, I rolled out of bed and made my way to the television, switching from network to network, slowly absorbing the news, not entirely unexpected, but shocking nonetheless: Toni Morrison had died. August 5, 2019, is now etched as much in my memory as is her birth date: February 18, 1931.

For the rest of that day in August 2019, I sat in my rumpled pajamas, my focus shuttling between the television screen and my handheld phone. Joining the worldwide Twitterverse, I engaged in a collective act of mourning and remembering one of the world's most venerated writers, who had just joined the ancestors. In between tweeting favorite passages from her voluminous body of work, I talked to one of the reporters assigned to my university's daily, *UVA Today*, who asked for an interview, having been told that I had taught Morrison's work in several classes over the years and had published an essay on her second novel, *Sula*. Breaking the ice, she asked me when and where I first met Toni Morrison. Oddly—then as now—I was at a loss to answer with any certainty, but "I think it was 1988," I told her, the year she was awarded the Pulitzer Prize for *Beloved*. That spring (or was it fall?), Cornell, from which Morrison received her MA degree, hosted a celebration in her honor, and I was privileged to be invited to join others in paying formal tribute to her in brief presentations about a work of our choosing. I selected *Sula*. Even if my memory is faulty, I've decided that this was the first time I met Toni Morrison "in the flesh." Long before that evening in 1988, however, I had been keeping company with Toni, conversing/communing with her through her writings, deepening my devotion to her work with each passing encounter.

I first encountered Morrison's fiction in the mid-1970s, when I began my doctoral program in the English department at a Big Ten university in Indiana. Newly transplanted there from an HBCU (Historically Black College and University) in Alabama, I enrolled with a scattering of other Black women in the schools and departments across the university, who were, like me, struggling to find intellectual footing on alien soil. Looking back on this period of my life, I recall Richard Wright's observation in *Black Boy*, "Whenever my environment had failed to support or nourish me, I had clutched at books," and the books I clutched at during this period were all written by Black American women. Their work was "extra-curricular," not found on any syllabus of any course

I was then taking, not even listed on the back pages as "optional" or "supplementary" reading for extra credit. I studied their writing just as avidly (perhaps more so) as I did the "canonical" work assigned in the courses I took.

Paradoxically, while their writing constituted for me a "shadow" curriculum, already by the time I entered graduate school in the 1970s, they had become what Hortense Spillers aptly termed, a "vivid new fact of national life." Through the sheer force and power of their writing, Toni Morrison, Alice Walker, Ntozake Shange, Gayl Jones, Toni Cade Bambara, Michelle Wallace, and many more were demanding that the world take notice, even if the notice it took was grudging, even sneering, at times. Indeed, their work was often roundly condemned in many quarters, notably among some Black men with public platforms as journalists, critics, and reviewers on the staffs of establishment literary publications. No matter the naysaying of this damned mob of scribbling male critics, many Black women had found a lifeline in the work of these prolific writers. Mary Helen Washington perhaps put it best in "The Darkened Eye Restored," when she wrote, "If there is a single distinguishing feature of the literature of black women … it is this: their literature is about black women; it takes the trouble to record the thoughts, words, feelings, and deeds of black women, experiences that make the realities of being black in America look very different from what men have written." For us, Black women, belated arrivals to the US academy, to be able to study, analyze, and interpret the work in which we saw ourselves so solidly affirmed was a gift from the universe. From that point in the 1970s, I dedicated myself to the study of this work, and Toni Morrison's novels had pride of place. Encountering her work reshaped my literary world, challenged my training, and compelled me to question everything I thought I knew and much of what I had been taught up to that point. I devoured her novels as soon as they were published, along with any material about her I could get my hands on: interviews, magazine features, newspaper editorials. When the invitation arrived to pay tribute to her at Cornell that evening in 1988, it was "sheer good fortune," to borrow from the dedication of *Sula*.

In the years that followed, I was fortunate to be in Toni Morrison's presence on countless occasions, thanks to her gracious invitations and those of others. I joined her at the premiere of Spike Lee's film, *Malcolm X*; was present at Carnegie Hall for the premiere of the song cycle, *Honey and Rue*; was at the production of *Margaret Garner* in Detroit; and was at a reception in her honor hosted by the mayor of Paris in the elegant surroundings of city hall. But the standout occasions were the decade birthday celebrations: the sixtieth birthday celebration held at Princeton, where I sat next to Toni Cade Bambara, who kept me in stitches throughout the evening. Then there was the seventieth birthday party at the New York Public Library, where I met the prepossessing soprano, Jessye Norman, who wafted about the elegant lobby wearing a black silk taffeta gown featuring yards and yards of ruching, and a matching head wrap reaching toward the ceiling. When the eightieth birthday celebration rolled around, I was lucky to join others at the Library of Congress, after which we gathered back at the home of Eleanor Traylor, Toni's longtime friend, since their days at Howard University. That intimate, post-birthday gathering in 2011 lasted until the wee hours of the morning, as we told stories, traded gossip, cracked jokes, and laughed raucously.

There were many such gatherings over the years when Toni invited a small circle to hang out with her, to witness her razor-sharp wit and her comic timing, to absorb her legendary, smoky laugh that surged spontaneously from down deep in her throat, lingered in the air, and lightened the atmosphere. While it is tempting to continue reminiscing about the many other mornings, afternoons, and evenings I passed in the company of one whom I felt privileged to call a friend, I would rather seize the honor of this invitation to recount instead the many ways Toni Morrison was a friend of my mind. Here, I am obviously borrowing from Sixo's often-quoted rhapsody about the "Thirty-Mile Woman" in *Beloved:* "She a friend of my mind." I concede that it flirts with triteness to summon this passage, which has been "picked clean" by other scholars, reviewers, and fans of Morrison's writings—especially of *Beloved*—but from the moment I encountered her work, Toni became just that: a "friend of my mind," an intellectual lodestar, a chosen guide, and so she has remained for the last forty-plus years.

That Toni Morrison has remained a friend of my mind is due, in great part, to the fact that she was herself a friend of *the* mind, a friend of thinking. Whether in her eleven novels, her essays, published interviews, libretti, poems, public lectures, or addresses, Morrison held up to readers a mind at work, a mind reveling in, luxuriating in thinking. In a 1977 interview with Mel Watkins, Morrison noted that writing was, for her, "the most extraordinary way of thinking and feeling … (Watkins, "Talk with Toni Morrison," 48). And, in an interview with Nellie McKay, she indicated that she wanted, in turn, to spark that same experience in her audience: "I don't want to give my readers something to swallow; I want to give them something to feel and think about." And that she did. This desire imbued her work with a philosophical character, no matter the genre in which she was writing. At its essence—and etymologically—philosophy involves this familiar schema: *philos* (friend or lover) and *sophia* (wisdom or knowledge), thus making a philosopher a friend of knowledge or wisdom. While Morrison considered narrative among the most effective means of structuring knowledge, she understood that all knowledge begins with questions. She was a novelist who pursued (and was pursued by) provocative questions. As she noted in several interviews, including one with Bill Moyers in 1987: "All the books are questions for me. I mean they start out—I write them because I don't know something." And as she explained in a 2015 interview with Hilton Als, pursuing these questions constituted a "movement toward knowledge," for herself, for her characters, and for her readers.

From work to work, Toni pursued the timeless questions that have bedeviled philosophers for centuries. What constitutes a flourishing human life, a "good" life? What are the habits of the ideal good? How can we live abundant lives that extend beyond the finite boundaries of the self? Is goodness knowable? What is good? What is evil? Why are we here? What is our responsibility to one another? What do we owe one another? What are the kinds and modes of being in relation that humanize us, that fulfill our lives (or alternatively, diminish them)? What is the nature of friendship? What is the nature of love? These were among the questions Morrison pursued in her second novel, *Sula*, which was the first of her novels I read, as well as the first of her novels I taught. I can proudly say that I have made my way through Morrison's entire published corpus; it is to *Sula* that I have returned again and again, considering it, of all her works, the one that is perhaps the "best" friend of my mind. Often asked why *Sula* occupies such pride of place, I have sometimes answered by returning to the philosopher Stanley Cavell. In "The Avoidance of Love," a chapter in his collection *Must We Mean What We Say?*, Cavell poses an intriguing question: "What sends us back to a piece or a passage?—as though it is not finished with us" (Cavell 314). I would say this is one reason why I am sent back again and again to *Sula*: it is not finished with me. Over the years, it has been a book to think with, to quarrel with, to mull over and meditate on, precisely for the way it wrestles with the vexing, ancient philosophical imponderables without providing the reader any easy answers or assurances.

An eminently teachable book, *Sula* has proven an equally vexing text for the students who appreciate its hypnotic lyricism, its narrative elegance and economy, its humanity, and its exploration of female friendship, but are baffled by its refusal to resolve the moral quandaries it stages in multiple scenes. You can probably anticipate that they would include Hannah's habit of sleeping with the husbands of her friends and neighbors, Eva's setting her son Plum afire, Sula putting Eva in the old folks' home. But, from class to class, across the decades, the *pièce de résistance* is Sula's decision to sleep with Jude, the husband of her best friend. The students seek a judgment and condemnation of Sula. They want the narrative to establish clearly and unequivocally who is guilty and who is innocent. Who is good and who is evil. Who is right and who is wrong. Few who have studied Morrison's writings—particularly the novels—can overlook their tendency to touch a nerve, to provoke a complex of strong, unsettling responses, particularly those that force a shift in our basic assumptions and understandings about ourselves and the worlds we inhabit. Of all the books in Morrison's corpus that I have taught, it is *Sula* that provokes and unsettles. Few can understand why, even on her deathbed, Sula does not seem to muster any sympathy for Nel, her erstwhile friend. To Nel's question, "I was good to you, Sula, why don't that matter?" Sula can only answer, "Being good to somebody is just like being mean to somebody. Risky. You don't get nothing for it" (*Sula* 144, 145). It is significant that Sula's last words to Nel come in the form of a question:

> "How you know?" Sula asked.
> "Know what? ..."
> "About who was good. How you know it was you? ... I mean maybe it wasn't you. ... Maybe it was me." (146)

I have extracted pedagogical value from this text that studiously refuses to presuppose moral absolutes as given and understood, preferring instead to upend comfortable assumptions in order to provoke her readers to "think the unthinkable," an objective she has long held as writer. I agree with Jean Wyatt, who writes in *Love and Narrative Forms in Toni Morrison's Later Novels*, that the ethical concern of Morrison's writing is "to keep a dialogue on ideas going and to provoke a questioning and reevaluating of all fixed convictions and established ideas—even her own" (191).

Over the course of the forty-plus years that Toni Morrison has been a "friend of my mind," she has provided me with an education and a pedagogy grounded in questions, not simply those posed implicitly and explicitly in her novels, but also in the essays, interviews, and commentary on her work. I am struck by how frequently Morrison appealed to the language and metaphors of learning, education, and knowledge production in all of her writing. Literal references to "curricula" crop up in her novels and essays alike. In "The War on Error," for example, she noted the ways in which we remain mired in "the same old curricula," its language and its methods. We need "new curricula," she argues, "containing some powerful visionary thinking about how the life of the moral mind and a free and flourishing spirit can operate." In her view, knowledge, learning, and teaching must lead to wisdom, and wisdom was, for her, the foundation on which "the good life" of ancient philosophical reference could be built and sustained.

II

Morrison's writings were central to the establishment of "new curricula" in the US academy of the 1970s and 1980s, when I came of professional age. There are now forces afoot that bid to see her work erased, at least from the K-12 curriculum. As I was a few pages into writing this foreword, Glenn Youngkin was elected, in a fiercely contested race, Governor of the Commonwealth of Virginia. He rode to victory by exploiting the timeworn wedge issue of race. This time Morrison's *Beloved* was his target. The book, he alleged, should be removed from high school curricula in the commonwealth, and he promised parents that he would work to ensure that they, not teachers, should and would have the power to decide what their children read in school, the power to eliminate any piece of writing that threatened them with "trauma" or made them feel bad or guilty. Of course, we know that *The Bluest Eye* had already been banned, as had *Paradise*, from all prison libraries. Now the magisterial *Beloved* had succumbed to the censor's silencing, swept up in the general and manufactured hysteria over "Critical Race Theory."

Across the decades of her career, Morrison took up the question of censorship, in various contexts, perhaps nowhere more incisively than in "The Nobel Lecture in Literature." There, she spoke of the "censored and censoring" work of "statist language," which exists to perform "policing duties." Such language, she continued, "thwarts the intellect, stalls conscience, [and] suppresses human potential. It is, above all, "unreceptive to interrogation." Those who ban literature, she went on to say, do so because it tends to be "interrogative," because it asks questions that demand to be raised even when, as she suggests in "God's Language," they "become answerable only in the art of storytelling." Significantly, the "answers" Morrison's storytelling provides were open consistently to revision, to reinterrogation, for she understood that the mind and the imagination must remain open, engaged, restless, ever dissatisfied with complacency. Indeed, what Morrison said about James Baldwin when she eulogized him might be said, with equal aptness, about her: "You gave us ourselves to think about, to cherish." Here, Morrison is referring to Black people, writ large, but looking back on that period in the 1970s when I discovered Morrison's novels, we might interpret "ourselves" as the Black American women who had yet to be represented in fiction in a fashion that captured our complexities. As she noted in an interview with Gloria Naylor, "There were no books about me. I didn't exist in all the literature I had read … this person, this female, this black did not exist center self." And so, Morrison set about writing the books she wanted to read featuring characters she wanted to see. As she noted in an introduction to a recent edition of *Sula*, "Nobody was minding us, so we minded ourselves."

For the small group of Black women who came of professional age in the 1970s and 1980s, Toni Morrison was creating books in which we were cherished, as in taken seriously. We were on her mind. In a manner of speaking, she "gathered" us, much as did Sixo's Thirty-Mile Woman. Many of us may have been lonely and dispersed in academic institutions often hostile to our presence, if not our very beings, but we were confident in the knowledge that Toni Morrison saw us, and that in her eyes, we were beloved and she was ours. Of course, her work showed an intimate knowledge of the richness and beauty of Black people, of Black culture, in general. Her treatment of Black life and culture came with love and celebration, free of apology. As she often put it herself, she worked to free herself as a writer from "the white gaze." She was right in noting that much African American writing seemed historically to be pleading with some imaginary white reader, defending Black people against some assumed pathology or deficiency, but she herself felt no need to explain Black people to white people. We who read and taught her work saw ourselves—our frailties, delights, our brilliance. As she was wont to say, "I write about Black people, about African American culture—the good, the bad, the indifferent." I would argue that she wrote about Black people "mindfully," in all our abundance, bound and free.

ACKNOWLEDGMENTS

We thank all the contributors who wrote essays for this collection. Their writerly excellence and their deep understanding of Toni Morrison's work—and its role in contemporary culture—are matched only by their patience. We appreciate the invitation of the Bloomsbury series editor, Ben Doyle, to prepare this volume and his careful preparation of these materials for publication. Sarah Shuler provided able and appreciated research assistance. Kelly would also like to thank the English Department at Western Kentucky University for a course release to work on this project.

Kelly L. Reames and Linda Wagner-Martin

Introduction

KELLY L. REAMES AND LINDA WAGNER-MARTIN

It would be no exaggeration to claim that *The Bloomsbury Handbook to Toni Morrison* has been in development for the past fifty years. As many of these essays show, Morrison's first novel, *The Bluest Eye*, published in 1970, remains a central part of readers' fascination with Chloe Ardelia Wofford's career as one of the world's most enduring novelists. America's most recent novelist to receive the Nobel Prize in Literature (awarded in 1993), Toni Morrison began her publishing history with a somewhat accidental name: she had submitted the manuscript of *The Bluest Eye* with no title page, and the editor who received the work knew her from publishing circles as the Random House editor Toni Morrison. This use of her married name, presaged by her family nickname,[1] might not have been her choice: she was as proud of her family name, Wofford, as she was of having been given her grandmother's name, Ardelia. The choice, however, did not rest in her hands.

Published by Holt, Rinehart, and Winston, a competitor of Random House, the publisher for which she worked as an editor, *The Bluest Eye* received few reviews. The slim first book set the stage for the ten novels to come, but at first glance—for readers new to thinking of her as a novelist—it seemed "difficult." *The Bluest Eye* was itself a puzzling title. When a prospective reader opened the book, its pages looked unusual. The name *Toni Morrison* was completely unknown in writerly circles. Yet it seems clear now, in retrospect, that the novel served as an accurate introduction to Morrison's *oeuvre*: innovative yet accessible, comic yet poignant, using the voices of two innocent young African American sisters to tell the story of a less fortunate African American girl, one whose tragic life was no anomaly. In many ways simple and yet compelling, *The Bluest Eye* also succeeded in telling a *new* story: the life of African American poverty and abuse told in idiomatic language, without nostalgia or sensationalism, deeply rooted in a quick-paced contemporary narrative that revealed its authenticity in every sentence.

Morrison as author would become *the* living writer able to convey the heart of African American culture, her language representing the colloquial, the strikingly bold idioms, the passions, and the proud diffidence. Just as she told one detailed story in *The Bluest Eye*, she would continue to mine segments of African American life in each of the successive novels she published. As a researcher, as a student of various kinds of African American and American and, in some cases, African experience, she would work her way through history, never editorializing but rather capturing background and foreground as well as elemental human experiences with infallible accuracy and conviction. As she would later write about the role of the African American author,

---

[1] When she had joined the Catholic Church in her youth, she had chosen St. Anthony as her patron saint—"Toni" became a reference to that allegiance.

Black writers who are committed to the renewal and refreshment of values can be identified by their taste, by their judgments, by their intellect, and by their work. They do not use black life as exotic ornament for pedestrian nonblack stories. The *essence of black life* is the substance of their work. Their work turns on a moral axis that has been forged among black people. They do not impose alien moralities about broken homes, and house-bound fathers, and petite power, and what is or is not gainful employment on their characters. (*Source* 225, emphasis in original)

To this prolegomenon, she adds, but never as a secondary consideration, "They do not regard black language as dropping *g*'s or as an exercise in questionable phonetics and inconsistent orthography. They know that it is much more complicated than that" (225).

Of relevance to this decade's fascination with culture wars comes the concluding paragraph to this quotation, when Morrison acknowledges the defensive position most writers of color have had to adopt: "And they waste no time explaining, explaining, explaining away everything they feel and think and do—to the other culture. They are challenged by and concerned with the enlightenment of their own, even when the enlightenment includes painful information … they do not view the habits and customs of their people with the eye of a charged-up ethnologist examining curios" (*Source* 225).

This practical mantra was little known when Morrison began her writing career: bookstores in 1970 had no separate sections housing African American writers. When Ralph Ellison's *Invisible Man* was published in the early 1950s, the race of the author was seldom mentioned. But by the 1970s, writings by African American men were becoming accepted—were being included in syllabi for courses in contemporary literature. But it took Maya Angelou's *I Know Why the Caged Bird Sings*, the first of her several memoirs, to create readership for works by African American *women* writers. The immediate success of the Angelou memoir, never out of print since that first publication, opened doors for the Morrison novels that were soon to appear on the shelves she was creating for Random House books—by Toni Cade Bambara, Paule Marshall, Angela Davis, Lucille Clifton, and Gayl Jones, as well as many male writers.

The synergy of African American women's writing that began with 1970 was fueled by the writings of Alice Walker, whose first novel, *The Third Life of Grange Copeland*, had also appeared in 1970, followed by her important 1973 story collection, *In Love & Trouble: Stories of Black Women*. The feminist emphasis in that collection paralleled what Morrison had achieved in her second novel, *Sula*, a flamboyantly nontraditional story of the woman as protagonist, a woman who flouts respectable behavior and takes on the unexpected power of living her own sexually free life, an "outlaw" woman. As the publications grew, as readers became accustomed to reading books by African American *women*, Alice Walker's most controversial novel, *The Color Purple*, appeared, unleashing a world of controversy over the appropriate sexual roles of both women and men. In 1983, Walker capped that excitement with her collection of essays, *In Search of Our Mothers' Gardens: Womanist Prose*. From Walker's essays came the vocabulary that gave women readers of all races and cultures the tools of language: womanist—a word that could rise *above* the limitations of gender. Alongside countless books of poems by both Walker and Maya Angelou, and a flood of novels that included more books by Walker and Toni Morrison (as well as Zora Neale Hurston's works from the 1930s and 1940s, discovered and brought back into print by Walker and her publisher), writing by African American *women* had begun to penetrate bookstores, classrooms, and cultural life. Those works became the mainstays for the new courses called "women's studies" that developed during the 1980s and the 1990s in US secondary schools, colleges, and universities—and throughout the world.

Throughout the 1970s, Toni Morrison had also been quietly writing her way into contemporary intellectual history. Her book reviews began appearing in the *New York Times* and the Washington papers as early as 1971, and she maintained that presence whenever she was asked for essays, opinion pieces, or reviews. Such a presence led to her later compiling essay collections that were of immediate cultural interest and laid the foundation for her to begin her hegira as a public intellectual.

More importantly for Morrison's early visibility were her second and third novels: *Sula*, published in 1973, and *Song of Solomon*, which appeared in 1977. *Sula* was reviewed reasonably well and was nominated for the National Book Critics Circle Award as well as the Ohioana Award. But it was *Song of Solomon* that crashed through the resistance that books about women characters often met: *Song of Solomon* with its Biblical sweep—focusing on not only male characters but also on their ancestral families, especially the wise older women of those families—*won* the National Book Critics Circle Award as well as the American Academy and Institute of Arts and Letters Award. Perhaps more significant for Morrison's progression to the eventual acclaim her novels would receive was the book's being chosen as a Book-of-the-Month Club selection. Would-be readers did not have to search to find copies of this important novel: it was everywhere.

Whereas both *The Bluest Eye* and *Sula* were focused on the lives of women and girls, *Song of Solomon* was seen as a more traditional novel. The protagonists were men, their lives were spent in search of their occupational quests, and those quests took them to various sites, geographical as well as emotional (even into African social and religious beliefs, even to mythic locations). Morrison had written a uniquely expanded bildungsroman. In part to honor the life of her beloved father, who had recently died, Morrison moved from what she called "a female locus" to that of male experience: "To get out of the house, to de-domesticate the landscape that had so far been the site of my work. To travel. To fly. In such an overtly, stereotypically male narrative, I thought that straightforward chronology would be more suitable than any kind of play with sequence and time I had employed in my previous novels" ("Foreword" xii). This intentionality that became the aesthetic hallmark of a Morrison novel shows clearly in her comment that

> the first two books were beginnings. I start with the childhood of a person in all the books, but in the first two, the movement, the rhythm is circular, although the circles are broken. If you go back to the beginnings, you get pushed along toward the end ... *Song of Solomon* is different. I was trying to push this novel outward; its movement is neither circular nor spiral. The image in my mind for it is that of a train picking up speed. (*Conversations* I, 124)

One of Toni Morrison's strengths as a writer is her ability to explain her often difficult writing to readers: as several of her essay collections show (particularly her last published work, *The Source of Self-Regard*), she is her own best critic. The life of Morrison as novelist becomes the life of Morrison as person as well as Morrison as intellectual. The themes of her novels reflect the cultural attitudes as well as the history of their appropriate times. Yet no matter the historical setting, her works maintain an immediacy, a currency that saves them from the dulling of mere historical fact. With *Tar Baby*, her fourth novel published in 1981, she explored both national identities and gendered ones. She was elected to the American Academy and Institute of Arts and Letters and appeared in a more popular venue on the cover of *Newsweek*. Then, after six years of exploring the anathema of slavery, she finally published *Beloved* in 1987. That novel won the Pulitzer Prize for Fiction, the Robert F. Kennedy Award, the Melcher Book Award, the Before Columbus Award, and the Elizabeth Cady Stanton Award from the National Organization of Women. The following year she won the Modern Language Association's Commonwealth Award in Literature and the Chianti Ruffino Antico Fattore International Literary Prize.

Because she had originally conceived of *Beloved* as one part of a trilogy, in 1992, she published what she considered the second part, the novel *Jazz*, her provocative study of American modernist life. The third book in the trilogy, the novel *Paradise*, would appear in 1998. But in 1993, she was awarded the Nobel Prize for Literature—the first American woman since Pearl Buck (in 1938) and the first American writer since John Steinbeck in 1962, following its awarding to William Faulkner in 1949 and to Ernest Hemingway in 1954. The award had never before been given to an African American.

Much sought after then for lectures, teaching positions, and whatever honors the literary world could bestow, Toni Morrison maintained her balance through her well-researched and evocatively written novels. In 2003, appeared *Love*, a provocative depiction of a middle-class Black society in which gender faded into voiced enigmatic narrative, something on the order of her attempts to create an unmarked consciousness in her introduction to the invaluable compendium of African American history, *The Black Book*. In 2008 appeared *A Mercy*, which grew from Morrison's creation of a colonial world in which skin color fused with morality to find actionable life choices. Here, race became less predictive; gender, along with sexual choices, was more determinative.

In 2012, she published *Home*, a work that ostensibly studied the harm of wars but focused more centrally on the wars of attrition wearing away African American self-worth, and in 2015, *God Help the Child*, with its return to the role of parenting and the development of any child, especially a child trapped in the social stigma too long associated with skin color and other racial perils. As many of the essays included in this collection suggest, *Home* has become one of the most important Morrison works in today's classrooms.

As Morrison's readers followed her writing through these many paradigm shifts, as she worked and reworked history into plots that were often surprisingly contemporary, her following grew. What occurred between Toni Morrison as author and the readers who followed her every book, her every essay, was a healthful symbiosis of reading. Like much else about Morrison's fiction, reading Morrison became in itself a unique act. In "Toni Morrison: A Friend of My Mind," the essay that opens this collection, Deborah E. McDowell adroitly calls Morrison "a friend of the mind, a friend of thinking." She explains that in everything Morrison wrote, "she held up to readers a mind at work, a mind reveling in, luxuriating in, thinking." One of Morrison's most engaging skills as a writer was to lead her readers to the unlimited heights of true intellectual capacity. She never made understanding easy, as she demanded that her readers recognize that understanding was the pathway to participating in a capacious, satisfying life.

The last two novels, *Home* and *God Help the Child*, are the shortest works Morrison published. There has been some dismay at that development, but in other respects, in these shorter works,

Morrison forced readers to assume for themselves more of the books' narratives. She had long stated that, as a writer, she wanted to physically *involve* her readers. In 1984 she had written, "To make the story appear oral, meandering, effortless, spoken—to have the reader *feel* the narrator without *identifying* that narrator ... to have the reader work with the author in the construction of the book—is what's important" ("Rootedness" 59, emphasis in original).

The organization of this *Handbook* follows this fifty-year progression of Toni Morrison's creation of a distinctly new pattern of American and African American letters. What Morrison created as she wrote her life into the most esteemed calendar of African American and American letters provides the map for the organization of these essays. Part One, Morrison's Novels, treats the works of her inspired and diligent creativity. Part Two, Morrison and the Contemporary World, attempts to describe the impact both Morrison the person and Morrison the writer have had on international thought, culture, and writing. Part Three, Morrison Teaching, Teaching Morrison, explains the way Morrison conceived of writing as this conjoined process between writer and reader, with practical applications for classroom reading of key Morrison works. In the concluding essay to this third section, Professor Trudier Harris provides apt illustration of the *kind* of reading Morrison would have enjoyed as she creates a new sensibility for readers of Morrison's novel *Home*.

PART ONE: MORRISON'S NOVELS

This longest segment of the *Handbook* exhibits various critical approaches, each essay aiming to cast new light on the intricate aesthetic practices Toni Morrison so carefully designed and implemented. Most of her novels appear in this section (as well as, often, in the essays within Parts Two and Three). The first three essays here show the possible successful critical methods that might be used to read Morrison's first novel, *The Bluest Eye*.

Corinne Bancroft's "The Sight and Sound of Intersectionality in *The Bluest Eye*" draws from the important scholarship of Kimberle Williams Crenshaw to emphasize the paradigms of Black aesthetics and language. When Morrison fuses gender with race and gender, and then moves on to class and gender, she fits *The Bluest Eye* within Crenshaw's compounded discrimination, "intersectionality." Placing the 1970 novel within the cultural and legal strategies of the 1990s allows Bancroft to perform a careful textual reading with modern cultural relevance.

A wide-ranging thematic reading marks Trudier Harris's "Revisiting the Unspeakable: Can Soaphead Church Be Redeemed?" Within what Harris sees as Morrison's unconventional moral axis, Soaphead Church can be read as a less-offensive, predatory character. He becomes, rather, the product of a family's "anglophilia," an attitude that condemns him to a life of only dissatisfaction. Harris uses comparisons with such other of Morrison's characters as Cholly, Guitar, Sethe, and Frank Money to illustrate the author's shifting value paradigms as she makes readers understand the great range of Morrison's moral understanding.

For James A. Crank, *The Bluest Eye* (along with the later *Beloved*) can be read alongside Michelle Obama's speech at the 2013 "Black Girls Rock Awards." "Do You Believe in Magic? #BlackGirlMagic in *The Bluest Eye* and *Beloved*" elevates Twitter chatter and today's strong social media presence to provide an interesting perspective on the ways in which Morrison creates her many-sided Black women characters. Crank's discussion of the magic—both figurative and literal—of positive reinforcement for maturing girls creates new sympathy for Pauline Breedlove as well as a new emphasis (in *Beloved*) on the roles of both Beloved and Denver, as well as the townspeople who manage to save both Sethe and Denver.

Thomas Fahy, too, provides a different perspective for readers of *Sula* in his "'Is? My Baby? Burning?': Segregation, Soldiers, and Civil Rights in Toni Morrison's *Sula*." Using the fulcrum of Nel's relationship with Sula, he provides a complex history of both military action and racial politics through the decades the novel covers. By giving readers the backgrounds of African American men's failed lives, using "Shadrack's haunting presence through his holiday National Suicide Day and his various encounters with Sula and Nel," Fahy creates a crucial timeline from 1919 to 1965. Readers benefit from this detailed information.

Justine Baillie places Morrison in the midst of today's controversies about Black women's rights and opportunities in her essay, "Toni Morrison's Female Epistemology: Post-Nationalism, Diaspora, and Postcolonial Futures in *Tar Baby*, *Mouth Full of Blood*, and *Paradise*." Using the British publisher's title, *Mouth Full of Blood*, instead of the US title, *The Source of Self-Regard*, Baillie tilts reader expectations about Morrison's 2019 collection, which is subtitled "*Essays, Speeches, and Meditations*." Through her positive readings of Jadine in *Tar Baby*, contrasted with the mono-national Son, Baillie places Jadine in an internationally vibrant culture, providing her with worlds of possibility. This reading, as the essay's title suggests, brings Morrison's often undervalued fourth novel into a prominence contemporary theory (by such critics as Paul Gilroy, Homi K. Bhabha, and Faith M. Avery) can support. As she does with both *Tar Baby* and *Paradise*, Baillie opens a new pathway into Morrison's oeuvre.

In "'How Can I Say Things that Are Pictures?': Foregrounding in *Beloved*," Jennifer Larson discusses Morrison's novel *Beloved* in tandem with the Jonathan Demme film of that work. As she explains what she means by Morrison's "unique vision for language," she employs Roger Fowler's *Linguistic Criticism*. Syntactic comparisons relate passages from the novel (taken from *Beloved*'s origin sequence) to the film: Larson calls her critique "foregrounding" and suggests in this taut essay at least one reason for the film's comparative ineffectiveness.

For Keith Clark, a revealing methodology to employ with Morrison's fiction is a much more contemporary approach. In "Rootlessness: Afro-Pessimism as Foundation in *Paradise*," he describes the theories of Frank Wilderson and Jared Sexton, linking their work to the earlier writings of Franz Fanon, Orlando Patterson, and Hortense Spillers. One might call "Afro-Pessimism" the immersion of a reader's consciousness in "a continuous lens of perpetual slavery." Clark's subsequent close reading of *Paradise* presents the reader with fresh, always pertinent insights.

Jameela F. Dallis creates a new and inclusive paradigm for Morrison's somewhat controversial novel. In "*Love*: Toni Morrison's African American Gothic," Dallis provides ample history for readers eager to contextualize the sometimes mysterious characters and events portrayed in the near-fantastic community of Silk, the African American seaside resort. Her emphases on the roles of history, portraiture, and gender privilege, as well as her discussions of the author's aesthetic choices, substantiate her conclusions.

For Leslie Elaine Frost, comparing Morrison's tenth novel *Home* with key works from Richard Wright strengthens the backstory, often omitted, about Frank Money. In "'A Home for the Heart': Rootlessness, Richard Wright, and Toni Morrison's *Home*," Frost draws throughout on such Wright texts as *Black Boy*; *White Man, Listen!*; and his edited collection, *Twelve Million*

Voices. She also draws on sources both literary and popular, from *Rolling Stone* and *Culture Trip* to modern music and such television series as *M*A*S*H*. Frost's informative allusions are both helpful and enriching.

In Janine Bradbury's "The Ancestor, Passing, and Imagination in Toni Morrison's *God Help the Child* (2015)," this British critic draws together the pervasive theme of reverence for the ancestor figure—often a woman—and the cultural miasma of colorism. Wide-ranging in application, these principles of her reading of Morrison's last novel, which was less often reviewed than most of her fiction, lead backward and forward into pervasive themes of the *oeuvre*. She also shows the importance of using trauma theory to explicate some of Morrison's characters, even as contemporary culture may try to negate society's emphasis on skin color.

In "Arcs of Transcendence: The Religious Imagination of Toni Morrison," Gurleen Grewal combines the personal with the scholarly. Her essay relates to both Professor McDowell's foreword and Professor Baillie's far-reaching international reading of Morrison's fiction and provides readers with a poignantly new reading of Morrison's work. Professor Grewal ties together what she sees as originary backgrounds for Morrison's aesthetic: classical lore, African beliefs, other religious beliefs—and the heresies related to those, Gnosticism and the Nag Hammadi texts, the Eleusinian Mysteries, witchcraft, and a category she defines as "eros and the sanctity of the body and the spirit." Grewal discusses *Desdemona* and the author's poem "Eve Remembering" as well as many of the novels. Her discussion accordingly leads readers to a wider realization of Morrison's astute, learned understanding, as she developed her own unique "religious imagination."

PART TWO: MORRISON AND THE CONTEMPORARY WORLD

Just as Morrison did in her own fiction, she as person and aesthetician became a touchstone for memorializing historical truth for the wider culture today. It was not only that she was awarded the Nobel Prize in Literature in 1993 that gave her this cultural prominence. From Michael Eric Dyson's many references to her in his 2022 book, *Entertaining Race*, like her presence in *Read Till You Understand, The Profound Wisdom of Black Life and Literature* by Farah Jasmine Griffin (2021), the name *Toni Morrison* has grown to be a touchstone for wisdom, capability, unprejudiced attitudes, and—perhaps most important—sanity. Or as critic Kirk Curnutt said, Morrison appears everywhere, as if illustrative of issues of literary tourism and the oddball ways literature and its creators get refracted into uplift, self-help, and popular history.

As Curnutt's essay in this section suggests, a writer's centrality to contemporary culture outlives not only that artist's physical presence but sometimes even the presence of an *oeuvre*.

As the essays in this segment show, much of the cultural criticism that derives from studying Morrison's work relates to contemporary politics. Such an inclusion was signaled by Morrison herself in even her earliest essays, and more definitively within the amalgam of essays she purposefully collected in her 2019 *The Source of Self-Regard*. As she wrote there, "What I want my fiction to do is to urge the reader into active participation in the nonnarrative, non-literary experience of the text … It is important that what I write not be merely literary" (264).

Both Professors Curnutt and Groover attend to the remarkable use made of Morrison's words from *Beloved* in the National Museum for Peace and Justice in Montgomery, Alabama. Opened in 2018, this magisterial building (see Groover's photographs) commemorates the thousands of victims of lynching throughout American history.

Kristina K. Groover's essay, "'Unforgetting': Toni Morrison's *Beloved* and the National Memorial for Peace and Justice," rehearses the recent history of the theoretical study of memorialization. Drawing from the work of Judith Butler, Drew Leder, Tanya Schult, Dora Apel, and others, she assesses the critical response to what she calls "counter-movements" of commemoration, like this "lynching museum" and Maya Lin's Vietnam Veterans Memorial, and then moves to discussing Morrison's novel *Beloved* as its own commemoration of slavery. Unexpected in several respects—particularly with regard to Morrison's creation of Schoolteacher—Groover adds much sensibility to readers' understanding of this crucial work, calling *Beloved*'s final chapter Morrison's "metanarrative commentary on the malleability of history."

Andrew Scheiber uses the scaffolding of music criticism to discuss Morrison's second book of what she considered her trilogy. In "Blues Lives Matter: Reading *Jazz* in the Era of George Floyd," Scheiber confronts various problems with police behaviors today, singling out Joe Trace's killing of Dorcas as one example. His scrutiny falls as well on the narrative strategies Morrison chooses to create a novel based partly on historical fact and partly on ambivalence. His attention to both Alice and Violet counters what have become conventional readings of this work.

Kristine Yohe reminds readers of what Saidiya Hartman called "critical fabulation" as she rehearses the influence on Morrison of the history of Margaret Garner—often discussed in literary criticism as one starting point for the character of Sethe in the novel *Beloved*. "Margaret Garner in History, Opera, and as Inspiration for *Beloved*" does its detailed diligence with history, the role of Morrison's project *The Black Book* for Random House in 1974, Morrison's *Beloved* in relation to her writing the libretto for the opera *Margaret Garner*, and the more immediate fallout after the premiere of that work in northern Kentucky/southern Ohio. Yohe's essay is the definitive telling of the way Morrison drew from history but spun a truly imaginative narrative from that starting point.

Frequently associated in readers' minds with Toni Morrison, William Faulkner—particularly in his guise as Southern novelist, premier American modernist, and critic of the conventional attitudes toward both race and gender—becomes one protagonist in David H. Krause's study of the contemporary relationship between Morrison and the older writer. In "Faulkner after Morrison," Krause sets Morrison, as the central protagonist, against Faulkner; playing secondary roles are James Baldwin, Sherwood Anderson, Cornell University, Emmett Till (and Morrison's play *Dreaming Emmett*), and Charles Bon (of *Absalom, Absalom!*). In his dynamic counterpointing of information and insight, Krause provides a plethora of both information and insight that answers many questions about the roles of these most significant American authors. With an easy competence, this essay speaks a great deal about what each author thought about the process of reading and the ways in which each created writing strategies to tell their complicated, and often ambivalent, stories.

Kirk Curnutt, writing in "Prospects for the Public Uses of 'Toni Morrison'," presents a cornucopia of various methods for demonstrating the cultural importance of writers. Focused specifically on Morrison, this essay yet demands that readers contextualize how little has been created in memorialization of both her body of work and its influence.

In "Going to Ground in *Home*: Morrison's Mid-Century Political Modernism," Thadious M. Davis focuses specifically on the contemporary political scene in relation to the American 1950s (the setting for Morrison's tenth novel). She describes Morrison here as "an architect, a mid-century modernist builder of narrativity that heralds a set of strategies designed for living Black in a time of transition." Focused on the American 1950s, this sweeping yet meticulous essay provides information as well as a prolegomenon for personal action. One of the premier speakers for the best of American Studies approaches, Davis places *Home* in the revealing company of Lorraine Hansberry, Senator Joseph McCarthy, and other now-historical figures. She concludes that *Home* is "a novel of radical thought," "a work of aesthetic and political resolve."

Returning in some respects to the opening essay of this collection, Marijana Mikić and Derek C. Maus move the use of intersectionality to an international contemporary fiction scene. Taking Morrison's novel *Home* as a starting point, they discuss such writers as Brit Bennett, Bryan Washington, Kaitlyn Greenidge, Akwacke Emezi, and others in "'Only White Folks Got the Freedom to Hate Home': Strategic Empathy and Expanded Intersectionality since Morrison's *Home*." Drawing as well on Suzanne Keen's concept of authorial strategic empathy, these coauthors create a new paradigm to help readers understand that fiction in the last decade may be judged as much by its sensibility as by its aesthetic force.

PART THREE: MORRISON TEACHING, TEACHING MORRISON

One of the themes that grew more and more apparent as Toni Morrison published more and more nonfiction was her passionate interest in helping readers learn how to read. Her attention often fell on the difficulty of anyone's approaching material that was multilayered, pertinent to contemporary truths that might in themselves be divisive, or personally painful. Accustomed as good readers are to absorbing the full range of emotional currency, for readers in this time of acknowledged chaos, reading per se has become even more difficult.

Morrison often wrote about the various difficulties of being a good reader. She early explained that the process of reading accurately allows the mind to move "from data to information to knowledge to wisdom" (*Source* 307). Acknowledging that one may never reach wisdom, she admitted how difficult writing—wrestling with language—could be: "The practice of writing puts demands on me that nothing else does. The search for language, whether among other writers or in originating it, constitutes a mission" (255). Lest readers forget how crucial the apt uses of language are, Morrison stated, "Literature, sensitive as a tuning fork, is an unblinking witness to the light and shade of the world we live in" (126).

It is no accident that the last essay Morrison included in her 2019 collection, *The Source of Self-Regard, Selected Essays, Speeches, and Meditations*, is her essay about the power of language and of reading. In "Invisible Ink: Reading the Writing and Writing the Reading," she draws significant threads of this pervasive attention into a grave and important message. She repeats again that reading is both a skill and an art. Her reference here is to "what lies under, between, outside the lines, hidden until the right reader discovers it." To clarify, Morrison used an analogy with singing, explaining that "there are the lyrics, the score, and then the performance, which is the individual's contribution to the piece" (*Source* 346–8).

The essays collected in this section exemplify both the practical uses of critics' thinking about teaching Morrison and, the editors hope, a kind of scaffolding for readers who are themselves interested in helping other readers read the Morrison *oeuvre*. Each essay here presents elements germane to this wide, and sometimes unwieldy, process.

As Michael Nowlin theorizes in his essay "Toni Morrison and the Politics of Literary Generosity," the author's useful directions in a number of her nonfiction writings create an atmosphere of kindly instruction—which Nowlin's essay replicates. In his discussion of what "political" means for the Morrison reader, as well as his unpacking her fascination with the reading process and her personal critical practices, Nowlin distances his considerable insight from the sometimes petty distinctions made by critics intent on only pushing their own insights.

Jennifer Haytock's "Soldiers, Identity, and Trauma: Teaching *Home* in a War Literature Course" provides the reader with the curriculum for such a course as well as one philosophy for the current interest in war and peace studies. In her detailed discussion of emergent useful theories about the business of war, she creates a sympathetic atmosphere for understanding Frank Money in Morrison's important novel.

Professor Janie Hinds creates a much wider context for her selection of Morrison's novel *Paradise*. Placing this twenty-first century work within a schematic "American literature" semester, Hinds shows its parallels with Mather's *Wonders of the Invisible World*. In "Cotton Mather's Witches and Toni Morrison's *Paradise*," she details similar themes—"continuities of power differentials across American history" among them. In a wide-ranging discussion, Hinds does not rely simply on uses of what we might today consider "gothic."

The strategy chosen by Christopher S. Lewis is a more eclectic approach to helping students realize the centrality of Morrison's uses of the political. In "'What Are You without Racism?': Toni Morrison on Perfectionism and White Supremacy," Lewis traces what he sees as Morrison's positions on a writer's responsibility to "the white gaze." In parallel, he discusses the facets of "perfectionism" through both Morrison's nonfiction and her fiction. Drawing from works by Baldwin as well as Zadie Smith, Lewis provides a structure for various arguments.

Marc K. Dudley's essay, "Teaching Toni Morrison's *Sula* in a 'Post-Racial' Moment," follows many of Lewis's concepts. For Dudley, who takes his reader argument by argument through several days of discussing Morrison's second novel, the teacher's role is provocative, not authoritative. Working primarily through imaginary dialogue, this essay conveys both the problems and the satisfactions of actual teaching.

For Catherine Seltzer, the difficulties with presenting Morrison's writing for students may well be inherent in the written work. Her essay, "'Understand[ing] All Too Well What Is Meant': Teaching Toni Morrison's 'Recitatif,'" focuses on the intentionally disruptive strategies Morrison chooses in creating the story. Here, the aesthetics derive from the themes as Morrison meant readers to feel bewildered when their usual clues for deciphering an author's intention did not work. Judging from the practical teaching essays within this segment, one finds that the intricacies of teaching Morrison have many sources.

As mentioned early in this Introduction, Trudier Harris's essay, "Toni Morrison's *Home*: One Scene, Four Takes," is a surprising yet effective close to readers' thinking about how to read the intricacies of Morrison's writing. In her focus on a single scene from this late novel—the scene of Black men on the porch, discussing the fight to the death between Jerome and his father—Harris presents a sorrowful story from the points of view her title suggests. Reflecting the dynamism of *Home* itself, this closing essay serves as a kind of resting point for the varied critical discussions presented within this collection.

WORKS CITED

Morrison, Toni. *Conversations with Toni Morrison*, edited by Danille Taylor-Guthrie. University Press of Mississippi, 1994.

Morrison, Toni. "Foreword," *Song of Solomon*. Vintage, 2004, p. xii.

Morrison, Toni. "Rootedness: The Ancestor as Foundation," *What Moves at the Margin: Selected Nonfiction*, edited by Carolyn C. Denard. University of Mississippi Press, 2008.

Morrison, Toni. *The Source of Self-Regard: Selected Essays, Speeches, and Meditations*. Knopf, 2019.

PART ONE

Morrison's Novels

CHAPTER ONE

The Sight and Sound of Intersectionality in *The Bluest Eye*

CORINNE BANCROFT

Reflecting on her exigency for writing *The Bluest Eye* (1970), Toni Morrison recalls,

> I wanted to show how painful this constructed horrible racism was on the most vulnerable people in the society: girls, black girls, poor girls. And that it really and truly could hurt you. So that's what I was looking for, and no one, I thought, had written that book, so since I really wanted to read it, I thought I should write it.

Morrison's move from gender, to race and gender, to class and gender offers an apt gloss for what many would today call "intersectionality," a term coined in 1989 by Kimberlé Williams Crenshaw to make visible the "compound-discrimination" that Black women might experience at the intersection of race and gender ("Demarginalizing the Intersection" 148). Crenshaw's concept is widely celebrated as one of the most important contributions of Critical Race Theory, the legal movement in the 1980s and 1990s that marked a key shift in thinking about racism as the denial of "formal equality" to an understanding of it as an institutional power structure that is ingrained in and perpetuated by the law. Right-wing operatives have since co-opted the term "Critical Race Theory" in their attempts to ban a broad spectrum of race-conscious thought from public schools. Morrison, whose works have often been the subject of such attacks, has pointed out that the "fear of unmonitored writing is justified because truth is trouble. It is trouble for the warmonger, the torturer, the corporate thief, the political hack, the corrupt justice system, and for a comatose public" (*Burn This Book* 2). From this perspective, right-wing efforts to ban knowledge prove the power of words, ideas, and knowledge even as these attempts expose their own totalitarian agenda. As this censorship movement indicates, the troubling intersectional truth that motivated Morrison to write her first novel continues to threaten systems of marginalization today.

I am grateful to Ellen Graham and Trevor Cook for providing invaluable research assistance; to Nancy Sorkin Rabinowitz for her advice on a draft; and, to Ewa Czaykowska-Higgins for her advice on the possible origins of the name Yacobowski. Toni Morrison has shared this story many times and made this particular comment in an interview on *The Colbert Report* Nov. 19, 2014.

The Bluest Eye introduces intersectionality as a lens that exposes how traditional lines of power, race, gender, class, and age can intersect to render "the most delicate member of society" vulnerable to violence (Morrison 211). This interpretation, certainly invited by the text, has become standard, if not required, after Crenshaw's concept became common parlance. However, *The Bluest Eye* also models intersectionality as activist practice, survival strategy, and community foundation. This understanding of intersectionality resonates more with the radical women of color who experimented with revolutionary forms of community in the 1970s and 1980s—such as the Combahee River Collective—than with the later writings of legal scholars. The radical anthology *This Bridge Called My Back* (1981) edited by Cherríe Moraga and Gloria Anzaldúa details the thinking behind this activist practice. In both writing and organizing, intersectionality as praxis is constituted by the coming together of different voices, different experiences that gain strength and power not only from what they have in common but, more importantly, from what distinguishes them. Morrison represents this type of intersectionality through the recurring motif of music that offers a vital sort of recognition for her characters and through the braided form of her novel, which, like the *Bridge* anthology, sets multiple experiences side by side in generative tension. This essay examines how *The Bluest Eye* introduces intersectionality as both sight (Crenshaw's lens that renders vulnerability visible) and sound (the radical women of color's emphasis on collectivity and the choral quality of their writing). Such a project requires a more accurate historical reading that situates Morrison's 1970 novel as a possible source for both the radical organizing of the 1980s and the legal movement of the late 1980s and 1990s. While it is common to use Crenshaw's 1989 framework as an analytic to return to texts like *The Bluest Eye*, I argue that the novel itself offers an earlier origin for intersectional thought.[1]

While the Critical Race Theory movement emerged in the legal sphere and takes the law as its horizon, Morrison refuses to depict the law as even a potential mechanism for justice. She locates legal crimes such as rape and assault on the same scale as interpersonal wrongs such as the refusal to see another person and collective scapegoating. In place of legal punishments like incarceration, Morrison emphasizes communal responses and collective judgments. Felice Blake argues that authors like Morrison use fiction to create alternative and more productive arenas for a communal accounting. In *Black Love, Black Hate: Intimate Antagonisms in African American Literature* (2018), Blake writes,

> Creative Black artists have used expressive culture as a means of convening a town meeting that cannot meet anywhere else. They recognize cultural work as one of the few endeavors where it is possible to forge textual and ideological critiques of White supremacy and its extensive effects on Black people, but also as a site where Black people can take stock of the degree to which they have internalized elements of the poisonous pathologies used to press them. In a society that suppresses organic oral traditions, commodifies culture, co-opts grassroots creativity, and shrinks institutions open to Black voices and interests, this is a serious challenge. Black literature is a crucial forum for devising, airing, and evaluating these terms. (7)

---

[1] Richard Schur (2000, 2004) has detailed how Morrison's nonfiction and fiction developed alongside and in dialogue with the Critical Race Theory movement: Morrison edited *Race-ing Justice, En-gendering Power* (1992) and coedited, with Claudia Brodksy Lacour, *Birth of a Nation'hood; Gaze, Script, and Spectacle in the O.J. Simpson Case* (1997), which feature Morrison's own thoughts on contemporary legal issues along with those of Critical Race Theorists such as Kimberlé Williams Crenshaw and Patricia Williams. This essay recognizes that Morrison published *The Bluest Eye* several years before the movement began and proposes a more expansive understanding of intersectionality.

The Bluest Eye creates such a public forum that is not confined by the conservative assumptions of the legal system. As Blake argues, fiction and art can imagine spaces of justice outside the courtroom, and this very imagining can draw on the traditions of Black art. Morrison's revelation of intersectionality situates interpersonal encounters within a broader framework of social hierarchies. Her braided narrative channels the aesthetics of blues and gospel music to propose a collective mode of accountability and acknowledgment.

INTERSECTIONALITY AS SIGHT

Intersectionality's recent[2] history might begin in 1977 when the Combahee River Collective, a radical group of Black feminist lesbians in Boston, dedicated themselves to "struggling against racial, sexual, heterosexual, and class oppression, and see as our particular task the development of integrated analysis and practice based upon the fact that the major systems of oppression are interlocking" (9). The Collective's organizers understood that an analysis of the way systems of power intersect must accompany a lived practice. This understanding of "interlocking" oppressions also informs the "Theory in the Flesh" at the core of the *Bridge* anthology. As Moraga explains in her preface to the fourth edition, this theory "makes sense of the seeming paradoxes of our lives; that complex confluence of identities—race, class, gender, sexuality—systemic to women of color oppression *and* liberation" (xix). Like the Combahee River Collective, the contributors to *Bridge* saw their lived experiences not only as evidence of vulnerability, but also as essential sources of knowledge that would lead to liberation. These ideas began to enter academia through the anthology *All the Women Are White, All the Blacks are Men, But Some of Us Are Brave* (1981), edited by Gloria T. Hull, Patricia Bell Scott, and Barbara Smith, a founding member of the Combahee River Collective. However, the term we use today to describe this understanding that one's experience is forged at what Moraga calls "the confluence of identities" comes from Crenshaw, who proposed the term "intersectionality" in 1989 to address a gap in antidiscrimination law.

While the radical women of color and Crenshaw have a lot in common, their visions differ in ways that correlate with Morrison's figures of sight and sound. *Bridge*'s contributors seek "nothing short of a revolution" (xliv), while Crenshaw keeps the legal sphere as her horizon. The total overhaul of social and political relations imagined in *Bridge* requires a choral telling. Moraga and Anzaldúa assert that the anthology's strength depends on the fact that "the works combined reflect a diversity of perspectives, linguistic styles and cultural tongues" (xlv). The radical women of color who contributed to *Bridge* used their writing, theorizing, and storytelling to give voice to experiences

---

[2]Importantly, the radical feminists, Black academics, and Crenshaw all situate themselves within a deeper history that acknowledges that enslaved women first experienced and articulated its nuances of intersectionality. In her foreword to the original edition of *Bridge*, Toni Cade Bambara evokes the images of the Middle Passage, chattel slavery, and Dr. King's civil rights rhetoric to describe the revolutionary work of the anthology: "*Bridge* lays down the planks to cross over onto a new place where stooped labor cramped quartered down pressed and caged up combatants can straighten the spine and expand the lungs and make the vision manifest" (xxx). The Combahee River Collective named themselves in honor of Harriett Tubman, one of these freedom combatants, who designed and led a military action that freed over 750 people from slavery. Further, Crenshaw cites and the *Brave* anthology includes Sojourner Truth's 1851 speech "Ain't I a Woman." Truth referenced her own strengths during slavery not only to argue that women are strong enough to vote, but also to argue that Black women ought to be extended that right as well.

left at the margins of other streams of thought and social organizing. In her introduction to the "Theory in the Flesh" Moraga explains,

> Here, we attempt to bridge the contradictions in our experience:
> We are the colored in a white feminist movement.
> We are the feminists among the people of our culture.
> We are often the lesbians among the straight.
> We do this bridging by naming our selves and by telling our stories in our own words. (19)

Like Morrison, who makes power from speaking "an unspeakable thing," *Bridge*'s contributors find words, names, and theories that can transform their own "flesh and blood experiences" into a healing vision (19). For these activist artists, narrating their lived contradictions builds bridges across difference. As a legal scholar, Crenshaw begins her analyses in the legal sphere and works her way out toward social practice. Crenshaw concentrates on ameliorating a legal blindless toward those whose grievances fall between the lines of protected classes. This essay will focus first on Crenshaw's concept because her emphasis on vulnerability seems to be the theme on which Morrison begins. Then, I'll turn to the radical women of color's radical vision because *The Bluest Eye*'s form resonates with their interest in the transformative potential of intersectional thinking and organizing.

Crenshaw sees how the "single-axis framework" of antidiscrimination law fails those whose experiences fall between protected classes associated with single identity categories ("Demarginalizing the Intersection" 139). In Crenshaw's initial example of *DeGraffenreid v. General Motors* (1976), five Black women attempted to sue General Motors for discriminatory hiring practices, but because General Motors hired white women, the court found no evidence of sex-based discrimination and encouraged the plaintiffs to join a contemporaneous suit brought by Black male mechanical workers. As Crenshaw explains,

> Discrimination, like traffic through an intersection, may flow in one direction, and it may flow in another. If an accident happens in an intersection, it can be caused by cars traveling from any number of directions and, sometimes, from all of them. Similarly, if a Black woman is harmed because she is in the intersection, her injury could result from sex discrimination or race discrimination. (149)

The analogy of the traffic accident emphasizes that, for Crenshaw, intersectionality is about seeing the multifaceted ways in which Black women can be injured, both legally and physically. Crenshaw demonstrates how the same processes of marginalization can play out "in shaping structural, political, and representational aspects of violence against women of color" ("Mapping the Margins," 358). For instance, structurally, "women burdened by poverty, child care responsibilities, and lack of job skills" may find it more difficult to escape domestic violence (358); politically, women from communities whose men have been historically maligned as sexually deviant may be less likely to speak out about domestic abuse; and, representationally, women willing to share their experiences may be "rhetorically disempowered in part because [they fall] between dominant interpretations of feminism and anti-racism" (376). Although Crenshaw grounds her analysis in the experience of Black women, she makes clear that multiple axes of oppression—not only race and gender, but also class, sexuality, citizen status, and so on—might converge, rendering the person standing at that juncture increasingly vulnerable to harm and injury. Intersectionality, then, is a theoretical frame that makes visible the way subordination and violence become concentrated on and compounded for society's most vulnerable members.

Morrison frames the inability to see those at the intersection as a perceptual problem in Pecola's encounter with Mr. Yacobowski, the owner of the "Fresh Veg. Meat and Sundries Store" (*Bluest Eye* 48). Morrison describes Mr. Yacobowski's failure to see Pecola, not as a conscious choice or cognitive choice, but a function of his eyes:

> Somewhere between retina and object, between vision and view, his eyes draw back, hesitate, and hover. At some fixed point in time and space he senses that he need not waste the effort of a glance. He does not see [Pecola], because for him there is nothing to see. How can a fifty-two-year-old white immigrant store-keeper with the taste of potatoes in his mouth, his mind honed on the doe-eyed Virgin Mary, his sensibilities blunted by permanent awareness of loss, *see* a little black girl? (48, emphasis in original)

Mr. Yacobowski's eyes enact his revulsion almost without his awareness. While Mr. Yacobowski takes her request for candies, he "senses," the way he might smell or taste, that "the effort of a glance" would be wasted in this transaction. The narrator's rhetorical question makes clear that it is Mr. Yacobowski's social position as a white adult store owner that renders Pecola, at the intersection of her age ("little"), race ("black"), and gender ("girl"), invisible to him. Morrison criticizes this "total absence of human recognition" that works to negate "the flux and anticipation" of a child waiting to be seen (49).

Although Mr. Yacobowski fails to "see" Pecola, Morrison does not fail to "see" him. Morrison gives this two-page character his own background and history of struggle. By giving the shopkeeper a Slavic, possibly Polish, surname,[3] Morrison references a history of racial formation that initially excluded some Eastern Europeans from the category of whiteness.[4] As a Catholic, he may have immigrated to the states to escape persecution abroad and found further prejudice here. Morrison does not reduce this character to a flat white villain, but rather gives him his own history of suffering that sits at the intersection of immigration status and religion. But Mr. Yacobowski's own "awareness of loss" does not build a bridge to Pecola. Instead, it further dulls his "sensibilities," foreclosing the possibility of recognizing the child.

For Morrison, the inability to recognize those at the intersection manifests as physical as well as ocular violence, a truth she reveals most devastatingly, perhaps, through the scenes of rape: what Morrison calls "Cholly's 'rape' by the whitemen" and the "almost-rape" of Darlene that set the stage for the incestuous rapes that Pecola endures (215). After Aunt Jimmy's funeral, white hunters interrupt Cholly's sexual initiation with Darlene, his willing partner. The two teens had just transitioned from foraging the not-quite-ripe muscadine to the joys of discovering each other's bodies. In the novel's "Afterword," Morrison categorizes the white hunters' perverted command to "get on wid it" as rape and positions Cholly as its victim (215). In the piercing gaze of the whiteman's flashlight, Cholly's "body remained paralyzed," and, even when he attempts

---

[3] My colleague, linguist Ewa Czaykowska-Higgins, explains that the "owski" ending is Polish, but the beginning "Yac" looks more like a "transliteration from Russian or Ukrainian by someone who is an English speaker" because "Y" never appears at the beginning of a word in Polish spelling, and the "c" "would be pronounced as a 'ts' sequence."
[4] The surname of Claudia's "next-door friend" Rosemary Villanucci makes a similar connection to the history of Italian assimilation.

to obey the whiteman's demand, he moves "with a violence born of total helplessness" (148). While Cholly can only "simulate what had gone on before" by miming the sexual act, Morrison describes the whitemen's phallic tools as penetrating his body: "The flashlight wormed its way into his guts and turned the sweet taste of muscadine into rotten fetid bile" (148). Cholly's emasculation registers on multiple levels: he cannot continue making love, convert the act to rape, or protect his partner. Instead, he becomes what Morrison describes as a "feminized" victim of white supremacy (215).

But Morrison not only exposes the sexual nuances of racial oppression, but she also reveals the intersectional elements of this violence through Cholly's thoughts toward Darlene. Although Cholly cannot violate her with the whitemen watching, "he almost wished he could do it—hard, long, and painfully, he hated her so much" (148). Blake analyzes this scene to introduce her concept of "intimate, intraracial antagonisms," which captures the way that "the fierce imposition of White supremacy positions Black people as witness to and symbols of each other's degradation" (2). The symbolic weight of the whitemen's flashlight turns Cholly's muscadine-sweet sexual curiosity into a bile-bitter hatred that motivates Cholly to inflict his own pain onto his once-willing partner. The intersection of racism and sexism subjects Darlene to the same violent flashlight beam that violated Cholly and to the aggression it spawned inside him. This misogynist violence born of racist hate shapes many of Cholly's subsequent sexual acts even outside the penetrating beam of the whitemen's flashlight.

The final scene of Cholly's section, which describes one of the times he raped his daughter, refers to the hatred, violence, and even tenderness of this initial experience with Darlene. Cholly's desire for Pecola begins not with the image of his wife in his daughter's form but with his "revulsion" to her "young, helpless, hopeless presence," which he interprets as a condemnation of his own "guilt and impotence" (161). Cholly first felt this hatred for Darlene, "the one who bore witness to his failure, his impotence. The one whom he had not been able to protect, to spare, to cover from the round moon glow of the flashlight" (151). In Cholly's mind, Darlene and Pecola, both Black girls, come to represent his masculine failure to protect and to provide. White supremacy forged the sexual threat to Darlene, Pecola's wish for whiteness that Cholly must have sensed if not known, and his own inability to measure up on these rigged scales of race and gender. The narrator poses the rhetorical questions that taunt Cholly: "What could he do for her—ever? What give her? What say to her? What could a burned-out black man say to the hunched back of his eleven-year-old daughter?" (161). These questions echo, in a different key, that of Mr. Yacobowski: "How can a fifty-two-year-old white immigrant store-keeper ... *see* a little black girl?" (48, emphasis in original). While the immigrant, assimilated as white, cannot recognize the child as human, the father, targeted as Black, sees only a reflection of his failures. The novel thus far has shown us that even if Cholly were not often drunk and unemployed, he could not give Pecola the blue eyes she wants just as he could not resist the perverted whitemen who assaulted him and Darlene. In the absence of a conceptual framework that would allow Cholly to "consider directing his hatred toward the hunters" (150), he turns his hatred on Black girls, so when he sees the foot-scratching echo of his wife in Pecola's gesture, his "tenderness" manifests as violence (162). The single act of racist hate captured in a flashlight's beam perverts Cholly's experience of sex, and the related structure of white supremacy makes it difficult for him to provide the kind of protection and life for Pecola that he himself aspires to. At the intersection of race, gender, class, and age, Pecola bears the compounded violence of Cholly's frustration.

Importantly, as Blake explains, Morrison interposes that instance of an "intimate, intraracial antagonism" against a scene that celebrates the Black community and the strong women at its core: Aunt Jimmy's funeral. For Blake, this juxtaposition makes it possible for Morrison to resist both narrow narratives of normativity associated with respectability politics and discourses that pathologize Black relationships. Instead, Blake argues that these recurring scenes of "intimate, intraracial antagonisms" in Black literature "fracture the boundaries that reinforce the hegemony of the traditional nuclear family (normativity) or its incestuous opposite (pathology)" (6). Such engagement with "portrayals of intimate antagonisms, in all their complexity and discomfort," Blake continues, "[is] key to an adequate reassessment of Black literature's life-affirming possibilities. Each fracture and fissure creates within these fictional texts a more capacious notion of freedom than before" (12). As I understand Blake's analysis, liberation in *The Bluest Eye* does not only entail equal protection from violence, but also demands the recognition and care that Cholly denies Darlene and that was denied him as a child and teen.

INTERSECTIONALITY AS FORM

Morrison makes this argument not only through juxtaposed scenes but also through the narrative structure of her novel. Just as Morrison interposes the rape of Cholly and Darlene against the backdrop of the Black matriarch's funeral, she sets the stories of Claudia, Frieda, and Pecola side by side with those of Pauline, Cholly, and other members of the community like Geraldine and Elihue Micah Whitcomb, also known as Soaphead Church. Such a structure not only makes visible the intersectional pathways of violence but also invites an inquiry into the relationship among the stories. Morrison does not center the novel on any one target of white supremacy, but rather moves between narrators and among characters to reveal different manifestations of power and different strategies of resistance. Concerned that concentrating "the weight of the novel's inquiry on so delicate and vulnerable a character [as Pecola] would smash her and lead readers into the comfort of pitying her rather than into an interrogation of themselves for the smashing," Morrison decided to "break the narrative into parts that had to be reassembled by the reader" (211). While Morrison assesses this technique as a failed strategy—"many readers remain touched but not moved" (211)—I argue that the formal structure she developed for *The Bluest Eye* helps to shape a subtype of the novel that I call the braided narrative, which can push readers toward the sort of self-interrogation that Morrison envisions. I have described the braided narrative as a genre where "different narrators tell distinct stories that twine together to form a single novel ... braided narratives afford writers a set of strategies that help train readers to hold multiple, often incommensurate, subjectivities in our minds simultaneously, pushing us to embrace new channels of responsibility that recognize many distinct subjects" (Bancroft 263).

The Bluest Eye can be considered a braided narrative because Morrison twists together three types of narrative threads to form the novel. Each of these three narrative threads can be differentiated using the classical understanding of narrative as a story represented in discourse. First, Morrison channels the voice of mid-century basal readers to tell the simple story of Jane's search for a friend, a story she repeats three times in the preface and a fourth time in fragments as the titles of her omniscient sections. Second, Morrison switches to character–narrator Claudia MacTeer for a second preface, the opening chapter of each of the novel's four seasonal parts, and the novel's final paragraphs (212). Wavering between the perspective of a reflective adult and innocent child, Claudia narrates a series of memories from her ninth year in an effort to explain the "how" of Pecola's violation. Third, in each of the novel's four seasons, Morrison follows Claudia with one or more third-person stories that focalize the experience of different members of the community (the Breedlove family; the three prostitutes Marie, China, and Poland; and "the sugar-brown Mobile girls" like Geraldine, Pauline Williams, Cholly Breedlove, and Elihue Micah Whitcomb; 82). This third thread itself comprises distinct stories each of which has a different protagonist and narrative progression, but I subordinate them under the third thread because they share the same third-person narrator (although Pauline's section has italicized first-person segments). Morrison disrupts this pattern most significantly in "Summer," the novel's final season, which replaces the third-person section with a dialogue between Pecola and her imagined friend and allows Claudia's voice to close the novel rather than that of the third-person narrator.[5]

Through this formal braiding, Morrison moves beyond intersectionality as lens that makes visible compounded injury to intersectionality as sound, a collective speaking or singing that builds strength from the difference among the voices. To my mind, this difference sounds first in the ethical claims that the various narratives pose. Each of these multiple narratives places an ethical claim on readers, as Adam Zachary Newton says all narratives do. Like a human face, narratives demand recognition. Each of these narrative threads creates different "ethical situations," a four-part taxonomy that James Phelan has developed to analyze ethics in narrative. In Morrison's novel, some of these ethical claims and situations take on a legal tone even as no one gets to be heard in court. Morrison's rendition of the Dick and Jane primers draws attention to the way these pedagogical stories not only teach children to read words and race but also interpellate the children who look like the watercolor white family as citizens. As Debra T. Werrlein explains, "The Elson-Gray curriculum surrounding Dick and Jane ... plac[es] responsibility for the nation's future prosperity and security squarely on the shoulders of middle-class children" (57). She cites the introduction of one of these Basic Readers: "Come with me, your book-comrade, I can carry you into the homes of some brave and true American boys and girls. They will tell you how you too, may become a helpful American citizen" (57). While Morrison's source material invites certain young readers to recognize their civic responsibilities, Morrison's novel compels her "presumably adult reader[s]" to interrogate the relationship between this constructed ideal and the nuanced lives of Morrison's Black characters (Morrison 214).

Claudia's preface moves the legal connection closer to the courtroom by disclosing the novel's central crime, incestual rape, and positioning herself as a potentially culpable witness. Even when age reveals her innocence, her interest still turns on questions of culpability: Claudia writes, "Our guilt was relieved only by fights and mutual accusations about who was to blame" (5). On Phelan's first level of ethical situations, that of "characters within the storyworld," Cholly, a clear offender, commits a reprehensible wrong (23). On the second level of "the narrator in relation to the telling, to the told, and to the audience," a child "underreports" the crime and "misinterprets" her own

---

[5]While some critics such as Carl D. Malmgren interpret this shift as evidence that Claudia is the third-person narrator, I don't find that argument very compelling. The third-person narrator knows very intimate details about each protagonist's life that Claudia could not possibly have known such as Geraldine's wish that "the necessary but private parts of the body [were] in some more convenient place—like the armpit, for example, or the palm of the hand" (84), the colors Pauline associates with good sex, Cholly's love for Blue, or the contents of Elihue Micah Wihitcomb's letter to God.

responsibility for it.[6] In the context of the contemporary classroom, a fictional child's disclosure of rape might remind readers of the mandatory reporting laws that obligate teachers to report such cases of suspected abuse. While these laws seek to help children like Pecola, they may contribute to the sort of silence that Morrison countered by creating an environment in which children fear the legal consequences for their parents if they share such information. On the third level, "that of the implied author in relation to the telling, the told, and the authorial audience," the implied Morrison speaks "an unspeakable thing," which she knew would shock her audience (Morrison 214). Wagner-Martin reports of the actual audience, "Among Morrison's 1970s readership—regardless of their skin color—*The Bluest Eye* was considered a sensational and sensationalized novel" (11). On the fourth level of "the flesh-and-blood reader in relation to the set of values, beliefs, and locations operating in situations 1–3," we encounter as many responses as there are readers (Phelan 23). Some students might connect with Claudia because of their awareness of a wrong they cannot control, others might share the shock of the 1970s audience, others might feel themselves the subject of Claudia's "back fence" gossip, and still others might respond as adults, possible caregivers in Claudia's life, who would comfort her and explain that it is not her fault (212). Although Phelan does not share Newton's language of claims, each of these potential responses stands as a type of recognition—even the refusal to read or the decision to dismiss the novel register on a scale with various forms of recognition on one side and negation on the other.

While the US justice system assumes the sort of singularity (single victim, single perpetrator, single crime) that we might identify in Claudia's opening, Morrison's novel troubles such a singular focus. Unlike a trial that would debate and dispute these facts, *The Bluest Eye* never questions their veracity. Morrison never offers oppositional stories or counter-stories, one of Critical Race Theory's solutions to this singular focus of the law that would tell the story from another perspective. Instead, the third-person narrative thread introduces other plaintiffs, asserts different wrongs, and accuses additional people. This strategy is perhaps most clear in "Mother," the third-person section detailing Pauline's coming-of-age, which Morrison opens as if it were a legal case: she writes, "The easiest thing to do would be to build a case out of her foot" (110). Given what we know about Pecola's violation, this first sentence might position Pauline as a defendant, a negligent mother needing to prove her innocence (110). The italicized first-person statements that Morrison intersperses throughout might shore up this interpretation but might also situate Pauline as a witness in Cholly's trial.

As "Mother" progresses, however, her status as defendant or witness becomes increasingly nuanced with her experiences as a victim. The first sentence suggests that Pauline herself might blame her hardships on her injured foot, but the third-person narrator makes clear that her experience is forged at the intersection of her (dis)ability, race, class, gender, and even migrant status. The narrator explains how, after moving north with Cholly, the "cocoon of her family's spinning" gets replaced with a deep loneliness caused by the "goading glances and private snickers" of the other Black women she meets in Lorain (111, 118). In her own words, Pauline testifies to how love ("all of them colors was in me" [115]) and sexual pleasure ("laughing between my legs" [131]) gives way to abuse ("Cholly commenced to getting meaner and meaner" [118]) and rape ("most times

---

[6]Phelan also identifies three axes of reliability that correlate to the functions of a narrator: reporting, reading/interpreting, and regarding/evaluating. Unreliable narrators can either under-function or misfunction on any one of these axes. For more, see pages 50–3 in *Living to Tell about It: A Rhetoric and Ethics of Character Narration*.

he's thrashing away inside me before I'm woke" [131]). While none of these experiences justifies the way she treats her children, they do position Pauline as an aggrieved party in her own right. Some of these injuries are grievable in a court of law, such as the white woman's refusal to pay Pauline's wages unless she leaves Cholly, but others manifest on a communal level like the social refusal of the Black women. This section allows Pauline to make her claim for recognition in her own voice. Unlike Claudia's first-person account, Pauline's italicized confessions adopt the second person. Pauline implores her unspecified audience to understand what it was like "when I first seed Cholly, *I want you to know* it was like all the bits of color from that time down home" (115, emphasis added). Pauline's first words about Cholly do not condemn him as a rapist but frame him in a positive light that connects him to the colors and pleasures of her childhood. While Pauline does censure Cholly, the shape of the story positions blame elsewhere as well: on the patronizing white women, on the cold reception of the Black community, and on her "education in the movies" (122). "Mother" does not deny Cholly's guilt but adds additional wrongs and implicates additional people.

Morrison's strategy of posing layered claims continues in "Father," the third-person section that focuses on Cholly's youth. By narrating Cholly's backstory sympathetically, Morrison invites readers to recognize Cholly's claim even as we remain committed to the condemnation of the crimes he commits. Cholly's mother abandons him as an infant "on a junk heap by the railroad," and when, fourteen years later, he tracks down the person he believes to be his father, the man rejects him cruelly, saying "get the fuck outta my face!" (132, 156). This repeated parental rejection causes Cholly to regress to infancy: the fourteen-year-old "soiled himself like a baby" (157). When the teenager collects himself to escape the public street, he crouches under a pier: "He remained knotted there in fetal position, paralyzed, his fists covering his eyes, for a long time. No sound, no sight, only darkness and heat and the press of his knuckles on his eyelids. He even forgot his messed-up trousers" (157). In the warm, womb-like space under the pier, Cholly curls into himself with the pre-birth helplessness of a fetus. These scenes cast Cholly as a child like Claudia or Pecola who crave adult attention, acknowledgment, and care. These scenes frame Cholly as a victim before he becomes the aggressor. Morrison uses the braided narrative to make these claims for Cholly without negating the claim that Claudia makes on Pecola's behalf. As Donald Gibson writes, "Morrison allows Cholly to be something other than simply evil ... Morrison does not tell us what Cholly does to Pecola is all right; rather she says that what happens is very complicated, and that though Cholly is not without blame for what happens to Pecola, he is no less a victim than she" (27). By twining together multiple narrative threads, Morrison layers competing claims that all must be acknowledged and cannot be simply resolved.

Differing claims arise in "Cat" as well, which illustrates further cruelty to Pecola while at the same time offering explanation but not excuses for the perpetrators. While the "Cat" climaxes with another poignant negation of Pecola (Geraldine curses her to leave their house and Pecola sees "Jesus looking down at her with sad and unsurprised eyes" [92]), that is not the story's only ethical dilemma. Morrison also invites ethical concern for the cat, who has been hurled against the window, Junior, the boy who harmed it, and Geraldine, who represents a whole class of "thin brown girls" who choose to disappear into a type (81). As others have observed, the violence that the black, blue-eyed cat endures portends Pecola's fate, and this omen gains strength from the very recognition that the cat's sentient status ought to protect it from being swung by its leg into a window. But this story, like the novel in general, is not only about "how" the violence was done, but also "why" (6). Junior, the third-person narrator takes care to explain, became a bully because he "discovered the difference in his mother's behavior to himself and the cat" and because she had indoctrinated him with a sense of a rigid hierarchy within the Black community (87). Geraldine denies Junior the love that could be the foundation of kindness and instead equips him with a supercilious sense of hate, so it is an easy slide between vengeful violence toward the cat and cruel harassment of Pecola.

While working backward from the story's climax makes it seem that Geraldine, the cold mother, is ultimately responsible, the third-person narrator spends the first half of the story in a social voice explaining her type of woman. This exposition simultaneously criticizes the careful cultivation that constructs this identity and mourns the loss of the "funkiness of passion, the funkiness of nature, the funkiness of the wide range of human emotions" that such a performance requires (83). Even as the narrator's tone chastises such a woman for the punishing lengths she goes through to maintain her image, Morrison builds a sense of pity for the sort of woman who considers her husband an "intruder" and never experiences an orgasm, except for when "her napkin slipped free of her sanitary belt" (85). The behaviors Morrison associates with this type demonstrate a sort of self-hatred that is not the same as, but not completely separate from, the self-loathing that causes Pecola's wish for blue eyes. Even as Morrison implicates Geraldine and Junior in "smashing" Pecola, she gives them a narrative that makes space for their own claims.

Just as the third-person narrator spends so much time with Geraldine in "Cat," the novel's second season, the third-person voice dwells with Elihue Micah Whitcomb in "Dog" in its penultimate. Better known as Soaphead Church, this "cinnamon-eyed West Indian" shares with Geraldine an internalized rejection of blackness (167). Elihue, like the other members of his family, cultivated an "anglophilia" that prized their white ancestry (168). Geraldine suppresses her own sexuality to achieve the constructed standard of "colored people" (87), and Elihue loses his own Beatrice because of his commitment to melancholy. However, unlike Geraldine who rejects Pecola as one of the "fly"-like little girls she had seen "all of her life" (91) and unlike Mr. Yacobowski who fails to see her, Elihue recognizes the child's desire for blue eyes. As Gurleen Grewal points out, "servile to white supremacist values, [Elihue] finds it perfectly understandable that Pecola should want blue eyes" (123). When Pecola voices her nervous request, "a surge of love and understanding swept through him, but it was quickly replaced by anger. Anger that he was powerless to help her ... For the first time he honestly wished he could work miracles" (174). Elihue responds differently to Pecola than he does to the other little girls whom he molests and to the adult clients whom he simply appeases. Both the third-person narrator and Elihue himself in his letter to God characterize this response as love. While he chooses to fulfill Pecola's wish by tricking her to murder the dog, he is the only adult to hear her desire, and he satisfies it in a way that, like the marigolds, would have been convincing to a child. Elihue recognizes and even loves Pecola because of their shared sense of self-hatred.

INTERSECTIONALITY AS SOUND

Morrison proposes a figure for this braided narrative structure through the music that wafts through her pages: the blues songs sung by Mrs. MacTeer and Poland and Ivy's Gospel solo that captivates Pauline. Like the aesthetic tradition of the Sorrow Songs, singing in *The Bluest Eye* simultaneously testifies to suffering and acts as a release of pain. As Frederick Douglass explains in his *Narrative*,

"The songs of the slave represent the sorrows of his heart; and he is relieved by them, only as an aching heart is relieved by its tears" (9). Claudia describes a similar power in her mother's voice: "Misery colored by the greens and blues in my mother's voice took all of the grief out of the words and left me with a conviction that pain was not only endurable, it was sweet" (26). The nine-year-old understands that there is something about the sound that can both express and relieve grief. Morrison's prose is almost like the "greens and blues" of Mrs. MacTeer's songs. The author, like her character, gives voice to misery in a way that endows it with a melty-eyed beauty that makes it speakable, bearable, and powerful. Morrison channels this power of music through the braided narrative of *The Bluest Eye*. Just as music relies on different instruments, different notes, and different chords that can all be heard at the same time, the braided narrative depends on different experiences, different stories, and different ethical claims that overlap, harmonize, and even clash.[7]

The power of song might stem from the different kind of recognition it affords. The third-person narrator describes how Pauline finds recognition in gospel music and in "a woman named Ivy who seemed to hold in her mouth all of the sounds of Pauline's soul" (113). This sexual image moves away from the visual, from the challenge of "see[ing] a little black girl" as the narrator puts it in the case of Pecola (48), toward the aural, to the project of acknowledging, recognizing, and speaking "the dark sweetness that Pauline could not name" (113). This sort of recognition is not about sameness but relies on difference, harmony, and resonance. Ivy sings in the church chorus about Jesus Christ and salvation, but Pauline experiences a sexual awakening aroused by the "songs [that] caressed her" and made "her body tremble for redemption, salvation" (113). When "the Stranger" comes for Pauline, he is not the "Precious Lord" that Ivy sings to, but Cholly Breedlove, who whistles his own music, kisses Pauline's foot, and makes her laugh. In the same vein, Mrs. MacTeer's songs provide relief and comfort even though she is not, as her naïve daughter yearns to be, "grown without 'a thin di-i-ime to my name.' … [L]ook[ing] forward to the delicious time when 'my man' would leave" (26). For Mrs. MacTeer and Pauline, the power of music does not rely on sameness or identification, but rather depends on difference.

Morrison situates her young girls as the contented audience of songs even as they become the subject of her song—in both senses, the image of a mother holding her child in song or a woman holding another's pain in her voice figures Morrison's narrative project. As Cat Moses argues, "The narrative's structure follows a pattern common to traditional blues lyrics: a movement from an initial emphasis on loss to a concluding suggestion of resolution of grief through motion" (623). Moses notes that Morrison's movement among multiple voices channels the "Classic Blues" that features a soloist and accompanying instruments. Building on this interpretation, we can see how the various narrative threads create what Moses describes as "the blues chorus that mediates against

---

[7] Linda Dittmar recognizes the role music plays in Morrison's novel. Dittmar writes,

> Like a griot, preacher, or blues singer, Morrison uses inventories and variations to make her case. The richness of her language, organized as it is into infinitely expandable sequences, suggests a wealth of possibilities and an ungovernable verbal fecundity which belie the social desolation she depicts. Such regenerative writing is not about retrieving and explaining, as *The Bluest Eye*'s opening claims, but about saying as cure. (150)

However, Dittmar argues that the "formal devices partly deflect but never quite extinguish the wish for a plot-based judgement. It is this tension between the two [theme and form] that makes *The Bluest Eye* a problematic novel" (140). I argue that this tension and difference among the voices is precisely what constitutes Morrison's intersectional and ethical argument.

the buzzing voices that condemn Pecola" (633). The third-person stories each voice a different experience, they each stage a different opportunity to acknowledge Pecola, and they each harmonize with each other. Morrison braids together with Claudia's narrative thread, which Moses thinks of as the soloist amid accompaniment, and the Dick and Jane sequence.

This juxtaposition enacts a sort of intersectionality as sound that resonates more with the radical women of color who contributed to *Bridge* than with Crenshaw's legal definition. Even as Morrison reveals how intersecting lines of power render people vulnerable in different ways, she layers those experiences and finds power in the naming, speaking, and singing. Anzaldúa writes for *Bridge*'s collective of contributors when she says, "We wield a pen as a tool, a weapon, a means of survival, a magic wand that will attract power, that will draw self-love into our bodies" (161). Anzaldúa traces the way in which writing one's own narrative generates power over that experience that can resist the very forms of dominance that forged the shape of that story. In their coediting of the anthology, Anzaldúa and Moraga recognized a further power in setting those narratives, poems, essays, and artworks side by side where the differences in the contributors' experiences become the strength at *Bridge*'s core. More than a decade before *Bridge*'s publication in 1981, Morrison, in drafting *The Bluest Eye*, imagined a collection of stories that each focused on a different experience of suffering that somehow twine together to tell the story of a community. Intersectionality in this sense is not only an analytic that makes visible overlapping systems of oppression, but also a liberatory practice, an action that draws power from difference. As Anzaldúa writes, "Our vulnerability *can* be the source of our power—*if we use it*" (195; emphases in original). While Crenshaw's work focuses on the vulnerability, she hopes that intersectionality might also reveal the way that "the organized identity groups in which we find ourselves are in fact coalitions, or at least potential coalitions waiting to be formed" (377). In this concluding note, Crenshaw proposes that the recognition that one's experience is different because of race and gender (or another factor) ought not to divide traditional groupings but instead make them stronger.

While many critics read Morrison's fragmented structure as an indictment of the community for using Pecola as a scapegoat[8] and thus shattering her, looking at these stories for their own claims can highlight an accompanying imperative for care, concern, and love for Black life. Claudia puts it best in *Summer* when she imagines Pecola's baby:

> I thought about the baby that everybody wanted dead, and saw it very clearly. It was in a dark, wet place, its head covered with great O's of wool, the black face holding, like nickels, two clean black eyes, the flared nose, kissing-thick lips, and the living, breathing silk of black skin. No synthetic yellow bands suspended over marble-blue eyes, no pinched nose and bowline mouth. More strongly than my fondness for Pecola, I felt a need for someone to want the black baby to live—just to counteract the universal love of white baby dolls, Shirley Temples, and Maureen Peals. (190)

---

[8]This idea of individual petitions for recognition that accrue into a collective demand does not negate the central theme of scapegoating that Claudia articulates toward the novel's end and that many critics have examined (see Michael Awkward, Jerome Bump, Edward Friedman, Jennifer Gillan, and Chikwenye Okonjo Ogunyemi). As Claudia writes, "All of us—all who knew her—felt so wholesome after we cleaned ourselves on her" (205). Instead, these two interpretations sit side by side, juxtaposed against each other in the same way that the narrative threads brush up against each other, sometimes harmonizing and sometimes creating discord.

Against the current of the adult women's consensus at the novel's close that there "ought to be a law: two ugly people doubling up like that to make more ugly. Be better off in the ground," Claudia and her sister want to imagine the baby's life as desirable, livable, lovable (190). Claudia situates her "need for someone to want the black baby to live" within her narrative about white dolls. She imagines Pecola's child as lovable and touchable in a way that white dolls are not. In place of the doll's "bone-cold head" and fake flat hair, Claudia sees a cushion of thick curly wool (20). In place of the hard hands that scratch, Claudia can feel the soft and smooth aliveness of Black skin. In place of a mouth pursed like a weapon, Claudia describes kiss-inviting lips. This imagined child's nose even opens itself to the world in ways foreclosed by the scrunched up almost sneer of the white doll.

Across the narrative threads, this wish for Black life resonates with Cholly's own abandonment: like the gossiping women, Cholly's mother may have thought that he was "better off in the ground." Claudia's impulse to demand love for Black children speaks to Junior's need for loving attention from his own mother. For Claudia and her sister, the problem is the misalignment of "universal love," the acute awareness that the world prefers white plastic and the girls that those dolls represent to the real lives of Black babies (190). Claudia explains, "We did not dwell on the fact that the baby's father was Pecola's father too; the process of having a baby by any male was incomprehensible to us—at least she knew her father. We thought only of the overwhelming hatred for the unborn baby" (191). In their naivety about where babies come from, Claudia and Pecola overlook the individual crime—the father's act of incestuous rape—at the expense of the social wrong—the conceptual annihilation of Black children.

By *Summer*, we realize that the wrong Claudia announces in her preface is not the crime of incest but the loss of Black life. Through Claudia's narration, Morrison moves away from the common understanding of the law, as rules that protect rights and prevent wrongs by mandating what not to do, toward a sense of responsibility, the instinct to act, to care for, to love another. This transition is apparent in the ease with which the gossiping women frame their condemnation in ethical and legal terms of "ought" and "law" while Claudia positions her wish that the child should live in the realm of "our own magic," responsibility, and marigolds (5). Although they are not culpable for the crime they do not understand, the sisters take responsibility for its result. They sacrifice their bicycle savings in the hopes that they can "change the course of events and alter a human life" (191). This youthful impulse to care for another person even, and perhaps especially, when it is completely out of their control opens up another way of looking at the third-person stories. Perhaps, they not only offer evidence of complicity in the smashing or the phenomenon of scapegoating, but also stage opportunities for responsibility and care. We have seen these opportunities refused by Geraldine and Junior in "Cat" and by Cholly in "Father," but they are accepted by the three whores in "House" and, as we have seen, by Elihue in "Dog." Although the third-person narrator only allows that the prostitutes "didn't despise" Pecola, the terms of endearment they use to address her (Miss Marie's favorite foods) and the way they entertain her questions implies a deeper affection (51). While Claudia and Frieda never "initiate talk with grown-ups" (23), Morrison uses the same verb to describe Pecola's routine with the prostitutes: "Pecola always took the initiative with Marie" (52). Like Mrs. MacTeer's laughter and song, the prostitutes' revelry creates a warm space where Pecola feels comfortable enough to lead conversation and not try to become invisible as she does in her own home.

This dialectic of seeing and not seeing, of recognition and refusal culminates in Pecola's own voice in the novel's final season. Where we might expect a third-person story, Morrison inserts a dialogue between Pecola and the friend she has imagined for herself: a friend only she can see and the only friend who can see her. The topic of the girls' conversation focuses on sight, but Morrison's dialogue pushes readers to imagine sound. The discordant call and response of different voices connects to the conflicting interpretations at stake in their exchange. While readers might attribute Pecola's psychic break to the father's violation, Pecola's imaginary friend asserts that she appeared "right after" Pecola got her blue eyes (196). While both interpretations work simultaneously, the order of the novel's threads shores up the imaginary friend's alternative interpretation; "Friend" follows "Dog" not "Father." Further, Pecola confesses that "every time I look at somebody, they look off" (195), which the friend explains as jealousy for her eyes, but readers interpret as shame or pity for Pecola. This painful conversation crystallizes the dual tension in the novel: it both centers on the "unspeakable" wrong that Pecola has endured and the politics of sight, the potential of relationships, the need for another voice. The injuries in this latter category cannot be arbitrated in a courtroom but must be dealt with in community. The only way Pecola can narrate her own story is by fracturing her psyche and creating multiple voices. Likewise, Morrison chooses, as she puts it, to "break the narrative into parts," into multiple narratives that she braids together to both condemn the crime and to call for recognition for all of the multiple subjectivities she narrates.

The recognition figured by the various notes of blues and gospel music is the truer chord sounded by *The Bluest Eye*. The novel testifies to the truth of intersectionality—that certain individuals are rendered more vulnerable than others by the confluences of power. The same social mechanisms that make Pecola invisible to the immigrant shopkeeper facilitate the incestuous violence that breaks her. As Claudia understands, the refusal enacted by the community compounds these injuries. Juxtaposed with this critical social reflection, however, the novel offers layered invitations for recognition and demands that Black life be valued. The novel's tragedy occurs in all the scenes where these demands go unmet from the "total absence of human recognition" at a candy shop to "the hatred mixed with tenderness" on the kitchen floor (48, 163). But we can hear the refrain of hope in the acceptance of the invitation, a mother's song and laughter, friendly banter with adult Black women, and the children's wish for living and loved Black babies. The novel's braided structure is itself such an invitation for recognition. By moving between different narrative threads, Morrison demands a concern, care, and an acknowledgment for multiple characters, even those who have damaged others. In this way, *The Bluest Eye* "convenes a town meeting" as Blake puts it, where Morrison proposes a sort of justice that asks readers to both hold characters accountable for their role in the shattering of another and to see the ways in which those characters have been harmed. The braided narrative asks readers to hold multiple experiences of suffering in our mind simultaneously rather than canceling one out with a worse wrong. This countenancing of differing claims allows for a more holistic recognition that, like the women's songs, can create a healing vision and sound.

WORKS CITED

Awkward, Michael. "'The Evil of Fulfillment': Scapegoating and Narration in *The Bluest Eye*." *Inspiriting Influences: Tradition, Revision, and Afro-American Women's Novels*. Columbia UP, 1989.

Bancroft, Corinne. "The Braided Narrative." *Narrative*, vol. 26, no. 3, 2018, pp. 262–81.

Blake, Felice D. *Black Love, Black Hate: Intimate Antagonisms in African American Literature*. Ohio State UP, 2018.

"Combahee River Collective Statement: Black Feminist Organizing in the Seventies and Eighties." *Freedom Organizing Series*: #1. Kitchen Table: Women of Color P, 1986.

Crenshaw, Kimberlé Williams, et al. *Critical Race Theory: The Key Writings that Formed the Movement*. New P, 1995.

Crenshaw, Kimberlé. "Mapping the Margins: Intersectionality, Identity Politics, and Violence against Women of Color." *Critical Race Theory: The Key Writings that Formed the Movement*, edited by K. Crenshaw et al., New P, 1995, pp. 357–83.

Crenshaw, Kimberlé. "Demarginalizing the Intersection of Race and Sex: A Black Feminist Critique of Antidiscrimination Doctrine, Feminist Theory and Antiracist Politics," *University of Chicago Legal Forum*, vol. 1989, no. 1, pp. 139–67.

Dittmar, Linda. "'Will the Circle Be Unbroken?' The Politics of Form in *The Bluest Eye*." *Novel: A Forum on Fiction*, vol. 23, no. 2, 1990, pp. 137–55.

Douglass, Frederick. *Narrative of the Life of Frederick Douglass, An American Slave*. The Anti-Slavery Office. 1945. Penguin, 1982.

Gibson, Donald B. "Text and Countertext in Toni Morrison's *The Bluest Eye*." *LIT: Literature Interpretation Theory*, vol. 1, no. 1–2, Dec. 1989, pp. 19–32.

Grewal, Gurleen. "'Laundering the Head of Whitewash': Mimicry and Resistance in *The Bluest Eye*." *Approaches to Teaching the Novels of Toni Morrison*, edited by Nellie Y. McKay and Kathryn Earle, Modern Language Association of America, 1997, pp. 118–26.

Hull, Gloria T., et al. *All the Women Are White, All the Blacks Are Men, But Some of Us Are Brave*. Feminist P, 1981.

Moraga, Cherríe, and Gloria Anzaldúa, editors. *This Bridge Called My Back: Writings by Radical Women of Color*. Fourth Edition. State U of New York P, 2015.

Morrison, Toni, editor. *Burn This Book: Notes on Literature and Engagement*. HarperCollins, 2012.

Morrison, Toni. *The Bluest Eye*. Plume, 1970.

Moses, Cat. "The Blues Aesthetic in Toni Morrison's *The Bluest Eye*." *African American Review*, vol. 33, no. 4, 1999, pp. 623–37.

Newton, Adam Z. *Narrative Ethics*. Harvard UP, 1995.

Phelan, James. *Living to Tell about It: A Rhetoric and Ethics of Character Narration*. Cornell UP, 2005.

Schur, Richard. "Locating 'Paradise' in the Post-Civil Rights Era: Toni Morrison and Critical Race Theory." *Contemporary Literature*, vol. 45, no. 2, 2004, pp. 276–99.

Schur, Richard. "The Subject of Law: Toni Morrison, Critical Race Theory and the Narration of Cultural Criticism." *49th Parallel*, vol. 6, 2000. https://fortyninthparalleljournal.files.wordpress.com/2014/07/5-schur-the-subject-of-law.pdf. Accessed Aug. 8, 2022.

"Toni Morrison." *The Colbert Report*. Nov. 19, 2014. http://www.cc.com/video-clips/9yc4ry/the-colbert-report-toni-morrison. Accessed Aug. 8, 2022.

Wagner-Martin, Linda. *Toni Morrison: A Literary Life*. Palgrave Macmillan, 2015.

Werrlein, Debra T. "Not so Fast, Dick and Jane: Reimagining Childhood and Nation in *The Bluest Eye*. *MELUS*, vol. 30, no. 4, Winter 2005, pp. 53–72.

CHAPTER TWO

Re-Visiting the Unspeakable: Can Soaphead Church Be Redeemed?

TRUDIER HARRIS

Toni Morrison is adept at using a variety of strategies to get her readers to identify with characters who are themselves despicable or who commit antisocial, despicable, immoral, inhuman, or just disgusting acts. Readers can admit from the outset that Soaphead Church, a character in Toni Morrison's *The Bluest Eye* (1970) who lures young girls into his apartment and gives them candy while he fondles their private areas and nibbles on their budding breasts, is not exactly a person we would like to have living next door to us. There is no question that what he does is unacceptable and equally no question that, from whatever base of morality we define human behavior, we condemn his actions. Yet, there he is, a significant character in a significant novel that one of America's and indeed the world's best-known novelists has created. He is the person who welcomes the distraught Pecola, however briefly, understands her plight, and "gives" her the blue eyes for which she longs so fervently. He does not, in this instance, attempt to caress the visibly pregnant Pecola or in any other way act out his usual pattern of sexual transgression with an underage girl. He simply provides her with the pathway, the formula, the ritual through which she can acquire her blue eyes. He sends her on the successful journey for which no other adult or child in the novel has been willing to serve as guide. His self-confessed prior pedophilia is thus the backdrop against a fleeting moment of generosity that is simultaneously altruistic and selfish; Pecola is primed to believe that she will have blue eyes once Bob, the repulsive dog that belongs to Soaphead Church's landlady, eats and reacts to the poisoned meat that Soaphead provides Pecola to give to the dog as the necessary trial that she must undergo to reap the reward of blue eyes.

Misguided middle-class values, pedophilia, selfishness, and misanthropy combine to make Soaphead as repulsive as he believes the dog Bob to be. Yet, there, near the end of *The Bluest Eye*, he serves a crucial role and provides the pathway to a crucial gift. He functions for Morrison, and there is little in the text to suggest that she rejects him in that functioning. Indeed, with the creation of Soaphead Church, Morrison joins significant literary predecessors, such as Richard Wright, Gwendolyn Brooks, Ted Shine, and Pearl Cleage, in offering to their readership characters whose redeemability is questionable but who ultimately earn reader sympathy (Wright, *Native Son*).[1] And she extends the trajectory of sympathetic engagement throughout the corpus of her

---

[1] In *Native Son* (1940), Richard Wright uses a history of victimization and violence against Blacks, narrative point of view, comments on a biased legal system, and customs and sexual stereotypes surrounding Black males to elicit sympathy for Bigger Thomas as he is in the process of committing murder as well as during his trial following the murder. Gwendolyn

works. Consider her treatments of antisocial, questionable, or violent characters in *Sula* (1973), *Song of Solomon* (1977), *Beloved* (1987), *Home* (2012), and *God Help the Child* (2015). In each of these texts, characters commit acts that, without Morrison's expert guiding hand, readers could reject rather easily and thereby condemn the characters in the process. In each instance, however, Morrison succeeds in lifting her characters from judgment into some kind of understanding.

Antisocial behavior is the guiding force in *Sula*, where Shadrack, the shell-shocked First World War veteran, earns a reputation for exposing himself publicly as well as for instituting National Suicide Day, a move that many consider the mark of insanity. Yet, Shadrack is allowed the space he needs in his community, and, thought to be basically harmless, he is generally left to his own devices. By presenting his backstory in the First World War and by providing intimate details of his return to civilian life, Morrison gets readers to understand the complexity of Shadrack's anti-sociability and the private demons that guide his life. Even with the man-stealing Sula, Morrison enables readers not to dismiss her, but to understand—if they do not totally accept—her faults. After all, it would be difficult to dismiss completely the character in an eponymous text. So, Morrison guides readers through understanding Sula's lack of creative options in the small Ohio town in which she resides. It is other characters, including Sula's best friend Nel, who come up more lacking in reader sympathy than Sula. As the catalyst for many events in the novel and, arguably, as a faithful friend to Nel (which Nel recognizes at the end of the text), Sula survives the accidental killing of Chicken Little as well as the infidelity of her affair with Nel's husband Jude to emerge as a character who has explored life to the fullest, even when there were severe consequences for doing so. Most readers would find this an admirable trait.

Far less admirable are the actions of Bride in *God Help the Child*. Her bordering-on-criminal behavior when she joins in falsely accusing a kindergarten teacher, Sofia Huxley, of sexual abuse lingers throughout the text. However, even this despicable action gets mitigated against the backdrop of the pigmentocracy that has dominated the imaginations of people of color since their arrival in America and a system of value based on skin color was instated. Readers can conclude that her mother Sweetness's hatred of Bride's (Lula Ann's) jet-black skin positions Bride as a victim as much as a history of lynching positioned Black folks generally to be victims. In echoing Pauline Breedlove's reaction to the dark-skinned Pecola in *The Bluest Eye* but in taking it many degrees beyond Pauline's poisonous mothering, Morrison posits that Bride is so psychologically and emotionally crippled by her mother's rejection that she points the finger at Sofia in an effort to get her mother to hold her hand, to show even the slightest affection for her. When she finally responds to why she accused Sofia, she says: "So my mother would hold my hand! … And look at me with proud eyes, for once" (*Child* 153). To portray a child who is orphaned even in her mother's presence, who knows that the only way she can get her mother to "like" her, even temporarily, is to fabricate an accusation, certainly earns reader sympathy. The desire for attention is also understandable. Most important in not dismissing Bride's taking of fifteen years from Sofia's life by having her imprisoned is the

---

Brooks, in "The Mother," succeeds in getting readers to listen to and perhaps understand why a mother has had at least three abortions (7–8). In his short play, "Contribution," Ted Shine depicts a septuagenarian who poisons a sheriff in a small southern town during a Civil Rights demonstration and who garners reader sympathy for her action (365–89). To save a small western community and the future of its Black residents, Pearl Cleage allows a group of Black exodusters to poison a man who attempts to sell their property away from them in *Flyin' West*; there is no remorse and no censure expressed against these characters. What Morrison does with her characters in *The Bluest Eye*, therefore, has a history as well as a future in African American literature.

fact that readers get to see Sofia's point of view. She has undoubtedly been damaged, but, in her own narrative sections of the text, she thanks Bride for doing her "a favor" and "thanks" Bride for having enabled her to arrive at a place of peace, a "release" that has the potential for a future (*Child* 70, 77). Without the strategy of showing the impact of the violator upon the violated, readers might have been less inclined to understand Bride's point of view. We also sympathize with Bride—as well as with Sofia—when Sofia beats the crap out of Bride when she comes, with cash and the equivalent of trinkets, trying to repay Sofia for the fifteen lost years of her life. Most important to reader sympathy for Bride is the fact that she is pregnant at the end of the narrative; the possibility that she could become a better mother than her own mother portends a future that is more optimistic than the falsely accusing unloved child might have deserved.

More challenging in terms of gaining reader sympathy are Guitar's actions in *Song of Solomon* and Frank Money's actions in *Home*. Both characters commit murder, and Morrison provides extenuating circumstances in each instance. Echoing Richard Wright in *Native Son* (1940), Morrison uses history and the violent victimization of Black people as the backstories against which she extends sympathy to Guitar. As a member of *The Seven Days*, Guitar and his six partners undertake the task of killing a white person each time a white person murders a Black person. Morally, that is as reprehensible as the actions of the whites who kill Blacks. Yet Morrison succeeds in getting readers to understand why Guitar pursues this course by referencing the history of violence against Blacks. In urging readers not to dismiss Guitar, Morrison uses the strategy of summarizing instead of portraying the grisly or gruesome deaths in which Guitar and his partners are involved. Her strategy here is similar to the one she employs in the case of Cholly Breedlove's killing of three white men. By not showing the murders, essentially by letting the action occur offstage, so to speak, Morrison enables readers not to be thrust into the position of making a judgment from the immediacy of the crimes; they can only judge from a brief synopsis, a synopsis that carries much less force than brute confrontation. This is not to suggest that Morrison condones murder; it is to suggest, however, that evaluations of murder can be mitigated under the right circumstances if a writer wields the narrative force to achieve that purpose, as Morrison certainly does. It is also significant that Guitar is Milkman Dead's best friend. The contrast between Guitar, the man with a purpose—though a deadly one—and Milkman, who has stretched out his "carefree" and at times aimless existence for more than thirty years, arguably favors the purpose-driven choice. Even when Guitar mistakenly pursues Milkman with the intent of killing him because he believes Milkman has cheated him and The Seven Days out of the gold they hoped to use to fund their purpose, readers still do not, thanks to Morrison's skills at narrative, dismiss Guitar completely.[2]

I argue that Morrison is less successful in getting readers to ignore the murder that Frank Money commits during the Korean War. Perhaps it is because the narrative focuses less on Frank or perhaps because his character is less developed; whatever the reason, Frank earns less sympathy than Guitar—though readers certainly do not dismiss him completely. Of course, readers are shocked to learn that it is Frank—not the previously claimed soldier who released him from guard duty— who kills a young Korean girl as a result of her touching his crotch. War, readers might believe, as with Shadrack, is the villain here. But Morrison presents more than that. Here is a genuinely

---

[2]For other instances—before and after Morrison's *The Bluest Eye*—in which characters commit murderous actions in African American literature and still elicit reader sympathy, see Chesnutt, Griggs, Wright (*The Outsider*), Petry, Walker, Cleage, and Gaines. For an example of a text in which a character kills but does not garner sympathy for that act, see Phillips.

psychologically disturbed man who cannot confront his own complex sexual humanity when the child touches him. His recognition that the child arouses something in him that he did not believe existed leads him to shoot the girl instead of allowing whatever she stirred in him to reach action. He shoots her to save himself, so to speak, and that action is strikingly reprehensible. It certainly is not mitigated completely, but it is tempered by where Morrison places it in the text, by reader knowledge of Frank's having lost not one but his two best friends in the war, and by Frank's being on his way to Georgia to rescue his younger sister from a quack white doctor who experiments on unsuspecting young Black women. The large chunks of the narrative surrounding other portions of Frank's life squeeze the horrible action in Korea into far less page space than those other events. Also, the fact that Frank finally remembers the Black man that he and his sister had seen whites bury when they were children and that he digs up the body and reinters it in a place of respect is also a mitigating factor. It may not completely redeem Frank, but it forces readers to see the totality of his existence instead of judging him by a single action that might be attributed to the immorality and cruelty of war, during which even "good" men commit atrocious acts.

More clearcut in terms of judgment is Sethe's killing of Beloved. Many scholarly publications have argued for understanding how an enslaved mother could claim motherhood during the oppressive system of slavery and claim her children in spite of the slaveholders' desires to label them as property.[3] In Sethe's dramatic assertion of a movement from "thingafication" to human being, from property to flesh, readers immediately engage with her plight. Again, history is the backdrop against which Morrison succeeds in urging readers to reevaluate their senses of morality, to set judgment aside, and to engage fully with the dilemma in which this enslaved mother finds herself. Is it better for her to allow her children, especially her daughters, to be remanded to slavery, to be placed at the sexual whims of white slaveholders, or is it better to send them to a place of safety—or at least quiet—that dying ostensibly offers? In that rhetorical question is the stance that Morrison takes in making it impossible for her readers to judge Sethe without qualification. Readers who are mothers would certainly identify with Sethe's plight. Any reader who abhorred slavery would be drawn to a mother's refusal to allow the system to control her or her children's destiny. The complexity of the situation therefore gives way to a basic human act: a mother saves her child the best way she knows how. Again, the fact that the action takes place offstage, so to speak—though we do see the bloody consequences—is important in evaluating Sethe. Also, the fact that the narrative begins after the killing and continues for years beyond it is also significant in denying judgment. Morrison allows this mother the forgiveness of time, a forgiveness that Paul D is not able to sully with his rejection; indeed, his ultimate return to Sethe is another measure of the extent to which readers are not allowed to dismiss this long-suffering woman. Instead, Morrison urges them to understand her plight if they do not fully forgive her actions.

Morrison's other novels, therefore, help to provide context for viewing Soaphead Church in terms of his positioning in a literary tradition where characters commit atrocious acts and still retain sympathetic reader engagement. However, Soaphead, as noted, appears late in the novel and in only one significant scene. Before his appearance, Morrison is tasked with getting readers to follow along as she presents another despicable character, namely Cholly Breedlove. Cholly has much more space in the novel and much more impact upon other characters. His rape of his

---

[3]For a sample of such arguments in understanding of Sethe's actions, see Harris (*Fiction and Folklore*; "Reconnecting Fragments"), Solomon, Beaulieu, and Andrews and McKay.

daughter Pecola comes after a series of events that echo the conditions of African Americans about which Richard Wright writes in *Native Son*. Cholly is a product of the deep South's sullying of Black humanity that defines the era in which Wright's Bigger Thomas was conceived and that is no more clearly demonstrated than in the instance in which Cholly has his first sexual encounter. Having left the repast following his great Aunt Jimmy's funeral for a secluded spot in the woods, Cholly and Darlene, a neighbor girl, begin to explore each other sexually. As Cholly is finally beginning to understand the movement and urges of his body during this, his first sexual encounter, armed white men discover his and Darlene's location and spoil what might have been a successful sexual initiation. Instead, the interaction is aborted, and Cholly is stunted permanently as a result of what occurs. It begins with laughter from one of the men:

> "Hee hee hee heeeee." The snicker was a long asthmatic cough.
> The other raced the flashlight all over Cholly and Darlene.
> "Get on wid it, nigger," said the flashlight one.
> "Sir?" said Cholly, trying to find a buttonhole.
> "I said, get on wid it. An' make it good, nigger, make it good." (Morrison, *The Bluest Eye* 147–8)

Cholly's embarrassment continues long after the men are gone and eventually evolves into a hatred toward Darlene, for, as the omniscient voice points out, "never did he once consider directing his hatred toward the hunters. Such an emotion would have destroyed him. They were big, white, armed men. He was small, black, helpless"; thus Darlene is the easier target, the cowardly compromise that becomes exemplary of how Cholly will operate for the remainder of his days (*The Bluest Eye* 150).[4] We could view the incident as lucky; after all, the men could have dismissed Cholly and raped Darlene. Nonetheless, the forced exposure of both youngsters warrants sympathetic consideration from readers. The idea that Black bodies should only provide entertainment for a racist white gaze is one that readers join with Morrison in rejecting.[5]

Following his great Aunt Jimmy's death, the encounter with the armed white hunters, the false belief that he may have impregnated Darlene, and the rejection by his father (who tells Cholly to "get the fuck outta [his] face"), Cholly earns sympathy from readers as being an orphan in the world (*The Bluest Eye* 156). He grows up careless and carefree, with the text claiming that "he had already killed three white men" by the time he meets, courts, and marries Pecola's mother Pauline, and he is "dangerously free" (*The Bluest Eye* 159). In this scheme of sympathetic consideration, it is crucial that Morrison does not dramatize Cholly's killings of the white men; any such vivid brutality might have tainted possible sympathy for Cholly. On the other hand, by the time he kills three white men, Cholly Breedlove has moved a long way from his fourteen-year-old victimization at the hands of the armed white hunters. Throughout this section of the novel, the narrator emphasizes how "free" Cholly is and enumerates a series of such freedoms: "Free to feel whatever he felt—fear, guilt, shame, love, grief, pity. Free to be tender or violent, to whistle or weep. Free to sleep in doorways or between the white sheets of a singing woman. Free to take a job, free to

---

[4] As African American literary scholar Delia Steverson points out, "That scene is soooo traumatizing and emasculating," which highlights again the sympathetic response it evokes in readers. Note to the author on May 15, 2018. I express my thanks to Steverson for reading and offering insightful responses to an earlier version of this essay.

[5] This is another point on which Morrison and Wright intersect. Consider numerous instances in Wright's essay, "The Ethics of Living Jim Crow," in which Blacks are subjected to white gazes. Note from Delia Steverson on May 15, 2018.

leave it"—and the extensive list of freedoms goes on for several more sentences (*The Bluest Eye* 159). The impression is that Cholly has an agency that has moved him beyond victimization but that has nonetheless warped his sense of being in the world. There is an aura of deliberateness in his "dangerous" freedom, an aura that suggests that Cholly is a willful murderer, one who is detached and cool enough to effect a kind of execution of the white men he encounters. Thus, if readers were to see the dramatization of that implicit power, they might take a step or two back from sympathetic engagement with Cholly.[6]

So, the narrator denies readers the graphic details of the suggested horrors of Cholly's killings in order not to run the risk of possibly mitigating sympathetic responses to Cholly; the summary statement makes the point without unseemly or bloody clutter. Instead, the narrator focuses on the sexual exposure and the father's rejection, both of which offer readers points of entry into identification with Cholly. American society generally does not expect fourteen-year-olds, even if they are six feet tall, to fend for themselves, as Cholly is forced to do when his father rejects him. Nor does it expect private moments, especially one's first sexual encounter, to be so publicly exposed. While response to neither of these reactions extends to Cholly's alcoholism and brutal fisticuffs with Pauline, they are nonetheless a part of the narrative, a part of how readers react to Cholly Breedlove. When Cholly rapes Pecola, those reactions are there, and readers cannot erase Cholly's history from his present actions, no matter how despicable those later actions might be. This is certainly not in any way to suggest that Morrison condones incest; it is rather to suggest that even repulsive and despicable actions earn their time of consideration with readers.

So, too, with Soaphead Church. On a despicable meter, it would be hard to say if Cholly or Soaphead Church ranks higher. Arguably, though, Morrison primes readers to grant an iota of tolerance to Soaphead Church through her portrayal of Cholly. Is a father who rapes his daughter to be rejected more swiftly than a stranger who bribes little girls with candy so that he can nibble on their breasts and play with their vaginas?[7] Is a pedophile capable of executing an altruistic act, of having a positive influence upon a needy child? In the fictional world that Morrison has created, the answer to this latter question is "Yes." In an early interview with literary scholar Robert Stepto, Morrison comments on the necessity of having Soaphead Church in the text:

> I had to have someone—her mother, of course, made her want it in the first place—who would give her [Pecola] the blue eyes. And there had to be somebody who *could*, who had the means; that kind of figure who dealt with fortune-telling, dreaming-telling and so on, who would also believe that she was right, that it was preferable for her to have blue eyes. And that would be a person like Soaphead. In other words, he would be wholly convinced that if black people were

---

[6]There is also the possibility of gender having an impact upon presentation with Wright and Morrison. Wright had been disappointed that reader response to his 1938 collection of short stories, *Uncle Tom's Children*, had been to weep over the characters and therefore not do anything to change society. He wanted to make Bigger Thomas hard, he said, so hard that no one would cry over him. Still, not crying and sympathizing are two different things, and I maintain that readers do manage a measure of sympathy for Bigger. On the other hand, Morrison even presents Cholly's rape of Pecola in such an artful way that the violence seems almost poetic. Blood and guts are generally not as prominent in her works as they are in those of Wright.

[7]Susmita Roye suggests that, not only does Cholly rape Pecola, but that her mother Pauline rapes her as well. "The unpalatable truth is that Pecola is raped by both her parents: Cholly rapes her physically and Polly, to borrow Furman's words, 'ravishe[s] the child's self-worth' (18)." See Roye (219) and Furman. Allen Alexander also notes: "His [Cholly's] rape of Pecola is reprehensible, but he does not rape her mind the way that Pauline and Soaphead do" (301).

more like white people they would be better off. And I tried to explain that in terms of his own West Indian background—a kind of English, colonial, Victorian thing drilled into his head *which he could not escape*. I needed someone to distill all of that, to say, "Yeah, you're right, you need them. Here, I'll give them to you," and really believe that he had done her a favor. Someone who would never question the request in the first place. (Stepto 223; emphases added)

That "Yes," therefore, comes from a consideration of Soaphead's background as well as Soaphead's present circumstances.

Born into a family of fair-complexioned West Indians who lauded their skin color and educational opportunities over their darker-skinned neighbors and relatives, Elihue Micah (he added his middle name) Whitcomb (aka Soaphead Church) avoids the plight of Cholly Breedlove by soulfully embracing the pollution that a "decaying British nobleman" has sown into one of his ancestors to begin the line of which he is the result (*The Bluest Eye* 167). He and his family were not discriminated against; indeed, they were the sources of discrimination against others. He has had post–high school educational advantages, numerous ones, that extended over six leisurely years, and he has studied everything from psychiatry to sociology to physical therapy, and ending with a stint in the ministry, before he declines into "a rapidly fraying gentility, punctuated with a few of the white-collar occupations available to black people, regardless of their noble bloodlines, in America: desk clerk at a colored hotel in Chicago, insurance agent, traveling salesman for a cosmetics firm catering to blacks" (171). Finally having settled in Lorain, Ohio, Soaphead enters into the healer-adviser profession that served so many newly migrated Blacks from the South. It is in his presumed capacity to transform fortunes and lives that Pecola comes to him requesting her blue eyes.

At a quick glance, Soaphead Church might not seem to be the victim of a constricting system of racial discrimination, violence, and limited opportunities. Arguably, however, his very skin color and so-called privileges and opportunities have victimized him. The family line from which he comes is such that all of the descendants are stunted by the poisons instilled in them through their white ancestors. While other antisocial characters might have tangible lacks, such as not being able to find jobs, what Soaphead Church lacks lurks in the deep recesses of his mind. The fastidiousness that his ancestors practiced has produced in him an inability to be spontaneous and natural in anything; indeed, when the women of Lorain learned of his celibacy and could not understand his rejection of them, they concluded that "he was supernatural rather than unnatural" (171). Everything must be studied, considered, and reconsidered before he acts. If actions occur too quickly, there is the risk for censure from judging eyes, including one's own; one must ever uphold the reputation of the Whitcombs. Consequently, Soaphead Church is a victim of his family's embracing of its own violation; one of Soaphead's ancestors, the text notes, "regarded as his life's goal the hoarding of this white strain" (167). By believing so willingly in the pollution that they witnessed in their mirrors every day, Soaphead's ancestors have continued an inadvertent decay in their family line, one that has no healthy resolution. It is that buying into history and that lack of hope for the future that earns Soaphead a bit of sympathy from readers. He has not only been victimized by the decaying British nobleman, but he, without the option of separating himself from them early enough and forming his own notions of the world, has been victimized by his family. They have infected him with an incurable disease, "Anglophilia," that instills in him a false sense of superiority to Blacks who are not as light-skinned as he and his relatives are. They also instill in him an unhealthy sense of sexuality, along with a peculiar disposition toward melancholy that serves as much a point of separation from others as does skin color. It is not surprising, then, that Velma, the fun-loving woman whom he married, got away from him as quickly as she could once she discovered his preference for his own melancholy state, not to mention that "he equated lovemaking with communion and the Holy grail" (170). Not only has Soaphead been shaped in excruciatingly limited ways, but he has no prospects for transforming himself. It is reader witnessing of that Frankensteinian creation and its consequences that enables identification with — and perhaps even sympathy for—Soaphead Church.

As far as his pedophilia is concerned, even Soaphead Church's reason for becoming a pedophile is relevant to reader sympathy. After considering an assortment of options, the narrator relates, Soaphead settled on little girls, and the third-person limited narration aligns with the perceptions that Soaphead offers in his letter:

> He could have been an active homosexual but lacked the courage. Bestiality did not occur to him, and sodomy was quite out of the question, for he did not experience sustained erections and could not endure the thought of somebody else's. And besides, the one thing that disgusted him more than entering and caressing a woman was caressing and being caressed by a man. In any case, his cravings, although intense, never relished physical contact. He abhorred flesh on flesh. Body odor, breath odor, overwhelmed him. The sight of dried matter in the corner of the eye, decayed or missing teeth, ear wax, blackheads, moles, blisters, skin crusts—all the natural secretions and protections the body was capable of—disquieted him. His attentions therefore gradually settled on those humans whose bodies were least offensive—children. And since he was too diffident to confront homosexuality, and since little boys were insulting, scary, and stubborn, he further limited his interests to little girls. They were usually manageable and frequently seductive. His sexuality was anything but lewd; his patronage of little girls smacked of innocence and was associated in his mind with cleanliness. He was what one might call a very clean old man. (*The Bluest Eye* 166–7)

To Soaphead's mind—and if the reader follows this logic—Soaphead has settled upon the lesser of any number of evils. He does not elect to be promiscuous with women; nor does he rape young boys or girls (however, his recognition that young girls are "manageable" is an indication of the non-altruistic power he has over them). He does not engage in sex with other men, and he is not a public nuisance who might expose himself on the streets, as Morrison's Shadrack sometimes does in *Sula*. Instead, he selects what his distorted mind tells him is the lesser of all the sexual aberrations, perversions, and even normal interactions in which he could have participated. Readers see Soaphead making a choice that he deems the most logical, and that process of thinking invites engagement. However, readers need also to keep in mind that Soaphead violates little girls in part because he cannot get past Velma's desertion (*The Bluest Eye* 170). The girls become "A Thing to Do Instead" (179).

In further considering the pedophilia, an additional important factor shapes reader response to Soaphead. The omniscient narrator mentions, in a mere three sentences, Soaphead's settling on little girls for his sexual outlet. Then, in his letter to God, Soaphead elaborates and offers his own assessment of his involvement with little girls. This first-person narrative, this positioning of the reader as if looking over the shoulder of the writer and learning surreptitiously information that is addressed to someone else, creates an aura of unbared truthfulness, of untainted confession. Since the letter is addressed to God, toward whom Soaphead at times has the inexplicable audacity to feel superior, there is little need for artifice. Soaphead can bare his soul, and, in that baring, readers can witness unadorned self-confession. That witnessing, comparable to what Gwendolyn Brooks effects in a mother's confession of aborting several fetuses in "The Mother" (1945), pushes the reader outside of judgment and into sympathy. Brooks's persona addresses her confession to her aborted children (at least three), recognizes that she has robbed them of countless options for fulfilling their life's potential, and remains staunchly committed to the course of action she has taken (readers quickly conclude that, should another pregnancy ensue, the speaker will seek yet another abortion). Consider these lines:

> If I stole your births and your names,
> Your straight baby tears and your games,
> Your stilted or lovely loves, your tumults, your marriages, aches, and your deaths,
> If I poisoned the beginnings of your breaths,
> Believe that even in my deliberateness I was not deliberate. (Brooks 17–21)

Brooks's persona ends by asserting her love for her aborted children—"Believe me, I loved you all"—just as Soaphead expresses his special affection for and appreciation of the young girls he violated. When he dies, he says, "little girls are the only things" he will miss (*The Bluest Eye* 181). He then elaborates on his perverted relationships with them:

> Do you know [he writes to God] that when I touched their sturdy little tits and bit them—just a little—I felt I was being friendly? I didn't want to kiss their mouths or sleep in the bed with them or take a child bride for my own. Playful, I felt, and friendly. Not like the newspapers said. Not like the people whispered. And they didn't mind at all. Not at all. Remember how so many of them came back? No one would even try to understand that. If I'd been hurting them, would they have come back? Two of them, Doreen and Sugar Babe, they'd come together. I gave them mints, money, and they'd eat ice cream with their legs open while I played with them. It was like a party. And there wasn't nastiness, and there wasn't any filth, and there wasn't any odor, and there wasn't any groaning—just the light white laughter of little girls and me. And there wasn't any look—any long funny look—any long funny Velma look afterward. No look that makes you feel dirty afterward. That makes you want to die. With little girls it is all clean and good and friendly. (*The Bluest Eye* 181)

With their designations of specified audiences (dead children and God), Brooks's speaker and Soaphead Church cast readers outside the trauma of sinful commission and into the realm of voyeur. As voyeurs, readers are engaged whether they wish to be or not. A commitment to read is therefore a commitment to entertain the possibility of sympathizing. In both instances, self-confession precludes allowing listeners or readers to pass judgment on what is being confessed—except perhaps at a distance that has little impact upon the confessor. After all, Soaphead, like Brooks's persona, is not seeking forgiveness from readers—or from God; nor is he making excuses. He is simply recording significant events of his life and the how and why of his having effected those events. He provides explanation and, to some extent, justification, all within his own perverted realm of logic. Just as readers cannot condemn the mother in Brooks's poem for aborting her children, similarly, from this perspective, readers will have a difficult time in condemning Soaphead. He is guilty, and he admits his guilt. What, then, is there left for readers to speculate about? Outside his logic, of course, we can shout to the heavens that grown men, by virtue of their authority as adults, cannot claim innocence in sexually violating children. Soaphead might not have raped the girls, but he was in a superior position of power over them. Trying to excuse himself by calling his engagement with the girls a "party," or by contextualizing his actions within his previous history with his ex-wife Velma, can all be rendered useless excuses from that outside abstract system of moral behavior—or lack thereof. However, by containing his logic within his confessions and by addressing his specified audience only, Soaphead, echoing Brooks's mother, succeeds in rendering irrelevant all those readers who could possibly pass judgment upon him—or at least he takes their comfortable moral platforms away from them.

In both instances, it is noteworthy that the audiences are silent, incapable of responding in the case of the deceased children and unlikely to respond in Soaphead Church's conceptualization of God. Silence means that both narrators have an uncontested stage for performance, an arena in which they experience no challenges to the accuracy or truthfulness of what they relate. As performers, they are the masters of illusion, masters of what observers take away from their performances. Their arenas do not allow censorship or editing; they, exclusively, are in charge. The price of admission for readers, so to speak, is to listen to what they have to say, hear them out, and realize that their narratives are outside the purview of revision and mostly outside the purview of judgment. These characters take full advantage of their time on stage and retain authorial control over their narratives as well as over their actions.

A further note about Soaphead's silent audience is in order. Are there ways in which we can see Soaphead's interaction with Pecola as a direct result of Soaphead's lost affection for and inability to ever realize a true relationship with God? Is Soaphead's helping Pecola a way for Soaphead to work through his own religious crisis, if he is even religious? Is he blaming God for his own situation, his inability to escape outcast/outsider status and move into normalcy/the status quo, a duplication of which he now sees in Pecola? Even before Pecola arrives at his door, Soaphead had faulted God for the lacks in his own life and for the general disorder he sees in the world:

> He was aware, of course, that something was awry in his life, and all lives, but put the problem where it belonged, at the foot of the Originator of Life. He believed that since decay, vice, filth, and disorder were pervasive, they must be in the Nature of Things. Evil existed because God had created it. He, God, had made a sloven and unforgivable error in judgment: designing an imperfect universe … God had done a poor job, and Soaphead suspected that he himself could have done better. It was in fact a pity that the Maker had not sought his counsel. (*The Bluest Eye* 172, 173)

Pecola's arrival verifies his impressions and increases his antipathy toward God. After all, he, unlike most worshippers, has no expressed fear of God. And not only does he question God, but he approaches the sin that Nathaniel Hawthorne's Ethan Brand commits in daring to put himself in a position superior to God.[8] He writes to God:

> You forgot, Lord. You forgot how and when to be God.
> That's why I changed the little black girl's eyes for her, and I didn't touch her; not a finger did I lay on her. But I gave her those blue eyes she wanted. Not for pleasure, and not for money. I did

---

[8] In the short story "Ethan Brand—A Chapter from an Abortive Romance."

what You did not, could not, would not do: I looked at that ugly little black girl, and I loved her. I played You. And it was a very good show! (*The Bluest Eye* 182)

What he has done, he asserts implicitly, makes him better than/superior to an ineffectual or uncaring supernatural being, and he gets bragging rights (though he neglects to mention that his reward is a dead dog and though the narrator has pointed out that Soaphead is a master of "the fine art of self-deception"; *The Bluest Eye* 169). In his daring to have done something that God could/would/did not do, Soaphead elevates himself and positions Pecola as a supplicant who approaches the only deity that could possibly grant her wish ("Suffer little children to come unto me, and harm them not," he quotes in his letter; 181). By asserting that God is unloving and/or uncaring, and that He definitely does not answer prayers, Soaphead questions the roots of a Christianity that serves a God that allows for the creation of a Pecola Breedlove and even a Soaphead Church. He undermines basic Christian beliefs in his willingness to move out of his assigned place in the Great Chain of Being, and he even goes so far as to claim boldly that he "weeps" for God, when it is usually human beings who go weepingly before the throne of Grace (180). As this reasoning goes, he may be a faulty human being, but he is the perfect "supernatural" vessel for bestowing blue eyes upon an "ugly little black girl."

Soaphead Church's first-person narrative, even couched in the form of a letter, is therefore a classic execution of the genre, one in which readers are locked into the mind of the narrator—his actions, responses, justifications. Whether they desire to do so or not, readers make the journey of confession with Soaphead, and they make it on his terms. By not pleading or asking for forgiveness and by assuming an autonomy that is outside normal social structures, Soaphead inspires a kind of marvel in readers. That inspiration of wonder, curiosity, or whatever we want to call it carries with it some engagement with Soaphead and his point of view. He has readers in his creative clutches, so to speak, just as Toni Morrison does, and he takes us where he wants us to go, that is, into contemplating what he has done and the logic of his explanation. If we commit to reading the text, therefore, we commit to engagement with Soaphead, and we are not allowed to dismiss the pedophile as readily as external social circumstances and our own codes of morality might dictate.

In reporting his case to God, Soaphead Church shares kinship with another famous literary raconteur who uses the power of the word to shape his version of reality: Trueblood in Ralph Ellison's *Invisible Man* (1952). Through the sheer force of language, Trueblood is almost able, in his first-person narrative, to excuse his incest with his daughter. As he tells his tale of sexual transgression to the white Mr. Norton, both Norton and the narrator sit entranced. As with Soaphead Church and as with the lack of dramatizing Cholly Breedlove's murders of three white men, the action that Trueblood relates occurred offstage, at a previous moment, long enough ago so that both his wife and the daughter he violated are now visibly pregnant. Only Trueblood's mastery of language brings the story to life, and the power of the telling proves entrancing for readers as well as for Norton and the narrator. Even more linguistically abled than Soaphead, Trueblood lifts his incest to the category of art. He narrates without shame or apology, a feat that Soaphead will approach sufficiently enough to engage readers as well. Recollective or summary narration pushes action into the background and emphasizes the *telling* of the action, and telling seems less horrible than the actual events (though certainly not from the wife's or the daughter's perspective, neither of which readers get access to in *Invisible Man*). Soaphead's summation of his actions has implicit in it the same motivation as in Trueblood's: a desire for innocence. If both narrators can tell what happened *their way*, from *their perspective*, then perhaps their sins might not seem so egregious. Soaphead, then, undertakes the task of making the monstrous seem normal, or at least not as despicable as biased observers would make it out to be.

Soaphead therefore becomes one of the *seemingly* extraordinary characters that Morrison talks about creating when reviewers, readers, and critics question her about various portrayals. She has asserted that no character she creates is larger than life; rather, life is large enough to accommodate all kinds of characters that readers might judge to be unusual or repulsive or even monstrous. Morrison made the comment in reference to her creating Sula, but it may just as well apply to a number of Morrisonian characters: Cholly Breedlove and Soaphead Church in *The Bluest Eye*; the eponymous character in *Sula*, as well as Shadrack; Guitar and Pilate, among others, in *Song of Solomon*; Golden Gray in *Jazz*; and a host of others whose lives seem to defy conventional conceptions of literary creations. Such characters often operate by a logic that boggles the minds of so-called normal/regular people. How, readers ask, could Sula have slept with her best friend Nel's husband Jude? How could Guitar have attempted to kill Milkman? Is Shadrack really insane, or does he exist in a world, comparable to Pecola, where his logic of existence ultimately defies all those around him?

The seeming differences in such creations do not separate these characters as dramatically from those around them as casual readers might suppose. Soaphead Church, despite his eccentricities, is integrally tied to the community in Lorain, Ohio (as is M'Dear, the conjurer-healer, another outsider who provides help to characters in need). As a healer-adviser, Soaphead has faithful clientele from throughout the community. He is a "Reader, Adviser, and Interpreter of Dreams" who embodies many of the hopes that those newly arrived to the cities so desperately needed, and he is a stable source of advice to longtime city residents (*The Bluest Eye* 165). The narrator sums up his profession and his place in the community: "His hours were his own, the competition was slight, the clientele was already persuaded and therefore manageable, and he had numerous opportunities to witness human stupidity without sharing it or being compromised by it, and to nurture his fastidiousness by viewing physical decay" (165). No matter his disdain for his clientele or his seeming aloofness from the very profession that sustains him, Soaphead Church provides a valuable service to his community, and the community in turn provides satisfaction to his sense of superiority. It is a mutual dependency, the success of which depends upon the clientele's willingness to believe.[9]

Relevant as well in terms of Soaphead's fitting into and providing a service to the community is the mere fact of his physical appearance and his speaking ability. Not only is he light-skinned and holds himself aloof from his neighbors, but he has inherited a British accent from his West Indian background and his family's imitation of British manners. Picture, then, the exoticism associated with a tall, slim, light-skinned man with a foreign accent in the small town of Lorain, Ohio. Soaphead's sheer physical presence provides a kind of exoticism, a foreignness, to which most of the newly arrived Southern Blacks and many of those who have been in the North for some time are probably not accustomed. Soaphead's very physical features and speech thus give

---

[9]In this context, consider Min in Ann Petry's *The Street* and her visit to Prophet David. She wants the Prophet to prevent Jones, the Super of a building and the man with whom she is currently living, from putting her out because he has become so enamored of Lutie Johnson, the beautiful young protagonist of the novel. Min, like Pecola, *believes* that the Prophet can help her, and he does.

him a kind of visual-oral advantage among the regular Black folks over whom he already considers himself having a distinct advantage. This line of reasoning might extend to suggest that, not only is Soaphead "freakish" in his sexual habits, but he is also freakish, unusual, weird in his very physical appearance. That appearance is characteristic of persons—conjurers, healers, advisers—in or near African American communities who are believed to have special powers to affect the fortunes of those who seek their assistance.[10] His body and his profession work to his advantage in carving out a place in the community, a place that positions him uniquely to help Pecola.

Soaphead's profession and Pecola's desire therefore join hands in a perfect concoction of functionality and belief. Soaphead serves, and Pecola believes. His interaction with Pecola showcases one of the few instances in the novel in which an observer has not rendered Pecola invisible, frowned upon her with disdain, run her away from a schoolyard or a house, or violated her sexually. Soaphead Church *really listens* to Pecola (which few in the novel have ever tried to do), *hears* what she says, recognizes the intensity of her desire, and attempts to do something about it. It is perhaps the first time in her life that someone has actually heard Pecola and has in turn responded to what they heard. In that interval before Soaphead turns Pecola into an instrument for his own cruel purposes, he sees her request for what it is:

> He thought it was at once the most fantastic and the most logical petition he had ever received. Here was an ugly little girl asking for beauty. A surge of love and understanding swept through him, but was quickly replaced by anger. Anger that he was powerless to help her. Of all the wishes people had brought him—money, love, revenge—this seemed to him the most poignant and the one most deserving of fulfillment. A little black girl who wanted to rise up out of the pit of her blackness and see the world with blue eyes. His outrage grew and felt like power. For the first time he honestly wished he could work miracles. (*The Bluest Eye* 174)

This is perhaps the highest moment of sympathetic engagement with Soaphead in the text. In his seemingly genuinely altruistic response to Pecola, one that is shaped by a recognizable human desire, he sees a heartfelt longing that perhaps echoes something out of his own background. In this moment, he responds to Pecola as many readers do—with sympathy and pity, which in turn leads readers to respond to him similarly. In this moment, his history disappears, and there stands before us a man who is without guile, without a desire to use or take advantage. Obviously, we can question the reliability of this narration, but, given Soaphead Church's brutal honesty in so many of the arenas of his life, the presentation here does not appear to be intentionally misleading.

That moment of unvarnished focus on Pecola and her problem, of course, does not last, and it is not necessary that it do so. What is important here is that Soaphead has reached into his dysfunctional, befuddled soul and found a chord that responds to Pecola. His desire simply to grant her wish places him in a category of helpfulness that most other characters in the text do not achieve—nor do we have any evidence that they wish to do so—with Pecola. Arguably, the lack of first-person narration from many of these other characters precludes definitive conclusions about their motives and intent (Claudia is the exception), though we do see, through omniscient and limited narration, what some of their inclinations might be, including those of Cholly. Readers need but contemplate Geraldine's ordering Pecola out of her house and her prankster son Junior's

---

[10]For commentary on such descriptions, see Puckett.

throwing a cat into Pecola's face to gauge how far Soaphead is removed from that. And, of course, Soaphead is a long way from Cholly Breedlove, whose rape of his daughter proves to be emotionally fatal to her. Unlike his predecessors, Soaphead hears, he listens, and he hurts for Pecola. In this posture, he is better than her mother, her father, her teachers, her fellow students, and even, to some extent, the MacTeer sisters—Claudia and Frieda. It is Pecola's encounter with Soaphead that readers might consider holding on to as they contemplate the novel and its cruel consequences for a child whose only faults are being born dark-skinned and, by the standards of those around her, unattractive.

No matter how repulsive Soaphead Church may be, he *helps* Pecola when no one else does. By playing the little god who grants Pecola her blue eyes through her killing of his landlady's dog, Soaphead sets Pecola on her final journey in the novel.[11] The last few pages feature her conversing with an imaginary friend who constantly reassures Pecola that she has the bluest eyes of all. Some would argue that this wish fulfilled is an escape from reality, a movement into insanity, and those inclined to argue such might see Pecola as a lost soul at the end, blighted beyond restoration to normality. I assert that the final glimpse we get of Pecola in the novel pictures her as perhaps the happiest she has ever been.[12] She was happy when she ate Mary Jane candies and imagined herself being Mary Jane, and she was especially happy at the MacTeers when she drank three quarts of milk in a very short period of time so that she could gaze upon the blue-eyed image of Shirley Temple. Claudia reports, "We [Claudia and her sister Frieda] knew she [Pecola] was fond of the Shirley Temple cup and took every opportunity to drink milk out of it just to handle and see sweet Shirley's face" (*The Bluest Eye* 23). Now, Pecola is happy to have Shirley Temple transmogrified from the cup she held so lovingly and into the realms of her imagination. She had to give up the cup with its hypnotizing image and leave the MacTeer household. She can now, whenever she wants, conjure her friend who compliments her blue eyes. Though the friend may disappear for a time, she returns again and again to assure Pecola that she has the bluest eyes of all. That companionship—even if it is only in her mind—is something that Pecola has not consistently had before. The friend, therefore, fills a crucial lack that has been made possible by Pecola's belief that Soaphead Church had the power to grant blue eyes. Soaphead Church has thus helped Pecola formulate a strategy for existing in a cruel and mostly unsympathetic world. We can chastise him for the perversion of trust that brought about this result, but there is no denying that the result serves a purpose for a child

---

[11]Ramona L. Hyman reads Pecola's receipt of blue eyes as the culmination of a process through which she has defined herself into a new existence. Hyman posits that "Soaphead Church is also an accoucheur if one accepts him as the figure who aids Pecola in her new birth" (262). Morrison has remarked that she was inspired to write about a young black girl's wanting blue eyes partly in response to hearing one of her elementary school classmates mention her fervent prayers over a two-year period for that result; the girl was convinced that God did not exist because He did not grant her wish. Morrison comments:

> What I later recollected was that I looked at her and imagined her having them and thought how awful that would be if she had gotten her prayer answered. I always thought she was beautiful. I began to write about a girl who wanted blue eyes and the horror of having that wish fulfilled; and also about the whole business of what is physical beauty and the pain of that yearning and wanting to be somebody else, and how devastating that was and yet part of all females who were peripheral in other people's lives. (Ruas 95–6)

[12]Roye agrees with this position to an extent. She offers that Pecola "seems to find her happiness only after losing her mind" and "this might almost be seen as the state of perfect happiness for Pecola" before moving on to qualify her assessment in various ways. See "Disrupted Girls," 222.

who has been abused by people who should have loved her and battered by a society that has no nurturing role for her to fill.

So ... can demons profess the word of God? Without a doubt.

WORKS CITED

Alexander, Allen. "The Fourth Face: The Image of God in Toni Morrison's *The Bluest Eye*." *African American Review*, vol. 32, no. 2, Summer 1998, pp. 293–303.

Andrews, William L., and Nelly Y. McKay, eds. *Toni Morrison's Beloved: A Casebook*. Oxford UP, 1999.

Beaulieu, Elizabeth Ann. *Black Women Writers and the American Neo-Slave Narrative: Femininity Unfettered*. Greenwood P, 1999.

Brooks, Gwendolyn. "The Mother." *Selected Poems of Gwendolyn Brooks*. HarperCollins, 1963, pp. 7–8.

Chesnutt, Charles. *The Marrow of Tradition*. 1901. U of Michigan P, 1969.

Cleage, Pearl. *Flyin' West*. Dramatists Play Service, Inc., 1995.

Ellison, Ralph. *Invisible Man*. Random House, 1952.

Furman, Jan. *Toni Morrison's Fiction*. U of South Carolina P, 1999.

Gaines, Ernest J. *The Tragedy of Brady Sims*. Vintage, 2017.

Griggs, Sutton. *The Hindered Hand*. 1905. West Virginia UP, 2017.

Harris, Trudier. *Fiction and Folklore: The Novels of Toni Morrison*. U of Tennessee P, 1991.

Harris, Trudier. "Reconnecting Fragments: Afro-American Folk Tradition in *The Bluest Eye*." *Critical Essays on Toni Morrison*, edited by Nellie Y. McKay, G. K. Hall, 1988, pp. 68–76.

Hyman, Ramona L. "Pecola Breedlove: The Sacrificial Iconoclast in *The Bluest Eye*." *CLA Journal*, vol. 52, no. 3, Mar. 2009, pp. 256–64.

Morrison, Toni. *Beloved*. Alfred A. Knopf, 1987.

Morrison, Toni. *The Bluest Eye*. Holt, Rinehart & Winston, 1970.

Morrison, Toni. *God Help the Child*. Alfred A. Knopf, 2015.

Morrison, Toni. *Home*. Alfred A. Knopf, 2012.

Morrison, Toni. *Jazz*. Alfred A. Knopf, 1992.

Morrison, Toni. *Song of Solomon*. Alfred A. Knopf, 1977.

Morrison, Toni. *Sula*. Alfred A. Knopf, 1973.

Petry, Ann. *The Street*. 1946. Beacon, 1985.

Phillips, Delores. *The Darkest Child*. 2004. Soho, 2018.

Puckett, Newbell Niles. *Folk Beliefs of the Southern Negro*. 1926. Negro UP, 1968.

Roye, Susmita. "Toni Morrison's Disrupted Girls and Their Disturbed Childhoods." *Callaloo*, vol. 35, no. 1, Winter 2012, pp. 212–27.

Ruas, Charles. "Toni Morrison." *Conversations with Toni Morrison*, edited by Danille Taylor-Guthrie, U of Mississippi P, 1994, pp. 93–118.

Schreiber, Evelyn Jaffe. *Race, Trauma, and Home in the Novels of Toni Morrison*. Louisiana State UP, 2010.

Shine, Ted. "Contribution." *Black Drama: An Anthology*, edited by William Brasmer and Dominick Consolo, Charles E. Merrill Publishing Company, 1970, pp. 365–89.

Solomon, Barbara H. *Critical Essays on Toni Morrison's Beloved*. G. K. Hall, 1998.

Stepto, Robert. "Intimate Things in Place: A Conversation with Toni Morrison." *Chant of Saints: A Gathering of Afro-American Literature, Art, and Scholarship*, edited by Michael S. Harper and Robert B. Stepto, U of Illinois P, 1979, pp. 213–29.

Steverson, Delia. Note to the Author. University of Florida. May 15, 2018.
Walker, Joseph. *The River Niger*. Hill and Wang, 1973.
Wright, Richard. *Native Son*. 1940. Basic Books, 2008.
Wright, Richard. *The Outsider*. Perennial, 2003.
Wright, Richard. *Uncle Tom's Children*. Harper and Row, 1938.

FURTHER READING

Bump, Jerome. "Racism and Appearance in *The Bluest Eye*: A Template for an Ethical Emotive Criticism." *College Literature*, vol. 37, no. 2, Spring 2010, pp. 147–70.

Byerman, Keith. "Intense Behaviors: The Use of the Grotesque in *The Bluest Eye* and *Eva's Man*." *CLA Journal*, vol. 25, no. 4, June 1982, pp. 447–57.

deWeever, Jacqueline. "The Inverted World of Toni Morrison's *The Bluest Eye* and *Sula*." *CLA Journal*, vol. 22, no. 4, June 1979, pp. 402–14.

Middleton, Joyce Irene. "Confronting the 'Master Narrative': The Privilege of Orality in Toni Morrison's *The Bluest Eye*." *Cultural Studies*, vol. 9, no. 2, May 1995, pp. 301–17.

Moses, Cat. "The Blues Aesthetic in Toni Morrison's *The Bluest Eye*." *African American Review*, vol. 33, no. 4, 1999, pp. 623–37.

Portales, Marco. "Toni Morrison's 'The Bluest Eye': Shirley Temple and Cholly." *The Centennial Review*, vol. 30, no. 4, Fall 1986, pp. 496–505.

Rosenberg, Ruth. "Seeds in Hard Ground: Black Girlhood in *The Bluest Eye*." *Black American Literature Forum*, vol. 21, no. 4, Winter 1987, pp. 435–45.

Tally, Justine. *The Cambridge Companion to Toni Morrison*. Cambridge UP, 2007.

Taylor-Guthrie, Danille, editor. *Conversations with Toni Morrison*. U of Mississippi P, 1994.

Wong, Shelley. "Transgression as Poesis in *The Bluest Eye*." *Callaloo*, vol. 13, no. 3, Summer 1990, pp. 471–81.

CHAPTER THREE

Do You Believe in Magic? #BlackGirlMagic in *The Bluest Eye* and *Beloved*

JAMES A. CRANK

Inspired by Michelle Obama's enthusiastic speech at the 2013 "Black Girls Rock Awards," activist CaShawn Thompson created a phrase highlighting Black women's accomplishments—Black Girl Magic; the expression was meant to "celebrate the beauty, power and resilience of Black women" ("Why Are"), who triumphed in spite of systemic racism, misogyny, and disenfranchisement. By celebrating the "magic" of Black women's success in the face of entrenched systems meant to subjugate them, Thompson hoped to reframe Black femininity as a tenacious and powerful identity actively contesting conventional/stereotypical notions of helplessness: "We're using [Black Girl Magic] to celebrate ourselves because historically black women haven't had the type of support that other groups have … Black Girl Magic tries to counteract the negativity that we sometimes hold within ourselves and is sometimes placed on us by the outside world" ("Why Are"). A few months later, #Black Girl Magic had become an immensely popular hashtag on twitter, Instagram, and Facebook, but the response from African American intellectuals and cultural critics was not entirely positive.

In one of the most memorable rebukes of #BlackGirlMagic, Linda Chavers writes,

> Here's my problem with Black Girl Magic … Black girls aren't magical. We're human … The "strong, black woman" archetype, which also includes the mourning black woman who suffers in silence, is the idea that we can survive it all, that we can withstand it. That we are, in fact, superhuman. Black girl magic sounds to me like just another way of saying the same thing, and it is smothering and stunting. It is, above all, constricting rather than freeing. ("Why Are")

Chavers found "magic" a troublesome description of the real lives of Black girls; to her, Black Girl Magic suggested that, to be considered extraordinary, Black women had to manifest superhuman strength and endurance. Moreover, Chavers felt that, by emphasizing magic, Thompson's phrase glossed over the lived-lives and brutal realities of what it meant to be a Black female in America.

Other African American writers and intellectuals took issue with Chavers's literalism; Akiba Solomon wrote,

> I strongly disagree with Chavers … "Black girl magic" isn't some Johnetta Henry bag of bricks we're dragging around the Internet. It's fun, efficient, and intimate … It's our way of loving each other up while we're going about the business of staying sane, creative, fly, and faithful. It's a salve for the thousands of puncture wounds that sloppy, resentful and racist police keep making in our collective skin.

While Chavers contests the word "magic" to describe the harsh realities of Black women/girls, those who champion #BlackGirlMagic see the phrase as a way to celebrate the humanity of Black women; more importantly, proponents of #BlackGirlMagic seek to make the lived-lives of Black women/girls visible to a public that refuses to acknowledge their struggles and successes. Even now, unresolved conversations about representations and celebrations of Black female successes and survival persist, especially regarding the dissonance between magical narratives and the very real existence of systemic oppression.

The conversation and controversy surrounding Thompson's drive to make visible the lives of Black girls and reframe their survival/successes as "magic" reminds me, of course, of Toni Morrison. In her novels, Morrison frequently animates, celebrates, and exposes the struggles, triumphs, and failures of Black women/girls who struggle in systems designed specifically to disenfranchise, humiliate, and wound them. And magic, enchantment, and the supernatural are key elements in many of her books. The tension between representing the reality of being a Black girl in America and using magic as a framing device is not lost on Morrison, who frequently bristled at the phrase "magic realism" to describe her work. In an interview just after the publication of *Beloved*, Morrison argues that critics use a phrase like that to dismiss her work and, ultimately, cover "up what was going on" (Davis 143). Her comments echo Chavers's anxiety over Black Girl Magic; Morrison argues calling her books magical realism is really

> a way of *not* talking about the politics. It was a way of *not* talking about what was in the books. If you could apply the word magical then that dilutes the realism but it seemed legitimate because there were these supernatural and unrealistic things, surreal things, going on in the text. But for literary historians and literary critics, it just seemed to be a convenient way to skip again what was the truth. (Davis 143–4, emphases in original)

Morrison's aversion to magical realism stems, in part, from a recognition that "magic" has all sorts of connotations that can be weaponized against a Black author, especially one focused on exploring the harsh realities of Black American existence. She notes that a magical way of seeing is a part of multiple cultural contexts, but

> it's just that when it comes from discredited people it somehow has some other exotic attachment: thus the word "magic." I remember many people were very upset when some major journalistic work was done on my work and the heading was "Black Magic": that is to say, my work was black magic. It was a favorable heading to them but the implication was that there was no intelligence there, it was all sort of, you know, "the panther does not know he is graceful because it is his nature to leap that way." (Davis 145)

But, for Morrison, magic was still an important element of the truth of Black experience that deserved to be represented: "My own use of enchantment simply comes because that's the way the world was for me and for the black people that I knew." Magic was another "knowledge or perception" that worked in concert, not opposition to "the very shrewd, down-to-earth, efficient way in which they did things and survived things" (144). Remembering the importance of magic to her as a child, she recalls that

> it formed a kind of cosmology that was perceptive as well as enchanting, and so it seemed impossible for *me* to write about black people and eliminate that simply because it was "unbelievable" ... that *is* the reality. I mean, it's not as though it's a thing you do on Sunday morning in church, it's not a tiny, entertaining aspect of one's life—it's what *informs* your sensibility. (Davis 144, emphases in original)

She concludes, "without [magic], I think I would have been quite bereft."

Situating Morrison's literary tension between real representations of Black femininity and magical elements of her books within contemporary conversations over #BlackGirlMagic is a useful way to think through how "magic" operates in Morrison's works and what possibilities magical thinking opens and forecloses for her characters. Though they were published decades before Thompson's celebration of Black femininity, Morrison's *The Bluest Eye* (1970) and *Beloved* (1987) benefit from a critical reappraisal in the wake of the #BlackGirlMagic's popularity, especially because, in the time between the novels, Morrison seems to have evolved in her thinking about "magic." By situating both these novels in the context of contemporary articulations and celebrations of #BlackGirlMagic, we can see how Morrison engaged in similar efforts to redefine the viability and legibility of Black girlhood by articulating and contesting what kind of "magic" makes such stories visible and redemptive.

Paying careful attention to #BlackGirlMagic's emphasis on empowerment and community, I find that *The Bluest Eye* and *Beloved* investigate ways that narratives of trauma (especially trauma inflicted by family) obfuscate possibilities for self-possession for female characters—and, in the case of the main characters, Pecola and Sethe, virtually destroy any conceptions of self-worth. However, Morrison undergoes an evolution about what kind of "magic" might heal Black women over the seventeen years between her first novel and *Beloved*; in the latter, Morrison emphasizes self-possession as a key spiritual element allowing Black women and girls to see, celebrate, and begin to heal themselves. Morrison's literary #BlackGirlMagic also connects with some central questions that seem to bother Chavers, such as, Why are Black girls/women only visible to a (white) public when they are in the familiar roles of survivor or victim? How do we make legible stories of abuse and trauma without taking away the agency of their victims? And, maybe more crucially for Morrison, how might we renegotiate Black girlhood's visibility into a celebration of an enduring magic, a story not of pain but of transformative love?

Morrison's first novel, *The Bluest Eye*, explores the limitations of "magic" to heal the wounds of Black women/girls. The plot follows the lives of several little girls living in Lorain, Ohio, in 1941, but it is the central figure of the book, Pecola Breedlove, whom Morrison examines in depth. The product of two parents victimized by virulent racism and poverty, Pecola's childhood is full of misery. Ostensibly, the novel tells the story of terrible events Pecola is forced to endure, but Morrison is far more interested in what is more "difficult to handle ... why" (7). Through Pecola, Morrison exposes the brutal stories of Black women's survival in twentieth-century America—stories that, in a world defined by white patriarchy, inherently resist visibility. Morrison suggests that understanding the circumstances that *create* a tragic life like Pecola's offers potential magical narratives effectively repositioning Black femininity as a supernatural/magical force of profound creativity and pushing back against conventional notions of weakness and helplessness. However, Morrison ultimately concludes that spirit, magic, or the supernatural cannot cure Pecola's deep wounds and transcend her realities; rather, magic becomes just another snare binding her to dominant cultural beliefs defining her as worthless and ugly.

When we meet Pecola, we understand her tragedy is intimately bound up in her family, especially because she is born to parents who are dangerous to/for one another. More importantly, Pauline, Pecola's mother, has internalized the harsh lessons about what it means to survive as a Black girl; she inevitably passes these lessons on to her daughter, who is, in turn, wounded by them. Born into a family of eleven children, Pauline is destined to be just another invisible Black girl, living a life of "total anonymity" (*The Bluest Eye* 110); she is only "saved" by a gruesome wound: "a rusty nail … punched clear through her foot" at two years old. In Pauline's earliest moments, she learns a lesson that Morrison comes back to often in her work: in order to be seen, Black girls must be hurt—they are only legible through their continuous wounding, only visible through scars, traumas, and (re)victimizations. For Pauline, the wound becomes a narrative, a story through which she comes to understand her value. More than just a site of trauma, her injured foot explains "why she never felt home anywhere, or that she belonged anyplace. Her general feeling of separateness and unworthiness she blamed on her foot" (111). In short, Pauline's wound operates less as a marker of inferiority and more as a special kind of interiority, a critical self-awareness, a way of seeing. Morrison emphasizes Pauline's self-awareness by offering us something few characters get in the novel: her own voice. Throughout the chapter about Pauline, the third-person narration splits into italicized first person as Pauline tells us her story in concert with a detached narrator. Unlike some characters in the book, Pauline talks back to those who try to own her story.

Morrison uses Pauline's wounds as an objective correlative for the emotional and psychological wounding of American Black women. Beyond her scarred foot, Pauline is marked by another more obvious deformity, the loss of her front tooth. In explaining how the tooth fell out, Morrison explains that it was not a single traumatic event, but a gradual decaying and erosion that rotted the root:

> There must have been a speck, a brown speck easily mistaken for food but which did not leave, which sat on the enamel for months, and grew, until it cut into the surface and then to the brown putty underneath, finally eating away to the root, but avoiding the nerves, so its presence was not noticeable or uncomfortable. Then the weakened roots, having grown accustomed to the poison, responded one day to severe pressure, and the tooth fell free, leaving a ragged stump behind. (116)

Like the insidious disenfranchisement and misogyny that plagued Black women during the 1930s and 1940s, the problem causing the decay of Pauline's tooth was largely invisible, "even before the little brown speck" had begun. To understand the power of the wound, Morrison suggests we must first make visible "the conditions, the setting that would allow [the poison] to exist in the first place"—just as to articulate systemic injustices faced by Black women, one must first examine "root" causes.

Losing her front tooth is deeply upsetting for Pauline. Unlike a wounded foot, the loss of her tooth is highly visible, a significant deformity defined not by what is there but what is not, of what is no longer visible. Her gap tooth marks her as valueless, especially for the Black women of Ohio she lives among. There is no Black Girl Magic of community or mutual celebrations of successes, only "goading glances and private snickers" (118) about how Pauline talks and dresses. The gap in her tooth becomes "the end of her lovely beginning" (110), an impossible wound that she cannot recover from because it cannot be concealed. But the wound is far more psychic than physical; we learn later that Pauline is taught that feminine beauty is inexorably tied to physical appearance, the basis for "romantic love" (122). Morrison's narrator explains that "romantic love" and "physical beauty" are, quite simply, "the most destructive ideas in the history of human thought. Both originated in envy, thrived in insecurity, and ended in disillusion" (122). For one critic, the two concepts are damaging precisely because of their relationship to visibility: "each [is] defined according to what they exclude and ... destructive to the extent that they are made definitionally unavailable" (Kuenz 424). Pauline's conception of her self-worth—especially in relation to her capacity to be loved and taken care of—is bound to the perfect image of feminine beauty; in losing her tooth, she feels completely worthless, both as a woman and a wife: "In equating physical beauty with virtue, she stripped her mind, bound it, and collected self-contempt by the heap. She forgot lust and simple caring for" (*The Bluest Eye* 122). Moreover, Pauline finds herself hardwired to understand beauty only through the perfect bodies and faces of white celebrities: "she was never able, after her education in the movies, to look at a face and not assign it some category in the scale of absolute beauty ... one she absorbed in full from the silver screen" (122). With the impossible archetypes of feminine beauty before her, Pauline becomes a woman for whom love means only "possessive mating" (122).

The only "magic" Pauline experiences exists decidedly outside herself, when she can lose herself in watching movies. But movie magic further muddies an understanding of her intrinsic value or ability to be loved: it only emphasizes how different she is from white paragons of beauty and morality. In the movies, "white men [are] taking such good care of they women," she explains in her own italicized section, "them pictures gave me a lot of pleasure, but it made coming home hard" (123). When her tooth falls out during an afternoon visit to the theater, Pauline abandons any pretense of living life vicariously through the magic of the screen: "Everything went then. Look like I just didn't care no more after that. I let my hair go back, plaited it up, and settled down to just being ugly ... the meanness got worse. I wanted my tooth back" (123). Completely devastated by a cultural archetype of beauty that emphasizes physical perfection and whiteness, Pauline settles into a magic-less life; she has "no time for dreams and movies" (126) any longer. She rejects the magic of the silver screen, romance, and gives up her obsession with mystery by "develop[ing] a hatred for things that mystified her." She finally decides to assign "herself a role in the scheme of things" (126) at the bottom, where she believes ugly women belong.

Pauline connects physical beauty with worthiness and "ugliness" with worthlessness, and that is the central legacy she passes on to her daughter, Pecola, the main character of Morrison's novel. Pauline's ideology is virulent; Rosenburg argues, "the socialization patterns thoughtlessly transmitted from mother to daughter, from Pauline Breedlove to Pecola, are fatal to that child's self-esteem" (440). Throughout *The Bluest Eye*, Pecola comes back to her mother's definitions of beauty—archetypal, white, unblemished—to assign inner values to things and people. Like her mother, Pecola believes fervently in the connection between perfect human beauty and inner worth, but, unlike Pauline, Pecola is young enough to believe in magic and mystery. She assumes she can transform herself through spiritual or supernatural magic. When Pecola moves in with Frieda and Claudia, she is obsessed with one specific child actress—she has endless "loving conversation[s] about how cu-ute Shirley Temple was" (19). Pecola longs for Shirley's features, not just her whiteness, but everything about her appearance, encapsulated by the "blue-eyed, yellow-haired, pink-skinned doll" (20) that the girls get for Christmas. Recognizing that she looks nothing like the paragon of beauty the doll represents, Pecola does not become cynical and hopeless like Pauline; rather, she turns to magic.

At first, she wishes for simple invisibility—she begs God to "please make me disappear" (45) and closes her eyes to see if that will speed up the process. Though she knows she can imagine all of her dissolving, "try as she might, she could never get her eyes to disappear. So what was the point? They were everything. Everything was there, in them" (45). In Pecola's mind, her eyes told the story of her worthlessness and her inability to escape: "as long as she looked the way she did, as long as she was ugly, she would have to stay with these people. Somehow she belonged to them" (45). Pauline's legacy of conflating physical beauty with worth infects Pecola and dooms her to view herself as trash; the girl's only escape is magical thinking. Unlike her mother, Pecola believes she can discover a secret way to become beautiful, worthy of love. She spends "long hours" at the mirror "trying to discover the secret of the ugliness, the ugliness that made her ignored" (45). Pecola believes that if her "eyes were different, that is to say, beautiful, she herself would be different," and "each night, without fail, she prayed for blue eyes" (46). Pecola's belief that something might change her is a key distinction between girlhood innocence and her mother's adult despair. Though Pecola might be slightly discouraged, "she was not without hope. To have something as wonderful as that happen would take a long, long time" (46). Pecola believes she can change, that God has the power to mutate her from the "ugly" anonymous girl she sees in the mirror to the beautiful blue-eyed Shirley Temple visible on posters all over town. And just as Pauline equates physical beauty with a worthiness for romantic love, Pecola begins to understand the answer to her question at the beginning of the novel—"How do you do that … get somebody to love you?" (32)—for her, the answer is simple: *look* lovable.

Unfortunately, the answer to her prayers is a poisonous, sick love given by her father, Cholly, who feels affection for the girl only after going through a range of emotions: "revulsion, guilt, pity, then love" (161). As he watches her do the dishes, Cholly realizes with disgust that, despite all he has done to her and the hurt he has caused his family, she still loved him—significantly, he knows because he can see it in her eyes: "Those haunted loving eyes … the love would move him to fury. How dare she love him?" (161). In a toxic mixture of "hatred" and "tenderness" (162), he grabs and rapes her. Deeply wounded by her father's sexual assault, Pecola turns to prayer for a final physical change that will make her worthy of a purer kind of love, but she receives no answer. The hope she placed in religious spirituality is bankrupted, and all Pecola has left is the secular supernatural.

Pecola's final hope is the trickster figure Soaphead Church, a former Anglican priest who has abandoned organized religion to become a "Reader, Adviser, and Interpreter of Dreams" (165), but his "magic" is nothing more than self-deception and trickery. "A cinnamon-eyed West Indian with lightly browned skin" (167), Soaphead names himself after his hair style, though "no one knew where the 'Church' part came from" (167). He claims to have special powers and the ability to speak to God, but he is just as infected as Pauline by the diseased notion equating blackness with worthlessness. As the distant descendent of "some decaying British nobleman" (167), he is taught to believe "DeGobineau's hypothesis that 'all civilizations derive from the white race, that none can exist without its help'" (168). If Pauline's belief in white beauty is physical, Soaphead's belief in white superiority is academic, philosophical.

Pecola finds one of Soaphead's cards that reads, "If you are overcome with trouble and conditions that are not natural, I can remove them" (173) and comes to ask for help, for she believes he can give her the blue eyes that will finally make her lovable. But just as the answer to her prayer is cruelly warped, so too is her request of Soaphead, who confesses to her, "I am not a magician" (174). In a rambling letter that closes the chapter, Soaphead writes to God that he has been able to do what He could not: "I gave her the eyes. I gave her the blue, blue, two blue eyes. Cobalt blue." He confesses, "No one will see her blue eyes. But *she* will. And she will live happily ever after" (182, emphasis in original). However, Pecola's story is not a fairy tale, and Soaphead has done nothing but force her to commit a gruesome act, killing his landlady's dog. When Pecola turns to both spirituality and magic to change her situation, she is only selfishly used by men warped by entrenched racism and misogyny.

In *The Bluest Eye*, magic is neither redemptive nor freeing but an insidious way to oppress, subjugate, and (re)violate Black girls and women. The tragedy of Pecola Breedlove is that she believes in magic. Because her magical thinking only wounds her more deeply, Pecola sinks into madness. For one critic, simply existing in the real world is no longer a "viable option for a female child like Pecola, whose dream is to vanish or to somehow magically acquire blue eyes, which, she thinks, will make her more lovable. Neither desire is possible" (Roye 219). Both Pecola's prayers and her appeal to Soaphead only confirm her belief that Black is ugly, worthless, and that, because of her body, she will never be able to be free from self-hatred. Pecola ends the novel changed, but not the way she had hoped: in the final chapter, we see that she has changed inside, dialoguing in her mind in multiple personalities. Claudia, the sometimes narrator of the book, notes that "she spent her days … walking up and down, up and down, her head jerking to the beat of a drummer so distant only she could hear" (*The Bluest Eye* 204). Believing the magic of Soaphead's transformation has not given Pecola a sense of self-possession and confidence, it has wounded her profoundly, broken her spirit, and left her fractured.

Because magic and spirituality traffic in the language of love—whether the potential love of a parental deity or social love/affection—they promise a way for Pecola to imagine herself loveable. But imagination is not reality, and the love Pecola receives is toxic. Claudia suggests that the only one who truly loved Pecola was Cholly, "but his touch was fatal, and the something he gave her filled the matrix of her agony with death" (206). The truth of what love means for Black women and girls is different than what it means for anyone else, for Black females were at the bottom of everything: "Everybody in the world was in a position to give them orders" (138). They are not free, and so, are not free to love. In that cruel radiance of bondage, the love Black girls receive is, likewise, not for them but for the one giving it. In such an instance when "the lover alone possesses his gift of love" and "the loved one is shorn, neutralized, frozen in the glare of the lover's inward eye," there is nothing of value for the Black woman/girl who is loved. Claudia puts it simply, "There is no gift for the beloved" (206). Even as Pecola turns endlessly to magic and spirituality to change her, the gift she longs for is not hers to possess. As "the beloved," she has no ownership over herself or, indeed, her capacity to be loved.

Claudia does not believe in magic, and, by the end of the novel, though still poor and Black, she survives precisely because she refuses to suffer the illusions that Pecola does. She and her sister Frieda recognize the futility of magic to change anything fundamental about their lives. In the opening of the novel, when the sisters were younger and more naïve, she tells how they planted marigold seeds hoping to restore Pecola's sanity, but

> there were no marigolds in the fall of 1941 … we could think of nothing but our own magic: if we planted the seeds, and said the right words over them, they would blossom, and everything would be all right. It was a long time before my sister and I admitted to ourselves that no green was going to spring from our seeds. (5)

Nothing comes from believing in such fantasies, Morrison suggests, because all fantasy and magic do is obscure and distort the reality of being a Black girl/woman:

> Fantasy it was, for we were not strong, only aggressive; we were not free, merely licensed; we were not compassionate, we were polite; not good, but well behaved. We courted death in order to call ourselves brave, and hid like thieves from life. We substituted good grammar for intellect; we switched habits to simulate maturity; we rearranged lies and called it the truth, seeing in the new pattern of an old idea, the Revelation and the Word. (205–6)

The magic of Black girls does not make visible the cruelties of their stories but instead fractures and possesses them; magic is not redemption in *The Bluest Eye*, it is deception, a dodge, a con, a mean trick that wounds in more insidious ways than Pauline's foot or lost tooth. In her first novel, Morrison rejects any notion that "magic" might transform the life of a poor Black girl born to parents like Pauline and Cholly; on the contrary, a belief in spirit and the supernatural brings only ruin.

Between the publication of *The Bluest Eye* and *Beloved*, Morrison seems to have evolved in her thinking of what kinds of possibilities magic might offer Black women, for *Beloved* represents a powerful reclamation of magical thinking—not as an escape from the realities and suffering of a girl like Pecola but as a re-narrativization of Black feminine pain, a story offering a means for self-possession. Written seventeen years after *The Bluest Eye*, Morrison's *Beloved* renegotiates the bankrupt promises of magic given to Black girls like Pecola by offering the "magic" of self-possession as a true "gift for the beloved." For Morrison, self-love is a truer form of magic than any external spiritual or supernatural force.

Beloved certainly deals in a much more explicit way with "magic" and the "supernatural" than *The Bluest Eye*. At its heart a ghost story, *Beloved* is nominally about the haunting of a woman and her daughter, Sethe and Denver, by a mysterious young woman that may or may not be the ghost of "Beloved," the young daughter Sethe murdered to save from being enslaved. As the novel begins, the house that Sethe, Denver, and Baby Suggs—Sethe's mother-in-law—live in, 124 Bluestone, is disturbed by a "spiteful" spirit that manifests itself in dark ways, "a mirror shattered," "two tiny hand prints … in the cake," "soda crackers crumbled and strewn in a line next to the doorsill" (3). Believing the haunting to be the spirit of her dead child, Sethe desperately wants to connect with her, to communicate. She asks Denver to do a séance with the baby, to contact the spirit, but attempting to talk with the ghost of a baby is fruitless: "She wasn't even two years old when she died," Sethe explains to Denver, "Too little to talk much" (4). Even so, Sethe is desperate to explain to her ghost daughter the reasons behind her actions, and she wishes there were some way she could bring her daughter back in the flesh. Unlike Pecola's wish, Sethe's supernatural dream comes true.

At first, the baby's haunting is mildly benevolent. When Sethe suggests that maybe they can move from the haunted house, Baby Suggs responds, "What'd be the point … Not a house in the country ain't packed to its rafters with some dead Negro's grief. We lucky this ghost is a baby" (5). In *Beloved*, it is not just the house that is haunted by memories of trauma, but the entire region.

However, Paul D—a man who was enslaved on the same plantation as Sethe—resurfaces and breaks the spell held on the house by the ghost baby. Seeing Paul D again reignites traumatic memories in Sethe that cannot be so easily exorcised. What Paul D and Sethe endured at their former plantation—Sweet Home—haunt their minds in far more insidious ways than the baby does at 124. Though the spirit of the baby gets displaced, the exorcism does not rid Sethe of her memories or Denver of her loneliness. The women mourn the loss of the ghost, who, though spiteful and full of rage, was "the only other company" the two can remember. When Paul D moves into the house days after his exorcism, he likewise fractures bonds among the women—Sethe, Denver, and the ghost baby—by his presence. A few days later, a mysterious young woman appears on the steps of the house. The same age her daughter would have been had Sethe not murdered her, the young woman appears to be the answer to Sethe's prayers. She quickly captivates Sethe, who believes that her appearance is some kind of magical way she might ease her suffering, finally confess to her deeds, and ask for her daughter's forgiveness.

The young woman, who calls herself "Beloved"—the one-word epitaph on Sethe's dead daughter's gravestone—is a welcome presence for both women. They see in her an opportunity to solidify a familial bond broken by the brutal world of Sweet Home. However, like Soaphead's magic, Beloved's supernatural potential is self-serving and toxic. Sethe is doubly haunted by the ghost woman and "haunted by her own actions" (Clough 187), but both forms of supernatural haunting do not invite transformation and healing, only (re)wounding. At first, Beloved's ravenous need for Sethe's attention is intoxicating; the young woman's affection is flattering, even though "the same adoration from her daughter (had it been forthcoming) would have annoyed her … but the company of this sweet, if peculiar, guest pleased her the way a zealot pleases his teacher" (*Beloved* 57). But Beloved's desire is not for Sethe to grow stronger and more independent; rather, she parasitically feeds on Sethe's traumatic memories and dark feelings.

Beloved's magic seems to grow stronger when she consumes narratives of trauma: "It became a way to feed her," the narrator writes, "Sethe learned the profound satisfaction Beloved got from storytelling. It amazed Sethe (as much as it pleased Beloved) because every mention of her past life hurt. Everything in it was painful or lost" (58). And yet, Sethe continues to feed the supernatural Beloved because watching her grow was "an unexpected pleasure" salving her guilt. Eventually, the two women develop a relationship that supersedes all others in Sethe's world. Because "Beloved yearns to possess her mother exclusively, irrespective of her sister, Denver, and her mother's lover, Paul D" (Ngom 198), Sethe is forced to choose between her roles as mother to Denver/lover to Paul D and her attachment to the magical young woman. The magic that Beloved offers Sethe promises healing and forgiveness, but, in actuality, her magic is a toxic solipsism that feeds itself on trauma: the more Sethe wallows in guilt, jealousy, anger, fear, or self-pity, the more powerful Beloved becomes.

If Beloved is somehow the supernatural fulfillment of Sethe's wish to explain to her daughter why she did the things she did, the answer to her prayer is poisoned—for Beloved does not offer Sethe forgiveness or understanding, only a bottomless appetite for Sethe's darkest fears and memories. Having her ghost daughter back in her life promises peace—"I couldn't lay down nowhere in peace, back then. Now I can"—she tells Beloved, but the kind of peace she receives is "like the drowned" (*Beloved* 204). Like Pecola in *The Bluest Eye*, Sethe's magical thinking ends up ensnaring her in a web of re-wounding that fragments her. Morrison emphasizes Sethe's brokenness in a chapter late in the novel where she alternates between speaking to herself and to/for Beloved: "Beloved, she my daughter. She mine. See. She come back to me … I also mean I'm yours. I wouldn't draw a breath without my children" (200–3). Beloved does not become a vessel through which Sethe can achieve forgiveness and self-possession but instead an identity that threatens to consume her. In Beloved's stream of consciousness section, she conflates Sethe's identity with her own and uses the language of possession to suggest that her final goal is to dissolve their two identities into one: "I am Beloved and she is mine … I am not separate from her … her face is my own and I want to be there in the place where her face is and to be looking at it too" (210). By conjuring Beloved from the grave, Sethe receives not a magical means of healing but a supernatural wounding that eventually overtakes her very identity.

The magic of Beloved's return promises self-possession but brings only actual possession. By the end of the novel, Beloved's hold on Sethe has become fatal. Denver notices that, "it was Beloved who made demands. Anything she wanted she got, and when Sethe ran out of things to give her, Beloved invented desire" (240). More insidiously, the ghost woman begins to dress "in Sethe's dresses … she imitated Sethe, talked the way she did, laughed her laugh and used her body the same way down to the walk, the way Sethe moved her hands, sighed through her house, held her head" until it is difficult for Denver to even "tell who was who" (241). Gradually, Beloved's existence begins to sap Sethe of her vitality. "The bigger Beloved got, the smaller Sethe became; the brighter Beloved's eyes, the more those eyes that used to never look away became slits of sleeplessness" (250). The parasitic relationship Beloved forms with Sethe becomes, by the end of the novel, vaguely consensual, with "Sethe trying to make up for" killing her daughter and "Beloved making her pay for it" (251). Recognizing there will be no end to that torment, Denver enlists the town to help her exorcise the woman from their house.

Significantly, the "magic" Denver and the townsfolk use to rid Sethe of Beloved is a familiar form of spirituality connected to Baby Suggs, Sethe's mother-in-law. When Sethe arrived at 124 after escaping Sweet Home, Baby Suggs takes her to a special place, the Clearing—"a wide-open place cut deep in the woods nobody knew what for" (87). There, Suggs holds a kind of church service, not based around an organized theology or dogmatic, teleological principle. Her "religion" speaks only of self-acceptance and love:

> She did not tell them to clean up their lives or to go and sin no more. She did not tell them they were the blessed of the earth, its inheriting meek or its glorybound pure. She told them that the only grace they could have was the grace they could imagine … "Here," she said, "in this here place, we flesh; flesh that weeps, laughs; flesh that dances on bare feet in grass. Love it. Love it hard … Love your hands! Love them. Raise them up and kiss them. Touch others with them, pat them together, stroke them on your face … *You* got to love it, *you!* (88, emphases in original)

When Beloved first comes to 124, Sethe returns to Suggs's Clearing to try to get clarity. She asks her mother-in-law for guidance and her cooling touch and feels the woman's fingers, "no more than the strokes of bird feather, but unmistakably caressing … Baby Suggs's long-distance love was equal to any skin-close love she had known" (95). Slowly, almost imperceptibly, the massaging hands become bolder and more dangerous until Sethe feels herself being choked. Denver and Beloved interrupt her before she passes out, and later, alone with Beloved in the woods, Denver confesses what she saw: "You did it, I saw you," she says, "I saw your face. You made her choke" (101). Morrison bifurcates "magic" into a healing world of spirituality and self-possession (Baby Suggs's cool touch) and a wounding, crippling possession that threatens to consume the self (Beloved's choking hands).

The struggle between Beloved's toxic magic and Suggs's healing spirituality is the crux of Morrison's *Beloved*. When the townsfolk come to sing and pray away Beloved's evil spirit, Sethe feels "as though the Clearing had come to her with all its heat and simmering leaves, where the voices of women searched for the right combination, the key, the code, the sound that broke the back of words" (261). When they do find the secret chords, it is a powerful magic, "a wave of sound wide enough to sound deep water and knock the pods off the chestnut trees. It broke over Sethe and she trembled like the baptized" (261). Morrison's use of religious/spiritual imagery here is significant in that it breaks Beloved's spell over Sethe. Only the redemptive power of Baby Suggs's self-acceptance can heal Sethe. At the end of the novel, when Paul D comes to visit Sethe one final time, he offers her the magic of Suggs's spiritual ethos, first in his gentle touch and washing of her feet, and finally by his assertion, "You your best thing, Sethe. You are" (273).

Morrison's *Beloved* rejects magic that feeds on despair and conjures parasites, and it also rejects the burden Black women are forced to accept in a world that asks them to own all their failures without celebrating their successes or survival. Such a magic is compelling because it promises visibility and closure by asking women to tell their own stories and gather their memories, but those narratives and memories are saturated in trauma and recriminations. Baby Suggs's promise of self-acceptance through self-possession—especially in the way it forms community—is the only magic that saves Sethe from complete destruction and makes possible a future Paul D could never have seen: "We need some kind of tomorrow," he tells Sethe as he caresses her (273). Unlike the end of *The Bluest Eye*—where Pecola disintegrates into pieces and loses any sense of herself—Sethe and Paul D share a hope that they can be gathered back together again, as Paul D joyfully recounts the refrain from Sixo's love song, "She gather me, man. The pieces I am, she gather them and give them back to me in all the right order" (272–3). If Beloved's magic offers trauma and fracturing, Baby Suggs's Black girl magic offers wholeness, healing, and community. Beloved's supernatural magic is divisive, lonely, and painful, but the affirmation of Suggs and Paul D that ends the novel reverberates strongly with Thompson's articulation of #BlackGirlMagic.

Thinking through the popularity of #BlackGirl Magic clarifies Morrison's evolution on the possibilities of magic from *The Bluest Eye* to *Beloved*, from rejection of magic, spirituality, or enchantment as something that obscures and ensnares Black women in a cycle of abuse and victimization (for Pecola) to a magic of legibility, visibility, celebration, and love (for Sethe). Morrison suggests that the successes of Black women—their survival in the face of inhuman odds, their thriving as mothers, sisters, daughters, citizens, or preachers, even their dogged failures and regrets—are magical, a love that moves away from possessing something or someone, as Pauline imagines it, and into a love of a self that is ultimately freeing and meaningful. And Morrison's #BlackGirlMagic operates simultaneously as a recognition, not a rejection, of the human realities of what it means to be a Black girl/woman in America; her novels expose the harshness of the lived realities of growing up as a Black girl even as they traffic in the language of the supernatural.

I want to conclude my analysis of Morrison's #BlackGirlMagic by suggesting how important it is that cultural and literary critics acknowledge how narratives of Black women's survivals and struggles are *still* being mediated by white patriarchy—even during the months I wrote and revised this essay. As I was working through my piece, I watched the public outcry after Naomi Osaka withdrew from the 2021 French Open and Simone Biles decided not to compete in certain events at the 2021 Olympics. Both women's decisions to prioritize their health (physical and emotional) were read by white, male commentators as the ultimate failure—selfishness. Piers Morgan condemned Boles in an essay for *The Daily Mail*: "Sorry Simone Biles, but there's nothing heroic or brave about quitting … you let down your team-mates, your fans and your country." In the reprehensible opinion piece, he goes on to applaud Biles's cockiness and grit by declaring herself the greatest Olympian of all time but excoriates her for taking care of her health first before doing her "duty" to her team.

Commentary like Morgan's shows how vital #BlackGirlMagic is, why it is necessary to emphasize self-acceptance and love, not in spite of but *because* of "failures." Because whatever Biles or Osaka might achieve as successes in the world of sports and beyond, they will routinely be defined by what they didn't do, not by their visibility in the winner's circle, but by the times when they were not there. As long as we continue to ask Black women and girls to own all of their shortcomings without ever celebrating their successes or making visible their narratives of survival and endurance, we risk fragmenting and wounding them; we continue the cycle of narratives in which Black women are visible only through their suffering. Toni Morrison's novels remind us, like Thompson's #BlackGirlMagic, that Black women are enough, that their existence and survival is a success, and that the spirit that animates them is magic. And perhaps, more than anything, Morrison and Thompson not only gave us books, words, and phrases to soothe our soul, but they also gave us something far more important: something to believe in.

WORKS CITED

Clough, Patricia Ticineto. "After Slavery." *Women's Studies Quarterly*, vol 42, nos. 1/2, Spring/Summer 2014, pp. 185–9.

Davis, Christina, and Toni Morrison. "Interview With Toni Morrison." *Présence Africaine*, Nouvelle Série, no. 145, 1er Trimestre 1988, pp. 141–50.

Kuenz, Jane. "*The Bluest Eye*: Notes on History, Community, and Black Female Subjectivity." *African American Review*, vol. 27, no. 3, Fall 1993, pp. 421–431.

Morgan, Piers. "Sorry Simone Biles." *The Daily Mail*, July 28, 2021. https://www.dailymail.co.uk/news/article-9835069/PIERS-MORGAN-Sorry-Simone-boast-GOAT-selfishly-quit.html. Accessed Aug. 6, 2021.

Morrison, Toni. *Beloved*. Knopf, 1987.

Morrison, Toni. *The Bluest Eye*. 1970. Plume, 1994.

Ngom, Ousmane. "Magic Realism as Postcolonial Aesthetics in African and Afrodiasporic Literatures." *Canadian Review of Comparative Literature*, vol. 47, no. 2, June 2020, pp. 196–214.

Roye, Susmita. "Toni Morrison's Disrupted Girls and Their Disturbed Girlhoods: *The Bluest Eye* and *A Mercy*." *Callaloo*, vol. 35, no.1, Winter 2012, pp. 212–27.

Solomon, Akiba. "The Real Problem With the #BlackGirlMagic Backlash is That You're Missing the Point." *Colorlines*, Jan. 13, 2016, https://www.colorlines.com/articles/real-problem-blackgirlmagic-backlash-youre-missing-point. Accessed Aug. 6, 2021.

"Why Are People Arguing about 'Black Girl Magic'?" *BBC*, Jan. 16, 2016, https://www.bbc.com/news/blogs-trending-35263240. Accessed Aug. 6, 2021.

CHAPTER FOUR

"Is? My Baby? Burning?": Segregation, Soldiers, and Civil Rights in Toni Morrison's *Sula*

THOMAS FAHY

The drowning death of Chicken Little creates a barrier between Sula and Nel, the central characters of Toni Morrison's novel *Sula* (1973). At his funeral, they do not "touch hands or look at each other … There was a space, a separateness, between them" (64). Only in the cemetery, "some distance away from the grave," does this divide dissolve (66). In many ways, this tension between intimacy and space characterizes their relationship. The closeness of the girls begins preternaturally—"as they had already made each other's acquaintance in the delirium of their noon dreams" (51)—and it continues throughout their adult lives. This bond stems, in part, from an understanding of racial and gendered oppression: "Because each had discovered years before that they were neither white nor male, and that all freedom and triumph was forbidden to them … they found in each other's eyes the intimacy they were looking for" (52). Yet significant gaps offset this connection. Sula leaves the Bottom for a decade without sending word to anyone. The women do not speak for three years after Sula's affair with Nel's husband. And only twenty-five years after Sula's death does Nel come to understand the importance of their friendship.

These spaces mirror numerous gaps in the text that underscore Morrison's social and political commentary about segregation. She first anchors the divisions between Black and white in the origin story of "the Bottom," an African American community nestled above the valley town of Medallion. As the narrator explains, a master convinced his slave to labor in exchange for freedom and some inhospitable land in the hills described as "the bottom of heaven—best land there is" (5). This backstory provides the historical touchstone for the way Black lives have been shaped by inequity, injustice, and exploitation throughout American history. In fact, Jim Crow laws permeate almost every aspect of life in the Bottom—from First World War soldiers serving in segregated units and "colored only" train cars to the racist hiring practices that prevent African Americans from working on New River Road.

The spaces in the novel get linked with violence as well, and Morrison uses veterans and the specter of war to examine the fraught relationship between the Black community and segregationist America. The townspeople of the Bottom exist in an embattled state: "They determined (without ever knowing they had made up their minds to do so) to survive floods, white people, tuberculosis, famine and ignorance" (90). Eva, for example, leaves her children for eighteen months with a neighbor, and like an injured veteran, she returns without a leg. Chicken Little goes missing for three days because the whites who discover him cannot be bothered to ferry a Black boy across the river. And after vanishing for ten years, Sula returns to the Bottom accompanied by a plague of dead robins. These temporal gaps point to some of the untold stories of Black America and cast war as a metaphor for various forms of racial oppression.

Specifically, the role of the First World War veterans and the allusions to other wars in the novel highlight the hypocrisy of asking African Americans to fight for democracy abroad while denying them basic freedoms at home. Plum, for example, serves in the First World War for two years before returning as a heroin addict. The most prominent veteran in the novel, Shadrack, remembers only eight days of his lengthy hospitalization for shellshock. He does not begin to recover until the early days of the Second World War when he "improved enough to feel lonely" (155). Shadrack's haunting presence, through his holiday National Suicide Day and his various encounters with Sula and Nel, spans 1919 to 1965. These damaged characters, along with the dates that serve as chapter titles, become a vehicle for Morrison to examine the historical relationship between military service and segregation—from the sacrifices of African American soldiers in combat to the eventual fracturing of the civil rights movement as a result of Vietnam.

In many respects, *Sula* fits into the tradition of the American war novel from Willa Cather's *One of Ours* (1922) to Tim O'Brien's *The Things They Carried* (1990). In the context of the late 1960s and early 1970s, Morrison's depiction of First World War veterans would have invited comparisons with the ongoing military conflict in Vietnam. On one level, Shadrack's experiences draw attention to the costs of war for the Black community—costs that did little to change the social realities of segregation, economic exploitation, and racial violence. On another level, by framing the novel with Shadrack's National Suicide Days in 1919 and 1941, as well as his observations about pollution in 1965, Morrison comments on the various hypocrisies undergirding US foreign and domestic policies. She challenges contemporary readers to consider the harmful impact of the Vietnam War, in part, by inviting them to recognize the dual conflict facing African Americans as they battled for civil rights at home and democracy abroad. The escalation in Vietnam and the burgeoning anti-war movement also had the effect of undermining the fight for social justice, and Morrison uses the violence at the end of the novel as an image for the fracturing of civil rights coalitions. In this way, the text suggests that the battle for racial equality would need to extend far beyond the accomplishments of the Civil Rights Act of 1964 and the Voting Rights Act of 1965.

Finally, the spaces in *Sula* challenge binary thinking. As more time passes, Eva, Sula, and ultimately Nel raise questions about the labels "good" and "evil," and the ambiguity surrounding these terms condemns the kind of binary political discourse (good/evil, right/wrong) used to justify war. This type of rhetoric ultimately placed some of the most vulnerable in society (people of color, the poor) on the front lines, and it exposed the country's failure to live up to its own purported values of fairness and freedom. By inverting binaries within the novel, particularly the way characters vacillate between viewing themselves and each other in moral absolutes, Morrison condemns the facile political discourse that fostered racial prejudice, downplayed the devastating human costs of war, and fomented social unrest at home in the name of democracy.

FILLING IN THE GAPS: AFRICAN AMERICAN SOLDIERS AND THE FIGHT FOR FREEDOM

Most scholars have interpreted Toni Morrison's *Sula* through the lens of Black Feminist Criticism. In fact, the novel became a touchstone for this field with the publication of Barbara Smith's essay "Toward a Black Feminist Criticism" in 1977. Her discussion of the ways race, class, and sexuality intersect to devalue the work of Black women established the foundation for her reading of *Sula* as a Black lesbian text. Though she views Sula and Nel's relationship as "suffused with an erotic romanticism" (162), lesbian desire can only be inferred. It exists in one of the many gaps that challenge readers to consider the unseen, missing layers of Morrison's work.

Numerous scholars have noted this feature of *Sula*. As Robert Grant argues, "*Sula* in form and content is 'about' gaps, lacks, 'missing' subjects, and ambiguous psychic space, all of which must be 'filled' and interpreted by the reader" (94). Likewise, Lucille P. Fultz ponders the "gaping hole" of Sula's ten-year gap between 1927 and 1937 in similar terms, arguing that this provocative decision on Morrison's part prompts the reader "to wonder about Sula's whereabouts and activities ... to fill in the gaps about [her] life" (5–6). Yet Morrison's emphasis on dates, titling each chapter with a specific year, draws attention to the curious holes in the novel's historical timeline as well. These missing years raise questions about aspects of the Black experience that often remain obscure to white America. In particular, the specter of the First World War, Second World War, and Vietnam invite broader discussions about the hypocrisy of segregationist policies in the United States and the relationship between military service and civil rights.

In her essay "Unspeakable Things Unspoken," Morrison acknowledges that "*Sula* was begun in 1969 ... in a period of extraordinary political activity" (24), and in many respects, the novel can be viewed through the lens of the 1960s—as a commentary on the struggle for civil rights as it intersected with US foreign policy and the military. She goes on to note her interest in exploring "the traumatic displacement this most wasteful capitalist war had on black people in particular" (26). Most of the scholarship about the character, Shadrack, however, focuses on African American veterans in the immediate aftermath of Armistice. Manuela López Ramírez, for example, links the madness of war with racist ideology in the early twentieth century. In her reading of *Sula*, she draws a parallel between the "appalling ordeals of war" and discrimination and oppression in American culture at the time: "In Morrison's shell-shocked soldiers, mental distress is connected both to the horrors of war and to the horrors of racist Jim Crow times" (130). Similarly, Chuck Jackson offers a compelling reading of *Sula* that weaves together its wartime commentary with contemporary lynching practices. He argues that the imagery throughout the novel, such as burned and maimed bodies, grotesque public spectacles, and National Suicide Day, alludes to lynching narratives. As such, this imagery helps "historicize and contextualize African-American participation in the war overseas with the undeclared war against African Americans at home" (Jackson 375). Ultimately, for Jackson, the lynched Black soldier becomes "a horrific reminder of how black men (still) represented a visible disruption of national, political, and racial uniformity in the early twentieth century" (376). Morrison even hints that the other damaged veteran in *Sula*, Plum, has witnessed racial violence in his travels throughout the United States. As Carlyle V. Thompson has noted, Plum visited several cities that witnessed race riots during the Red Summer of 1919 before returning to the Bottom.

Given the historical scope of the novel, however, its military narrative does not merely address Jim Crow laws, domestic terrorism, and rioting in the early twentieth century. If we take the ending of the novel as a starting point, which the prologue encourages, we must consider the intersection between the military and civil rights throughout the twentieth century. The battle among First World War veterans for benefits, the integration of the military after the Second World War, and the fracturing of the civil rights movement during Vietnam fill in some of the important historical gaps in Morrison's text. They give insight into the national events that influenced life in the Bottom. And they enable readers to examine the corrosive history of segregation and the failure of US culture to live up to its own ideals about democracy, opportunity, and justice.

President Woodrow Wilson famously claimed that the First World War would "make the world safe for democracy," and US involvement in this conflict included over 360,000 African American servicemen. Within the Black community, many perceived military service as a way to change racist attitudes at home and to create greater social and economic mobility. Even W. E. B. Du Bois viewed the war as a possible vehicle for transforming race relations. As he argued in "The African Roots of the War" (1915), a real commitment to peace demanded a recognition of the global oppression of people of color and the application of democratic ideals to everyone: "We shall not drive war from this world until we treat them [black men] as free and equal citizens in a world-democracy of all races and nations" (712). He—along with other civil rights organizations and activists such as journalist James Weldon Johnson—viewed the war as intertwined with civil rights. After the lynching of five Black men in Georgia in 1917, for instance, Johnson wrote about the incongruity between American outrage over German atrocities in Belgium and their tacit support for the wholesale violence against African Americans in the South. According to historian Jonathan Rosenberg, this "explicit parallel between the violation of human rights overseas and at home" was designed "to grab the attention of [Johnson's] readers and deepen their commitment to the domestic struggle, a strategy that [he] and others used repeatedly in order to garner support for the movement" (35). Johnson's writings, along with Harlem Renaissance works such as Claude McKay's "If We Must Die" (1919) and Jean Toomer's "Blood-Burning Moon" (1923), captured the anger of the Black community over lynching, and this type of literature and journalism became a powerful tool for calling on white America to act.

Despite these appeals, the country watched over twenty-five cities burn from race riots in the "Red Summer" of 1919, in which hundreds of African Americans died. Seventy-seven were lynched in 1919 alone, including several Black men in uniform (see McWhirter 71). According to McWhirter in *Red Summer*, these atrocities inspired civil rights activism, and soon National Association for the Advancement of Colored People (NAACP) leaders pressured Congress to pass anti-lynching legislation. Several Congressmen even crafted bills proposing a constitutional amendment to prevent lynching (35). Yet widespread rumors about the sexual threat that Black men posed to white women undermined many of these efforts. Mob violence continued to flare up across the country, and such rioting ratcheted up tensions that transformed "everyday places where blacks and whites intersected—trains, work, restaurants, bars, and the street—into potential battlegrounds" (74).

The most significant civil rights gains at the time, however, came from the government itself—particularly through its efforts to support veterans. The US Employment Service promised assistance to those who served in the armed forces through medical care, job training, and educational opportunities. Yet it failed to anticipate the degree to which racist ideology would stymie these efforts. Many hospitals, for example, turned away African American veterans because they did not have segregated wards. White medical examiners often denied disability claims for Blacks.

Culturally biased tests, labeling African American soldiers as inferior, limited access to occupational training programs and higher education. And African Americans who did not indicate race on job applications often found themselves fired on sight. In response, the US Employment Service began pressuring companies to reserve jobs for these men. It provided scholarships for veterans at Black colleges. It even funded separate hospitals. When Congress finally approved neurosis and shellshock as illnesses that qualified for disability benefits in 1921, it "guaranteed black veterans eligibility to receive treatment in a government-run hospital" (Keene 160).

Disabled Black veterans, in particular, occupied a unique position with regard to government support. As Jennifer D. Keene points out, "Securing the economic rights of disabled black veterans, the only group of African Americans that the federal government had officially pledged to help, became a critical part of this larger campaign to enlist the federal government as an ally in the struggle for civil rights" (151). By seeking the help of organizations such as the NAACP and even former commanding officers, Black veterans fought for their benefits, and their successes became cause for celebration. Activists worked tirelessly to support these men, and as Keene persuasively argues, "Rather than viewing them as a special group with unique problems to overcome, the civil rights movement linked the disabled veteran struggle to the obstacles that every person of color faced in the United States" (166). In these ways, the government helped advance the fight for racial justice, and the Black community held firm to its view of military service as a vehicle for social and economic advancement.

The Second World War provided another opportunity for furthering the cause of civil rights. President Franklin Roosevelt altered some of the racial biases influencing the draft through the Selective Service Act of 1940, which prohibited racial discrimination. As such, the military was forced to draft African Americans in numbers that reflected their overall population (roughly 10 percent). By 1945, of the nearly 2.5 million African Americans who had registered for the draft, over one million were inducted into military service, or 10.7 percent of overall inductees (see Westheider 21). Yet when the Selective Service Act expired in 1947, Congress replaced it with a new law that did not prohibit racial quotas or segregation. The Senate also resisted President Harry Truman's calls to enact anti-lynching and anti–poll tax laws. In response, Truman signed Executive Order 9981 in the summer of 1948 to outlaw segregation in the military and to create a committee with oversight to ensure its desegregation. The order begins by stating that the armed services must uphold the "highest standards of democracy, with equality of treatment for all of those who serve," and it goes on to specify that this equality must be provided "without regard to race, color, religion, or national origin" (see "Executive Order 9981"). As James Westheider notes, the Selective Service officially announced the end of racial quotas for the draft and prevented restrictions on Black enlistments (21).

Yet the Korean War proved to be the watershed moment for civil rights in the military, though a costly one. African Americans now volunteered and were drafted in high numbers, making up approximately 25 percent of all inductees between 1950 and 1954, and they were more likely to see combat and die in battle than their white counterparts (see Knauer 167). Initially, Blacks fought in segregated units, but these units fully integrated by the end of the war. As Christine Knauer points out, however, this process was uneven. The navy and air force seemed willing to accept government calls to desegregate, but the army proved more intractable under General MacArthur's leadership (167). Nevertheless, the Korean War did end the Jim Crow military, and this policy change resonated powerfully within the African American community. According to Daniel S. Lucks, the armed forces—as "the most integrated institution in American society"—held "an esteemed place in the minds of black America" (6). It offered professional and economic opportunities, including "the chance to leave their impoverished urban ghettos or provincial southern hamlets" (6). This attitude toward the US military continued into the 1960s, and it created significant tension among African Americans over Vietnam.

In the first half of the 1960s, civil rights remained at the forefront of American life. In 1960, the sit-in at a Woolworth's segregated lunch counter in Greensboro, North Carolina, inspired thousands of students to organize similar protests throughout the South. In Birmingham, Alabama, in 1963, images of dogs attacking African American children and the police spraying crowds with firehoses were seared into the public imagination. A few months later, at the March on Washington, Martin Luther King's "I Had a Dream" speech echoed in the nation's ears—only to be followed two weeks later by the death of four Black girls in the 16th Street Baptist Church bombing in Birmingham. The culmination of this fight for civil rights—a fight that had been waged since the Civil War—occurred in 1964 and 1965 with the Civil Rights Act and the Voting Rights Act, respectively. In the wake of milestone 1950s legislation such as *Brown v. Board of Education* (1954), the Civil Rights Act of 1964 prohibited discrimination based on race and gender, ending segregation in schools and public accommodations. It also established the Equal Employment Opportunity Commission and gave the Office of Education authority to help desegregate schools. The Voting Rights Act, as Rosenberg explains, "gave the attorney general the power to order federal examiners to register black voters in places where local officials refused to do so and banned literacy tests and other tactics states and counties had used to prevent blacks from voting" (217). By the end of the year, nearly a quarter of a million African Americans registered to vote.

At the very moment of these monumental accomplishments, the rise of the anti-war movement in 1965, the same year President Johnson first sent combat troops to Vietnam, began fracturing these domestic efforts for racial justice. By the end of 1965, "The Vietnam War would supplant civil rights as the nation's most pressing issue and polarize the struggle for racial justice at home" (Lucks 71). In fact, the violence abroad only seemed to deflect attention away from the ongoing racial strife in the United States. Until Lyndon Johnson's Gulf of Tonkin Resolution on August 4, 1964, which allowed the president to use military force in Southeast Asia without declaring war, most Americans paid little attention to Vietnam. One Gallup poll in 1964 found two-thirds of the public uninformed or without an opinion about the events unfolding in Southeast Asia, and a University of Michigan poll revealed that one in four Americans knew nothing of the fighting (see Lucks 60 and 67). African Americans seemed even less interested. They were focused more on the significance of the Civil Rights Act and the ongoing violence in the South. Front page news coverage of the Gulf of Tonkin Resolution, for example, appeared alongside an account of the bodies of three missing civil rights workers discovered in Mississippi. Likewise, 3,500 marines arrived to defend Da Nang air base on the same day as Bloody Sunday in Selma, Alabama, on March 7, 1965.

Nevertheless, with its positive view of the military, the Black community initially considered the Vietnam War an opportunity. "Consequently, blacks joined the service in great numbers and reenlisted at over twice the rate of whites," as Westheider notes. "Many black leaders around the nation lauded the military for its advances and held it up as a model for the rest of the nation to emulate" (2). Civil rights organizations, however, disagreed over the best way to handle the war. Younger, more radical groups, such as the Student Nonviolent Coordinating Committee and the Students for a Democratic Society, publicly condemned the hypocrisy of a government that would send troops 8,000 miles away in the name of democracy but do little to crack down on segregationist violence and bloodshed in the Deep South. However, more moderate members warned against such criticisms. African American leaders did not want to squander their newfound access to power through the Civil Rights Act and the Voting Rights Act, and they harbored fears that President Johnson might withdraw his support for racial justice if the Black community did not support his administration's stance on Vietnam (Lucks 84).

These internal divisions came at a time when much of white America viewed the battle for civil rights as over. This attitude dovetailed with many white activists turning their attention from civil rights to Vietnam. According to Lucks, the milestone legislative acts in 1964 and 1965

> [created] the erroneous impression that the civil rights issue had been resolved. They believed that it was now the responsibility of African Americans alone to improve their plight. The euphoria over the eradication of de jure segregation in the South would be short-lived and would give way to confusion over how to tackle the more tenacious issues of poverty, despair, and illiteracy in the northern ghettos. (93)

Certainly, the problems of racial inequity were far from over as the riots in New York City in 1964 and Watts in 1965 illustrated. The Watts riot, which started just days after the Voting Rights Act had been signed into law, proved to be the largest in US history at the time. It resulted in thirty-five deaths, thousands of injuries, and nearly 4,000 arrests. As the civil rights movement struggled to find a path forward, many leaders feared retribution for any anti-war activism. Even Martin Luther King, Jr., after his first public critique of the war in 1965, drew the ire of various US Senators and FBI director J. Edgar Hoover, who considered him a Communist. The subsequent personal and public attacks shocked King, and they deterred him from pursuing anti-war activism at that time.

As African Americans enlisted and were drafted into the military, they soon found their prospects for a better future dashed. They not only experienced systemic racism within the military itself, but they were also dying in disproportionately high numbers. African Americans constituted 25 percent of all combat deaths in 1965 alone (see Westheider 12). The problem, as Westheider explains, did not stem from overrepresentation but the fact that so many African Americans served in combat units. They were also ineligible for the types of exceptions available to millions of whites such as attending college. Many African Americans had gone to poorly funded segregated schools, which made college a near impossibility, and "those with lower than a high school education were three times as likely to be drafted as those with a college education" (23). Such discrepancies raised issues about the racial fairness of the draft, chipping away at support for the war within the Black community. The hypocrisy of fighting the evils of communism and upholding the values of democracy in Southeast Asia became increasingly difficult to reconcile with urban riots and the rise of the Black Power movement at home. While the end of segregation marked the culmination of a struggle that had been waged throughout the twentieth century, the civil rights movement needed a new strategy for dealing with racial inequity as evidenced by poverty, substandard housing, and limited opportunities in education and employment. Yet the war consumed the Johnson Administration and splintered this movement, leaving the more insidious and intractable problem of institutional racism in place even at the height of civil rights accomplishments.

SEGREGATION, SOLDIERS, AND THE PROBLEM OF "EVIL" IN *SULA*

As Morrison's portrait of veterans and the historical scope of *Sula* demonstrate, military service for African Americans mostly led to trauma, disillusionment, and self-destruction. Black soldiers found themselves on a two-front war: fighting against both foreign enemies in the name of democracy and systematic racism at home. In the context of the novel, the link between segregation and war captures the Black community's embattled quest for equality. Through Morrison's depiction of segregated public accommodations, Plum's drug addiction, Shadrack's invention of National Suicide Day, and the specter of war in 1965, *Sula* captures the horrors of segregation and places the history of Black military service at the heart of the nation's struggles for civil rights. What emerges is a damning portrait of American hypocrisy over the failure to achieve its democratic ideals and the need to address the underlying problems of racist ideology.

Early in the novel, Morrison captures the vile indignities of institutional racism through the experiences of Helene Wright and several Black veterans on a segregated train. Helene, with her daughter Nel in tow, feels apprehensive about travelling to the Deep South for her grandmother's funeral. She believes "a beautiful dress" and a refined bearing will shield her from the humiliations of Jim Crow America (*Sula* 19). Almost immediately, however, the insults from a white conductor bring back "all the old vulnerabilities," and she resorts to "an eagerness to please," smiling at him "dazzlingly and coquettishly" (20, 21). Her behavior inspires the disgust of two African American soldiers in the car: "Their faces tighten, a movement under the skin from blood to marble" (21–2). This transformation stems partially from the double standard of fighting for democracy abroad while suffering the daily humiliations of institutional racism in the United States. At the same time, they also seem to be hardening themselves against the implications of Helene's obsequiousness, which is inspired by fear and the ugly imprint of racial hierarchies on Black identity. Blackness was something to apologize for in America, and veterans, like these men, hoped military service would change that. Not surprisingly, Morrison describes them as wearing "shit-colored uniforms" (21), transforming clothing that should have afforded them dignity into an image for the filthy hypocrisy of segregation.

Plum, Eva's son, returns to the United States after the First World War with a similar sense of hopefulness until he witnesses some of the more explosive consequences of racial injustice. Between 1919 and 1920, Plum travels around the country, visiting major northern cities that all experienced race riots: "He returned to the States in 1919 but did not get back to Medallion until 1920. He wrote letters from New York, Washington, DC, and Chicago full of promises of homecomings, but there was obviously something wrong" (45). The "something wrong" has multiple sources here. First, these cities were among the over twenty-five that experienced race riots in the Red Summer between April and November of 1919. Several riots broke out in New York City throughout the summer months of 1919, for example. In Washington, DC, the July riot involved drive-by shootings and attempted lynchings. African Americans were being dragged from streetcars and beaten in front of the White House, forcing President Wilson to mobilize 2,000 marines to patrol the streets (McWhirter 109). Plum would have also likely witnessed either the massive riot or its aftermath in Chicago. After an African American teenager was drowned for drifting into a whites-only beach on Lake Michigan, a riot erupted when police refused to arrest anyone other than a Black man at the scene. The violence lasted several days until the state militia intervened. Over 1000 Black families had their homes burned to the ground. Stores and streetcars were vandalized and looted. Over 500 people were injured. And thirty-eight people lost their lives (McWhirter 147). The gaps surrounding Plum's experiences during the war and the Red Summer link the violence of trench warfare with racial violence in the United States. Both leave Plum devastated and hopeless, driving him to isolation and heroin addiction.

Eva responds to Plum's condition by burning him to death—a metaphor for both the fires of war and racial divisiveness in the United States. Her rationale for this act has to do with his masculinity. According to Eva, "I done everything I could to make him leave me and go on and live and be a man but he wouldn't and I had to keep him out so I just thought of a way he could die like a man, not all scrunched up inside my womb, but like a man" (*Sula* 72). War, segregation, and drugs have infantilized Plum, leaving him unable to discuss his past or his hopes for the future. In fact, Plum remained doggedly silent about his experiences: "Everybody ... waited for him to tell them whatever it was he wanted them to know. They waited in vain" (45). Nevertheless, the domestic conditions for African Americans give some insight into Plum's condition. Poverty, dilapidated housing, and limited access to education and employment opportunities characterized Black life in the aftermath of the First World War. Morrison captures this dynamic in the Bottom, in part, through the emasculation of Nel's husband, Jude. When his skin color prevents him from getting work on the New River Road, for example, Nel realizes that "rage, rage and a determination to take on a man's role" inspired him to marry. Subsequently, he relies on her to sooth his wounded pride, "to care about his hurt" (82). The consequences of prejudice and disillusionment cause both men to suffer. Eva hints at this after Hannah confronts her in a panic about Plum burning: "Is? My baby? Burning?" (48). Eva's three-part question links this moment with Morrison's broader themes. The verb "is" invites readers to ask, "What is the truth about Plum's experiences and the lasting impact of racism on black identity?" The reference to "my baby" becomes Eva's way of asking whether or not the man who witnessed war and race riots is still her child, still the Plum she knew, raised, and "floated in a swaddle of love and affection" until 1917. Finally, the question of "burning" challenges readers to think about the sources burning the Black community in America—whether military service for a country denying them civil rights or racist practices robbing them of dignity and opportunity.

Finally, Morrison connects the most prominent veteran in the novel, Shadrack, whose Biblical namesake links him with fire,[1] to the devastating consequences of racism as well. During his "first encounter with the enemy" in 1917, Shadrack witnesses the face of a Black infantryman "fly off ... The rest of the soldier's head disappeared under the inverted soup bowl of his helmet. But stubbornly, taking no direction from the brain, the body of the headless soldier ran on" (8). Certainly, this faceless, headless body becomes an image for the incomprehensible losses of war in which casualties can too easily become statistics. In the context of this segregated unit, however, this moment also represents the countless casualties of racism in the United States from the atrocities of slavery to the practice of lynching in the Jim Crow era. Not surprisingly, this soldier's facelessness creates a longing in Shadrack to verify his own existence, and this crisis of identity resonates with Du Bois's

---

[1] The name Shadrack alludes to the third chapter in the Book of Daniel in which Shadrach, Meshach, and Abednego refuse to worship the gold idol of King Nebuchadnezzar. Infuriated by their defiance, the King has them cast into a fiery furnace, but it does not harm them. Unlike his biblical namesake, Morrison's Shadrack does not come out of the fiery furnace of war unsinged, but he does survive literally.

famous notion of "double-consciousness" in *The Souls of Black Folk* (1903)—the awareness among African Americans of always being viewed through the lens of white racism, of being both Negro and American, both American and not American. The Black soldier had to reconcile his experiences with inequality both in and out of uniform, and Morrison captures the devastating consequences of this through Shadrack.

Discrimination immediately marks Shadrack's postwar experiences during his convalescence in a military hospital. He finds comfort, for example, in the meticulously divided food trays: "the white, the red, and the brown, would stay where they were—would not explode or burst forth from their restricted zones" (*Sula* 8). The language of violence here not only reflects his wartime trauma but also the blood-red risks associated with integration—or the mixture of brown and white—in America. This may explain his panic while hallucinating that his fingers are "[growing] in higgledy-piggledy fashion" (9). These ever-growing hands suggest a desire to reach or strive for more in a country unwilling to offer opportunity to African Americans. Only in a straitjacket, with his hands bound and hidden from sight, does Shadrack feel "relieved and grateful" again (9). His sense of equilibrium, in other words, gets restored only within the familiar confines of being a Black man in America. Not surprisingly, the end of his medical care has nothing to do with wellness but with a hospital directive to create more space—a reminder both of the military's lag in granting health care services for those with shellshock and of the inequitable treatment of Black veterans more broadly. Aimless, disoriented, and traumatized, Shadrack finds himself arrested for intoxication and vagrancy. Only when he sees his Black face reflected in the toilet water of the cell does he regain control of his hands. This reflection, like the shit-colored uniforms of the veterans on the train, becomes an image for the disgraceful treatment of African Americans. The recognition of his blackness stops the uncontrollable growth of his fingers and his subconscious desire for recognition as a US soldier. Instead, Shadrack resigns himself to the imprisonment of being Black in America, and he chooses to isolate himself from country and community.

Morrison also links Shadrack with the segregationist violence inflicted on Chicken Little's body. Shadrack's home, which Sula enters to find out if he witnessed Chicken Little's drowning, has a meticulous neatness that strikes her as incongruous with his public persona: "The only black who could curse white people and get away with it, who drank in the road from the mouth of the bottle, who shouted and shook in the streets. This cottage? ... With its made-up bed" (62). This contrast can be understood, in part, through the tension between control and chaos that shapes Shadrack's life. The order of the cabin, an environment he can fully control, contrasts the chaos of dealing with the indignities of Jim Crow America. His encounters with whites devolve into shouting because they serve as reminders of the failed promises of democracy and decency. After the exchange in Shadrack's cabin, a white bargeman discovers Chicken Little's body, and this man's interior monologue captures the legacy of racist ideology. He views African Americans as animals and mules, and he even references "Ham's sons," one of the Biblical stories used to justify slavery (63). Upon seeing Chicken Little's body, for example, the sheriff merely claims that "they didn't have no niggers in their county" (64). Neither he nor the bargeman, who does not want to return two miles upriver to deliver the body to Medallion, care about this boy because of his skin color. Instead, the body gets dragged in the water and does not get returned for three days. His condition is so horrifying that Chicken Little's mother goes into shock upon seeing him: "Her mouth flew wide open again and it was seven hours before she was able to close it and to make a sound" (64). In a sense, she is witnessing a war-ravaged body. His death even inspires some of the townswomen to think of their own sons who died in the First World War: "Or they thought of their son newly killed and remembered his legs in short pants and wondered where the bullet went in" (65). Once again, the war becomes a metaphor for the embattled state of Black lives in the early twentieth century, and Chicken Little's burial in the "colored part of the cemetery" offers a chilling reminder of the intractability of white prejudices.

Shadrack's subsequent association with the devastation surrounding New River Road links the disillusionment of the Black community with both world wars. When construction begins in 1927, the optimistic mood in Medallion is predicated on a falsehood: "The war was over, a fake prosperity was still around" (81). This fakeness stems from the gap between the economic hopes of this project (trade possibilities and "a hunger for more and more") and the racist practices that prevented African Americans from sharing in this prosperity. Jude Green, for example, longs to be part of this undertaking "not just for the good money, more for the work itself ... More than anything he wanted the camaraderie of the road men: the lunch buckets, the hollering, the body movement that in the end produced something real, something he could point to" (81–2). Like many men in the Bottom, Jude desires a job that can provide a sense of accomplishment and community, and Morrison makes freedom, as represented by body movement here, a prerequisite for enabling African Americans to build something real. However, such freedom is denied to Jude, and he soon realizes that African Americans will never be chosen for the crew—only "thin-armed white boys ... and the bull-necked Greeks and Italians" (82). Once again, prejudice emerges as the corrosive force that limits African Americans, leaving nothing behind but "rage, rage," hurt, and "raveling edges" (82, 83).

In 1941, the year the United States enters the Second World War, Shadrack's National Suicide Day attracts the attention of almost everyone in town, and this event once again connects America's war abroad with racial violence at home. As a spontaneous parade forms, the community feels a false sense of hope:

> The same hope that kept them picking beans for other farmers; kept them from finally leaving as they talked of doing; kept them knee-deep in other people's dirt; kept them excited about other people's wars; kept them solicitous of white people's children; kept them convinced that some magic "government" was going to lift them up, out and away from that dirt, those beans, those wars. (*Sula* 160)

Decades of economic and social oppression have left this community resentful over tireless labor "in other people's dirt," unequal racial hierarchies, and war itself. All of these forces have kept them "from finally leaving." They do not have dirt/land of their own to cultivate, and the description of wars as "other people's" alludes to the government's ongoing hypocrisy in asking Black men to sacrifice their lives in the name of rights denied to them. The primary war for the Black community, in other words, is over equality, dignity, and fairness within the United States. Ironically, the inability of the government to "lift them up" does involve magic, a sleight of hand that promises opportunity but remains unwilling to make the necessary changes to enable it.

The destructive climax of National Suicide Day in 1941 not only foreshadows the incomprehensible losses of the Second World War, which African American soldiers will share, but it also becomes a reminder of the social forces that continue to devastate the Black community. As Shadrack's parade gets closer to New River Road, the entrance to the unfinished tunnel reminds them of their own disenfranchisement: "Their hooded eyes swept over the place where their hope had lain since

1927. There was the promise: leaf-dead. The teeth unrepaired, the coal credit cut off, the chest pains unattended, the school shoes unbought, the rush-stuffed mattresses, the broken toilets, the leaning porches, the slurred remarks and the staggering childish malevolence of their employers" (161). Not a single aspect of Black life has been untouched by the systemic denial of economic opportunity: medical health, basic necessities, household repairs, and personal dignity (under the cruelty of employers). The reference to school shoes also captures the way poverty traps generation after generation in similar conditions.

When the crowd sees the tunnel, they lash out with anger and resentment, and Morrison associates this moment with war to include military service as another false promise by white America:

> led by the tough, the enraged, and the young they picked up the lengths of timber and thin steel ribs and smashed the bricks they would never fire in yawning kilns … They killed, as best they could, the tunnel they were forbidden to build … but in their need … to wipe from the face of the earth the work of the thin-armed Virginia boys, the bull-necked Greeks and the knife-faced men who waved the leaf-dead promise, they went too deep, too far. (161–2)

Their desire to eradicate what the tunnel represents—segregation, racism, and the false promises of opportunity—leads to an act of self-destruction. The description of going too deep suggests that the ideology of racism is too deeply wedded into the foundation of American culture to destroy. Yet Shadrack's haunting presence over this spectacle, as he stands there "ringing his bell," adds another layer to this tragedy. With the country on the cusp of entering the Second World War, African Americans will join the US military, and like those people in the Bottom trying to prevent others from drowning in the tunnel, more Black soldiers will be "pulled to their deaths" (162). A new generation of Shadracks will be forged by the horrors of war only to return to a home shaped by racial injustice and violence.

The novel ends in 1965, on the hundredth anniversary of the end of the Civil War and in the year of the Voting Rights Act, yet Morrison opens this chapter with uncertainty about the extent of Black freedom in America: "Things were so much better in 1965. Or so it seemed" (163). African Americans worked in stores, wearing keys for the cash register around their necks, and one Black man even taught math at a local school. Yet Nel reflects on postwar prosperity in the 1940s and 1950s through the lens of loss. Her romantic relationship with a sergeant, for example, ends when he gets "called away," and she resigns herself to experiencing love only as a parent. She also notes radical changes in the town: "The Bottom had collapsed. Everybody who had made money during the war moved as close as they could to the valley" (165). As whites become increasingly interested in living in the hills, the value of real estate soon keeps African Americans away: "Those black people who had moved down right after the war and in the fifties couldn't afford to come back even if they wanted to" (166). These changes fracture the community, causing an increased sense of isolation: "Now there weren't any places left, just separate houses with separate television and separate telephones and less and less dropping by" (166). Morrison makes clear that the economic hierarchies that limited Black opportunity in America persisted in 1965, and the Black community left behind in the Bottom is no longer cohesive. In the context of the civil rights movement at the time, this dynamic can be viewed as emblematic of the state of Black activism. The seeming accomplishments of civil rights, as embodied by the legislations in 1964 and 1965, brought about positive changes, but as activists struggled to pursue a cohesive domestic agenda alongside the escalation in Vietnam, the movement faltered. Many, including Martin Luther King, Jr., feared alienating the support of President Johnson by criticizing the war. As *Sula* suggests, US foreign policy left African Americans without a clear path forward for achieving equality.

At this very moment in the text, Morrison returns to the character of Shadrack, and his presence serves as a reminder of the forthcoming sacrifices by Black Americans in yet another war. After Nel visits Sula's grave, she encounters Shadrack upon leaving "the colored part of the cemetery." He was "a little shaggier, a little older, still energetically mad" (173). He can't recall her, in part, because he is too preoccupied with the loss of his fish: "He hadn't sold fish in a long time now. The river had killed them all. No more silver-gray flashes, no more flat, wide, unhurried look. No more slowing down of gills. No more tremor on the line" (174). These two images of death involve forces outside of one's control—social and environmental. The colored cemetery and the toxic river become images for the victimization of the Black community through the ongoing legacy of segregation and environmental racism. Yet Shadrack's presence adds another dimension to this moment. The description of fish dying from his fishing line sets up a contrast between a natural death ("the slowing down of gills") and an unnatural one (the toxic river). Through Shadrack's status as a veteran, Morrison casts him as a reminder of a new generation of African Americans who will die prematurely (who will die an unnatural death, so to speak) in Vietnam while race riots rage across the United States. Over 300,000 African Americans would serve in the conflict, and the positive assessment among African Americans of the military for its historical role in integration would vanish as "racial problems rent the armed forces" (Lucks 6). Not only were African Americans drafted in higher percentages than whites, but they were also dying in larger numbers, making up a 30 percent higher death rate than other members of the armed forces in Vietnam (Westheider 13). In 1965 in particular, African Americans constituted one out of four deaths—a number so high that the Pentagon modified its policy about front-line positioning of Black soldiers (12). For Morrison, Shadrack becomes a reminder of the disproportionate number of African American deaths early in Vietnam and of the ongoing problems with racism in the US military.

CONCLUSION: EVIL AND THE RHETORIC OF WAR

After Eva accuses Nel of complicity in Chicken Little's death for watching and doing nothing, Nel asks herself a disturbing set of questions: "Why didn't I feel bad when it happened? How come it felt so good to see him fall?" (*Sula* 170). One of the more destabilizing elements of *Sula* comes from its challenge to simple binaries such as good and evil. Sula's return to the Bottom, for example, is accompanied by an evil omen—a plague of robins—yet her presence inspires good. Negligent mothers become committed caretakers. Indifferent wives start caring for their husbands. And folks begin to "repair their homes and in general band against the devil in their midst" (117–18). Sula even challenges Nel's presumption of herself as the "good" one: "How do you know? ... About who was good? ... How you know it was you? ... I mean maybe it wasn't you. Maybe it was me." (146). Moments such as these capture Morrison's critique of binary thinking and language, and each inversion of categories such as good/evil and right/wrong reinforces her message that such labels do not adequately capture the complexity of human experience. As Deborah McDowell explains, *Sula* blurs "glories in paradox and ambiguity beginning with the prologue that describes the setting, the Bottom, situated spatially in the top. We enter a new world here, a world where we never get to the 'bottom' of things, a world that demands a shift from an either/or orientation to one that is both/and, full of shifts and contradictions" (80). These shifts and contradictions have significant implications for the novel's war narrative as well.

Throughout the text, Morrison's references and allusions to US wars capture the tension between the types of binaries used to justify it: good/evil, right/wrong, freedom/oppression. From the First World War onward, the ostensible justification for US involvement involved the importance of fighting for the good of democracy, yet such idealistic rhetoric offered a stark contrast with the denial of civil rights for African Americans at home. The Black solider, in particular, became a powerful image for these contradictions. Whether fighting and dying on the front lines or returning home injured, these warriors sacrificed themselves in the hope that such service would provide greater opportunity and respect. In actuality, these veterans came back to a country divided by segregation and shaped by racist hatred and systemic violence. They fought for benefits. They were championed by civil rights activists, and many celebrated the military's efforts to integrate the armed forces. But after the first few years of the Vietnam War, which followed the milestone accomplishments of the Civil Rights Act and the Voting Rights Act, disillusionment within the Black community about the United States reached new lows. The rise of the Black Power Movement, the assassinations of Malcom X and Martin Luther King, Jr., and the sacrifices of Black soldiers in Vietnam seemed to do little to change decades of economic and social inequality.

Certainly, the role of African American soldiers brought national and international attention to America's hypocritical treatment of people of color. It undercut the simplistic rhetoric of good and evil that justified the Cold War and the escalation in Vietnam. Interestingly, Morrison also addresses the problem of good and evil through the consequences of inaction. The characters in the novel repeatedly witness atrocities and do nothing. Sula, for instance, watches her mother Hannah burn to death "not because she was paralyzed, but because she was interested" (78). Likewise, Nel feels good about watching Chicken Little drown, and she never questions her response because of assumptions about her own goodness relative to Sula. Binary thinking, in other words, not only becomes a way of justifying harm, but it also becomes a way of tacitly condoning it. Just as the atrocities of the Second World War raised questions about the complicity of the German public in the extermination of millions of people, Morrison uses inaction and the problem of complicity to critique white Americans not involved in the battle for civil rights. When Nel visits Sula's grave in the closing moments of the novel, she notes that none of the headstones for the Peace family include first names: "Peace 1890–1923, Peace 1910–1940, Peace 1892–1959. They were not dead people. They were words. Not even words. Wishes, longings" (171). For Morrison, the wishful longing for peace is not enough. It involves engagement and the recognition of sacrifice. It involves recognizing the dangers of binaries that justify war, segregation, and prejudice. Just as war functions as a metaphor for Black life in America, the literal sacrifices of African Americans in the US military become a clarion call for systemic social change. They become, in Morrison's deft hands, a clarion call for this nation to live up to the promise of its founding principles and to strive for peace, justice, and equality for all its citizens.

WORKS CITED

Du Bois, W. E. B. "The African Roots of the War." *Atlantic Monthly*, May 1915, pp. 707–14.

"Executive Order 9981: Desegregation of the Armed Forces (1948)." *Our Documents: 100 Milestone Documents from the National Archives*. https://www.ourdocuments.gov/doc.php?flash=false&doc=84#. Accessed Aug. 8, 2022.

Fultz, Lucille P. *Toni Morrison: Playing with Difference*. U Illinois P, 2003.

Grant, Robert. "Absence into Presence: The Thematics of Memory and 'Missing' Subjects in Toni Morrison's *Sula*." *Critical Essays on Toni Morrison*, edited by Nellie Y. McKay, G. K. Hall, 1988, pp. 90–103.

Jackson, Chuck. "A 'Headless Display': *Sula,* Soldiers, and Lynching." *Modern Fiction Studies*, vol. 52, no. 2, Summer 2006, pp. 374–92.

Keene, Jennifer D. "The Long Journey Home: African American World War I Veterans and Veterans Policies." *Veterans' Policies, Veterans' Politics*, edited by Stephen Ortiz, Florida UP, 2015, pp. 146–70.

Knauer, Christine. *Let Us Fight as Free Men: Black Soldiers and Civil Rights*. U of Pennsylvania P, 2014.

Lucks, Daniel S. *Selma to Saigon: The Civil Rights Movement and the Vietnam War*. UP of Kentucky, 2014.

McDowell, Deborah E. "'The Self and Other': Reading Toni Morrison's *Sula* and the Black Female Text." *Critical Essays on Toni Morrison*, edited by Nellie Y. McKay, G. K. Hall, 1988, pp. 77–89.

McWhirter, Cameron. *Red Summer: The Summer of 1919 and the Awakening of Black America*. Henry Holt, 2011.

Morrison, Toni. "Unspeakable Things Unspoken: The Afro-American Presence in American Literature." *Michigan Quarterly Review*, vol. 28, no. 1, 1989, pp. 1–34.

Morrison, Toni. *Sula*. 1973. Plume, 1982.

Pruitt, Claude. "Circling Meaning in Toni Morrison's *Sula*." *African American Review*, vol. 44, no. 1-2, 2011, pp. 115–29.

Ramirez, Manuela López. "The Shell-Shocked Veteran in Toni Morrison's *Sula* and *Home*." *Journal of the Spanish Association of Anglo-American Studies*, vol 38, no. 1, June 2016, pp. 129–47.

Rosenberg, Jonathan. *How Far the Promised Land? World Affairs and the American Civil Rights Movement from the First World War to Vietnam*. Princeton UP, 2006.

Smith, Barbara. "Toward a Black Feminist Criticism." Reprint in *All the Women Are White, All the Blacks Are Men, But Some of Us Are Brave: Black Women's Studies*. Feminist P, 1982, pp. 156–70.

Thompson, Carlyle V. "'Circles and Circles of Sorrow': Decapitation in Toni Morrison's *Sula*." *CLA Journal*, vol. 47, no. 2, 2003, pp. 137–74.

Westheider, James E. *Fighting on Two Fronts: African Americans and the Vietnam War*. New York UP, 1997.

CHAPTER FIVE

Toni Morrison's Female Epistemology: Post-Nationalism, Diaspora, and Postcolonial Futures in *Tar Baby*, *Mouth Full of Blood*, and *Paradise*

JUSTINE BAILLIE

Toni Morrison has been considered primarily as a writer concerned to recover the ancestor in charting specifically African American histories, and yet contemporary theorizations of diaspora, cosmopolitanism, and transnationalism may now be employed to illuminate her work as both novelist and as public intellectual. For example, we can approach her fourth novel *Tar Baby* (1981) as being Morrison's presentation of a female protagonist, Jadine Childs, an emblematic transnational figure, one who eventually returns to Paris, the site of diasporic transnationalism, to engage at last with her diasporic, female identity.[1] It is in *Tar Baby*, set in the period in which it was written, that Morrison anticipates twenty-first-century debates around identity and what it means to be a Black, educated, and mobile woman. In this regard, Morrison's reflections in her essays and addresses on feminism, education, and postcolonialism, brought together in *Mouth Full of Blood* (2019), also help enable nuanced readings of *Tar Baby* and offer new possibilities for diasporic futures. In this chapter, I am concerned, firstly, with Morrison's engagement with Black

---

[1] Toni Morrison, herself, in "Rootedness: The Ancestor as Foundation" emphasizes the significance of the ancestor in the African American writing tradition. Ancestors are "timeless people whose relationships to the characters are benevolent, instructive, and protective, and they provide a certain kind of wisdom" and without whom we are "lost" (62–3). Readings of *Tar Baby*, that valorize the ancestor, tradition, and the folk, include Keith Byerman, claiming that the novel marks a positive "immersion into the black folk world" (84), Judylyn Ryan arguing that "the novel convincingly discredits Jadine's agenda … because it is undergirded by a materialist and self-alienating consciousness which recommends selling one's cultural inheritance" (83). Marilyn Sanders Mobley notes that Jadine's "sense of self is based on a denial of her own cultural heritage" (135). J. Brooks Bouson writes that "part of the text's mission is to undermine Jadine's elitist attitudes and put her in vital contact with her African-American roots" (118). Criticism more sympathetic toward Jadine includes Elliot Butler-Evans acknowledging "the need for Black women to construct their own identities without having to submit to a dominant myth of racial authenticity" (157). Pelagia Goulimari recognizes Jadine's "rejection" of an "essence of black womanhood predicated on sexuality and fertility" (77) and regards Son as espousing a "black essentialism" (74).

nationalism in the post–civil rights era of the late 1970s and early 1980s, as represented in the gendered "contentions" (*Tar Baby*, Epigraph) between Jadine, the assimilationist Black model and Son, the Black nationalist. I also consider Morrison's nonfiction, as collated in *Mouth Full of Blood*, and the ways in which Morrison mediates marginalized, peripheral knowledge into an effective and counter epistemology to challenge established hegemonic knowledge claims and nationalisms. I conclude by arguing that Morrison's critique of Black nationalism, first evident in *Tar Baby*, becomes the main concern of her *fin de siècle* novel, *Paradise* (1998).

In *Tar Baby*, Jadine's resistance to female ancestral tradition leaves Morrison's character open to criticism as an inauthentic individualist committed to a career in the vanguard of consumer capitalism, a career she pursues at the expense of her community and its history. Thus, early readings of *Tar Baby* generally viewed the novel as constituting Morrison's own critique of her protagonist; yet such interpretations may now be inflected with understanding of the diverse positionalities of diasporic experience as expressed in contemporary debates about authenticity, tradition, transnationalism, and the relationship between the individual and community. As Yogita Goyal put it in 2006: "Viewing Morrison through diaspora theory does not simply involve reading her work retroactively, but recognizing that her turn to the black diaspora in *Tar Baby* accompanies growing interest in diaspora and helps us define its conceptual coordinates more effectively" (395). Reading *Tar Baby* in this way, Jadine's rejection of Son's monocultural perspective, as expressed through his valorization of the ancestral past and his idealizations of Black womanhood, allows us to signal Jadine's own mobile, diasporic indeterminacy as being anti-essentialist and cosmopolitan. It is toward the end of the novel that Jadine, having been shaken from her complacent position of privileged entitlement by Son's arrival on the Isle des Chevaliers, contemplates her heritage, not when in America, or in the Caribbean, but while in Paris, where she had earlier been "derailed" by an African woman in yellow, a figure representative of authentic blackness (*Tar Baby* 42–4). For Faith Avery, Jadine's "return to Europe suggests a cultural re-approachment that is not available to her in the United States or the transitive space of the Isle des Chevaliers" (7).

Tar Baby is also an island narrative, a biopolitical text in which nature is feminized by the presence of the wild and ancient swamp women who threaten to drag Jadine back to her ancestral past, and who also serve, metaphorically, as indicative of how man's exploitation and rationalization of the natural world have distorted the ecosystem of the Caribbean. Once a flowing river, the swamp has now become a repository for the psychosis brought to the island by imperial and colonial expansion: "Poor insulated, brokenhearted river. Poor demented stream. Now it sat in one place like a grandmother and became a swamp the Haitians called Sein de Vielles. And witch's tit it was; a shrivelled fog bound oval seeping with a thick black substance that even mosquitoes could not live near" (8). Here, Morrison evokes a connection between environmental destruction and the receding authority of those women in possession of "ancient properties" (308) women to whom she in fact dedicates *Tar Baby*. To respect such properties as being expressive of a historical, originary trauma and its manifestations in diasporic experience, but without becoming entrapped or overdetermined by them, is the tension that runs throughout Morrison's reclamation of the *Tar Baby* story by which she is, in her own words, in her essay, "The Writer Before the Page," "recollecting the told story. Refusing to read a modern or westernized version of it" (268).[2] Jadine's individualistic quest

---

[2] Craig Werner notes that Morrison "apprehends myth both as a tool of Euro-American power and as a reservoir of historical knowledge capable of resisting that power" (151). For a wider discussion of Morrison's use of folklore, see Trudier Harris (1991).

means she is indifferent to such properties and to any insight they may bequeath and, thereby, impervious to the imperious culture of Valerian Street's household and its command over the Isle des Chevaliers. Indeed, she returns to the island in the hope of dispelling the disturbance brought by her encounter, as a successful model living in Paris, with the African woman in a supermarket in the nineteenth arrondissement, only to be confronted, once on the island, by the same sticky substance—her "skin like tar" (*Tar Baby* 42)—the woman represents. Dressed in canary yellow and with tribal markings scored into her cheeks, she appears again and again in Jadine's consciousness, possessed of transcendent beauty and grace that speak, as she disappears from Jadine's view, of "a moment before the cataclysm, when all loveliness and life and breath in the world was about to disappear" (43). Morrison reclaims and inverts the tar baby myth by turning the negative image of the tar baby as a racial slur into one in which tar becomes invested with sacred and positive racial qualities, albeit essentialized in ways that threaten Jadine's modern constructions and affirmations of herself. Jadine resists contact with her racial past as she is fearful of sticking to it, of losing "the person she had worked hard to become" (264). Trapped in tar, Jadine resists the permanent embrace of the ancestors, represented this time by the tree women of the swamp on the Isle de Chevaliers:

> This girl was fighting to get away from them. The women hanging from the trees were quiet now, but arrogant—mindful as they were of their value, their exceptional femaleness; knowing as they did that the first world of the world had been built with their sacred properties; that they alone could hold together the stones of pyramids and the rushes of Moses's crib; knowing their steady consistency, their pace of glaciers, their permanent embrace, they wondered at the girl's desperate struggle down below to be free, to be something other than they were. (184)

AUTHENTICITY

In the nineteenth arrondissement, before her flight to the Caribbean, Jadine assumes a mask of authenticity when choosing her dinner party recipe ingredients in a district of Paris heavily populated by subjects of the African diaspora.[3] Her reaction to the woman in yellow is so extreme precisely because, when shopping in the nineteenth arrondissement, Jadine believes she is being authentic, her ingredients the last word in world cuisine, but which are in fact culled from recipes in glossy magazines (*Tar Baby* 41). Her performance is suddenly exposed by the woman in yellow, leaving Jadine with the suspicion that she is "inauthentic" (45). This is a consequence of her position as an international model in a world becoming increasingly globalized and in which diverse diasporic identities, by the early 1980s, already existed in close enough proximity to threaten either the retreat into essentialized cultural identities, or its opposite, the assimilation of the diasporic subject into western metropolitan centers. Jadine believes her choice is a binary one, limited to either "blackening up or universalling out" (62); she cannot, of course, benefit from the insight afforded by those postcolonial theorizations of authenticity, difference, and subjectivity that emerged in the 1990s. For Homi Bhabha, for example, a meaningful, politically engaged, postcolonial subjectivity

---

[3]In "Unspeakable Things Unspoken" Morrison writes, "The Tar Baby tale seemed to me to be about masks ... For Son, the most effective mask is none. For the others the construction is careful and delicately borne, but the masks they make have a life of their own and collide with those they come in contact with" (193).

can be initiated by thinking "beyond narratives of originary and initial subjectivities and [focusing] on those moments or processes that are produced in the articulation of cultural differences" (1), and he goes on to emphasize that the "presentation of difference must not be hastily read as the reflection of pre-given ethnic or cultural traits set in the fixed tablet of tradition" (2). Unable to revel in her hybridity, nor assume a politicized consciousness that would position her as existing within Bhabha's space of "in-betweeness," Jadine instead remains an orphan, forever inauthentic, or so she herself believes, once her self-constructions had dissolved before the "powerful" (*Tar Baby* 42) eyes of the African woman in the supermarket.

Shopping for ingredients, Jadine appropriates the cultural heritage of diasporic others for her dinner party menu, and, indeed, the African woman is, fleetingly, another of Jadine's appropriations, just one more element in her Parisian fantasy of authenticity; the woman in yellow, however, deflects Jadine's gaze with the resistant "force" (*Tar Baby* 44) of her own stare, assured of her "unphotographable" beauty and confidence as "mother/sister/she," a "woman's woman" possessed of "ancient properties" that threaten to overwhelm Jadine (41–4). As the woman in yellow resists appropriation, it is Jadine herself, the exoticized "copper Venus" (115), the literal and metaphorical orphan, without either a secure sense of self or the sustenance of maternal tradition, who must, therefore, reinvent herself. This Parisian encounter is the catalyst for Jadine's existential crisis, the point of fracture in her existence as a postmodern, postcolonial subject, the life before and life after the episode. Jadine must now confront life after the "cataclysm" (43), as she becomes newly conscious of her racial heritage as a Black woman and must now understand the present as that which the past has bequeathed, history accounted for in a revelatory moment in time for Jadine as an orphan of the diaspora. As the "loveliness" (43) of her old world evaporates, so too do the certainties and affirmations of her private education and life of privilege as she senses the weight of the past as embodied by the ancestral-like figure of the woman in yellow.

The complexities of ancestral return are evoked by Saidiya Hartman in *Lose Your Mother* (2007) in which she describes her journey along Ghana's slave route as a "returnee" African American woman in search of an ancestral past and identity:

> Circling back to times past, revisiting the routes that might have led to alternative presents, salvaging the dreams unrealized and defeated, crossing over to parallel lives. The hope is that *return* could resolve the old dilemmas, make a victory out of defeat, and engender a new order. And the disappointment is that there is no going back to a former condition. Loss re-makes you. Return is as much about the world to which you no longer belong as it is about the one in which you have yet to make a home. (100, emphasis in original)

Jadine remakes herself repeatedly throughout *Tar Baby* and, on visiting Son's hometown in the American South, she learns that to return will not in itself resolve the dilemmas of identity with which she struggles. Again, as Hartman puts it, "To lose your mother was to be denied your kin, country, and identity. To lose your mother was to forget your past" (85). For Ondine, who has raised her niece, Jadine's motherlessness does not mean she cannot be a "daughter," and yet, knowing how to be a daughter is a necessary precondition for learning how to be a "real woman: a woman good enough for a child; good enough for a man—good enough even for the respect of other women" (*Tar Baby* 283). Crucially, "A daughter is a woman that cares about where she come from and takes care of them that took care of her" (283).

Jadine returns to the island, however, not to find herself, but for a vacation, to consider her career, and to decide whether she should marry the besotted white European man, Ryk. She will only *play* the role of daughter to Sydney and Ondine and that of companion to Margaret, Valerian's wife, but Son's arrival disrupts her plans and unsettles her self-image. Morrison asks of the reader to consider whether we accept Ondine's privileging of the maternal as the route to self-knowledge, endorse Son's valorizations of the ancestor Thérèse as the essence of Black authenticity, or validate Jadine's mobility and economic independence, her transnational adventure by which she spans continents and transcends nationhood. Speaking just before the publication of *Tar Baby* to the young female students of Barnard College, in an address, "Cinderella's Stepsisters," Morrison recognizes female ambition as empowering but suggests that "we pay as much attention to our nurturing sensibilities as to our ambition. You are moving in the direction of freedom and the function of freedom is to free somebody else. You are moving toward self-fulfillment, and the consequences of that fulfillment should be to discover that there is something just as important as you are" (111–12).

Morrison leaves Jadine without such a nurturing sensibility, but perhaps moving toward a freedom that is not dependent upon economic and professional stability, but rather an unsteady, risky freedom achieved through self-knowledge. As Morrison tells her female audience: "In your rainbow journey towards a realization of personal goals, don't make choices based only on your security and your safety" ("Cinderella's Stepsisters" 112). Returning finally to Paris, Jadine recalibrates, accepts risk, and may yet find her way to such a consciousness (*Tar Baby* 292). Morrison makes clear in her lecture, "Unspeakable Things Unspoken," that *Tar Baby* is about safety, about risk, and its gains and losses; "Safety itself is the desire of each person in the novel. Locating it, creating it, losing it" ("Unspeakable" 193). Indeed, the novel begins with Son's misplaced sense of security, "He believed he was safe" (*Tar Baby* 1), an opening line that evokes the indeterminacy and ambivalence underlying *Tar Baby*, a device by which Morrison exposes the contingency of diasporic existence. By the end of *Tar Baby*, both Jadine and Son embrace risk and uncertainty, in their own ways, and it is risk itself that Morrison endorses, not the wildness of the briar patch nor the flight to cosmopolitan Paris, neither character fixed in history or geography and their proscriptions. Morrison conveys new possibilities for African Americans negotiating identity and freedom in ways no longer exclusively inscribed by the traumas of slavery, the essentializations of *Négritude* and pan-Africanism, or the collective solidarity of the civil rights movement. New possibilities arise for the mobile cosmopolitan subject, and the novel ends with Jadine contemplating her reinvention, not within the feminized currents of the sea, in which Son himself is reborn, but instead flying through the air aboard a flight bound for Paris where she will, after all, "tangle with the woman in yellow—with her and with all the night women who had *looked* at her. No more shoulders and limitless chests. No more dreams of safety. No more. Perhaps that was the thing—the thing Ondine was saying. A grown woman did not need safety or its dreams. She *was* the safety she longed for" (292; emphases in original).

THE BLACK ATLANTIC

Paris, as a city of "diasporic convergence" (Braddock and Eburne 2) is the appropriate site for a reinvention that necessitates Jadine's conscious reengagement with that represented by the woman in yellow—namely, Africa as the source from which the complexities of diasporic being originate. The imperial and colonial incursions of France into both Africa and the Caribbean, and consequent circulations of diasporic generations, has seen Paris evolve as the capital of the Black Atlantic: "From the Haitian revolution to the war for Algerian independence, the role of Paris as the metropolitan seat of colonial power has been necessarily complemented, and contested, by the forms of agitation and dissent that have circulated through it" (3). Jadine knows her options in America are proscribed by race, limited to marriage, modeling, or school teaching, whereas Europe offers her a "fourth choice" (*Tar Baby* 226). What this choice may be remains open for Jadine, her future as yet undetermined in all its possible multiplicities, except that of its transnationality. It does, however, entail her confrontation with the artifice of her Parisian existence, and, by extension, her encounter with the "black as tar" woman is revelatory as to the artifice of Paris itself, a city built on colonial adventure, consumer capitalism, and exoticizations of the Black female body in its literature and figurative art. What at first appears as a Baudelairian encounter with the "passerby" in Paris, in its apparently transitory passivity, becomes instead the catalyst for Jadine's confrontation of herself. Jadine cannot move on as Parisian *flâneur* and simply forget the fleeting encounter; rather, she becomes mired in the "ancient properties" that radically destabilize her sense of self. Tyler Stovall, while mindful of the complexities of the African American presence in Paris, nevertheless concludes, in *Paris Noir*, that migration to the French capital has proffered African Americans both escape from, and critique of, American racial structures:

> The idea of Paris as a city that receives blacks with dignity and respect should be considered not just a statement of objective reality (although much evidence supports it), but equally as a conceptual strategy for criticizing continued discrimination in the United States. Color-blind Paris is a city of the mind, a legendary place of refuge whose boundaries correspond only in part to those of earthly urbanity. As long as racial hierarchies remain central to life in America, the importance of the black expatriate experience as a symbolic escape from, and critique of, racism will endure. (Stovall 300)[4]

Jadine, viewed from a transnational perspective, now comes into focus as a figure of the Black Atlantic, situated by Morrison in a cultural, historical, and geographical arena necessarily heterogeneous in its accommodation of difference. Paul Gilroy's 1993 conceptualization of the diaspora in *The Black Atlantic* has become the touchstone for any contemplation of transatlantic cultural production. Gilroy's work marks a turn in postcolonial studies to thinking in terms of diasporas and, by extension, toward theorizations of "cosmopolitanism" and the "transnation." The flexibility of Gilroy's model of diaspora as emanating from slavery helps us to relate to the conceptual and philosophical foundations of Morrison's work in general, as she articulates the diversity of diasporic experience through an increasingly transnational, globalized, poetics. *Tar Baby* represents a transitional point in Morrison's work after which, in *Beloved* (1987), she turns to nineteenth-century slavery to explore the hold a traumatic past has on the present and how such trauma may be worked through for the negotiation of the future. The past, and especially slavery, permeates all Morrison's novels but, in *Tar Baby*, truth is obfuscated by a mythical quest for an

---

[4]In "The Woman in Yellow in Toni Morrison's *Tar Baby*," Angela Shaw-Thornburg concludes that "Jadine's decision to return to Paris can be read as a decision to begin exploring the 'new properties' of an African-American identity shaped by encounters with other people of African descent" (56).

undefined racial authenticity, and the novel can be seen as Morrison's clearing of the terrain of racial identity before her direct, visceral engagement with slavery as undertaken in *Beloved*.

In what Gilroy calls an evolving "non-traditional tradition" (*Black Atlantic* 101), Black Atlantic writers and artists explore the ambivalence of Black subjectivity. They provide a transnational and intercultural perspective through creative expressions that reflect the fluidity of diasporic existence and the consciousness arising from such experience. Gilroy appropriates Walter Benjamin's dialectics of past and present (xii), expressed in Benjamin's sailing imagery: "Being a dialectician means having the wind of history in one's sails. The sails are the concepts. It is not enough, however, to have sails at one's disposal. What is decisive is knowing the art of setting them" (Benjamin 473, cited in *Black Atlantic*, epigraph). Gilroy's purpose is to locate the ship as the focal point for his analysis of the transnational, transcultural creative expressions of the Black Atlantic, expressions that constitute a counterculture to modernity, its linear time, and the dualism that informs the Enlightenment's separation of politics and ethics. Artists and intellectuals working within this aesthetic employ memory and alternative histories to disrupt the linearity of history as unbroken progression. Existing within modernity itself, its expressive culture originating in the slave system so integral to the development of the West, the Black Atlantic nevertheless transcends modernity in its delineations of history, memory, and time and is, to return to Benjamin, the corrective that resets the sails of history. In its "hybridity," the "intermixture of ideas" (*Black Atlantic* xi) that finds expression in both Western and non-Western artistic and philosophical traditions, the Black Atlantic is inherently anti-nationalist and provides a utopian model in its creative articulations of trauma, memory, and survival. The dislocation engendered by the Middle Passage can thus be reformulated; the sea, borderless, flowing, and unidirectional, serves as a metaphor for the wide-ranging and multiple explorations of emerging subjectivities. For Gilroy, *Beloved* reformulates the relationship between "rational, scientific, and enlightened Euro-American thought and the supposedly primitive outlook of prehistorical, cultureless, and bestial African slaves" (220), a reformulation of the African American experience as being what Gilroy calls the "slave sublime" (220).

Discussing *Tar Baby*, in "The Writer Before the Page," Morrison explains how she reaches back in the novel to the creation myth, to the paradise lost. She talks about how she wanted to evoke the "earth that came out of the sea and its conquest by modern man" ("Writer" 269). Son reaches the Isle des Chevaliers by way of the ocean as a disruptive, destabilizing presence, "the man born out of the womb of the sea accompanied by ammonia odors of birth" (269). He is borne by a mythic female presence, guided through the water in a feminized current, "like the hand of an insistent woman," a rootless, "undocumented" (*Tar Baby* 167) itinerant who yet, ironically, has fixed notions about identity, tradition, and women as the bearers of culture. It is instead Jadine, prosaically associated with commercial air travel, and not with water—itself an inversion of stereotypical gendered associations on Morrison's part—who represents diasporic identity, not as "some invariant essence" but rather as a dynamic expression of diasporic existence. As Gilroy writes in his later work, *Between Camps* (2000),

> It is ceaselessly reprocessed. It is maintained and modified in what becomes a determinedly non-traditional tradition, for this is not tradition as closed or simple repetition. Invariably promiscuous, diaspora and the politics of commemoration it specifies challenge us to apprehend mutable forms that can redefine the idea of culture through a reconciliation with movement and complex, dynamic variation. (129–30)

For Gilroy, there is no authentic identity to which one can return—the transnationalism of the Black Atlantic does not denote an essentialized route back to Africa in search of racial origin, but is instead multidirectional, often atemporal, in its literary, metaphorical, and physical journeying. This allows for the Middle Passage to be remembered in new, creative evocations that help ameliorate trauma through liberatory reclamations of recovery and healing, rather than in the static remembrance of an originary loss. Morrison's own reclamations of the Middle Passage, across her work generally, are feminized. Sula, in *Sula* (1973), for example, is linked to water and fluidity, and Beloved in *Beloved* reimagines the Middle Passage in a stream of fractured memory. The sea is also significant in *Love* (2003)—Celestial's dive into the water constitutes her assured, free reclamation of the sea, and in *A Mercy* (2008), shipwrecked Sorrow's identity originates from water and is imbued with fluidities of race and gender.

Morrison brings together the ship at sea, art, memory, and history in her reading of French artist Théodore Géricault's 1819 painting, *Raft of the Medusa*. In her 2006 address at the Louvre, "The Foreigner's Home," Morrison reads the painting as a "moment" (23, translations by Justine Baillie) between borders, a French naval ship, wrecked between imperial France and colonial Africa, Géricault's raft of survivors in peril, but where hierarchies of rank and racial inscription dissolve in the face of shared mortality. From her globalized, transnational perspective, art now exceeds the boundaries of its frame (22) as new meaning emerges from Morrison's excavation at the Louvre into what she has called elsewhere "the cellar of time" ("Future of Time" 122) and by which Géricault's realist documentation of the historical event reverberates throughout time to speak profoundly to present-day patterns of migration, exile, belonging, and exclusion ("Foreigner's Home" 24). In Paris, Morrison's curatorship is an appropriation of Western art that invests the exhibits she selects with new transnational and postcolonial meaning that enrich the art of the Louvre, itself another site replete with narratives of conquest. Morrison's rereading can be contrasted with her knowing characterization, twenty-five years earlier, of Jadine as a naïve student of art history, one who has internalized Western notions of creativity and originality to the point of being embarrassed by Black artistic expression: "Picasso *is* better than an Itumba mask. The fact that he was intrigued by them is proof of *his* genius, not the mask-makers'" (*Tar Baby* 72; emphases in original). As an art history student of the Sorbonne, Jadine appears to have learned nothing that speaks to her own heritage and its appropriation at the heart of European culture. In an essay on Gertrude Stein and modernism, Morrison discusses how modernist visual art is dependent upon racial categories for its radical non-realist mode, expressive of the fragmentation and fissuring of the modern experience: "The imaginative terrain upon which this journey took place was and is in a very large measure the presence of the racial "Other" ("Gertrude Stein" 208).

In its borderlessness, the sea offers possibilities for the diasporic individual that are unbound by nationhood and externally imposed definitions of identity in relation to family, gender, and community. Jadine, then, may be seen as a nascent member of the transnation, a figure who, in choosing Paris, identifies, in Bill Ashcroft's postcolonial theorization, "with no 'nation', ethnic group, cultural or immigrant group completely, if at all" (Ashcroft, "Globalisation" 18). For Ashcroft, "The transnation exists within, beyond, and between nations. It is a collectivity comprised of communities who may be drawn in one way or another to the myth of a particular nation state, but who draw away perpetually into the liberating region of representational undecideability" ("Globalisation" 22). He writes elsewhere that it is a space "in which national and cultural affiliations are superseded, in which binaries of centre and periphery, national self and other, are dissolved" (Ashcroft, "Borders" 11). Liberation for Jadine means not being defined by her European lover's racialized exoticization of her body, Ondine's maternal expectations, or Son's prescriptions of Black womanhood. Jadine muses, "I want to get out of my skin and be only the person inside—not American—not black—just me" (*Tar Baby* 45). In financing her private education, Sidney and Ondine facilitate Jadine's cosmopolitanism as a privileged traveler of the diaspora with choices, including being unfettered by nationality, race, community, or family. Yogita Goyal refers to Jadine's rejections of rootedness as constituting "a gendered critique of black nationalism," one that is "legible within the logic of postessentialist diaspora identities" (Goyal 396). Ironically, Sydney and Ondine's labors have enabled an individualistic modern woman whose European education has meant her alienation from the racial past, community, and family. With some bitterness Ondine speaks of Jadine the orphan, "Another one not from my womb, and I stand on my feet thirty years so she wouldn't have to" (*Tar Baby* 285). Ondine understands how Jadine's advantages have been won at the expense of her own servitude, how Jadine's freedoms enable her to enjoy "a whole bunch of stuff they can do that we never knew nothing about" (285). In effect, Ondine situates her niece within what we today may call the "new" or "post" Black category (Touré), one in which positionality can reside "beyond belongingness and, in many respects, embrace a condition of illegibility" (Murray 35). This impulse, however, contains the potential for reduction to an individualistic expression of identity—Jadine's "just me"—that bypasses the collective past and depoliticizes its struggles. There is the danger that this impulse is merely "indicative of a contemporary perception that the collective strategic essentialism of earlier expressions of black empowerment is no longer necessary" (Baillie 290) when, in fact, the twenty-first century, so far at least, has revealed an imperative for renewed collective resistance to the brutality inflicted upon the Black body.

MORRISON'S POSTCOLONIAL FUTURES

It is productive to turn our attention to Morrison's nonfiction, a substantial body of work recently collected in *Mouth Full of Blood* (2019), as her essays and addresses are testimony to her long-standing vigilance concerning matters of politics, race, and gender. To read Morrison's nonfiction in parallel with her novels reveals an ongoing dialogue between her fiction and her reflections on feminism, subjectivity, and the practice of writing itself. For example, as we have seen, in "Cinderella's Stepsisters," Morrison provides instruction on how to bear the responsibilities of being a young, educated woman in ways that illuminate our reading of Jadine's individualistic impulse in *Tar Baby*. In later nonfiction, Morrison's scope has global dimensions, as she highlights the urgency of millennial crises and discusses the dangers of nationalism, warnings that build upon her critique of Black nationalism in *Tar Baby*. In "Racism and Fascism" (1995), she anticipates the neoliberal present and its links to racism and fascism in a discussion of the criminalization of the other within the borders of the nation-state and the increasingly apparent propensity for the repetition of racist and fascistic practices of the past. For Morrison, racism, fascism, and misogyny are the interrelated consequences of patriarchal nationalisms that continue to operate, albeit in new guises: "Criminalize the enemy. Then prepare, budget for, and rationalize the building of holding arenas for the enemy—especially its males and absolutely its children" ("Racism and Fascism" 15). The reestablishment and normalization of the detention camp is a contemporary echo of colonial and totalitarian practice, and, notably, Morrison discusses the American prison system as a modern version of institutional slavery that exploits the labor of a disproportionate number of African Americans ("Slavebody" 77).

For Morrison, the narratives by which such practices are justified must be challenged by the academy generally, artists, human rights organizations, and women. On women, she has much to say in *Mouth Full of Blood*, on their creativity and scholarship, and on the complicity of some women in the building of patriarchal structures ("Cinderella's Stepsisters" 111). Women are central to Morrison's articulation of the future, and she invokes the importance the civil rights movement had for feminism in America during the 1960s and the 1970s ("Women, Race" 87). Meaningful and progressive agency means the dismantling of the divisions between women that threaten their future, the deconstruction of the language of male supremacy that shares much with racialized language, and, importantly, recognition of the inequalities of social class that perpetuate the reactionary present (86–94). In her 1989 address, titled "Women, Race, and Memory," Morrison speaks of finding liberating promise in the work of women artists and scholars as expressions that do not merely replicate the strictures of patriarchal subjugation:

> It may be the first hint of a possible victory in being viewed and respected as human beings without being male-like or male dominated. Where self-sabotage is harder to maintain; where the worship of masculinity as a concept dies; where intelligent compassion for women unlike ourselves can surface; where racism and class inequity do not help the vision or the research; where, in fact, the work itself, the very process of doing it, makes sororicide as well as fratricide repulsive. (94)

The deployment of controlled, mature language is paramount for the challenge to the neoliberal discourse underpinning the contemporary landscape, "the regime, the authority of the electronically visual, the seduction of 'virtual'" (Morrison, "Literature and Public Life" 100). Any redemptive or "alleviated" future ("Literature and Public Life" 100), Morrison argues, will mean the generation of new language that refuses to replay over and again the old themes—individualism, racial constructions, misogyny, insider/outsider dichotomies—and the rejection of the "passionate juvenilia" of exclusionary, reactionary discourse ("Wartalk" 24). The racialized language of what Morrison called, in her titular keynote at the Race Matters Conference, Princeton, "a racial house" ("Race Matters" 132), must be deciphered in ways that do not replicate entrenched structures but rather provide an inclusive arena for the purposeful deconstruction of language deployed in the name of violence and control ("Nobel Lecture" 103–5). Belonging entails the creation of an "intellectual" and "spiritual home" ("Race Matters" 133), a space of creativity as the response to globalism and displacement, one that equates with Ashcroft's conceptualization of the transnation in its transcendence of national and racial borders.

MORRISON AND "HOME"

In her opening address to the Race Matters Conference in 1994 at Princeton University, Morrison talked about how she wishes to contest, and at the same time "domesticate," the architecture of racialized discourse. Morrison conceptualizes a "race-specific yet non-racist home" ("Race Matters" 133), one that embraces borderlessness as it "imagines safety without walls" (139). Morrison recognizes current literary and academic discourses on race, including her own, as discourses about home and homelessness; as "creative responses to exile, the devastations, pleasures, and imperatives of homelessness as it is manifested in discussions on globalism, diaspora, migrations, hybridity, contingency, interventions, assimilations, exclusions" (133). Morrison's notion of home is therefore diasporic; a place in which race matters, but also a place that must be constructed beyond racialized discourse. Importantly, this includes resisting nationalism and spurious notions of identity:

> Nationhood—the very definition of citizenship—is marked by exile, refugees, guest arbiter, immigrants, migrations, the displaced, the fleeing, and the under siege. Hunger for home is entombed among the central metaphors in the discourse on globalism, transnationalism, nationalism, the break-up of nations, and the fictions of sovereignty. Yet these dreams of home are frequently as raced themselves as the originating racial house that has defined them. When they are not raced, they are, as I suggested earlier, landscape, never inscape; utopia, never home. (138)

The arguments Morrison makes in "Race Matters" resonate, in other ways, in her millennium novel *Paradise* in which she attempts a reformulation of race for the twenty-first century through the construction of de-raced language to resist those dominant forms of "language that can powerfully evoke and enforce hidden signs of racial superiority, cultural hegemony, and dismissive 'othering' of people and language" (*Playing in the Dark* xii–xiii). Famously, the novel begins with the sentence, "They shoot the white girl first" (*Paradise* 3)—we never learn which of the girls is the white girl and are thus compelled to confront the ways in which race is socially constructed as well as consider its accompanying hierarchies.

In "Race Matters" Morrison recognizes the "hopeful language" of Martin Luther King as part of an unrealistic project to construct "a world free of racial hierarchy" as such a world could only be visualized by King and his followers "if accompanied by the Messiah" (131). In *Paradise*, however, Morrison revives and revises King's Christian humanism through her characterization of the Reverend Richard Misner, a progressive, liberal minister who recognizes the dangers of Ruby's racial exclusivity and its links with nationalist thinking. Misner's understanding of "true home" (*Paradise* 213) clearly incorporates his Christianity as a spiritual space, one not constructed on domination or fear, but transglobal and transhistorical in its metaphorical reach to the pre-lapsarian origins of humanity.

Misner's image of "home" preempts the conceptualization of paradise/home with which Morrison ends the novel. But crucially, Misner's vision is an attempt to reverse Western history, whereas the paradise attained at the end of the novel is a futuristic one in which the confrontation of history is a necessary precondition for its existence. Paradise is not a place marking the end of history or a place looking backward to an imaginary wholeness before history, "a protected preserve, rather like a wilderness park … a failed and always failing dream," (Morrison, "Race Matters" 131–2) but one that, once cleared of "racist detritus" (137), has liberatory potential for the future of history in Morrison's attempt to "destabilize the racial gaze altogether" (137).

In Morrison's paradise, the ways in which to be Black, to be human, are multiplied, and possibilities of peace and security exist beyond intolerance. Morrison's vision is indeterminate, one which relies, in its resistance to closure, upon the reader's engagement and interpretation. It could be regarded as utopian, a useful novelistic, aesthetic conceit allowing the writer the luxury of two endings. A politicized reading is, however, much more productive in its emphasis upon a diasporic space traversing race, class, and sexuality—the transnation. The Convent women's reincarnation and repossession of their own past lives, after their massacre, leads them to the "paradise" of Morrison's title, and yet this paradise is not a secluded and idyllic island; rather, it includes worldly detritus that is somehow imbued with a certain shimmering beauty: "Around them on the beach, sea trash gleams. Discarded bottle tops sparkle near a broken sandal. A small dead radio plays the quiet surf" (*Paradise* 318). To exist in paradise is not to simply escape from the twentieth-century world and its realities of oppression, violence, and inequality that are sustained by the language and culture of the "race house." Rather, to be in paradise means to have attained the knowledge to recognize, "domesticate," and transcend the malignant ideologies of Western power. Paradise is realizable when responsibility for language and culture is seized, not only in oppositional ways, but also in genuinely new, vital, and imaginative ways that bypass the malady of culture. Paradise is not a fantastical, other worldly, or heavenly existence but, as aesthetically rendered by Morrison—for whom narrative is "radical, creating us at the very moment it is being created" ("Nobel Lecture" 108)—it offers possibilities for ways of being in the real world that recognize oppression yet provide the cognitive and imaginative tools for its transcendence.

For Morrison, the issue is one of how to define identity and achieve civic and social equality without duplicating modernity's hierarchies of race, gender, and class. This effort is especially significant in her late work—in the context of global, genocidal mechanisms of nationalism and fundamentalism that imply new forms of exclusion as the promise of transnational flows of markets, technologies, and labor dissipated post-9/11. For Morrison, categories of religion, nation-state, and race can no longer affect the construction of meaningful identities or lasting political and social change.

Morrison has consistently worked to recover that which would otherwise be lost or remain unspoken from the traumatic past. The official historical record, "manifest destiny," "progress," and the American literary canon itself, are all problematized by such excavations of recovery. It is from within transnational cultural expression that Morrison finds hope, in its "informed vision based on harrowing experience that nevertheless gestures toward a redemptive future" ("Future of Time" 126). Such imaginings of a future to be sustained beyond the nation-state are now found in post-realist, post-national expressions that are themselves responses to nation building and its failure to accommodate the trauma instigated in the very act of constructing national identity. The nation-state, in its monumental and ceremonial inscriptions of its own narrative can, for Morrison, only repeat the past. History is closed here, to be opened only by literature emanating from an understanding of history that is "race inflected, colonialized, displaced, hunted" (126).

Literature is crucial for resisting the appropriation of language, temporality, space, identity, and belonging. Salman Rushdie and Ben Okri are among authors cited by Morrison as sources of literature as remembrance and empathy, as reading constitutes "a social act" that helps create the foundations for informed and meaningful citizenship of the world ("Literature and Public Life" 100).[5] Literary creation and its reception can alleviate the pessimism of much contemporary meditation on time and its future and resist the "rush into the past" ("War on Error" 30) that

---

[5]Ben Okri, the postcolonial writer referred to by Morrison, writing in the context of the global climate crisis, proposes an "existential creativity," which entails developing "a new art to waken people both to the enormity of what is looming and the fact that we can still do something about it" (4).

such an unimaginable horizon has encouraged. For Morrison, time does have a future worthy of imagination:

> Perhaps it is the reality of a future as durable and far-reaching as the past, a future that will be shaped by those who have been pressed to the margins, by those who have been dismissed as irrelevant surplus, by those who have been cloaked with the demon's cape; perhaps it is the contemplation of that future that has occasioned the tremble of latter-day prophets afraid that the current disequilibria is a stirring, not an erasure. That not only is history not dead, but that it is about to take its first unfettered breath. ("Future of Time" 126)

Morrison insists upon the promotion of beauty and art as the best response to the imposition of borders, labels, or categories as mechanisms for rule and control. This means using difference not as a weapon of subjugation, or as the mirrored response to oppression that can only replicate it, but rather as the source of transnational possibilities embedded in an "alternate language [that] does not arise from the tiresome, wasteful art of war, but rather from the demanding, brilliant art of peace" ("Wartalk" 25). It is impossible to speak well with "a mouth full of blood" ("The Dead of September 11" 3), and so Morrison strives for composed reflection on diasporic, migratory experience from its early incarnation as the slave ship to its contemporary manifestation as the boat of refugees on the perilous sea.

It is the sea, in all its ambiguities as the site of danger, rescue, and nourishment that informs our readings of the indeterminate endings of both *Tar Baby* and *Paradise*. In *Tar Baby*, we have Son returned to the Isle de Chevaliers by the maternal, "nursing sound of the sea" (309) to join the ancestral, mythic realm of the blind horseman; the alternative ending available is a realist one, in which Jadine is airborne, en route to Europe.[6] *Paradise* ends with the possibility that the women of the Convent have been massacred in the realist world of Ruby; or, they are returned to the sea, in another island narrative that has them awaiting rescue by "another ship, perhaps, but different, heading to port, crew and passengers, lost and saved, atremble" (*Paradise* 318), another evocation of Géricault's *Raft of the Medusa* and Morrison's inversion of the Middle Passage, her Afrofuturist ending in which rescue of the diasporic refugee is enabled by the ancestor Piedade. It is in such "rhythms of water" ("Literature and Public Life" 318) that liberation may be found if history's repetitious delineations of borders, nationhood, and race are deciphered to enable the construction of alternative and reachable postcolonial futures.

WORKS CITED

Ashcroft, Bill. "Globalisation, Transnation, and Utopia." *Locating Transnational Ideals*, edited by Walter Goebel and Saskia Schabio, Routledge, 2010, pp. 13–29.

---

[6]It is worth noting here how it is not until her last novel, *God Help the Child* (2015), that Morrison brings another ambitious female protagonist, and purveyor of the beauty myth, Bride, to a full recognition of the female ancestor and her ancient powers. In *Tar Baby* however, Morrison leaves Jadine's dilemma unresolved, her concern being to present a modern woman struggling with authenticity in a cosmopolitan space, whose response is an ambiguous and complex one that does not essentialize blackness but, rather, recognizes its transnational manifestations in ways that, furthermore, serve to undercut the patriarchal impulse behind nationalist ideologies.

Ashcroft, Bill. "Borders, Bordering, and the Transnation." *English Academy Review*, vol. 36 no. 1, 2019, pp. 5–19. https://doi.org/10.1080/10131752.2019.1584261. Accessed June 28, 2022.

Avery, Faith M. "'Let Loose the Dogs': Messiness and Ethical Wrangling in Toni Morrison's *Tar Baby*." *Iowa Journal of Cultural Studies*, vol. 16, issue 1, article 3, 2014, pp. 4–21.

Baillie, Justine. "Morrison and the Transnation: Toni Morrison, *God Help the Child* and Zadie Smith, *Swing Time*." *Contemporary Women's Writing, Special Issue: Global Morrison*, edited by Justine Baillie, vol. 13, no. 3, 2020, pp. 287–306. https//:doi.org/10.1093/cww/vpaa009. Accessed June 28, 2022.

Bhabha, Homi, K. *The Location of Culture*. Routledge, 1994.

Benjamin, Walter. *The Arcades Project*. Translated by Howard Eiland and Kevin McLaughlin. The Belknap P of Harvard UP, 1999.

Bloom, Harold, editor. *Toni Morrison: Modern Critical Views*. Chelsea House, 1990.

Bouson, J. Brooks. *Quiet As It's Kept: Shame, Trauma, and Race in the Novels of Toni Morrison*. State U of New York P, 2000.

Braddock, Jeremy, and Jonathan P. Eburne. "Introduction." *Paris, Capital of the Black Atlantic: Literature, Modernity, and Diaspora*, edited by J. Braddock and J. P. Eburne, Johns Hopkins UP, 2013, pp. 1–14.

Butler-Evans, Elliott. *Race, Gender, and Desire: Narrative Strategies in the Fiction of Toni Cade Bambara, Toni Morrison, and Alice Walker*. Temple UP, 1989.

Byerman, Keith. "Beyond Realism: The Fictions of Toni Morrison." *Toni Morrison: Modern Critical Views*, edited by Harold Bloom, Chelsea House, 1990, pp. 55–84.

Denard, Carolyn C., editor, *What Moves at the Margin: Selected Nonfiction of Toni Morrison*, Mississippi UP, 2008.

Gilroy, Paul. *The Black Atlantic: Modernity and Double Consciousness*. Verso, 1993.

Gilroy, Paul. *Between Camps: Race, Identity and Nationalism at the End of the Colour Line*. Allen Lane, 2000.

Goulimari, Pelagia. *Toni Morrison*. Routledge, 2011.

Goyal, Yogita. "The Gender of Diaspora in Toni Morrison's *Tar Baby*." *MFS Modern Fiction Studies*, vol. 52, no. 2, 2006, pp. 393–414. doi:https//10.1353/mfs.2006.0046. Accessed June 28, 2022.

Harris, Trudier. *Fiction and Folklore: The Novels of Toni Morrison*. 1991. U of Tennessee P, 1993.

Hartman, Saidiya. *Lose Your Mother: A Journey along the Atlantic Slave Routes*. Farrar, Straus and Giroux, 2007.

Mobley, Marilyn Sanders. "Narrative Dilemma: Jadine as Cultural Orphan in *Tar Baby*." *Folk Roots and Mythic Wings in Sarah Orne Jewett and Toni Morrison: The Cultural Function of Narrative*, edited by Marilyn Sanders Mobley, Louisiana State UP, 1991, pp.134–67.

Morrison, Toni. *Sula*. 1973. Picador, 1991.

Morrison, Toni. "Cinderella's Stepsisters." 1979. *Mouth Full of Blood: Essays, Speeches, Meditations*, edited by Toni Morrison, Chatto & Windus, 2019, pp. 110–12.

Morrison, Toni. *Tar Baby*. 1981. Picador, 1991.

Morrison, Toni. "The Writer Before the Page." 1983. *Mouth Full of Blood: Essays, Speeches, Meditations*, edited by Toni Morrison, Chatto & Windus, 2019, pp. 263–70.

Morrison, Toni. "Rootedness: The Ancestor as Foundation." 1984. *What Moves at the Margin: Selected Nonfiction of Toni Morrison*, edited by Carolyn C. Denard, Mississippi UP, 2008, pp. 56–64.

Morrison, Toni. *Beloved*. 1987. Picador, 1988.

Morrison, Toni. "Unspeakable Things Unspoken: The Afro-American Presence in American Literature." 1988. *Mouth Full of Blood: Essays, Speeches, Meditations*, edited by Toni Morrison, Chatto & Windus, 2019, pp. 161–97.

Morrison, Toni. "Women, Race, and Memory." 1989. *Mouth Full of Blood: Essays, Speeches, Meditations*, edited by Toni Morrison, Chatto & Windus, 2019, pp. 86–95.

Morrison, Toni. "Gertrude Stein and the Difference She Makes." 1990. *Mouth Full of Blood: Essays, Speeches, Meditations,* edited by Toni Morrison, Chatto & Windus, 2019, pp. 205–19.

Morrison, Toni. *Playing in the Dark: Whiteness and the Literary Imagination.* 1992. Picador, 1993.

Morrison, Toni. "The Nobel Lecture in Literature." 1993. *Mouth Full of Blood: Essays, Speeches, Meditations*, edited by Toni Morrison, Chatto & Windus, 2019, pp. 102–9.

Morrison, Toni. "Race Matters." 1994. *Mouth Full of Blood: Essays, Speeches, Meditations*, edited by Toni Morrison, Chatto & Windus, 2019, pp. 131–9.

Morrison, Toni. "Racism and Fascism." 1995. *Mouth Full of Blood: Essays, Speeches, Meditations*, edited by Toni Morrison, Chatto & Windus, 2019, pp. 14–16.

Morrison, Toni. "The Future of Time: Literature and Diminished Expectations." 1996. *Mouth Full of Blood: Essays, Speeches, Meditations*, edited by Toni Morrison, Chatto & Windus, 2019, pp. 113–26.

Morrison, Toni. *Paradise.* Vintage, 1998.

Morrison, Toni. "Literature and Public Life." 1998. *Mouth Full of Blood: Essays, Speeches, Meditations*, edited by Toni Morrison, Chatto & Windus, 2019, pp. 96–101.

Morrison, Toni. "The Slavebody and the Blackbody." 2000. *Mouth Full of Blood: Essays, Speeches, Meditations*, edited by Toni Morrison, Chatto & Windus, 2019, pp. 74–8.

Morrison, Toni. "The Dead of September 11." 2001. *Mouth Full of Blood: Essays, Speeches, Meditations*, edited by Toni Morrison, Chatto & Windus, 2019, pp. 3–4.

Morrison, Toni. "Wartalk." 2002. *Mouth Full of Blood: Essays, Speeches, Meditations*, edited by Toni Morrison, Chatto & Windus, 2019, pp. 21–5.

Morrison, Toni. *Love.* Chatto & Windus, 2003.

Morrison, Toni. "The War on Error." 2004. *Mouth Full of Blood: Essays, Speeches, Meditations*, edited by Toni Morrison, Chatto & Windus, 2019, pp. 26–32.

Morrison, Toni. "Étranger chez soi"/"The Foreigner's Home." *Toni Morrison: Invitée au Louvre Étranger chez soi*, edited by Christian Bourgeois, Musée du Louvre, 2006, pp. 13–26.

Morrison, Toni. *A Mercy.* Knopf, 2008.

Morrison, Toni. *God Help the Child.* Vintage, 2015.

Morrison, Toni. *Mouth Full of Blood: Essays, Speeches, Meditations,* Chatto & Windus, 2019.

Murray, Derek Conrad. "The Blackest Blackness: Slavery and the Satire of Kara Walker." *Slavery and the Post-Black Imagination*, edited by Bertram D. Ashe and Ilka Saal, U of Washington P, 2020, pp. 21–42.

Okri, Ben. "Artists Must Write as if These Are Our Last Days on Earth." *The Guardian*, Nov. 13, 2021, p. 4.

Peterson, Nancy J., editor. *Toni Morrison: Critical and Theoretical Approaches.* Johns Hopkins UP, 1997.

Ryan, Judylyn S. "Contested Visions/Double-Vision in *Tar Baby*." *Toni Morrison: Critical and Theoretical Approaches*, edited by Nancy J. Peterson, Johns Hopkins UP, 1997, pp. 63–87.

Shaw-Thornburg, Angela. "The Woman in Yellow in Toni Morrison's *Tar Baby*." *The Explicator*, vol. 70, no. 1, 2012, 53–6, doi:10.1080:00144940.2012.663417. https://doi.org/10.1080/00144940.2012.663417. Accessed June 28, 2022.

Stovall, Tyler. *Paris Noir: African Americans in the City of Light.* Houghton Mifflin, 2012.

Touré. *Who's Afraid of Post-Blackness?: What It Means to Be Black Now.* Free P, 2011.

Werner, Craig H. "The Briar Patch as Modernist Myth: Morrison, Barthes and *Tar Baby* As-Is." *Critical Essays on Toni Morrison*, edited by Nellie Y. McKay, G. K. Hall and Co., 1988, pp. 150–67.

CHAPTER SIX

"How Can I Say Things that Are Pictures?": Foregrounding in *Beloved*

JENNIFER LARSON

Toni Morrison's unique vision for language distinguishes her work and offers critics a shared, productive entry point into her texts. Naomi Mandel explains, for example, that "while critical readings of Morrison understandably offer a variety of opinions on just what determines the cultural identity of her writing, this investment in language's limits remains a crucial common denominator" (602). Thus, in highlighting the experiences that language cannot signify, Morrison's texts push readers to reconsider the boundaries of both language and linguistic analysis.

One especially fruitful method for such reconsideration is foregrounding analysis, a traditionally reader-response-focused approach to literary criticism that, by nature of its name, also translates well to visual interpretation, specifically of film. In *Linguistic Criticism*, Roger Fowler explains that foregrounding applies to any linguistic structure or event that stands out in a work: "Whenever some item or construction appears in a text with unusual or noticeable frequency and apparently for some valid reason, then cumulatively, a distinctive effect emerges" (95). That is to say, simply, that redundant linguistic structures or events—by nature of their difference from their contexts (or backgrounds)—have the potential to make language mean more than what is stated, to move beyond the basic sign-signifier relationships of the individual words or constructions.

Since "foregrounding uses a visual metaphor to explain a linguistic technique," it inherently highlights language's limits—reminding audiences of what language alone cannot be and of what cannot (or perhaps should not) be spoken (Fowler 96). Foregrounding analysis, then, fits Morrison's work in general, and *Beloved* in particular, especially well. Morrison explores language's boundaries in other novels, but in *Beloved*, this exploration is especially prominent and especially useful for interpreting the narrative. Specifically, foregrounding analysis helps illuminate how Morrison recreates the unspeakable while still leaving it unspoken, and it helps to resolve some of the text's mysteries, including the mystery of Beloved's identity.

Morrison herself even uses foregrounding analysis for her discussion of the novel's first lines in the 1988 lecture-turned-essay, "Unspeakable Things, Unspoken: The Afro-American Presence in American Literature." She describes how, even in these initial sentences, she is mindful that something as seemingly simple as rearranging clauses or embedding numerals can lead to the kind of productive disorientation that creates "a sound just beyond hearing," one that might even be "unsettling" to readers (31–2). The discussion points to Morrison's use of language as experience creator, a method of setting the stage for the reader's immersion into the novel and into its characters' unspeakable thoughts and emotions. Morrison explains that, through the text's language, "the reader is snatched, yanked, thrown into an environment completely foreign"; thus, readers are "snatched just as the slaves were from one place to another, from any place to another, without preparation and without defense" (32). Since words alone do not usually reenact such visceral experiences, Morrison's unique vison for and use of language simultaneously reveals and challenges language's traditionally perceived limits. According to Naomi Mandel, "for Morrison, evoking language's limits redeems it from [complicity in historic subjugation], reinstating language as a recuperative and healing force," and "when language foregrounds its limits" new and deeper meanings can be revealed (605). Knowing and then pushing against language's limits are the first steps toward changing or removing those limits and, therefore, creating possibility.

But Beloved's iconoclastic moves aren't limited to the opening lines. Passages throughout the novel immerse readers in the unfamiliar and the uncomfortable. The most prominent of these passages is what critics sometimes refer to as the "poetic" or "soliloquy" section—the first-person passages that represent the interior dialogues of Sethe, Denver, and Beloved. We are introduced to these chapters through the eyes of Stamp Paid, who watches the three women through a window and who, the narrator explains, is able to recognize but not decipher "the thoughts of the women of 124, unspeakable thoughts, unspoken" (199).

This entire poetic/soliloquy section itself is foregrounded within the novel as a whole because of the shift in narration. According to Fowler's point-of-view definitions, the narration in the section is first-person type A or "internal" narration, while the narration for most of the novel would be a third-person type A told "from the point of view of someone who is not a participating character but who has knowledge of the feelings of the characters—a narrator, or the so-called 'omniscient' author" (170). Within this section, Beloved's individual chapter (third in the series of four) is foregrounded because of its shifts in both form and content and because Beloved's identity and origins/history challenge the limits of language.

Rebecca Ferguson asserts that Beloved's speech is "complex in its shifting of pronouns, identities, and bodily parts; hers is an opening, seeking, concentrated language of elision" (117). As Morrison promises in "Unspeakable Things Unspoken," the novel is not just telling us what is said; rather, the challenging and innovative grammar, focus, concentrated presence, and even absence, allow it to *say* more and to *be* more. Mandel points out that Beloved and her language become a living embodiment of "unspeakable thoughts, unspoken" because "Beloved names Sethe's own frustrations and desires and it is precisely these frustrations and desires that come back to haunt her, rendering language simultaneously superfluous and crucial, and positioning the relation between speech and the unspeakable as the crux of the novel" (589).

A foregrounding analysis of Beloved's chapter in the poetic/soliloquy section, then, begins to unlock the mysteries of her identity and origins. While her past is essentially unknown, the novel suggests five possibilities, as explained by Teresa Heffernan: "She is the voices of the slaves in the Middle Passage; she is the brutalized girl who escapes from the white man's cabin; she is the daughter looking for her lost mother; she is the ghost of Sethe's baby girl and the sexual female who torments Paul D; she is among the freed slaves wandering the roads" (569). The third-person narration in the rest of the novel provides some clues about which of these potential identities is most likely, but ultimately, Beloved's first-person chapter offers the most clarity. Indeed, foregrounding analysis of this key passage reveals that Beloved is both an observer along a traumatic timeline of African and African American experience and a participant in the tragic story of 124: she is inextricably and inexplicably connected to a communal past while also being the individual physical manifestation of the (already crawling?) baby's ghost.

I will begin the discussion of foregrounding in this chapter by looking at the images that are foregrounded in the sections within the chapter as well as throughout the chapter as a whole. The two most important elements found throughout the chapter are underlexicalizations and the repeated focus on body parts. Fowler defines underlexicalization as "the lack of a term or set of terms" (216). He notes that, according to his psycholinguistic approach, "such gaps, in an individual's lexical repertoire, mean that the individual does not have access to the concepts concerned, or has difficulty of access" (216). For texts such as *Beloved*, in which linguistic experimentation is prevalent, underlexicalization appears as "either a noticeable suppression of a term, or the substitution of a noticeable complex expression for what in other registers would be a simple term" (216). Many of the underlexicalizations in Beloved's chapter are difficult, if not impossible, to decipher—readers may glean myriad possible meanings from them based on their own experiences and knowledge. Other underlexicalizations such as "the men without skins" are more easily identified and more likely to be interpreted more uniformly by readers.

Beloved's underlexicalizations might be ascribed to her early stages of linguistic development had she not demonstrated—in this chapter and elsewhere—that she was clearly capable of sophisticated metaphor, such as when she speaks of the man on the ship with the "body which is a small bird trembling" (211). Therefore, underlexicalizations are more likely foregrounded as part of the text's emphasis on the language's limits and possibilities. Rachel Lee points out that "in *Beloved*, language and expression in general fall short because the experiences they strive to capture are peculiar—always circumscribed by the legacy of having been owned" (577). The normative signs and signifiers of language cannot capture the nuances of the individual slaves' experiences. Also, historically, written and spoken language (in this case English), was used by oppressors to subjugate the enslaved. In the novel, therefore, "Morrison highlights the lack of vocabulary available to speak the experience of the enslaved self as well as the often perilous relation of the former enslaved to a historically specific language which commodifies African Americans" (Lee 577).

The chapter uses an emphasis on body parts to highlight language's limits by replicating absence and disembodiment. Beloved rarely speaks of the body as a whole, and when she does, she speaks of wanting to distance herself from it, for she says, "We are all trying to leave our bodies behind" (210). During slavery, families and personal histories were fragmented as mothers were separated from their children, husbands from wives. The fragmented body thus becomes a metaphor for this separation. Beloved is also preoccupied with faces, and she points to the face as the place where lost familial connections can be found since she believes she knows her mother because they have the same face. She says "face" 30 times in the chapter, and the body parts that follow in frequency of use are also associated with the face (four "teeth," five "eyes," three "ears," and two "mouths"). Other body parts, "shoulders" and "legs" are mentioned only once each, "feet" twice, while "neck," notable because of how Sethe killed her baby, is mentioned four times.

For ease of discussion, I have divided the chapter into seven sections based on the spaces between each section in the printed text: Section two begins with "All of it is now" (210); section three begins with "We are not crouching now" (211); section four begins with "In the beginning I could see her"

(211); section five begins with "I cannot lose her again" (212); section six begins with "They are not crouching now" (212), and section seven begins with "I am standing in the rain falling" (212).

Looking at the sections individually, each provides images that represent one or more of Beloved's possible identities. For example, the first suggests that she is the daughter of an enslaved woman harvesting crops on a plantation. Beloved speaks of a kind of labor as she watches the "she" in the text "take flowers away from leaves." However, it is clear that the labor is not for the woman's own use or from her own land because "the leaves are not for her" (210). Also, Beloved must be related to this woman—and based on the earlier images, the woman is likely Beloved's mother—because Beloved states, "her face is my own" (210).

In the second section, new imagery suggests a shift in place and time to the middle passage. She describes "others," "crouching," "men without skin," "rats," hunger and thirst, "trembling," and the "dead man on [her] face" (210). Among the atrocities mentioned, the tightness of the space is specifically foregrounded in this section as "crouching" is mentioned three times in the first three lines, and later, she notes that "someone is thrashing but there is no room to do it in" and that "there is no room to tremble" (210–11). Although most of the chapter is present tense, Beloved introduces this section with the time marker "All of it is now it is always now," indicating that she is speaking of a time distinct from the time in the first section but still part of her present (211).

The third section strengthens Beloved's connection to the middle passage. Beloved again speaks of hunger and death, but she also alludes to the water and to chains. First, "the bread is sea colored" (211). She is likely on deck because "the sun closes [her] eyes," and she watches women "fall into the sea which is the color of the bread" noting that "the women with [her] face is the sea" (211). At the same time, this woman wears, "a circle around her neck," perhaps an underlexicalized iron collar. With the mention of this woman who shares Beloved's face, the text brings the reader back to the first section, and Beloved's histories begin to overlap.

And indeed, in the following section, the enslaved daughter and the middle passage narratives intertwine completely. This section, however, occurs at a different point in the present tense; now Beloved speaks of events "in the beginning," which is also used as part of the "hungry suffering" in section two ("in the beginning we could vomit"; 211, 210). She again speaks of the flower picking as the mother "wants her round basket," the one that she originally used for flowers but could also be an underlexicalization of the baby basket that enslaved mothers used to carry their children in while working (211). Yet, Beloved is also still clearly on the slave ship, for "the storms rock us," the dead man is still with her, and the woman "is crouching" nearby (211–12).

The fifth and sixth sections follow similar patterns, mixing the images of the women with those of the middle passage. In the seventh section, though, there is a new "him" that Beloved tells us, he "hurts where I sleep" (212). Beloved notes that "he puts his finger there" but that there is no one in this story "to say me my name" (212). These passages use the same language as the earlier sexual passages with Paul D.; this section thus links Beloved's identity and memory with those of Ella, who escaped from a white man's sexual prison. Yet, nods to the other histories are also still present. The sun again "closes [her] eyes" as it did in the middle passage section, and there is water here (212). However, "no boats go on this water," and her "dead man is not floating here," so we know that she is no longer on the slave ship (212). The mother also returns, but this time "her face comes through the water" (213). Beloved then builds on this mother connection to link specifically with Sethe, for she concludes, "Sethe's is the face that left me" (213).

The foregrounded images are complemented by the chapter's foregrounded pronouns. Pronoun use changes significantly from section to section, and Fowler labels such changes "syntagmatic shifts" or changes in "the linear ordering of sounds and of words constructing a sentence" (98). In the first section, there are seven "I"s, four "she"s, and six "her"s, of which four are used as objects and two as possessives. In the second section, Beloved introduces the "we" and uses it six times; the associated "us" object is used three times. She also adds two "he"s, along with the possessive "his" (seven), and "they" and "their," both used twice. "I" is used six times. The third section incorporates most of the individual, feminine (no masculine), and collective pronouns used in the first two, with eight "I"s, two "she"s, two "her"s in the possessive slot, two "we"s, and one "they." In the fourth section, however, there is a significant increase in the number of "I"s to seventeen. There is also an increase in "her"s to twelve, five in the object position, and "she"s increase to five. "He" and its related pronouns are prominent in this section as well, with four occurrences of "he," one of "him," and seven of "his." At the same time, "we" and "us" lose prominence, with only one mention each.

The fifth and sixth sections, the shortest in the chapter, again scale down the use of "I," while favoring the "they." Each of these sections has only two "I"s versus three "they"s. The fifth also eliminates the "we" but offers six "she"s and two "her"s in the object position, while the sixth brings back the "we," though there is only one occurrence, and scales the "she"s back to two and the "hers" to one possessive.

Finally, in the seventh section, we see significant change. There are 43 "I"s, fifteen "she"s, and six "her"s—four in the adjective slot, two in the object; one "we," two "he"s, one "him," and two "his"s.

The table below summarizes the list above:

	Section						
	1	2	3	4	5	6	7
I	7	6	8	17	2	2	43
She	4	0	2	5	6	2	15
Her	6	0	2	12	2	1	6
He	0	4	0	4	0	0	6
His	0	7	0	7	0	0	2
Him	0	0	0	1	0	0	2
We	0	6	2	1	0	1	1
Us	0	3	0	1	0	0	0
They	0	2	2	0	3	0	0
Their	0	2	0	0	0	0	0

Although this pronoun-focused foregrounding analysis admittedly seems overly methodical at first glance, the exercise proves especially valuable when considering the potential implications of this pronoun use alongside each section's foregrounded images. Specifically, the number of "I"s in a section demonstrates the level of personal investment that Beloved brings to the history with which that section is aligned. The omnipresence of the first-person pronoun indicates that she has some level of investment in all the histories, but the "I"s dominate in the first, fourth, and seventh sections. All of these sections share the round basket image that correlates with the daughter of the enslaved mother. The most "I"-heavy section, section seven, adds the direct link to Sethe, thereby showing that Beloved feels the strongest personal connection to Sethe's story in general and to Sethe as mother in particular.

The prominence of the "I" in section four is also significant because "she" and "he" (and their related possessive pronouns and objects) are also more common in this section, so this dual foregrounding links the three. "She" refers to the woman who shares Beloved's face, the enslaved mother, and "he" refers to the man who dies near Beloved. The section's images still evoke the middle passage, but the communal pronouns of the other middle passage sections are less prominent, thus indicating a partial shift to an alternate, and more individual, history that is nevertheless still tethered to the communal past. So Beloved's saying that the man "dies on [her] face" encourages readers to consider the meaning that "face" signals for her. Based on the use of "face" in previous sections and elsewhere in the novel, he is likely related to her. As such, he could be Halle, who probably died around the same time as Sethe's (already crawling?) baby, or he could be Beloved's grandfather, who Ma'am recalls that Sethe's mother met and loved aboard the slave ship. Either explanation also fits because Beloved connects the man with the mother through the round basket image when she says, "his singing is of the place where a woman takes flowers away from their leaves and puts them in the round basket" (211).

Beloved's personal versus communal investment in each section's history is also illuminated in the foregrounded verb tense and agency. Present-tense verbs are prominent in the chapter, but the number of direct active action verbs—that is, action verbs that are not hedged with a modal, not negated, and not softened by the present-perfect tense—fluctuates slightly from the first to the sixth sections, with each section having no more than three. The seventh section, however, features eighteen active action verbs, of which only five occur in the present participle form. Nearly all have "I" as the subject. Thus, in the final section's history—the history that suggests she really is Sethe's child—Beloved is an active participant and an agent rather than an observer or a passive actor.

But the chapter's foregrounding is not limited to parts of speech images; unique sentence-level constructions also stand out from the text's background. The most noticeable foregrounded constructions are compound sentences and sentence fragments, which appear as stand-alone repeated phrases or merely single words. Since most of the chapter's sentences follow the basic English subject–verb–object word order, the compounds and fragments are paradigmatic shifts, introducing a change in linguistic pattern (Fowler 98).

Fragments appear primarily as noun phrases and prepositional phrases; only two fragments are verb phrases, one set adverbs. The first fragment, the repeated noun phrase "a hot thing," is found in the chapter's first section (*Beloved* 210). No fragments appear again until section three, where there are seven. "A hot thing" appears twice, along with the noun phrases "the one whose teeth I loved," "the little hill of dead people," and "the face that is mine," the verb phrase "bite it away," and the preposition "inside" (211). The fourth section, although just slightly longer than the third, has only three fragments: the noun phrases "a hot thing" and "the shining in her ears" and the prepositional phrase "before the clouds" (211). The fifth and sixth sections, the two shortest in the chapter, have only one fragment each, "a hot thing" and the prepositional phrase "with my face," respectively (212). The passage then concludes with a sudden increase to ten fragments in the seventh section: the only adverbs come with four fragments together in "again again night day night day," the second verb phrase (still only partial as it is missing its helping verb), "doing it at last," as well as three instances of "a hot thing" and the other noun phrases "no men without skin" and "the face that is going to smile at me" (212–13).

While there are no obvious significant thematic connections among these fragments—either within or among sections—taken together, the fragments still have rhetorical value as foregrounded elements. A fragment is missing some element that would make it a complete sentence; therefore, fragments create a sense of absence for readers. By presenting us with only part of the sentence, usually the noun phrase, Beloved speaks to the gaps in both her experience and her expression. These linguistic gaps also complement the aforementioned focus on body parts as symbols for absences as well as the graphic spacing gaps in the text on the printed page. This visual spacing receives much critical attention: Ferguson, Mandel, and Lee all address it. Abdellatif Khayati (1999) also links these gaps to Morrison's use of the neo-slave narrative genre, noting that "where the tradition of the slave narratives is concerned, Morrison is attentive to silences and gaps in these narratives" (1). Ferguson claims that the gaps are crucial to an understanding of African American experience and to Beloved's communal as well as individual history. She writes that because "Beloved brings the whole traumatic experience of slavery with her, she not only knows more than she could otherwise have known in her previous short life, but she also contains the *effects* that slavery had, its profound fragmentation on the self and the connections the self might have with others" (114; emphasis in original). Thus, her chapter's fragments highlight how Beloved's identity—and perhaps Beloved herself—emerges from pieces (fragments) of history and self that she remembers and that she has collected from lost/found/forgotten/stolen narratives.

Compound sentences appear far less frequently than the fragments (no passage has more than two), so their purpose reads as more focused; they emphasize connection and relationship. And this emphasis starts with the chapter's first sentence—"I am Beloved and she is mine," a compound (210). There is one other in the first section, "her face is my own and I want to be there in the place where her face is and to be looking at it too," as well as two in the second section, "his mouth smells sweet but his eyes are locked" and "daylight comes through the cracks and I can see his locked eyes" (210). The third, fifth, and sixth sections have no compounds, but the fourth has one, "In the beginning the women are away from the men and the men are away from the women" (211–12). Finally, the seventh has two, "there is night and there is day" and "Sethe sees me see her and I see the smile." All of these compounds point either to origins—such as the men and women coming together on the slave ship and the biblical allusion of night and day—or to figures associated with parents, such as the women with the face like Beloved's and the man with the pretty teeth who rests on Beloved's face. As they are foregrounded, the compounds also bring additional attention to these relationships, reinforcing the personal investment foregrounded by the "I" pronoun and the active verbs.

Considering all of these foregrounded elements together, then, shows that Beloved's origin story is rooted simultaneously in both the communal/collective history as well as the individual experience of Sethe's baby. The foregrounded elements suggest that Beloved clearly took part in multiple possible historical identities, even though she has the strongest personal investment in and connection to the trauma of 124. However, because Beloved does engage so directly with all of the possible histories, and because the chapter uses language to both obscure and reveal Beloved's fragmented past, present, and future, the text compels readers to also consider language's role in creating as well as shaping individual and communal identity. Lee, for example, explains, "*Beloved* does not take for granted that there is only one language (i.e., that defined by semioticians or that practiced by Schoolteacher and his nephews)" or that language is benign since it "has hitherto effectively constructed black subjects as less than human" (582). More broadly, Fowler, building on Mikhail Bahktin's idea of "multiaccentuality," says that "all words are inherently double voiced or double valued" (Fowler 104). In other words, the novel in general, and this chapter in particular, reiterates and enacts that there be more than one signifier for a given sign, and Beloved literally embodies this idea through the identities her language helps resurrect.

Finally, since foregrounding analysis borrows its central metaphor from the visual, foregrounding analysis also offers a productive lens through which to consider the relationship between the novel and its 1998 film adaptation, directed by Jonathan Demme and produced by/starring Oprah Winfrey. Whereas foregrounding analysis of the novel shows Beloved to have both a central individual identity—the resurrected baby spirit that is "beloved" by Sethe—as well as a series of communal identities drawn from the shared African American traditions of which the spirit is a part, the film focuses less on solving the mystery of Beloved's identity and instead uses visual elements to highlight the psychological journeys that Beloved prompts the story's other characters to take. In the film, there is little to cast any doubt that Beloved is the baby spirit come to life. Nevertheless, the film adaptation employs many of the same foregrounded images as the novel. These images encourage viewers to believe that Beloved is an undead girl at the same time as they evoke the novel's emphasis on the communal by showing how Beloved—and her emphasis on storytelling in particular—acts as a catalyst through which Denver and Sethe confront and begin to heal from the past's open wounds.

Jemelian Hakemuler explains that when considering a work's film adaptation, "Examining foregrounding requires a distinction between possible causes and possible effects: the devices of film that we can point out in a text that might also draw readers' or spectators' attention and make them reflect on the significance of form" (127). There are no scenes in the film that correspond directly to the novel's poetic/soliloquy chapters; however, there are a number of origins-focused scenes with foregrounded images and sounds that parallel the novel's foreground text. For example, when Beloved first appears in the film, the camera focuses first on the flowers that surround her, then on the insects that surround her and eventually gather (in a swarm that looks like blood) on her neck. The camera eventually settles on a close-up of her face with its nearly flawless skin—all in a quick succession of short jump cuts. This progression links Beloved's rebirth to both the natural and the supernatural. Her body appears almost merged with the flora and insects, as if she were a part of a universal consciousness similar to that which the novel suggests when it connects her to multiple timelines and narratives.

The close-ups, though, also create a disembodied effect, just like the novel's foregrounding of body parts and sentence fragments. For example, when Sethe, Denver, and Paul D. see Beloved for the first time, the film initially shows only a close-up of her shoe. And when they take her into the house, the camera repeatedly comes back to her feet and hands. In one of these moments, Paul D. says, "Look at her feet, they ain't walking feet. More like she ride from somewhere all the way here." By foregrounding specific parts of Beloved's seemingly impossible body, the camera separates the parts from the whole and Beloved's fragmented body becomes a metaphor for her fragmented identity and history.

Close-ups are also often a precursor to what is perhaps the film's most important foregrounded elements: flashbacks. Beloved consistently encourages Sethe and Denver to tell her stories. "Tell me," she repeats, her flawless face filling the screen. The request is almost always followed by a story told in flashback, even if the teller was not actually witness to the recounted events—such as when Denver tells the story of her own birth. Flashbacks are rife for foregrounding analysis because they are fundamentally paradoxical: they provide narrative *background* by bringing up the past, a temporal element outside of the story's linear chronology; yet, in so doing, they *foreground* that past as the flashback disrupts that chronology. In the novel and the film, the stories force characters to resurrect and confront the past, often to facilitate healing. The result is a conflation of the past and the present that complicates traditional notions of memory and history.

The flashbacks also offer a valuable site of comparison for the page and screen versions of *Beloved*. According to Angela Christie, "Morrison's text is innately visual through her inclusion of a series of cinematic flashbacks where the past intrudes on the present. Yet, while Morrison's pen was able to omnisciently zoom in and out of her characters' minds, Demme's camera was confined to third-person observation, calling for selective scene adaptations and shifting close-ups to accommodate visual art" (para. 15). This key difference shows the limits of visual representation by highlighting what the screen leaves unseen: "Things that are pictures" cannot always be said, but pictures, similarly, cannot always say the things that words can.

Overall then, foregrounding analysis for both the novel and its film adaptation reveals that although there is a dominant signifier, the baby ghost that is "beloved" by Sethe, the sign "beloved" also refers to a series of identities and shared African American traditions of which the spirit is a part. Beloved, Heffernan posits, "mocks the desire to represent, to categorize, and to name. She is both adult and child, woman and ghost; at the same time that she is the unspeakable and the unknown, she is culturally and historically situated" (569). By crafting this identity for Beloved that is both singular and plural, the text renders futile any attempt to "use words as if they have only one meaning: to suppress critical and paradoxical values in favor of the main which is convenient for the ideology of the current discourse" (Fowler 104). Foregrounding then becomes the vehicle for both exposing and overcoming the boundaries of language: it speaks the unspeakable of multiple histories, while leaving them all unspoken, preserving the beauty, complexity, and synergy of both individual and communal Black identity and Black experience.

WORKS CITED

Christie, Angela. "A *Beloved* Performance: Reading between the Lines." *Babel*, vol. 24, 2011, pp. 105–20.

Ferguson, Rebecca. "History, Memory, and Language in Toni Morrison's *Beloved*." *Feminist Criticism*, edited by Susan Sellers, U of Toronto P, 1991, pp. 109–27.

Fowler, Roger. *Linguistic Criticism*. Oxford UP, 1996.

Hakemuler, Jemelian. "Tracing Foregrounding in Responses to Film." *Language and Literature*, vol. 16, no. 2, 2007, pp. 125–39.

Heffernan, Teresa. "*Beloved* and the Problem of Mourning." *Studies in the Novel*, vol. 30, no. 4, 1998, pp. 558–73.

Khayati, Abdellatif. "Representation, Race, and the 'Language' of the Oneffable in Toni Morrison's Narrative." *African American Review*, vol. 33, no. 2, 1999, pp. 313–24.

Lee, Rachel. "Missing Peace in Toni Morrison's *Sula* and *Beloved*." *African American Review*, vol. 28, no. 4, 1994, pp. 571–83.

Mandel, Naomi. "'I Made the Ink': Identity, Complicity, 60 Million, and More." *Modern Fiction Studies*, vol. 48, no. 3, 2002, pp. 581–613.

Morrison, Toni. *Beloved*. Plume, 1987.

Morrison, Toni. "Unspeakable Things, Unspoken: The Afro-American Presence in American Literature." *Michigan Quarterly Review*, vol. 28, no. 1, 1989, pp. 9–34.

CHAPTER SEVEN

Rootlessness: Afro-Pessimism as Foundation in *Paradise*

KEITH CLARK

In this meditation on *Paradise*, I draw upon the critical notion of "Afro-Pessimism" as my primary interpretive framework. The scholars chiefly associated with this critical discourse, Frank Wilderson and Jared Sexton, foreground and build upon the writings of seminal thinkers/scholars Frantz Fanon and Orlando Patterson in formulating their own hypotheses. Informed by Sexton's and Wilderson's exegeses, I will explore how *Paradise* can be limned through an Afro-Pessimism critical lens, given the novel's depiction of the ill-conceived and ultimately calamitous enterprise of constructing a racially "pure" refuge in an America for which virulent antiblackness functions as desideratum.

AFRO-PESSIMISM: A PROLEGOMENON

With the 2020 publication of *Afropessimism*, Wilderson has emerged as its principal architect, enumerating what the book's dust jacket copy describes as "an increasingly prominent intellectual movement that sees blackness through the lens of perpetual slavery." Though this recent book constitutes his fullest rendering of it, Wilderson has explored it in previous works, most notably in "Afro-Pessimism and the End of Redemption," published in 2015. While heavily influenced by Fanon and Patterson—most directly the former's *Black Skin, White Masks* (1967) and the latter's *Slavery and Social Death* (1982)—Wilderson also draws upon the pioneering work of literary critic/theorist Hortense Spillers:

> Afro-Pessimism is premised on an iconoclastic claim: that Blackness is coterminous with Slaveness. Blackness *is* social death, which is to say that there was never a prior meta-moment of plentitude, never a moment of equilibrium, never a moment of social life. Blackness, as a paradigmatic position (rather than an ensemble of identities, cultural practices, or anthropological accoutrement), cannot be disimbricated from slavery. The narrative arc of the slave who is Black (unlike Orlando Patterson's generic slave who may be of any race) is *not an arc at all*, but a flat line, what Hortense Spillers [in her 1987 essay "Mama's Baby, Papa's Maybe: An American Grammar Book"] calls "historical stillness": a flat line that "moves" from disequilibrium to a moment in the narrative of faux equilibrium, to disequilibrium restored and/or rearticulated. (Wilderson, emphases in original)

I would like to thank my colleague, Dr. Stefan Wheelock, for his astute suggestions on a draft of this essay.

The neologism "Slaveness" is the linchpin here, as Wilderson designates slavery as the matrix of Blackness; ergo, Blackness and Slaveness can never be disaggregated. Any notions of progress are vitiated by the permanency of the derogated, subjugated position where blackness will be forever circumscribed by and synonymous with slaveness. Afro-Pessimism's other key theorist, Jared Sexton, complementarily avers,

> The slave, in other words, is the anoriginal figure of difference in the articulation of the human being, the pivot or hinge or fulcrum of its machinations, associated with all that is abjected by its collective organization in order to lend coherence to its internal conflicts (e.g., race, class, gender, sexuality) and definition to its external boundaries (e.g., animal, machine, object, spirit). (Sexton 99)

Hence, the slave becomes the sine qua non in the architectonics of being itself, the object upon and against which the autonomous subject's very essence—that is, the indivisible symbiotic identities white and American—is formulated.

If American slavery is the *Ur*-moment of Black abjection, Morrison's own nomenclative alloys, reflected in the title of her 2000 essay, "The Slavebody and the Blackbody," adumbrate Afro-Pessimism's discursive matrix. On the one hand, she makes the following delineation: "When I use the term 'slavebody' to distinguish it from 'blackbody,' I mean to underscore the fact that slavery and racism are two separate phenomena. The origins of slavery are not necessarily (or even ordinarily) racist" ("Slavebody" 74). Her subsequent enumerations, however, signal the concepts' coaxial qualities:

> Much of what made New World slavery exceptional was the highly identifiable racial signs of its population in which skin color, primarily but not exclusively, interfered with the ability for subsequent generations to merge into the nonslave population. For them there was virtually no chance to hide, disguise, or elude former slave status, for a marked visibility enforced the division between former slave and nonslave (although history defies the distinction) and supported racial hierarchy. The ease, therefore, of moving from the dishonor associated with the slavebody to the contempt in which the freed blackbody was held became almost seamless because the intervening years of the Enlightenment saw a marriage of aesthetics and science and a move toward transcendent whiteness. In this racism the slavebody disappears but the blackbody remains and is morphed into a synonym for poor people, a synonym for criminalism and a flash point for public policy. (76–7)

Within the context of Afro-Pessimism, my gloss on Morrison's race theorizing is this: while codified, de facto slavery may have had a finite temporality, the continually denigrated blackbody shatters spatiotemporal boundaries. The Slave Codes, the Black Codes, Jim Crow, the New Jim Crow, the Prison Industrial Complex, anti-Black extrajudicial violence, Black Lives (Don't) Matter: the connective filament here that traverses space and time elucidates how dark skin has always functioned as the metonym for racial abjection—"poor people," "a synonym for criminalism."

Anglo-American historical discourse and African American literature evidence how the slavebody and the blackbody are mutually constitutive. To be sure, a cursory perusal of Anglo-American racio-judicial history and foundational writings evinces how erasure, dispossession, and derogation reify the symbiotic connection between nominally liberated blackbodies and their legally disenfranchised progenitors. Founding patriarch Jefferson's infamous primer on inveterate black wretchedness, "Query XIV," is replete with such prevailing certitudes:

> Add to these [features establishing superior white physical beauty], flowing hair, a more elegant symmetry of form, their [negroes] own judgment in favour of the whites, declared by their preference of them, as uniformly as is the preference of the Oran-ootan for the black women over those of his own species. The circumstance of superior beauty, is thoughtworthy attention in the propagation of horses, dogs, and other domestic animals; why not in that of man? (Jefferson 138)

Inarguably, the father of the Declaration of Independence was "a thoroughgoing and unabashed Anglo-Saxonist" (Douglas 11). The tentacles for such anti-Black dogma reached well into the nineteenth century, borne out by the 1857 Dred Scott decision. In denying the enslaved Scott's petition for liberation based on his having lived in free territory, chief justice Roger B. Taney concluded on behalf of the court's majority: "They had for more than a century before been regarded as beings of an inferior order, and altogether unfit to associate with the white race, either in social or political relations; and so far inferior, that they had no rights which the white man was bound to respect; and that the negro might justly and lawfully be reduced to slavery for his benefit" ("The Dred Scott Decision"). Such baneful statutory rhetoric situates blackness as judicially outside of economies of the human(e). In the aggregate, Jefferson's and Taney's archetypal racial rhetorics are the stanchions for the "social death" upon which Afro-Pessimism is constructed; the Black object is consigned to an immutable state of debasement and nonbeing.

African American literature, whether historical or fictional, abounds with Black ontological despair and erasure, the bedrock of Afro-Pessimist critical discourse. The writings of the enslaved are often heralded as counternarratives to demeaning inscriptions of blackness as irredeemably benighted and alien (re: Jefferson and Taney). Indeed, narratives of enslavement and liberation have been extolled as written testaments to African Americans' dogged endurance and resourcefulness, the apogee of the hallowed *American* value of individual self-making and the ensuing reward of life and liberty. Consider, for instance, the autobiography of America's foremost male slave author-cum-abolitionist-cum-statesman, Frederick Douglass. Ostensibly, one might read the 1845 *Narrative*'s opening passage as a recuperation and dismantling of Jefferson's bestializing "Query XIV": "By far the larger part of the slaves know as little of their ages as horses know of theirs" (17), Douglass here countering and recasting the founding father's literal subhumanizing sentiments with an equine metaphor exposing the depths of white brutality and Black victimization, with its attendant epistemological deprivation. Subsequently, Douglass exclaims how his physical subduing of the brutal overseer Mr. Covey inaugurated a revitalized self: "I felt as I never felt before. It was a glorious resurrection, from the tomb of slavery, to the heaven of freedom ... and I now resolved that, however long I might remain a slave in form, the day had passed forever when I could be a slave in fact. I did not hesitate to let it be known of me, that the white man who expected to succeed in whipping, must also succeed in killing me" (74–5). But however psychically resuscitative physical violence might be, such declarations position blackness as tenuous and contingent, the blackbody perpetually facing the specter of metaphorical and literal death as the price for establishing Black subjectivity. Regardless of Douglass's liberation from mental bondage, his "slaveness" juridically and in the white American imaginary remains unalterable.

Dred Scott's "rightless-ness" reverberates in the escaped Harriet Jacobs's lament in *Incidents in the Life of a Slave Girl* (1861), when her owners attempt to reclaim their human inventory once she's escaped to putatively "free" New York. Though Jacobs rebuffed her white benefactress's offer to purchase her freedom outright, Mrs. Bruce nevertheless intervened unbeknownst to Jacobs, née the pseudonymous "Linda Brent." Though she jubilantly entreats Jacobs to return to North Carolina—"I am rejoiced to tell you that the money for your freedom has been paid"—and after another white abolitionist/friend in New York informs Jacobs that he has "seen the bill of sale," the now-liberated bondwoman ruminates on the odious terms on which Black "freedom" is garnered: "I well know the value of that bit of paper; but much as I love freedom, I do not like to look upon it … I despise the miscreant who demanded payment for what never rightfully belong to him or his" (348–9). Slavebodies as transactional; blackbodies as objects whose extrication is brokered *between* whites—Jacobs fully grasps that even the magnanimous act of abolitionist allies securing her freedom gives tacit legitimacy to Taney's ignominious claim consigning Blacks to "an inferior order." The very mercantile verbiage—"paid," "bill of sale"—speaks to Black "thingification" and the patina of bondage that continues to circumscribe the blackbody, even when the status of slavebody is nominally removed. The recent commemoration of the first captured Africans' arrival to America in 1619, coupled with the interminable torrent of brutality inflicted upon "free" African American bodies in the twentieth and twenty-first centuries regardless of age or gender—from George Stinney and Denise McNair to Tamir Rice and Breonna Taylor—exposes how the blackbody remains the ineludible site of otherness deserving of eradication, the 400-plus intervening years notwithstanding.[1]

THE DISALLOWERS AND THE DISALLOWED: INADMISSIBLE, UNASSIMILABLE BLACKNESS

Recall the moment in *Beloved* when four marauding subjugators arrive on horseback to capture and re-enslave the escaped Sethe Suggs and her children—an action that effectuates a bloodbath, as Sethe commits what one character calls the "rough choice" of murdering the eponymous "crawling-already?" baby and the attempted killing of Beloved's siblings. Morrison invokes the mononymic modifier "The Misery" to capture the unfathomable horror of this moment. Though not nearly as calamitous in terms of infanticide and the psychic violence it engenders, "The Disallowing" in *Paradise* is another watershed moment in which the author enacts a deft appellative maneuver. Like a poet bending a word's case, inflection, mood, or semantic function, Morrison transforms the verb into a noun that simultaneously describes an act of rejection and the generative ontological moment for a formerly enslaved community's search for a home in the "Indian Territory" of late-nineteenth-century Oklahoma.

---

[1] Though not often acknowledged in the annals of the nation's most vicious anti-Black crimes, the killing of fourteen-year-old George Stinney is nevertheless abhorrent. He remains the youngest person ever executed in the United States, convicted of killing two white girls in his hometown of Alocu, South Carolina, in 1944. His sentence was vacated in 2014, as authorities concluded that he had not received a fair trial. For a recounting of this case, see "In 1944, George Stinney Was Young, Black and Sentenced to Die." South Carolina's executing of Stinney for a murder that many insisted he did not commit is especially appalling: while Dylann Roof was sentenced to death for murdering nine members of an African American church in the state in 2015, he was reportedly treated to a Burger King meal by the officers who took him into custody. Better known in the history of American anti-Black terrorism is the 1964 bombing of the 16th Street Baptist Church in Birmingham, where eleven-year-old Carol Denise McNair was the youngest of the four slaughtered "little girls" (Addie Mae Collins, Cynthia Wesley, and Carole Robertson were all fourteen years old).

Just as a near factoid of a newspaper's account of an enslaved mother's infanticide provided the catalytic shoot that germinated into *Beloved*, her 1987 magnum opus, another piece of historical miscellany from the book then Random House editor Morrison shepherded into being provided the creative seedling for *Paradise*. Though not nearly so startling or gruesome as the reprinted snippet from a Kentucky newspaper recounting Margaret Garner's manifold tragedy, another historical artifact contained in *The Black Book* of 1974, a prodigious compendium of African American history and folk culture, so piqued Morrison's attention that it too became the germ for another labyrinthine novel. Captivated by advertisements in the nineteenth-century's numerous "colored" newspapers beckoning newly freed African Americans to venture west as a viable alternative to northward migration, Morrison was particularly struck—or more accurately, taken aback—by what she considered the crux of those solicitations: "Prominent in their headlines and articles was a clear admonition: Come Prepared or Not at All" (Morrison, "Foreword," xii). From this she extrapolated two less-than-hospitable caveats: "1) If you have nothing, stay away. 2) This new land is Utopia for a few. Translation: no poor former slaves are welcome in the paradise being built here" (xii). Morrison foregrounds here not African American (comm)unity and collaborative effort in the wake of the nation's most repugnant crime but their antithesis: clannishness, hierarchization, policing, maligning. While some may pinpoint the novel's rather lurid opening line as the key to unlocking its core meanings, I identify another event, the aforementioned "The Disallowing," as the cataclysmic event that occasions my Afro-Pessimist reading.

During the nomadic flight in which a band of formerly enslaved persons trek across Mississippi and Louisiana and find themselves in Fairly, Oklahoma, these wayfaring families assume they have found a potential home amid another enclave of Black families who share their past as chattel. Yet as it did in *The Bluest Eye*, pigmentation becomes the touchstone by which admission or rejection is determined: the lighter-skinned Fairly-ites conclude that their darker-skinned *non*-brethren/sistren are worthy of a night's respite and even food, but their phenotypic excrescence makes them unassimilable and precludes permanent cohabitation. As handed down to twins Deacon and Steward Morgan by their grandfather Zechariah ("Big Papa") and their father Rector ("Big Daddy"), the collective history of the Haven-cum-Ruby-ites after Reconstruction consists of itinerancy and protracted experiences of longing and rejection. While the questing "one hundred and fifty-eight freedmen" might have been despondent over but unsurprised by the inhospitableness suffered at the hands of "rich Choctaw and poor whites" (13), it is their fellow Blacks' pungent "come-prepared-or-not-at-all" ethos that becomes a millstone around the families' collective necks: "They were nevertheless unprepared for the aggressive discouragement they received from Negro towns already being built" (13). These rejections take a withering psychic toll, as the families' sense of their own subjectivity is diminished and invalidated by those with whom they share a destabilizing history of institutional bondage:

> It stung them into confusion to learn they did not have enough money to satisfy the restrictions the "self-supporting" Negroes required. In short, they were too poor, too bedraggled-looking to enter, let alone reside in, the communities that were soliciting Negro homesteaders. This contemptuous dismissal by the lucky changed the temperature of their blood twice. First they boiled at being written up as "people who preferred saloons and crap games to homes, churches and schools." Then, remembering their spectacular history, they cooled. What began as

overheated determination became cold-blooded obsession. "They don't know we or about we," said one man. "Us free like them; was slave like them. What for is this difference?" (14)

This early reference to generic disallowings or disavowals in the novel—as opposed to "The Disallowing" explicated much later—is intriguing in that it appears grounded in a classism and othering that are paradoxically raced *and* non-raced. As far back as her groundbreaking debut novel *The Bluest Eye*, Morrison has consistently highlighted how middle-class African Americans' self-regard stems from their ability to assimilate generally and to imbibe undilutedly a material-centric, even fetishistic American dream ideology. A core underpinning of this uplift/success ideology is Black respectability: not only must successful Blacks commit to a philosophy of acquisitiveness, but they must simultaneously repudiate those African Americans whose behavior is deemed disreputable to or runs afoul of white sensibilities. This is dramatized most prominently in the character Geraldine, who vehemently eschews "funkiness"—that is, behavior deemed stereotypically "black" and thereby incompatible with white definitions of American success and, conterminously, citizenship.[2] Thus, the passage quoted above encapsulates a manicured, antiseptic notion of "blackness," where disreputability—"people who preferred saloons and crap games"—precludes entry into a community of Black aspirants who valorize the argot of American selfhood (self-supporting, thrift, bootstrap self-lifting) in which American identity was/is rooted. As the passage's final sentence connotes, the ability to shed the yoke of "slaveness" is not enough; one must also have ingested a distinctly Americanized liberation theology that measures the degree to which one has moved "up from slavery" by the inculcation of such sacrosanct principles of domesticity, piety, and education ("homes, churches and schools")—all of which in the historical Anglo-American consciousness are foreign to "funky," disrespectful/disrespected African American culture.

As *Paradise* progresses, the identity-shattering moment of repudiation comes more sharply into focus: "There were nine large intact families who made the original journey, who were thrown out and cast away in Fairly, Oklahoma, and went on to found Haven" (188). Thus, the culminative, etiological repudiation and disclamation in/by the ironically named Black enclave becomes the most execrable one and, consequentially, the cohering narrative for the deracinated ex-slaves deemed unassimilable. While economic status and the twin scourge of antiblackness informed the sojourners' lamentation "Us free like them; was slave like them," the omnipresent scourge of skin-color stratification becomes the ultimate benchmark for determining Black *unbelonging*. Though grand patriarch Zechariah's wounded foot prevents him from engaging and directly petitioning the men of Fairly once the sojourners arrive, the narrative privileges his point of view:

---

[2] In contextualizing Geraldine and the arid white bourgeoise ideology she and other African American middle-class wannabes have swallowed whole—an indoctrination that, importantly, occurs at historically Black colleges and universities such as the unnamed one Geraldine attended (eliciting comparisons to the unnamed Tuskegee Institute in *Invisible Man*, which both its author and the novel's eponymous protagonist attended)—Morrison writes in *The Bluest Eye*:

> They go to land-grant colleges, normal schools, and learn how to do the white man's work with refinement: home economics to prepare his food; teacher education to instruct black children in obedience; music to soothe the weary master and entertain his blunted soul. Here they learn the rest of the lesson begun in those soft houses with porch swings and pots of bleeding heart: how to behave. The careful development of thrift, patience, high morals, and good manners. In short, how to get rid of the funkiness. The dreadful funkiness of passion, the funkiness of nature, the funkiness of the wide range of human emotions. (83)

Blacks like Geraldine, therefore, are the progeny of Fairly's puritanical fair-skinned denizens, mimicking their ardent repudiation of anything that runs counter to Anglo-America's straitlaced notions of betterment and respectability.

> He missed witnessing the actual Disallowing; and missed hearing disbelievable words formed in the mouths of men to other men, men like them in all ways but one. Afterwards the people were no longer nine families and some more. They became a tight band of wayfarers bound by the enormity of what had happened to them. Their horror of whites was convulsive but abstract. They saved the clarity of their hatred for the men who had insulted them in ways too confounding for language: first by excluding them, then by offering them staples to exist in that very exclusion. (189)

The underpinnings of the (un)Fairly-ites' rejection, made all the more scalding by what the men view as pity-impelled charity, ultimately come into sharp relief a few pages later:

> This time the clarity was clear: for ten generations they had believed the division they fought to close was free against slave and rich against poor. Usually, but not always, white against black. Now they saw a new separation: light-skinned against black. Oh, they knew there was a difference in the minds of whites, but it had not struck them before that it was of consequence, serious consequence, to Negroes themselves. (194)

While the notorious and nefarious Black Codes became postbellum edicts consigning putatively freed Blacks to the Pattersonian realm of "social death" befitting their status as formerly enslaved, what Zechariah and his male coterie find more insidious is their brethren's inculcation of unexpressed *White* Codes, the pigmentary gauges that Fairly's all-Black denizens have recalibrated and hypostatized.

It is that definitive, tectonic moment of repudiation that becomes what Haven's founding "Old Fathers" deem their generative narrative—at once collectively affirming and abnegating, the (hi)story of their rejection as "the controlling one" (13) kept alive from generation to generation. This consequential act of phenotypic-based *disclamation* becomes the ontological basis for the nomads' eventual founding of their homeland in 1890: "Haven"—their new-world heaven, the titular "paradise." The once rejected families now reimagine themselves as "8-rockers," as one character explicates their newly formed sable-centric homespace: "eight-rock, a deep home space level in the coal mines. Blue-black people, tall and graceful, whose clear, wide eyes gave no sign of what they really felt about those who weren't 8-rock like them" (193). In their inverted hue hierarchy, the self-anointed "8-rock" families elevate their darkest-skinned selves to the apex of the skin color totem, with those failing to meet that parochial standard assigned to the lower rung. Their "Misery"-tinged "Disallowing" has been alchemized into a hallowed, exclusionary H(e)aven, notwithstanding the necessity of relocating and renaming their idyll in light of a post–Second World War downturn. But Haven-cum-Ruby, based on a mimetic albeit inverted ideology of racial purity and consanguinity that informed the founding of Anglocentric America, is a blighted pastoral. Mark Tabone makes this point trenchantly: "Although in Ruby this American version of a dystopian white supremacist longing for a racially purified 'paradise' has been turned inside-out in terms of its racial content, its form remains largely intact" (135). As Morrison herself solemnly concludes, "isolation" invariably "carries the seeds of its own destruction because as times change, other things seep in, as it did with Ruby" (Denard 156).[3]

---

[3]Other critics have echoed Tabone's point about the Rubyites' inculcation and (re)deployment of white supremacist ideology, coupled with Morrison's admonition that adopting such a corrosive framework will ultimately lead to a community's implosion. This white supremacist hermeneutics coheres with what many of the novel's critics have deemed "American exceptionalism"—syllogistically, white supremacy is to American exceptionalism what the Black Codes are to Jim Crow. For

In a 1998 interview, Morrison reflected on a blood-sodden history's potential to subsume and consume: "You can find it so overwhelming and so frightening and so wicked that you can't separate yourself from its wickedness—say, slavery, for example—so that you feel sullied and stained and incompetent and hurt all of your life" (Denard 164). As a result, *all* of those formerly enslaved represented on a palate of skin color are inexorably "stained" and perpetually "hurt for the entirety of their lives." This is evidenced in the cruel actions perpetuated by the "Disallowers" and the correlative responses of the Disallowed, who transmogrify the event into the bases of both their individual personhood and inviolable clannishness. The enduring crippling psychic impact of this episode continues some five decades later, when the Haven-ites are forced to relocate their deteriorating neo-Camelot to a town they christen "Ruby" in 1950. The pain of the most piercing rejection remains "a burn whose scar tissue was numb by 1949, wasn't it?" (194)—the interrogative mood punctuating the openness of a wound not salved by time. Though time and relocation may have cauterized the wound, it cannot be excised; this dovetails with the discourse of Afro-Pessimism, the undergirdings of which are primordial Negrophobia/Afrophobia and irremediable sub-humanity—the very pillars of Anglo-American subjectivity.

Permanently blemished by and freighted with this self-negating ideology, Black subjects inculcate antiblackness—Afrophobia—and its symbiotic scourge, Anglophilia. Slavery's scaffolding apparatus—epidermal debasement—(re)ensues in "The Disallowing," with lighter-skinned Blacks *performing* whiteness in an act of racial appropriation and transvestism; this enactment engenders an inversion of the racial hierarchy on the part of "8-rockers," who recast themselves as "chosen" and "pure"—the sinews of the hegemonic, Anglocentric national corpus. In this re(in)scripted/reimagined version of what James Baldwin termed a "fantasy revenge," light-skinned Blacks function as surrogates for the enslavers, whose belief system—if not vicious practices—the Disallowers have adapted and adopted.[4] Ultimately, to invert the color chain-of-value by repositioning dark skin as a

---

an insightful interpretation of the novel from this perspective, see Holly Flint's "Toni Morrison's *Paradise*: Black Cultural Citizenship and the American Empire," where she contends,

> Regardless of its explicit rejection of white society, Ruby's isolationist historiography merely accommodates the larger imperial agenda of American settler colonialism when it justifies its place outside white society using a rhetoric of exceptionalism. By mimicking white exceptionalism, proclaiming itself the 'one allblack town worth the pain,' Ruby attempts to secure its place in the American frontier; however, this rhetoric only sows the seeds of the town's eventual destruction and gives carte blanche, at least symbolically, to the rest of American society to proceed with its own imperial destiny. (604)

[4] In his inimitable fashion, Baldwin invoked the term "fantasy revenge" in *Notes of a Native Son* to capture his fellow Christian Harlemites' unshakable faith in an Old Testament–wielding avenging God whose divine laws supersede earthly, Anglo-centric ecclesiastical doctrines that enshrined white supremacy and black misery. Conceiving of God as a celestial bulwark against American racism, Black supplicants, according to Baldwin, held fast to a belief that whites who violated Biblical edicts consecrating brotherhood and sisterhood irrespective of pigmentation would have to ultimately pay for their racial trespasses. The following "testimonial" is rooted in Baldwin's widely known upbringing in a fanatically fundamentalist household, in a Harlem dotted with zealous, "holiness" churches:

> These churches range from the august and publicized Abyssinian Baptist Church on west 138th Street to resolutely unclassifiable lofts, basements, store-fronts, and even private dwellings. Nightly, Holyroller ministers, spiritualists, self-appointed prophets and Messiahs gather their flocks together for worship and for strength through joy. And this is not, as *Cabin in the Sky* would have us believe, merely childlike emotional release. Their faith may be described as childlike, but the end it serves is often sinister. It may, indeed, "keep them happy"—a phrase carrying the inescapable inference that the way of life imposed on Negroes makes them quite actively unhappy—but also, and much more significantly, religion operates here as a complete and exquisite fantasy revenge: white people own the earth and commit all manner of abominations and injustice on it; the bad will be punished and the good rewarded, for God is not sleeping, the judgment

higher coordinate on an epidermalized axis is to implicitly accept blackness as the nadir, the apogee of abjectness, something requiring restoration and elevation. Stated slightly differently, undergirding this valorizing of dark skin is a core acceptance of the very hierarchies of differentiation, blackness as irredeemably conflated with "slaveness." This repellent colorism, stratifying, and displacement demonstrate how, "according to Afro-pessimism, the modern world was created by Black slavery. The world of White Masters and Black Slaves is the world we have inherited and the world we live in today" (Poll 69). Hence, the historical fetters of Anglocentrism and Afrophobia extend all the way to 1976, America's Bicentennial and the year in which *Paradise* opens. Therefore, though the mise en scène for most of the narrative action is post-Reconstruction, *Paradise* ultimately foregrounds the ubiquity of the blackbody as an a priori and irreversible slavebody, obdurately static in a country that champions opportunity, mobility, and ascendancy.

OF MULES AND MISOGYNISTS: AFRO-PESSIMIST INEXORABILITY

It is crucial to reiterate the omnipresence of slavery and its debilitating, devitalizing discourse as the loci of *Paradise*'s Afro-Pessimist iterations. As noted in the Prolegomenon, The Founding Fathers' subhumanizing racial convictions find their most unvarnished articulation in the writings of Jefferson. Recall the ferine-laced language of "Query 14"—the conflation of "negroes" and "the Oran-ootan." Jefferson's bestializing racial declensions inform Afro-Pessimism's critical morphology. Sexton extrapolates from this cartography of difference the slavebody's irreversible and necessary otherness—re: as *the* figure of difference/abjection which "lend[s] coherence to its internal conflicts (e.g., race, class, gender, sexuality) and definition to its external boundaries (e.g., animal, machine, object, spirit)." Through Sexton's hermeneutic lens, Jefferson's—and concomitantly, the nation's—founding grammar situates blackness as the nadir and touchstone not only for white civil(ized) society but for humanness itself. Thus, the fungible slavebody/blackbody are antonymous, the binary opposite of and around which whiteness coheres and takes its human(e), civil form. And if we allow that the cardinal "Disallowing" functions analogously, then it and subsequent acts can be read as a series of displacements in which befouling blackness is projected and re-projected in what might be called a series of proxy *niggerizations*, the negated blackness becoming the sine qua non around which orthodox, hegemonic identity is constructed and consolidated. A central question, then, emerges: Will the rebuffed and exiled "8-rockers" brand another group abject to, in Sexton's lexicon, "lend order to its internal conflicts"—to scapegoat, otherize, demonize? The answer can be found, again, in the fraught words of Sally Heming's owner and father of their six "disavowed" children.

When Jefferson alleges that "negroes"—his appellation for Black men—favor white women on the basis of "a more elegant symmetry of form," then it follows that, vis his group stratifying, "the preference of the Oran-ootan for the black women over those of his own species." This positioning of Black women as something so alien that they cannot even be found on the "Great Chain" casts them as mongrelized, a type of human-beast hybrid. Thus, it is only fitting that a creative writer and anthropologist would most eloquently theorize the derogated status of Black women: "De nigger woman is de mule uh de world so fur as Ah can see" (Hurston 14). The most evocative quotation

---

is not far off ... All these topics provide excellent springboards for sermons thinly coated with spirituality but designed mainly to illustrate the injustice of the white American and anticipate his certain and long overdue punishment. (65–6)

from Zora Neale Hurston's most famous novel has reverberated through the decades: the mule's hybridity, its different-species status a corollary for Jefferson's debased and debasing taxonomies. Given that Morrison names so purposefully, I don't believe it accidental that Ruby's founders are referenced by the sobriquets of its patriarch Zechariah "Big Papa" Morgan and his son Rector "Big Daddy" Morgan. Thus, the Haven architects' appellation of "Old Fathers" and that of their male progeny as "New Fathers"—Rector's sons Steward and Deacon, who lead the 1949 relocation to and the creation of Haven—is paradigmatic, their lexical proximity to "Founding Fathers" iterating and thereby valorizing heteropatriarchal hegemony. If white male supremacist sovereignty provides a blueprint for the towns' founding fathers' subjectivity, then it should not be surprising that a masculinist prerogative will have a calamitous impact on the "mule[s] of de world," Black women. As Wilderson's neologism "slaveness" functions as lexical metonym for historical and interminable Black erasure and nonbeing, then "New Father" Deacon's outrage when a younger Black man refers to the Morgan twins' ancestors as "ex-slaves" is revelatory. In defending the tenacity and commitment it took for the Old Fathers to construct the communal "Oven," Deacon indignantly counters, "Nothing was handled more gently than the bricks those *men—men*, hear me? not *slaves*, ex or otherwise—the bricks those men made" (85; emphasis added). The insolubility of "slave" and "men" thus betokens further displacement and degradation: through a hideous transmutation, Black women become the newly "Disallowed," neo-*mules* meriting not only expulsion, but worse. A brief look at what Saidiya Hartman aptly calls "one of the most well-known scenes of torture in the literature of slavery" (3) will help limn the quasi-slaving of Black women in the novel, which becomes the grounds for their extermination.

In her signal 1987 essay "The Site of Memory," Morrison deemed the slave narrative African American literature's generative genre. In enumerating its admirable aesthetic aims, however, she also trained her attention on a glaring lacuna prevalent throughout the genre: "Over and over, the writers pull the narrative up short with a phrase such as, 'But let us drop a veil over these proceedings too terrible to relate'" (Morrison, "Site," 237); she continues, "But most importantly—at least for me—there was no mention of their [bound persons'] interior life." While *Beloved* became her most profound fictive rendering of enslaved persons' elided interiority, the first and most famous of Douglass's triptych of autobiographies, the 1845 *Narrative*, is especially germane in my meditations on *Paradise*'s Afro-Pessimist reverberations. Recall Douglass's recapitulation of the sado-erotic beating of his "Aunt Hester" at the hands of her master, Anthony Auld—what the author deems "this most horrible exhibition" and "a most terrible spectacle" (20–1).[5] While clearly meant to index the depths of slavery's inapprehensible depravity, Douglass's interpolating it into his decidedly male-centric self-portrait has nevertheless been a bit problematic with respect to the scene's gendered inflections: for instance, does it pornify Black women, (re)presenting their physical flagellation and sexual degradation in the service of his broader abolitionist project?

---

[5] For what remains an immensely compelling reading of the brutalization of Douglass's aunt, whom he pseudonymously refers to as "Hester"—actually, Esther—and the vexed and vexing racio-gendered ways in which he frames it, see Jenny Franchot's "The Punishment of Esther: Frederick Douglass and the Construction of the Feminine." My point here recapitulates hers, where she argued that

> starkly opposing the white father-owner to the black mother-surrogate, the scene outlines bitterly conflicted racial and gender identifications. If the masculine is vitiated by its identification with the white slaveholder, so is blackness contaminated by its identification with the exposed and degraded woman. To achieve "manhood," then, is to forsake not only the mother but her race, whereas to achieve "blackness" is to forsake the father and his virility. (142)

But another vexing issue is Douglass's positionality during this episode (recall that he's a child, possibly six years old, hiding in the closet), as words such as "exhibition" and "spectacle" insinuate the episode's spectatorial dimensions. Given that Auld is not only Hester's sexual tormentor and policer of her desire but also Douglass's father, the scene obliquely manages to highlight Douglass's affiliative conundrum: does he identify with the insuperable white male/patriarch to whom he's connected consanguineously, or does his allegiance lie with the distaff side of his miscegenized lineage—with the disempowered, ravaged relative-object of the white man's juridical, economic, physical, and sexual brutality? The identitarian, racio-gendered "double consciousness" besetting Douglass here evinces itself in a brief but portentous story lodged in Steward Morgan's memory, his interpretation prefiguring what might be consequently described as his and the other town Fathers' latent Master Anthony.

Though Morrison has never explicitly alluded to the grisly "exhibition" scene and Aunt Hester's multiple silences—within the moment itself, within the pages of her nephew's inscription of it—*Paradise* nevertheless offers a haunting if unintentional signification on it. Steward fondly recollects a story fashioned by his older brother Elder Morgan, a First World War veteran who shared the following anecdote from 1919 as he disembarked in Hoboken upon returning from England:

> Taking a walk around New York City before catching his train [back to Haven], he saw two men arguing with a woman. From her clothes, Elder said, he guessed she was a streetwalking woman, and registering contempt for her trade, he felt at first a connection with the shouting men. Suddenly one of the men smashed the woman in the face with his fist. She fell. Just as suddenly the scene slid from everyday color to black and white. Elder said his mouth went dry. The two whitemen turned away from the unconscious Negro woman sprawled on the pavement. Before Elder could think, one of them changed his mind and came back to kick her in the stomach. Elder did not know he was running until he got there and pulled the man away. He had been running and fighting for ten straight months, still unweaned from spontaneous violence. Elder hit the whiteman in the jaw and kept hitting until attacked by the second man. Nobody won. All were bruised. The woman was still lying on the pavement when a small crowd began yelling for the police. Frightened, Elder ran and wore his army overcoat all the way back to Oklahoma for fear an officer would see the condition of his uniform. (94)

Given her commitment to providing "places and spaces" for readers in/of her fiction, Morrison neither comments on this vignette's dramatis personae nor provides expository details.[6] Is the Black woman a victim of wanton violence meted out to Blacks of any gender whose very presence white men deem an affront?[7] If we trust Elder's interpretive gaze, are the men dissatisfied johns who

---

[6]In her aesthetic treatise on the indispensable role the reader plays in the oracular "call-and-response," she attempts to replicate—what she conceives as a reciprocal exchange between herself as writer and each individual reader of her fiction—see "Rootedness: The Ancestor as Foundation": "And, having at my disposal only letters of the alphabet and some punctuation, I have to provide the places and spaces so that the reader can participate" (341).

[7]This scene is richly evocative of one Richard Wright describes in his Zeitgeist-capturing 1938 essay, "The Ethics of Living Jim Crow." In just a few stark pages, he encapsulates the quotidian but miasmic terror subsuming the lives of black Mississippians in the 1920s and 1930s. Note the parallels between the following encounter Wright, then a young man working as a porter at a clothing store, recreates involving a Black woman battered (and likely sexually assaulted) by the proprietor and his son and the scene depicted in *Paradise*:

> One morning, while polishing brass out front, the boss and his twenty-year-old son got out of their car and half dragged and half kicked a Negro woman into the store. A policeman standing at the corner looked on, twirling his nightstick.

attacked the woman over a discrepancy between her price and the "services" they received? Are they outraged that they have to pay at all, given what Hartman identifies as whites' imperishable conceptions of "black female 'excess'—immoderate and overabundant sexuality, bestial appetites and capacities that were most often likened to those of the orangutan"? (86). Steward's recapitulation of his brother's story continues:

> He never got the sight of that whiteman's fist in that colored woman's face out of his mind. Whatever he felt about her trade, he thought about her, prayed for her till the end of his life … Steward liked that story, but it unnerved him to know it was based on the defense of and prayers for a whore. He did not sympathize with the whitemen, but *he could see their point, could even feel the adrenaline, imagining the fist was his own.* (94–5; emphasis added)

Both brothers countersign and rehearse the vertical architectonics by which value is antipodally determined: white/Black; male/female; moral/immoral; human/bestial. Despite the almost Pavlovian response to the woman's assault that stems from a sense of racial solidarity and/or a quasi "code" of chivalry, both brothers filter their responses through abnegating Anglocentric *and* Androcentric epistemologies: the victim here is assumed to be lascivious and in need of divine moral intervention, cleansing, and correction; she is their moral inferior on the basis of what they presume to be her sexual immodesty and immorality. And perhaps most repugnantly and revealingly, they not only sanction white male bloodlust but vicariously imagine inhabiting the white pummeling male bodies in order to experience the psycho-orgasmic pleasure of (way)laying the prostrate "whore" deserving of her fate. To be sure, this scene bears out Andrew Read's succinct assessment of raced and gendered hegemonies: "Morrison's ultimate indictment of Ruby's patriarchy is that it reproduces ideologies and practices of racist white men" (538).

The brothers' blinkered ways of seeing and interpreting hearken back to Jefferson's nascent raced polarities and inhere what Sexton enumerated as "the rank ordering of life asserted in the *scala naturae* or 'Great Chain of Being,'" around which other forms of difference are vertically arrayed (99). As prefigured in the Aunt Hester/Master Auld/man-child Douglass triangulation, the Morgan brothers have solved the quadratic of racio-gendered double consciousness by rechanneling what I earlier deemed their latent Anthony Auld. Like that inaugural moment of concupiscent violence, devaluation, and exclusion, the Black woman becomes a surrogate new nigger in the Black men's mimetic economies of (de)valuation—she the neo-Disallowed, they the neo-Disallowers. In their raced and gendered hermeneutics, whiteness generally and white maleness distinctly are sovereign, the apogee of moral, racial, and gendered superiority, while the trammeled beating victim is cast as Aunt Hester's sister-sinner, the quintessence of slaveness and abjection. In Elder and Steward's inconsonantly borderline gleeful telling and retelling, this beating becomes a variation on America's

---

> I watched out of the corner of my eye, never slackening the strokes of my chamois upon the brass. After a few minutes, I heard shrill screams coming from the rear of the store. Later the woman stumbled out, bleeding, crying, and holding her stomach. When she reached the end of the block, the policeman grabbed her and accused her of being drunk. Silently, I watched him throw her into a patrol wagon.

"Boy, that's what we do to niggers when they don't pay their bills," [the boss] said, laughing. When Wright recounts this story among his male peers during their lunch break, one incredulously asks, "Huh! Is tha' all they did t' her?" and observes, "Shucks! Man, she's a lucky bitch! … Hell, it's a wonder they didn't lay her when they got through" (136). Both the white men's brutality and Wright's coworker's chauvinistic, disdainful attitude adumbrate the Morgan brothers' disaffiliation with the besieged Black "whore" and their coterminous veneration of white heteropatriarchal racial and sexual license.

inaugural Disallowing, which generations of Morgan men have "carried like a bullet in the brain" (109)—the pain that they now have no qualms relieving through the analgesic of a Black woman's abasement and brutalization.

Instances in which the Black woman's body serves as the site of physical, rectitudinous, and rhetorical violence resurface throughout the novel in what might be deemed gynophobic eruptions. The Disallowed men of Ruby, for which "New Fathers" Deacon and Steward Morgan become the primary transmitters of their defiled history as well as its principal avengers, displace their own disempowerment and impotence onto Black women. In a slight variation of the above-mentioned episode, pathogenic antiblackness metastasizes into a gynophobia that mimics the Disalloweds' inverted phenotypic hierarchy. Again, Steward serves as articulator and arbiter of this pernicious commingling of the anti-woman/anti–ersatz-whiteness ethos, now represented in the form of a "hazel-eyed girl" whom one of his fellow New Fathers secretly married while away from Haven. While serving in the First World War and stationed in Tennessee, Roger Best wed Delia, with whom he bore a daughter, Patricia. When a heartsick Roger implores his new wife to join him in Haven, his fellow Rubyites are barely as hospitable as the lighter-skinned formerly enslaved who forsook them in Fairly. Not only do Roger's parents bristle at their son's violation of the rigid sable-centric color code—the gall of his taking "a wife of sunlight skin, a wife of racial tampering" and producing a little girl with "light-brown hair"—but Steward dares to utter the heteropatriarchs' enmity, which most of the women passively cosign: "Only Steward had the gall to say out loud, 'He's bringing along the *dung* we leaving behind'" (201; emphasis added). When Delia (along with their second child) perishes in childbirth upon the relocation to Ruby, an embittered adult Pat Best somberly surmises, the "good brave men ... had the satisfaction of seeing the dung buried" (197, 202).

As postcolonialism's most perspicacious theorist whose writings provide Afro-Pessimism its discursive substructure, Frantz Fanon has made at least two references to excrement in his pioneering works, specifically integrating the words of fellow Martinican intellectual Aimé Césaire to buttress his own hypotheses. He writes from the perspective of the colonized, "native" African, first, in *Black Skin, White Masks*:

> In other words, I begin to suffer from not being a white man to the degree that the white man imposes discrimination on me, makes me a colonized native, robs me of all worth, all individuality, tells me that I am a parasite on the world, that I must bring myself as quickly as possible into step with the white world, "that I am a brute beast, that my people and I are like a walking dung-heap that disgustingly fertilizes sweet sugar cane and silky cotton, that I have no use in the world." (98)

Fanon re-invokes the fecal simile in *The Wretched of the Earth*, quoting a line from Césaire's poem *Les armes miraculeuses* ("The Miraculous Weapons"); here the colonized, in the persona of "The Rebel," combats his white colonizers: "We had attacked, we the slaves; we, the dung underfoot,/ we the animals with painted hooves" (88). In Fanon's rhetorical register, *slave-as-dung* functions as lexical synecdoche for abnegated identity—the position of the disempowered, the nonbeing, blackness itself.

Within the novel's raced and gendered hierarchies, such *wretched* identities are reconfigured and reassigned. As Dana Williams posits, "Rather, Ruby's men perform as white men—America's founding fathers and their descendants to be exact—first and foremost by declaring themselves exceptional" (186). Conjunctively, then, Haven's sepia-hued Founding Fathers install themselves as the neo-white male colonizing forces in a perverse bit of racial transvestism or minstrelsy.[8] In their warped reordering of the Sexton's *scala naturae*, lightly melanated women are relegated to the slave-as-dung status to which they themselves were reduced in the psychically traumatic and ineradicable Disallowing.[9] What amounts to an *excremantalizing* of *t(a)inted* Black womanhood becomes the basis of the Haven/Ruby heteropatriarchs' collective subjectivity. Steward's pronouncement, in the form of a scatological verbal excretion—re: Roger Best is "bringing along the *dung* we leaving behind"—is reinforced in the men's willful neglect of Delia, whose eventual death during childbirth they indirectly caused, as recalled by daughter Patricia. Though her father refuses to believe that the hegemony of "New Fathers," which ostensibly includes Roger himself, could have been guilty of such incalculable cruelty, Pat's interpretation, in the form of an apostrophe to her dead mother, is nevertheless a more plausible version given the event that opens the novel and the men's fervent denigration of women: "He doesn't agree with me that those 8-rock men didn't want to go and bring a white [doctor] into town; or else they didn't want to drive out to a white's house begging for help; or else they just despised your pale skin so much they thought of reasons why they could not go" (198). In simulating and repurposing the very white enslaving apparatus that enshackled their ancestors, this act of medical/maternal maleficence—collective matricide and infanticide?—replicates an earlier catastrophic instance of *excrementalization*, visited upon the Morgan Twins' cherished late sister for whom the newly relocated Haven is named.

During the relocation from Haven, youngest-sibling Ruby—"that sweet, modest laughing girl"—falls ill but is refused treatment at hospitals where "colored people were not allowed in the wards" (113). This callous treatment takes a more malicious turn at another hospital, where "no regular doctor would attend them": "When the brothers learned the nurse had been trying to reach a veterinarian, and they gathered their dead sister in their arms, their shoulders shook all the way home." Alas, if the New Fathers' spiteful treatment of Delia reflects a type of communal sororicide, then its fraternal leaders, Steward and Deacon, experience firsthand racio-gender–based violence in the form of their sister's nightmarish experience. Thus, this medicalized Jim Crow tragedy becomes the Morgans' more intimate, personally lacerating version of the Disallowing, sister Ruby's effaced personhood more in line with Jeffersonian epistemologies that delineated

---

[8] For an insightful reading of the novel through the critical/historical lens of blackface minstrelsy, see Dana Williams's "Playing on the 'Darky': Blackface Minstrelsy, Identity Construction, and the Deconstruction of Race in Toni Morrison's *Paradise*."

[9] While Ruby, as enforced by its martinet-like leaders the Morgan Twins, has codified an inverted skin color hierarchy, I would be remiss in not acknowledging that the Twins' personal past and even present actions have gainsaid their fetishistic idolizing of "coal-black" skin. As Candice Jenkins perceptively argues in "Pure Black: Class, Color, and Intraracial Politics in Toni Morrison's *Paradise*,"

> It would seem, then, that Ruby's citizens have created a neat reversal of the Western color hierarchy that privileges whiteness and derides blackness and ranks those in-between according to how they fall on the phenotypic spectrum … A more nuanced reading of the text is not only possible, however, but necessary, for the reverse color hierarchy that exists in Morrison's all-black town of Ruby is neither an exact equivalent to white racism nor a consistently applied arbiter of light skin. In fact, at key points in the text, light skin, and the racial commingling that creates it, is admired, even idealized. To understand this is to begin to understand the complex relationship between race, color, and class that Morrison's novel outlines. (280)

As evidence, Jenkins dissects the Twins' boyhood pedestalizing of the fair-skinned "nineteen Negro ladies" being photographed at the town hall of an all-black town: in their adult recollections, they continue to idealize these white-clad women as paragons of virtuous black womanhood and idealized beauty, with their "skin, creamy and luminous in the afternoon sun" (Morrison, *Paradise*, 109) and "creamy, sunlit skin" (110).

Negrohood as alien, beneath the realm of the human. The calcified race hatred that underlies the bestializing of Ruby's Black female body becomes the model for the New Fathers' own pigmentary and gendered hierarchializing. Inculcating and sanctioning these jaundiced praxes, the men disavow Delia in her hour of prenatal need, thereby reinscribing the same corrosive hermeneutics that rendered the Morgan Twins' own ailing sister *dung* unworthy of human(e) care. No amount of sacralizing their own "blue-black skin" or nomenclating homage to their deceased/murdered sister can mitigate the entrenched Anglophilic designation of Negro inferiority and mongrelization (from Jefferson: "the preference of the Oran-ootan for the black women over those of [the Oran-ootan's] own species"). The Ruby-/Havenites' putative self-deification of dark skin cannot dislodge their latent if unconscious belief that their own *dung-tinged* skin is ineradicably contaminated, its color conferring the derogated, nonentity status that Anglo-American culture ascribes to all Blacks regardless of where they fall on the skin color palate.

As inferred in the central tenet of Afro-Pessimism, blackness as alien, inadmissible, unassimilable—as excremental—belies space and time; this is Spillers' notion of the temporal "flat line" that Wilderson invokes, which he adduces "moves from disequilibrium to a moment in the narrative of faux equilibrium, to disequilibrium restored and/or rearticulated." Thus, the pernicious nineteenth-century protocols of race and gender remain implacable and are accordingly "rearticulated" in the late 1940s, the time of the relocation from Haven and young Ruby's homicidal disallowal. The men's malignant attempts to redirect and reimpose/reassign the degraded, abject identity upon fair-skinned women like Delia Best—to neo-enslave them—cannot remove the indelible dark stain that they loathe in themselves. As Consolata (Connie), the Convent's spiritual loadstar, professes early in the novel, "Scary things not always outside. Most scary things is inside" (39). Subsequently, the mere presence of Consolata and the collective of women she harbors at her gyno-centered edifice will engender the novel's most heinous enactment of misplaced and displaced hatred.

The disdain and malicious neglect that resulted in Delia Best's natal death becomes a harbinger for direct, full-scale butchery, which the novel's pregnant opening line portends: "They shoot the white girl first" (3). Delia's and Ruby's deaths, grounded in race and gender abjection, become vestibular acts of gynocidal terror that presage the slaughter at the Convent. The novel's deliberately coy and deceptive opening line belies the author's own diagnoses regarding the *sui generis* brand of misogyny visited upon African American women. In an interview with novelist Salman Rushdie about her then recently published Harlem Renaissance-era novel *Jazz* (1992), Morrison expounds,

> Black women always felt themselves to be the most vulnerable in that society, and some of them prepared themselves and refused to be lightly attacked, refused to be—I think the word in the book is "easy prey." It may happen because rape, abuse, sexual assault was understood to be the *menu* of Black women, in particular a slave or post-reconstruction society. There was no protection. Black men who wanted to protect them were all strung from trees, so you had to make decisions about these things. (Denard 57, emphasis in original)

Not insignificantly, she began this response to Rushdie's query with an equally piercing declaration: "Our lives have been lived in what has got to be one of the world's most violent countries." As my primary critical proposition has been how America's originary act of disallowance—slavery—spawns manifold reenactments of repulsion and rejection throughout *Paradise*, then the execution of the predominantly Black Convent women evinces the ultimate act of disavowal, hatred, and extermination.

That the semiotics of eugenics undergird the New Fathers' climactic gynocide shocks but does not surprise. Indeed, the Haven-cum-Ruby-ites' self-mythologizing, through their inverted valorization of dark skin and derogation of those less melanated, approximates the discourse of "race science," which held sway after the Civil War and through the 1940s. In their zealous inverting of the skin color totem, which devalues if not quite demonizes the darker-complexioned, they weaponized the metric upon which whites and fair-skinned Blacks deemed them inalienably other and inadmissible. Roger Best is disdained for violating "the blood rule" in marrying Delia (195), her hue the indelible scarlet letter rendering her very being evidence of "racial tampering" (197); her daughter Pat provides a pungent gloss on this reconfigured racial axis and makes unassailably legible the 8-rockers' sacralizing of their "blue-black," uncontaminated bloodlines: "The generations had to be not only racially untampered with but free of adultery too. 'God bless the pure and holy' indeed. That was their purity. That was their holiness" (217). The New Fathers' lexicon of racial immaculacy is the lingua franca connecting their mindset not only to Founding Father Jefferson's language of Black subalternity, but also to purveyors of baleful pseudoscientific racial postulates such as Madison Grant, Josiah Nott, and George Gliddon; in the especially execrable words of one such adherent, Charles Carroll, "When we turn upon this statement the light of [the apostle] Paul's declaration that 'there is one kind of flesh of men, another flesh of beasts,' etc., it becomes plain that the horse and the ass and the negro all belong to one kind of flesh—the flesh of beasts."[10] This man-to-beast conjugation not only becomes the template for the derogation of such women as Elder Morgan's unnamed battered "whore," Delia Best, and Ruby Morgan; most grievously, it provides the rationale for the expulsion of any woman classified as "beastly"—in the New Fathers' self-appointed godhead status, any woman deemed excessively or lasciviously carnal.

The culminative violence that the quasi-Black male lynch mob inflicts upon the Convent women thus marks the zenith of perverted devolution and displacement, its slave origins speaking to Blackbodies' perennial slaveness. As their brazen, cocksure actions bear out, "In the minds of the patriarchs of Ruby, the Convent women represent a viral infiltration of their perfect town. The focus on infiltration is certainly in keeping with racist, homophobic, or sexist discourses of creating communities through the exclusion of the other" (Grattan 273). Hence, in Ruby's heteropatriarchs' re-pathologizing, the Convent women function as neo-niggers, violent misogyny the byproduct of their fetishizing of racial purity and masculinist hegemony. Consider the litany of examples—from the points of view of various members of the lynching party—attesting to how their condemnatory language approximates/replicates the debasing idiom Jefferson, Carroll, and others deployed to underwrite Black nonbeing and animality: "His saliva is bitter and although he knows this place is *diseased*, he is startled by the whip of pity flicking in his chest. What, he wonders, could do this to women? How can their plain brains think up such things: revolting sex, deceit and the sly torture of children?" (8; emphasis added). "Something's going on out there, and I don't like any

---

[10]I am indebted to the recuperative scholarly labor of the late literary critic J. Lee Greene. In his pathbreaking historical/theoretical study *Blacks in Eden: The African American Novel's First Century*, he assiduously interprets novels by nineteenth-century African American writers such as William Wells Brown and Charles Chesnutt as fictive rejoinders to the writings of what Greene labels "racist propagandists" (64)—scores of rabidly Negrophobic thinkers, including Madison Grant, Josiah Nott, and George Gliddon. Especially noteworthy is Greene's inclusion of Charles Carroll, a lesser known but equally vituperative promulgator of biblically rooted beliefs of Black inferiority and bestialness; it is through Greene's work that I learned of Carroll's *"The Negro A Beast" ... Or "In the Image of God."*

of it. No men. *Kissing on themselves*" (276; emphasis added). The women's frailties are ultimately summarized in this montage of abominations:

> Before those heifers came to town this was a peaceable kingdom. The others before them at least had some religion. These here sluts out there by themselves never step foot in church and I bet you a dollar to a fat nickel they ain't thinking about one either. They don't need men and they don't need God. Can't say they haven't been warned. Asked first and then warned. If they stayed to themselves, that'd be something. But they don't. They meddle. Drawing folks out there like flies to shit and everybody who goes near them is maimed somehow and the mess is seeping back into *our* homes, *our* families. (276, emphases in original)

Explicitly, the very same rhetoric Anglo-American "Founding Fathers" marshalled to legitimize their impugning, vilifying, and if necessary, killing of the Rubyites' very own enslaved forebears reverberates in this compendium of calumnies. Noteworthy from the outset is the simultaneous infantilizing of women—"plain brains"—and pathologizing—"diseased." This conflation hearkens back to slavery and reconstruction, when Black men were incongruously deemed guileless, childlike "Sambos" and savage, sexually rapacious "brutes." Like reputedly benevolent slaveholders, Ruby's policing agents imagine themselves as a God-anointed, beneficent patri-hegemony presiding over their own "peaceable kingdom," their sable neo-Eden, which casts the improperly feminine Convent denizens as sacrilegious "sluts."

Thus, the men who enact the pogrom fashion themselves a deific exorcising force. The women's homo-gendered anti-Haven is a veritable hotbed of fleshly excess, homosexuality a timeless emblem of perhaps the most flagrant violation of Christian verities and the heteroideology the men have enshrined. The aspersive, sexualizing language here hearkens back to Jefferson's Query IV's abjectifying of the enslaved, which specifically hypersexualized "Negro" male bodies: "They are more ardent after their female: but love seems with them to be more an eager desire, than a tender delicate mixture of sentiment and sensation" (139). But in the heteropatriarchs' re-schematizing of America's foundational discourse of abjection, their multipronged transferences and displacements recast Black women as "ardent" or intemperately libidinal, made all the worse by the specter of same-gendered lust. Further, the men brand the women's beatific shepherdess, Consolata, the literal embodiment of unbridled carnality. A kiss that she bestows upon the married Deacon during their brief affair pierces his lip and produces blood; his response as presented from the third-person narrator's point-of-view is revelatory and adumbrative: "'Don't ever do that again.' But his eyes, first startled, then revolted, had said the rest of what she should have known right away" (*Paradise* 239). This description prefigures his brother's, spoken on the eve of the male insurgents' attack on the Convent. Affixing blame for his brother's affair solely on Consolata, Steward hypothesizes that her gender-based predilection for bloodsucking and her lighter complexion are incontrovertible evidence of her animaloid traits and attendant propensity for predation: "An uncontrollable, gnawing woman who had bitten his lip just to lap the blood it shed; a beautiful, golden-skinned, outside woman with moss-green eyes that tried to trap a man" (279).[11] Like Carroll's "negro

---

[11] Steward's attribution of Connie's ability to seduce his twin and pollute Deacon's presumed unimpeachable virtue to her beguiling, Anglicized appearance—"green eyes," "tea-colored hair" (*Paradise* 223)—and a mystical, "black-magic"-imbued cunning hearkens back to another tale of proscribed racio-sexual desire. Given that the incarnation of white virtue, Desdemona, would never deign to consort with "a black Moor" of her own volition, Brabantio conjectures that his daughter must have fallen prey to Othello's hypnotic conjuration and degenerate sexual wiles.

beast" and Jefferson's "ardent" Black male, in Deacon's and eventually his brethren's collective imagination, she is alchemized into woman as *todos as coisas parasitas*—potentially sirenic *and* vampiric. The eradicating mob's subsequent recuperation, commingling, and redeployment of historically encoded language for Black sexuality and gay desire—"defilement and violence and perversions beyond imagination," "filth," "sea of depravity" (287)—thus dovetail with Anglo-inflected foundational discourses that rendered blackness as pestilential and gayness as sodomitic, both incompatible with Anglicized, heterocentric notions of paradise.

Accordingly, Consolata becomes another iteration of Delia Best, the exemplar of female epidermalized mongrelization, her blackness adulterated by the scourge of whiteness, as borne out when Sister Mary Magna is captivated by the abused and orphaned nine-year old in Brazil: "for by then she had fallen in love with Consolata. The green eyes? the tea-colored hair? ... Perhaps her smoky, sundown skin?" (223). Moreover, apropos of Delia Best's earlier denomination—"dung"—the men also employ this gyno-excremental metaphor to the Convent women, who are "drawing folks out there like flies to shit"; note too Consolata's geospatial association with excrement, when the narrator describes how Mary Magna "rescues" her from "the shit-strewn paths" of Connie's native Brazil. This idiomatic stigmatizing reinforces the binary of human(e) and animal, recalling Julia Kristeva's theorizing of the abject: "Polluting objects fall, schematically, into two types: excremental and menstrual ... Excrement and its equivalents (decay, infection, disease, corpse, etc.) stand for the danger to identity that comes from without: the ego threatened by the non-ego, society threatened by its outside, life by death" (71). Cumulatively, such derogating lexical indices and codes concretize the classification of the Convent women as "this new and obscene breed of female" (279), their ontological alterity rendering them undeserving of sympathy vis-à-vis Hurston's "black-woman-as-mule" metaphor. Quite the contrary: Benighted, unnatural, amoral, feral, licentious, unconstrainable—the women ultimately become the repository for everything deemed dangerous, the pinnacle of what Anglophilic America has perennially cast as (its) *nigger*, the quintessence of the unassimilable and impermissible. As Sean Grattan asserts in his interpretation of the novel, "They are instead monstrous to the men of Ruby ... In the United States raced and gendered bodies have a long history of being further marked as monstrous" (374). Their monstrousness, accordingly, provides the justification for their eradication.

The unbridled violence that marks the novel's climax, then, is grounded in the Ruby heteropatriarchs' inculcation and replication of self-debasing dominant narratives; the uncontrollable Convent denizens "lend coherence to its internal conflicts," according to Afro-Pessimism's core principles as Sexton outlined. Put another way, Ruby's patrihegemony is unable to valorize blackness without a crystallizing, externalized figure of difference. Correlatively, as Consolata emerges as the Convent's spiritual doyenne, her merciless execution at the hands of Steward—"The bullet enters her forehead" (289)—is especially abhorrent and reverberant. In another of her major essays, "Rootedness: The Ancestor as Foundation," Morrison expounds upon that archetype's inestimable roles—spiritual, epistemological, pedagogical—in African American culture. She finds them omnipresent in canonical African American literature, describing them as "elders" who are "sort of timeless people whose relationships to the characters are benevolent, instructive, and protective, and they provide a certain kind of wisdom" ("Rootedness," 343).

However, that the novel opens with the men's incursion and violation of the gynophilic refuge demonstrates their disregard for women's ancestral value, which Consolata comes to embody. Armed with guns and their censorious condemnation of the women, the men "blew open the Convent door, the nature of their mission made them giddy. But the target, after all, is detritus: throwaway people" (4). "Detritus," "throwaway people"—in the lexicon of Afro-Pessimism, the space of nonvalue to which Blacks are relegated, irrespective of time and space. As Wilderson explains, "But just as there is no time for the slave, there is no *place* of the slave. The slave's reference to his or her quarters as home does not change the fact that it is a spatial extension of the master's dominion" (emphasis in original). Given the cosmological power and wisdom she ultimately assumes across time and space—specifically dramatized in her lineal connections to the first New World slaves brought to Brazil and her mystical and transformative encounter with one such ancestral figure—she is a maligned ancestral presence, disavowed/disallowed as a threat to androcentric hegemony. Just as distinctions partitioning past and present are collapsed in rendering blackbodies as perpetual, a priori slavebodies, so too do the men conceive of Consolata and her charges as nonentities—"detritus"—irrespective of time and space. Thus, the seventeen miles separating Ruby and the Convent, like the contemporaneity of slave past and Black present, is easily traversed, the female place(lessness) easily annexed, just as the slave quarters were inseparable from the master's omnivorous plantation. Counterpoising the heteropatriarchs' religion of androcentrism and domination, Consolata—Consolidate?—must therefore come "under the master's dominion," her slaughter amounting to a type of ancestral sororicide in the men's attempts to shed or displace the yoke of their own slave past. If this "ancestorcide" strikes a familiar chord, then it should: recall the Black Nationalist manqué Guitar Bains's inexplicably cruel execution of the matri-ancestor Pilate Dead in *Song of Solomon* (1977). Analogously, the Ruby posse's annihilative violence becomes a form of cultural suicide, emblematizing their inability to consolidate their slave past and their supposed present-day freedom. Ultimately, then, their "final solution" becomes an analog to the physical, mental, and economic violence that rendered their forebears dispossessed and deracinated—if not outright exterminated.

CONCLUSION

"*Human Life is dependent on Black death for its existence and for its conceptual coherence*" (Wilderson, emphases in original). Given that this is one of Afro-Pessimism's cardinal premises, the thanatotic imperative that undergirds America (and *The* Americas, for that matter) can neither be elided nor transcended. *Afrophobia* is inexpungable, congenitally constitutive in the nation's and region's very physiology. In *Paradise*, then, "Black death" is multivalent: though clearly rooted in the generative derogation of Black (and Brown) peoples as sub-beings and nonbeings thereby deserving of enslavement if not complete extirpation, such a malevolent ethos becomes de rigueur in the process of group identity (de)formation. Consequently, the Disallowed mutate into the Disallowers, those repudiated and displaced invariably establishing surrogates upon whom to project the contaminative, excremental qualities on which their own inadmissibility was decided. The geo-spatial freedom, instantiated in the founding of Haven-Ruby, is ultimately both ephemeral and chimerical: slavery's Manichean divisions and death-bound logics are lodged in the New Fathers' psyches, eventuating in a microscopic reenactment of the type of grand-scale annihilative violence on which the Founding Fathers' American project was conceived.

WORKS CITED

Baldwin, James. *Notes of a Native Son*. 1955. Beacon, 1984.

Carroll, Charles. *"The Negro A Beast" … Or "In the Image of God."* American Book and Bible House, 1900.

Denard, Carolyn C., editor. *Toni Morrison: Conversations*. U of Mississippi P, 2008.

Douglas, Kelly Brown. *Stand Your Ground: Black Bodies and the Justice of God*. Orbis Books, 2015.

Douglass, Frederick. *Narrative of the Life of Frederick Douglass, An American Slave*. 1845. *Narrative of the Life of Frederick Douglass, An American Slave* and *Incidents in the Life of a Slave Girl*. The Modern Library, 2000, pp. 1–113.

"The Dred Scott Decision." https://www.digitalhistory.uh.edu/disp_textbook.cfm?smtID=3&psid=293. Accessed July 2020.

Fanon, Frantz. *Black Skin, White Masks*. Grove, 1967.

Fanon, Frantz. *The Wretched of the Earth*. Grove, 1963.

Flint, Holly. "Toni Morrison's *Paradise*: Black Cultural Citizenship in the American Empire." *American Literature*, vol. 78, no. 3, 2006, pp. 585–612.

Franchot, Jenny. "The Punishment of Esther: Frederick Douglass and the Construction of the Feminine." *Frederick Douglass: New Literary and Historical Essays*, edited by Eric J. Sundquist, Oxford UP, 1990, pp.141–65.

Grattan, Sean. "Monstrous Utopia in Toni Morrison's *Paradise*." *Genre*, vol. 46, no. 3, Fall 2013, pp. 367–92.

Greene, J. Lee. *Blacks in Eden: The African American Novel's First Century*. UP of Virginia, 1996.

Hartman, Saidiya V. *Scenes of Subjugation: Terror, Slavery, and Self-Making in Nineteenth-Century America*. Oxford UP, 1997.

Hurston, Zora Neale. *Their Eyes Were Watching God*. 1937. U of Illinois P, 1978.

"In 1944, George Stinney Was Young, Black and Sentenced to Die," *The Post and Courier* (South Carolina), Mar. 25, 2018, https://www.postandcourier.com/news/special_reports/in-1944-george stinney-was-young-black-and-sentenced-to-die/article_a87181dc-2924-11e8-b4e0-4f958aa5ba1c.html. Accessed June 2020.

Jacobs, Harriet. *Incidents in the Life of a Slave Girl*. 1861. *Narrative of the Life of Frederick Douglass, An American Slave* and *Incidents in the Life of a Slave Girl*. The Modern Library, 2000, pp. 115–389.

Jefferson, Thomas. *Notes on the State of Virginia*. 1787, edited by William Peden, W. W. Norton, 1972.

Jenkins, Candice M. "Pure Black: Class, Color, and Intraracial Politics in Toni Morrison's *Paradise*." *Modern Fiction Studies*, vol. 52, no. 2, Summer 2006, pp. 270–96.

Kristeva, Julia. *Powers of Horror: An Essay on Abjection*. Columbia UP, 1982.

Morrison, Toni. *The Bluest Eye*. 1970. Plume, 1994.

Morrison, Toni. Foreword. *Paradise*, by Toni Morrison. Vintage International, 2014, pp. xi–xvii.

Morrison, Toni. *Paradise*. 1997. Vintage International, 2014.

Morrison, Toni. "Rootedness: The Ancestor as Foundation." *Black Women Writers (1950–1980): A Critical Evaluation*, edited by Mari Evans, Anchor, 1980, pp. 339–45.

Poll, Ryan. "Can One *Get Out*? The Aesthetics of Afro-Pessimism." *Midwest Modern Language Association*, vol. 51, no. 2, Fall 2018, pp. 69–102.

Read, Andrew. "'As if Word Magic Had Anything to Do with the Courage It Took to Be a Man': Black Masculinity in Toni Morrison's *Paradise*." *African American Review*, vol. 39, no. 4, 2005, pp. 527–40.

Sexton, Jared. "Affirmation in the Dark: Racial Slavery and Philosophical Pessimism." *The Comparist*, vol. 43, 2019, pp. 90–111.

Tabone, Mark A. "Rethinking *Paradise*: Toni Morrison and Utopia at the Millennium." *African American Review*, vol. 49, no. 2, Summer 2016, pp. 129–44.

Wilderson, Frank B. III. "Afro-Pessimism and the End of Redemption." *Humanities Futures*. Franklin Humanities Institute, Duke University, 2015. https://humanitiesfutures.org/papers/afro-pessimism-end-redemption. Accessed June 2020.

Williams, Dana A. "Playing on the 'Darky': Blackface Minstrelsy, Identity Construction, and the Deconstruction of Race in Toni Morrison's *Paradise*." *Studies in American Fiction*, vol. 35, no. 2, Autumn 2007, pp. 181–200.

Wright, Richard. "The Ethics of Living Jim Crow." 1938. *The Norton Anthology of African American Literature*. 3rd ed., vol. 2, edited by Henry Louis Gates, Jr., and Valerie A. Smith, W. W. Norton, 2014, pp. 132–40.

CHAPTER EIGHT

Love: Toni Morrison's African American Gothic

JAMEELA F. DALLIS

It is easily the most empty cliché, the most useless word, and at the same time the most powerful human emotion—because hatred is involved in it, too. I thought if I removed the word from nearly every other place in the manuscript, it could become an earned word. If I could give the word, in my very modest way, its girth and its meaning and its terrible price and its clarity at the moment when that is all there is time for, then the title does work for me.

—Toni Morrison (qtd. in Hudson 2)

Set primarily in Silk, an African American eastern seaboard community, *Love* (2003) is mournful, elegiac, and Gothic. *Love* is about loving and living in times and spaces touched and shaped by circumstances and legacies that exemplify a particular kind of Gothic—one recognized through familiar aesthetics but is uniquely African American. We witness the deterioration of Black entrepreneur and patriarch Bill Cosey's Hotel and Resort, which in the 1930s to 1960s was an upscale destination for Blacks, but by the 1990s is only a boarded-up, decayed memory of a lost age. *Love* is "not about the civil rights movement not being a good idea," says Morrison, for the movement was "absolutely necessary"; but, she adds, "there was a price":

> There were these fabulous black schools, high schools, insurance companies, resorts, and the business class was very much involved. They worked very hard to have their own resorts ... they were all black and very upscale. Those stores are gone; those hotels are gone. (qtd. in Langer 43)

As the nonlinear, short, yet labyrinthine, novel reveals, love in all its complexity *is* the price. Similar to other Morrison novels, *Love* circles, spirals out and in, and covers a large swath of time. The past erupts in surprising ways, and characters' intentions and words are not always clear and certain—they are hybrid and furtive. *Love*'s main plot centers on two older protagonists—both with traits of the conventional Gothic heroine—Christine Cosey, Bill's granddaughter, and Heed the Night Cosey (née Johnson), Bill's widow. The women were best friends as children, but are

---

For Randall Kenan and James W. Coleman.
It is with deep gratitude that I acknowledge my dissertation advisors Minrose Gwin and Shayne L. Legassie along with committee members Ruth Salvaggio, María DeGuzmán, and the late James W. Coleman and thank them for their original comments on and responses to this work. I have adapted this chapter from my dissertation wherein I write about several

now doomed to occupy the Cosey mansion on One Monarch Street where they scheme against one another, vying to be the unidentified "sweet Cosey child" of Bill's will (79).[1] Throughout their lives, Christine and Heed are susceptible to the wiles and plans of family, socioeconomic circumstances, the desires of men, and, most significantly, the devices of Bill, a man who is loving, lustful, abusive, and haunting. *Love* is also a novel about Junior Viviane, a trickster, heroine, and antiheroine whom Heed hires as a personal assistant to help write Heed's memoir, dye her hair, bathe her, and ultimately fabricate a will explicitly naming her the rightful beneficiary.[2] Junior is desperate, reckless, and sinister, and her mechanisms ultimately lead to Heed's death. Romen Gibbons, a brief hero at the novel's beginning and end, is a young man learning to navigate the world outside his protective grandparents: Sandler and Vida. Romen does handyman chores for the Cosey women; both his grandparents worked at the Cosey Hotel, and his grandfather Sandler was Bill's confidant. Romen and Junior have a passionate, sometimes sadomasochistic sexual relationship.

There are other characters, ghostly, yet essential to the novel, such as L, Bill's faithful cook. Although her full name is withheld from readers, we may assume it is Love as she is named for "*the subject of First Corinthians*" (199; emphasis in original).[3] Celestial, the "sporting woman" with whom Bill falls deeply in love, is another ghostly character (188). (May, Christine's mother, tells Christine and Heed, "Stay as far away from her as you can … Cross the road when you see her coming your way … Because there is nothing a sporting woman won't do" [188].) Arguably, there is the ghost of Bill himself. Bill is the most Gothic element of the novel; its remaining objects and circumstances become more Gothic because of their relationship to him. One of the most complex and telling objects Morrison incorporates from a Gothic literary past is a portrait of Bill. It is animated and haunted; it is a posthumous presence of the founding patriarch. The presence and influence of this portrait, along with the novel's characters and setting, compose an arresting Gothic narrative as Morrison draws out and exaggerates familiar Gothic aesthetics in her novel that reflect the conditions and themes that have governed Gothic narratives since the first Gothic novel, Horace Walpole's *The Castle of Otranto* (1764).[4] Bill's actions and the way the community perceives them embody the multifaceted nature of power and influence, law and lawlessness, society and family, and sexuality. These themes are familiar in the Gothic text, but Morrison adapts and builds on these themes in an African American context that examines their troubling expressions before, during, and after segregation in the US South.

---

contemporary women, including Toni Morrison and Angela Carter who incorporate eighteenth- and nineteenth-century Gothic aesthetics into their work. In this text, I capitalize Black when referring to people of African descent, I do not use a hyphen in African American, and I capitalize Gothic, but I do respect the original capitalization and punctuation used in the sources I cite.

[1] There is confusion about the identity of the "sweet Cosey child" in part because Heed, the wife, refers to Bill as "Papa" and Bill is Christine's grandfather, Christine being the daughter of his late son.

[2] For a reading of Junior as a trickster figure, see Susana Vega-González's article, "Toni Morrison's Love and the Trickster Paradigm."

[3] In this chapter, all of L's words are presented in their original italics unless otherwise noted.

[4] *Love* is Gothic in several ways: its structure, its events, and characters. There is the imprisoning or otherwise Gothic house (the house on Monarch Street and the Cosey Hotel), the doppelgänger (e.g., Junior), and the active, animated ghost (Bill). Morrison also incorporates and revises Southern Gothic themes.

THE AFRICAN AMERICAN GOTHIC

In *Love*'s 2005 foreword, Morrison writes, "Beneath (rather, hand-in-hand with) the surface story of the successful revolt against a common enemy in the struggle for integration (in this case, white power) lies another one: the story of disintegration—of a radical change in conventional relationships and class allegiances that signals both liberation and estrangement" (parentheses in original, xi). As Fred Botting (1996) explains, "uncertainties about the nature of power, law, society, family and sexuality dominate Gothic fiction ... [and] are linked to wider threats of disintegration manifested most forcefully in political revolution" (*Gothic* 5). The 1964 Civil Rights Act that ended *de jure* segregation sent reverberations through culture in the throes of sociopolitical revolution where disintegration and, ultimately, integration, were dueling forces. Morrison employs the Gothic mode because of its ability to reveal, disrupt, and provoke powerful emotional responses through its juxtaposition of the nonrational and rational, love and hate, and past and present. With disturbance and unease comes the potential for action.[5] Although Morrison and other Black writers and critics dislike the term Gothic and its connotations, I use Gothic with care and intention. Teresa A. Goddu discusses the latter in *Gothic America: Narrative, History, and Nation* (1997): "The gothic's typical association with the 'unreal' and the sensational ... has created a resistance to examining African American narratives in relation to the gothic" (139). She cites Alice Walker who dislikes the label because it "conjures up the supernatural," and Walker says what she writes has "something to do with real life" (Walker qtd. in Goddu 140). Morrison, too, is "reluctant to have her writing described as gothic," and in a 1988 interview says she "dislikes the term *black magic* used in conjunction with her work" because it implies the absence of intelligence (140; emphasis in original). Thus, Goddu explains, the Gothic's "apparent lack of connection to reality and intellectual purpose has made it troubling to use in conjunction with African-American writers" (140). Yet, five years earlier, before the publication of *Beloved* (widely described as a novel with strong Gothic overtones), Morrison explains,

> I also want my work to capture the vast imagination of black people. That is, I want my books to reflect the imaginative combination of the real world, the very practical, shrewd, day to day functioning that black people must do, while at the same time they encompass some great supernatural element ... it does not bother them one bit to do something practical and have visions at the same time. So all parts of living are on an equal footing. (Morrison qtd. in McKay 153)

Certainly, the idea that the supernatural or nonrational somehow lessens the serious endeavors of fiction is unwarranted as Gothic texts often deal explicitly with serious issues of the abuse, oppression, and marginalization of women and social minorities—the Gothic becomes necessary because it reflects the realities of those forced to suffer under the weight of its confining mansions and lecherous villains. Ultimately, the Gothic is a "mode intimately connected to history" (Goddu 139).

Goddu explains that African Americans (and I add Blacks in the Caribbean and other slave-holding and colonized counties) have endured the realities of Gothic horrors for centuries. Goddu endnotes Gladys-Marie Fry's study *Night Riders in Black Folk History* (1975) as one example of how the Gothic has "long been allied with reality" in Black American's lives (187). Goddu

---

[5] I am beholden to Angela Carter for this phrasing. Carter maintains the Gothic mode is one that "retains a singular moral function: that of provoking unease" while asserting, "I think that it is immoral to read simply for pleasure" ("Notes" 134).

explains that Fry's study details how during slavery and Reconstruction, the "supernatural was used by whites as a form of psychological control of African Americans … a master designating haunted places or the Ku Klux Klan riding as ghosts through the night, the supernatural kept African Americans literally and figuratively in their place" (Goddu 187). Rather than the master's "stage effects" it was "the institutionalized power that lay behind" such effects (187). Thus, Goddu proposes that

> instead of accepting traditional readings of the gothic as unrealistic and frivolous, thereby excluding African-American narratives from this genre, we should use the African-American gothic to revise our understanding of the gothic as an historical mode. Re-viewing the gothic through the lens of African-American transpositions and recognizing that the gothic itself is a dynamic and contradictory mode whose tropes and conventions can be used for a variety of ends makes visible the American gothic's relationship to history. (140)

In a similar vein, Maisha L. Wester in *African American Gothic: Screams from Shadowed Places* (2012) argues that rather than "borrow" Gothic aesthetics from Anglo writers, Black writers use "appropriation," which "implies a determination to reconfigure—to make [the genre] suitable—for black experience" (28). For Wester, this reconfiguration gives space for Black writers to shift signifiers and "introduce profound variations that make the gothic something new," and insisting that Black "texts must be read through African (American) forms and traditions unique to the black experience … ignores the complexity of African American existence" and such insistence only "reaffirms the need to recognize black use of gothic tropes" (28, 29). Reading Morrison through the lens of an African American Gothic that uses, subverts, and revises known Gothic aesthetics and tropes opens new ways to critical pathways.

MORRISON AND MONSTROUS LOVE

"*Beloved* unleashed a host of ideas about how and what one cherished under the duress and emotional disfigurement that a slave society imposes," writes Morrison in *Jazz*'s 2004 foreword. "One such idea—love as perpetual mourning (haunting)—led me to consider a parallel one: how such relationships were altered, later, in (or by) a certain level of liberty" (parentheses in original, xvi). This exploration of love and haunting continues in *Love*:

> For among the things Christine, Heed, and Junior have already lost, besides their innocence and their faith, are a father and a mother, or, to be more precise, fathering and mothering. Emotionally unprotected by adults, they give themselves over to the most powerful one they know, the man who looms even larger in their imagination than in their lives. (Foreword xii)

The three women lack protective ancestor figures and fall victim to the power and desire of Bill—someone at least one critic identifies as "classic Gothic hero-villain" (Heise-von der Lippe 176). The ancestor, as well as the wisdom the figure represents, has been an important trope since Morrison's beginnings. Morrison's fiction reminds readers—specifically African Americans—of the dual responsibility to listen to ancestors and act as protective conduits for future generations. In her well-known essay, "Rootedness: The Ancestor as Foundation" (1984), Morrison argues that the presence of an ancestor becomes a paradigmatic symbol in and distinctive characteristic of African American literature. When present, these ancestors warrant success and happiness (61–2).

An ancestor's absence is "frightening ... threatening" and leads to "destruction and disarray" (62). Morrison complicates this idea in *Love* through its chapter titles: Portrait, Friend, Stranger, Benefactor, Lover, Husband, Guardian, Father, and Phantom; throughout the novel, Bill plays the titular role of each chapter at one time or another.

Love revisits and builds on themes from Morrison's oeuvre, including *The Bluest Eye* (1970), *Song of Solomon* (1977), *Beloved* (1987), *Jazz* (1992), and *Paradise* (1997). *Love* also names the subject of so many of Morrison's novels, and a subject familiar to the Gothic narrative: love. In *The Bluest Eye*, love becomes perverse, corrupted, and too closely tied with lust and desire. As a result, Pecola Breedlove and her rapist father Cholly turn to self-hate. In *Song of Solomon*, self-love is achieved through connecting with one's ancestors, which leads to family love and the love of one's community. Morrison's trilogy, *Beloved*, *Jazz*, and *Paradise*, immediately precedes *Love* and centers on the theme of who is the beloved, or who or what is the object of love and loving in each novel. In *Beloved*, "mother-love"; in *Jazz*, "couple-love"—the "reconfiguration of the 'self' in such relationships" and the "negotiation between individuality and commitment to one another" (xviii). In *Paradise*, it is self-love, woman-love, community-love, and the love of the divine. *Love* combines the many textures of love we find in Morrison's work and acknowledges the slippage that occurs in the space of love amid the real-life terrors of being Black in the United States. In *Love*, love has time to grow, be haunted by history and shaped by circumstances, and mutate into a monstrous construct. And if, as Wester argues, Black writers began appropriating the Gothic with slavery, then revising the genre "proves a powerful insurgent act" (256–7). "Through their gothic (anti-)heroes, haunting specters, and distressed damsels," Wester points out that Black writers reveal how "racial injustice inevitably contributes to and overlaps with other oppressions," which makes the Gothic "a tool capable of expressing the complexity of black experience in America" (257). Through Morrison's exploration of love and haunting from enslavement to the near-contemporary moment, her commitment to telling more than one type of Black story is clear.

LOVE'S FIRST PAGES: L'S PROLOGUE AND AFRICAN AMERICAN HISTORY

Love opens with L's italicized words. At first encounter, L's voice is reminiscent of the narrator in *Jazz*: omniscient yet opinionated, knowledgeable yet detached, intimate yet longing. L's prologue feels mournful as she tells the reader of changing times, the history of Silk and Up Beach—its people, its land, its politics. Throughout the novel, readers are presented with scenarios related to the shades of love. The first words are full of lust and desire: *"The women's legs are spread wide open, so I hum. Men grow irritable, but they know it's all for them. They relax. Standing by, unable to do anything but watch, is a trial, but I don't say a word. My nature is a quiet one, anyway"* (3, emphasis in original). These five sentences are full of meaning—meaning that doesn't become fully clear until one reads the novel again. Here, L reveals the sexual freedom of the contemporary age—perhaps a gentlemen's club or nightclub. It isn't as if these places haven't existed in the American landscape for some time; but rather, beginning a novel with such a scene speaks to the moment: sex sells, sex is no longer something we hide as it may have been in the early days of Silk. L laments, *"Before Women agreed to spread in public, there used to be secrets—some to hold, some to tell. Now? No"* (3). But this opening also speaks to the nature of one of the novel's main conflicts and to one of its elements that renders it Gothic. Bill is a sexual predator who like so many other

Gothic villains is driven by his desire and violates an innocent woman (or women).[6] In 1942, Bill, the wealthiest Black man in the town marries eleven-year-old Heed in a public ceremony and then entrusts her with important aspects of his hotel business. Through this pedophilic marriage, Bill initiates Heed, 41 years his junior, into adult sexuality and relationships and steals her childhood and her ability to learn on her own what secrets are hers to hold, or hers to tell.

L views the present with contempt and longing:

> *They* [Christine and Heed] *live like queens in Mr. Cosey's house, but since that girl* [Junior] *moved in there a while ago with a skirt short as underpants and no underpants at all, I've been worried about them leaving me here with nothing but an old folks' tale to draw on. I know it's trash: just another story made up to scare wicked females and correct unruly children. But it's all I have. I know I need something else. Something better. Like a story that shows how brazen women can take a good man* [Bill] *down. I can hum to that.* (10, emphasis in original)

The prologue introduces *Love* and Silk, a small, isolated African American town experiencing significant changes in the twentieth century. The prologue also sets the reader's expectations for the novel and centers on Bill and his demise that relates to his relationships with "brazen"—dangerous, bold, independent—women. By the end, we understand that L herself is a brazen woman through her involvement with Bill's death and his will. We're left to question what makes a "good man" and reevaluate narratives of identity and history.

Recovering parts of African American history often neglected or suppressed, the Cosey Hotel, Silk, and their environs are modeled on Florida's American Beach.[7] Founded in 1935, American Beach provided African Americans with "beach access in a resort atmosphere" during racial segregation (Chase). In its founding year, Jacksonville's Afro-American Life Insurance Company (AFRO) Pension Bureau bought 33 acres of Amelia Island's shorefront property where A. L. Lewis, AFRO's president, hosted company events and invited employees to use the beach. The Bureau subdivided the land and sold parcels to shareowners, company executives, and community leaders. AFRO bought 183 more acres over the years and in 1940, with many lots unsold, began selling property to the wider African American community. After the end of the Second World War and the building boom, American Beach was an attractive location for entrepreneurs who began building restaurants, motels, guest homes, and night clubs. Many African Americans had summer homes there as well. American Beach drew patrons and residents from all over the United States, and on the beach, in a friendly environment, Blacks could enjoy small snacks, ice cream, "surf fishing and shell gathering, beauty contests and automobile races" (Chase) Excursion buses operated between nearby minority communities and American Beach, so day visitors benefited from its proximity. The A. L. Lewis Motel, Williams's Guest Lodge, and Cowart's Motel and Restaurant were the main lodging establishments, but vacationers could also room with or rent out homes from locals. After nightfall, visitors enjoyed dining and live entertainment at the Ocean-Vu-Inn.

---

[6]Bill's determination to eventually reproduce a male heir to maintain his empire, as it were, brings to mind the ruthless behaviors of Faulkner's Thomas Sutpen and Manfred in Walpole's *The Castle of Otranto*, for example.

[7]My sincerest thanks to the late Randall Kenan for saying that the town I described in *Love* reminded him of American Beach. For an in-depth history of American Beach and A. L. Lewis, see Justine Tally's 2011 chapter, "Toni Morrison's *Love*: The Celestial Whore and Other Female 'Outlaws.'"

When Hurricane Dora destroyed many homes and businesses in 1964, it was also transformed by the Civil Rights Act (Chase). According to historian Marsha Dean Phelts (1997),

> The civil rights legislated in 1964 ... opened all public facilities to African Americans. Former American Beach vacationers and day-trippers now frolicked on Miami Beach ... and rode high at St. Simons Island. All along the shores of the East Coast, blacks explored areas that had once been off limits. The three-day weekends at American Beach shrank to one day; the Sunday visitors and day-trippers no longer stayed overnight. Loaded buses no longer caused a bottleneck at the crossroads. With so little business most of the restaurants and resort establishments closed. (120)

It is a painful, dark irony that the same legislation that allowed Blacks more freedom and equality damned the community that had catered to and provided safety, culture, entertainment, and comfort for thirty years. By the 2000s, American Beach is mostly bereft of motels and restaurants; property taxes and land values continue to rise, and many properties are for sale. Some of the community's original homeowners' descendants have maintained properties, but most have sold. A portion of the land is now a part of the Timucuan Ecological and Historic Preserve (Chase). The result is the "price" Morrison bemoans, and it seems the story of places like American Beach is best told in the Gothic mode.

Forty years prior, the hotel was *"full of visitors drunk with dance music, or salt air, or tempted by starlit water"*—the *"best and best-known vacation spot for colored folk on the East Coast"* (6, emphases in original). In the novel's present, however, that image has transformed into a scene of decay and dilapidation, but there is a latent beauty—a sort of nostalgic romantic image so germane to the Gothic novel. L observes,

> *Up Beach is twenty feet underwater; but the hotel part of Cosey's Resort is still standing. Sort of standing. Looks more like it's rearing backwards—away from hurricanes and a steady blow of sand. Odd what oceanfront can do to empty buildings ... Hills of sand piling in porch corners and between banister railings ... Foxglove grows waist high around the gazebo, and roses, which all the time hate our soil, rage here, with more thorns than blackberries and weeks of beet red blossoms. The wood siding of the hotel looks silver-plated, its peeling paint like the streaks on an unpolished tea service. The big double doors are padlocked ... No matter the outside loneliness, if you look inside, the hotel seems to promise you ecstasy and the company of all your best friends. And music. The shift of a shutter hinge sounds like the cough of a trumpet; piano keys waver a quarter note above the wind so you might miss the hurt jamming all those halls and closed-up rooms.* (7, emphases in original)

The decaying hotel conjures the familiar Gothic image of a decaying estate and imbues it with life despite its state of disintegration; despite its once-grand architecture, the building is full of "hurt" from the immorality of Bill's pedophilic marriage to the origins of his wealth that built the hotel and resort, as his father was a police informant working against his own people.

As in other Gothic works, there's also meaning in the flora surrounding the hotel. Foxglove is known for its beauty and poison. In regulated doses, foxglove or digitalis is medicinal and used for heart health. It is also associated with "youth and stateliness" and when given as a gift, conveys wishes that the recipient will "heal from any ailment or trauma, and to regain [her] happy, youthful vitality" ("Foxglove Flowers"). Later, the dilapidated hotel proves to be a place of passion, danger, and death, but it is also the scene of recovery and positive transformation—it is the place where Heed and Christine experience a healing of their hearts.

In L's prologue, readers may not immediately recognize her mention of flora, but rather that this early description of the abandoned hotel is deliberate and woven together to produce the specific feeling of loss. *Love* is many things, and it is most certainly a novel about the widespread effects of social (and environmental in this example) change. Morrison's use of Gothic aesthetics here and in the novel proper speak to Ellen Malenas Ledoux's (2013) central argument that Gothic writing's complex relationship between authorial intention and readers' response wields the power to impact social policy. In *Love*, Gothic conventions represent the aftermath of racial integration in the United States in towns like Silk, Up Beach, and American Beach while drawing attention to the fact that what was lost was once grand because of patriarchy, racist policies, and the basic human needs to survive and love. That is, Blacks went to American Beach and places like it because they were not welcome anywhere else and places like American Beach fostered happiness and conviviality.[8]

LOVE'S GOTHIC WOMEN: JUNIOR, HEED, AND CHRISTINE

In the first chapter, Portrait, Junior enters Christine and Heed's world seeking freedom from poverty and abuse. The third chapter, Stranger, reveals her history. Born in Settlement, Junior was one of the "rurals" (53). Settlement girls are discouraged from attending school, and people born there are shunned for leaving and are generally feared by outsiders (53–5). Junior's father, who her mother says "weren't nothing … Nothing at all" abandons the family, and her longing for a father makes her more susceptible to Bill's influence (55). The trajectory of Junior's life changes when she gives a baby cottonmouth snake to her Jewish friend, Peter Paul Fortas (who lives outside of Settlement), and her teenage uncles demand she return the snake to "its rightful home" (57). Her uncles threaten to "break [her] pretty little butt" and "hand [her] over to Vosh," an "old man in the valley who liked to walk around with his private parts in his hand singing hymns of praise," and chase her into the woods (57). Thinking she will find Peter's house, she leaves the cover of the woods and ventures out into the road—the space of men and violence—where her uncles, "idle teenagers whose brains had been insulted by the bleakness of their lives," run over her with their truck (57–8). Her uncles lie about what happened and make themselves heroes. At ten, Junior's toes are crushed and her foot is forever disfigured like a hoof.

Junior's disfigurement is the birth of her trickster self and the catalyst that leads to her decision to run away at eleven. When Junior runs away, she commits the "settlement version of crime: leaving, getting out" (59). Junior enters "Correctional" for shoplifting and remains there until she is eighteen. When released, she adds an "e" to Junior Vivian "for style" (59). Susana Vega-González (2005) points out that her decision to change her name, at one point considering "June," mirrors the "mutability" of the Yoruba trickster god Esu whose names include Legba, Esu/Eshu Elegbara (278). Esu is the "guardian of the crossroads" (Gates qtd. in Vega-González 278). (And, Junior's injury happens in a road that leads to a crossroads in her life.) The fact that trickster gods are associated with heightened sexuality is reflected in Junior's relationship with Romen (278). More pertinent

---

[8] According to the American Beach Museum, this is made evident in A. L. Lewis's motto for American Beach, which was "recreation and relaxation without humiliation" ("About Us").

to the Gothic aesthetics of the novel is considering the hoof's allusions to Pan, the "Greek god of forests and wilderness" or the Devil, the familiar Christian antagonist. Vega-González footnotes,

> Junior epitomizes the female wilderness, freedom and transgression that Morrison is so interested in; on the other hand, the implicit reference to the devil would imply Junior's embodiment of evil and sin in a patriarchal system. However ... Morrison dismantles the borders between evil and good, blurring the received clear-cut notions of such binarism. (286–7)

The latter half of that passage becomes clearer as the novel progresses, but the freedom wilderness is associated with brings to mind the early Gothic heroine's journey into the forest to escape a sexual predator or to seek out some hidden truth about her identity. Junior is chased into the woods like an eighteenth-century Radcliffean heroine.

Junior's childhood is Gothic. Virtually imprisoned within her community, she is physically abused and lives under the threat of sexual violence (e.g., from Vosh). Her uncles act as an aggregated symbol for the conventional older male villain who imprisons the heroine, stalks her movements, and abuses her psychologically, physically, or sexually—most often the abuse is a combination of all three. This trope reaches back to Walpole's *Otranto* when heroine Isabella escapes antagonist Manfred's advances into a "subterraneous passage which led from the vaults of the castle" to a church (27). George Haggerty (2006) argues that in Gothic writing, "Terror is almost always sexual terror, and fear, and flight, and incarceration, and escape are almost colored by the exoticism of transgressive sexual aggression" (2). The same is true for Junior. Settlement invokes the isolated town familiar to the Southern Gothic with its grotesque characters and its themes of violence, alienation, and futility (Boyd 311). Settlement embodies classic Southern Gothic themes in a way that embodies an African American experience updated for the mid-1980s. Instead of a white patriarch or heir struggling with the effects of such history, Black people navigate the world that long-dead plantation society and its tenets bequeathed them. The intransigence of the community conveyed through Junior's uncles and her own mother's actions are the result of the long history of de facto and de jure segregation and other forms of institutionalized racism. *Love*'s narrator (not L) reveals that Settlement is

> quite the way it was in 1912 when the jute mill was abandoned and those who could leave left and those who could not (the black ones because they had no hope, or the white ones who had no prospects) lolled on, marrying one another, sort of, and figuring out how to stay alive from day to day. They built their own houses from other people's scraps ... and if they hired out in a field or kitchen, they spent the earnings on sugar, salt, cooking oil, soda pop, cornflakes, flour, dried beans, and rice. If there were no earrings, they stole. (54)

Settlement is a virtual prison of despair. It represents the people and ways of life many US citizens would like to forget exists. It is the wound that cries out; it bears the taint of the collective shame of the United States.[9] Settlement's persistence into the late twentieth century is an encounter with the uncanny.

Another iteration of the uncanny is the doppelgänger or double. Originally a "defence against annihilation" and an "insurance against the extinction of self," according to Freud (1919), the

---

[9] I borrow the image of a wound crying out from Cathy Caruth's discussion of the nature of trauma in *Unclaimed Experience* (1996).

double has become an "uncanny harbinger of death" (142). It is no coincidence that Junior responds to Heed's advertisement for "COMPANION, SECRETARY SOUGHT BY MATURE, PROFESSIONAL LADY. LIGHT BUT HIGHLY CONFIDENTIAL WORK," because Junior is Heed's doppelgänger.[10] Common in Gothic writing, the doppelgänger

> in demonic form can be a reciprocal or lower bestial self … Gothic doppelgängers often haunt and threaten the rational psyche of the victim to whom they become attached. (Frank 435)

Heed marries Bill at eleven, the same age Junior flees Settlement. Each woman's mannerisms and diction reveal to the other the impoverished origins from which she has escaped (24–8). Furthermore, Heed cannot write or perform many basic tasks for herself, as arthritis has deformed her hands. Perhaps this deformity marks her as someone who has been affected by the weight of her past as Junior's deformed toes attest to her own desolate history. After Junior lists all the things she can do for Heed ending with, "I need a job and I need a place to stay. I'm real good, Mrs. Cosey. Really real good," Heed subconsciously recognizes a sort of kinship with Junior, but she does not fully realize it: "[Junior] winked, startling Heed into a momentary recall of something just out of reach, like a shell snatched away by a wave. It may have been that flick of melancholy so sharply felt that made her lean close to the girl and whisper, 'Can you keep a secret'"? (27). Here, Heed not only sees her younger self in Junior's eagerness, but she also mourns for her broken friendship with Christine—the main person from whom she wants Junior to keep secrets. (Her words also echo L's prologue: "*there used to be secrets—some to hold, some to tell*" [3, emphasis in original].) By the end of the novel, Junior does become demon-like; she manipulates and takes advantage of Heed's desperation.

Heed is from Up Beach, a town that in the 1940s was akin to Junior's hometown, Settlement. Her parents are characterized as unapologetically shiftless; and for her family, the Johnsons, "*shiftlessness was not a habit, it was a trait; ignorance was destiny; dirt lingered on by choice*" (138, emphasis in original). They are "*poor and trifling*," and the Johnson girls are "*mighty quick in the skirt-raising department*" (139). Yet, when light-skinned, grey-eyed, "slippery"-haired Christine meets seven-year-old dark-skinned kinky-haired Heed, who is wearing a man's undershirt, on Silk's white sand beach—all because she "wander[s] too far … down to big water and along its edge where waves skidded and mud turned into clean sand"—the friendship is instant (191, 78). Even though May (who later blames integration for ruining the Cosey Hotel's business [104]) initially tells her, "Go away now. This [beach] is private," Christine calls for her to "Wait! Wait!" (78). The two girls fall in love and experience *philia*—a type of love that encompasses deep friendship and loyalty. Yet, things change when fifty-two-year-old Bill marries Heed. Frightened that Heed's status as wife and the sex matrimony demands will taint Christine, she sends the girl to boarding school, and Heed learns how to navigate her new life the best she can (139).

---

[10]Arguably, Heed and Christine are also doppelgängers. Elaine Showalter sees similarities to Brontë's *Wuthering Heights* and points out,

> More or less sold to the old man by her shiftless parents, the illiterate Heed learns to be a lady and to fight with Christine for primacy in the Cosey family; as adults their childhood roles are reversed, with Heed the heiress and Christine her servant. Their relationship is almost gothic in its ferocity and passion, as if they were African-American female versions of Cathy and Heathcliff.

Like Junior, Heed will do anything to survive. Morrison uses Christine and Heed's relationship to demonstrate that, within a racially segregated society, African Americans had a complex system of social stratification. Boundaries were maintained to keep the trace of poverty—a condition that marks a direct connection to the abolished plantation society—at bay. The Coseys and their hotel guests sought to separate themselves from that reality, and Heed emerges to become a constant reminder of what they would have rather buried. Bill marries Heed because he wants to have another son; both his first wife and son died. To marry Heed, Bill pays Heed's father "two hundred dollars" and gives her mother a "pocketbook" (193). Christine says to Heed in their secret language, pig Latin, that Bill bought her with a year's rent and a candy bar (193). When Heed is sold to Bill, the transaction reveals that no one is truly acting in Heed's best interest. Her parents are no better than Junior's uncles. Bill, the community's benefactor, seems no better than Vosh holding his genitals and singing hymns.

Morrison draws on familiar Gothic and Southern Gothic motifs, as well as those found in *The Bluest Eye* such as pedophilia and incest. Bill is both hated and loved by the people around him. Susan Neal Mayberry (2007) argues that Morrison connects *The Bluest Eye*'s Cholly, Mr. Henry, and Soaphead Church and *Love*'s Bill to "the most heinous of crimes against nature" and "contextualize[s] their pedophilia in terms of white Western tenets of sexual repression, competitive ownership, physical beauty, and romantic love" (14).[11] Mayberry points out that Bill is reactionary to his father's actions and legacy: he employs Black people from Up Beach, but has to pay off white policemen and the liquor man during prohibition to keep his resort operating, which contrasts with his father's status as a *"well paid, tipped off, and favored"* courthouse informer for fifty-five years (68). Thus, the *"cops paid off the father; the son paid off the cops"* (68, emphases in original). Bill spends his inheritance on things his father "cursed": *"good times, good clothes, good food, good music, dancing till the sun came up in a hotel made for it all"* (68). Bill is a patriarch and his marrying a prepubescent girl proves he feels he is above basic moral expectations. It also may reflect this desire to atone for the originary trauma he experiences while he spies for his informant father (44–5). Bill's report that a man has left by the back door of the house his father tells him to watch leads to that man being "dragged through the street behind a four-horse wagon"; a group of crying children run after the wagon and a little girl as "raggedy as Lazarus" trips in "some horse shit and fell" (45). People laugh and Bill says he does "nothing at all" (45).[12]

This incident haunts Bill, perhaps reflecting his desire to remove the shame from his complicity in the original girl's humiliation (and if he did indeed laugh with the others—that shame as well). He may have seen Heed as an incarnation of that "raggedy as Lazarus" girl, for he admits after marrying Heed that his attraction had to do with wanting to "raise her and [that he] couldn't wait to watch her grow" (148). In short, he is the "classic Gothic hero-villain"; L suggests as much: *"You could call him a good bad man, or a bad good man. Depends on what you hold dear—the what or the why ... He was an ordinary man ripped, like the rest of us, by wrath and love"* (Heise-von der Lippe 176; Morrison, *Love* 200, emphasis in original). But, as in *The Bluest Eye*, pedophiles and rapists are not excusable.

---

[11] Mayberry's chapter "Laying down the Law of the Father: Men in *Love*" in her book, *Can't I Love What I Criticize?: The Masculine and Morrison*, provides Lacanian readings of the men and their relationships in the novels.

[12] Bill's character is even more complex when we consider that Junior's mom describes her father as "Nothing at all" (55). Is saying "nothing at all" equal to being "nothing at all"? This is yet another instance of doubling with Heed and Junior.

Before his marriage to Heed, Bill touches her inappropriately. Christine and Heed are enjoying a day at the beach when Heed goes to retrieve playing jacks from Christine's room in the Cosey Hotel. On the way, she bumps into Bill, "the handsome giant who owns the hotel and who nobody sasses" (190). He then proceeds to "[touch] her chin, and then—causally, still smiling—her nipple, or rather the place under her swimsuit where a nipple will be if the circled dot on her chest ever changes" (191). Heed runs to tell Christine what happened, but Christine has seen her grandfather standing "in her bedroom window, his trousers open, his wrist moving with the same speed L used to beat egg whites into unbelievable creaminess"; he does not see her with his eyes closed, and Christine cannot assimilate what she has just witnessed (192). She vomits and neither girl can talk about what has happened: "It was the other thing. The thing that made each believe, without knowing why, that this particular shame was different and could not tolerate speech—not even in the language they had invented for secrets" (192). It is important to note that the location where Bill masturbates, Christine's room, and the closeness of the girls' relationship gestures toward incestuous desire. This type of unfulfilled incestuous desire is akin to Quentin Compson's desire for Caddy in Faulkner's *The Sound and the Fury* (1929) and *Absalom, Absalom!* (1936). By *Love's* present time, Heed and Christine's relationship seems irrecoverably broken, and even though Bill has been dead for more than twenty years, his influence continues to haunt them through his contested will and Junior's relationship with his portrait.

PORTRAITURE AND THE GOTHIC NOVEL: *LOVE'S* ANACHRONISM

Bill's portrait is one of the most Gothic elements of the novel. An anachronistic portrait helped bring Horace Walpole's authorship of *Otranto* to light, and an enduring tradition of portraits in various shapes and sizes persists in Gothic writing. In *Portraiture and British Gothic Fiction: The Rise of Picture Identification, 1764–1835* (2012), Kamilla Elliott examines the variety of forms and functions of portraiture in Gothic literature from Walpole to Jane Austen. Portraiture has long been associated with wealth, status, power, and inheritance, and portraits have helped police "access to spaces, resources, and privileges" (3). As the middle class grew alongside the literary Gothic from 1764 to 1835, they began commissioning portraits, and by adopting the practice of commissioning portraits, as Elliott explains, the middle class utilized "ideologies of portraiture [to] infiltrate and co-opt as well as debunk and assault aristocratic ones" (5). Thus, like the Gothic novel, the middle class's use of portraiture was subversive—to varying degrees. Bill's portrait represents the persistence of the past into the present and polices the politics of inheritance through Junior. Elliott argues Gothic narratives may "remythologize and revolutionize picture identification" by granting portraiture "unprecedented and unsurpassed authority as a site of power, entitlement, access, knowledge, identity, desire, terror, criminalization, and social revolution" (9).

Readers first encounter Bill's portrait in "Portrait." Heed's room is crowded with furniture: "a chaise, two dressers, two writing tables, side tables, chairs high-backed and low-seated" (25). And, all of these items are "under the influence of a bed behind which a man's portrait loomed" (25). The latter seems to anthropomorphize the portrait and ascribe to it a threatening, ominous quality. Morrison calls attention to the portrait through its first description, the name of the chapter, and through its anachronistic presence, as commissioning portraits ties Bill to a former age and wealth or social ascendancy. When Junior goes to sleep in Heed's bed, she feels a "peculiar new thing: protected," which is far removed from the terror she experienced at Correctional (29). In reality, Junior moves from one space of imprisonment to another. Junior has been searching for a home and a sense of belonging her entire life. At Correctional, the "nights were so terrifying" with dreams of "upright snakes on tiny feet [that] lay in wait, [with] their thin green tongues begging her to come down from the tree" (29). Thus, Correctional is akin to Eden, but it is a dangerous, fallen Eden invoking the danger associated with many gardens in Gothic writing.

In Junior's dreams, "once in while there was someone beneath the branches standing apart from the snakes, and although she could not see who it was, his being there implied rescue" (29). She would endure and freely enter these nightmares if only for a "glimpse of the stranger's face"—a face she never saw as he eventually "disappeared along with the upright snakes" (30). But, now, at One Monarch Street, something has shifted:

> Deep in sleep, her search seemed to have ended. The face hanging over her new boss's bed must have stated it. A handsome man with a G.I. Joe chin and a reassuring smile that pledged endless days of hot, tasty food; kind eyes that promised to hold a girl steady on his shoulder while she robbed apples from the highest branch. (30)

Thus, the new space begins to become the home she never had. But the imagery is suggestive of another possibility: it seems that Junior does not consider the fact that the stranger she longed for in her Correctional dreams eventually disappears with the menacing, "upright snakes." (Upon a second reading of the novel, here, readers will perceive Morrison's deft foreshadowing.)

For Junior, the Cosey house on Monarch Street is a diametrically opposite space to Correctional, and the legacy of Bill solidifies her sense of security: "As soon as she saw the stranger's portrait she knew she was home" (60). He stands in for the father she never knew, and in her dream, she rides his "shoulders through an orchard of green Granny apples heavy and thick on the boughs" (60). The Cosey house becomes the new Eden where she can eat boldly from forbidden fruit—or the comfortable life that Settlement and Correctional had denied her—supported by her deity-like father figure, Bill. Correctional taught her to "gauge the moment. Recognize a change" and to say to herself, "It's all you. And if you luck out, find yourself near an open wallet, window, or door, GO! It's all you. All of it. Good luck you found, but good fortune you made" (118).

Junior thinks that Bill, her "Good Man" in the portrait agrees; and "as she knew from the beginning, he liked to see her win" because they "recognized each other the very first night when he gazed at her from his portrait" and became acquainted in her dream (118). That same morning, she longs to see him again; she borrows a suit from Heed's closet, wanting to "undress right there in Heed's bedroom while he [Bill] watched" (118). But, Junior does not. Instead, Heed directs her to eat breakfast and return right away, but on her way back, she receives another sign that Bill is interested in her:

> On her way back to Heed … she knew for sure. In the hallway on the second floor she was flooded by his company: a tinkle of glee, a promise of more; then her attention drawn to a door opposite the room she had slept in. Ajar. A light pomade or aftershave in the air. She stepped through. Inside, a kind of office … She stroked ties and shirts in the closet; smelled his shoes; rubbed her cheek on the sleeve of his seersucker jacket. Then, finding a stack of undershorts … [undresses and] stepped into the shorts, and lay on the sofa. His happiness was unmistakable. So was his relief at having her there, handling his things and enjoying herself in front of him. Later

… Junior looked over her shoulder toward the door—still ajar—and saw the cuff of a white shirtsleeve, his hand closing the door. Junior laughed, knowing as she did that he did too. (119)

Immediately after this encounter, Junior sees Romen outside and considers him a "gift" from Bill (116). She then seduces Romen, introduces him to rough sex, and ultimately lies to and manipulates him (62). She only sees him as a "bonus" on her path to ultimately convince the rivaling women to "leave things to her" (120).

It is unclear if Bill's portrait has come to life, if he is haunting the Cosey house, or both; however, it is clear that Bill becomes an entity that actively haunts Junior while he lives on through the memories of those who knew him. Elliot argues that "theories of immanence governing portraiture tighten" the relationship between subject and image, image and ghost, and that "subject and image, sign and substance" inherit in each other (109). She explains further, "Since imaging and inherence *themselves* inhere in each other, when the portrait images the body, which images the soul, such imaging attests to their inherence" and the "ghost" is "always already in the portrait" (109, emphasis in original). In other words, the historical portrait adds not only legitimacy to one's person or status, but it also ensures immortality (akin to the first type of doppelgänger); therefore, in the early Gothic novel, for example, the portrait is always haunted by the person (and ultimately the lineage) it represents. When Junior first encounters the portrait, Heed tells her, "That's him. It was painted from a snapshot, so it's exactly like him" (26). This line and Elliot's claims about portraiture suggest that Bill's ghost may have indeed emanated from its painted frame. Junior is immediately taken with the portrait, but other characters react in different ways. In the novel's present, Christine tries not to "shiver before the 'come on' eyes in the painting over that grotesque bed" (97). Yet, like Junior, years before, Vida, Romen's grandmother, needed the security of a job, so she "believed a powerful, generous friend gazed out from the portrait hanging behind the reception desk" (45). Perspective matters because the narrator says Vida's reaction "was because she didn't know who he was looking at" (45).

The portrait was painted from a photograph in which Bill is gazing off to someone else—Celestial, the woman he loved and had an affair with for many years who was also a prostitute (188). In the final pages of *Love*, L reveals that Celestial was the true beneficiary of the will and that L killed Bill and changed his will to preserve his legacy and pride lest his love and desire win out (200–1). Here, L takes on the role of arbiter and executioner:

I just had to stop him. Had to … They never saw the real thing—witnessed by me, notarized … leaving everything to Celestial. Everything. Everything. Except a boat he left to Sandler Gibbons. It wasn't right … There wasn't but one solution. Foxglove can be quick, if you know what you're doing, and doesn't hurt all that long. (200–1, emphasis in original)

Significantly, the foxglove returns to the text. Only referenced in L's prologue and in these final words, it seems fitting that she uses the plant, a cardiac toxin that can kill and heal, to bring death to the man whose heart's desire was a request with which she disagreed. L admits that if she had read the will in 1964 instead of 1971, she would have realized what she thought was "*self-pity and remorse was really vengeance, and that his hatred of the women in his house had no level. First they disappointed him, then they defied him, then they turned his home into a cautionary lesson in black history*" (201, emphasis in original). The Cosey women dared to disappoint the patriarch, they dared to do other than he demanded, and they dared to challenge his desire.

By deeming Celestial undeserving of his wealth, L inserts herself into the politics of property—specifically "women's status as property vs. women's control over property," a theme central to the Gothic, especially the female Gothic (Sweeney qtd. in Heise-von der Lippe 175). To L, Celestial was not a worthy beneficiary. L acts out of a sense of loyalty to Bill's legacy—to the image he created for himself and the image she cherished. Yet, at the same time, L acknowledges that he is not the good man she thought he was. At the moment she decides to kill him, it seems for L, the idea that Bill is a "good bad man" or a "bad good man" crystalizes (200). Fearing change, L seeks to maintain some level of status quo through altering the will. Maintaining or restoring the status quo is a common theme in many eighteenth- and nineteenth-century novels. That is, after chaos and terror, there is a return to the status quo. Yet Morrison does not allow for such an easy conclusion, as the status quo was already broken. Morrison uses Junior to unsettle and disturb the Cosey women, and ultimately, to have a role in repairing the primary love relationship that was severed by a man's lust for power and women—the *philia* love between Heed and Christine.

(RE)DISCOVERING LOVE

The final scenes of *Love* exhibit the continual push and pull of annihilation and transformation in Gothic writing. Desperate to forge the will and identify herself as the "sweet Cosey child," Heed asks Junior to take her to the abandoned Cosey Hotel to look for a menu in the hotel's attic (like the one L used to forge Bill's will). While they search for a menu, "Junior smells baking bread, something with cinnamon" and asks if Heed smells something; Heed admits, "Smells like L" (175). Thus, another ghostly presence inserts herself into the characters' lives. Here, L seems to inhabit the role of Morrison's benevolent ancestor. Christine notices that Heed and Junior have left the house at Monarch Street; and because Heed never leaves the house, she can surmise what Heed is planning to do. Christine confronts Heed and Junior and when her eyes meet Heed's in the attic, "opening pangs of guilt, rage, fatigue, despair are replaced by a hatred so pure, so solemn, it feels beautiful, almost holy" (177).

Here is the moment of transformation. Heed falls through the attic into Christine's childhood bedroom, Christine runs to Heed's rescue and then holds her in her arms. Each woman "searches the face of the other. The holy feeling is still alive … but it is altered now, overwhelmed by desire. Old, decrepit, yet sharp … in a little girl's bedroom an obstinate skeleton stirs, clacks, refreshes itself" (177). The room is like a grave, its "solitude … like the room of a dead child, the ocean has no scent or roar" (184). The furniture in the room is "disintegrating along with the past," and the "landscape beyond this room is without color. Just a bleak ridge of stone and no one to imagine it otherwise" (184). Albeit only for a short time, this Gothic space in *Love* becomes a space of positive transformation.

The women reconcile and let go of the broken love turned to hatred by circumstance, by conniving, and by perverted lust. Heed reveals that, although she had no say in the matter, she hoped marrying Bill would allow her to be with Christine: "I wanted to be with you. Married to him, I thought I would be" (193). In Heed's last moments, they recover their childhood language and the most secret of code phrases, "Hey, Celestial" (187). This phrase holds within it radical power. As children, Heed and Christine hear a man call out, "Hey, Celestial" to a young woman wearing a red sundress. Celestial turned instead to look at them instead of Bill, "Her face was cut from cheek to ear … Her eyes locking theirs were cold and scary, until she winked at them, making their toes clench and curl with happiness" (188).[13] From that point on, whenever either girl wants to say "Amen" or "acknowledge a particularly bold, smart, risky thing, they mimicked the male voice crying, 'Hey, Celestial'" (188). In the end, Celestial is the type of "*brazen*" woman who can take a "*good bad man*" down (10, 200, emphasis in original). And so is Junior. Her scheming leads to the rediscovery of love between Heed and Christine. In her final moment, Heed reflects on the beauty of the stars at the beach when they were children: "Love," she says, "I really do" (194). Christine's last words to Heed are, "Ush-hidagay. Ush-hidagay. [Hush. Hush]" (194).

As Heed and Christine rediscover their love, Junior encounters romantic love—a feeling beyond the sexual attraction she feels for Romen. Overcome by the aroma of L's ghostly "baking bread," Junior returns to One Monarch Street to seek out her "Good Man" (177). Junior cannot tell what he thinks, but she is convinced "he would laugh when she told him, showed him the forged menu his airhead wife thought would work, and the revisions Junior had made in case it did … It was a long shot … but it might turn out the way she dreamed" (178).[14] But, she cannot find him in any of the usual places, so she goes "directly to him" and "there he was. Smiling welcome above Heed's bed. Her Good Man" (178). She seeks Bill's approval, and her anxiety reveals the possibility that she knows she has disappointed him. After abandoning Christine and Heed at the hotel, she invites Romen to have sex in Heed's bed, underneath Bill's portrait. Romen resists because of "that face hanging on the wall," and later admits that he "hate[s] that picture. Like screwing in front of your father" (179). Romen resists the gaze of the portrait, which suggests that he is not susceptible to the destructive influence of the past that Bill represents. Romen's character holds promise for a different type of man, one governed by discretion over lust and power because when Junior tells Romen what happened at the hotel, he comes to the women's rescue. The revelation is engendered by Junior's transformation. Perhaps as Heed opens to love, she is able to as well—she is her doppelgänger after all. Reflecting on her blossoming, unexpected love for Romen, Junior feels the "jitter intensified and suddenly she knew its name. Brand-new, completely alien, it invaded her, making her feel wide open and whole, already approved and confirmed" (196).

In a 2003 interview with Pam Hudson in which Morrison talks about her new novel, *Love*, she says,

> The idea of a wanton woman is something I have inserted into almost all of my books … An outlaw figure who is disallowed in the community because of her imagination or activity or status—that kind of anarchic figure has always fascinated me. And the benefits they bring with them, in spite of the fact that they are either dismissed or upbraided—something about their presence is constructive in the long run … In *Love*, Junior is a poor, rootless, free-floating young woman—a survivor, a manipulator, a hungry person—but she does create a space where people can come with their better selves. (2)

This is one message of *Love*: an encounter with otherness can inspire us to create something greater or better in ourselves; and perhaps through that inspiration, we can work to shape a better world. Both Celestial and Junior are "wanton," "rootless, free-floating" women. Some characters are

---

[13] The fine scar indicates that Celestial is the same nine- or ten-year-old girl from whose face Billy (Bill's late son) removes a homemade fishhook under the watchful gaze of his father, Bill (101). I am indebted to Mayberry for noting this connection in her chapter on *Love*.

[14] Junior revises the will and names herself as beneficiary in the event of Heed's death.

fascinated by them and others fear them. It is important to consider that Heed and Christine's most secret code phrase is "Hey, Celestial." This phrase embodies the two girls' acceptance of otherness, which mimics their original openness to one another despite their difference in socioeconomic status and speaks to the complexity of Black life and experience in the United States. *Love* mourns a period many did not realize was lost or repressed. L's spectral voice conveys the message in kind while bringing to light the specific struggles that haunt and permeate the lives of African Americans and African American communities in the twentieth century and beyond.[15]

WORKS CITED

"About Us." *American Beach Museum*. http://www.americanbeachmuseum.org/. Accessed Nov. 8, 2015.

Botting, Fred. *Gothic*. Routledge, 1996.

Boyd, Molly. "Gothicism." *The Companion to Southern Literature: Themes, Genres, Places, People, Movements, and Motifs*, edited by Joseph M. Flora, et al. Louisiana State UP, 2002, pp. 311–16.

Carter, Angela. "Notes on the Gothic Mode." *The Iowa Review*, vol. 6, nos. 3/4, 1975, pp. 132–4.

Caruth, Cathy, ed. *Unclaimed Experience: Trauma, Narrative, and History*. Johns Hopkins UP, 1996.

Chase, Larry. "History of American Beach." *National Park Service*. Apr. 2003. http://www.nps.gov/foca/learn/history culture/ambch_history.htm. Accessed April 28, 2015.

Dallis, Jameela F. *Haunted Narratives: The Afterlife of Gothic Aesthetics in Contemporary Transatlantic Women's Fiction*. 2015. Department of English and Comparative Literature, The University of North Carolina at Chapel Hill, PhD dissertation.

Elliott, Kamilla. *Portraiture and British Gothic Fiction: The Rise of Picture Identification, 1764–1835*. Johns Hopkins, 2012.

"Foxglove Flowers." *FlowerInfo.Org*. http://flowerinfo.org/foxglove-flowers. Last accessed Nov. 8, 2015.

Frank, Frederick S. *The First Gothics: A Critical Guide to the English Gothic Novel*. Routledge, 1987.

Freud, Sigmund. *The Uncanny*. Translated by David Mclintock, Penguin, 2003.

Fry, Gladys-Marie. *Night Riders in Black Folk History*. University of Tennessee Press, 1975.

Goddu, Teresa. *Gothic America: Narrative, History, and Nation*. Columbia, 1997.

Haggerty, George E. *Queer Gothic*. U of Illinois P, 2006.

Heise-von der Lippe, Anya. "Others, Monster, Ghosts: Representations of the Female Gothic Body in Toni Morrison's *Beloved* and *Love*." *The Female Gothic: New Directions*, edited by Diana Wallace and Andrew Smith, Palgrave Macmillan, 2009, pp. 166–79.

Hudson, Pam. "The Truest Eye." *O, The Oprah Magazine*, Nov. 2003, Apr. 28, 2015. http://www.oprah.com/omagazine/Toni-Morrison-Talks-Love.

Langer, Adam. "Star Power." *Book*. Nov./Dec. 2003, pp. 40–6.

Ledoux, Ellen Malenas. *Social Reform in Gothic Writing: Fantastic Forms of Change, 1764–1834*. Palgrave Macmillan, 2013.

Mayberry, Susan Neal. *Can't I Love What I Criticize?: The Masculine and Morrison*. U of Georgia P, 2007.

---

[15]In one reading, *Love* calls for a reevaluation of our grand narratives of domestic bliss and the American Dream. It seems that in a stratified, racist society, the achievement of such dreams or the adherence to such narratives comes at a costly price corrupting Bill, Heed, Christine, and Junior in the process. In *Love* we see that costly price is the disintegration of the family unit—incest and pedophilia and the elevation of one man's desire over the needs of a girl for whom he should be a benevolent ancestor figure.

McKay, Nellie. "An Interview with Toni Morrison." *Conversations with Toni Morrison*, edited by Danille Taylor-Guthrie, UP of Mississippi, pp. 138–55.

Morrison, Toni. *Beloved*. Vintage, 2004.

Morrison, Toni. *Jazz*. Vintage, 2004.

Morrison, Toni. Foreword. *Love, by Toni Morrison*. Vintage, 2005, pp. i–xii.

Morrison, Toni. *Love*. Knopf, 2003.

Morrison, Toni. "Rootedness: The Ancestor as Foundation." *Black Women Writers (1950–1980): A Critical Evaluation*, edited by Mari Evans, Anchor, 1984, pp. 339–45. Rpt. in *What Moves at the Margin*, edited by Carolyn C. Denard, UP of Mississippi, 2008, pp. 56–64.

Morrison, Toni. *The Bluest Eye*. Quality Paperback Book Club, 2003.

Phelts, Marsha Dean. *An American Beach for African Americans*. UP of Florida, 1997.

Showalter, Elaine. "A Tangled Web." *The Guardian*. Nov. 28, 2003. http://www.theguardian.com/books/2003/nov/29/fiction.tonimorrison.

Tally, Justine. "Toni Morrison's *Love*: The Celestial Whore and Other Female 'Outlaws.'" *Cultural Migrations and Gendered Subjects: Colonial and Postcolonial Representations of the Female Body*, edited by Silvia Pilar, et al., Cambridge Scholars P, 2011, pp. 13–26.

Vega-González, Susana. "Toni Morrison's *Love* and the Trickster Paradigm." *Revista Alicantina de Estudios Ingleses*, vol. 18, 2005, pp. 275–89.

Walpole, Horace. *The Castle of Otranto*, edited by W. S. Lewis, Oxford UP, 2008.

Wester, Maisha L. *African American Gothic: Screams from Shadowed Places*. Palgrave Macmillan, 2012.

CHAPTER NINE

"A Home for the Heart": Rootlessness, Richard Wright, and Toni Morrison's *Home*

LESLIE ELAINE FROST

Keep the home fires burning,
While your hearts are yearning.
Though your lads are far away
They dream of home.
There's a silver lining
Through the dark clouds shining,
Turn the dark cloud inside out
Till the boys come home.

"Keep the Home Fires Burning (Til the Boys Come Home)"
Ivor Novello/Lena Guilbert Ford, 1914

Toni Morrison's taut tenth novel *Home* is set at the end of the first global conflict in which American troops were integrated and at the beginning of legal jurisprudence's upending of the Southern Jim Crow system of apartheid. The story centers on Black Korean War veteran Frank "Smart" Money, who returns "home" to the United States from war only to be called "home" to Georgia to save his only sister. In a novel whose title is so richly evocative of place, it is a story filled with movement and, significantly, movement symbolic of Black history and experience. Money's trip South to save his sister Cee and bring her back to Lotus, Georgia, reverses their childhood experience of being terrorized and driven with their neighbors from their homes. His travel by rail with his safety dependent on the bearings provided by the "Green Book" recalls and reverses the nineteenth-century Underground Railroad escapes of the enslaved north to freedom.[1] Physically on the move,

---

[1] Frank Money copies out addresses from this book, a guide written by a Harlem postal worker named Victor Green. Its full name was *The Negro Motorist Green Book: An International Travel Guide*, and it was published from 1936 to 1967 (Ribaud 111).

Money is also on a path of psychological healing. He has been traumatized by the violence and loss he experienced of wars waged both abroad and at home, and he bears deep grief and guilt over his murder of an innocent. Frank Money is a wandering Odysseus; he is a broken Hawkeye Pierce; never described as Black, Money's responses to the world mark him as a Black man raised in and returning to the stifling confines of the American apartheid system. As Morrison's place-name of "Lotus" suggests, Money's experiences in Asia and America are intimately paralleled, and the psychological damage wrought by war balanced precariously on the fragile social scaffolding protecting the poor, Black, Southern self in Jim Crow, mid-century America. Frank "Smart" Money is a soldier of his time and place, a man whose experiences abroad reshape the meaning of his life at home.

A twenty-first-century America looking back to 1950s-era mass-media representation as history, as well as what politics are created by such nostalgia, animated Morrison's decision to write *Home*. If in book after book, Morrison "reimagines the lost history of her people," as early critic John Leonard notes (*Toni Morrison: Critical Perspectives* 37), in numerous interviews, Morrison describes how she fits *Home* into that larger project. "I was trying to take the scab off the 50s, the general idea of it as very comfortable, happy, nostalgic. *Mad Men*. Oh, please. There was a horrible war you didn't call a war where 58,000 people died. There was McCarthy" (Brockes). The main themes that she wanted to touch upon, Morrison said, were war, anti-communism, and the medical experimentation on Black people, prisoners, and soldiers. But moreover, as she said in her Cornell conversation with colleague and friend Claudia Brodsky, "When I heard these people for the first election of Barack Obama they were saying we want to take our country back and I was wondering, 'Back to where?' and it was really the '50s. I mean I think that's what the 'back' meant" (Brodsky).

Nostalgia for a "comfortable, happy" era carries powerful political weight in America. As scholar Erin Penner notes: "Such narratives only inhibit political and social progress by ignoring the through-line of social friction in America" (343). Reviewers picked up on Morrison's theme: "'*Home*,' Morrison's latest novel, is a comparatively brief tale set in the early 1950s, a concentrated look at a time many people—especially politicians—use as a symbol of America as a powerful, peaceful paradise, where families were stable and "home" was a word that meant nothing but goodness and safety" (Churchwell). Of *Home* (2012), *Washington Post* reviewer Ron Charles writes, "This scarily quiet tale packs all the thundering themes Morrison has explored before. She's never been more concise, though, and that restraint demonstrates the full range of her power." Not all critics or readers appreciated Morrison's departure from what Margaret Atwood called her "antiminimalist lyricism" (Leonard 35). *Home* received generally positive but mixed reviews. Popular critical consensus seems to be that what *Home* does, *Beloved* does better. It was not listed on the New York Public Library's list of six novels to start with when reading Morrison; it was ranked tenth of eleven by news and entertainment site *Inquisitor*. It was left off of lists of both travel blog *Culture Trip's* "Five Essential Toni Morrison Classics You Should Read" and *Rolling Stone's* 2019 "9 Most Essential Works by Toni Morrison." Weaned on *Beloved's* evocation of trauma, critics seem bemused by the redemption of *Home*. "*Home* should be relentless, unsparing, but Morrison relents halfway through, and spares everyone—most of all herself," concludes Sarah Churchwell for *The Guardian* (2012). Yet *Home* continues Morrison's work with characterization, in which she does, as early reviewer Ann Snitow writes, "what Dickens did: create wild, flamboyant, abstractly symbolic characters who are at the same time not grotesques but sweetly alive, full of deep feeling?" (29) And if its almost allegorical structure curtails the rich pleasures of her previous works, what remains central is Morrison's lifelong project: to memorialize the history of the Black American experience.

In yoking the international to the national through the figure of the soldier returning home, *Home* astutely recalls a shifting Black American experience and identity that undergirds Money's odyssey. Often visually recalled through the homogenized white vision of American television and aurally remembered for the explosion of Black sound in rock and roll, the 1950s saw profound change. *Brown v. Board of Education* heralded new American civil rights at home while American troops in conflict in Korea solidified the American international presence in a Cold War abroad. Both events contributed to movement in America's racial culture. Historian Benjamin Quarles notes in his 1964 *The Negro in the Making of America* that international communities formed in the 1950s offered great hope to and, in a sense, internationalized Black Americans: "Negroes welcomed the U.N. because it would sensitize the world to the problems of race and color and provide a sounding board for yellow, black, and brown people to press their case" (230). As the United States took its position as the leader of the Western world, and Black soldiers returned home from the Korean conflict, Black Americans demanded it fulfill its democratic promise at home.

With its place name of Lotus as the "battlefield" of Frank Money's childhood, Morrison gestures toward this 1950s-era globalized perspective, one expressed by American novelist Richard Wright in another slim book, 1957's *White Man, Listen!* In his dedication, Wright expresses post–Second World War Black hopes for a national reckoning at home through global solidarity. He internationalizes the meaning of place, memory, self, and family when he invokes home as both reward and solace for those struggling to build meaningful lives out of the poverty, cultural displacement, and oppression that are the legacies of slavery and colonialism. *White Man, Listen!* is a collection drawn from a series of European lectures given by a "rootless man" who can "make myself at home almost anywhere on this earth and can, if I've a mind to and when I'm attracted to a landscape or a mood of life, easily sink myself into the most alien and widely differing environments" (*White Man*; xvi–xvii). Wright attributes this ability neither to the technology of his era nor to a particular facility of his. "I must confess that this is not personal achievement of mine; this attitude was never striven for … I've been shaped to this mental stance by the kind of experiences that I have fallen heir to" (xvii). Wright dedicates *White Man, Listen!* to Westernized people of color, the

> lonely outsiders who exist precariously/on the clifflike margins of many cultures—men who are distrusted, misunderstood, maligned, criticized by Left and Right, Christian, and pagan—men who carry on their frail but indefatigable shoulders the best of two worlds—and who, amidst confusion and stagnation, seek desperately for a home for their hearts: a home which, if found, could be a home for the hearts of all men. (xvii)

Wright was in Korea in the 1950s, though not as a soldier. He attended what he called the "meeting of the rejected" (*The Color Curtain* 12): members of Asian and African states, many of which were newly independent, who gathered in Bandung, Indonesia, in 1955. Wright understood that the Black American experience found corollary in the experiences globally of all peoples of color.[2]

---

[2]Developing countries in the Middle East and newly independent nations in Africa and Asia sent representatives to Bandung, Indonesia, in April 1955 for the Afro-Asian Conference to discuss issues relating to global power relations and postcolonialism.

Frank Money returns from Korea seeking desperately for a home for his heart. Both in his later writings and in his novelistic autobiography *Black Boy*, Wright is an insistent presence haunting the margins of *Home*. Yet his voice raised against a Western world that marginalized people of color was itself marginalized in the American popular culture of *Home*'s setting. Disavowed by former protégés Ralph Ellison and James Baldwin, Wright was living in Paris and struggling to make a living. His voice—its political tenor linked to both the Communist Party affiliation of his youth and its unyielding rhetorical intensity—was out of vogue in the new Cold War. Moreover, Americans were tired of war and the economy was booming. Although 78 percent of Americans supported sending aid to Korea, support quickly eroded, and the "police action" was called "The Forgotten War" even in its own time.[3] Americans got down to the business of building highways and making money in a postwar boom. The new mass media entertainment of television programming reflected a comfortable world of white mobility and aspiration, subsuming both historic racial, social, and political fissures and the current events of change.[4]

Literary allusions from Morrison's previous novels and more populate *Home* like a community of friendly spirits. As Vicent Cucarella-Ramon notes, "As in many of her novels, Morrison resorts to intertextual allusions within her own narrative to burnish or simply ruminate about key concepts such as racism, healing, spirituality, or, as in this case, masculinity" (2017). Morrison spoke often about *Home*, answering many of the interpretive questions raised by the novel's allusive and elliptical style, at least as concerning authorial intention. But as clearly as symbolic trees recall Paul D's journey north and medical experiments recall Sethe's horror at the hands of Schoolteacher and as much as the couple bloodied and humiliated on the train recall Cholly Breedlove's humiliation and the slicing of honeydew reminds us of the corn in *Beloved*, as clearly or perhaps more does Frank Money's character and world of Lotus, Georgia, step outside of Morrison's fiction to recall the self and world of Richard Wright. Like Frank, Wright was a rootless boy who became a rootless man. And if *Home*'s allusions are as diverse as *The Odyssey*, *Invisible Man*, *M*A*S*H*, and *Bailey's Café* and if it evokes symbols, characters, and themes from *Beloved* and *The Bluest Eye*, the rootlessness that is the heart of Frank's struggle, and his disconnection from community find their source and the full extent of their meaning in Wright's works, particularly *Black Boy*.[5] The lens of Wright's experiences he had "fallen heir to" and recounted in *Black Boy* as well as his mid-century considerations of white oppression of "colored mankind," a grouping of Black, Asian, and Brown cultures and peoples, focuses our analyses of the places, time, and characters of *Home*. Drawing on Wright, *Home* is filled in; the literary history of Black books, the creation-as-remembrance, that is Morrison's project is deepened.

Wright is perhaps most powerfully evoked in *Home* through the description of Frank and Cee's childhood experiences in the fictional Georgia town of Lotus. First published in 1945, *Black Boy*

---

[3]According to *The Gallop News Brief*, "President Harry S. Truman sent U.S. ground troops into Korea on June 30, 1950. At that time, 78% of Americans said they approved of Truman's decision to send military aid, and 15% disapproved. By the following year, however, public support had eroded, and it fluctuated thereafter, in response to events in the war" (Crabtree).

[4]News media carried coverage of major civil rights events and white backlash violence of the decade, including the Montgomery bus boycott and other nonviolent civil rights action, the murder of Emmett Till in 1955, and the 1957 integration of Central High School in Little Rock, Arkansas.

[5]The phrase is from Wright's text for *Twelve Million Black Voices: A Folk History of the Negro in the United States* published in 1941.

remembers Wright's Southern boyhood and young manhood. Born in 1908 on a former plantation in Mississippi, Wright moved with his family again and again in search of the economic stability that would provide enough food for his mother and her two sons. Wright describes his family's peripatetic life moving from house to house as they teetered at the edge of disaster. After his father left them, his mother sought various jobs that would provide stability, but was finally forced to move in with her extended family. At home with his aunt and uncle who would provide the first table to satiate young Richard's ever-present hunger, he glimpses another, more stable world. But after his uncle was murdered by white men who wanted his thriving business, the family flees to his grandmother's house. After years of peripatetic schooling, poor diet, and alienation from both his family and the life of the mind he connects with through books, Richard makes his way to Memphis where he works to earn money to move out of the South.

Wright describes a childhood rooted in fear and alienation. His mother beat him to teach him how to do right. His grandmother's ferocious and unrelenting Seventh Day Adventism and fear for the state of her grandson's soul would ever cement Richard's indifference to religion and religious practice.[6] Rarely able to attend school for a full year, he writes his first story for publication in eighth grade. Richard forges a card to borrow the books where he discovers a world of ideas where he wants to live. But to help the family, he takes on a variety of odd jobs that seemingly invariably lead to the petty dishonesty and thievery that he describes as one of the few open opportunities available in the Southern Black working world. As Richard sees himself falling into the life of petty crime that sustains others, he resolves to escape the South and moves alone to Memphis "making the first lap in my journey to a land where I could live with a little less fear" (*Black Boy* 207). Richard condemns the South he is leaving behind: "This was the culture from which I sprang. This was the terror from which I fled" (*Black Boy* 257).

Black Boy unflinchingly details the emotional and physical deprivations placed upon young Richard by his own family as it chronicles the force of Southern racism that conditioned his upbringing. It identifies the fear that shadows the adults of his young world, fear which they, of necessity, try to instill in their children. *Black Boy* follows and deepens Wright's 1940 novel *Native Son*'s searing indictment of racism on the moral and psychological development of young Black men. Some critics and friends have contended that Wright did not live the bleakness imposed on his childhood in *Black Boy*. Writes Claudia Tate, "Although it is probably true that Black Boy contains many exaggerated and even fictitious incidents, the emotions that they excite within Richard truthfully adhere to Wright's emotional existence" (119). Importantly, the events of *Black Boy* adhere to the emotional existence of others: in his foreword to the 2006 edition of *Black Boy*, novelist Edward P. Jones, who grew up in the early 1960s, writes of his identification with Richard's experiences. "Wright was living a southern life I knew in the city: one of constant moving from one slum house to another—the heart wears out in having to pick itself up and make a new home so often" (ix).

The privation, beatings, and the terror Richard experiences are only glimpses of the conditions that undergird, as footings uphold a house's foundation, the individual emotional existence and a history of Black masculinity presented in *Home*. In its major elements of character and plot, *Black*

---

[6]Wright would have four Bibles in his library, according to Michel Fabre *in Richard Wright: Books and Writers* (12–13). Fabre's note: "A few years under the care of his religious grandmother left Richard Wright steeped in the language of the Bible—he says that he has never known a Negro who didn't read the Bible" (Cameron).

Boy parallels *Home*. A mother's love diminished by the effort of provision. A grandmother's stony heart. Forced migration. The horror of sadistic, ritualized lynching. *Black Boy* fills in the gaps of Frank Money's painful childhood. Morrison writes, "Money ... hated Lotus. Its unforgiving population, its isolation, and especially its indifference to the future were tolerable only if his buddies were there with him" (16). The character Frank Money tells her "*Lotus, Georgia, is the worst place in the world, worse than any battlefield*" (83, emphasis in original). *Black Boy* narrates stories that fill in the ellipses of *Home*; Morrison's almost allegorical minimalism is informed by the lyrical, rich interiority of Wright's novelistic autobiography.

The absence of the domestic home is at the heart of Wright's childhood memories and Money's childhood. As Wright's later description of a "home for the heart" and Jones's identification with *Black Boy*'s rootlessness attest, the home that is missing creates both an ontological lack and psychological trauma. Wright described this psychology of poor Southern Black people in his 1941 essay for *Twelve Million Black Voices* published by the Farm Security Administration thusly:

> THE WORD "NEGRO," the term by which, orally or in print, we black folk in the United States are usually designated, is not really a name at all nor a description, but a psychological island whose objective form is the most unanimous fiat in all American history ...
> This island, within whose confines we live, is anchored in the feelings of millions of people, and is situated in the midst of the sea of white faces we meet each day; and, by and large, as three hundred years of time has borne our nation into the twentieth century, its rocky boundaries have remained unyielding to the waves of our hope that dash against it. (30)

What Wright refers to as a "psychological island" is an alienated individual life lived apart from communal support and without familial refuge. It is the condition of being profoundly existentially adrift. Wright argues that race, held in his time as a scientific category determined by biological criteria and immersed in a logic of empirical inquiry, is instead a projection of the psychology of, the "feelings of," white people upon the lives of Black folk. These white feelings, buttressed by laws and traditions, form a kind of psychotic force field. This field of force circumscribes the lives and possibilities of Black Americans for generations. There is no shelter nor protection; there is no safe home as sanctuary.

An opposition to this psychological state is that of the individual rooted in community and secure in the possibility of reflection that is the foundation of a political life, or a life engaged in civic individual and communal activity. In the fictional spaces of Morrison's worlds, home can be a refuge and site of communal engagement, but it is not safe. As critic Nancy Jesser notes of *Beloved*, her most powerful examination of the meaning of home, "Morrison, through a complex interweaving of peopled spaces, shows how homes and communities serve as places to gather strength, formulate strategy, and rest, even as they are insufficient to the task of 'solving' institutional and social ills" (325). The story of *Beloved* is inextricably tied to a rootedness in place; the exploration of the limits of home is predicated on 124 Bluestone Road belonging to Sethe and her family and being the site of both Beloved's murder and the memorial of her existence. The story of *Home*, told in media res, begins with the story of forced migration of his family when Frank Money was five and his mother was pregnant with his sister Cee. Driven out of Banderas County, Texas, by a white mob, the whole town leaves everything behind but what they can carry. The migration and the loss of the established community, its wealth, and its stability, is the beginning of memory for Frank.

Both *Black Boy* and *Home* begin stories of Black masculinity with memories of individual transgression against home.[7] With his grandmother lying ill in the next room and having been admonished to be good, young Richard becomes curious to see what will happen if he brings the leaping yellow light of the fire to the intricate lace of the curtains. "My idea was growing, blooming. Now I was wondering just how the long fluffy white curtains would look if I lit a bunch of straws and held it under them" (*Black Boy* 4). Warned against it by his brother, he lights the drapes on fire. "Red circles were eating into the white cloth, then a flare of flames shot out. Startled, I backed away. The fire soared to the ceiling and I trembled in fright" (4). As the flames shoot into the room and smoke fills his lungs, Richard flees in terror to the crawlspace under the house. "Nobody would find me there. I crawled under the house and crept into a dark hollow of a brick chimney and balled myself into a tight knot. My mother must not find me and whip me for what I had done" (5). Lying still despite his mother's frantic calls and the wailing arrival of the fire engine, Richard stays curled up against the chimney, certain that if he is found he will be beaten. He *is* found and dragged out by his father. He *is* beaten by his terrified mother, so badly, he writes, that he nearly dies.

Home also begins with a childhood transgression. Money and his sister Cee slip through a hole under the fence to go outside of town. "We shouldn't have been anywhere near that place. Like most farmland outside Lotus, Georgia, this one here had plenty of scary warning signs. The threats hung from wire mesh fences with wooden stakes every fifty or so feet" (*Home* 3). Money and his sister Cee witness—though they don't understand it—a burial. "Never lifting our heads, just peeping through the grass, we saw them pull a body from a wheelbarrow and throw it into a hole already waiting" (4). When he thinks later of their adventure, he represses his memory of the murder, remembering vividly not a *"black foot with its creamy pink and mud-streaked sole being whacked into the grave,"* but two stallions fighting gloriously over a herd of mares (4). *"They rose up like men. We saw them. Like men they stood"* (3, emphases in original). Like Wright's young Richard, Frank and Cee stay quietly curled up together as they watch the body buried, certain that if found they will be in trouble. Unlike Richard, when they get home, they are not discovered. Some event about which they are not told has focused the adults' attention.

Both transgressions are dangerous, and, in both cases, children escape a full accounting. Both begin with children's curiosity about a world of which they know little and remind adults of that remarkable childhood capacity for heedless bravery that we spend the rest of our lives shaking our heads over. But setting the transgression of *Black Boy* beside that of *Home* draws as much attention to difference as to similarity. The child of Wright's *Black Boy* is telling a story of Black masculinity in which transgression against family and home, begun in exploratory wonder, sets him at odds and apart from his family. His "I," the strong and insistent focus of so many declarative sentences, is alone. The first pages of Wright's narrative serve to demonstrate how the transgressive childhood acts of Black boys do not create an irrevocable arc toward criminality. As Maurice Wallace notes, Black masculinity has often been made visible to a racialized gaze only through particular rigidly defined categories, the most prominent of which is transgression (7). In the context of *Black Boy*, the anecdote showcases the void in which young Richard forms his earliest sense of self. This transgression, later contextualized by conditions of Black life defined by powerlessness, fear, and want, takes on particular intensity within the autobiography. Set against omnipresent, brutalizing

---

[7]Maurice O. Wallace writes of Wright's enduring interest in crime, criminality, and Black juvenile delinquency as a function of white racism (134).

forces, transgression becomes an act of self-definition. Wright's curious "I," living a childhood without positive guidance, growing up in a South of lynchings, poor schooling, poverty, and hunger, wants to burn down the house. Addressing critiques that this bleak world overshadows the development of this "I," Ralph Ellison wrote in "Richard Wright's Blues" that

> Wright assumed that the nucleus of plastic sensibility is a human heritage—the right and the opportunity to dilate, deepen, and enrich sensibility—democracy. Thus the drama of *Black Boy* lies in its depiction of what occurs when Negro sensibility attempts to fulfill itself in the undemocratic South. Here it is not the individual that is the immediate focus, as in Joyce's Stephen Hero, but that upon which his sensibility was nourished. (267)

Yet, as Ellison also notes, Wright's conflict with his community was in the assertion of the individual. And in both the particulars of this undemocratic South and in the individual separate from community, Morrison rewrites Black masculinity. In *Home*, Cee and Frank, forming a unified "we," want only to remain unnoticed together. They are bonded in both the adventure of transgression and the trauma of their experience. This "we" will be split both by the passage into adulthood and in italicized chapters in which Frank Money as character seems to be confiding in Toni Morrison, author, about the story she is writing. "*Since you're set on telling my story, whatever you think and whatever you write down, know this: I really forgot about the burial. I only remembered the horses. They were so beautiful. So brutal. And they stood like men*" (5; emphases in original). This memory both sets up the story's theme of displacement and foregrounds the separation between the two bonded siblings when Frank leaves Lotus to enlist in the Army.

But it will be his bond with his sister and to reconnect with that formative "we" that initiates his return. When he receives a note that she is in danger ("Come fast. She be dead if you tarry" [*Home* 8]), he returns to the South. The story of the soldier returning home is one of the oldest stories in the Western tradition. But while Money is a soldier and returning to the land of his birth, his is a very modern retelling. He brings the trauma of his experiences with him to a world that did not yet understand the psychological effects of war. In addition, as a Black soldier he is exchanging one battlefield for another. This second reality is expressed plainly in Frank's character telling the author in one of the italicized chapters, "*Lotus is the worst. Worse than any battlefield. At least on the field there is a goal, excitement, daring, and some chance of winning* (83). The only reason he is returning to the place that is not a home of Lotus, Georgia, is to help save his sister. Of this choice, Money's character tells Morrison his author, "*Don't paint me as some enthusiastic hero. I had to go, but I dreaded it*" (84). Home is not home. "*There was no goal other than breathing, nothing to win and, save for somebody else's quiet death, nothing to survive or worth surviving for. If not for my two friends I would have suffocated by the time I was twelve*" (83, emphases in original). No meaning adheres to any Lotus connection outside of his family except the friends who will go to war with him. Frank's remembrance of a place both barren and bleak connects his character to the puzzling epigraph in which the speaker asks, "Whose house is this?/Whose night keeps out the light, in here?/Say, who owns this house?/It's not mine" (109). As Emmanuelle Andres notes, "The overwhelming feeling in the epigraph is that something is off someplace, that something doesn't belong" (110). That something that does not belong is the unfamiliarity of a house whose lock fits one's key but is not home, the South of Frank's childhood. Money is unable to live in community, existing far from home as a lonely outsider on the margins of others' cultures, others' communities. "The war still haunted him" (*Home* 76), we are told. The death of his best friends, and that of a young Korean girl, still haunt him, he tells us in italicized chapters. In his journey back to where he came from where his critically ill sister needs him to care for her, Money struggles with the ghosts of the dead to whom he feels responsible. These ghosts stem both from his childhood and from his violent Korean War encounters with the broader marginalized world. It is only when he returns home to his heart and fully confronts his memories and their meanings that he becomes whole.

Frank's war trauma parallels that of one of the most popular television characters of all time. On the last episode of *M*A*S*H*, Hawkeye Pierce has been hospitalized for erratic behavior and sudden outbursts. Over the course of the episode, through conversations with the show's longtime psychiatrist character, Hawkeye gradually remembers the truth of a memory: that on a bus ride back to the beach in which the M*A*S*H unit picks up refugees and comes under shelling, he frightens a mother into smothering her child. First remembering the trip as a fun journey with just the members of the unit, he then adds a woman with a chicken that he yells at to keep quiet. Through going over the bus ride over and over with the psychiatrist, he finally realizes what he has done and in confronting his grief and his guilt, begins to heal.

We had already met psychologist Sidney Freedman in earlier episodes. The sixth season "War of Nerves," written and directed by Alan Alda, aired on October 11, 1977. In this episode, Freedman has gone to the front to check up on a former patient. Both are caught in artillery fire and end up at the 4077th M*A*S*H unit where Freedman finds a camp descended into squabbling and divisiveness; he is enlisted to help people talk through their anxieties and fears. Personnel turn the task of burning diseased clothes into a massive bonfire and as they watch the fire burn, the 4077th (and entire cast) sings "Keep the Home Fires Burning." This visually and aurally haunting evocation of community emphasizes how distant the war is from home.

A poor Black man, Frank does not get a psychiatrist, and in fact his only experience in the mental hospital is when he is arrested, robbed, and wakes up drugged up and restrained. In distinct contradiction to wartime relationships on television, both of his friends die and his comradeship with other soldiers is sundered. But he has not only experienced terrible things, but has done them. Frank confides his shame and horror to the author; he has Morrison to hear his story. In a poignant twist on the best-known evocation of the Korean War, she sits with him; she listens to his words and in italicized chapters she transcribes them. They are a circling of the truth. Guarding a garbage dump, Frank sees a Korean girl child scavenging among the piles of rotting food and garbage. She comes to pick through trash and she first reminds him of Cee and then of homey things, a bird feeding her young or a hen scratching in the dirt. And then another soldier appears:

> *As he approaches her she raises up and in what looks like a hurried, even automatic, gesture she says something in Korean. Sounds like "Yum-yum." She smiles, reaches for the soldier's crotch, touches it. Yum-yum! As soon as I look away from her hand to her face, see the two missing teeth, the fall of black hair above eager eyes, he blows her away. Only the hand remains in the trash, clutching its treasure, a spotted, rotting orange.* (95, emphasis in original)

It is a terrible story, and one that readers, even those not conditioned by watching the final episode of *M*A*S*H* with the rest of America[8] or seeing it on ubiquitous reruns, might well suspect covers up a more terrible truth. Morrison lets him tell the story he remembers until he can tell the story

---

[8] The final episode of *M*A*S*H* is the most watched television episode in history by many millions. Only nine Superbowls have had more viewers.

that is true—that it was his crotch that the little girl touched, his finger that pulled the trigger, his horrified knowledge that he had been aroused—and take responsibility for his action and fully realize the intensity of his grief and guilt. The novel is, then, in a sense, an extended series of therapy sessions. Through the act of listening, the novelist lets flower the sensibility of her character and the significance of his life, two fundamental aspects of humanity denied her ordinary Black soldier by a white America that constrained the possibilities of his life.

Morrison deploys language to depict the psychic and spiritual pain of living in a white world. The novel literally withholds color from the text until the end. Morrison has discussed how she has had to free herself from the "white gaze." "I have had reviews in the past that have accused me of not writing about White people … as though our lives have no meaning and no depth without the White gaze. And I've spent my entire writing life trying to make sure that the White gaze was not the dominant one in any of my books" (Charlie Rose interview). In *Home*, Money's trauma manifests in his vision fading to white and in the landscape he travels, as well as of his memories in Korea, and descriptions range almost solely in a color palette of whites and grays. Morrison has discussed the stylistic choice to wash color from the dangerous white world Money has to negotiate in *Home.* She linguistically traps Money in that white gaze until he goes to Atlanta and frees his sister, and arrives in Lotus, feverish sister Cee in his arms. Once back in Lotus, he discovers a landscape awash in color under a "menacing" and "malevolent" sun (117). "Every sidewalk sported flowers protecting vegetables from disease and predators—marigolds, nasturtiums, dahlias. Crimson, purple, pink, and China blue. Had these trees always been this green?" (117). Cee has begun quilt making as she heals from her wounds, and she will make a quilt of "lilac, crimson, yellow, and dark navy blue" (143).

Poor Black men like Frank Money did not get a therapist, but Richard Wright helped open the Lafargue Mental Hygiene Clinic in Harlem in 1946 to counter the devastating psychic toll of American racism that Morrison encodes in her erasure of color (Doyle). In *Black Boy* he writes,

> Whenever I thought of the essential bleakness of black life in America, I knew that Negroes had never been allowed to catch the full spirit of Western civilization, that they lived somehow in it but not of it. And when I brooded upon the cultural barrenness of black life, I wondered if clean, positive tenderness, love, honor, loyalty, and the capacity to remember were native with man. I asked myself if these human qualities were not fostered, won, struggled and suffered for, preserved in ritual from one generation to another. (37)

Wright would build upon this idea in *White Man, Listen!* as he argues that the "ultimate effect of white Europe on Asia and Africa was to cast millions into a spiritual void; I maintain that it suffused their lives with a sense of meaninglessness" (34). This meaninglessness drives a search for an idea that will alleviate the pain it induces; Wright argues that

> the dynamic concept of the void that must be filled, a void created by a thoughtless and brutal impact of the West upon a billion and a half people, is more powerful than the concept of class conflict, and more universal. (35)

And yet, directly after recounting the tale of his arsonist tendencies in *Black Boy*, Wright describes childhood thusly: "Each event spoke with a cryptic tongue" (*Black Boy* 7). He then recalls, in a series of gorgeously realized images, the surrounding world that molded his being and aspirations. "There were the echoes of nostalgia I heard in the crying strings of wild geese winging south against a bleak autumn sky" (7). "There was the aching glory of masses of clouds burning gold and purple from an invisible sun" (7). In image after image, Wright links his complex, sensitive inner life with the beauty of the natural world. With color.

In *White Man, Listen!*, Wright wrote, "Recently a young woman asked me: 'But would your ideas make people happy?' and before I was aware of what I was saying, I heard myself answering with a degree of frankness that I rarely, in deference to politeness, permit myself in personal conversation: 'My dear, I do not deal in happiness; I deal in meaning'" (1957, xvii). Richard Wright is most remembered for his association with the Communist Party ideals and aesthetics of his youthful writings. Indeed, he continued to write politically engaged fiction and nonfiction for the rest of his life. But as his concerns became increasingly philosophical, a year and a half before his death in 1960, Wright was introduced to haiku by Beat poet Sinclair Beiles. Wright read R. H. Blyth's 1949 anthology *Haiku*.[9] In the last eighteen months of his life, he wrote more than 4,000 haiku. He collected 817 for *Haiku: This Other World* (Ogburn), which was published posthumously in 1998. As John Zheng writes, "Reading and writing haiku gave Wright an opportunity to get in touch with Asian literature and culture, to discover a new way of examining the relationship of human beings with nature, and to rediscover his poetic spirit. Wright's zeal in haiku writing also showed his willingness to accept the influence of Japanese aesthetics and Zen philosophy" (127).

In his writing, Wright's life comes full circle. In *Black Boy*, one "event that spoke with a cryptic tongue ... was the love I had for the mute regality of tall, moss-clad oaks" (8). His haiku penned in the final months of his life return to this regard of nature with awareness of the meaning of his being a part of this world:

Suddenly mindful
The tree was looking at me
Each green leaf alive (Beinecke Library)[10]

Wright wrote in *White Man, Listen!* of his rootlessness, "I'm a rootless man, but I'm neither psychologically distraught nor in any wise particularly perturbed because of it. Personally, I do not hanker after, and seem not to need, as many emotional attachments, sustaining roots, or idealistic allegiances as most people" (xvi). Perhaps. But perhaps too, he was a man worn from exile and longing for a home of the heart. Perhaps his soul was bruised by a life spent fighting against injustice with his head and his heart and his hands. Perhaps he longed to look again on the aching glory of gold and purple clouds. Where else might such a man return but to a place named Lotus?

Having faced his guilt and shame over the murder of the Korean child, Frank seeks out his grandfather to find out the truth about the Black man he had seen buried when he lay still and scared with Cee in the long grass. His grandfather is with a group of old men gathered to play checkers and chess. Together, they remember the story detail by detail. The man had been forced to fight his son for sport "they brought him and his daddy from Alabama. Roped up. Made them fight each other. With knives" (118). The fight was to the death. "The game was set up so only the one left alive could leave" (119). The man had ordered his son to kill him. "Obey me, son, this one last time. Do it" (119). All the men of Lotus knew about it because the son had come to them, hysterical and bloody, and the townspeople gathered to give him money and clothes. "If the sheriff had seen

---
[9]Ellen bought him a copy of *Haiku* by Reginald Blythe in 1959, according to Michel Fabre.
[10]The haiku was tweeted on June 24, 2019, by the Beinecke Library at Yale University.

him dripping in blood, he'd be in prison this very day" (119). This was the matter that kept the adults from noticing that two children had gone very far from any place that was safe.

Home was published the year Trayvon Martin was murdered and at the beginning of a decade when brutality against Black men was widely captured and shared on cell phone cameras and across social media. The ever-present danger to Black boys and men in America was finally widely viewed. When protests erupted across the United States in the wake of George Floyd's murder on May 25, 2020, and white people tut-tutted about the burning of buildings, YA novelist Kimberly Jones captured Black anger and grief at the centuries of unmet hopes in a profoundly passionate speech on inequality that went viral. She concludes,

> There's a social contract that we all have. That if you steal or if I steal then the person who is the authority comes in and they fix the situation. But the person who fixes the situation is killing us! So the social contract is broken![11] And if the social contract is broken, why the fuck do I give a shit about burning the fucking football Hall of fame … about burning a fucking Target? You BROKE the contract when you killed us in the streets and didn't give a fuck. You broke the contract when for 400 years we played your game and built your wealth. You broke the contract when we built our wealth again on our own by our bootstraps in Tulsa and you dropped bombs on us … when we built it in Rosewood and you came in and you slaughtered us. You broke the contract.
>
> As far as I'm concerned, they could burn this bitch to the ground. And it still wouldn't be enough. And they are lucky that what Black people are looking for is equality and not revenge.

Jones yokes her grief and anger to Black democratic idealism, lashing out against the unbearable burden of trying to live and love and hope and dream in the face of systemic, unrelenting violence and injustice. The beauty and humanity and history of the struggle are what Morrison memorializes in her novels. Like Wright, Morrison does not deal in happiness; she deals in meaning.

Richard Wright should be the name of a character in a Morrison novel. Wright (archaic): definition, a maker or builder. It is a good, sturdy homonym to the making work that he trained himself to do. Out of his childhood years of physical privation and psychological pain, Wright taught himself to write. And writing not only took him out of hardship and into renown, but like Frederick Douglass before him, Wright made/built the writer, and the writer was a man. Wright describes a moment in *Black Boy* where he goes to visit his father working as a sharecropper on a plantation:

> Standing alone upon the red clay of a Mississippi plantation, a sharecropper clad in ragged overalls, holding a muddy hoe in his gnarled, veined hands—a quarter of a century during which my mind and consciousness had become so greatly and violently altered that when I tried to talk to him I realized that, though ties of blood made us kin, though I could see a shadow of my face in his face, though there was an echo of my voice in his voice, we were forever strangers, speaking a different language, living on vastly different planes of reality … I stood before him, poised, my mind aching as it embraced the simple nakedness of his life, feeling how completely his soul was imprisoned by the slow flow of the seasons, by wind and rain and sun, how fastened were his memories to a crude and raw past, how chained were his actions and emotions to the direct, animalistic impulses of his withering body. (34)

---

[11] She refers in these lines to Trevor Noah's Facebook Live video posted May 29, 2020.

"Here stands a man," writes Frank Money on a sign he posts at the base of the sweet bay tree at the end of *Home*. He has commemorated the dead by burying the stranger; he has embraced the value of Black womanhood by asking for and receiving the gift of Cee's colorful quilt as shroud. These tasks accomplished, he writes himself into being. And with his words, Toni Morrison enfolds with the wide arms of her beautiful prose the Black men of literary history—yes, Richard Wright but by extension Frederick Douglass, W. E. B. DuBois, James Weldon Johnson, James Baldwin, Ralph Ellison, and so many more—who with voice and pen declared their manhood and remade the world.

WORKS CITED

Andres, Emmanuelle. "From Korea to Lotus, Georgia: Home, Displacement, and the Making of Self in Toni Morrison's *Home* (2012)." *Cultures in Movement*, edited by Martine Raibaud, et al., Cambridge Scholars Publisher, 2015.

@Beinecke Library. "Wright, Richard. Haiku. 1959." *Twitter*, June 24, 2019. Richard Wright Papers.

Brockes, E. "Toni Morrison: 'I Want to Feel What I Feel. Even if It's Not Happiness.' An Interview with Toni Morrison." *The Guardian*, Apr. 13, 2012, https://www.theguardian.com/books/2012/apr/13/toni-morrison-home-son-love. Accessed July 11, 2022.

Brodsky, Claudia. "Reading the Writing: A Conversation between Toni Morrison and Claudia Brodsky." *Cornell University Africana Studies*. Mar. 7, 2013, https://www.cornell.edu/video/toni-morrison-on-language-evil-and-the-white-gaze.

Cameron, May. "Author, Author!" *Conversations with Richard Wright*. 1938, edited by Keneth Kinnamon and Michel Fabre, UP of Mississippi, 1993.

Charles, Ron. "Book Review: Toni Morrison's *Home*, a Restrained but Powerful Novel." *Washington Post*, Apr. 30, 2012. https://www.washingtonpost.com/entertainment/books/book-review-toni-morrisons-home-a-restrained-but-powerful-novel/2012/04/30/gIQAKiWSsT_story.html. Accessed July 11, 2022.

Crabtree, Steve. "The Gallup Brain: Americans and the Korean War." *Gallop News Brief*. Feb. 4, 2003, https://news.gallup.com/poll/7741/gallup-brain-americans-korean-war.aspx.

Churchwell, Sarah. "Home by Toni Morrison—Review." *The Guardian*, Apr. 27, 2012, https://www.theguardian.com/books/2012/apr/27/toni-morrison-sarah-churchwell-home.

Cucarella-Ramon, Vicent. "Any Man's Blues: Exposing the Crisis of African-American Masculinity in the Delusion of a Post-Racial United States in Toni Morrison's *Home*." *Studies in the Literary Imagination*, vol. 50, no. 2, 2017, pp. 91–109. http://libproxy.lib.unc.edu/login?url=https://www-proquest-com.libproxy.lib.unc.edu/scholarly-journals/any-mans-blues-1-exposing-crisis-african-american/docview/2313018993/se-2?accountid=14244.

Doyle, Dennis. "'A Fine New Child'": The Lafargue Mental Hygiene Clinic and Harlem's African American Communities, 1946–1958." *Journal of the History of Medicine and Allied Sciences*, vol. 64, no. 2, 2009, pp. 173–212. http://www.jstor.org/stable/24631987.

Ellison, Ralph. "Richard Wright's Blues." 1945. *The Antioch Review*, vol. 57, no. 3, 1999, pp. 263–76.

Fabre, Michel. *Richard Wright: Books and Writers*. UP of Mississippi, 1990.

"Goodbye, Farewell, and Amen." *M*A*S*H*, directed by Alda, Alan, Season 11, episode 16, directed by Alan Alda, CBS, Feb. 28, 1983.

Jesser, Nancy. "Violence, Home, and Community in Toni Morrison's *Beloved*." *African American Review*, vol. 33, no. 2, 1999, pp. 325–45. https://doi.org/10.2307/2901282.

Jones, Kimberly. "Police." *LastWeek Tonight with John Oliver*. Video. 33:32 (31.55) https://www.youtube.com/watch?v=llci8MVh8J4. Accessed July 12, 2022.

Leonard, John. "Jazz." *Toni Morrison: Critical Perspectives Past and Present*, edited by Henry Louis Gates, Jr., and K.A. Appiah, Amistad, 1993, pp. 36–49.

Morrison, Toni. *Home*, Alfred A. Knopf, 2012.

Morrison, Toni. Interview by Charlie Rose. *Charlie Rose*. PBS. May 7, 1993. Video. 55:11. https://charlierose.com/videos/18778. Accessed July 12, 2022.

Novello, Ivor, and Lena Lena Guilbert Ford. "Keep the Home Fires Burning (Til the Boys Come Home)" [song]. 1914. Chappell and Co, 1915.

Ogburn, F., Jr., "Richard Wright's Unpublished Haiku: A World Elsewhere." *MELUS*, vol. 23, no. 3, 1998, pp. 57–81.

Quarles, Benjamin. *The Negro in the Making of America*. Collier Books, 1964.

Ribaud, Martine, Micéala Symington, Ionut Untea, and David Waterman, eds. *Cultures of Movement*. Cambridge Scholars Publishing, 2015.

Snitow, Ann. "*Beloved*." *Toni Morrison: Critical Perspectives Past and Present*, edited by Henry Louis Gates, Jr., and K. A. Appiah, Amistad, 1993, pp. 26–32.

Tate, Claudia. "*Black Boy*: Richard Wright's Tragic Sense of Life." *Black Literature Forum*, vol. 4, no. 1, 1976, pp. 117–19.

Wallace, Maurice O. "'I'm Not Entirely What I Look Like': Richard Wright, James Baldwin, and the Hegemony of Vision; or, Jimmy's FBEye Blues." *Constructing the Black Masculine: Identity and Ideality in African American Men's Literature and Culture, 1775–1995*, Duke UP, 2002.

"War of Nerves." *M*A*S*H*, directed by Alda, Alan, Season 6, episode 5, CBS, Oct. 11, 1977.

Wright, Richard. *12 Million Black Voices: A Folk History of the Negro in the United States*. Viking P, 1941.

Wright, Richard. *Black Boy*. 1945. HarperCollins, 2006.

Wright, Richard. *The Color Curtain*. World, 1956.

Wright, Richard. *White Man, Listen!* Doubleday, 1957.

Zheng, John. "Zen in Richard Wright's I AM NOBODY." *Explicator*, vol. 68, no. 2, 2010, pp. 127–30.

CHAPTER TEN

The Ancestor, Passing, and Imagination in Toni Morrison's *God Help the Child* (2015)

JANINE BRADBURY

In her essay "Rootedness: The Ancestor as Foundation" (1984), Toni Morrison writes, "It seems to me interesting to evaluate Black literature on what the writer does with the presence of an ancestor" (61). This ancestor, she explains, could be "a grandfather as in Ralph Ellison, or a grandmother in Toni Cade Bambara" but more generally these "timeless people" are characterized by a presence that is "benevolent, instructive, and protective" (61–2). They provide, she suggests, "a certain kind of wisdom" (62). This said, Morrison recognizes that Richard Wright "had great difficulty" with this figure in his work, while James Baldwin seemed "confounded and disturbed" by the prospect in his (62). Upon reflection, she decides that "It was the absence of the ancestor," in particular, "that was frightening, that was threatening" and that "caused huge destruction and disarray in the work itself" (62). For Morrison, the ancestor is a touchstone; they orient us; "If we don't keep in touch with the ancestor," she warns, "we are, in fact, lost" (63).[1] It is this sense of ancestral loss or disorientation—as well as the confoundment and narrative disarray accompanying it—that Morrison confronts at the very beginning of her final novel *God Help the Child* (2015), a tale of trauma, colorism, and intergenerational disconnect. In this chapter, I, like Morrison, also "evaluate … what the writer does with the presence of an ancestor." Specifically, I focus on Morrison's invocation of ancestral figures who are racially ambiguous or racially incongruent, or who pass for white. Such figures, I argue, represent or symbolize gaps, spaces, and ancestral fissures that affect our ability to narrate and recuperate our connection to the past in any definitive, linear, teleological, or holistic sense. In Morrison's work, I suggest, the tropes of passing and racial ambiguity often serve to rupture ancestral lineages and communal connections—and *God Help the Child* is no exception. But the ancestor is also conjured in ways that present opportunities for transitory restoration.

Joy James notes that "Speech about the ancestors … enables critiques of historical oppression (such as the references to slavery made in *Beloved* and *Song of Solomon*)" (219). The way that

---

[1] Joy James notes that "Morrison uses the term 'ancestor' to refer to physically living elders and ancestral spirits," while James "reserve[s] the term for ancestral figures" (216). Also see Sandra Pouchet Paquet's "The Ancestor as Foundation in Their Eyes Were Watching God and Tar Baby" (1990) for a similar summary of Morrison's "Rootedness" (1984).

Morrison's narrator Sweetness speaks about the passing ancestor in *God Help the Child* similarly enables a critique of a particular type of oppression—colorism, defined by Alice Walker as the "prejudicial or preferential treatment of same-race people based solely on their color" ("If the Present" 290). Morrison's initial references to the ancestors suggest that colorism has a deleterious effect on matrilineal connection and harmony and locates colorism itself as a phenomenon that is itself encoded through genealogy and ancestry. Two clear matrilineal fissures are introduced in the opening chapter of the novel, both of which are framed as being caused by ancestral loss: the first between Sweetness and her daughter Bride/Lula Ann and the second between Sweetness and her unnamed maternal grandmother. Morrison conveys the narrative disarray caused by the loss of an ancestor in this novel through her characteristic use of multiple narrators and choice to begin the novel in media res, which unsettle the reader. In the opening line, Sweetness declares, "It's not my fault. So you can't blame me. I didn't do it and I have no idea how it happened" (3). The "error" that light-skinned Sweetness excuses here, we soon learn, is the birth of her own dark-skinned child, Bride/Lula Ann, whose color (in her mother's opinion) represents both a fault (as in mistake) as well as a fault line (as in fracture or discontinuity) in Sweetness's genealogy given that both of Sweetness's parents are light enough to pass for white (3–4). The disturbance, the fright, the threat that Morrison observes in Wright's and Baldwin's invocations of the ancestor are in this instance associated with or projected onto the figure of the child, who connotes ancestral uncertainty and indeterminacy. Sweetness expresses fright at Bride's appearance recounting without shame that "She was so black she scared me" (3). She is also confounded and "thought she was going crazy when [Bride] turned blue-black right before my eyes" (5). Bride's arrival is also a threat to Sweetness's marriage; indeed, Bride's father "just up and left" when Sweetness suggests that perhaps "the blackness must be from his own family—not mine" (6). Children traditionally (to the point of cliché) represent the future, the unknown, what lays ahead somewhere, out there, ahead of where we are now. But of course the child is also a physical manifestation of all that has gone before, a literal embodiment and personification of the past, a culmination of history, of what happened sometime back then. The body of the child is the site for genealogical inheritance. We recognize this from the ways we might talk about a child having his grandmother's eyes or father's smile. The child is thus the ancestor—uncanny and reanimated.[2]

Bride/Lula Ann's arrival signifies on the horror of recessive ancestral blackness found in conventional passing narratives,[3] such as Kate Chopin's "Désirée's Baby" (1894), in which the titular (white) character gives birth to a child who "is not white" (541), even though her husband is of "old" and "proud" Southern "stock" (539). When her husband disowns her, Désirée takes her child and "disappeared among the reeds and willows ... of the deep, sluggish bayou, and did not come back again" (542). Weeks later, her "white" husband discovers a letter from his own mother to his father revealing that it is she who "belongs to the race that is cursed with brand of slavery" (542). In turns out, to borrow Sweetness's words in *God Help the Child*, that "the blackness must be from his own family" (6). In Nella Larsen's *Passing*, Clare explains to her girlfriends over tea that

---

[2]In fact, Maxine Lavon Montgomery suggests that Bride herself is seen by Booker as "a semidivine female ancestor" with "hair like a million black butterflies asleep on her head" (111).
[3]By signifying, I refer to those literary mechanisms of intertextual "revision," "repetition," and "pastiche" outlined by Henry Louis Gates Jr. (685–6).

she "nearly died of terror the whole nine months before Margery was born for fear that she might be dark" because the "strain"—a double entendre for stress and blood—"is simply too-too hellish" (49). Indeed, as Stephanie Li summarizes, "Even when marks of racial difference are not visible on the skin, as explored in many passing narratives ... there is always the threat that the color of a child may betray its mother or more subtle marks like hair texture or fingernails may give away one's true racial identity" (68). Even as Larsen's Gertrude explains that any resurgent blackness "might go way back" and a child might "turn out dark no matter what colour the father and mother are" (49), this is something that Sweetness and her husband Louis in *God Help the Child* refuse to believe. Sweetness reflects with bemusement,

> I'm light-skinned with good hair, what we call high yellow, and so is Lula Ann's father. Ain't nobody in my family anywhere near that colour ... You might think she's a throwback, but throwback to what? (4)

A throwback without a referent, Bride is seen as a racial anomaly, without family, without lineage, but who actually exists outside of a real genealogy that Sweetness does not care to remember. Sweetness views her own daughter as an aberration who throws her family's light-skinned lineage and ancestry into disrepute. Sweetness is so ashamed of her daughter's darkness, that "once—just for a few seconds—[she] held a blanket over her face and pressed" (4), a symbol of her desire to smother, repress, and contain the past which her skin evokes. As Shirley A. Stave explains,

> Bride's color, then, functions as the return of the repressed, the visible marker that demands the acknowledgement of an enslaved past, even as it underscores what Sweetness also would not choose to concede—that her own light skin bespeaks the rape(s) of her foremothers. (6)

The lost Black ancestor, who in Bride is the ancestor returned, is a presence who can testify to the widespread rape of enslaved Black women by white men. The emergence of a light-skinned "class" of African Americans (such as Sweetness and her parents) and the patriarchal and racist valorization of their proximity to whiteness have their genetic and ideological genealogy in the systemic abuse of enslaved women. As Caroline Randall Williams startlingly phrases it in her piece for the *New York Times*, "My Body is a Confederate Monument. I have rape-colored skin. My lightbrown-blackness is a living testament to the rules, the practices, the causes of the Old South" (n.p.). As Stave notes, "In her family's dedication to 'whitening up', what must remain unacknowledged is the plight of those ancestors who were seen as subhuman because of their color, even as project of 'whitening up' began with the rape of their female progenitors" (6). In Morrison's world, the arrival of the ancestral child ushers in with it a collapsing of time and space. Bride's body invokes nobody (and no body) that Sweetness knows of in her family tree. And yet, Bride can be read as ancestral revenant, a woman whose body reanimates a figure long since gone, the emblem of an irrecoverable and traumatic history. Her phenotype emblematizes and signals the loss of the/her Black maternal foremother, a repressed Africanist presence, an ancestral specter whose experiences Sweetness wishes to deny so forcefully that she not only forbids her child to call her "mama" or "mother" but considers suffocating her at birth.

The discomforting, latent, repressed Black foremother (who when invoked in the context of a light-skinned family represents racial dissonance and incongruity) is not the only progenitor that is missing, presumed lost, in this text. The maternal passing ancestor also haunts the text. "You should've seen my grandmother" Sweetness boasts,

> She passed for white and never said another word to any of her children. Any letter she got back from my mother or my aunts she sent right back, unopened. Finally they got the message of no message and let her be. Almost all mulatto types and quadroons did that back in the day—if they had the right kind of hair that is. Can you imagine how many white folks have Negro blood running and hiding in their veins? (3)

Sweetness, then, has also lost her own grandmother who crossed the color line and passed for white, disowning her children, just as Sweetness disavows her own daughter. Colorism casts a long shadow over the relationship between light-skinned Sweetness and her dark-skinned daughter Bride. Morrison explains, "The principal thing [in this book] was the pain of being very, very Black in a house that has spent a lot of their energy on passing or being very, very light" (Griffin, "Toni Morrison's" n.p.). The author is unequivocal in her message: Sweetness's colorist attitudes are inextricably linked to a cultural penchant for passing, and we know passing and colorism are phenomena born(e) out of the widespread sexual exploitation of enslaved Black women.

Morrison, adding to this sense of temporal collapse, revisitation, and déjà vu, evokes a genre that like the ancestral figures in the text is supposed to be dead and buried. As Michele Elam explains, by the turn of the new millennium, many thought passing "had quaintly, almost nostalgically, gone the way of gramophones, congolene, and flappers," fading away, passing away into obscurity (Elam 749). And yet ironically, this novel—which critics celebrate as the most contemporary of all of Morrison's works—opens with an unsympathetic narrator harking back to a supposedly long-lost, unfashionable, and archaic past. As Elam notes, passing is "reanimated," and "born again," a revenant genre "resurrected to assume a spectacular new life" (750).[4] Sweetness invites her twenty-first century reader to pass back in time with her and imagine the lightness of her grandmother's skin and the texture of her hair (*God Help the Child* 3), and she calls upon the antiquated language of passing novels such as James Weldon Johnson's *The Autobiography of an Ex-Coloured Man* (1912/1927), Charles Chesnutt's *The House Behind the Cedars* (1900), and William Wells Brown's *Clotelle* (1867), speaking of "mulatto types," "quadroons," and "Negro blood" (3–4). She recalls the language of one-drop hypodescent, wondering "how many white folks have Negro blood running and hiding in their veins" (3). In a particularly startling flashback to a traumatic past, Sweetness pictures herself as an inverse and peculiar white antebellum "mammy," claiming, "for me, nursing [Bride] was like having a pickaninny sucking at my teat" (5–6). The collapse of temporal, historical, and racial positionalities are, again, a confounding effect of the loss of the ancestor. There is a sad irony in Sweetness's remembrance of a grandmother who "never said another word to any of her children," refusing to accept their letters, offering only the paradoxical "message of no message" (3). Sweetness's desire for others to bear material witness to a woman who cannot be witnessed, who has vanished by passing out of reach and out of sight is bittersweet. While her children "let her be" (3), Sweetness, in her remembrance, cannot.

The mulatta ancestor (and the generic discourse accompanying her invocation) thus additionally haunts the text. Both Sweetness's grandmother and her unknown Black foremothers represent

---

[4]Elam's article focuses on works published in the wake of what Danzy Senna describes as "The Mulatto Millenium" (1998), such as Senna's *Caucasia* (2001), Philip Roth's *The Human Stain* (2001), and Colson Whitehead's *The Intuitionist* (1999). We are, I would argue in a second post-millennium wave of passing (most recently exemplified in Brit Bennett's novel *The Vanishing Half* (2020), Misha Green's television series *Lovecraft Country* (2020), and Rebecca Hall's adaptation of Larsen's *Passing* (2021).

spectral presences that, to borrow from Jacques Derrida's description of hauntology, "desynchronises and recalls us to anachrony" (6). As Katy Shaw explains, "The critical practice of hauntology turns to the past in order to make sense of the present" (3); in order for Sweetness to make sense of Bride (the present), she revisits the ancestral past (although she ultimately fails to process the significance of the past, the ancestor is lost, so is she, for there is "no conscious historical connection" [Morrison, "Rootedness" 64]). Morrison's oeuvre as a whole is deeply concerned with this mode of hauntological enquiry, and *God Help the Child* is in many ways a text that constitutes (to borrow Merlin Coverley's words) a "return and repetition of the past in the present [which is] manifested through the figure of the revenant," who is in this case, Bride, "which returns each time as if it were the first, unchanging and insistent, demanding a reckoning for a message that went unheard or was ignored" (11). This message is ultimately one of intergenerational trauma caused by the sexual abuse of enslaved Black women in the antebellum era and colorism. The message Bride presents to the reader, of colorism, of the trauma of slavery, becomes desperately contorted in its retelling and projection when Bride falsely accuses Sophia Huxley of sexual abuse (when in fact it is her mother who has abused her psychologically). Bride falsely testifies against Sophia, but as the novel's revenant, as one who repeatedly returns from the violence and pain that threatens to vanquish her—her mother's rejection and fantasy of infanticide, Sophia's assault, and additionally, as Delphine Gras reminds us, "a car accident," "a shooting," "a slap," and "a burn" (8)—Bride regenerates until she can testify to the pain of the past, until she can truly reconcile her place in the world.

The ancestral figures in the text also facilitate a process of "rememory." Coined by Morrison in her novel *Beloved* (1987), the word "rememory" is used by the character Sethe to describe how "some things go" or "pass on" while "some things just stay" (43). The term has since been theorized by Ashraf Rushdy as a "conceptual device for understanding the sometimes direct, sometimes arbitrary relationship between what happened sometime and what is happening now" or "a way to understand how we can share in the prior experiences of others," a way of understanding that "historical events have enduring afterlives" (7). In the case of *God Help the Child*, the historical event of passing has an enduring afterlife in Sweetness's colorism, and her Grandmother's disavowal of her descendants calls into question the strength of the bond between Sweetness and her own child and grandchild. Brenda K. Marshall's definition of rememory as "constitution by absence," a "present absence, a remembered absence, not a void" is also an apt description of the ancestors in the text (191). Jeong-eun Rhee poetically describes rememory as "both forgetting and remembering" as "both doing and (non)being," "transcending the temporality of past, present, and future" (2). As Morrison herself explains, "Rememory" is a process of "recollecting and remembering as in reassembling the members of the body, the family, the population of the past" ("Rememory" 324). In Sethe's case, this pertains to her daughter Beloved and in Sweetness's, her grandmother. "The pitched battle between remembering and forgetting," Morrison continues, "became the device of [Beloved's] narrative" and "the effort to both remember and not know became the structure of the text" ("Rememory" 324). The opening of *God Help the Child* is similarly attentive to these techniques. Sweetness both attempts to remember and yet cannot know her kin or the people of her past, because they have "passed on" into whiteness. What remains is Sweetness and her "blue-black" daughter Bride whose skin bears no trace of her great-grandmother even as she, as descendent, stands as testament to her existence. And so when Morrison invokes a history of passing here, it is to contextualize what is happening in the novel's present. It sheds some light on Sweetness's preference for light skin, and passing comes to metaphorically represent an elision between the mother and the child.

While critics often describe Morrison's novels as ones that celebrate the ancestor as a foundation for community and the discovery of heritage (indeed Morrison herself uses the language of "roots" and "foundations"), she undoubtedly invokes mulatta/o ancestors as emblems of the difficulties of recuperating the past. In his reading of another Morrison novel, *Song of Solomon* (1977), John Brenkman veers toward a reading of the ancestor as foundational, as recoverable, as discoverable. He suggests that Milkman Dead's "quest is bathed in irony … because what [he] keeps finding instead of the gold is the genealogy of his own family" (65). Family, genealogy, and ancestry are figurative and representational devices, which, Brenkman argues, represent "the path, not the hindrance, to the truth" (65). Even though Brenkman uses the novel to reconstruct (literally, in a chart) the "dead family tree" (66; a phrase that in itself suggests fruitlessness rather than anything generative), Juda Bennett questions our ability to trace heritage in the novel. In "Toni Morrison and the Burden of The Passing Narrative" (2001), Bennett reads the passing ancestor (Sing) as being "associated with the familiar themes of the fractured family and the conflicted identity," who is presented "indirectly through memories that are partially lost, distorted, or made ambiguous in the telling" and who represents "a problematic and partially lost essence" (206). Not only is her name unknown for much of the novel's narrative, even once her name is recovered, "the mystery of whether or not Sing did pass for white … doubles her significance" and she "continues to be shrouded in mystery" (209). "The past," Bennett concludes, "can never be fully retrieved, and the act of passing for white presents special challenges to those who need [it]" (206). The ancestral passing figure is thus a figure of ambivalence. They are both present and absent, rememories of a past that is both ultimately irrecoverable and still somehow knowable and imaginable, if that is, we are willing to embrace what Morrison describes as other "ways of knowing."

Saidiya Hartman grapples with this tension (of how to describe and reconstruct what is ultimately irretrievable) in her interrogation of the Black archive, asking,

> How can narrative embody life in words and at the same time respect what we cannot know? How does one listen for the groans and cries, the undecipherable songs, the crackle of fire in the cane fields, the laments for the dead, and the shouts of victory, and then assign words to all of it? Is it possible to construct a story from "the locus of impossible speech" or resurrect lives from the ruins? Can beauty provide an antidote to dishonor, and love a way to "exhume buried cries" and reanimate the dead? (3)

These questions are of course ones that Morrison grapples with too. She recognizes that in order to convey "the interior life" of the historical Black subject and "as a writer who is black and a woman" she must first be willing to "rip that veil drawn over 'proceedings too terrible to relate,'" proceedings that the mainstream [white] discourse has made oblique or refuses to name ("The Site of Memory" 71). Second, Morrison suggests that she must trust her own "recollections" and "memories" as well as those of others. And finally, she invokes that other way of knowing: the imagination. She writes,

> Memories and recollections won't give me total access to the unwritten interior life of these people. Only the act of the imagination can help me. If writing is thinking and discovery and selection and order and meaning, it is also awe and reverence and mystery and magic. (92)

Morrison's process is not far removed (if removed at all) from what Hartman describes as "critical fabulation," a "re-presenting [of] the sequence of events in divergent stories" in order to "imagine what might have happened or might have been said or might have been done" by "throwing into crisis 'what happened when' and by exploiting the 'transparency of sources' as fictions of history" (11–12). Moreover, Morrison's description of imagination as "another way of knowing," as rich with "magic" chimes with her descriptions of ancestral connections to people who "formed a kind of cosmology that was perceptive as well as enchanting" even as they were "shrewd" and "down-to-earth":

> I grew up in a house in which people talked about their dreams with the same authority that they talked about what *really* [sic] happened. They had visitations and did not find that fact shocking and they had some sweet, intimate connection with things that were not empirically verifiable. (Davis and Morrison 144)

The enchanting, mystical, and magical processes by which we can reconnect to the past (even as we recognize this can never be a "verifiable process") and that characterize the ancestor and their other "ways of knowing" can help us in our reading of Morrison's alternative ancestral figure, Queen.

Morrison suggests that the ancestor should be "benevolent, instructive, and protective" or "not necessarily as a parent but as an abiding, interested, benevolent, guiding presence that is yours and is concerned about you, not quite like saints but having the same sort of access" (Davis and Morrison 145). This is an apt description of Queen. Gras argues that "Bride's final step in her transformation is to overcome her alienation and develop healing bonds instead," and we can "situate Queen as a key ancestor" who facilitates this process. Susana Vega-González suggests that "the reader immediately notes that Queen resembles the ancestor mother-wit figure that Morrison introduces in many of her novels" and is crucial to "the healing process" (81). And Maxine Lavon Montgomery implies that Queen embodies the same contradictory dynamic of rememory in that she is both "forgetful but all-knowing" and is "a timeless, benevolent ancestral figure" (115). While Sweetness and Bride remain separated in the text both in terms of narrative voice and geography (we never witness or hear their reconciliation), Bride turns to Queen (who is her partner Booker's aunt) to find the maternal love she has been craving. Queen is a complex figure ushering in destructions and endings as well as chances for reconciliation and recovery. Queen serves as a symbolic other-mother for Bride. Even though she has lost her own children to former husbands, even "as the smarts came too late for her children," having had "no opportunity to raise a child beyond the age of child" (158), she provides shelter and nourishment for Bride. Her home, decorated with symbolic quilts and other hand-stitched items, ostensibly represents a maternal and ancestral home for Bride, much in keeping with Alice Walker's vision in *In Search of Our Mothers' Gardens* in which the anonymous quilt maker is both "a person of powerful imagination and deep spiritual feeling," and "one of our grandmothers" whose "creative spark" and "genius" we must witness "for the sake of our children, and if necessary bone by bone" ("Mothers' Gardens" 239–40; "Zora Neale Hurston" 92). We read that

> Queen sewed, knitted, crocheted and made lace. Curtains, slipcovers, cushions, embroidered napkins were elegantly hand made. A quilt on the headboard of an empty bed, whose springs were apparently cooling outside, were pieced in soft colours and, like everything else, cleverly mismatched ... One whole wall was covered with photographs of children. (145)

It would be easy to romanticize and idealize the connection between Queen and Bride—to draw a sense of resolution from the fact that they find each other. Bride on the one hand, so desperately in need of maternal connection; Queen on the other, with a wall of photographs of her lost children. However, the kinship between Queen and Bride is short-lived, as less than a day after Bride's arrival, in dramatic scenes evocative of Morrison's 1973 novel *Sula*, Queen's mobile home goes up in flames. Even though Queen is rescued from the building, Morrison foreshadows the dangers of holding onto an ancestral past; as her devoted nephew Booker desperately attempts to resuscitate his aunt, "Suddenly a spark hiding in Queen's hair burst into flame, devouring the mass of red hair in a blink" (165). Morrison subtly hints that Queen's presence as ancestral mother-figure is transitory—she is on her way out. When Bride first encounters Queen, she is preempting the arrival of parasitic life by destroying the eggs of the bedbugs, her own children have moved on, her marital bed is empty, and its burning bedsprings ultimately lead to the fire responsible for her demise. Bride's imminent journey toward motherhood is contrasted with Queen's exit from this realm. And yet Queen is not a pernicious or destructive presence, she is creative and generative, a homemaker, a quilter. Writing about the quilt as motif in African American women's writing, Houston A. Baker, Jr. and Charlotte Pierce-Baker observe that

> A patch is a fragment. It is a vestige of wholeness that stands as a sign of loss … As a remainder or remnant, the patch may symbolize rupture … it may be defined by the faded glory of the already gone. But as a fragment, it is also rife with explosive potential of the yet-to-be-discovered. Like woman, it is a liminal element between wholes. (706)

When Bride arrives at Queen's home, she is fragmented, a "a sign of loss" of the ancestor, "a remainder or remnant" of an enslaved past who "rupture[s]" Sweetness's world. But not only is Queen's home "rife with explosive potential" (her house implodes in flame), but her nurturing of Booker and Bride ushers in the potential of the future, symbolized through their unborn child. Queen is a "liminal element"—knowing and not knowing, the ancestral mother and an unrealized mother, here and safe and then in the flash of an eye, engulfed in flames. But Vega-González reads the quilt in *God Help the Child* as "a metaphor for the final putting together of the patches that compose fragment characters" arguing that the "idea of putting a person back together is metaphorically portrayed in Queen's quilt" (82). Quilts, she observes, "have traditionally been made and used by the African American community and have likewise been employed in literature to signify the healing of fragmented characters" (82). And so Queen, as a "benevolent, instructive, and protective" ancestor "not necessarily as a parent but as an abiding, interested, benevolent, guiding presence," substitutes for the maternal ancestors whose presence has been denied or dismissed or who are themselves denying or dismissive.

Crucially Queen is herself a figure of racial ambiguity, an allusion to the ancestral passing figure of Sweetness's grandmother. Not only does she share a name with Alex Haley's eponymous mulatta grandmother (in *Queen: The Story of an American Family* [1993]), but her last name "Olive" denotes light skin. She has "woolly red hair" (*God Help the Child* 144), lives in a "pale-yellow" mobile home (142), and her skin tone is never specified. If Queen is indeed an ancestral figure, and a racially ambiguous ancestral figure at that, in tending to her on her deathbed, Bride revisits and makes peace with old trauma, lays old ghosts to rest, and (re)connects with the ancestor who would see fit to reject her. As Montgomery summarizes, "In a ceremonial moment resonant with loss, mourning, and celebration, Booker delivers a final musical tribute to his deceased aunt as the newly reunited couple pay homage to the female ancestor" (117). While Queen fights for her life in hospital, Booker and Bride unwittingly prepare her body for death. Queen "had to be scoured, oiled, and rewrapped," and Bride, "not trusting the indifferent hands of the nurse, did [it] herself as tenderly as possible. And she bathed her one section at a time, making sure the lady's body was covered in certain areas after cleansing" (*God Help the Child* 166). Similarly, Booker, "insist[ing] like a daily communicant at Easter, on the duty of assuming that act of devotion," "soaped then rinsed Queen's feet, finally massaging them slowly, rhythmically with a lotion that smells of heather" (167). Tragically, just as the couple plan to get "a place where all three [of them] could be together," Queen passes away (172). But in preparing her so tenderly, Bride and Booker make peace with the past.

In letting go of the past—symbolized by Queen's demise—Booker and Bride turn to embrace their future as parents. In the closing scenes of the book, Bride learns she is pregnant and in a refiguring of the letter motif from the start of the novel, writes to her mother, without leaving a return address, to share the news. Bride looks forward to "A Child. New Life. Immune to evil or illness, protected from kidnap, beatings, rape, racism, insult, hurt, self-loathing, abandonment. Error-free, All goodness. Minus wrath" or "so they believe" (175). Merlin Coverley argues that hauntology does not only harken back to the past, but also speaks to the future, "the not yet," a haunting of "the present from the future, through the unfulfilled promise of that which never came to pass but which may yet do so" a prospect alluded to through the renewed symbol of "the child" (and foreshadowed by what Baker and Pierce-Baker describe as "the yet-to-be-discovered" [706] potential of the quilt). The impending arrival of Bride's child circles back to the novel's opening detailing Bride's own birth. Morrison (and Sweetness) are quick to remind us that time, like life, is cyclical, elliptical. Sweetness's final lines are apt: "Good luck and God help the child," who is destined to orbit the same path as the parent, fated to reencounter rememories of ancestral lives gone by (*God Help the Child* 178).

Passing is invoked in many of Morrison's other works to create a sense of discord, to allude to trauma, or to disrupt notions of a singular and definitive truth. In *The Bluest Eye* (1970), Pecola, who fantasizes about having blue eyes by way of protecting herself from her father's abuse and mother's neglect, is a signifying revision of Fannie Hurst's character Peola from *Imitation of Life* (1933). As Bennett explains, in *The Bluest Eye*, Morrison revises the traditional passing narrative "ignoring biology and phenotype for fantasy and the imagination of passing" ("Toni Morrison" 208), and I would add that this is in order to convey the irreparable damage inflicted on the child by the parent. In "Recitatif" (1983), which is Morrison's sole short story, the author withholds the racial identities of her two principal characters as they in turn argue about the racial identity of a woman they knew from their time at a children's home, a time when their parents were unable to care for them. As we attempt to guess the racial identities of the dual protagonist, Morrison "recasts the drama of passing between text and reader" (J. Bennett, "Toni Morrison" 206). Again, passing is invoked in part to convey matrilineal fracture. But in *God Help the Child*, the additional inclusion of Queen (and not just the absent ancestors) signals an opportunity to heal from trauma. Vega-González reads the novel as being one of several of Morrison's works, in which "characters undergo the effects of traumatic experiences," which in turn "triggers mechanisms of defence" but "after a metaphorical and physical journal, and usually with the assistance of an ancestor figure, those characters finally heal and recover" (70). While Bride can never fully recuperate the maternal ancestors and forebears she has lost, she does repair and regenerate.

As Bennett observes in *Toni Morrison and the Queer Pleasure of Ghosts* (2014), "the passing figure," alongside "the invisible man, the zoot suit, [and] the lynched corpse," is a ghost that haunts the African American literary tradition (18). The passing figure is a specter, a haint, a ghost, a vision, a threat to the status quo, an anachronism, and an apparition. They represent that which is lost, disappeared, and vanished. They sound like silence. The passing ancestor is a manifestation of what Kathleen Brogan describes as a text of "cultural haunting," which "explor[e] the hidden passageways not only of the individual psyche, but also of people's historical consciousness" (152), which in this case is slavery and colorism. Although by Brogan's definition the ghosts of passing are metaphorical rather than literal (there are not actual apparitions who appear to the characters), the fantastical elements of *God Help the Child* do constitute a "turn to the supernatural in the process of recovering history," which "emphasizes the difficulty of gaining access to a lost or denied past, as well as the degree to which any such historical reconstruction is essentially an imaginative act" (Brogan 152). The mystical ancestor, whose invocations present "another way of knowing" offer a connection to the past, illustrate the difficulties we encounter when we attempt to recuperate history, and are rendered—in part—through the literary imaginary. Because Morrison positions her evocation of the ancestor as part of a broader cosmology that is not of this—white, European, empirical—world, the ancestor is more than a biological or genetic antecedent, a name on a family tree or a historical factoid. As Joy James explains, "Toni Morrison's dissection of racist paradigms is framed by a world view that testifies to African American ancestral spirits" (210). She continues, "Extending through time and space to include our predecessors, contemporaries, and future generations, community" in Morrison's work "is not bound by physical or temporal limits; its relationships are transcendent" and "this transcendence is marked by the presence of ancestors" (218). Morrison's rendering of the passing ancestor as a personification of a history that can only be imagined, that has been "lost" and "denied" is a key characteristic of *God Help the Child*, even as the passing ancestor is only a transitory presence in the text. Morrison undoubtedly begins the novel with an exploration of what happens when the ancestor is lost. Sweetness's Black maternal ancestor whom her daughter resembles is disavowed, and the passing maternal ancestor that she reveres, has ironically abandoned her kin. Because of this, Morrison implies, both Bride and Sweetness are themselves lost, because when "we don't keep in touch with the ancestor, we are, in fact, lost" (63). They destroy possibilities of generation and hope—Sweetness in her aberration of her own child and Bride in her "punish[ment] of one of the only individuals who had actually accepted Lula Ann/Bride prior to her makeover," Sophia Huxley (Gras 10). In Sweetness's disdain for Bride, and Bride's punishment of Sophia, they in turn lose people who present opportunities for connection. But in the fantastical, imaginative, and racially ambiguous ancestral figure of Queen, Morrison skillfully represents an opportunity for reconciliation, community, and connection, as fleeting as this may be.

WORKS CITED

Baker, Houston A., and Charlotte Pierce-Baker. "Patches: Quilts and Community in Alice Walker's 'Everyday Use'." *Southern Review*, vol. 21, no. 3, 1985, pp. 706–20.

Bennett, Juda. "Toni Morrison and the Burden of the Passing Narrative." *African American Review*, vol. 35, no. 2, 2001, pp. 205–17.

Bennett, Juda. *Toni Morrison and the Queer Pleasure of Ghosts*. SUNY P, 2014.

Brenkman, John. "Politics and Form in Song of Solomon." *Social Text*, vol. 39, 1994, pp. 57–82.

Brogan, Kathleen. "American Stories of Cultural Haunting: Tales of Heirs and Ethnographers." *College English*, vol. 57, no. 2, 1995, pp. 149–65.

Chopin, Kate. "Désirée's Baby." *The Norton Anthology of American Literature: 1865–1914*, vol. C, edited by Robert Levine et al., W. W. Norton & Company, 2017, pp. 538–42.

Coverley, Merlin. *Hauntology: Ghosts of Futures Past*. Oldcastle Books Ltd, 2020.

Davis, Christina, and Toni Morrison. "Interview with Toni Morrison." *Presence Africaine*, vol. 145, 1988, pp. 141–50.

Derrida, Jacques. *Specters of Marx*. Routledge, 2006.

Elam, Michele. "Passing in the Post Race Era: Danzy Senna, Philip Roth and Colson Whitehead." *African American Review*, vol. 41, no. 4, 2007, pp. 749–68.

Gates, Henry Louis, Jr. "The 'Blackness of Blackness': A Critique of the Sign and the Signifying Monkey." *Critical Inquiry*, vol. 9, no. 4, 1983, pp. 685–723.

Gras, Delphine. "Post What? Disarticulating Post-Discourses in Toni Morrison's *God Help the Child*." *Humanities*, vol. 5, no. 4, article 80 (2016). doi:10.3390/h5040080.

Griffin, Farah Jasmine. "Toni Morrison's '*God Help the Child*': An Instant New York Times Best-Seller." *Essence*. Oct. 27, 2020. http://www.essence.com/2015/05/01/toni-morrisons-god-help-child-new-york-times-best-seller. Accessed July 12, 2022.

Haley, Alex, and David Stevens. *Alex Haley's Queen: The Story of an American Family*. William Morrow & Company, 1993.

Hartman, Saidiya. "Venus in Two Acts." *Small Axe*, vol. 12, no. 2, 2008, pp. 1–14.

James, Joy. "Politicizing the Spirit: 'American Africanisms' and African Ancestors in the Essays of Toni Morrison." *Cultural Studies*, vol. 9, no. 2, 1995, pp. 210–25.

Larsen, Nella. *Passing*. Modern Library, 2002.

Li, Stephanie. *Specifying Without Signifying: Racial Discourse in the Age of Obama*. Duke UP, 2012.

Marshall, Brenda. *Teaching the Postmodern*. Routledge, 2013.

Montgomery, Maxine Lavon. "'You Not the Woman I Want': Toni Morrison's *God Help the Child* and the Legend of Galatea." *New Critical Essays on Toni Morrison's God Help the Child: Race, Culture, and History*, edited by Alice Knox Eaton, et al., UP of Mississippi, 2020, pp. 106–20.

Morrison, Toni. *Beloved*. 1987. Vintage, 2005.

Morrison, Toni. *The Bluest Eye*. 1970. Vintage, 1999.

Morrison, Toni. *God Help the Child*. Chatto and Windus, 2015.

Morrison, Toni. "Rememory." *The Source of Self-Regard: Selected Essays, Speeches, and Meditations*. Knopf, 2019, pp. 322–5.

Morrison, Toni. "Rootedness: The Ancestor as Foundation." *What Moves at the Margin: Selected Non-Fiction*, edited by Carole C. Denard, U of Mississippi P, 2008, pp. 56–64.

Morrison, Toni. "The Site of Memory." *What Moves at the Margin: Selected Non-Fiction*, edited by Carolyn C. Denard. U of Mississippi P, 2008, pp. 65–81.

Morrison, Toni. *Song of Solomon*. 1977, Vintage. 1998.

Morrison, Toni. *Sula*. 1973. Vintage, 1998.

Paquet, Sandra Pouchet. "The Ancestor as Foundation in Their Eyes Were Watching God and Tar Baby." *Callaloo*, vol. 13, no. 3, 1990, pp. 499–515.

Rhee, Jeong-eun. *Decolonial Feminist Research: Haunting, Rememory and Mothers*. Routledge, 2020.

Rushdy, Ashraf. *Remembering Generations: Race and Family in Contemporary African American Fiction*. U of North Carolina P, 2001.

Senna, Danzy. "Mulatto Millennium." *Half and Half: Writings on Growing Up Biracial and Bicultural*, edited by Claudine C. O.'Hearn, Pantheon Books, 1998, pp. 12–27.

Shaw, Katy. *Hauntology: The Presence of the Past in Twenty-First Century English Literature*. Springer, 2018.

Stave, Shirley A. "Skin Deep: Identity and Trauma in *God Help the Child*." *New Critical Essays on Toni Morrison's God Help the Child: Race, Culture, and History*, edited by Alice Knox Eaton, et al., UP of Mississippi, 2020, pp. 5–29.

Vega-González, Susana. "'Let the True Note Ring Out Loud': A Mindful Reading of *God Help the Child*." *New Critical Essays on Toni Morrison's God Help the Child: Race, Culture, and History*, edited by Alice Knox Eaton et al., UP of Mississippi, 2020, pp. 67–86.

Walker, Alice. "If the Present Looks Like the Past, What Does the Future Look Like?" *In Search of Our Mothers Gardens: Womanist Prose*. The Woman's P, 1984, pp. 290–312.

Walker, Alice. "In Search of Our Mothers Gardens." *In Search of Our Mothers Gardens: Womanist Prose*. The Woman's P, 1984, pp. 231–43.

Walker, Alice. "Zora Neale Hurston: A Cautionary Tale and a Partisan View." *In Search of Our Mothers' Gardens: Womanist Prose*. The Woman's P, 1984, pp. 82–92.

Williams, Caroline Randall. "You Want a Confederate Monument? My Body is a Confederate Monument." *New York Times*, June 26, 2020, https://www.nytimes.com/2020/06/26/opinion/confederate-monuments-racism.html. Accessed Oct. 28, 2021.

CHAPTER ELEVEN

Arcs of Transcendence: The Religious Imagination of Toni Morrison

GURLEEN GREWAL

NYACK-ON-THE-HUDSON

For years I had wanted to visit this house on the Hudson River, the one inhabited by a black woman. Quarrying native stone as the various early settlers of Nyack did, she had been building houses, building bridges across chilly waters—but only as writers can do. Setting marks in the stone, benchmarks gleaned from a tradition of transmutation from ancestors having forded rivers, having "waded through the waters troubled by God."

She even quarried blue stone to pave the road for that fictive house on 124 Bluestone Road, shelter given by abolitionists to an old and tired freed woman, Baby Suggs (free to take in endless wash, to cobble and mend shoes), the same house where her ancient heart finally broke, as Sethe, her daughter-in-law, reckless, did things no mother should, to protect her beloved baby girl from slavery. The rest is history, Margaret Garner's, which this Black woman entered and reshaped—but only as certain writers can do.

I had longed to enter that home down by the riverside where lived this shaman storyteller who knew how to direct the potency of words to wounds, who knew how to "convert the outrage of the years/Into a music, a sound, and a symbol," à la Jorge Luis Borges's poem, "Ars Poetica."

May 18, 2015: I am in the village of Nyack (Rockland County, New York), named after one of the Indian tribes whose home it was prior to the Dutch in the 17th century. I am in the company of Toni Morrison Society (TMS) members, here for a day-long celebration of installing a "bench by the road," a ritual inspired by Toni Morrison's poignant remark: "There is no place you or I can go ... to summon the presences of, or recollect the absences of slaves; nothing that reminds us of the ones who made the journey and of those who did not make it. There is no suitable memorial or plaque or wreath or wall or park ... There's no small bench by the road" ("The Slavebody and the Blackbody," 75). Emblematic canary yellow umbrellas bobbing above figures dressed in white, our procession walks from the Church towards Nyack Memorial Park, where to the sound of ceremonial drums is unveiled a bench—the 15th bench placement—in honor of Cynthia Hesdra, a Nyack resident, one of the many remarkable women who escaped slavery and served as an Underground Railroad Conductor assisting others in going north to freedom.

Before the day's end, just as our group is dispersing, we are serendipitously invited to her home.

It is past 6 p.m. when I enter that old boathouse-renovated-almost burnt down-then remodeled into an elegant multi-story house of light and glass, wood and steel, with a long-railed pier white and luminous in the Hudson, its waters dusky, the color of warm stone now burnished silver.

At the end of the pier, afloat on rods, a pergola shelters a white bench. Squinting into the light I see on the pergola a plaque in memoriam, the initials KSM, for son Kevin Slade Morrison (1965–2010). Surrounding that sky room in the Hudson are jutting cypress knees, where a cormorant sits sunning its wings.

I notice the quiet elegance of the terraced garden sloping to the rocks, hear the waves lapping the rocks, the swing on the lower deck, the potted jade and rocking chair … the waters turning color in the light that pervades everything.

In her living room, with its tall glass windows framing the garden shrubs and trees on one wall, the Hudson on the other, we gather for some pictures. Her presence fills the spacious room with its comfortable beige sofas, books, Kevin's paintings, hand carved African art. She regales us with small anecdotes that evoke laughter. Signs some books at the table. It didn't occur to me to bring books for her to autograph.

Standing before her living room window, I behold the Grand View-on-Hudson through glass. A fluid expanse of silence reflects the changing light in a transparent moment that stays forever.

Who are you Toni, and what are you to me?

A partly rhetorical question I now begin to contemplate.

FINDING TONI MORRISON

It's the mid-1980s.

Three years into the PhD program, I have switched my thesis topic three times: my statement of purpose said I had come to research the transcendent in Thoreau and Whitman; I was interested in that cosmic song of the Self, the *Bhagavad Gita* as it morphed and became accessible to the poetic imagination in English. But newly arrived in America, I found myself challenged by history, one that I could not easily transcend; I was living the conundrums of the "postcolonial." The first two years of graduate school I attended classes despondent about *doing* English in a town where I had to explain why I spoke such good English.

Indian, I explained.

Which tribe came the well-meaning query.

Philosophical questions became historical ones: Why am I here? How come …?

Stung by the belatedness of grasping a certain subject position in history, I would find out with Morrison that *belatedness* itself was a condition of traumatic knowing and not knowing.

It was while researching the myth in literature of Demeter-Persephone—the mother-daughter goddesses central to the cosmic Eleusinian mysteries revealed in the religious cult at Eleusis in ancient Greece—that I was led to this item on my list in the library stacks: *The Bluest Eye. Here is the house … There were no marigolds … the earth itself unyielding … the seasons.* Standing, I began to read. The words, intimate and iconoclastic, sorrowful and singing, enchanting and uncanny.

Tired from holding the books, I lay them on the floor and, sitting beside them, keep reading in the aisle until I realized I had a stomach and that it hungered too.

I soon went back for *Sula*; savoring it between classes, I was smitten. I recalled why I had gravitated to literature in high school at fourteen. What perplexing mysteries awaited. The ride, by no means easy: dead men and a song of songs, a trickster at the crossroads, and that living tome as tomb, a talking book of jazz, more dead bodies, shootings, dying and spectral bodies to inter and enter, more burials ... *dear God!*

Enjoy, said the storyteller, narrating and breaking taboos with revelatory relish.

Now I understand that Morrison was compiling her own wisdom stories of liberation from the bonds of the past. The denouement of each novel, departing from its staged catastrophic beginning, rests in what has been accomplished or realized in the wake of the literal and metaphoric death and dying. Reviewing her oeuvre, across novels, essays, and plays, one can trace a shamanic project of individual and collective self-making in a literature where confrontation with the past, with an unjust social order, takes place in realms that are intimate, nonrational, embodied, spectral, and spiritual.

"We go to art" for many reasons, writes Morrison, among them being "anticipation with certainty that the art form will take us past our mundane selves into a deepness where we also reside" (*Source of Self Regard*, 287–8). I have come to appreciate Morrison's undertaking to be a religious one if, following Paul Tillich, "being religious means asking passionately the question of the meaning of our existence and being willing to receive answers, even if the answers hurt," if by religious we mean engaging the "dimension of depth" at the heart of experience (1).

THE MINISTERIAL VISION OF CHLOE–TONI MORRISON

Morrison's imagination, literary and spiritual, is a confluence of many waters. We know that Chloe Ardelia Wofford chose to be baptized Catholic at 12, that she took the middle name Anthony, after the Franciscan patron saint of the lost, St. Anthony.

Chloe Anthony Wofford went to Howard University, married, became Toni Morrison, and remained so since she divorced and became a writer, but she never ceased to be Chloe. I learn that *chloē* is a Greek word meaning "a green shoot of grass or grain," that "Demeter, the Greek goddess of agriculture, is sometimes referred to as Chloē ("Verdant")." In the same post "exploring the biblical theology of Christian egalitarianism," Marg Mowesko suggests that Chloe is a "prominent female minister" who engages Paul out of her genuine concern for the Corinthian church.

A self-appointed guardian of lost things, Toni Morrison's names aptly point to the convergence of spiritual traditions as expressed in her writings. The Bible, the spirituals of the African American tradition along with African diasporic religious tradition(s), the sermons of Black churches, the music of the Catholic liturgy, and that quintessentially Black diasporic and *modern spiritual* art form in music, jazz—these constitute Morrison's religious heritage. She invigorates the roots of her mixed heritage by claiming them all.

She reclaims the discredited epistemology and cosmology of the West African traditions and centers them in her novels where the spirit world is as real as the living, and where communication takes place with the seen and unseen worlds that include ancestral and sacralized nature spirits—where one divinized source is the origin of all the varied and sacred worlds.[1]

I thank Deborah G. Plant for her careful reading of an earlier draft of this essay.
[1] See Zauditu-Selassie's *African Spiritual Traditions in the Novels of Toni Morrison*.

She reclaims the *gnosis* (knowledge) upheld by the divine feminine principle subordinated within Christianity itself, but prominent in the gnostic gospels of the Nag Hammadi texts (Coptic translations of ancient manuscripts) discovered in 1945, one of whose editors is Elaine Pagels, a scholar of early Christianity and a colleague of Morrison's at Princeton. Pagels sums up as follows the differences between the gnostic texts and the Christianity that became consolidated by AD 200:

> Orthodox Jews and Christians insist that a chasm separates humanity from its creator: God is wholly other. But some of the gnostics who wrote these gospels contradict this: self-knowledge is knowledge of God; the self and the divine are identical.
>
> Second, the "living Jesus" of these texts speaks of illusion and enlightenment, not of sin and repentance, like the Jesus of the New Testament. Instead of coming to save us from sin, he comes as a guide who opens access to spiritual understanding. But when the disciple attains enlightenment, Jesus no longer serves as his spiritual master: the two have become equal—even identical … Does not such teaching—the identity of the divine and the human, the concern with illusion and enlightenment, the founder who is present not as Lord, but as spiritual guide—sound more Eastern than Western? … Could Hindu or Buddhist tradition have influenced gnosticism? (xx–xxi)

Pagels admits to such a possibility, adding, "What we call Eastern and Western religions, and tend to regard as separate streams, were not clearly differentiated 2,000 years ago" (xxi). At any rate, Pagels notes that the gnostic understanding, "suppressed and condemned by polemicists like Irenaeus," was branded as heresy by orthodox Christians (xxii). After two centuries of diverse Christian belief and practice, "by A.D. 200," Pagels informs us, "Christianity had become an institution headed by a three-rank hierarchy of bishops, priests, and deacons, who understood themselves to be the guardians of the only 'true faith'" (xxiii). She asks the basic questions feminist scholarship must ask: "According to tradition, a heretic is one who deviates from the true faith. But what defines that 'true faith'? Who calls it that and for what reasons?"

The epigraphs of both *Jazz* and *Paradise*, invoking a poetic voice of wisdom, are taken from one of the fifty-two Nag Hammadi texts retrieved: *Thunder, Perfect Mind*. In this gnostic text, a feminine wisdom proclaims the nullity of dichotomies in her eternal I am-ness:

> I am the whore and the holy one.
> I am the wife and the virgin …
> I am the silence that is incomprehensible …
> I am the utterance of my name. (Pagels, xvii)

Toni Morrison has heretical women and heresy as the subject and subthemes of several novels: Sula (*Sula*), Pilate (*Song of Solomon*), Consolata Sosa and the Convent women (*Paradise*), and Widow Ealing and her daughter Jane, targets of the Puritan witch hunt in the early 1690s (*A Mercy*). In both *Paradise* and *A Mercy*, Morrison decries dualistic, misogynistic, and otherworldly constructs that inform the conceptions of morality, church, and paradise as such an ordering of the world has negative consequences upon life and relationships on earth. It allows a split male psyche to "love the idealized virgin while raping her whore body," in Jungian analyst Marion Woodman's pithy formulation of the problem. If we add commodity capitalism to a dualistic, patriarchal mindset we have the apocalyptic war on life-forms that Morrison critiques, covertly or overtly, in every novel.

In *Paradise*, Morrison's gnostic understanding of God as being not "a peevish Lord" (146), not a force to be placated outside oneself but as a presence to be known within, is signaled to the congregation through Reverend Misner who "held the crossed oak in his hands, urging it to say what he could not: that not only is God interested in you; He *is* you" (emphasis in original). That this is an unorthodox Christian point of view is underscored by Misner wondering, "Would they see? Would they?" (147). At Save Marie's funeral, Misner finds himself articulating the ever-present intelligence of God: "It is our own misfortune if we do not know in our long life what she knew every day of her short one: that although life in life is terminal and life after life is everlasting, He is with us always, in life, after it and especially in between, lying in wait for us to know the splendor" (307).

Eros and the sanctity of the body and the spirit is central to Morrison's imagination and to her revised understanding of Christianity in *Paradise*. Consolata must unlearn what she learns from the nun Mary Magna: "My body is nothing my spirit everything" (263). A reformed Consolata, "a new and revised Reverend Mother" (265), voices her own gnostic gospel: "Hear me, listen. Never break them in two. Never put one over the other. Eve is Mary's mother. Mary is the daughter of Eve" (263). Morrison would agree with Alexander Irwin's assessment, "Christianity has not been kind to eros" (ix). Theologians like Paul Tillich and contemporary womanist and feminist ones have attempted to reinstate its integral function in all aspects of life. Lone DuPres rebukes the lopsidedness of Consolata's convent education: "You need what we all need: earth, air, water. Don't separate God from His elements. He created it all. You stuck on dividing Him from His works. Don't unbalance His world" (244). The observation of Woodman is cogent here: "The point of feminine consciousness is not to resolve matter into spirit, or spirit into matter. Rather it is to see spirit in matter and matter in spirit" (170).

In this ambitious novel of religious truth-making at the crossroads of the diaspora, Morrison expands to include the Afro-Brazilian religious practice Candomblé with its West African cosmology of life forces called the orishas.[2] In *Paradise*, Connie evolves into Consolata Sosa, a syncretic high priestess who enacts a ritual of purification and release for the tormented women in her charge. She becomes a shaman guiding the women across a psychic and spiritual terrain from soul loss to soul retrieval. *Paradise* ends with evocations of Yemanjá, Yoruba Goddess of the Ocean, of Piedade as the Black Madonna, of Demeter and Persephone, fulfilling the gnostic epigraph's promise of eternal life: "And they will live, and they will not die again."

Morrison's gnostic affirmation of feminine consciousness in Christianity is further expressed in poetry. "Five Poems," the brief collection of free verse published in a limited edition issued in 2002, begins with the poem "Eve Remembering":

> 1
>   I tore from a limb fruit that had lost its green.
> My hands were warmed by the heat of an apple
> Fire red and humming.
> I bit sweet power to the core.
> How can I say what it was like?
> The taste! The taste undid my eyes

---

[2] For a detailed analysis of related themes, see Marouan.

>   And led me far from the gardens planted for a child
>   To wildernesses deeper than any master's call.
>   2
>   Now these cool hands guide what they once caressed;
>   Lips forget what they have kissed.
>   My eyes now pool their light
>   Better the summit to see.
>   3
>   I would do it all over again:
>   Be the harbor and set the sail,
>   Loose the breeze and harness the gale,
>   Cherish the harvest of what I have been.
>   Better the summit to scale.
>   Better the summit to be. (1–18)[3]

The stanza's first line allies the plucking of the apple with eros; ignorance is associated with the virginity of not knowing, whose loss of green is a desirable thing—what attracts is the fire red. The "heat" and "sweet power" of passionate knowledge has consequences that are not bad: something to do with a mature vision that leads her beyond the child's contained garden (whose innocence is limiting) to unknown terrain far removed from obedience to any authority but her own. The next two stanzas progress from eyes envisioning and scaling the summit, to being it. In the last stanza, Eve has no regret in pursuing this odyssey that has been hers; the harvest is not something external but the enrichment of her own being. As Pagels points out, the serpent "appear[s] in gnostic literature as the principle of divine wisdom" (xvii).

Just as the gnostic Christian points of view were eclipsed by Orthodox Christianity, so the Eleusinian Mysteries and their sanctuaries were closed when Roman Christianity was imposed upon the Hellenist world. A longtime student of the Greek Classics, Chloe Morrison reclaims the Greek myths of the divine feminine that encode insight into the secrets of nature. It turns out that Morrison's writing had more than a minor relationship to the Greek goddesses Demeter and Persephone of the Eleusinian mysteries. In that encoding of the artist as a girl, we see an attunement to the mysteries of the sacred rites of Demeter–Persephone.

According to William Savage, the Eleusinian Mysteries were "religious practices characterized by initiation rites, cathartic and ecstatic practices, and a code of silence. *Eleuseos* means 'the coming,' so the word Eleusinian refers to a spiritual advent." According to Thomas Taylor, "the Lesser Mysteries signified the miseries of the soul while in subjection to the body. The Greater Mysteries obscurely intimated, by mystic and splendid visions, the felicity of the soul, both here and hereafter, when purified from the defilements of a material nature and constantly elevated to the realities of intellectual [spiritual] vision" (88).

Toni Morrison acknowledges rapport with the ritual cathartic and communal character of Greek tragedy and cosmology:

---

[3]For an extended analysis of the poems, see Li's essay.

> A large part of the satisfaction I have always received from reading Greek tragedy, for example, is in its similarity to Afro-American communal structures (the function of song and chorus, the heroic struggle between the claims of community and individual hubris) and African religion and philosophy. In other words, that is part of the reason it has quality for me—I feel intellectually at home there. ("Unspeakable Things Unspoken," *The Source of Self-Regard* 163)

The story of Demeter's separation from the daughter, Persephone's abduction and experience of the dark underworld in Hades, and her return to light in the order of seasons structures not only *The Bluest Eye*, but also informs the story of Sethe and Beloved in *Beloved* (1987), Consolata and Piedade in *Paradise* (1997), Florens and her *minha mae* in *A Mercy*, and even Desdemona and her surrogate mother Barbary in the play *Desdemona* (2011). It is the archetypal template through which Morrison gives voice to both the primal loss experienced in the Black diaspora and to the transcendent wisdom possible through the terrifying descent and the eventual ascent.

Woodman explains that the ancient rituals honoring and surrendering to the goddess are "performed … in the full knowledge that the instinctual energy pouring through them did not belong to them personally":

> Instead they honored it as the transpersonal energy of the Goddess. Having once surrendered to that energy, they were "virginal," incapable of usurping goddess energy as a personal attribute. In other words, psychological virginity, which releases an individual from selfish, possessive clinging, was attained, as is attained, through surrender to a god or goddess. (168)

Such an understanding illumines both the Yoruba-inspired Afro-Brazilian Candomblé (alluded to as the "dreaming" in *Paradise*) and the ancient Eleusinian Mystery cults, even as it points to the appeal of the transpersonal dimension of sacred myths that Morrison inscribes.

THE PRESENT AND THE PAST: ACHIEVING A SPIRITUAL INTEGRATION

Faulkner once said, *"The past is a foreign country"* (emphases in original).

For writers whose collective history as African Americans is eclipsed in the shadow of a dominant one, *whose present sometimes feels like a foreign country*—W. E. B. DuBois wrote of double consciousness, James Baldwin wrote mostly from outside the United States, Morrison about "the foreigner's home"—it becomes imperative to reclaim the past so that neither the past nor present remain estranged. When a stigmatized past or a discredited epistemology both shapes the life of the present *and* is repressed at the personal, generational, or national level, it exerts a force, offering compelling symbols and cryptic silences. This collective symbolic crypt is what Morrison enters and gives imaginative voice to, while honoring the lives of her ancestors.

When the present honors the past, and the past informs the present, neither is any longer the foreign country it once was; it holds few existential terrors. It equips Milkman to ride the air on freed wings in *Song of Solomon*; Sethe to learn she is her "own best thing" in *Beloved* (273); violent Violet to have some peaceful years with Joe in *Jazz*. In *Home* with the actual and metaphoric burial of bones, resting not haunting, Frank Money is freed to come home in a healing of masculine embodiment, as his sister Cee comes to be at home in her own body.

Morrison writes of ancestral lines on both sides of her lineage in the American South. She can sense and see, enter the liminal worlds. Like Pilate, that memorable daughter, sister, and aunt in *Song of Solomon*, Morrison "paid close attention to her mentor—the father who appeared before her sometimes and told her things" (*Song*, 150). She had a vision of a woman (like Beloved) rise out of the waters of the Hudson. One might say Morrison had clairvoyant abilities. In their tribute to the "special magic" of thirty women writers, Taisia Kitaiskaia and illustrator Katy Horan consider "the mantle of 'Literary Witch' [as] the highest honor [they] can bestow upon an author" (4). Toni Morrison is named "Queen of Miracles, Generations, and Memory," who "sees—cleaving from the skin of every person—the child they were, their parents, great-grandparents … She can see this ancestor's original hurt, carried around in the generations like a splinter in the spleen" (31). Her narratives of feminine and masculine wounding lift repressions, haunt absences, trace inhibitions, and dramatize dysfunctions. A writer who chronicles the subjective effects of socially sanctioned inequities, Morrison's genius is to enter the rifts of the psyche in an amorous and therapeutic telling.

"With her mind, Toni ferries her people's unsettled ghosts across hostile rivers," writes Taisia Kitaiskaia describing Morrison's witchery (31). Indeed, Morrison even turns to literary characters whose fictional death or absence, or neglect, needs some redress. Shakespeare's *Othello* gets a musical makeover in *Desdemona*, featuring the doomed heroine, her nursemaid Barbary, and Iago's wife, in addition to Othello, their dialogues or soliloquies in concert with African music staged by the Malian singer-storyteller Rokia Traoré.

Desdemona (2011) is emblematic of Morrison's revisioning the past to align it with the truths that escaped representation in literature or history for ideological reasons, such as the truth about African "Barbary," and the Black man Othello, and the silent doomed women. By highlighting the perspective of the spectral, where the dead freely speak to each other and to us, her play restores the integrity of the Black text to the race-biased white, of the feminine and feminist text to the masculine and sexist one, and the text of class elided in Desdemona's relationship to her maid Barbary. In Morrison's script, the perspective of life beyond death enables the expression of spiritual and spectral dimensions that have been registered freely since Sula observed her own death in *Sula*: "Well, I'll be damned she thought, it didn't even hurt. Wait'll I tell Nel" (149).

In an interview with Pip Cummings in 2015, Morrison recounts an early encounter with death, an astral body experience, that altered her perspective:

> Toni Morrison is telling me about the time she died several decades ago, and making it sound strangely appealing. "I left my body and I was only eyes and mind, that's all," she says. "I could think and I could see. I didn't try to speak because I was so fascinated with this experience."
>
> "I was moving down the street—sometimes slowly but, if I wanted to, I could go fast," she says. "Everything around me just looked incredible. I didn't want to come back but I had kids, so I tried to come back … Morrison mimes a struggle as she describes the difficulty of "getting back inside" her body, moving "from weightlessness to weight." She raises an index finger slowly from the arm of her chair, as if made from lead.
>
> "The attraction! Ooh, it was better than anything I'd ever felt. It was free, it was intelligent and I was in control. And the only other time that happens—those three things—is when I write."

Desdemona's description of the afterlife could well serve as that of the writing life that Morrison extols above:

"Late" has no meaning here. Here there is only the possibility of wisdom. Of knowing the earth is not quiet nor waiting. In the screech of color and the whisper of the lightless depths of the sea, it boils, breaks, or slumbers. And in this restless rest human life is as unlimited and miraculous as love. Here the infidel can embrace the saint just as sunlight creates the air we breathe. (*Desdemona*, 60)

Toni Morrison's achievement on a national and transnational register has been to mourn and celebrate African American experience in novels that chronicle resilience and despair, invoking both ancestral wisdom and trauma. The height and depth of the heroic, the tragic, and the lyric are measured by unforgettable characters who through their most vulnerable and glorious moments shape a living mythology for the Black diaspora.

THE SPIRITUAL DIMENSIONS OF TONI MORRISON'S OEUVRE

Morrison's oeuvre records an interior journey that can be called a spiritual one, its register distinct from the social; we could also refer to it as an archetypal inner journey of transformation. In Morrison's art, within the works and also across them, we witness an alchemical journey from the proverbial leaden states of lack and loss to transformation in a gnostic fire of suffering toward a more expansive allowing of *being*: toward love, mercy, belonging, to resume one's rightful place in an earthly *paradise* as home. No single character embodies the full vision, but Consolata of *Paradise* and Desdemona in the afterlife of Morrison's play come close.

We see the call to wholeness in Sula who had "seen ... the slant of life that made it possible to stretch it to its limits." Her disappointment with Nel was that she had become "one of them":

One of the spiders whose only thought was the next rung of the web, who dangled in dark dry places suspended by their own spittle, more terrified of the free fall than the snake's breath below. But the free fall, oh no, that require—demanded—invention: a thing to do with the wings, a way of holding the legs and most of all a full surrender to the downward flight if they wished to taste their tongues or stay alive. But alive was what they ... did not want to be. Too dangerous. (*Sula* 120)

In *Sula*, the "always" alluded to by Shadrack that made an impression upon her as a girl, eludes Sula as a woman, who encounters in the sexual act "a stinging awareness of the endings of things: an eye of sorrow in the midst of all that hurricane rage of joy ... in the center of that silence ... not eternity but the death of time and a loneliness so profound the word itself had no meaning" (123).

Lying alone on her death bed, she experiences a profound disenchantment with the world: "Nothing was ever different. They were all the same. All of the words and all of the smiles, every tear and every gag just something to do ... I didn't mean anything." In a stunning Black feminist encoding of dust to dust, the "Clabber Girl Baking Powder lady," a household symbol of whiteness and feminine domesticity is associated with death in her dream: "Smiling and beckoning to her ... she disintegrated into white dust" (147). Between the glimpse of "always" and the nihilistic "death of time," Sula dies to the world in a detachment that underscores the weariness described in the Bible: "What has been will be again, and what has been done will be done again; there is nothing new under the sun" (Ecclesiastes 1:9). However, such weariness with the repetitive quotidian can also lead one to engage with questions of ultimate meaning, what Paul Tillich would consider "the dimension of depth."

In *Song of Solomon*, Milkman Dead accomplishes the "full surrender" and "flight" that Sula yearns for. We see the disillusioned and lonely stance that was Sula's transform into a relational one that gestures toward giving and loving:

> "Here I am!"
> *Am am am am*, said the rocks.
> "You want me huh? Huh? You want my life?"
> Life life life life …
> "You need it? Here." Without wiping away the tears … Or even bending his knees—he leaped. As fleet and bright as a lodestar he wheeled toward Guitar … For now he knew what Shalimar knew: If you surrendered to the air, you could ride it. (emphases in original)

Milkman no longer allies himself with his father's deadly ambitions of accumulation and dominance over the vulnerable—"Own things. And let the things you own own other things. Then you'll own yourself and other people too" (55), which is the enslaved and enslaving mindset of the plantation owner who killed his grandfather. In *A Mercy* (2008), Morrison traces this mindset back to the colonial settler of the 1690s who wants to grasp what he sees as mine, mine, mine—an attitude leading to ecocide and the dispossession of peoples, poor white, native, and Black.

Enabling Milkman's transformation and central to this novel is another unconventional woman, Pilate, who

> threw away every assumption she had learned and began at zero … When am I happy and when am I sad and what is the difference? … What is true in the world? Her mind traveled crooked streets and aimless goat paths … Throughout this fresh, if common, pursuit of knowledge, one conviction crowned her efforts: since death held no terrors for her (she spoke often to the dead), she knew there was nothing to fear. (149)

Pilate pursues the path of self-knowledge or "insight"—to quote Pagels, "gnosis involves an intuitive process of knowing oneself" (xix). In Pilate's granddaughter Hagar we see the broken self that needs shoring, for the spiritual journey needs a stable container. This is the work that Morrison undertakes in *Beloved*.

Literary critics, including myself, have discussed at length the multiple registers of meaning represented in the figure of Beloved; here I wish to comment on an unnoticed aspect pertaining to the religious dimension of the wound of abandonment that Morrison enters fully in the groundbreaking novel *Beloved*. "The Song of Songs," the song cycle of Hebrew love poetry at the center of the Bible, evokes sensual pastoral imagery to describe the longing for the beloved. In the devotional Christian poems of St. John of the Cross, we can hear the echoes of the former. In the dialogue between the bride and the bridegroom in "The Spiritual Canticle" of St. John of the Cross, the "vexing afflictions" of the "wound of love" invite a comparison of *Beloved*'s exploration of the same. Ernest E. Larkin describes the context of the composition by St. John of the Cross:

> The poem opens with a statement of intense desire for the beloved. The life situation of the author at the time of composition was the painful experience of the Toledo prison that mirrored interior desolation … The desolation describes the interval between the … dark night and the

spiritual betrothal and marriage ... There is the experience of the infinite emptiness of the human spirit and the felt absence of the only Reality than can fill this cavity. The desire for God is at a fever pitch, the pain overwhelming.

Of course, the beloved for the Spanish mystic was Christ, and while Morrison's Beloved/*Beloved* does not represent the unitive experience of the spiritual life, it prepares the ground for it in the experience of the soul's desolation and in Sethe's gaze inward to the realization that she is her own "best thing," not the Beloved that leaves. Stanza 8 could well describe Sethe's condition of desolation in *Beloved*:

So, why do I go on like this,
Not living where you live, O life?
I die shot through
With arrows sharpened
By all my heart conceives of my beloved.

Paul D's impatience with the restless ghost/woman, Beloved, is reminiscent of the bridegroom's concern, in the thirtieth stanza, that his bride's house no longer be shaken:

By the soft strumming of the harp,
By the enchantress' song, I conjure you:
Cease your raging,
Rattle not our walls, Let my bride sleep in peace

Stanzas 21, 22, 23, and 24, describing the erotic love of the bride and bridegroom suggests the encounter of the mother and child dyad (recall Beloved playing with Sethe's earring) that later spirals into Beloved's needy and destructive narcissism.

In the 1560s, along with his spiritual guide St. Teresa of Avila, St. John of the Cross was instrumental in reforming the Carmelite Order of monks into the Reformed Discalced Order, where the mendicants walked barefoot or wore sandals in cold weather to remind them of their spiritual calling. Several characters in Toni Morrison's novels walk *discalced* or *without shoes*, their shoes missing or stolen or inadequate. Motherless Florens in *A Mercy* and evicted veteran Frank Money in *Home* are dispossessed Black pilgrims, sojourners in the American wilderness who come to realize their inner worth and spiritual poise through enduring hardship. Florens inwardly matures: "Mãe, you can have pleasure now because the soles of my feet are hard as cypress" (189). At the end of *Paradise*, a chastened and *reformed* Deek (Deacon) walks through town in "a clean white shirt" toward his mentor Richard Misner's house: "No shoes. No socks" (300).

In Sethe, Morrison also alights upon the archetype of the devouring and dreadful feminine force known in the Indian tantric tradition as Mother Kali, the black goddess, who in one hand holds a severed head, in another the severing and bloodied cleaver. Divine Mother of creation and destruction, her representation is unique among the pantheon of Hindu goddesses, all of whom have a pleasing countenance allied with light: Kali alone is fearsome, wild, and unrestrained, beyond the order of the social. As David Kinsley notes, Kali's teaching is "that pain, sorrow, decay, death, and destruction are not to be overcome or conquered by denying them or explaining them away" (*Sword and the Flute*, 144).

In Morrison's work, the dark energy of the Kali archetype is the fierce eruption of what Woodman calls "the revolutionary energy of the outcast goddess," "the Black Goddess in whom spirit and instinct meet" and whose role is to "counterbalance" the "rational" (166). On the inner plane, Kali brings liberation from bondage through the force of annihilation of the felt sense of separation from the divine. One might say that St. John of the Cross was intimate with her archetype.

THE ARTFUL IMAGINATION

> What works of art testify to is the presence in this world of consciousness … It is not the artists's awareness I am speaking of but the awareness he or she makes. For that is what fine writing does: it creates a unique verbal consciousness. (William Gass, "The Literary Miracle")

In his essay, "Healing the Imagination: Art Lessons from Baldwin," James K. A. Smith reflects on imagination as the "acquired" faculty that guides "our habits of perception: what we make of the world before we ever think about it." If imagination is a "learned, bodily disposition to the world," then the arts play a very significant role as they shape our individual and collective imagination with profound consequences. "Grabbing hold of us by the senses, artworks have a unique capacity to shape our attunement, our feel for the world," or what "philosopher Charles Taylor … calls our collective "social imaginary," that is,

> "the way ordinary people 'imagine' their social surroundings" before they ever think about it, the way we perceive others and our collective life in an instant. Our "take" on others. Importantly, Taylor points out that our social imaginary is "not expressed in theoretical terms, but is carried in images, stories, and legends." In other words, the social imaginary is shaped by the ways artists show us the world: our storytellers, image-makers, and performers of all kinds *enact* a story about who we are. (emphasis in original)

The Bluest Eye shows the attenuating effect that Shirley Temple, Jean Harlow, and white middle-class primers had on the imaginations of Pecola and her mother Pauline Breedlove. The music, folk and ghost stories Chloe Wofford heard in her own extended family allowed her imagination to take root in Black culture and be nourished by world literature that awaited her in the libraries of Lorain, Howard University, Cornell, and other places. She would then bring to bear her own learned and embodied disposition to "creat[e] a unique verbal consciousness" that would shape the social imaginary of the nation and beyond. The restoration of a complex Black diasporic subjectivity to the imagination of world readers is no small thing. To her readers, Toni Morrison has opened all the private rooms of the stranger's home, the secrets, the taboos, the longings. Wandering through them, we find there is no stranger; or, in the mirrors of the artful text, we welcome the estranged as ourselves.

Morrison's Desdemona underscores both the manifesting power of life and the creative power of imagination:

> The world is alive and even if we kill it, it returns fresh, full-throated and hungry for time and space in which to thrive. And if we haven't secured the passionate peace we yearn for, it is

because we haven't imagined it. Is it still available, this human peace? In our privileged position in timelessness, our answer is a roar. (61)

Aligned to the cosmic feminine principle eclipsed for a millennium, Toni Morrison returns us to the shared enterprise of making peace with the crossings, the crossroads, the cross, that intersection of dimensions, phenomenal time horizontal with eternal time vertical.

WORKS CITED

Cummings, Pip. "'I Didn't Want to Come Back': Toni Morrison on Life, Death and Desdemona," *Sydney Morning Herald*, Aug. 7, 2015. https://www.smh.com.au/entertainment/i-didnt-want-to-come-back-toni-morrison-on-life-death-and-desdemona-20150804-giqaxu.html. Accessed Aug. 1, 2021.

Irwin, Alexander. *Eros Toward the World: Paul Tillich and the Theology of the Erotic*. Wipf and Stock Publishers, 2004.

Kinsley, David R. *The Sword and the Flute*. U of California P, 1975.

Kitaiskaia, Taisia, and Katy Horan. *Literary Witches: A Celebration of Magical Women Writers*. Seal P, 2017.

Larkin, Ernest E. "Contemplation in *The Spiritual Canticle*: The Program of St John of the Cross." *Carmel and Contemplation: Transforming Human Consciousness, Carmelite Studies VIII*, edited by Kevin Culligan and Regis Jordan, ICS Publications, 2000, pp. 267–80.

Li, Stephanie. "Five Poems: The Gospel According to Toni Morrison." *Callaloo*, vol. 34, no. 3, Summer 2011, pp. 899–914, 984.

Marouan, Maha. "'Thunder, Perfect Mind': Candomblé, Gnosticism, and the Utopian Impulse in Toni Morrison's *Paradise*." *Witches, Goddesses, and Angry Spirits: The Politics of Spiritual Liberation in African Diaspora Women's Fiction*. The Ohio State UP, 2013, pp. 71–102.

Morrison, Toni. *Beloved*. 1987. Vintage International, 2004.

Morrison, Toni. *Desdemona*. Bloomsbury Publishing, Kindle Edition. 2011.

Morrison, Toni. "Five Poems." Rainmaker Editions, 2002.

Morrison, Toni. Nobel Lecture of 1993. https://www.nobelprize.org/prizes/literature/1993/morrison/lecture/. Accessed July 20, 2021.

Morrison, Toni. "The Slavebody and the Blackbody." *Source of Self-Regard: Selected Essays, Speeches, and Meditations*. Knopf, 2019, pp. 74–8.

Morrison, Toni. *Song of Solomon*. 1977. Vintage International, 2004.

Morrison, Toni. *Source of Self-Regard: Selected Essays, Speeches, and Meditations*. Knopf, 2019.

Mowesko, Marg. "Who was Chloe of Corinth?" Apr. 26, 2015. https://margmowczko.com/who-was-chloe-of-corinth/. Accessed July 15, 2021.

Pagels, Elaine. *The Gnostic Gospels*. Vintage, 1989.

Savage, William. "Quest of the Soul: The Eleusinian Mysteries." *Sunrise Magazine*, Feb./Mar. 2006. https://www.theosociety.org/pasadena/sunrise/55-05-6/me-savage.htm. Accessed July 15, 2021.

Smith, James K. A. "Healing the Imagination: Art Lessons from James Baldwin." *Image Journal*, Issue 107. https://imagejournal.org/article/healing-the-imagination-art-lessons-from-james-baldwin/. Accessed June 30, 2021.

Taylor, Thomas. *The Eleusinian and Bacchic Mysteries*. 1891. https://www.sacred-texts.com/cla/ebm/index.htm. Accessed July 15, 2021.

Tillich, Paul. "Invocation: The Lost Dimension in Religion." *The Essential Tillich: An Anthology of the Writings of Paul Tillich*. U of Chicago P, 1999, pp. 1–10.

Woodman, Marion. *The Pregnant Virgin: A Process of Psychological Transformation*. Inner City Books, 1985.

Zauditu-Selassie, K. *African Spiritual Traditions in the Novels of Toni Morrison*. UP of Florida, 2009.

PART TWO

Morrison and the Contemporary World

CHAPTER TWELVE

"Unforgetting": Toni Morrison's *Beloved* and the National Memorial for Peace and Justice

KRISTINA K. GROOVER

In 1989, in a speech accepting the Melcher Book Award from the Unitarian Universalist Association, Toni Morrison characterized her novel *Beloved* as a kind of memorial, created in the absence of any monument recognizing the lives of millions of enslaved people who were sold, purchased, brutalized, and killed during 250 years of slavery in America. "It's almost as though the novel substitutes for something, that it exists instead of something else," Morrison stated. "There is no place you or I can go … to summon the presences of, or recollect the absences of slaves … And because such a place doesn't exist … the book had to" (Morrison, "Melcher Book Award"). In this essay, I read Morrison's "memorial" novel *Beloved* alongside the National Memorial for Peace and Justice (NMPJ)—the recently opened "lynching memorial" in Montgomery, Alabama. Both Morrison's novel and the NMPJ function as counter-monuments, challenging American metanarratives that have erased or distorted African American lives and stories. To name those whom history has not named and fill in the gaps and silences of their lives destabilizes a dominant national narrative shaped by ideologies of American exceptionalism and progressivism. Both Morrison's text and the NMPJ further inscribe a history that is "infinite," as Morrison has described it, and that is constantly being constructed. As such, the impact of the Memorial and the novel are not merely restorative, but potentially reparative—invoking, in Ta Nehisi Coates's definition of the term, a "full acceptance of our [national] biography and its consequences."

The NMPJ and its companion Legacy Museum opened in 2018 as projects of the Equal Justice Initiative (EJI), a public interest law firm in Montgomery. Bryan Stevenson, founder and director of EJI, conceived of the Memorial and Museum as extensions of the law firm's work against wrongful conviction, excessive sentencing, and abuse within the criminal justice system. Over time, the legal staff of EJI had recognized that the cases they were fighting would ultimately be determined not simply by questions of law, but by whether or not decision-makers valued the lives of the Black defendants standing before them. They realized that they were "fighting a broader historical narrative"—one that we as a country had created—about the relative value of Black lives.[1] To understand the source of that narrative, and to revise it, requires a communal descent into

---

[1] Sia Sanneh, interview with Kristina K. Groover, September 27, 2020.

a deliberately buried history. The NMPJ and the Legacy Museum bring the mostly forgotten history of racial terror lynching into the public sphere, while placing this record within the larger American history of slavery, convict leasing, Jim Crow laws, police brutality, and mass incarceration.

Viewed from a distance, the NMPJ looks like a somewhat conventional, even classical, monument.[2] The low colonnade, situated on a hill overlooking the state capital of Montgomery, is formed by hundreds of identical steel pillars apparently supporting the structure's roof. The pillars, each representing a county in the United States where documented racial lynchings took place, are engraved with the names of thousands of victims. This is a stately memorial for the dead.

Upon entering the Memorial, however, a viewer's experience transforms from spectator to participant.[3] Walking among the steel pillars and reading the names recalls the experience of wandering in a graveyard, even as the oversized markers create a sense of disorientation. As one proceeds through the Memorial on a downward-sloping walkway, the steel pillars seem to rise slowly overhead. They are not, in fact, holding up the roof, but rather are suspended from it. As visitors continue their descent, the columns finally, sickeningly, hang overhead, invoking bodies hung from trees or gallows, with spectators gaping up from below (Figure 12.1).

Exiting from the shadows of the Memorial into bright daylight, visitors encounter this quotation from Toni Morrison's *Beloved*, emblazoned on an enormous wall (Figure 12.2):

> And O my people, out yonder, hear me, they do not love your neck unnoosed and straight. So love your neck; put a hand on it, grace it, stroke it and hold it up. And all your inside parts that they'd just as soon slop for hogs, you got to love them. The dark, dark liver—love it, love it, and the beat and beating heart, love that too. More than eyes or feet. More than lungs that have yet to draw free air. More than your life-holding womb and your life-giving private parts, hear me now, love your heart. For this is the prize.

The passage comes from Baby Suggs's preaching in the Clearing, as she encourages the former slaves in her congregation to lovingly embrace their bodies that were used and abused as tools of slavery (Morrison 104). By reclaiming the community's "deeply loved flesh"—inextricable from their spirits—she restores their humanity, delivering them from the material claims of slave owners that reduced them to chattel.

The NMPJ enters into a tradition of counter-monuments established by Maya Lin's Vietnam Veterans Memorial in 1982. While traditional public monuments often aim to achieve a sense of closure by creating a singular, collective public memory, counter-monuments resist that aim. Rather, counter-monuments acknowledge what historian James Young terms "*collected* memory"—the diverse memories and experiences that make up a history and cannot be reduced to a single story. Counter-monuments emphasize that past events are not "frozen in time or static in space," but are continually animated, interpreted, and remade by present-day lives (Young 8, emphasis in original). Morrison's *Beloved* testifies to this infinite and malleable history.

---

[2]Commenting on the Memorial's classical structure, Tanja Schult argues that the monument "evokes architectonical references that can be read art historically as a critical reflection on Western civilization, with its imagined beginning in an idealized white Greek Antiquity" (12).
[3]Kirk Savage points out the "spatial turn in monumental design" was "confirmed and popularized" by the Vietnam Veterans Memorial, which opened in 1982. "At the beginning of the twenty-first century, national memorials are now expected to be spaces of experience … rather than exemplary objects to be imitated" (20–1).

EMBODIED HISTORY

Conceiving of Morrison's novel as a memorial isn't difficult. At the center of the text stands a tombstone, marked not with the name of the dead child buried there, but with the word "Beloved." The marker and the text both serve as memorials to the countless "beloved"—the "sixty million and more" lost to slavery, as Morrison reminds in her epilogue. The novel's spiritual and psychological center is a loss that haunts the living: literally, in the case of the "spiteful" baby ghost that disturbs Sethe's house; but, more broadly, in the countless homes and families grieving a lost "beloved." "Not a house in the country ain't packed to its rafters with some dead Negro's grief," Baby Suggs reminds her daughter-in-law (6). *Beloved* probes both memory and mourning: what is remembered; how memory is mediated by language, bodies, and places; the ways that mourning is allowed or disallowed; how memories and mourning construct the present.

Both the NMPJ and Morrison's novel explicitly connect the reclaiming of history and story with the reclaiming of physical bodies. Baby Suggs's preaching—the "gospel" at the heart of *Beloved*—focuses not on the afterlife, or the soul, but on the body. Her ministry, which evokes New Testament accounts of Jesus' ministry as he preached in outdoor spaces before large crowds, "both adheres to and critiques the tradition of Christianity in the black community" (Coleman 90). In keeping with the practice of call-and-response, Baby Suggs's sermon is less prescriptive than constructive; her teaching draws on her knowledge of Christian texts while adapting to the experiences and needs of her formerly enslaved congregants.[4] She invokes Jesus' Sermon on the Mount, only to reject parts of its message that have been used to subdue and control the Black community: "She did not tell them to clean up their lives or to go and sin no more. She did not tell them they were the blessed of the earth, its inheriting meek or its glorybound pure." Rejecting the political uses of religion to perpetuate slavery, she focuses not on her listeners' sins, nor on their salvation in the hereafter, but on reclaiming their embodied lives "in this here place," where "we flesh; flesh that weeps, laughs; flesh that dances on bare feet in grass" (103).

Highlighting the vulnerability of Black bodies—those "run off ... hanged ... rented out, loaned out, bought up, brought back, stored up, mortgaged, won, stolen or seized"—may seem to invite a focus on trauma, rather than reparation (Morrison 28). Indeed, a significant body of published criticism on *Beloved* has rightly focused on individual and collective trauma.[5] However, in *Precarious Life: The Powers of Mourning and Violence*, Judith Butler argues that the universally shared human vulnerability to physical harm shapes not only our psychological makeup, but also our political formation and identity. Because every person is subject to loss and harm, she writes, "each of us is constituted politically in part by virtue of the social vulnerability of our bodies" (20). Acknowledging the bodies of ourselves and others "implies mortality, vulnerability, agency: the skin and the flesh expose us to the gaze of others, but also to touch, and to violence, and bodies put us at risk of becoming the agency and instrument of all these as well ... The body has its invariably public dimension" (26). Butler thus defines human vulnerability to harm, as well as our role as agents of harm, as "social conditions of ... embodiment" (26).

---

[4]In *Transforming Scriptures: African American Women Writers and the Bible*, Katherine Bassard refers to this as literary "sampling." Baby Suggs shows knowledge of the scripture not to "'prove' a prior assumptions," but to create something new (52).
[5]See, for example, Schreiber, Bast, Vine, and Spargo.

In *Beloved*, Baby Suggs's sermon invokes this shared bodily vulnerability. Her ministry originates in her own physical brokenness: because "slave life had 'busted her legs, back, head, eyes, hands, kidneys, womb and tongue,' she had nothing left to make a living with but her heart" (102). Standing before her congregation, she takes the reclaiming of their broken bodies as her urtext:

> Yonder they do not love your flesh. They despise it. They don't love your eyes; they'd just as soon pick em out. No more do they love the skin on your back. Yonder they flay it. And O my people they do not love your hands. Those they only use, tie, bind, chop off and leave empty. Love your hands! Love them. Raise them up and kiss them.

The body thus serves as a record of slavery's atrocities—the flayed back, the bound hands—as well as a source of potential healing and reclamation for both the individual and the community: "Love your hands! ... Raise them up and kiss them. Touch others with them, pat them together, stroke them on your face" (103). Sethe's body, too, serves as both a record of her history and a potential site of healing. The tree-shaped scar on her back functions as both symbol and narrative, its roots and branches signifying the endless generational impact of slavery on her family line. As Paul D "reads" Sethe's history by touching his cheek to her scarred back, the tree discloses the unspeakable cruelties she has suffered: he "learned that way her sorrow, the roots of it; its wide trunk and intricate branches" (20). As he holds Sethe's breasts in his hands, she wonders whether being relieved of that maternal weight makes it possible to "feel the hurt her back ought to. Trust things and remember things because the last of the Sweet Home men was there to catch her if she sank" (21). Sethe's scarred body testifies not only to personal trauma, but to a shared history: of bodies vulnerable "to touch, and to violence," as well as bodies as the "agency and instrument" of that brokenness (Butler 26).

The NMPJ also invokes a shared sense of vulnerable humanity by placing embodiment—that of both victims and spectators—at its center. Gazing up at the suspended monuments inevitably recalls photographs of spectators gathered at public lynchings, observing heinous acts of brutality with seeming dispassion. These images give witness to the underlying narrative of Black inferiority constructed during slavery; only the failure to see Black victims of violence as human can explain the inured response to their suffering.[6] At the same time, the participatory nature of the memorial destabilizes the viewer's subject position; even as visitors gaze up at the monuments, they are surrounded by the names of thousands of victims, thus having the visceral experience of being on view themselves.[7] As Drew Leder writes in *The Absent Body*, embodied experience is "a profoundly social thing, arising out of experiences of the corporeality of other people and of their gaze directed back upon me ... My self-understanding always involves the seeing of what others see in me" (92). It is our own embodiment that, in Butler's terms, "expose[s] us to the gaze of others."[8] History is always embodied; to obscure or erase embodied lives is to erase history itself.

---

[6]A large collection of lynching photographs, which were often reproduced on-site as postcards, is found in James Allen's *Without Sanctuary*.
[7]Tanja Schult refers to the Memorial's "public shaming strategy" (36)—a reading that I resist as potentially reductive. Like any complex artwork, the Memorial will inspire a variety of emotional reactions among visitors, based on their own racial identities as well as many other factors. Likewise, while there is much that is *shameful* in Morrison's novel, it would be reductive to characterize its aim as one of *shaming*. For complex discussions of the role of shame in commemorating atrocities, see Neiman (2019) and Doss chapter 5, "Duluth's Lynching Memorial and Issues of National Morality" (2010).
[8]In *Monument Wars*, Kirk Savage points out that the reflective black granite of the Vietnam Veterans Memorial notably makes the visitor's experience central to constructing the meaning of the Memorial: "Seeing themselves reflected in the

SPACE, PLACE, AND HISTORY

Asked why he did not locate the NMPJ in Washington, DC, Bryan Stevenson states that "We want people to come here." From its vantage point on a hill overlooking downtown Montgomery, the Memorial surveys a city that was central to the nineteenth-century domestic slave trade. Beginning around 1840, Montgomery became a principal slave trading city of the deep south. Enslaved people were transported to Montgomery by steamship, by train, and on foot. They were held in warehouses and depots located throughout Montgomery's downtown before being sold, either privately or in public auction at the present-day Court Square. In the midst of this mercenary landscape stands Alabama's state capitol building, emblematic of the collusion of state and commerce in a landscape dominated—physically and financially—by slavery (*Slavery in America*). Once a visitor has that geographic knowledge, Stevenson points out, "your relationship to that space ... changes radically" (Stevenson, "Narrative Power").

While the slave trade fundamentally shaped its urban geography, Montgomery's memorial landscape largely erases the central role of slavery in the city's history and economy. Instead, Montgomery's memorials are devoted to a celebration of the Confederacy—and, more recently, to the city's role in central events of the civil rights movement.[9] On the grounds of the state capitol, a massive memorial mourns the lost lives of Alabama's Confederate soldiers; a larger-than-life statue of Jefferson Davis stands nearby. Davis's home, the "White House of the Confederacy," is one of Montgomery's major tourist attractions. At the riverfront, where thousands of enslaved people arrived by boat and train, a public information display installed in 2014 relates the history of Montgomery on narrative panels tracing the city's development. The display is mounted on the concrete remains of a "cotton slide"—a device that hastened the loading of cotton onto barges. While the cotton slide constitutes a literal, physical remnant of the architecture of slavery, the text of the display does not mention slavery—not even on the panel devoted to "A City Built on Commerce (1820–1865)."[10] The slave trade that formed the backbone of Montgomery's commercial rise is thus elided from the memorial landscape. In 2017, as other states and cities were removing Confederate memorials, Alabama passed the Alabama Memorial Preservation Act, making it illegal to remove any monument more than forty years old from public lands—a clear effort to safeguard a dominant political and cultural narrative.[11] This geographic knowledge is essential for

---

wall, mingled with the names and the scenery, would remind them that their own thoughts and reactions were as much the subject matter of the memorial as the soldiers being commemorated" (273). The National Memorial for Peace and Justice is similarly immersive.

[9] The Seal of the City of Montgomery features the words "Cradle of the Confederacy" and "Birthplace of the Civil Rights Movement"; the latter phrase was added by the Montgomery City Council in 2002. Montgomery features a number of tourist sites related to the civil rights movement of the 1950s and 1960s, including a Rose Parks Statue and Museum, a Freedom Riders Museum, and the historic Dexter Avenue Memorial Baptist Church where Martin Luther King, Jr. served as a young pastor and rose to leadership. Unlike these sites, the Legacy Museum "invites visitors to envision a much longer periodization of racial terrorism, beginning with the kidnapping of people of color from their homes in the seventeenth century and lasting for centuries" (Hasian and Paliewicz, 190).

[10] I photographed this display on a visit to Montgomery in October 2020. The panel titled "A City Built on Commerce (1820–1865)" reads, in part, "It was at this time that the first of many riverboats, the *Harriott*, arrived and transformed Montgomery into an important regional hub for the shipping, trading, and storing of cotton and many other important commodities." Only when I returned home and enlarged the photo did I see that a visitor had added an addendum; scratched into the display's plexiglass cover, below the word "commodities" is the phrase "AKA SLAVES."

[11] The Alabama Memorial Preservation Act "prohibits the relocation, removal, alteration, renaming, or other disturbance of any monument located on public property which has been in place for 40 years or more." (https://ahc.alabama.gov/

understanding the impact of the NMPJ, which both critiques and supplants Montgomery's built environment. The NMPJ disrupts a carefully constructed public narrative in which Confederate soldiers are memorialized while the lives of enslaved people are erased, and in which Montgomery became a wealthy commercial center of the booming cotton industry without a slave in sight. As James Young argues, such memorial iconography rests on a "precarious foundation" (155): "an old order that never existed in the first place" (130).[12]

Public monuments often serve as sites for articulating communal grief, whether that of a town or of a nation. On one level, both Montgomery's Confederate monuments and the NMPJ serve this role. However, Judith Butler argues that memorials have the further function of proclaiming which lives are grievable, and which are not. Writing of the public memorials and obituaries commemorating US lives lost on September 11, 2001, Butler questions "how certain forms of grief become nationally recognized and amplified, whereas other losses become unthinkable and ungrievable." To build memorials and write public obituaries for American lives lost while remaining silent about those whom the United States has killed creates a "differential allocation of grievability that decides what kind of subject is and must be grieved, and what kind of subject must not" (xiv). This "disavowed mourning," Butler continues, "operates to produce and maintain certain exclusionary conceptions of who is normatively human" (xv). The country's public memorializing of September 11 thus contributes to a hegemonic public discourse, not only about national mourning and memorializing of the dead, but also about the relative valuation of human lives.

Butler's analysis, although focused on the United States' actions in an international forum, is strikingly applicable to the memorialization that followed the US Civil War. After the end of Reconstruction, and in the following decades, supporters of the Confederacy erected a vast landscape of public remembrance: memorials, monuments, and place names honoring the Confederate cause.[13] This pervasive iconography establishes a public record of which lives are "grievable"—those of Confederate soldiers and supporters—and which are not—those of enslaved people, whose lives are erased from public view. As Paul Connerton argues in *How Societies Remember*, "Control of a society's memory largely conditions the hierarchy of power" (1). Clearly, widespread Confederate iconography has the intent and effect of asserting authority and power. But by Butler's analysis, the erasure of these lives in the public square goes further: lives not publicly represented are not only disempowered, but ungrievable—therefore, perhaps, not even human. Indeed, to maintain the American mythology of freedom and equality in the face of our indisputable history *requires* the de facto dehumanization of Black people—thereby placing them, in our national imagination, "beyond the realm of politics" (Coates).

The NMPJ alters this emplaced history—not only in its disruption of Montgomery's memorial landscape but, more radically, in its ambition to alter the memorial landscape of the country.

MonumentPreservation.aspx#:~:text=The%20Alabama%20Memorial%20Preservation%20Act,for%2040%20years%20or%20more.).

[12]In 2013, the Equal Justice Initiative installed three historic markers in Montgomery, noting the downtown locations of warehouses that held slaves as well as the railroad and river depots where enslaved people were imported into the city. These markers, like the National Memorial for Peace and Justice, disrupt narrative and geographic silence surrounding the history of racial violence.

[13]As many historians have noted, most Confederate monuments were erected in the early twentieth century, followed by a second wave in the early 1960s. As Susan Neiman writes, "The monuments were not innocuous shrines to history; they were provocative assertions of white supremacy at moments when its defenders felt under threat" (263).

Outside the NMPJ, laid out in long rows, are duplicate monuments for each of the more than 800 stelae that comprise the Memorial. They are there to be claimed by the hundreds of counties across the country where racial lynchings have been documented.[14] The Equal Justice Initiative works with local groups that want to uncover their own communities' hidden histories of racial terror violence and commemorate those lost lives with the placement of monuments. This Community Remembrance Project aims to "transform our national landscape into a more honest reflection of the history of America and reflect a community's ongoing commitment to truth-telling and racial justice" ("Community Remembrance"). Tanja Schult calls this project the Memorial's "take-away twin," comparing it to the decentralized Holocaust memorial formed by thousands of *Stolpersteine* across Europe.[15] Literally "stumbling stones," these small markers embedded in the pavement in front of homes and businesses commemorate individual lives at the places they were snatched up by the terrorist machine of the Third Reich. Similarly, the Community Remembrance Project translates the violent history documented at the NMPJ into losses that are both personal and local—providing stumbling stones that interrupt accepted and familiar histories.

Toni Morrison's historical novels, too, act as stumbling stones that disrupt America's national narratives. Morrison's deep engagement with history is well-known to readers of her work. In *Beloved*, her characters consciously insert themselves into the country's recorded history with their animated discussions of "the true meaning of the Fugitive Bill, the Settlement Fee, God's Ways and Negro pews; anti-slavery, manumission, skin voting, Republicans, Dred Scott, book learning, Sojourner's high-wheeled buggy, the Colored Ladies of Delaware, Ohio" (204). At the same time, Morrison's view of history is a distinctly postmodern one that rejects broad historical narratives. In *Beloved*, Sethe claims that she finds it hard to "believe in" time as a linear construct: "Some things go. Pass on. Some things just stay" (43). Here, Sethe articulates the malleability of a history in which some voices and events dominate, while others are forgotten or repressed. When Sethe's dead child reappears, Sethe's own long-repressed memories are triggered by the girl's questions; as Beloved's singsong refrain of "Tell me" punctuates Sethe's days, she recalls stories "she had forgotten she knew," events "that had seeped into a slit in her mind" (73). The novel thus turns on a malleable history that is continually being constructed and reconstructed. While the progressive narrative of American history focuses on 1865 as a historical end point, the "end" of slavery forms only a dim background to Sethe's story. Long after the conclusion of the Civil War and the passage of the Thirteenth Amendment, the suffering set in motion by slavery reverberates endlessly in her present and future. In 1873, the novel's present day, Sethe's losses remain staggering: she has lost her husband, the daughter she murdered to save her from enslavement, the traumatized sons who subsequently ran away, and the mother-in-law who died of heartbreak. Like the scar on her back, these losses are permanently etched into Sethe's life. Paul D's narrative, likewise, is not that of the heroic escaped slave on a linear journey from slavery to freedom—a literary trope that reflects a larger historical narrative of American exceptionalism and progressivism. Instead, Paul D endures

---

[14]Strikingly, Marouf Hasian and Nicholas Paliewicz state that the duplicate memorials are there to be "(*re*)claimed" (emphasis added) by local communities. This locution emphasizes the project's mission of encouraging communities to acknowledge and commemorate their history more fully and honestly—that is, (*re*)claiming a history that already belongs to them.

[15]Schult writes, "The take-away twin will travel to the scenes of the crimes to memorialize the specific act of horror and trauma *in situ*. The envisaged erection of single memorial markers in places throughout the US promises to refurnish and thereby fundamentally reshape American identity based on the acknowledgment of the country's history of racial violence" (2).

eighteen years of homeless wandering, separated from loved ones, his repressed memories locked within the rusted tobacco tin of his heart. In Morrison's construction, slavery has no end point and is not contained by a linear history.

Perhaps Morrison's most radical disruption of the American narrative about slavery is her depiction of slaveholders. Schoolteacher is not singularly, extraordinarily evil, but disarmingly ordinary. His actions are driven by detached economic calculation rather than overt hostility or hatred. When faced with the horrific specter of Sethe's dead child, he reacts by observing that "there was nothing there to claim."

> The three (now four—because she'd had the one coming when she cut) pickaninnies they had hoped were alive and well enough to take back to Kentucky, take back and raise properly to do the work Sweet Home desperately needed, were not. Two were lying open-eyed in sawdust; a third pumped blood down the dress of the main one—the woman schoolteacher bragged about, the one he said made fine ink, damn good soup, pressed his collars the way he liked besides having at least ten breeding years left. (175–6)[16]

Here Morrison undermines the trope of the slave master as exceptionally evil or pathological—a stereotype that informs the mythology of slavery as an aberrant chapter in the larger narrative of American goodness. Morrison makes clear that American prosperity and slavery are inextricably interwoven; the "aberration" here is not slavery, but the inconvenient fact that "there was nothing there to claim."[17]

For Morrison, both places and bodies are repositories of memory that are animated by present-day human lives. For this reason, Sethe works to shield her daughter Denver from sites of past trauma. Sweet Home, the farm where Sethe was brutalized while she was enslaved, is a real, material place; but it also transcends the material as the atrocities that happened there live on in "rememory." "It's never going away," Sethe tells Denver. "Even if the whole farm—every tree and grass blade of it dies. The picture is still there and what's more, if you go there—you who never was there—if you go there and stand in the place where it was, it will happen again; it will be there for you, waiting for you" (43–4). As Morrison's narrative demonstrates, while Sethe can keep Denver from the physical space of Sweet Home, she cannot shield her from inevitable encounters with the past. Like the tree-shaped scar on Sethe's back, "rememory" signifies the eternal present of slavery.

STORIES: THE WORD AND HISTORY

I want to turn, finally, to the idea of narrative and its relationship to memorializing and to reparation. Bryan Stevenson has often stated that he believes the "true evil" of slavery was not the enforcement of involuntary servitude, but the creation of a narrative of racial difference: the deep and persistent

---

[16] Dean Franco argues persuasively that Morrison makes "claiming" central to her novel: Schoolteacher's claim of ownership, facilitated by a slavecatcher and a sheriff, precipitates the novel's central tragedy; Sethe resists by claiming her right, as a mother, to "put my babies where they'd be safe" (193); Paul D is frightened away, less by Sethe's actions than by what she "claimed" (193).

[17] As Ta-Nehisi Coates has argued, while "Colored Only" signs are the de facto symbol of white supremacy, that symbol should instead be a pirate flag—signifying the enormous wealth generated through slave labor and its legacy.

narrative of Black inferiority and criminality that made slavery possible and that has informed a long history of discriminatory and inhumane practices. The South lost the Civil War but "won the narrative," Stevenson claims, by constructing a durable romantic history of the "Lost Cause" while largely erasing slavery and its legacy. Our willful inattention to correcting this narrative "is what has sustained the problems we've tried to overcome" ("Truth and Reconciliation," 22).

In *Beloved*, Morrison depicts language and narrative as tools both to enslave and to liberate. This is powerfully displayed in the character of the slaveholder Garner who, while he does not strike or otherwise brutalize his slaves, nonetheless uses language to define and control them. He revels in bragging to his neighbors that "at Sweet Home, my niggers is men every one of em. Bought em thataway, raised em thataway. Men every one" (12). His boast, however, is not of his slaves' humanity, but of his own manliness: he comes home from these arguments "bruised and pleased, having demonstrated one more time what a real Kentuckian was: one tough enough and smart enough to make and call his own niggers men" (12–13). As slaveholder, Garner holds the power of the definer to make his slaves either "niggers" or "men," according to his own will. Paul D recognizes that "they were only Sweet Home men at Sweet Home. One step off that ground and they were trespassers among the human race" (147–8). Schoolteacher's power and Garner's are much the same, both lying in the power of defining:

> For years Paul D believed schoolteacher broke into children what Garner had raised into men ... Now ... he wondered how much difference there really was between before schoolteacher and after. Garner called and announced them men—but only on Sweet Home, and by his leave. Was he naming what he saw or creating what he did not? ... Did a white man saying it make it so? (260)

Morrison thus shows the constructive power of language to assign subjectivity and to create what can be believed as real.

Schoolteacher reifies this power through his pseudoscientific study of the enslaved people living at Sweet Home, recording their "animal" and "human" characteristics in his notebook. His project both reflects and constructs an ongoing narrative about Black inferiority, animality, unintelligence—those beliefs essential to slavery as an institution. To challenge this narrative is to risk being literally and brutally silenced, as when Paul D is forced to wear a "bit" as punishment for an escape attempt. In an interview, Morrison explicates the power of the bit as a symbolic link between silencing and dehumanizing: "It is having no language, not being permitted to articulate anything, not being permitted to express anything, which is the final devastation ... And imposing that kind of restraint, little by little by little, atom by atom by atom, should destroy you—physically, spiritually—and all of your human qualities would evaporate." For Morrison, to silence is to dehumanize—to impose "the final devastation" (Benson). When Sethe kills her daughter, she saves her not only from the physical brutality of slavery, but also from the necessary and degrading narrative that perpetuates it: "No one, nobody on this earth, would list her daughter's characteristics on the animal side of the paper. No. Oh no" (296).

The power of narrative returns me to Baby Suggs's preaching, which Stamp Paid refers to as "the Word": "'Listen here, girl,' he told her, 'you can't quit the Word. It's given to you to speak. You can't quit the Word, I don't care what all happen to you'" (209). Stamp's language invokes the Gospel of John, which proclaims that, in the incarnation of Jesus Christ, the Word was "made flesh, and dwelt among us ... full of grace and truth." Like Baby Suggs's message, which is centrally about bodily healing and the inextricability of body and spirit, the scripture conflates text—a "Word ... full of grace and truth"—with embodiment—a Word that "was made flesh" in the person of Jesus. Stamp Paid regrets having forgotten this truth when he berated Baby Suggs for abandoning her ministry: he laments "the high tone he took; his refusal to see the effect of marrow weariness in a woman he believed was a mountain" (212). Baby Suggs is not a mountain, but an embodied and vulnerable human, worn to the breaking point by slavery's ravages. The Word—of hope, of history, of healing—is inextricably connected to the body. To save the one relies upon saving the other.

CONCLUSION: AGAINST REDEMPTION

Beloved's final chapter serves as a kind of postscript, a metanarrative commentary on the malleability of history. The character of Beloved is reconfigured as a memory: one "shaped and decorated" by those who had known her, or seen or heard about her, and then deliberately forgotten. Yet, like any seemingly forgotten story, she recurs again and again, returning in dreams and fleeting apparitions, resurfacing from the water where she emerged. Her footprints beside the stream "come and go, come and go. They are so familiar. Should a child, an adult place his feet in them, they will fit. Take them out and they disappear again as if nobody ever walked there" (324). Like the roots of a family tree, or a palimpsestic photograph, the past may fade to invisibility; but its reach is unending.

Ta-Nehisi Coates and others have argued that the primary mechanism of any reparations proceeding must be truth-telling about our history—a process that is critical to establishing a more just present and future.[18] As Coates writes,

> Perhaps no [monetary] number can fully capture the multi-century plunder of black people in America. Perhaps the number is so large that it can't be imagined, let alone calculated and dispensed. But I believe that wrestling publicly with these questions matters as much as—if not more than—the specific answers that might be produced. An America that asks what it owes its most vulnerable citizens is improved and humane. An America that looks away is ignoring not just the sins of the past but the sins of the present and the certain sins of the future.

Memorials can play a critical role in this confrontation with the past, their acts of "collected memory" bringing previously suppressed stories into the national narrative. To unflinchingly confront a deliberately repressed history makes possible what Dora Apel terms "a process of unforgetting ... in order to counter disbelief, construct a sense of empathy, and achieve a greater understanding of the roots of racial and ethnic oppression and of the ongoing struggles for equality and social justice" ("Calling Memory," 11).

Even those artworks that expose formerly neglected, ugly truths risk endorsing a progressive narrative that gives a sense of purpose to horrific crimes. As James Young asks, how can a memorial confront a horrific history "without filling it with consoling meaning?" (4) Both *Beloved* and the NMPJ avoid the progressive narrative in two ways: by emphasizing the inextricability of Black

---

[18]In *The Debt: What America Owes to Blacks*, Randall Robinson writes that our country's willful blindness to the past also blinds us "with the same stroke, to any common future" (6–7). In "Reading the Reparations Debate," Jacqueline Bacon argues that reparations advocates "fundamentally alter the nature of the debate about race in the U.S." simply by "challenging the traditional historical narratives" (172).

bodies from Black stories and by insisting on a history that is not linear and limited, but infinite. Morrison's novel refuses to allow slavery to become an abstraction. Despite the metaphorical possibilities offered by a ghost story, *Beloved* explicitly avoids this trope by employing a ghost who shows up in the flesh—a point that Morrison emphasizes in an incredulous exchange among the women who come together to plot Sethe's rescue:

> "Ella. What's all this I'm hearing about Sethe?"
> "Tell me it's in there with her. That's all I know."
> "The daughter? The killed one?"
> "That's what they tell me."
> "How they know that's her?"
> "It's sitting there. Sleeps, eats, and raises hell. Whipping Sethe every day."
> "I'll be. A baby?"
> "No. Grown. the age it would have been had it lived."
> "You talking about flesh?"
> "I'm talking about flesh." (301)

In *Beloved*, slavery remains relentlessly embodied, years after its ostensible "end." The bereaved mother and the child deprived of her own life still suffer, not metaphorically, but in the flesh. Like the NMPJ, *Beloved* forces a harrowing confrontation with the physical vulnerability of others—and thus with their grievability. Such an acknowledgment of suffering rejects a progressive or redemptive narrative. As Dora Apel writes, in confronting historic atrocities, "it must be understood that the wrong can never be righted, the death ... never made meaningful" ("Memorialization," 231).

If memorial art refuses redemption, what role can it then play in the work of reparation? Judith Butler argues that a recognition of the other's pain offers creative possibilities for reshaping collective identity, and thus the future. Acknowledging shared vulnerability can engender "another way of imagining community" by prompting recognition of "our collective responsibility for the physical lives of one another" (27, 30). This acknowledgment, and the grieving it necessitates, can have a transformative function. A collective mourning may reveal "something about who we are ... something that delineates the ties we have to others, that shows us that these ties constitute what we are, ties or bonds that compose us" (22).

Morrison viewed facilitating a constructive engagement with the past as part of her work as an artist. As she writes in "Memory, Creation, and Fiction," "If my work is to be functional to the group (to the village, as it were), then it must bear witness and identify that which is useful from the past and that which ought to be discarded; it must make it possible to prepare for the present and live it out and it must do that not by avoiding problems and contradictions but by examining them" (331). Any honest encounter with our country's racial history is sure to be painful—but Butler reframes mourning as a process that is also constructive. To collectively mourn, she argues, is to "[agree] to undergo a transformation ... the full results of which one cannot know in advance" (21).

Memorial art can facilitate such a collective mourning. Texts and memorials can repudiate historical narratives shaped by denial and obfuscation. They can offer public displays of collective grief and loss, refusing the silencing that compounds the historic violence against Black lives. They can raise the dead, restoring lost names and stories to our history. "Anything dead coming back to life hurts," Morrison warns in *Beloved* (42). But a reckoning with the truth, while deeply painful, is also profoundly hopeful—as the work of transformation is always hopeful.

FIGURE 12.1 National Memorial for Peace and Justice, Montgomery, Alabama, 2020
Source: Photo by Kristina K. Groover

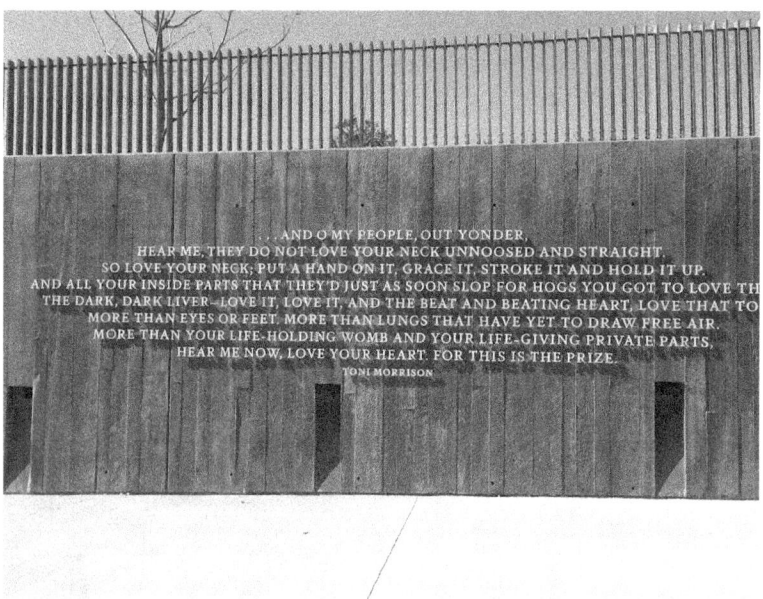

FIGURE 12.2 National Memorial for Peace and Justice, Montgomery, Alabama, 2020
Source: Photo by Kristina K. Groover

WORKS CITED

Allen, James. *Without Sanctuary: Lynching Photography in America*. Twin Palms, 2000.

Apel, Dora. "Memorialization and Its Discontents: America's First Lynching Memorial." *Mississippi Quarterly*, vol. 61, nos. 1–2, Winter–Spring, 2008, pp. 217–35.

Apel, Dora. *Calling Memory into Place*. Rutgers UP, 2020.

Bacon, Jacqueline. "Reading the Reparations Debate." *Quarterly Journal of Speech*, vol. 89, no. 3, Aug. 2003, pp. 171–95.

Bassard, Katherine. *Transforming Scriptures: African American Women Writers and the Bible*. U of Georgia P, 2010.

Bast, Florian. "Reading Red: The Troping of Trauma in Toni Morrison's *Beloved*." *Callaloo*, vol. 34, no. 4, Fall 2011, pp. 1069–87.

Benson, Alan, director. *Toni Morrison: Profile of a Writer*. Interview by Melvyn Bragg. RM Arts, 1987.

Butler, Judith. *Precarious Life: The Powers of Mourning and Violence*. Verso, 2004.

Coates, Ta-Nehisi. "The Case for Reparations." *The Atlantic*, June 2014, https://www.theatlantic.com/magazine/archive/2014/06/the-case-for-reparations/361631/. Accessed Aug. 13, 2022.

Coleman, James. *Faithful Vision: Treatments of the Sacred, Spiritual, and Supernatural in Twentieth-Century African American Fiction*. Louisiana State UP, 2006.

"Community Remembrance Project." *Equal Justice Initiative*. eji.org.

Connerton, Paul. *How Societies Remember*. Cambridge UP, 1989.

Doss, Erika. *Memorial Mania: Public Feeling in America*. U of Chicago P, 2010.

Franco, Dean. "What We Talk About When We Talk About *Beloved*." *MFS*, vol. 52, no. 2, Summer 2006, pp. 415–39.

Hasian, Marouf A., Jr., and Nicholas S. Paliewicz. *Racial Terrorism: A Rhetorical Investigation of Lynching*. UP of Mississippi, 2021.

Leder, Drew. *The Absent Body*. U of Chicago P, 1990.

Morrison, Toni. *Beloved*. 1987. Vintage, 2004.

Morrison, Toni. "Melcher Book Award Acceptance Speech." *UU World* Jan./Feb. 1989. https://www.uuworld.org/articles/a-bench-by-road. Accessed Aug. 13, 2022.

Morrison, Toni. "Memory, Creation, and Fiction." *The Source of Self-Regard: Selected Essays, Speeches, and Meditations*. Alfred A. Knopf, 2019, pp. 326–33.

Neiman, Susan. *Learning from the Germans: Race and the Memory of Evil*. Farrar Straus and Giroux, 2019.

Robinson, Randall. *The Debt: What America Owes to Blacks*. Dutton, 2000.

Savage, Kirk. *Monument Wars: Washington, D.C., the National Mall, and the Transformation of the Memorial Landscape*. U of California P, 2009.

Schreiber, Evelyn Jaffe. *Race, Trauma, and Home in the Novels of Toni Morrison*. Louisiana State UP, 2010.

Schult, Tanja. "Reshaping American Identity: The National Memorial for Peace and Justice and its Take-Away Twin." *Liminalities: A Journal of Performance Studies*, vol. 16, no. 5, 2020, pp. 1–45.

Slavery in America: The Montgomery Slave Trade. Equal Justice Initiative, 2018.

Spargo, R. Clifton. "Trauma and the Specters of Enslavement in Toni Morrison's *Beloved*." *Mosaic: An Interdisciplinary Critical Journal*, vol. 35, no. 1, Mar. 2002, pp. 113–31.

Stevenson, Bryan. "The Narrative Power of Slavery and Its Legacy." *YouTube*, uploaded by Andrew W. Mellon Foundation, Dec. 13, 2019, https://www.youtube.com/watch?v=ulhVyZUMcEA&t=146s. Accessed Aug. 13, 2022.

"Truth and Reconciliation." *Aperture*, Apr. 25, 2018. https://aperture.org/editorial/truth-reconciliation-bryan-stevenson-sarah-lewis/. Accessed Aug. 13, 2022.

Vine, Steve. "Belated Beloved: Time, Trauma, and the Sublime in Toni Morrison's *Beloved*." *Through a Glass Darkly: Suffering, the Sacred, and the Sublime in Literature and Theory*, edited by Holly Faith Nelson, Lynn R. Szabo, and Jens Zimmerman. Wilfrid Laurier UP, 2010, pp. 299–315.

Young, James Edward. *The Stages of Memory: Reflections on Memorial Art, Loss, and the Spaces Between*. U of Massachusetts P, 2016.

CHAPTER THIRTEEN

Blues Lives Matter: Reading *Jazz* in the Era of George Floyd

ANDREW SCHEIBER

As I wrote the first sentences of what would eventually become this essay, it was just a few weeks since the killing of George Floyd by Minneapolis police officers on a street corner a few miles from my house. That incident, captured on citizen cell phones for the world to see, laid bare the festering racial wound of policing in the American metropolis and brought to the surface long-standing (but chronically unheeded) calls for Americans to rethink their conceptions of "public safety," criminal justice, and the role of law enforcement in their communities. In Minneapolis at least, the slogan "defund the police" gained some temporary traction before political inertia blunted its urgency; but if nothing else, the summer of rage sparked by George Floyd's death raised questions in the wider society about the tenuous and racially fraught relationship between policing and justice, especially in communities of color.

"Same as it ever was," many might say, given the origins of American policing in the slave patrollers of pre-Emancipation South and the post-Emancipation policing of Black bodies in the Jim Crow era and beyond.[1] Sadly, racially asymmetrical practices in policing and in the criminal justice system have changed little since the Great Migration of Blacks to the Northern cities over a century ago. Yet in her 1992 novel *Jazz*, published the same year as the protests that followed the police beating of Rodney King, Toni Morrison presents us with a Black urban space (the Harlem of the mid-1920s) from which the police and the courts are largely absent and within which residents of the community are able to call on their own psychological and cultural resources to address offenses committed by their fellow members.

The central crimes around which the story revolves—the murder of a young woman, Dorcas, by a jealous older lover, and the desecration of her corpse by that lover's enraged wife—go uninvestigated, unprosecuted, and unpunished by the formal justice system, even though both occur in a public space and in the full view of multiple witnesses. At first glance this might seem like a curious narrative lacuna on Morrison's part; when we think of the fraught relationship between Black communities and the police, it's the problems created by police *presence* and *action* that generally come to the fore. But *Jazz* is not primarily concerned with the oppressive history of American policing; instead, Morrison focuses on the creative interventions performed by Black people and communities in the face of its betrayals and failures. That is to say, while *Jazz* contains

---

[1] See Lepore for an elegant overview of this history.

some powerful implicit critiques of American policing and justice, its primary energy is affirmative, focusing on the sustaining power of Black vernacular cultural resources.

Indeed, this affirmation of Black cultural power is central to Morrison's agenda as an artist. She once described her work as "village literature, fiction that is really for the village, the tribe," insisting that it be read in the context of the "confrontation between old values of the tribe and new urban values" that has been ongoing since the Great Migration began over a century ago. More particularly for our purposes here, she also acknowledges that her fiction depicts (at least in part) Black people's negotiation of a legal framework that marginalized their humanity and thus produced the necessity for a countercultural, even extralegal, response: "My work," she asserts, "suggests who the outlaws were, who survived under what circumstances and why, what was legal in the community as opposed to what was legal outside it" (LeClair).[2]

Though these comments were given over a decade before the publication of *Jazz*, they presciently anticipate the novel's main story arc: that of Black vernacular values and practices asserting themselves both within and against the constraints of dominating, even hostile, cultural institutions. This formulation is as paradigmatic in the 2020s as it was in the 1920s, and it applies now as then to Black conceptions of justice as well as to the vexed cultural locations of Black music in either era. In the discussion that follows, I will strive to show the multivalent significance of Morrison's treatment of questions of policing and justice in *Jazz*. This significance may be apprehended in terms of three basic valences of the story: first, its allusion to an ongoing crisis in American policing that reached an inflection point in the early 1920s; second, its implicit critique of some of the assumptions and practices that led to that crisis (and to the persistence of that crisis into the present day); and third, her depiction of an alternative response, informed by vernacular perspectives and practices, to the problem of crime and other bad acts in the community.

"HELPLESS LAWYERS AND LAUGHING COPS"

Whatever else one might say about *Jazz's* intricate narrative structure, no one can accuse Morrison of burying her lead, especially when it comes to her depiction of her characters' dismissive, even caustic, attitude toward the formal criminal justice apparatus. In the third paragraph of the novel, immediately after describing Violet's disruption of Dorcas's funeral, the unnamed narrator tells us,

> Like me, they knew who she was, who she had to be, because they knew that her husband, Joe Trace, was the one who shot the girl. There was never anyone to prosecute him because nobody actually saw him do it, and the dead girl's aunt didn't want to throw money to helpless lawyers or laughing cops when she knew the expense wouldn't improve anything. (4)[3]

Despite the subtle shifts in point of view, from the consciousness of the narrator to the community to "the dead girl's aunt," Alice Manfred, the main point of this case summary remains emphatic: while

---

[2]McKee aptly uses the distinction between "in-laws" and "outlaws" to parse this dynamic, which she characterizes as a conflict between an "organic sense of justice that functions as a kind village law" and an "inorganic law that has no mercy for its victims" (146).

[3]The narrator is factually inaccurate on one count: there were actually witnesses to Joe's shooting of Dorcas; she is literally shot in Acton's arms, surrounded by others at a dance party (see 192). But if we take "no one" to mean "no one whose testimony would count in court," we can read the narrator as referencing the historical marginalization and exclusion of Black witnesses and Black claimants from the American justice system.

crimes have been committed and the perpetrators are known, these are matters in which the police or the courts can or will offer no meaningful intervention.

A twenty-first century reader might wonder how the option of keeping the police and the legal system at bay even exists for Alice and others. Thanks to Foucault's widely influential *Discipline and Punish*, there is a tendency to think of the combined apparatus of courts and police as all-pervading, an Enlightenment-spawned dystopia[4] whose technologies of surveillance and sanction are nevertheless infected by (or perhaps even generated out of) long-standing racist biases. As Charles Scruggs wryly notes, in Morrison's work there is no clearer representative of this vision of the law than Schoolteacher, the cruel and soulless overseer of Sweet Home in *Beloved* (181). In his seeming omnipresence (even seeking out Sethe and her children in a supposed "free state"), he embodies the pervasive reach of the law and its reification of Black people as objects of its discipline. As such, he is the novel's principal agent of an all-encompassing prison-world to which Sethe's murderous deeds are a desperate rejoinder.

In marked contrast with its omnipresent reach in *Beloved*, the long arm of the law in *Jazz* is curiously withered and ineffectual. While the effects of American racism are still deeply and painfully felt, the novel offers us no post-Emancipation counterpart of Schoolteacher; it contains no *named* policeman, lawyer, judge, or other agent of the law to embody the legal superstructure of slavery and its legacy. Instead, the novel shines its light on a different mystery of the law: its impotence and irrelevance (one might go so far as to say its illegitimacy) in the face of the world it has largely wrought.

To grasp the nature and scope of this illegitimacy, it is helpful to understand the ad hoc, chaotic, and sometimes indifferent nature of actual law enforcement in Black urban communities of this time and place. It is true that well into the early decades of the twentieth century, American policing practices aimed at a comprehensive surveillance and control of Black bodies along the lines of the panoptical world described by Foucault. Even in the Northern urban centers, policing practices and attitudes toward Black citizens owed much to the slave patrols of the pre–Civil War South as well as to various legal and extralegal efforts to assert white privilege against the civic claims of immigrants, foreigners, and people of color. In the nineteen teens and twenties, police harassment of New York City's Black citizens was routine; and the beating of those residents (the latter often referred to as "the third degree") was a common tool of intimidation by which the police showed Harlem residents "who was in charge" (see King 153–86; Sacks 799). While, as Shannon King notes, "the string of race riots punctuating black America during the World War I era and throughout the 1920s somehow missed Harlem" (153), police provocations kept Black anger on a simmering boil that occasionally erupted in violent conflict between the community and law enforcement.

But in Harlem and other Black neighborhoods of early twentieth-century New York, an often-antagonistic police presence was complemented by a posture of negligent absence. As Marcy Sacks notes in her study of policing of the era, "while physical force helped policemen control black behavior that seemed to threaten whites, officers otherwise neglected black neighborhoods outright" (810); aside from taking their cut of the vice industries to which they turned a blind eye, police remained largely indifferent to criminal acts in which Blacks were the victims (Sacks 811).

---

[4]A representative sample of Foucault's discussion on this point: "With the police, one is in the indefinite world of a supervision that seeks ideally to reach the most elementary particle, the most passing phenomenon of the social body" (213–14).

Emblematic of these attitudes was a 1915 NAACP report, which found that "both in Harlem and in the San Juan Hill district, inspectors and captains said, without mincing their words, that they considered the colored people worthless, and that it was 'useless to bother with them'" (Blascoer 23; qtd. in Sacks 811).[5]

To some extent, this indifference of the police to Black communities was a matter of strained resources as well as toxic racial attitudes. Both at the local and national levels, policing in the 1920s was challenged by Prohibition and the criminal infrastructure it spawned, but rapid urbanization and underdeveloped social and physical infrastructure in the Northern cities was a factor as well. This was especially the case in places like Harlem, which attracted increasing numbers of Black people escaping poverty and oppression in the South. In any case, crime rates across the nation spiked dramatically in the period between 1900 and 1925; the homicide rate in particular "swelled by nearly 50 percent" in this period (Adler 36).

Under such conditions, prosecution and conviction rates plummeted nationally. Police found that even when they did make arrests, the overburdened justice system was more likely to discharge the arrestees than to prosecute them; in mid-1920s New York City, three-fourths of homicide cases were dropped before they reached grand juries. While some blamed this shortfall on "inadequate police work," others pointed to feckless prosecutors and lenient judges who had little time for or interest in common offenses (sometimes even murder), especially when they occurred within the Black community (Adler 37–8). This historical background is clearly reflected in Morrison's depiction of the City, which countenances "all sorts of ignorance and criminality" (8), and whose bays and estuaries conceal the detritus of its corruption, their murky depths littered with bootleggers' crashed airplanes, dead bodies and dirty money still trapped in their flooded interiors (35).

More critically for Morrison's characters in *Jazz*, policing resources were spread even more irregularly in Harlem than in other regions of the metropolis, resulting in a chaotic, almost frontier-like culture of law and [dis]order in which long-standing racial prejudices were deeply embedded. Given this historical context, it is not just a fictional extravagance on Morrison's part that so many criminal acts in *Jazz* go unnoticed and unpunished by the formal justice apparatus. Aside from the top count of homicide (Joe's killing of Dorcas) and Violet's collateral act of desecrating the dead girl's corpse, there are unadjudicated allegations of kidnapping (again, with Violet as the accused party) and thievery of various kinds: for instance, by Malvonne's nephew Sweetness (who after stealing from postal boxes graduates through a series of aliases to the full-on gangster name Little Caesar [41]) and by Felice's mother, who filches a ring from Tiffany's in revenge for being racially profiled by a store manager (202–3).

Compared with Joe's murder of Dorcas, these other acts are mostly small matters and may seem even more so in the context of police indifference to (and frequent complicity in) ongoing instances of white-on-Black mob violence like the East St. Louis riot in which Dorcas's parents are killed. But the relative lack of official response to even such minor offenses serves as a reminder of how the law, for all its claims of "coverage," is as conspicuous by its relative absence in the Black community as it is by its abiding role as an enforcer of racial inequalities. If "justice" for the murdered Dorcas (or for any other Black person in Harlem) is not likely to be found through formal policing and

---

[5]These "inspectors and captains," like virtually all officers, would have been white. New York's police force didn't commission its first Black officer, Samuel Battle, until 1911 (Browne 88), and the attitude of its rank and file toward Battle and toward Blacks in general ranged from dismissive to hostile well into the 1920s and beyond.

judicial processes, the historical record suggests that this owes as much to the justice complex's malign indifference to and neglect of Black lives as to any active racist interventions.

"I DON'T HAVE NO EVIL OF MY OWN"

I'd like to return for a moment to Alice's thought that involving the law "wouldn't improve anything"—a statement that addresses some problematical aspects of the conventional justice apparatus that often go unexamined, even as it suggests the alternative view of justice that Morrison's characters pursue. Given that no one, inside or outside the law, can bring Dorcas back to life, what would Alice regard as an "improvement"? And why in her view is it pointless to look to the legal system for such satisfaction?

A partial answer to the second question may be found in the operational and moral failures of the judicial apparatus previously noted—not only the long-standing racial biases embedded in the police and court systems, but also the incompetence and dysfunction that afflicted these institutions across the board in the early 1920s. But Alice's reflections on "improving things" also raise definitional or epistemological questions that are of urgent significance in the novel. For instance, What is "justice" supposed to look like or feel like? How are we to recognize when its outcomes are satisfactory? What exactly is the work of justice supposed to improve, and for whom?

Too often in the conventional justice system, these questions are answered in *retributive* terms, in which the ideal is to establish an equivalence between the gravity of the crime and the sanctions imposed on its perpetrator. Wai Chee Dimock refers to this as the "dream of objective adequation"; she goes on to insist that this principle—most famously embodied in the figure of Justitia with her balancing scales—is what "makes the concept of justice intelligible in the first place" (6). As Megan Sweeney notes, the effect of this is to treat justice as a ledger of accounts that must be balanced, "with punishment equal to the crime, redress adequate to the injury, and benefit corresponding to the desert" (442, 440). "Justice" thus becomes a currency of exchange in an all-encompassing political economy that effectively "reif[ies] and quantif[ies] both victims and perpetrators" (Sweeney 442), inviting uncomfortable comparisons with what Morrison has characterized as "the equating of human beings with commodity" in the Transatlantic slave trade ("Moral Inhabitants" 42).

An additional aspect of the formal justice system—one whose significance will become crucial later in this discussion—is the interposition of the State as the ultimate authority in determining what constitutes "adequate" or "commensurate" response to a criminal injury. That the State (and, by extension, the police and the courts) should be involved in this way is such a naturalized assumption that it is difficult to imagine "justice" being served otherwise. But as John Braithwaite notes, our present, almost exclusive reliance on State institutions is relatively recent in human history, and in the West, can be traced back to developments in the early Renaissance, in which crime was reconfigured as "a matter of fealty to and felony against the king, instead of as a wrong done to another person" (*Restorative Justice and Responsive Regulation* 5).[6] The "commensurate" aspect of Western justice noted by Dimock may also have its roots in this transformation; Howard Zehr for instance notes that the word "*guilt* may derive from the Anglo Saxon *geldan*, which, like the German word *Geld*, refers to payment" (Zehr; qtd. in *RJ&RR* 5, emphasis in original).

---

[6]Hereafter cited in the text as *RJ&RR*.

In direct contrast to the assumptions underlying the formal justice system, the desire to make Joe or Violet "pay" for their crimes—especially through the intermediation of the State—seems conspicuously beside the point among Morrison's characters. It is not that Joe's and Violet's transgressions are ignored or discounted; in the weeks after Dorcas's murder, Alice obsesses on "what she called the *impunity* of the man who killed her niece just because he could" (*Jazz* 73; emphasis in original). But even in her anger and sorrow, she doesn't thirst for legal or social sanctions against Joe and Violet. Rather, she comes to regard the Traces' unhappiness as punishment enough for their acts: "She found out the man who killed her niece cried all day and for him and for Violet that is as bad as jail" (4).

Black civil society, in the form of the Salem Women's Club, confers a similar assessment on Violet's and Joe's scandalous actions, focusing on help rather than on punishment. After considering whether Violet "needs assistance," they conclude that she does not—not because her and Joe's acts have placed her beyond the bounds of the community's concern and charity, but because the needs of others (including a family that has lost its home in a fire) are more urgent. And their judgment on Joe aligns with Alice's view that the misery Joe and Violet have brought on themselves is punishment enough: they conclude that Joe simply "needed to stop feeling sorry for himself" (4), implying that an attitude adjustment, not a prison sentence, is what Dorcas's killer most urgently requires.

It's hard to imagine a more dramatic asymmetry than the balancing of Joe's tears of self-pity against his murder of a sixteen-year-old girl. But the main consolation offered by the formal justice system—that of "adequation" through the punishment of the offender—is not one that is typically available to Black victims, regardless of the race of the perpetrator. Furthermore, these imputed ideals of balance and fairness might well seem hollow, even hypocritical, to a community against whom the formal justice system has been historically *unbalanced* in the extreme. (The question of Joe's "impunity," for instance, seems beside the point when compared with the impunity of the white mob whose ravages killed Dorcas's parents and so many others; or one might observe the crucial disconnect in which Blacks, while disproportionately subject to scrutiny and punishment by the law, are also disproportionately denied access to its protection.) We should not be surprised, then, that members of the community should seek different pathways, and perhaps different ideals of "justice," in dealing with the perpetrators of hurtful acts.

The second way in which the community response departs from the ideology of the formal justice system is more subtle; but it is also more significant because it goes to conflicting views of the nature and origin of criminal acts themselves. A quick glance at the conventional way of talking about crime and punishment—exemplified in the common idiom of "paying for one's crime"—reveals the percipience of Foucault's critique of the philosophical underpinnings of such rhetoric. It defines crime as an act of an individual person committed through the agency of an individual body. (In a parallel fashion, it is typical to think of the injuries resulting from bad acts as primarily affecting individual victims rather than groups or the whole community.) Accordingly, the "scales of justice" are balanced by imposing a punishment on that person's body (lashing, imprisonment, even death) in proportion to the severity of the crime.

Viewed from outside this framework, though, criminal acts are not solely, or sometimes even primarily, the fruit of personal motives or defects of individual character. Even when committed by identifiable individuals, such individual acts are symptomatic of complex social forces that extend deeper and further than the crime-and-punishment model's frame of individual responsibility. Such acts must also be read as indicators of what Polanyi calls "polycentric problems," which require a "harmonization of ... purposes" only possible through creativity and wisdom (176) rather than prescriptive procedure. As Braithwaite notes, such problems "are not well suited to the judicial model" (*RJ&RR* 90), whose tendency is to narrow rather than expand the possible considerations and outcomes. The negative effects of such acts on other individuals or on the community cannot be effectively redressed by the punishment of the perpetrator alone, even if the policing and judicial system were interested in doing so. Convicting and jailing one murderer—or a hundred of them—does little to mitigate any underlying social or historical conditions out of which such crimes arise, nor does it seem "commensurate" to focus redress on an individual *only* when these broader influences are in play.

An authentic response to Joe's and Violet's bad acts—a response that the judicial apparatus is incapable of providing—would involve recognition of those acts as part of the fabric of racialized violence, past and present, of which their own individual histories are intertwined threads. Interestingly, even as Alice mourns her murdered niece, her instincts trend in this direction. She is quick to apprehend the fact that the Traces' crimes are not just isolated phenomena but are rather embedded in historical and social contingencies. The chronicle of violence and suffering she obsessively follows in the Black newspapers of the day ("the *Age*, the *News*, *The Messenger*"; *Jazz* 80) is upsetting to be sure, but it allows her to fit what has happened to her own family into a broader context:[7]

> Idle and withdrawn in her grief and shame, she whittled away the days making lace for nothing, reading her newspapers, tossing them on the floor, picking them up again. She read them differently now. Every week since Dorcas' death, during the whole of January and February, a paper laid bare the bones of some broken woman. Man kills wife. Eight accused of rape dismissed. Woman and girls victims of. Woman commits suicide. White attackers indicted. Five women caught. Woman says man beat. In jealous rage man. (74)

As Knadler notes, these sensational stories of so-called "women with knives" are far removed from the world that the "staid and proper" Alice has tried to build around herself and her niece (99); but taken together, they represent a pattern, a network of hidden causation, that begins to afford her some insight on Violet's actions. The repetitive nature of the stories—killings, suicides, sexual and racial violence—underscores the pervasive, suprapersonal forces at work in shaping the misery of Black lives and Black peoples' responses to it.

But it is not just the pervasiveness of racial and sexual violence experienced (and sometimes acted out) by Black women that the newspapers register; there is also the impotence or indifference of the law with respect to those who are victims of, or vulnerable to, such violence. (Note that even when white perpetrators of racial violence *are* identified, they are only *indicted*, not *convicted*.)

---

[7] The significance of these newspaper stories has been noted by other critics, but with slightly different emphases than I give them here. Knadler discusses them as examples of a "tabloid" genre that "constituted one of the few discourses on domestic violence available to Harlem women" and that "were also meant to be functional and generative of African American women's performance of their own identity" (102). McKee reads the role of the newspapers differently, seeing them allied with "the legalistic world of the law" and conveying "the letter of the law" in contrast with the more organic and vernacular discourse exemplified in jazz performance (138). My view is that these Black newspapers provide an empirical basis for Alice's (and the reader's) understanding that crime and violence are structural and racial problems, not just individual ones—a view that points toward a very different view of justice than that encoded in "the letter of the law."

Alice thus intuits that an act of rage like Violet's is not a defect of character, not just the act of a dangerous "crazy woman"; it has structural and historical rather than just individual sources. Violet, like the other "women with knives" in the newspapers, is acting out a learned response to the predations of a racist social order that includes the order of the law itself:

> Read carefully, the news accounts revealed that most of these women, subdued and broken, had not been defenseless … All over the country, black women were armed. That, thought Alice, that, at least, they had learned. Didn't everything on God's earth have or acquire defense? Speed, some poison in the leaf, the tongue, the tail? (*Jazz* 74)

Reading these accounts, along with hearing "how torn up" Joe is, helps Alice to be "no longer frightened" of Violet (80, 79); and after a month of resisting the idea, she relents and lets the wife of her niece's murderer into her home. This first conversation between Alice and Violet begins a discursive process that will eventually produce a psychological and social outcome much more profoundly enabling than any arrest and trial would have. Violet strikes the keynote for this process when she assures Alice, "I'm not the one you need to be scared of" (80). The exchange that follows, beginning with Alice's retort, is telling and significant:

> "No? Who is?"
> "I don't know. That's what hurts my head."
> "You didn't come here to say you sorry. I thought maybe you did. You come here to deliver some of your own evil."
> "I don't have no evil of my own." (80)

Violet is making the point that her acts (and, by extension, Joe's) are not, as Gatsby once phrased it, "merely personal," but are highly determined by the pressures and influences of the surrounding world. And in the context of what Alice has seen, thought, and remembered in the weeks leading up to this encounter, Violet's statement has more the ring of truth than the stink of excuse. (Indeed, Alice's own murderous thoughts toward her own long-dead husband, who abandoned her for another woman, suggest that she shares with Violet a common root of experience.)

The question that Alice asks Violet remains largely unanswered. Who *should* be feared? What is the nature of the *real* threat, if that threat cannot be defended against merely by the identification of individual bad actors, or by submitting those individuals to the processes of the law? Dorcas may have died from a bullet fired by Joe Trace, but her fate was generations in the making, with the dead hand of history a more fearful and powerful force than the hands of any individual murderer. Alice's realization of this truth may relieve her fear of any immediate danger from Violet or Joe; but where does that leave the question of justice—for Dorcas, or for anyone else? If Violet "has no evil of her own," then how is the individual or the community to respond to admitted bad acts like Joe's and Violet's? If not arrest and trial, then what?

DON'T TAKE IT, MAKE IT

A starting point for an answer to this question would be first to follow the example of the Salem Women's Club and sidestep entirely the principle of "adequation" on which the formal justice system operates. One must accept that it is neither possible nor productive to try and achieve a symmetrical relationship between the injury and any punishment that might be levied as an adequate "payment" for Joe's and Violet's crimes. Perhaps counterintuitively—even in the context of more "restorative" models of justice—gestures of apology and forgiveness are not on the table, either. Violet has not approached Alice to make amends, either for herself or on Joe's behalf; and Alice notes that if "forgiveness" is what Violet is after, "I can't give you that. It's not in my power" (110).

It is not even clear at first that Violet has come to talk at all, let alone apologize; when Alice first lets her into the apartment, all Violet seems to want is to "sit down in [Alice's] chair" and stare at a photo of Dorcas—a photo that, in a gratuitously generous gesture, Alice gives to Violet at the end of their conversation (80, 82). But they soon settle into a process of mutual interrogation; in this process, the questions they ask one another are not aimed at determining responsibility, guilt, or innocence, but at eliciting each other's stories—stories that give context to the often-unspoken-of violence that Violet and Joe have inflicted on Alice's household. But more significantly, these encounters reveal the parallel wounds of history whose scars they share and bear as Black women of their place and time. As Alice reflects after a few of these encounters: "When Violet came to visit … something opened up" (83).

This "opening up" is possible because Violet's visits to Alice create discursive possibilities beyond the adversarial process of the courtroom, which almost invariably has the effect of "consolidating offenders and victims into opposed out-groups" (*RJ&RR* 90). Freed from the legally constructed roles of accused and complainant, Violet and Alice use Dorcas's murder as a focal point from which they can begin to understand the underlying patterns and intersections that link their destinies. Violet realizes that, under other circumstances, perhaps with just the slightest tweaking of personal history, Dorcas might have engaged her maternal instincts rather than her jealousy (*Jazz* 109); conversely, Alice is forced to recall her own murderous jealousy, a "starving for blood" never acted on, toward the woman for whom her own husband abandoned her decades earlier (88).

In *Jazz* as in *Beloved*, the characters' shared experience of having been "victims of the law" (see Scruggs 185) becomes the basis for a transformed sense of community. Crucially, this occurs because the parties involved put aside questions of punishment, of who hurt whom. Story replaces the compulsions of legal testimony; the distinctions between guilt and grievance, perpetrator and victim, are subsumed in a collective recognition of common suffering, aspiration, and renewed moral agency. As Violet contemplates her own feelings of betrayal, rage, and frustrated desire, she asks Alice, "Where the grown people? Is it us?"—the shift from the "I" to "we" perspective signaling an awareness of their shared state of suffering. Alice's spontaneous response—"Oh Mama"—mirrors Violet's own thoughts (*Jazz* 110), as both recall the struggles of their forebears and acknowledge the parallel histories that have shaped their own fateful connection in the present.

Morrison underlines this discursive process with a potent motif that conveys the values of healing and connection, as opposed to punishment and sanction, that suggests an alternative response to Violet's and Joe's criminal acts. By their second meeting, Alice is already noting the disheveled state of Violet's clothing and feels impelled to mend it—at first, not so much out of pity as out of her "irritation" at the other woman's disordered appearance (82). But eventually it becomes a habit; hardly a conversation goes by without some mention of Alice taking her needle and thread to Violet's clothing.

As others have noted, Morrison uses the sewing motif, with its imagery of "stitches and seams, traces and tracks" to make intertextual connections among her novels—inviting us, for instance, to see "traces" of Beloved in Joe's mother Wild (see Cutter 67–8). But this imagery also suggests another kind of linkage, one that emphasizes the "traces" that can be found between one life and another and, which, once recognized, can bind up the wounds on the communal body that crimes like Joe's and Violet's have inflicted. Like disordered clothing, disordered behavior is often the fruit of starved, even traumatizing circumstances, and in Alice's hands, the motifs of sewing and mending point toward a restoration of psychic and moral coherence that the wider world continues to undermine and degrade at every turn.

This restoration is not a matter of legal process, or of striking a commensurate balance between crime and punishment; if anything, it is a result of decidedly *incommensurate* behaviors. Alice, the surviving victim of Joe's and Violet's violence, stitches up Violet's frayed parts, repaying the latter's offense with mending care. Furthermore, the connection between them is, like Alice's needlework, something *made* or *done* rather than *proved* or *transacted*—created on the fly, as it were, out of the disparate yet entangled threads of their respective individual destinies. In a moment of climactic realization, Alice sees that Violet's and Dorcas's positions—as well as her own—are in the end more parallel than oppositional, with both suffering from the hungers and losses that history imposes. As she tells Violet,

> Fight what, fight who? Some mishandled child who saw her parents burn up? Who knew better than you or me or anybody just how small and quick this little bitty life is? Or maybe you want to stomp somebody with three kids and one pair of shoes. Somebody in a raggedy dress, the hem dragging in the mud. Somebody wanting arms just like you do ... Nobody's asking you to take it. I'm sayin make it, make it! (*Jazz* 113)

Alice's advice to Violet suggests above all that coming to terms with loss and injury is not a matter of evidentiary process and judicial compensation but rather of creativity, a "making" that is metaphorically represented in her own activity of sewing.

Not coincidentally, all this suggests another kind of "making"—specifically the making of music, particularly the music that gives the novel its title. Olly Wilson once asserted that the music of the African diaspora—not just, but perhaps especially, jazz—is distinguished by "a conceptual approach," a "way of doing something, not something that is done" ("Significance" 14). Morrison herself once said that she intended her work to do for her community of readers "what the music did for blacks, what we used to be able to do with each other in private" (LeClair). Her phrasing here implicitly emphasizes the importance of *intra-community* meaning-making, the kind that occurs in spaces not associated with the workings of institutional power—the kitchen, the church basement, the apartment-building stoop, or even (as in the case of music) the dance hall or the speakeasy (as opposed to the conservatory or the concert hall).

So, while many commentators have quite appropriately noted the way in which Morrison's text evokes the properties of Black music,[8] her take on the "jazz" part of the "Jazz Age" concerns not just the music per se, but the creative methodology (the "conceptual approach," in Wilson's phrasing) through which her characters create and express their own vision of the beloved community. Using jazz as both a metaphor and a model, Morrison imagines the powerful appeals of a similarly

---

[8]In addition to McKee and Sweeney, also see Jewett's discussion of *Jazz* as a "modal" performance (445); Rubenstein argues that Morrison uses "literary techniques that inventively borrow from blues patterns and the structure of jazz performance" (149); Gussow (159–94) and Scheiber ("*Jazz* and the Future Blues") both situate Morrison's novel in the context of the rise of blues as a popular recorded art form, beginning with Mamie Smith's transgressive valorization of Black-on-blue violence in her 1920 hit "Crazy Blues."

Black-specific set of creative impulses regarding the ways in which the notion of justice could or ought to be expressed. Not accidentally or coincidentally, this set of impulses presents a challenge to the moral and political norms of American justice in the same way that Black music disrupted long-standing Western, Enlightenment-based aesthetic assumptions.

While it is not my purpose to elucidate fully the parallels between Black music and Black justice suggested in Morrison's novel, a brief summary of the salient impulses underlying their common "conceptual approach" is in order:

1. The vernacular justice practices depicted by Morrison eschew formal procedure or written laws. Conceptions of justice are relational, organic, and rooted in specific circumstances, including the shared legacy of New World slavery and its post-Emancipation perseverations in American society.

2. These vernacular practices aim at "functional efficacy" (see Wilson, "Black Music" 3)—that is, justice-making must (as Alice puts it) "improve things" and not just in a theoretical or intellectually satisfying way.

3. Justice-making is improvisatory and open-ended; it must have a collaborative or dialogical component in which various players or stakeholders have an opportunity to participate and in which they are not locked into legally constricted roles (e.g., plaintiff, defendant, judge, jury).

4. Justice is seen not just in terms of the fate of individuals; rather, it must proceed from a standpoint that is "we-focused" rather than "I-focused," with an emphasis on "community values and ... community morale" (see Williams 543).

5. The "community values and morale" are served by a focus on the healing and restoration to the community of the involved individuals (including those responsible for bad acts) rather than on punishment or on formal determinations of guilt.

GEORGE FLOYD SQUARE AND "THE SHADOW OF THE AXE"

For some readers, the alternative ethos of justice that Morrison depicts in *Jazz* will call to mind the empirical and theoretical findings of recent and contemporary interventions aimed at the transformation of policing and criminal justice, especially insofar as those institutions affect communities of color.[9] But as Braithwaite has noted, these more recent innovations draw on practices that have a long historical precedent in vernacular cultural practices (*RJ&RR* 7ff), especially in colonial and postcolonial Africa, whose communities bear some filial relationship to the African American "villages" of Morrison's remarks.

Indeed, Morrison's own characterization of the "city/village" dynamic, in which Black indigenous practices are part of a "civilization that existed underneath the white civilization" (LeClair), uncannily resembles what legal scholars have observed of the bifurcated justice practices

---

[9] These interventions would include, among other examples, Braithwaite's seminal work on models of "restorative justice" (cited above) and the efforts of the postapartheid South African Truth and Reconciliation Commission (TRC). Though he has published often on the topic, Braithwaite's most fully developed and influential elucidation of his ideas may be found in his book *Restorative Justice and Responsive Regulation* (2002; cited above). For a more compact presentation of his ideas, see his article "Principles of Restorative Justice." For a firsthand explanation of the rationale behind the work of the South African TRC, see Desmond Tutu's *No Future Without Forgiveness* (1999).

in some postcolonial societies, especially in Africa. Such places, Elechi et al. note, have evolved "two parallel systems of social control—one based on African indigenous justice values and the other based on Eurocentric values." In the resulting tensions between the justice system imposed by the colonizer and the abiding justice practices of the colonized, such vernacular formations act "as a buffer between the predatory ... states and the people" (74); and they remain most relevant and vibrant in remote or highly tribalized settings—such as "villages"—where "access to the formal criminal justice system" either is limited or produces "inappropriate" outcomes in the community's eyes (Omale 44).

It would be hard to find a more apt account than this of the relationship between the Harlemites of Morrison's novel and the policing–justice complex. The police and the courts are not an extension of "the village" but a colonizing, even alien presence whose authority and power need to be mitigated or supplemented (if not actually resisted) by the community. Morrison's characters respond to the bad acts of those in their midst in ways that reject the premises and processes of State-sponsored justice, and which (not coincidentally, I think) remarkably emulate the attributes that Elechi et al. associate with vernacular African justice practices: "values and principles of restraint, respect, and responsibility" and a conception of "the goal of justice" as "the restoration of relationships and social harmony" (Elechi et al. 74).[10]

Thus, as Sweeney has argued, "Morrison's *Jazz* ... illustrates the consolation entailed in recognizing residues that remain unsubsumed by dominant narratives of justice" (444). But terms on which these "consolations" are available are highly contingent; while *Jazz* dramatizes the way in which members of the Black community seek justice by supplementing failed State institutions with tools of their own devising, this opportunity is not sanctioned at any official level. As we have seen, at least in 1920s Harlem, the opportunity to explore these alternative paths of justice owes much to the indifference, neglect, and disorganization of State institutions. But despite Morrison's characterization of this as "a time when the possibility of personal freedom, and interior, imaginative freedom ... could be engaged" for Black people ("The Source of Self-Regard" 318), the police and the legal system still hover, with the potential to reassert themselves at any time and to preempt more vernacular solutions. As one commentator notes, even robust alternatives to the formal justice system operate "in the shadow of the axe" of State power, which is always present and ready to fall (von Holderstein Holtermann 189).[11]

Morrison's vision of this tension between justice in its official, institutional forms and its vernacular underlife may reflect the historical reality of Harlem in the 1920s, but it also indexes the realities faced a century later, in the United States and elsewhere. One would be hard pressed to find a more palpable example of this tension than ongoing developments at the junction of 38th Street and Chicago Avenue in Minneapolis, the intersection directly adjacent to George Floyd's murder by police in May 2020. In the days and weeks after Floyd's death, an unofficial memorial

---

[10]Or, as Desmond Tutu summarized it in his own explanation of the goals of the TRC, "the central concern is not retribution or punishment but ... the healing of breaches, the redressing of imbalances, the restoration of broken relationships" (Tutu 51; qtd. in Allais 337–8).

[11]In its original context, this metaphor was used to describe the use of formal judicial process of trial and punishment as a "backstop" or threat to secure the perpetrator's adherence to the sort of discursive process that Violet and Alice adopt voluntarily (see Allais 348); but the phrase also captures the ever-present possibility that the State, in the form of the legal system, can impose itself upon, or preempt, such processes and thus disrupt or choke off the informal vernacular activity that proves so salutary for Morrison's characters.

sprang up at that location. Once a busy commercial corner, the intersection was closed to traffic for over a year, and the storefronts that frame it—including that of Cup Foods, whose clerk summoned the police because of his suspicion that Floyd was trying to pass a counterfeit $20 bill—were adorned with murals, posters, and other artwork dedicated to Floyd's memory. Almost since its inception, this makeshift memorial space has been dominated by a large sculpture of a raised fist, erected at the center of the intersection.

For over a year, the space was tended and guarded by an ad hoc group of community members, in a rare instance of a successfully sustained effort to impose the rhetoric of the community on a "public" space, of testifying to the lives whose existence is masked by the official map of the city. I would argue that, as such, it represents a signature expression of the community's vision of and aspiration toward "justice"—not just for George Floyd as an individual. It has attracted artwork and other objects that commemorate other victims as well; additionally, the vernacular place-making around the Floyd memorial has expanded beyond the corner of 38th and Chicago, developing an equally ad hoc annex in a near-adjacent green space, with makeshift grave markers memorializing many of the other victims of policing violence.

Taken together, these installations remind us that Floyd's death, uniquely vivid as it has become in the national imagination, is symptomatic of an ongoing history and part of the shared experience—both remembered and directly lived—of a community still striving for an official justice that seems ever deferred. But as I write this (in June 2021), bulldozers and orange-vested workers from the city of Minneapolis are in the process of asserting their official jurisdiction over the area, clearing away the makeshift barriers that demarcate the Square and making other preparations for the return of business as usual. It is not clear how much of the ad hoc installation will be incorporated into the restored street design, but one cannot help but be reminded of *Jazz*'s account of the City, whose "design" provides the appearance of convenience, mobility, orderliness, and opportunity (9), even as it grants these things to some while systematically excluding those who make up its vital underlife.

Despite the successful prosecution of former police officer Derek Chauvin for Floyd's murder, I think it is fair to say that few in the community will agree that it represents anything approaching the kind of closure that the legal system implicitly claims to provide (though, certainly, a "not guilty" would have been far more toxic). The twenty-two and a half years to which Chauvin was sentenced on June 25, 2021, seems at once too little and beside the point. Systemic problems of racialized policing remain, problems that have deeper roots than any individual prosecution, however successful, can root out—an abiding problem that points to the inadequacy of individual sanction and punishment as a way of restoring balance to the social body. In comparison, the unofficial judgment expressed in George Floyd square—an affirmation of humanity and solidarity in the face of the justice system's failures—resonates more powerfully, satisfyingly, and (dare one say it without stretching the definition?) *justly* than any individual legal verdict.

Similarly, the vernacular interventions performed by Morrison's characters are no less potent for being enacted in the interstices of official policing and judicial power, as a challenge and rebuke to its dominant assumptions and practices. If we think of Alice and Violet, sitting together in Alice's kitchen, or if we think of Felice, mounting the doorstep of her best friend's killer with the healing gifts of food and music, or if we think of the young men blowing their honeyed horns from the rooftops, we are looking at a kind of justice, one in which injury and poverty are repaid with acts of affirmation and healing grace and through which the shared bonds of community, often frayed by isolation and fear, are proclaimed in the open air. Like the created space of George Floyd Square, Morrison's novel offers a vision of Black self-love, self-forgiveness, and self-understanding that finds ways to grow and flourish, even in the shadow of the axe.

WORKS CITED

Adler, J. S. "Less Crime, More Punishment: Violence, Race, and Criminal Justice in Early Twentieth-Century America." *Journal of American History*, vol. 102, no. 1, 2015, pp. 34–46, doi:10.1093/jahist/jav173.

Allais, Lucy. "Restorative Justice, Retributive Justice, and the South African Truth and Reconciliation Commission." *Philosophy & Public Affairs*, vol. 39, no. 4, 2011, pp. 331–63, doi:10.1111/j.1088-4963.2012.01211.x.

Blascoer, Frances. *Colored School Children in New York*. Public Education Association of the City of New York, 1915, http://name.umdl.umich.edu/AGE2012.0001.001. Sept. 2, 2021.

Braithwaite, John. "Principles of Restorative Justice." *Restorative Justice and Criminal Justice: Competing or Reconcilable Paradigms?*, edited by J. A. R. Von Hirsch et al. Oxford, 2003, pp. 1–20.

Braithwaite, John. *Restorative Justice and Responsive Regulation*. Oxford UP, 2002.

Browne, Arthur. *One Righteous Man: Samuel Battle and the Shattering of the Color Line in New York*. Beacon P, 2015.

Cutter, Martha J. "The Story Must Go on and on: The Fantastic, Narration, and Intertextuality in Toni Morrison's *Beloved* and *Jazz*." *African American Review*, vol. 34, no. 1, 2000, pp. 61–75, doi:10.2307/2901184.

Dimock, Wai Chee. *Residues of Justice: Literature, Law, Philosophy*. U of California P, 1996.

Elechi, Oko O., et al. "Restoring Justice (Ubuntu): An African Perspective." *International Criminal Justice Review*, vol. 20, no. 1, 2010, pp. 73–85, doi:10.1177/1057567710361719.

Foucault, Michel. *Discipline and Punish: The Birth of the Prison*. Translated by Alan Sheridan. Vintage, 1979.

Gussow, Adam. *Seems Like Murder Here: Southern Violence and the Blues Tradition*. U of Chicago P, 2002.

Jewett, Chad. "The Modality of Toni Morrison's '*Jazz*.'" *African American Review*, vol. 48, no. 4, 2015, pp. 445–56, doi:10.1353/afa.2015.0052.

King, Shannon. *Whose Harlem Is This, Anyway? Community Politics and Grassroots Activism during the New Negro Era*. NY UP, 2015.

Knadler, Stephen. "Domestic Violence in the Harlem Renaissance: Remaking the Record in Nella Larsen's *Passing* and Toni Morrison's *Jazz*." *African American Review*, vol. 38, no. 1, 2004, pp. 99–118.

LeClair, Thomas. "'The Language Must Not sweat': A Conversation with Toni Morrison." *The New Republic*, March 21, 1981, https://newrepublic.com/article/95923/the-language-must-not-sweat. Accessed Aug. 13, 2022.

Lepore, Jill. "The Invention of the Police." *The New Yorker*, July 13, 2020, https://www.newyorker.com/magazine/2020/07/20/the-invention-of-the-police. Accessed Aug. 13, 2022.

McKee, Jessica. *Ghosts, Orphans, and Outlaws: History, Family, and the Law in Toni Morrison's Fiction*. 2014. University of South Florida, PhD Dissertation. https://login.ezproxy.stthomas.edu/login?url=https://www-proquest-com.ezproxy.stthomas.edu/dissertations-theses/ghosts-orphans-outlaws-history-family-law-toni/docview/1530237701/se-2?accountid=14756. Accessed Aug. 13, 2022.

Morrison, Toni. *Jazz*. Plume, 1993.

Morrison, Toni. "Moral Inhabitants." *The Source of Self-Regard: Selected Essays, Speeches, and Meditations*. Knopf, 2019, pp. 41–48.

Morrison, Toni. "The Source of Self-Regard." *The Source of Self-Regard: Selected Essays, Speeches, and Meditations*. Knopf, 2019, pp. 304–21.

Omale, Don John O. "Justice in History: an Examination of 'African Restorative Traditions' and the Emerging 'Restorative Justice' Paradigm." *African Journal of Criminology and Justice Studies*, vol. 2, no. 2, 2006, pp. 33–63.

Polanyi, Michael. *The Logic of Liberty: Reflections and Rejoinders*. U of Chicago P, 1951.

Rubenstein, Roberta. "Singing the Blues/Reclaiming Jazz: Toni Morrison and Cultural Mourning." *Mosaic*, vol. 31, no. 2, June 1998, pp. 147–63.

Sacks, Marcy S. "To Show Who Was in Charge: Police Repression of New York City's Black Population at the Turn of the Twentieth Century." *Journal of Urban History*, vol. 31, no. 6, 2005, pp. 799–819, doi:10.1177/0096144205278167.

Scheiber, Andrew. "*Jazz* and the Future Blues: Toni Morrison's Urban Folk Zone." *Modern Fiction Studies*, vol. 52, no. 2, Summer 2006, pp. 470–94.

Scruggs, Charles. *Sweet Home: Invisible Cities in the Afro-American Novel*. Johns Hopkins UP, 1993.

Sweeney, Megan. "'Something Rogue': Commensurability, Commodification, Crime, and Justice in Toni Morrison's Later Fiction." *Modern Fiction Studies*, vol. 52, no. 2, Summer 2006, pp. 440–69.

Tutu, Desmond. *No Future without Forgiveness*. Random House, 1999.

Von Holderstein Holtermann, Jakob. "Outlining the Shadow of the Axe—On Restorative Justice and the Use of Trial and Punishment." *Criminal Law and Philosophy*, vol. 3, no. 2, 2009, pp. 187–207, doi:10.1007/s11572-008-9069-y.

Williams, Sherley Ann. "The Blues Roots of Contemporary African American Poetry." *Massachusetts Review*, vol. 18, no. 3, Autumn 1977, pp. 542–54.

Wilson, Olly. "Black Music as an Art Form." *Black Music Research Journal*, vol. 3, 1983, pp. 1–22. http://www.jstor.org/stable/779487.

Wilson, Olly. "The Significance of the Relationship between Afro-American Music and West African Music." *Black Perspective in Music*, vol. 2, no. 1, 1974, pp. 3–22.

Zehr, Howard. "Rethinking Criminal Justice: Restorative Justice." Unpublished paper, 1995.

CHAPTER FOURTEEN

Margaret Garner in History, Opera, and as Inspiration for *Beloved*

KRISTINE YOHE

Like artists of all genres, Toni Morrison often draws upon history for inspiration and source material for her work. From recalling her personal family background growing up in the 1930s and 1940s in Lorain, Ohio, when creating the otherwise fictive world of *The Bluest Eye* (1970), to reaching back before the colonial European origins of the United States in *A Mercy* (2008), to reimagining the Korean War as the backdrop for *Home* (2012), Morrison's novels are steeped in history. And she profoundly situates her fifth novel, *Beloved* (1987), in the time period during and just after the end of slavery, in late nineteenth-century America. Yet when discussing how history has influenced her wider oeuvre, she explains, "I just tried to see what was already there, and to use that as a kind of well-spring for my own work." Rather than feeling a need to reinvent lore, she says, "I was just interested in finding what myths already existed. There already was a Margaret Garner, there already was a myth about flying Africans" (qtd. in Cecil Brown 114). It is noteworthy that, in this discussion and elsewhere, Morrison places the historical record on a par with the cultural influence of mythology and folklore, all of which undergird her works, including the flying Africans myth in *Song of Solomon* and the history of Margaret Garner and US slavery more generally for *Beloved*. In a 2002 interview, Morrison describes the influence of *Beloved*, which "takes, of course, the story of Margaret Garner, a story no one wanted to remember, the buried past, and resurrects it. But it is as much about the obsessive love of mothers and children in the context of slavery as it is about history" (qtd. in Hostetler 204). And in *Beloved*, as in all her novels, Morrison strives to reveal what she calls "the unwritten interior life of these people," which, she notes, is only accessible through "the act of the imagination" ("The Site of Memory" 238). This effort parallels critic Saidiya Hartman's ideas of "critical fabulation," where, she explains, "The intention here isn't anything as miraculous as recovering the lives of the enslaved or redeeming the dead, but rather laboring to paint as full a picture of the lives of the captives as possible" (Hartman 11). So while exploring this historical foundation is enormously enriching in understanding *Beloved*, we also benefit from trying to imagine what Morrison's fictional but still real characters would have thought, done, and felt. And seeking to know about Margaret Garner's unique and profound history is an essential step in this journey.

In the middle of the nineteenth century, Margaret Garner was a young Black woman entrapped in slavery on Maplewood Farm, legally considered to be the property of Archibald Gaines in Richwood, Kentucky, about twenty miles south of Cincinnati, Ohio. While she was able to marry an enslaved Black man on a neighboring farm, Robert Garner, there is ample evidence to support that she was repeatedly raped by a white man, likely Archibald Gaines, who fathered at least three of her four children. Eventually, Margaret, Robert, their four children, and his parents decided to escape on a snowy night in January 1856. Their plan was to stop in Cincinnati and then continue on to Canada with assistance from Underground Railroad activists, including Quaker abolitionist Levi Coffin. They made it to Covington, Kentucky, leaving the borrowed horses and sleigh in a livery stable, and then continued on foot over the frozen Ohio River and into Cincinnati. The refugees gathered at the home of a cousin, a free Black man named Simon Kite, near Mill Creek on the west side of Cincinnati. Very shortly thereafter, they were caught by the pursuing enslaver, Archibald Gaines, and a posse of federal marshals. A shoot-out ensued, and Margaret decided to kill one child—with plans to kill them all and herself—rather than allow a return to slavery. So she cut her toddler daughter Mary's throat with a butcher knife and struck the other children but didn't kill them. Before she could continue further, Margaret was stopped, and all of the family members were taken into custody.

In the next month, February 1856, Margaret Garner was visited in jail by P. S. Bassett, of Cincinnati's Fairmount Theological Seminary, who reported the following encounter in a publication called *The American Baptist*:

> She said, that when the officers and slave-hunters came to the house in which they were concealed, she caught a shovel and struck two of her children on the head, and then took a knife and cut the throat of the third, and tried to kill the other—that if they had given her time, she would have killed them all—that with regard to herself, she cared but little; but she was unwilling to have her children suffer as she had done.
>
> I inquired if she was not excited almost to madness when she committed the act. No, she replied, I was as cool as I now am; and would much rather kill them at once, and thus end their sufferings, than have them taken back to slavery and be murdered by piece-meal. She then told the story of her wrongs. She spoke of her days of suffering, of her nights of unmitigated toll [toil?], while the bitter tears coursed their way down her cheeks …
>
> * * * * *
>
> She alludes to the child that she killed as being free from all trouble and sorrow, with a degree of satisfaction that almost chills the blood in one's veins; yet she evidently possesses all the passionate tenderness of a mother's love. (qtd. in Harris et al. 10)

Bassett's description of this visit was later included in a scrapbook of Black American culture, *The Black Book*, edited by Middleton Harris, Morris Levitt, and Roger Furman, and published by Random House in 1974. Though not listed in this first edition, Toni Morrison was the book editor and quite actively involved in the creation of this amazing volume.

Margaret Garner's case went to trial in Cincinnati and lasted an unprecedented two weeks. A driving issue was whether the federal Fugitive Slave Law would prevail, and thus return the Garners, categorized as "property," back to the slave-owning state of Kentucky, or whether Ohio law would abide, which said that they could be considered free because they previously had been temporarily brought to the state by their enslavers. If the latter, abolitionists were especially eager for Margaret Garner then to be charged with murder under Ohio law, which would mean that the child she killed was considered a human being. During the proceedings, renowned white abolitionist and women's rights advocate Lucy Stone met with Margaret and spoke publicly at the trial, while alleging that the extremely fair skin of three of the enslaved woman's children was relevant to the case: "The faded faces of the negro children tell too plainly to what degradation female slaves submit. Rather than give her little daughter to that life, she killed it. If in her deep maternal love she felt the impulse to send her child back to God, to save it from coming woe, who shall say she had no right to do it?" (qtd. in Weisenburger 173). Lucy Stone makes clear that she recognizes that Margaret suffered sexual abuse by her enslavers and that she manages to retain her humanity and committed maternal love. In his influential 1998 book, *Modern Medea: A Family Story of Slavery and Child-Murder from the Old South*, Steven Weisenburger agrees with Stone's allegation and corroborates it with his research that indicates that Archibald Gaines was in residence at Maplewood during the relevant time periods before each of Margaret's three last pregnancies. Nevertheless, the judge presiding in the case, John L. Pendery, a US Commissioner for the Southern District of Ohio, soon ruled that the federal Fugitive Slave Law prevailed and the Garner family would be returned to slavery in Kentucky. Archibald Gaines verbally agreed that he would later bring Margaret Garner back to Cincinnati to be charged with murder by the State of Ohio, but instead he sold her south. As Delores Walters explains, "Pro-slavery proponents considered Margaret's act of infanticide evidence of the savagery of Black women, thus justifying slavery, while anti-slavery activists vilified slavery itself, not its victims," precisely because this violent response logically flowed from the evil system of slavery (Walters 4). Shortly after being sold south, Margaret survived a boat accident, in which her younger daughter perished; this enslaved mother apparently was relieved, as this child too was spared from living within the hell of slavery. Two years later, in 1858, Margaret Garner died of typhoid.

Although no direct primary sources from Margaret Garner herself are known to be extant, another contemporary report, also from 1856, comes from Reverend Horace Bushnell, a Congregationalist minister and abolitionist, who visited Margaret Garner during her incarceration in Cincinnati before the trial. He reported the following exchange:

Q: "Margaret, why did you kill your child?"
A: "It was my own," she said; "given me of God, to do the best a mother could in its behalf. I *have done the best I could!* I would have done more and better for the rest! I knew it was better for them to go home to God than back to slavery."
Q: "But why did you not trust in God—why not wait and hope?"
A: "I did wait, and then we dared to do, and fled in fear, but in hope:—hope fled—God did not appear to save—*I did the best I could!*" (qtd. in Taylor 74, emphases in original)

Nikki M. Taylor includes Bushnell's account of this interaction in her 2016 book, *Driven Toward Madness: The Fugitive Slave Margaret Garner and Tragedy on the Ohio*. Throughout this significant work, Taylor explores the trauma that Margaret Garner experienced under slavery and theorizes that this enslaved woman was the victim of psychological and physical abuse and specifically sexual assault and rape by her enslaver, Archibald Gaines, who likely fathered at least two of her children.

Margaret Garner's bold act, to take charge of her child Mary's life and death, inspired many Americans, including writers, artists, and abolitionists. Not only did this killing demonstrate the hell of slavery—if death for one's beloved child was preferable—but it also was a shocking move for an enslaved woman to assert such extreme agency. The resulting moral dilemma of contemplating the horror of infanticide within the horror of slavery has proven to be a compelling motivation for response. White Cincinnati artist Thomas Satterwhite Noble painted his interpretation of Margaret Garner's ordeal in his 1867 work, *The Modern Medea*, which now hangs in the National Underground Railroad Freedom Center. Although not technically accurate, as it shows the two older sons killed, the painting offers a stunning rendition of an indignant Margaret defiantly confronting the group of white men. In his 2010 book, *Who Speaks for Margaret Garner?* Mark Reinhardt explains that the painting was originally called *Margaret Garner*, but that it was renamed *The Modern Medea* when it was photographed by Matthew Brady and then turned into an engraving, which was published in *Harper's Weekly* in May 1867. Reinhardt explains that the original large painting, which had been commissioned by a New York businessman, was lost, and the one available today is a smaller version, painted in 1868 (Reinhardt 261). The killing of Mary Garner also inspired a number of literary responses, seven of which are included in Reinhardt's book.

Before *Beloved* was published in 1987, the most accomplished and famous literary work to come from Margaret Garner's deed appeared a year after the killing, in 1857, when renowned Black writer, abolitionist, and suffragist Frances Ellen Watkins Harper published a poem, "The Slave Mother: A Tale of the Ohio" (not to be confused with her similarly titled 1854 poem "The Slave Mother"). Here, she imagines how Margaret Garner, whom she does not name, would have felt, in a way that predicts the Morrisonian concept of an "interior life." In this poignant poem, Harper depicts Garner as a loving mother who feels great joy in her children: "the treasures of my soul / They lay like doves around my heart." But when she realizes their imminent danger, this enslaved mother seeks to escape across the icy Ohio River, only to soon realize that "The pursuer is on thy track, / And the hunter at thy door." As imagined by Harper, this woman, unnamed but clearly Margaret Garner, declares that she will protect her children by killing them: "I will hew their path to freedom / Through the portals of the tomb." And she ends her 64-line domestic narrative with an admonishment to her readers to respond with moral conviction and, "if there is any honor, / truth or justice in the land," then to decisively take a position "on the side of freedom" (Harper 23). First published in Harper's 1857 expanded reissue of *Poems on Miscellaneous Subjects*, which had originally appeared in 1854, this poem enjoyed a wide readership, with 10,000 copies in print (Reinhardt 249). Unlike the sometimes overwrought news accounts of Garner's act, Harper's poem strikes a chord of profound pathos, making its heroine sympathetic and admirable. Like many Morrison scholars, I have regularly found including this poem to be helpful when teaching *Beloved*, and it is included in Oxford University Press's 1999 *Toni Morrison's "Beloved": A Casebook*, edited by William L. Andrews and Nellie Y. McKay.

With few exceptions, the Garner case faded from public awareness in the century after its occurrence, only occasionally appearing in newspaper and journal articles. One of the most substantial was published in 1953 by Julius Yanuck in the *Mississippi Valley Historical Review*. As the recipient of a PhD in history from Columbia University in the same year, Yanuck was an expert on constitutional history, especially its intersections with the 1850 Fugitive Slave Law, which his treatment of the Margaret Garner ordeal clearly reflects. Yet his article also taps into the humanity of this case: "The constitutional issues were grave, if not dangerously close to insoluble, but the Garner case had yet other meanings for the nation. It demonstrated forcefully the deep personal tragedy of slavery. The way Margaret Garner's little girl died embarrassed the South and disturbed the North more than a hundred arguments of antislavery philosophers" (Yanuck 47). Yanuck describes the legal proceedings against Margaret Garner in clear and cogent detail in his article and ends it by explaining the high tensions resulting from the clash of who had legal authority—the State of Ohio or the federal government via the Fugitive Slave Law. That it was ultimately the latter becomes, Yanuck avers, the essential fabric of the era, leading to growing tension: "These circumstances could only result in a heightened conflict between Ohio and the federal government. It was out of cases such as that of Margaret Garner that friction between free states and the national government grew into increasingly bitter hostility" (Yanuck 66). The United States, of course, would plunge into Civil War less than a decade after the influential Margaret Garner case embodied some of the gravest divergences at stake. While all of these judicial intricacies remain in the background for Toni Morrison's later use of the Margaret Garner story, they provide essential context and balance for her fictional reinterpretation of this historical woman's life.

After becoming a textbook editor in 1965 with a Syracuse, New York, subsidiary of Random House and then later working as a senior editor at Random House in New York City, Toni Morison edited many celebrated Black authors, including Henry Dumas, Angela Davis, Gayl Jones, Leon Forrest, June Jordan, Toni Cade Bambara, and Muhammad Ali. As part of her work at Random House, she oversaw the production of the important 1974 text *The Black Book*, an archival collection of Black American history and culture, really a fusion of scrapbook, history and collage. Although Morrison's name does not appear on the book—which was officially coedited by Middleton Harris, Morris Levitt, Roger Furman, and Ernest Smith—she was heavily involved with its compilation. Some of the people thanked in the book's acknowledgements are her parents, Ramah Wofford and George Carl Wofford (who are not named as her parents in the book), who donated materials used in *The Black Book*, including a photograph of Morrison's mother, which is among many others pictured on the book's cover. A thirty-fifth-anniversary edition of the book was reissued by Random House in 2009 with a new foreword by Morrison. Here, *The Black Book*'s original back cover poem is now included inside as its preface, and now with its author listed: Toni Morrison, whose name also now appears on the book's front cover. Black American editor Chris Jackson said that he sees this book demonstrating the sweep of Morrison's influence and eye and that he appreciates its ambition. "*The Black Book* is not exactly a celebration of black life. It is a gathering together of artifacts. It's a sort of way of witnessing black life, but, again, it does feel like it's coming from the perspective within the black community ... almost a family history in a way" (qtd. in Ghansah 55). The work of creating this encyclopedic book—with its more than 500 items—exposed Morrison to influential relics of Black history, including first learning about the story of Margaret Garner, which would inspire both the 1987 novel *Beloved* and the 2004 opera *Margaret Garner*.

In reading the newspaper clipping of the account that P. S. Bassett wrote for *The American Baptist* in February 1856 (discussed above) and included in *The Black Book*, Morrison has stated that she was struck by the boldness and the claim of Margaret Garner, as an enslaved Black mother who dared to determine what happened to her children. In multiple venues, including a 1988 interview, Morrison has said that she sees Garner's bold act as evidence of "an outrageous claim for a slave woman" (qtd. in Darling 252). In a conversation with Gloria Naylor in 1985, Morrison explains that, in developing Sethe, she was inspired by Margaret Garner as a woman who "had placed all of the value of her life in something outside herself. That the woman who killed her children loved her children so much; they were the best part of her and she would not see them sullied. She would not see them hurt. She would rather kill them, have them die" (qtd. in Naylor 207–8).

Two other essays yield significant insights about *Beloved* and Margaret Garner. First, in "On *Beloved*," an undated and previously unpublished essay included in *The Source of Self-Regard* (2019), Morrison explains that the genesis of the novel sprang from her meditation on gender, motherhood, and choice. She tries to imagine an enslaved woman who "chose to be responsible for" her children, and who manages "to claim them," and who is, antithetically to the entire enterprise of slavery, "not a breeder, but a parent." Morrison recognizes this hypothetical woman as "an expression of intolerable female independence," who embodies freedom and whose "claim extended to infanticide." And then, she notes,

> These lines of thought came together when I recalled a newspaper article I had read around 1970, a description of an abolitionist cause célèbre focused on a slave woman named Margaret Garner who had indeed made such claims. The details of her life were riveting. But I selected and manipulated its parts to suit my own purposes. Still my reluctance to enter the period of slavery was disabling. The need to reexamine and imagine it was repellent. Plus, I believed nobody else would want to dig deeply into the interior lives of slaves. ("On *Beloved*" 282)

This historical stimulus leads Morrison into what she calls the excitement and possibility of creating "uncolonized territory," resulting in fiction. *Beloved*, thus, joins the openness of imagination with the contours of history and a deep respect for authenticity. In this same essay, Morrison next discusses the tensions that memory embodies in the novel: "The shared effort to avoid imagining slave life as lived from their own point of view became the subtheme, the structure of the work. Forgetting the past was the engine, and the characters (except for one) are intent on forgetting." And she notes that the novel's arc coalesces on her certainty that slavery "haunts us all" and that this haunting is "both what we yearn for and what we fear" ("On *Beloved*" 283–4).

Another essay where Morrison discusses how she wrote *Beloved* is the eponymous work in the collection *The Source of Self-Regard*, where she explains—in what originated as a 1992 speech in Portland, Oregon—what she sees as a necessary progression for anyone's "serious education," where, she says, "We move from data to information to knowledge to wisdom." She then states that she undertook this approach in her research for the novel but that she intentionally limited some of it: "So here I am appropriating a historical life—Margaret Garner's life—from a newspaper article, which is sort of reliable, halfway unreliable, not doing any further research on her, but doing a lot of research around her" ("The Source of Self-Regard" 308). Morrison further explains that she worked to keep the novel's focus not on slavery but instead centered on individual enslaved people. Here, she gives an insightful reading of how a historical tool of torture, the bit, becomes an overarching symbol in the novel to simultaneously reveal the brutal inhumanity of the institution while set against the very human experience of suffering through it. "I wanted it to remain indescribable but not unknown. So the point became to render not what it looked like, but what it felt like and what it meant, personally. Now that was the parallel of my attitude toward the history, toward the institution of slavery, that is, I didn't want to describe what it *looked* like, but what it *felt* like and what it meant" ("The Source of Self-Regard" 312, emphases in original). Morrison then quotes a long passage from the novel, the scene where Sethe and Paul D discuss how Halle is not able to defend Sethe from being assaulted and Paul D is unable to speak to Halle because he is wearing the bit. Rather than explain to Sethe how the bit felt, he ends up talking about Mister, the rooster "who was allowed to be and stay what he was. But I wasn't allowed to be and stay what I was" (*Beloved* 86). In this essay, Morrison next discusses her novel

Jazz and how she places it in its unique cultural moment. She then returns to *Beloved* and links the two works and how in both she is "looking at self-regard in both racial and gendered terms." She further explains,

> In *Beloved*, I was interested in what contributed most significantly to a slave woman's self-regard. What was her self-esteem? What value did she place on herself? And I became convinced, and research supported my hunch, my intuition, that it was her identity as a mother, her ability to be and to remain exactly what the institution said she was not, that was important to her. Moving into Reconstruction and beyond it, as difficult as it was to function as a mother with control over the destiny of one's children, it still became then, certainly, a legal responsibility after slavery. So this is where the sources of self-regard came for Margaret Garner or Sethe. And it is exaggerated because it's that important and that alien and that strange and that vital. But when Sethe asks, "Me? Me?" at the end of *Beloved*, it's a real movement toward a recognition of self-regard. ("The Source of Self-Regard" 317–18)

Through giving this valuable analysis, Morrison offers her readers enormous insights that not only enhance our experience of the novel, but also allow us to begin to comprehend the interior lives of enslaved people.

A final source where Morrison explains how the story of Margaret Garner influenced her writing of *Beloved* comes in the foreword included in the 2004 edition of the novel. Here, she explains that after leaving her editing job in 1983 to focus full-time on teaching and writing, she found herself consumed with ideas about freedom, gender, and choice. By contemplating her own relative freedom, she felt compelled to consider the almost total absence of freedom that enslaved women endured:

> Inevitably these thoughts led me to the different history of black women in this country—a history in which marriage was discouraged, impossible, or illegal; in which birthing children was required, but "having" them, being responsible for them—being, in other words, their parent—was as out of the question as freedom. Assertions of parenthood under conditions peculiar to the logic of institutional enslavement were criminal.
>
> The idea was riveting, but the canvas overwhelmed me. Summoning characters who could manifest the intellect and the ferocity such logic would provoke proved beyond my imagination until I remembered one of the books I had published back when I had a job. A newspaper clipping in *The Black Book* summarized the story of Margaret Garner, a young mother who, having escaped slavery, was arrested for killing one of her children (and trying to kill the others) rather than let them be returned to the owner's plantation. (*Beloved* foreword xvi–xvii)

It is fascinating to contemplate Morrison's juxtaposition of her own individual life against the history of enslaved Black women and then zooming in on Margaret Garner. Because she is thinking here about having just left her work in publishing, it follows that this profound example from that work life would surface. She explains that she was awestruck by Margaret Garner's "single-minded" focus and impressed that "she had the intellect, the ferocity, and the willingness to risk everything for what was to her the necessity of freedom." But, Morrison also explains, she was not interested in adhering too closely to the record, as she wished instead to imagine a life somewhat like Margaret Garner's but filtered through the auspices of fiction:

> The historical Margaret Garner is fascinating, but, to a novelist, confining. Too little imaginative space there for my purposes. So I would invent her thoughts, plumb them for a subtext that was historically true in essence, but not strictly factual in order to relate her history to contemporary issues about freedom, responsibility, and women's "place." The heroine would represent the unapologetic acceptance of shame and terror; assume the consequences of choosing infanticide; claim her own freedom. The terrain, slavery, was formidable and pathless. To invite readers (and myself) into the repellant landscape (hidden, but not completely; deliberately buried, but not forgotten) was to pitch a tent in a cemetery inhabited by highly vocal ghosts. (*Beloved* foreword xvii)

Clearly, Morrison succeeds in her project to combine these seemingly divergent threads so she can center her novel on gender and motherhood within the "terrain" of slavery. As Angelita Reyes argues, in *Beloved*, "Morrison is not as concerned with recording historical facts as she is with constructing meaning and emotional *truth* out of them" (77, emphasis in original). And it is interesting that, although she imagines an ecosystem that is not based in the historical record, Morrison's novel does give the Garner name to both enslavers and the enslaved. In addition, Sweet Home, the farm where the early action takes place, is set in the rolling Kentucky countryside much like the historical Maplewood Farm, where the historical Margaret Garner was enslaved.

Long after *Beloved* was published in 1987, Morrison returned to the Margaret Garner story in 2004, when she wrote and published the libretto for an opera called *Margaret Garner*, with music composed by Richard Danielpour. (Note that the specifics of this title can vary, with Morrison's libretto sometimes called *Margaret Garner: Opera in Two Acts* and the score by Danielpour named *Margaret Garner: A New American Opera*.) Here, Morrison's lyrics are more closely based on the documented facts than *Beloved*, but she nevertheless chooses to deviate from the historical record on behalf of her art. While the Garner story creates the contextual stimulus for *Beloved*, it provides a perhaps more intimate and internal spark for the opera. In an interview in May 2005 with Janelle Gelfand, Morrison explains how she used history in writing the opera libretto, but that she also drew upon her own creativity: "We're not doing a documentary. We're trying to wrestle with some of the larger questions of those incidents that took place at that time, in that place," culminating in the essential questions of "Is she human or is she property? The questions of, is she a murderer, or has she stolen something, is the crux of the whole thing" (qtd. in Gelfand A6). Morrison explains that, as she prepared to write the libretto, she struggled to return to this material. The program for the premiere of *Margaret Garner* at the Michigan Opera Theatre in May 2005 includes a short essay, "A Note on *Margaret Garner* from Toni Morrison." Here, Morrison comments on the difficulties she encountered in engaging with what she calls "Margaret Garner's ordeal" in order to write *Beloved*: "For more than five years I had been in thrall to the material, trying to do justice to the historical characters involved while exercising the license I needed to interrogate the dilemma Margaret both presented and represented." She explains that the experience of confronting this material had been intensely challenging, even depleting. Yet, Margaret Garner's story summoned her again: "Some ten years later, free of the exhaustion following the publication of *Beloved* I realized that there were genres other than novels that could expand and deepen the story. The topic, the people, the narrative theme, passion and universality made it more than worthy of opera; it begged for it" ("A Note on Margaret Garner" 8).

Morrison's *Margaret Garner* libretto encompasses a dramatic narrative arc that takes the titular heroine and her family from Kentucky enslavement to brief freedom in Ohio, and then back to Kentucky, where she is tried and convicted for theft, ultimately then choosing to hang herself at the opera's end. Morrison's powerful lyrics, paired with Richard Danielpour's soaring music, embrace a wide swath of emotion, ranging from the poignant love Margaret expresses for her children to the wrenching pain felt by the enslaved because of violent assaults on body and soul perpetrated by the enslavers. In an early exchange with Cilla, her mother-in-law, Margaret sings of her sleeping baby, "I need to see her eyes, her smile." Cilla's admonishing reply—which the stage directions note she delivers "*emphatically, as a warning*"—echo how *Beloved* shows Paul D's fear of Sethe's excessive love. Here, Cilla sings, "It's dangerous, daughter, / To love too much" (*Margaret Garner* 17, emphasis in original). Shortly thereafter, perhaps the most moving aria in the entire opera comes when Margaret thoughtfully contemplates her fate and how she understands the meaning of love:

No pretty words can ease or cure
What heavy hands can do.
When sorrow is deep,
The secret soul keeps its quality love.

Morrison vividly demonstrates the brutality of the institution of slavery when this tender aria is interrupted by the enslaver, here named Edward Gaines, who objects to her "fine sentiments," asserting that he can overcome them with his "many remedies" and immediately thereafter raping Margaret (*Margaret Garner* 25–6).

After the family escapes to Ohio, they have three weeks of relative peace before Gaines and a posse confront the Garners in their hiding place and forcibly overtake them. In the printed libretto, Morrison gives few details, but in the performances in Detroit, Cincinnati, and Philadelphia, as well as in New York, the ensuing plot developments are handled somewhat differently, but all involve Robert quickly being lynched, Margaret attacking Gaines with hot coals, and Margaret killing her two children while proclaiming, "Never to be born again into slavery!" (*Margaret Garner* 33). This highly dramatic scene is followed by a brief and still Intermezzo where a distraught Margaret appears alone. The opera then leads into the next scene, "In a courtroom, in early April 1861," where Edward Gaines asserts, three times, "I have committed no crime," when his daughter seeks to sway him to regard Margaret Garner as a human being and to "help change the debate / Raging the land," reflecting the rumbles of the imminent Civil War. The judges, however, issue their decision: "He has committed no crime ... / The charge is theft, / The sentence is just. / This one will be made ready / For execution" (*Margaret Garner* 35). Then the "*relieved*" chorus of white townspeople derisively proclaims of Margaret, "She is not like you or me!" Margaret "*quietly*" agrees and asserts, twice, "I am not like you. / I am me!" She then refuses to acquiesce to the judges' demand for her to be seated silently, and she repeats her claim a third time, now amplifying it to the courtroom:

You have no authority.
I am not like you.
(*defiantly*) I am me!
I am me!
I am! (*Margaret Garner* 36, emphases in original)

The operatic Margaret Garner's existential claim here echoes Morrison's 1992 interrogation of how her fictionalized Sethe—and the historical Margaret Garner—demonstrate their "sources of self-regard," discussed above, through their agency as mothers and their abilities to recognize themselves ("The Source of Self-Regard" 318). In this essay, Morrison connects Margaret's growing self-awareness to Sethe's incipient consideration at the end of *Beloved* that, rather than her children, maybe she could be, as Paul D suggests, her own "best thing." Thus, the way the opera's Margaret Garner asserts her identity deeply resonates with Sethe's last words in the novel: "Me? Me?" (*Beloved* 322).

The closing scene of the opera shows Margaret refusing the offered reprieve of her execution—which would return her to the clutches of the rapist-enslaver Edward Gaines—and choosing instead to die by hanging herself, demonstrating her insistence that she can choose the terms under which she will live or die, much as she does with the mercy killing of her children. But Morrison does not quite end it there. Instead, in a brief Epilogue, the chorus of "The Townspeople" joins the chorus of "The Slaves" to sing together, "Have mercy. Have mercy on us. / Help us break through the night." This mixed chorus sings together in the Epilogue for the first time in the entire opera, thus demonstrating the potential for healing and forgiveness. And the last words go to the enslaved chorus:

> Break through the night,
> Break through the night;
> Let her linger a while
> And ride the light,
> And ride the light.

In this final piece, the enslaved chorus first echoes what they have just sung together with the white townspeople, while then offering a prayer for Margaret's soul so that she can "linger" and, in a sort of benediction, "ride the light," into heaven. Here, as throughout the *Margaret Garner* opera, Morrison uses powerful symbols of dark and light to indicate the tensions of despair and hope. This closing scene also echoes how the first sung lines of the opera are issued by the "Slave Chorus" who emerge from *"total darkness,"* situated on an auction block, and demanding, "No, no more. / No more, not more. / Please, God, no more" (*Margaret Garner* 9, emphasis in original). Thus, the opera comes full circle from darkness and negation and—even after the tragic loss of the lives of Margaret, Robert, and their children—still manages to end with mercy, hope, and light. This redemptive catharsis embodies the dramatic possibility that Morrison long foresaw for Margaret Garner's story, especially within the genre of opera, thus allowing for this enslaved woman to transcend physical existence into spiritual triumph.

The way that Toni Morrison reacted when she first learned of Margaret Garner in the early 1970s stayed consistent when she was inspired by this history to write *Beloved* in the 1980s, and the intensity of her connection to this woman remained into the writing of the libretto. Similar to the novel, in the opera, an enslaved mother's protective infanticide is also in the spotlight, and Morrison is in awe of Margaret's singular courage, as she notes in an interview about the opera: "That black slave woman was a revolutionary who clung to freedom and said, 'I am in charge of my children'" (qtd. in Gelfand A6). It is evident that Morrison admires this historical woman's ability to assert herself and to claim her right to agency, including over her children, which, of course, she legally does not "own." Considering how Margaret Garner, an enslaved mother, could kill her child *out of love*, Morrison explains her reaction in a 1987 video interview with Alan Benson: "For me, it was the ultimate gesture of the loving mother. It was also the outrageous claim of a slave. The last thing a slave woman owns is her children" (qtd. in Benson). Morrison explores the import of these factors first in *Beloved* and then reconsiders them in writing the *Margaret Garner* libretto, which has, as noted above, several parallels to the novel as well as numerous differences. While both works depict an enslaved mother's bold acts of mercy killing, they engage vastly different circumstances. One significant way that the opera diverges from history is how Morrison depicts Margaret Garner's husband, Robert Garner. While the historical man fought for the Union in the Civil War and was interviewed in 1870 in Cincinnati, the operatic Robert Garner dies by lynching shortly after the family escapes. In real life, Robert raised two sons, whom Margaret had birthed, although he almost certainly was not their father—the white enslaver, Archibald Gaines, the owner of Maplewood Farm, likely was. In addition, the Margaret Garner of history died of typhoid two years after she killed her daughter, Mary, after having been moved to Mississippi. The operatic heroine, who receives a legal reprieve while standing on the gallows, nevertheless chooses to die by hanging herself in the opera's dramatic ending. Both history and the opera are set in Northern Kentucky and Cincinnati, Ohio, both within the horrific contours of slavery at Maplewood, and both are placed in a setting heading directly toward national disaster. This fraught context is further heightened in the opera as Morrison changes the time from 1856 to 1861, truly the brink of the Civil War.

Because of its place in Margaret Garner's history, Maplewood Farm, in Richwood, Kentucky, was the site for some of the public activities that came to Greater Cincinnati in 2005 as part of the programming leading up to the *Margaret Garner* opera's Cincinnati premiere in July of that year. I discuss in detail the contentious community interactions surrounding these events in my chapter, "Confronting *Margaret Garner* in Cincinnati: The Opera, The Toni Morrison Society Conference, and the Public Debate," which is included in the 2016 book, *"Margaret Garner": The Premiere Performances of Toni Morrison's Libretto*, edited by La Vinia Delois Jennings. Much of the controversy centered on the allegations by a white woman descendant of the Bedinger farm, which was next to Maplewood, Ruth Wade Cox Brunings, who long sought to restrict the narrative and access around this historical site. Her involvement goes back to the late 1990s, when Maplewood Farm became widely known as the place where Margaret Garner had been enslaved; this was in part because of the growing interest in this history following the publication of Steven Weisenburger's 1998 book about Garner, *Modern Medea*. Because of this attention, Brunings became, through her membership in the Boone County Historical Society, the Maplewood liaison, so that the landowner, George Budig, would not have to handle arrangements for anyone visiting the farm. Therefore, visits to this site had to go through Brunings, who sought to promote her personal vision of slavery. In particular, Brunings denied that Archibald Gaines raped Margaret Garner; instead, she claimed that Margaret was remorseful for entering into an "adulterous" relationship with the enslaver; many of us in the wider community regarded such a statement to be nonsense. Even the relatively conservative *Cincinnati Enquirer* newspaper issued an editorial just two days before the opera premiere, where they stated, among other strong arguments, "Enslaved women like Garner were the property of their masters and didn't have the power to say 'no.' They were rape victims" ("Garner Story Has Much to Teach"). Nevertheless, the opera cast members and crew visited Maplewood in June 2005, where I and others witnessed a heated exchange between some of the stars, notably Gregg Baker and Angela Brown, who are Black, and Ruth Brunings.

Thereafter, we took almost 300 Toni Morrison Society conference attendees to the farm when they came to Cincinnati and Northern Kentucky for the July 2005 conference; interactions with Brunings continued to be tense, but we got through it. That same week, the conference participants also attended, along with Professor Morrison, the Cincinnati premiere of the magnificent *Margaret Garner* opera, starring Denyce Graves, in Music Hall, as well as the opening night cast party at the National Underground Railroad Freedom Center.

By the end of that momentous summer, with the opera and the Toni Morrison Society conference all behind us, my former colleague Delores Walters led the way in negotiating, along with the former president of Northern Kentucky University (NKU) James Votruba, a new arrangement to allow for future educational visits to Maplewood Farm, which is on private property owned by George Budig, a member of a local business-owning and philanthropical family. Walters sought to ease future visits so that Brunings could be avoided, which was exactly what happened. Since Fall 2005, I have been able to take multiple groups of students—some from classes focused solely on Toni Morrison, and all of whom had just read *Beloved*—to Maplewood, an experience they find to be significant and enriching. Fortunately, unlike the circumstances before these negotiations transpired, we no longer must set up our trips through Brunings. To date, I have arranged many such visits not only for my NKU classes, but also for classes taught by other NKU colleagues as well as area high school classes, community groups, and more. Most recently, in June 2020, I helped to facilitate a Maplewood visit for a film crew working on a French documentary, *Toni Morrison, Black Matter(s)*, from Roche Productions and directed by Claire Laborey. Interest in this historical "site of memory" does not seem to be waning, not only for devotees of Morrison but for those interested in the fullness of history.

Visiting Maplewood Farm, reading *Beloved*, watching and studying the *Margaret Garner* opera, learning how the real Margaret Garner defied slavery—all of these experiences enhance our understanding of history and our ability to reckon with the past. The need for this work was brought into the foreground quite recently, when, in October 2021 in Virginia, the Republican gubernatorial candidate—now Governor-elect Glenn Youngkin—promoted a "controversy" over the teaching of Morrison's *Beloved*. When the novel was charged with obscenity, and it was said to have caused nightmares for a Republican activist's high-school-aged son, censoring *Beloved* became an apparently effective lightning rod in the heated culture wars of twenty-first-century America, especially within this particular election. It is striking to note that, in her 1992 essay "The Source of Self-Regard," Morrison describes her interaction with high school students who responded in a similarly limited way almost thirty years ago. She notes that these students "were either alarmed or offended by the explicit sexuality in *Beloved*," yet, she remarks, "nobody was offended or confused or unable to understand the context in which the story is set, which is slavery. The sexuality troubled them. But the violence and the criminality and the license in that institution did not alarm or offend them" ("The Source of Self-Regard" 306). All of these reactions and more demonstrate how essential *Beloved* is, how singularly formative it remains in enabling a discourse that is long overdue. In 1988, Morrison explained that, because at that time, as far as she knew, there was "no suitable memorial" where one could go to remember slavery, not even a "small bench by the road," that was why she had to write the novel ("A Bench" 44). She has also said that, as difficult as it was to write the novel, "If they can live it, I can write about it. I refuse to believe that that period, or that thing [slavery] is beyond art. Because the consequences of practically everything we do, art alone can stand up to. It's not the historians' job to do that" (qtd. in Caldwell 244). And, as I always tell my students, if they could live it and she could write it, then we can read it. So the ripple effects of Margaret Garner's singular life go far and wide, reverberating far into the future.

WORKS CITED

Bassett, P. S. "A Visit to the Slave Mother Who Killed her Child. Feb. 12, 1856." *The Black Book*, edited by Middleton A. Harris et al. Random House, 1974, p. 10.

Benson, Alan. Interview with Toni Morrison. *Profile of a Writer: Toni Morrison*. Alan Benson, dir. RM Arts, 1987.

Brown, Cecil. Interview with Toni Morrison. *Toni Morrison: Conversations*, edited by Carolyn C. Denard, UP of Mississippi, 2008, pp. 107–25.

Caldwell, Gail. "Author Toni Morrison Discusses Her Latest Novel *Beloved*." *Conversations with Toni Morrison*, edited by Danille Taylor-Guthrie, UP of Mississippi, 1994, pp. 239–45.

Darling, Marsha. "In the Realm of Responsibility: A Conversation with Toni Morrison." *Conversations with Toni Morrison*, edited by Danille Taylor-Guthrie, UP of Mississippi, 1994, pp. 246–54.

"Garner Story Has Much to Teach." Editorial. *The Cincinnati Enquirer*, July 12, 2005.

Gelfand, Janelle. "Author Brings Focus to Boone Slave's Life: Nobel, Pulitzer Prize Winner Reflects on Opera's Premiere." *The Cincinnati Enquirer*, July 11, 2005, pp. A1, A6.

Ghansah, Rachel Kaadzi. "What Toni Morrison Saw." *The New York Times Magazine*, Apr. 12, 2015, p. 55. https://www.nytimes.com/2015/04/12/magazine/the-radical-vision-of-toni-morrison.html. Accessed Aug. 13, 2022.

Harper, Frances Ellen Watkins. "The Slave Mother." 1854. *The Norton Anthology of African American Literature*. 3rd ed., vol. 1, edited by Henry Louis Gates, Jr., and Valerie A. Smith, Norton, 2004, pp. 450–1.

Harper, Frances Ellen Watkins. "The Slave Mother: A Tale of the Ohio." 1857. *Toni Morrison's* Beloved: *A Casebook*, edited by William L Andrews and Nellie Y. McKay, Oxford UP, 1999, pp. 21–3.

Hartman, Saidiya. "Venus in Two Acts." *Small Axe*, vol. 12, no. 2, June 2008, pp. 1–14. *Project MUSE*, muse.jhu.edu/article/241115.

Hostetler, Ann. Interview with Toni Morrison: "The Art of Teaching." *Toni Morrison: Conversations*, edited by Carolyn C. Denard, UP of Mississippi, 2008, pp. 196–205.

Jennings, La Vinia Delois, editor. Margaret Garner: *The Premiere Performances of Toni Morrison's Libretto*. U of Virginia P, 2016.

Laborey, Claire, director. *Toni Morrison, Black Matter(s)*. Roche Productions, 2020.

Morrison, Toni. *Beloved*. 1987. Vintage, 2004.

Morrison, Toni. "A Bench by the Road: *Beloved*." *Toni Morrison: Conversations*, edited by Carolyn C. Denard, UP of Mississippi, 2008, pp. 44–50.

Morrison, Toni. Foreword. *Beloved*, by Morrison. 1987. Vintage, 2004, pp. xv–xix.

Morrison, Toni. Libretto. *Margaret Garner*. Music by Richard Danielpour. Schirmer, 2004.

Morrison, Toni. "On *Beloved*." *The Source of Self-Regard: Selected Essays, Speeches, and Meditations*. Knopf, 2019, pp. 280–4.

Morrison, Toni. "The Site of Memory." *The Source of Self-Regard: Selected Essays, Speeches, and Meditations*. Knopf, 2019, pp. 233–45.

Morrison, Toni. *The Source of Self-Regard: Selected Essays, Speeches, and Meditations*. Knopf, 2019.

Morrison, Toni. "The Source of Self-Regard." *The Source of Self-Regard: Selected Essays, Speeches, and Meditations*. Knopf, 2019, pp. 304–21.

Naylor, Gloria. "A Conversation: Gloria Naylor and Toni Morrison." *Conversations with Toni Morrison*, edited by Danille Taylor-Guthrie, UP of Mississippi, 1994, pp. 188–217.

Noble, Thomas Satterwhite. *Modern Medea*. 1867, National Underground Railroad Freedom Center, Cincinnati, Ohio.

Reinhardt, Mark. *Who Speaks for Margaret Garner? The True Story that Inspired Toni Morrison's* Beloved. U of Minnesota P, 2010.

Reyes, Angelita. "Using History as Artifact to Situate *Beloved*'s Unknown Woman: Margaret Garner." *Approaches to Teaching the Novels of Toni Morrison*, edited by Nellie Y. McKay and Kathryn Earle. MLA, 1997, pp. 77–85.

Taylor, Nikki M., *Driven toward Madness: The Fugitive Slave Margaret Garner and Tragedy on the Ohio*. Ohio UP, 2016.

Walters, Delores M. "Introduction: Re(dis)covering and Recreating the Cultural Milieu of Margaret Garner." *Gendered Resistance: Woman, Slavery, and the Legacy of Margaret Garner*, edited by Mary E. Frederickson and Delores M. Walters, U of Illinois P, 2013, pp. 1–22.

Weisenburger, Steven. *Modern Medea: A Family Story of Slavery and Child-Murder from the Old South*. Hill and Wang, 1998.

Yanuck, Julius. "The Garner Fugitive Slave Case." *Mississippi Valley Historical Review* (now *Journal of American History*), vol. 40, no. 1, June 1953, pp. 47–66.

Yohe, Kristine. "Confronting *Margaret Garner* in Cincinnati." Margaret Garner: *The Premiere Performances of Toni Morrison's Libretto*, edited by La Vinia Delois Jennings, U of Virginia P, 2016, pp. 93–115.

Yohe, Kristine. "Enslaved Women's Resistance and Survival Strategies in Frances Ellen Watkins Harper's 'The Slave Mother: A Tale of the Ohio' and Toni Morrison's *Beloved* and *Margaret Garner*." *Gendered Resistance: Woman, Slavery, and the Legacy of Margaret Garner*, edited by Mary E. Frederickson and Delores M. Walters, U of Illinois P, 2013, pp. 99–114.

CHAPTER FIFTEEN

Faulkner after Morrison

DAVID H. KRAUSE

"CRAZY TO LEARN TO READ"

William Faulkner began his career writing fiction with a tall tale about a young man whose overwhelming passion for education and literacy turns deadly, a young man who dies learning to read. While living in the French Quarter of New Orleans in the spring of 1925, a few steps from both Sherwood Anderson's flat and the city's iconic bronze equestrian statue of Andrew Jackson, Faulkner competed with Anderson to invent—both orally and in writing—outrageous stories about less heroic members of the Jackson family. Two of Faulkner's letters to Anderson about imaginary Jackson descendants have long been accessible under the title "Al Jackson." Few readers of Faulkner pay much attention to these Jackson family letters, missing their absurdist humor, flickers of serious social commentary, and, most importantly, their pointed warnings about the problematics and risks of learning to read. In his second Jackson letter to Anderson, Faulkner claims authority for a new wild, intimate, and sad family story:

> I received most of this information from people at Herman Jackson's funeral the other day. Herman, you know, was a queer boy, with a passion for education. Old man Jackson didn't believe in education. But the boy Herman was *crazy to learn to read* * * * At last, at the age of eighteen he learned to read and he established a record. He read Sir Walter Scott's complete works in twelve and one half days. For two days afterward he seemed to be dazed—could not remember who he was. So a schoolmate wrote his name on a card which Herman carried in his hand, showing it to anyone who asked his name. Then on the third day he went into convulsions, passing from convulsion to convulsion and dying after days of terrible agony. ("Al Jackson" 478; emphases added)

Faulkner's casual, playful, satirical obituary for Herman Jackson represents a compelling allegory of reading, a disquieting parable of some dangers readers might encounter. Faulkner initially characterizes Herman as *"crazy to learn to read"* to convey the boy's urgent desire for his education, but along the way he provokes unsettling questions about literacy that animate his own reading and writing in complicated ways throughout his career: Why is it so important to learn how to read? How do we learn to read? How can we be taught to read—and by whom? How do we know what or whom to read? How might reading help us better know ourselves and others, rather than cause us to forget who we are or aspire to become? Is reading an individual or communal activity? Who defines what it means to be literate? Is reading inherently dangerous—a threat to our thinking, imagination, even our sanity, identity, and place in the world—or only if we read the wrong books in the wrong way at the wrong time? Maybe young Herman inherited cognitive deficiencies and vulnerabilities from Old Man Jackson, who, when he was eight, "had learned by heart one thousand verses from the new testament, bringing on an attack resembling brain fever"—a diagnosis ruled out by a veterinary who "said it couldn't be brain fever," suggesting he couldn't detect enough of a brain to catch fever ("Al Jackson" 475). Or maybe Herman, desperate to educate himself in the cultural norms of his community, becomes dazed and confused, convulsed, mad, lost to himself—and ultimately lost to the world—because he reads too many books by Sir Walter Scott too fast to comprehend or question anything in the books. Faulkner's cryptic parable raises more questions than it answers about how a particular human mind in a particular time and place engages (or fails to engage) the language of a particular written text.

Toni Morrison's first novel, *The Bluest Eye* (1970), begins by requiring readers to remember and forget how we originally learned to read Dick and Jane primers in school, defamiliarizing words and typography in ways that destabilize comfortable assumptions about cultural literacies, about who is included and who is excluded within the language and subject of the narrative: "Hereisthehouseitisgreenandwhiteithasareddooritisveryprettyhereisthefamily" (2).[1] The novel's strange, sad story of Elihue Michah Whitcomb (aka Soaphead Church) problematizes and contextualizes learning to read even more radically than Faulkner's tale of Herman Jackson. Elihue "had been reared in a family proud of its academic accomplishments and its mixed blood—in fact they believed the former was based on the latter," convinced by racist bogus science that "all civilizations derive from the white race, that none can exist without its help, and that a society is great and brilliant only as far as it preserves the blood of the noble group that created it" (*Bluest Eye*, 167–8). Like others in the troubled multiracial Whitcomb family who found it "difficult to maintain their whiteness," Elihue's father married "a sweet, indolent half-Chinese girl":

> Her son, named Elihue Micah Whitcomb, provided the schoolmaster with ample opportunity to work out his theories of education, discipline, and the good life. Little Elihue learned everything he needed to know well, particularly the fine art of self-deception. *He read greedily but understood selectively*, choosing the bits and pieces … of other men's ideas that supported whatever predilection he had at the moment.
>
> Thus he chose to remember Hamlet's abuse of Ophelia, but not Christ's love of Mary Magdalene; Hamlet's frivolous politics, but not Christ's serious anarchy. He noticed Gibbons' acidity, but not his tolerance, Othello's love for the fair Desdemona, but not Iago's perverted love of Othello. The works he admired most were Dante's; those he despised most were Dostoyevsky's. For all his exposure to the best minds of the Western world, *he allowed only the narrowest interpretation to touch him.* (169; emphases added)

Morrison delineates Elihue Whitcomb's fragile racialized and sexualized identity and his resulting failures reading with greater expansiveness and specificity than Faulkner explains Herman Jackson's problems, alerting her readers about how to engage literature authentically in order to avoid deceiving ourselves, losing ourselves and our place in the world in a kind of blindness or madness. Through Elihue, Morrison instructs us to learn to read differently: to participate in texts with an open mind and heart, even if they challenge our assumptions and convictions; to allow

---

[1] See Christian, "Contemporary Fables," 59–74 for an especially elegant and insightful discussion of reading *The Bluest Eye*.

ourselves to be affected intellectually *and* emotionally—to be touched—by what we read; to avoid interpreting literature narrowly; to explore worlds and minds beyond our own, and beyond the West; to transgress Eurocentrism; and, above all, *not* to privilege whiteness.

Faulkner's Herman Jackson, "*crazy to learn to read*," privileged whiteness, as represented within his community by the complete works of Sir Walter Scott. "Every Southern household when they bought books they bought Scott," Faulkner told students at the University of Virginia years after his adventures with Anderson and Herman Jackson in New Orleans. "That was because you got more words for your money," he continued flippantly, before adding more seriously, "But every household that [at] all pretended to be literate had Scott."[2] Learning to read books, then, and especially merely owning books, sometimes generates only an illusion of literacy. Only a few years before Faulkner wrote to Anderson about Herman, Mark Twain had lambasted the pretensions and delusions of Scott's "pernicious" books and their entitled white readers. Twain diagnosed "the Sir Walter disease" infecting Southern character and culture, claiming with characteristic hyperbole that Scott "did measureless harm; more real and lasting harm, perhaps, than any other individual that ever wrote." Twain charged that "Sir Walter had so large a hand in making Southern character, as it existed before the war ... that he is in great measure responsible for the war." The language of Scott's romances, according to Twain, "created rank and caste [in the South] and also reverence for rank and caste" and helped to sustain slavery through "jejune romanticism of an absurd past that is dead, and out of charity ought to be buried."[3] Although Faulkner would famously write that "the past is never dead. It's not even past" (*Requiem*, 73)—and would justifiably be criticized for his own lapses into jejune romanticism and, worse, for privileging whiteness and maleness, especially in his public life—as early as his 1925 letters to Anderson, he deliberately begins to leave Scott behind, tries to bury Scott when he buries Herman Jackson.

I begin this essay with two of the many scenes of reading embedded within the fictions of William Faulkner and Toni Morrison because these passages alert us to the authors' self-consciousness about their own practices of reading. These scenes represent some epistemological, ontological, and ethical uncertainties and risks inherent in our efforts to make sense, not only of language and literature, but also of ourselves, each other, and our world. Often, though not always, at least since the publication of *Song of Solomon* (1977), learning to read Faulkner after Morrison has meant pairing their novels, comparing and contrasting texts, and staging encounters and conversations between the architectures and languages of their narratives to make more visible their differing yet resonant strategies for investigating American identities, especially as inflected by race, class, and gender. Swerving away from that approach, while respecting its continuing value to me and others, this essay reimagines and rethinks how we might best respond *now* to a question succinctly posed by Patrick O'Donnell decades ago: "What does it mean, then, to read Faulkner in light of Morrison?" (225). *Why* should we read Faulkner after Morrison? *How* should we read Faulkner after Morrison? What are some of the possible consequences of reading—or not reading—Faulkner and Morrison *now*? My purpose here remains to stimulate further, deeper questions, rather than to determine or prescribe meanings—that is, to invite your (re)reading, not to privilege my own (re)reading.[4]

---

[2] See Gwynn and Blotner, *Faulkner in the University*, 135.
[3] *Life on the Mississippi*, chapter 46, "Enchanters and Enchanted," 400–502.
[4] Philip M. Weinstein's 1996 book-length study, *What Else But Love?*, establishes the pattern of intertextual encounters that illuminate the fictions of both Faulkner and Morrison, a proliferating and continuing approach further represented

"IF WE AMERICANS ARE TO SURVIVE"

Morrison's soaring and searing commentary in the *New Yorker* a few days after the 2016 presidential election pivots on two unblinking sentences: "So scary are the consequences of a collapse of white privilege that many Americans have flocked to a political platform that supports and translates violence against the defenseless as strength. These people are not so much angry as terrified, with the kind of terror that makes knees tremble." Morrison concludes her brief postelection commentary with three sentences, often overlooked: "William Faulkner understood this better than almost any other American writer. In *Absalom, Absalom!*, incest is less a taboo for an upper-class Southern family than acknowledging the one drop of black blood that would clearly soil the family line. Rather than lose its 'whiteness' (once again), the family chooses murder." Faulkner, as Morrison had been reading him since the 1950s, understood the terror and trembling caused by a collapse of white privilege ("the family chooses murder"), understood and represented the "Mourning for Whiteness" Morrison exposes in her title and throughout her essay: "If it weren't so ignorant and pitiful, one could mourn this collapse of dignity in service to an evil cause" (54). Morrison reads Faulkner, but does not mourn for whiteness.

Morrison also reads James Baldwin. She points us to Faulkner in "Mourning for Whiteness" at least partly because Baldwin inspires her message and inhabits her language. Most specifically, sixty years after Baldwin, she revoices Baldwin's fiery 1956 *Partisan Review* essay, "Faulkner and Desegregation." Morrison summons Baldwin, manifesting her gratitude for three gifts she had graciously accepted from him in her 1987 eulogy for him: a "decolonized" *language* to dwell in;" "the *courage* of one who could go as a stranger in the village and transform the distances between people into intimacy with the whole world;" and "a tenderness, a *vulnerability*, that asked everything, expected everything ... and provided us with the ways and means to deliver" ("Eulogy," 229–32, emphases in original). Reading Faulkner's fiction in 1952, Baldwin had discovered there, as Morrison knew, "the beginnings—at least—of a more genuinely penetrating search" to understand American racial politics within "its context; its context being the history, traditions, customs, and moral assumptions and preoccupations of the country; in short, the general social fabric" ("Autobiographical Notes," 8–9). By 1956, however, Baldwin had lost patience with Faulkner's increasingly clumsy, condescending, and inflammatory extra-fictional pronouncements about civil rights and desegregation, finding him, as Morrison also knew, "guilty of great emotional and intellectual dishonesty," yet insisting that "his statements demand our attention" ("Desegregation," 211).

In "Faulkner and Desegregation," Baldwin does more than simply refute Faulkner's incoherent politics and nearly incomprehensible moral equivocations. The first paragraph of Baldwin's essay maps his project, which, in turn, becomes what Morrison calls her own "serious project" in "Mourning for Whiteness," and which remains our project and responsibility after Morrison. "Any real change," Baldwin begins, "implies the breakup of the world as one has always known it, the loss of all that gave one an identity, the end of safety"; continuing, "And at such a moment, unable

---

by the collections *Unflinching Gaze* (1997) and *Faulkner and Morrison* (2013). John Duvall contributes influential essays introducing both volumes, establishing convincingly within an inevitably fraught literary culture "that one can validly read not only Faulkner's influence on Morrison, but also Morrison's influence on Faulkner—how her fiction and literary criticism may cause one to rethink Faulkner in a fundamental way" ("Anxiety" 4).

to see and not daring to imagine what the future will now bring forth, one clings to what one knew, or thought one knew; to what one possessed or dreamed that one possessed" (209). Baldwin says that he continues reading Faulkner as one "means of understanding what is happening in the minds and hearts of white Southerners today" (209). In his penultimate paragraph, Baldwin anticipates Morrison, sixty years later, giving her not just her thesis, but her language: "Faulkner is not trying to save Negroes, who are, in his view, already saved; who, having refused to be destroyed by terror, are far stronger than the *terrified white populace*; and who have, moreover, fatally, from his point of view, the weight of the federal government behind them. He is trying to save 'whatever good remains in those white people'" (214; emphases added). Baldwin reads Faulkner mourning for whiteness. He tries to understand; but he cannot mourn: "There is never time in the future in which we will work out our salvation. The challenge is in the moment, the time is always now" (214). Morrison reminds us, bluntly, that we have not yet met the moment or the urgency of now, recognizing, as had Baldwin, that "in order to limit the possibility of this untenable change, and restore whiteness to its former status as marker of national identity, a number of white Americans are sacrificing themselves" ("Mourning" 54). She sends us to Faulkner, who, as she reads him, understands these losses and sacrifices.

Specifically, Morrison sends us to *Absalom, Absalom!* (1936), demanding from us what she elsewhere said she admired in Faulkner's writing: "a sort of staring, a refusal-to-look-away approach". Faulkner, Morrison explained, "could infuriate you in such wonderful ways. It wasn't just complete delight—there was also this other quality that is just as important as devotion: outrage. The point is that with Faulkner one was never indifferent" ("Faulkner and Women" 298). In 1956, Faulkner infuriated and outraged almost everyone, not just liberals and progressives, and not just readers of the 1949 Nobel laureate's novels—including *The Sound and the Fury* (1929), *Light in August* (1932), and *Go Down, Moses* (1942), as well as *Absalom, Absalom!*—but any American or global citizen mindful of escalating conflicts over civil rights and desegregation. Reading Faulkner after Baldwin disrupts and distresses any easy assumptions about where and how and who we are in the world, at least as much now as in 1956. Faulkner published three famously disruptive and distressing commentaries in high-profile magazines in 1956, all embarrassing attempts to explain away a disastrous interview from February of that year in which he promised to shoot Negroes in the street if necessary to protect white privilege in Mississippi: "Letter to a Northern Editor" (*Life*, March); "On Fear" (*Harper's*, June); and "A Letter to the Leaders of the Negro Race" (*Ebony*, September). Baldwin—and Morrison—read *this* Faulkner in 1956. Baldwin responded quickly, angrily, eloquently, and persuasively, at the invitation of the *Partisan Review*, with "Faulkner and Desegregation," which circulated at the same time as Faulkner's letter in *Ebony*. Morrison, who had just finished writing about Faulkner at Cornell, responded differently and over time.

Ebony's editors published Faulkner's open letter under the title "If I Were a Negro," provocatively but fairly highlighting a phrase the author deploys frequently in his paternalistic lecture to Black leaders. Faulkner desperately tries to translate, justify, and even retract his March letter in *Life*. Unconvincingly claiming that his earlier letter had been motivated by concern for the safety of Autherine Lucy, the first African American student ever admitted to the University of Alabama, who "had just been compelled to withdraw temporarily ... by a local violence already of dangerous proportions," and that inevitable attempts to re-enroll Lucy would lead to increasing violence, Faulkner doubles down on his original advice to "go slow," insisting he really means "be flexible." "If I were a Negro," Faulkner writes, "I would advise our elders and leaders to make this our undeviating and inflexible course—a course of inflexible and unviolent flexibility" ("Letter to the Leaders" 109). After a weak flicker of self-awareness—"It is easy enough to say glibly. 'If I were a Negro, I would this or that.' But a white man can only imagine himself for the moment a Negro; he cannot be that man of another race and griefs and problems" (this from the man who wrote *Light in August*)—Faulkner returns to his message: "So if I were a Negro, I would say to my people: let us be always unflaggingly and inflexibly flexible. But always decently, quietly, courteously, with dignity, and without violence. And above all, with patience" (111). Still more offensively, Faulkner instructs his *Ebony* readers (as if he were one of them): "We must learn to deserve equality so that we can hold and keep it after we get it. We must learn responsibility, the responsibility of equality" (111). Faulkner's letter, rather than advocating for equality or responsibility, mourns whiteness: "You have shown the Southerner what you can do and what you will do if necessary; *give him space in which to get his breath* and assimilate that knowledge; to look about and see that … he himself *faces an obsolescence in his own land* which only he can cure" (108; emphases added). Faulkner's lesser-known essay "On Fear" also deserves to be read after Morrison's "Mourning Whiteness." He asks, without irony or self-consciousness, "What are we Mississippians afraid of? Why do we have so low an opinion of ourselves that we are afraid of people who by all our standards are our inferiors?" (100). Having read Baldwin reading Faulkner, Morrison sends us to Faulkner at the end of her 2016 *New Yorker* piece because he "understood this [mourning for whiteness] better than *almost* any other American writer" ("Mourning for Whiteness" 54, emphasis added). Morrison's precise "*almost*" opens a space for others, including Baldwin—and herself.

Morrison claimed a space for herself within Faulkner's world decisively in 1985 by reading from her then unpublished manuscript of *Beloved* (1987) at the fifteenth annual Faulkner and Yoknapatawpha conference.[5] Before reading, Morrison graciously, but not casually, stresses her desire to "associate myself in some real way with the Center for the Study of Southern Culture" and "to visit the campus of the University of Mississippi" (which, violently and under extreme pressure, had admitted its first Black student, James Meredith less than 25 years earlier). She explains that she had declined an invitation to interrupt work on her own new book to write a paper about the conference theme—"Faulkner and Women"—and that she hopes to learn about her own writing by reading it aloud. Morrison declines to contextualize in any way the narrative she will share. She does not say, *Here's a story about a woman that Faulkner did not have the authority, the courage, the tenderness, or the language to write; here's a story only I can write. Here's a story about a woman who refused to go slow, refused to be flexible*. The published conference proceedings (1986) can only bracket the main event, Morrison's boundary-shattering reading—"[The author read from her work-in-progress and then answered questions from the audience]" ("Faulkner and Women" 297)—recording only Morrison's moves around the margins. Her move immediately before reading from *Beloved* asserts her authority:

---

[5]Morrison's contribution to this conference, somewhat confusingly, has been titled "Faulkner and Women" both within the published proceedings and in *The Source of Self-Regard*. The most frequently cited excerpts from this publication of her self-introduction and comments during a question-and-answer period have focused on Faulkner and Morrison or on Morrison's thoughts about reading and writing, rather than on Faulkner and women or Morrison and women. By reading from her unpublished manuscript of *Beloved*, Morrison simultaneously subverted and transcended the conference theme in ways not usually acknowledged.

In 1956 I spent a great deal of time thinking about Mr. Faulkner because he was the subject of a thesis that I wrote at Cornell ... there was for me not only an academic interest in Faulkner, but in a very, very personal way, in a very personal way as a reader, William Faulkner had an enormous effect on me, an enormous effect.

Then, without any recorded pause, "The title of the book is *Beloved*, and this is the way it begins."

After Morrison's reading, the first questioner asks, "Ms. Morrison, you mentioned that you wrote a thesis on Faulkner. What effect did Faulkner have on your literary career?"—prompting a rich improvisational response from which a single sentence has often been cited out of context: "Well, I am not sure that he had any effect on my work" (297). Morrison deftly turns away from talking further about Faulkner's possible influence on her writing and returns to reflecting on how and why she read Faulkner at the time she wrote her thesis:

But as a reader in the fifties and later, of course (I said 1956 because that's when I was working on a thesis that had to do with him), I was concentrating on Faulkner. I don't think that my response was any different from any other student at that time, inasmuch as there was in Faulkner this power and courage—the courage of a writer, a special kind of courage. My reasons, I think for being interested and deeply moved by all his subjects had something to do with my desire to find out something about this country and that artistic articulation of its past that was not available in history, which is what art and fiction can do but sometimes history refuses to do. (297)

Morrison's "desire to find out something about this country" through literature, and specifically through Faulkner's fiction, reenacts Baldwin and charts the trajectory of her own career reading and writing. But how do we reconcile Morrison's "I don't think that my response [to Faulkner] was any different from any other student at that time" with her declaration before reading from *Beloved* that at Cornell she had more than an academic interest in Faulkner and that his influence on her reading was "enormous" and extremely personal? And why does Morrison twice locate her master's thesis in 1956, when all available evidence confirms that she received her degree in 1955?

As we have seen, in 1956, not just Toni Morrison, but much of the country, much of the world, was "thinking about," "concentrating on" Faulkner. This might at least partially account for Morrison's repetition of 1956 as the most important year of her early Faulkner reading. We need not speculate much about the politics of reading within Cornell's English Department between 1953 and 1955 to find it nearly impossible to imagine a brilliant, ambitious young Black woman fastidiously reading Faulkner, oblivious to the politics of race playing out loudly and violently across the country, with Baldwin and Faulkner near the center of public discourse. Representing a lingering consensus, Philip Weinstein writes that "Morrison's 1955 master's thesis, written at Cornell and titled 'Virginia Woolf's and William Faulkner's Treatment of the Alienated,' is a brief (thirty-nine pages) and strictly New Critical performance. Questions of race barely enter the discussion" (*What Else*, 218). Morrison was only twenty-four or twenty-five when writing her thesis, and we should proceed with caution when drawing inferences from what it does or does not say about Faulkner (or Woolf).[6] Nevertheless, as early as the 1950s, it now seems clear, Morrison was learning to write

---

[6] See Alessandra Vendrame for brief but helpful comments on Morrison's Cornell Master's thesis. See Barbara Christian's "Layered Rhythms" for extraordinary insights not only into Morrison and Woolf, but also into Morrison's experience at Cornell.

in what she would much later call "invisible ink." When Morrison began her undergraduate studies in English at Howard University in 1949 (coincidentally the same year William Faulkner received the Nobel Prize in Literature), she expected to find "a place where I could read." She found herself (happily, in general) at a historically Black institution where, to her great disappointment, "they wouldn't teach any black stuff in the English Department." At Howard, Morrison's Shakespeare teacher became "outraged" that she wanted to write about Black characters in Shakespeare's plays: "No, he wouldn't let me, so I wrote something else." Morrison soon became much more comfortable in Howard's drama department, where *they read things differently*—"you have to know the emotions, you have to know the conflicts, to know all these subtleties which are in the language, but you express them physically and so on. So I *always* preferred the drama department" (*Pieces*, emphases in original).[7]

Cornell may not have nurtured Morrison's desire to learn to read different "stuff" differently, but it did not deter her. The entire arc of her career traces her multiple strategies for learning and unlearning how to read—and how to *be read*—differently. Scolded even at Howard for wanting to write about an Africanist presence in Shakespeare, why would she risk writing explicitly about an Africanist presence in Faulkner at Cornell? Instead, Morrison again writes "something else." She writes about Quentin Compson and Thomas Sutpen, white men of different generations and temperaments, both terrified of losing their privilege, their identities, their whiteness—both isolated and alienated from any authentic community. Writing in invisible ink, Morrison accurately describes Quentin seeing others as "forms of behavior or reactions to various elements of the South" (12), without needing to explicate all the language of Quentin's self-conscious musings about race in *The Sound and the Fury*:

> I used to think that a Southerner had to be always conscious of niggers. I thought that Northerners would expect him to … When I first came East I kept thinking you've got to remember to think of them as colored people and not niggers … I learned that the best way to take all people, black or white, is to take them for what they think they are, then leave them alone. That is when I realized that a nigger is not a person so much as a form of behavior, a sort of obverse reflection of the white people he lives among. (57)

James Baldwin understood Quentin's radical fear of losing his identity if he could not define his whiteness against blackness: "In sum, the North, by freeing the slaves of their masters, robbed the masters of any possibility of freeing themselves of the slaves" ("Desegregation" 213). Morrison also understood.

Morrison did not tell her 1985 audience in Mississippi that, restless in the world and in her fiction, she had temporarily interrupted her work on *Beloved* to write a play, an extravagantly experimental and dream-like play through which Morrison poses the disturbing question: "What do you lose when a 14-year-old boy is killed?" Morrison's play interrogates the "ease with which black children are killed by other people" and, more specifically, the lynching of Emmett Till on August 28, 1955, a mere seventy-five miles south of Oxford, Mississippi, the site of the Faulkner conference. *Dreaming Emmett*, which premiered in Albany, New York, a few months after Morrison read from *Beloved* in Mississippi, resists any conventions of historical documentary. Morrison

---

[7]The well-conceived and well-edited documentary, *Toni Morrison: The Pieces I Am*, offers an exceptional opportunity to engage and pay attention to Morrison as a formidable voice and presence off the page and within cultural contexts.

described it at the time as "a play about a boy's imagination. If you unleash the imagination and intelligence of a young black kid, what would he do? What is it like if his dreams are fulfilled?" *A New York Times* review of the production describes how

> In a dream state [Emmett] suffers the pain of remembering his death 30 years before. Seeking revenge and a place in history, he summons up the perpetrators of his murder, as well as his family and friends, all to be characters in his dream. But his ghosts refuse to be controlled by his imagination; all see the past in their own way, as the boy doggedly searches for a meaning to his death—and thereby his life. (Croyden 221)

Another reviewer notes that "if there is a center to the play, it is the role of the mother ... She simply loved her son." This astute review ends with an uncanny insight into Morrison's moral and imaginative vision and the creative impulses shaping, in different but complementary ways, both *Dreaming Emmett* and *Beloved* (without the critic knowing what we know, or think we know, about the novel then in progress): "Toni Morrison's exquisite and yet biting drama reminds us that only if we allow the unspoken words of all the forgotten, living or dead, to be assimilated into our memories along with the words of those who are vocally present, can we really hear the sound of the world."[8]

James Baldwin, like Toni Morrison, heard the sound of the world; and like Morrison, he could not stop thinking about, dreaming about Emmett Till *and* the white men who lynched him. Twenty years before *Dreaming Emmett*, Baldwin wrote his own experimental play about a Mississippi lynching, *Blues for Mister Charlie* (1964). In his introductory "Notes for *Blues*," Baldwin claims that, "I do not know why this case pressed my mind so hard—but it would not let me go" (xiv), only to offer a sobering, and yet surprisingly hopeful, explanation: "What is ghastly and really almost hopeless in our racial situation now is that the crimes we have committed are so great and so unspeakable that the acceptance of this knowledge would lead literally to madness ... We are walking in terrible darkness here, and this is one man's attempt to bear witness to the reality and the power of light" (xiv–xv). Here Baldwin deliberately and repeatedly uses the inclusive pronoun "we," rather than "they," showing his own desire to understand why whiteness has become so terrified of blackness, to transcend or subvert differences, without ignoring them. He plays blues for Mr. Charlie (white men) as well as for the lynched Black youth. Both Baldwin's language and his subject were anticipated a decade earlier when he was reading and thinking and writing about Faulkner:

---

[8]Morrison posed the question about losing a teenage boy to Andrew J. Sherry at the time of the first (and only) production of *Dreaming Emmett*. Elizabeth Adams recognized the importance of Emmett's mother to the play as well as the profound value of listening to the sounds of the world (94). The University of Pennsylvania's Annenberg Center has posted this concerning its 2021–2 season:

> *Dreaming Emmett* is an abstract interpretation of the murder of a young black man named Emmett Till in 1955, and the subsequent trial and acquittal of the accused. After the initial performance, nearly all copies of the script were destroyed, the play was never again performed, and the only remaining artifacts of *Dreaming Emmett* were critical reviews. Now, 35 years after the original production, Morrison's estate has approved DNAWORKS to stage Morrison's original script of the historical retelling of the case that became a global paragon of Southern American racism at the start of the civil rights movement. This performance will be a world premiere of the original script by Toni Morrison, never seen by a public audience.

For the arguments with which the bulk of relatively articulate white Southerners of good will have met the necessity of desegregation have no value whatever as arguments, being almost entirely and helplessly dishonest, when not, indeed, insane … They have never seriously conceded that their social structure was mad. They have insisted, on the contrary, that everyone who criticized it was mad … [Faulkner] concedes the madness and moral wrongness of the South, but at the same time he raises it to the level of a mystique which makes it somehow unjust to discuss Southern society in the same terms in which one would discuss any other society. "Our position is wrong and untenable," says Faulkner, "but it is not wise to keep an emotional people off balance." ("Desegregation" 209–10)

Exhibiting this kind of racial blindness and madness, Faulkner's initial statement to the press about this sensational 1955 lynching not far from his own home refuses even to name Emmett Till. Faulkner does not really see Emmett Till. He looks away as he does not in his best fiction. Faulkner may mean what he says in his most quoted sentence about Till's lynching: "Because if we in America have reached the point in our desperate culture when we must murder children, no matter for what reason or color, we don't deserve to survive, and probably won't" ("Press Dispatch on the Emmett Till Case" 223). He may also mean what he tries to say in an earlier sentence: "Because if we Americans are to survive, it will have to be because we choose and elect and defend to be first of all Americans to present to the world one homogeneous and unbroken front, whether of white Americans of black ones or purple or green" (223). But this troubles us because America—as Faulkner's own fiction makes us confront—has never been homogeneous or unbroken—or indifferent to color. Faulkner, as the very first sentences of his solicited and, presumably, well-intentioned press release make excruciatingly clear, mourns whiteness, not Emmett Till: "When will we learn that … if America is to survive, the whole white race must survive first?" (222).[9]

"HOW DO I KNOW THAT WHAT YOU READ WAS IN THE BOOK?"

In one of her most direct and subversive comments on the kind of reading she aspired to write, Morrison acknowledged her efforts "to try to put the reader into the position of being *naked and quite vulnerable*, nevertheless trusting, *to rid him of all his literary experience and all of his social experiences* in order to engage him in the novel" (Ruas 109, emphases in original). But *how* can we learn to read books by Morrison or Faulkner—or anyone else—stripped of *all* our literary and social experiences, as the naked and vulnerable readers Morrison desires? Most of the time, most of us cannot. But we *can* recognize whenever encountering a book—or each other—that each of us carries our own assumptions about literature and our place in the world. Morrison knows that no two of us can or should read in exactly the same way, knows that she may not be writing to or for or about me, though I am welcome to participate, and expects that the way we read today will not (should not) replicate the way we read five or ten or more years ago, and will not (should not) anticipate how we may read next year or five years from today. *Playing in the Dark*, Morrison's most overt and influential attempt to theorize and map an agenda for reading (American) literature,

---

[9]Faulkner's "Press Dispatch Written in Rome, Italy for the United Press on the Emmett Till Case" was originally published in the *New York Herald Tribune* on September 9, 1955, and has been reprinted in his *Essays, Speeches, and Public Letters* (222–3).

encourages me to read in light of her interest "in what prompts and makes possible the process of entering what one is estranged from—and in what disables the foray, for purposes of fiction, into corners of consciousness held off and away from the reach of the writer's imagination" (4). How do readers, as well as writers, enter otherness? I learn more about how and why I read by risking "the process of entering what one is estranged from" through scenes of reading and writing within Morrison's fiction than from her forays into theoretical discourse. I find myself most vulnerable and most engaged, most bereft of my own literary and social assumptions, when reading Morrison writing her characters reading.

Late in *Beloved*, Stamp Paid reads a newspaper clipping to Paul D. Through this extended scene of reading (and not reading), Morrison simultaneously pulls us deeper into her book—"the reader, as part of the population of the text, is implicated"—and keeps us at a distance, as she imagines "what would be the response of the people in the book if they read the book?"[10] Long before we enter this self-reflexive scene, *Beloved* has reminded us repeatedly of the sometimes contradictory cultural, political, legal, and personal consequences of (il)literacy during slavery. On the one hand, "Lady Jones did what whitepeople thought unnecessary if not illegal: crowded her little parlor with colored children who had time for and interest in book learning" (102). On the other hand, slaves at Sweet Home could "even learn reading if they wanted to—but they didn't want to since nothing important to them could be put down on paper" (125). Still, nothing prepares us for the radical ways Stamp Paid irrevocably explodes the intimacy between Paul D and Sethe—and between Morrison and us—by reading.

Learning to read Faulkner after Morrison, for me, began in earnest with *Beloved* and Stamp Paid's clipping. For several years before reading *Beloved* in 1987, I had been thinking and teaching and writing about how *Absalom, Absalom!* self-reflexively interrogates literacy in frequent destabilizing scenes of reading that help subvert and expose any assumptions we may have about race and gender and class in the popular narrative of American history. In chapter 7 of *Absalom*, Quentin Compson imagines Thomas Sutpen "sent to school for about three months one winter—an adolescent boy of thirteen or fourteen ... where he learned little save that most of the deeds, good and bad both, incurring opprobrium or plaudits or reward either, within the scope of man's abilities, had already been performed and were to be learned about only from books" (227). Within my own classrooms, we often discussed these extreme claims for the value of books and literacy, not only for Sutpen and other characters in Faulkner's novels, but also, more self-consciously, for ourselves. We agreed that we learn in so many ways beyond reading books and yet value what can be learned through reading books. Students enjoyed challenging my authority and, implicitly, my veracity, when talking about *Absalom* together, borrowing and adapting young Sutpen's skepticism when questioning his teacher: "How do I know that what you read was in the book?" (196). How indeed? Through young Thomas Sutpen, more seriously and consequentially than he had through young Herman Jackson, Faulkner offers us a paradigm, parable, or allegory that problematizes the risks of reading, including reading *Absalom*. Whatever Sutpen's teacher read to him from the book sends him to the

---

[10] "Unspeakable" 185 and LeClair 121, respectively. Compare this meditation by Harry Wilbourne in Faulkner's *If I Forget Thee, Jerusalem*: "*Maybe I can read*, he thought. Then he cursed, thinking, *That's it. It's all exactly backward. It should be the books, the people in the books inventing and reading about us—the Does and Roes and Wilbournes and Smiths—males and females but without the pricks or cunts*" (44–5, emphasis in original).

West Indies, changing his life and damaging the lives of many others through a legacy of racism, sexism, and classism. We do not know what was in that book.[11]

Morrison does not tell us what is and is not in the clipping that Stamp Paid reads to Paul D. Meaning, nonetheless, emerges from the specificity of her language, from what words do and do not say. The specificity begins and ends with "that ain't her mouth."

> "I know Sethe's mouth and this ain't it." He smoothed the clipping with his fingers and peered at it, not at all disturbed. From the solemn air with which Stamp had unfolded the paper, the tenderness in the old man' fingers as he stroked the creases and flattened it out, first on his knees, then on the split top of the piling, Paul D knew that it ought to mess him up. That whatever was written on it should shake him. (*Beloved* 154)

Morrison economically generates multiple tensions even before Stamp Paid reads a word: she makes us see and feel the materiality of the clipping and its handling (smoothing, unfolding, stroking, flattening); she makes us see and feel Paul D peering at a sketch of a mouth, rather than at "whatever was written." In this moment, although Paul D "knew that it ought to mess him up," that the clipping should "shake" him, he remains "not at all disturbed"; he clings to an innocence enabled by his illiteracy. As this heart-stopping scene slowly unfolds, Morrison repeats and elaborates details, with subtle differences, specifying the "picture drawing" accompanying "black scratches" in the clipping, and deepening Paul D's resistance to what he does not want to know.

> He [Stamp] had made up his mind to show him this piece of paper—newspaper—with a picture drawing of a woman who favored Sethe except that was not her mouth. Nothing like it. Paul D slid the clipping out from under Stamp's palm. The print meant nothing to him so he didn't even glance at it. He simply looked at the face, shaking his head no. No. At the mouth, you see. And no at whatever it was those black scratches said, and no to whatever it was Stamp Paid wanted him to know. (156–7)

Encountering this scene within the contexts of our reading of *Beloved*, we understand why "Stamp Paid didn't say it all. Instead he took a breath and leaned toward the mouth that was not hers and slowly read out the words Paul D couldn't" (158)—and we understand that, for us, this scene of reading will remain a scene of not reading. Morrison has no intention of letting us read the clipping with Stamp Paid and Paul D, but rather depends on us to (not) read it in light of what we have already learned, or not learned, from our reading of *Beloved*, particularly from the violent scene immediately preceding Stamp Paid reading to Paul D: "And when he finished, Paul D said with a vigor fresher than the first time, 'I'm sorry, Stamp. It's a mistake somewhere 'cause that ain't her mouth'" (158). Despite his vehement denials, Paul D. confronts Sethe in an even

---

[11]When Sutpen interrogates what is and is not in the book, Faulkner may be remembering and flipping the script on Tom Sawyer, whose exchange with Ben Rogers in chapter 2 of *Adventures of Huckleberry Finn* anticipates the excruciating dynamics of emancipating Jim in the final chapters:

BEN: "Ransomed? What's that?"
TOM: "I don't know. But that's what they do. I've seen it in books; and so of course that's what we got to do."
BEN: "But how can we do it if we don't know what it is?"
TOM: "Didn't I tell you it's in the books? Do you want to go to doing different from what's in the books, and get things all muddled up?" (633)

See also chapter 35, especially 859 and 863.

more painful and elliptical scene of reading: "He only caught pieces of what she said—which was fine, because she hadn't gotten to the main part—the answer to the question he had not asked her outright, but which lay in the clipping he showed her" (161). Despite not wanting to hear the story again, and not wanting to know the answer, Paul D wants to ask Sethe—*does* ask her, without words—*Why*? Sethe, feels no obligation to explain her actions to Paul D, or "she would have said what the newspaper said she said and no more." Morrison writes *Beloved* to pull us as deeply as possible through language into intimate, communal, intellectual, and visceral participatory reading, "circling the subject." When reading *Beloved*, we do not need to know that, while compiling *The Black Book*, Morrison became haunted by the 1856 newspaper clipping about "A Visit to the Slave Mother Who Killed Her Child." Morrison writes Sethe's story, not Margaret Garner's. Sethe, we're told, "could recognize only seventy-five printed words (half of which appeared in the newspaper clipping), but she knew that the words she did not understand hadn't any more power than she had to explain" (161). We never see the contents of the clipping Stamp Paid passes on ("This was not a story to pass on."). We never see the words or the picture drawing. We never know which words Sethe can and cannot read. Morrison's scene of reading—full of holes and spaces, absences and silences, questions without answers, unspeakable things unspoken—helps us see ourselves reading *Beloved* more clearly than we see her characters reading and not reading a newspaper article. Morrison takes us beyond the limits of literacy yet trusts us to learn to read.[12]

Throughout chapter 4 of *Absalom*, Faulkner focuses our attention on a letter that Mr. Compson self-consciously holds before finally and almost ritualistically handing it to his Harvard-bound son, Quentin, to read. Compson cannot make sense of this letter—presumably written by Charles Bon to Judith Sutpen—partly because, like first-time readers of the novel, he does not see or imagine Bon as the mixed-race son of Judith's father, but mostly because he clings to his privileged, early twentieth-century white male assumptions about race, gender, and class: "It's just inexplicable. It does not explain … you re-read, tedious and intent, poring, making sure you have forgotten nothing, made no miscalculation, you bring them together again and again nothing happens: just the words, the symbols, the shapes themselves, shadowy inscrutable and serene, against the turgid background of a horrible and bloody mischancing of human affairs" (80). Decades ago, I argued in print that "all responsible readers of *Absalom* must sooner or later confront methodological, ontological, and epistemological uncertainties about reading, about what is and is not in the book, and thus, more radically—uncertainties about how we are and are not in the world" ("Reading Bon's Letter" 226).

My premise still seems reasonable to me, although today it offers a much less adequate, more limited intellectual, imaginative, and emotional account of my own readings of *Absalom* than it did at the time of writing. I do not repudiate my process of learning to read Faulkner through borrowed theoretical lenses; nor do I claim that I now read Faulkner differently *only* in light of Morrison. Rather, having read and lived a lot more within the volatile dynamics of American (and global) history, culture, and politics, I keep returning to Faulkner, with less theoretical baggage, confident that "attentiveness will always yield wonder," amplifying, rather than eliminating my "uncertainties about how we are and are not in the world." Faulkner's words haven't changed, but the world has changed. Every time I read *Absalom, Absalom!* I see differently: "like when you pass through

---

[12]Demme's film of *Beloved* reads this scene between Paul D and Stamp Paid with elegance and restraint, keeping the camera focused tightly on their handling of the clipping, as well as their faces.

a room fast and look at all the objects in it and you turn and go back through the room again and look at all the objects from the other side and you find out you had never seen them before" (186). Every time I read *Absalom, Absalom!* I change. So do most readers. Faulkner always frustrates our compulsive desire for even the illusion of narrative or historical closure in *Absalom, Absalom!*, insisting that we remain endlessly open to seeing differently—to changing our readings, our minds, our selves, and our world.

Compson cannot change. Although (or because) his own family has lost most of the material legacy of their antebellum white privilege, Compson clings to his fatalistic amoral illusions about the Civil War as "a horrible and bloody mischancing of human affairs" and "the shadowy paragons which are our ancestors born in the South and come to manhood and womanhood about eighteen sixty or sixty one" (80). Compson's precarious sense of his own identity in 1909 allows him to imagine himself only in a lost past, among "the people in whose living blood and seed we ourselves lay dormant and waiting, in this shadowy attenuation of time possessing now heroic proportions, performing their acts of simple passion and simple violence, impervious to time and inexplicable" (80). In chapter 4 of *Absalom*, Compson imagines his doomed hero, Charles Bon ("He is the curious one to me" [74]) in New Orleans, educating Henry Sutpen about the realities of slavery and white male privilege, realities that Henry willfully seems not to have seen or confronted at home with this father: "since Henry and Judith had grown up with a negro half sister of their own" (87). Through Compson's lurid and fatalistic imagination, Faulkner represents slavery more intimately and violently than he does anywhere else in his fiction, while simultaneously exposing the stunning failures of men like Compson to see the past—and its consequences in the present—with any understanding or empathy or guilt or responsibility. Compson does not look away, but he does not really see. He too easily imagines, "the slave girls, the housemaids neated and cleaned by white mistresses or perhaps sweating bodies out of the fields themselves and the young man rides up and beckons the watching overseer and says Send me Juno or Missylena or Chlory and then rides into the trees and dismounts and waits" (87). He imagines Bon justifying himself to Henry in New Orleans:

> But we do save that one, who but for us would have been sold to any brute who had the price, not sold to him for the night like a white prostitute, but body and soul for life to him who could have used her with more impunity than he would dare to use an animal, heifer or mare, and then discarded or sold or murdered when worn out or when her keep and her price no longer balanced. (92)

And he even coldly imagines Bon's "child, the boy, sleeping in silk and lace to be sure yet complete chattel of him who, begetting him, owned him body and soul to sell (if he chose) like a calf or puppy or sheep" (91). Faulkner gives Compson language for the inhumanity of slavery that shocks us, but does not shock Compson or—as far as we can tell—even Quentin, because neither of them can yet imagine himself outside the destructive legacy of white male privilege, though Quentin, in his way, tries to free himself from that legacy throughout *Absalom, Absalom!* (and *The Sound and the Fury*).

In chapter 4, Compson imagines Bon confronting Henry: "Have you forgot that this woman, this child are niggers? You, Henry Sutpen of Sutpen's Hundred in Mississippi?" (94). At the end of chapter 8, Quentin and Shreve reimagine this confrontation, intensifying rather than changing its racialized and sexualized stakes: "*I'm the nigger that's going to sleep with your sister. Unless you stop me, Henry*" (286, emphasis in original). Henry stops Bon. According to Quentin and Shreve—as well as Morrison and most readers of the novel—Henry chooses murder to protect his family's whiteness. In this persuasive reading, Henry cannot change. He cannot protect whiteness. He cannot stop the legacy of slavery in his own family, let alone within his country, leading to Shreve's final disturbing racial calculus: "You've got one nigger left. One nigger Sutpen left" (302). Faulkner, however, does not unambiguously authorize this single motive for Henry's murder of Bon, emphasizing instead that it emerges from the feverish imaginings of two young men at Harvard trying to make sense of a violent past event that remained inexplicable to others before them. Compson, Rosa Coldfield, and others within Faulkner's narrative have failed to make the story their own: "like five or six people all trying to make a rug on the same loom only each one wants to weave his own pattern into the rug" (101). As readers of the novel, we find ourselves participating, even competing, in this search for a coherent and meaningful pattern. What Morrison and the rest of us read in *Absalom, Absalom!*, however, may or may not be in the book. Quentin and Shreve do not ultimately get the last word. We do. And yet we do not.[13] Reading Bon's letter and Faulkner's *Absalom, Absalom!* at this moment in the twenty-first century—and in light of Morrison and all that she represents and questions—renews our urgent responsibility to risk learning to read the unreadable, to imagine the unimaginable, to speak the unspeakable, and to change the unchangeable.

WORKS CITED

Adams, Elizabeth. "Morrison's *Dreaming Emmett*." *Theater*, vol. 17, no. 3, Nov. 1986, pp. 92–4.

"Annenberg Center Remounts Toni Morrison's *Dreaming Emmett* with Artist-in-Residence DNAWORKS." https://sachsarts.org/grant-awards/annenberg-center-remounts-toni-morrisons-dreaming-emmett-with-artist-in-residence-dnaworks/. Accessed Sept. 20, 2021.

Baldwin, James, "Autobiographical Notes." *James Baldwin: Collected Essays*, edited by Toni Morrison, Library of America, 1998, pp. 5–9.

Baldwin, James. *Blues for Mr. Charlie: A Play*. 1964. Vintage International, 1995.

Baldwin, James. "Faulkner and Desegregation." *James Baldwin: Collected Essays*, edited by Toni Morrison, Library of America, 1998, 209–14.

Demme, Jonathan, director. *Beloved*. Buena Vista, 1998.

Christian, Barbara. "The Contemporary Fables of Toni Morrison." *Toni Morrison: Critical Perspectives Past and Present*, edited by Henry Louis Gates, Jr. and K. A. Appiah, Amistad, 1993, pp. 59–99.

Christian, Barbara T. "Layered Rhythms: Virginia Woolf and Toni Morrison." *Modern Fiction Studies*, vol. 39, no. 3/4, Fall/Winter 1993, pp. 483–500.

Croyden, Margaret. "Toni Morrison Tries Her Hand at Playwriting." *Conversations with Toni Morrison*, edited by Danille Taylor-Guthrie, UP of Mississippi, 1994, pp. 218–22. Reprinted from *New York Times*, Dec. 29, 1985.

Duvall, John N. "Tony Morrison and the Anxiety of Faulknerian Influence." *Unflinching Gaze: Morrison and Faulkner Re-Envisioned*, edited by Carol A. Komerton, Stephen M. Ross, and Judith Bryant Wittenberg, UP of Mississippi, 1997, pp. 219–27.

---

[13] Michael Gorra acknowledges that, paradoxically, "We shouldn't believe any of it; we believe all of it" (247). In "Reading Shreve's Letters," I acknowledged my failures reading *Absalom, Absalom!*, concluding that these "failures of writing and reading [,] are necessary and liberating: they free writer and reader to re-write and re-read" (168). For many years I have embraced and learned from my freedom to fail.

Duvall, John N. "Morrison and the (Faulknerian Dark) House of Fiction." In *Faulkner and Morrison*, edited by Robert W. Hamblin and Christopher Rieger, Southeast Missouri State UP, 2013, pp. 19–35.

Faulkner, William. *Absalom, Absalom!*. 1936. Vintage International, 1990.

Faulkner, William. "Al Jackson." *Uncollected Stories of William Faulkner*, edited by Joseph Blotner, Random House, 1979, pp. 474–79.

Faulkner, Willian. *If I Forget Thee, Jerusalem*. 1939. Vintage International, 1995.

Faulkner, William. "A Letter to the Leaders in the Negro Race, 1956." *William Faulkner: Essays, Speeches, and Public Letters*, edited by James B. Meriwether, Random House, 1965, pp. 107–12. Reprinted from *Ebony*, Sept. 1956.

Faulkner, William. "Letter to a Northern Editor, 1956." *William Faulkner: Essays, Speeches, and Public Letters*, edited by James B. Meriwether, Random House, 1965, pp. 86–91. Reprinted from *Life*, Mar. 5, 1956.

Faulkner, William, "On Fear: Deep South in Labor: Mississippi, 1956." *William Faulkner: Essays, Speeches, and Public Letters*, edited by James B. Meriwether, Random House, 1965, pp. 92–106. Reprinted from *Harper's*, June 1956.

Faulkner, William. "Press Dispatch Written in Rome, Italy for the United Press on the Emmett Till Case, September 9, 1955." *William Faulkner: Essays, Speeches, and Public Letters*, edited by James B. Meriwether, Random House, 1965, pp. 222–3.

Faulkner, William. *Requiem for a Nun*. Vintage, 2011, p. 73.

Gwynn, Frederick L., and Joseph L. Blotner, editors. *Faulkner in the University*. Vintage, 1959.

Gorra, Michael. *The Saddest Words: William Faulkner's Civil War*. Liveright, 2020.

Krause, David. "Opening Pandora's Box: Re-Reading Compson's Letter and Faulkner's *Absalom, Absalom!*" *The Centennial Review*, vol. 33, no. 3, Summer 1986, pp. 358–82. Reprinted in *William Faulkner: Six Decades of Criticism*, edited by Linda Wagner-Martin, Michigan State UP, 2002, pp. 271–92.

Krause, David. "Reading Bon's Letter and Faulkner's *Absalom, Absalom!*" *PMLA*, vol. 99, Mar. 1984, pp. 225–41.

Krause, David. "Reading Shreve's Letters and Faulkner's *Absalom, Absalom!*" *Studies in American Fiction*, vol. 11, 1983, pp. 153–69.

LeClair, Thomas. "The Language Must Not Sweat: A Conversation with Toni Morrison (1981)." *Conversations with Toni Morrison*, edited by Danille Taylor-Guthrie. UP of Mississippi, 1994, pp. 119–28.

Morrison, Toni. *Beloved*. Alfred A. Knopf, 1987.

Morrison, Toni. *The Bluest Eye*. Holt, Rinehart and Winston, 1970.

Morrison, Toni. "Faulkner and Women." *The Source of Self-Regard: Selected Essays, Speeches, and Meditations*, Knopf, 2019, pp. 296–303.

Morrison, Toni. "Invisible Ink: Reading the Writing and Writing the Reading." *The Source of Self-Regard: Selected Essays, Speeches, and Meditations*, Knopf, 2019, pp. 346–50.

Morrison, Toni. "James Baldwin Eulogy." *The Source of Self-Regard: Selected Essays, Speeches, and Meditations*, Knopf, 2019, pp. 229–32.

Morrison, Toni. "Mourning for Whiteness," *The New Yorker*, November 21, 2016.

Morrison, Toni. *Playing in the Dark: Whiteness and the Literary Imagination*. Harvard UP, 1992.

Morrison, Toni. "Unspeakable Things Unspoken: The Afro-American Presence in American Literature." *The Source of Self-Regard: Selected Essays, Speeches, and Meditations*, Knopf, 2019, pp. 161–97.

O'Donnell, Patrick. "Faulkner in Light of Morrison." *Unflinching Gaze: Morrison and Faulkner Re-Envisioned*, edited by Carol A. Komerton, Stephen M. Ross, and Judith Bryant Wittenberg, UP of Mississippi, 1997, pp. 219–27.

Ruas, Charles. "Toni Morrison (1981)." *Conversations with Toni Morrison*, edited by Danille Taylor-Guthrie, UP of Mississippi, 1994, pp. 93–118.

Sherry, Andrew J. "Award-Winning Novelist's First Play Premieres in Albany." *AP News*, Jan. 12, 1986. https://apnews.com/article/2a12d0d107bdc03ecfcb7520ef32bb98. Accessed Aug. 13, 2022.

Greenfield-Sanders, Timothy, director. *Toni Morrison: The Pieces I Am*. PBS American Masters, 2020.

Twain, Mark. *Adventures of Huckleberry Finn*. In *Mark Twain: Mississippi Writings*, edited by Guy Cardwell, Library of America, 1982, pp. 617–912.

Twain, Mark. *Life on the Mississippi*. In *Mark Twain: Mississippi Writings*, edited by Guy Cardwell, Library of America, 1982, pp. 217–616.

Vendrame, Alessandra. "Toni Morrison; A Faulknerian Novelist?" *Amerikastudien/American Studies*, vol. 42, no. 4, Winter, 1997, pp. 679–84, http://www.jstor.org/stable/41157341.

Weinstein, Philip M. *What Else but Love? The Ordeal of Race in Faulkner and Morrison*. Columbia UP, 1996.

CHAPTER SIXTEEN

Prospects for the Public Uses of "Toni Morrison"

KIRK CURNUTT

Throughout her later career, when she was at once an institution, an industry, and a bona fide celebrity, the writer born Chloe Ardelia Wofford often noted the distance she felt from the name "Toni Morrison." "People who call me Chloe are the people who know me best," she told *New York* interviewer Boris Kachka in 2012. "Chloe writes the books ... I still can't get to the Toni Morrison place yet."[1] Provocatively titled "Who is the Author of Toni Morrison?," Kachka's profile highlights Morrison's at times playfully indifferent, at times readily apparent concern about whether her work would "pass the test [of posterity] that begins only after Chloe Wofford is gone, and Toni Morrison is all that's left." Yet except for a brief reference to "a scholarly fan club known as the Toni Morrison Society," the article never defines how legacies are maintained. Kachka implies that "her place in the pantheon" depends upon whether she continues to be studied and taught (Kachka). In reality, writers' standing in the academy constitutes only one aspect of the literary afterlife—although, as was demonstrated when *Beloved* (1987) became a surprisingly decisive flash point in the 2021 Virginia gubernatorial race, a political controversy over the classroom value of canonical authors tends to command exorbitant amounts of media attention.[2] Ultimately, though, the pantheon is simply a reflection of the forum magnum, the public marketplace in which the broader inheritances of literature are honored and curated.

The simplest answer then to the question of who authors "Toni Morrison" since Chloe Wofford's August 5, 2019, passing is that our public uses of her do. By this term I mean the ways in which authors are invoked either to commemorate, to inspire, or to shape public opinion on an issue—functions that generally have little to do with critical exegesis and more with strategic

---

[1] Some variation of this quote appears in countless interviews and in Greenfield-Sanders's film *Toni Morrison: The Pieces I Am* (2019), a congenial, career-overview documentary that, because it was released only weeks before Morrison's death, served for most fans as a comforting requiem.

[2] In 2016, then governor Terry McAuliffe vetoed Virginia's so-called *Beloved* bill that would have required schools to notify parents of K-12 students when violent and sexually explicit literature was assigned in classes. Five years later, as McAuliffe ran for a second (nonconsecutive) term, his Republican opponent, Glenn Youngkin, campaigned with a commercial featuring the mother, Laura Murphy, whose complaint about the trauma her son suffered upon reading Morrison's novel in an Advanced Placement class in 2013 inspired the proposed legislation. In what conservative forces heralded as a victory for parents' rights in education, Youngkin won the election; progressives argued that Murphy's commercial was a racist dog whistle that conflated *Beloved* with campaigns to ban Critical Race Theory and limit discussions of the history of slavery and Black oppression in secondary curricula. See Nierenberg.

deployments of a name, image, or quotation. In my adopted hometown of Montgomery, Alabama, for example, the Equal Justice Initiative, a nonprofit legal advocacy organization spearheaded by Bryan Stevenson, the author of *Just Mercy: A Story of Justice and Redemption* (2014), displays a wall-sized engraved excerpt from *Beloved* as a centerpiece of its profoundly moving six-acre site honoring the 4,400 victims of racial terrorism throughout the United States from 1877 to 1950. Opened in 2018, the National Memorial for Peace and Justice quotes Morrison's self-taught preacher Baby Suggs, who in a sermon teaches the novel's Black community how to endure the long national nightmare of white supremacy:

> And O my people, out yonder, hear me, they do not love your neck unnoosed and straight. So love your neck; put a hand on it, grace it, stroke it and hold it up. And all your inside parts that they'd just as soon slop for hogs, you got to love them. The dark, dark liver—love it, love it, and the beat and beating heart, love that too. More than eyes or feet. More than lungs that have yet to draw free air. More than your lifeholding womb and your lifegiving private parts, hear me now, love your heart. For this is the prize. (*Beloved* 122)

Popularly known as the Lynching Memorial, this solemn landmark sits less than two hundred yards from my office at Troy University's Montgomery campus. Several times a year I lead students through its 800 six-foot steel columns that document victims' names and murder dates. Pausing at the Morrison inscription, I always invite classes to speculate why a passage from *a novel* is featured instead of a nonfiction oration by Ida B. Wells, W. E. B. DuBois, James Weldon Johnson, or another prominent member of the contemporary anti-lynching crusade. As I suggest, the use of *Beloved* may just be the most moving example they will ever encounter of a passage of fiction memorializing a real-world atrocity.

Not all public uses of a writer prove so stirring, however. Some may even risk stereotyping authors for the exact reasons they are venerated. In the case of Ernest Hemingway or Sylvia Plath, uses may overemphasize the biography to the detriment of the art. In other cases, they may sand off the rough edges of a corpus, ossifying an evasive, personally secretive figure such as Langston Hughes—one whose career wove through stages of political radicalism and renunciation—into a paragon of sentimental uplift. Perhaps most dangerously, readers may have little interest in literature's ability to illuminate history, culture, and other grand concerns and use it strictly to look inward as a tool of self-help.

In Morrison's case, the attribute most endangered by these uses is her complexity, whether the formal challenges posed by the stylistic density she inherited from the modernist influence of Woolf and Faulkner, the evasiveness and contrarianism of her public persona that marked her unwillingness to be "known" or easily summed up, or her refusal to resolve with convenient bromides and contrived resolutions the tangled issues of race, motherhood, "Otherness," and related topics she dramatized. As Namwali Serpell wrote shortly after the author's final birthday, Morrison's "imperiousness" both intimidates and inspires: "Morrison incenses people. How dare she be difficult *and* a black woman? ... How dare she refuse to comfort or seduce or translate? It cannot be easy to be Toni Morrison. And yet I aspire to it ... I, too, yearn for that specific, human, black, female freedom: to feel at ease to be difficult" (Serpell, emphasis in original). Kachka's profile quotes the writer's friend Claudia Brodsky on the opposing frustrations general audiences feel because her work is neither easily consumed nor consoling: "White women have a very strong—'You are the wise black wom[a]n who will take care of my innermost'—relationship with her. They're like, 'How dare she not be this mammy?' That [role] works if there's one book and it's life-affirming in this very obvious way. I think it's because you can't quite mammy-ify her entirely that there's a great resentment" (qtd. in Kachka). How Morrison's literary difficulty is preserved and packaged within broader celebrations of her accomplishments will thus prove a major challenge of stewarding her legacy. For the moment, this challenge is best traced through uses of her name and quotations from her work. These uses predate her passing but continue to shape how she is revered.

WHAT'S IN A NAME?

A starting point for assaying these public uses of "Toni Morrison" dates back to January 22, 1995, when her hometown library dedicated a space in her honor. The Lorain (Ohio) Public Library System's Toni Morrison Reading Room was the first such physical site named for her and came about specifically through a request from the author as the city of Lorain debated how best to recognize its newly crowned Nobel laureate. As a one-time employee of the library in her late teens, Morrison preferred to see her name attached to the building at 351 W. Sixth Street to the city's suggestion that it either rechristen its main artery, Broadway Avenue, after her, erect a statue, or name a public park in tribute. As Morrison said at the time,

> [The room] felt fine to me. Much better than the alternatives. I remember working at the library ... I spent long, long hours reading there, so I wanted one place available in the neighborhood with a quiet room and comfortable chairs. I hope that people spend forty-five minutes, or an hour or two there. Not for entertainment. Not for rest. The point is, in books lie real knowledge. (qtd. in Sagert)

Alongside various family members, her friend the poet Sonia Sanchez, and then Congressman (and future Senator) Sherrod Santos, Morrison attended the dedication ceremony, coverage of which was widely promulgated in national newspapers thanks to a syndicated dispatch (Associated Press).

More than twenty-five years later, the Morrison room, located on the ground floor of the library's main branch, remains a charmingly unassuming tribute to the writer. Despite a 2020 renovation and rededication timed to commemorate the state of Ohio's official adoption of her February 18 birthday as Toni Morrison Day, the space has changed little in the intervening quarter century. Shortly after her death, the website Atlas Obscura, the self-proclaimed "definitive guide to the world's hidden wonders," offered its travel-enthusiast audience a tour while explaining the significance of the room for the writer herself:

> In the years after the dedication, books and memorabilia trickled into the library from Morrison's office in Princeton, eventually taking the form of a small but formidable altar ... The Lorain librarians assiduously saved nearly every clipping of stories about Morrison in local and national papers and stowed them in a dedicated file. While Morrison donated the bulk of her personal papers, including notes, corrected proofs, and early manuscripts, to Princeton, the Lorain Public Library had, over the years, built up its own record of how dearly the author was cherished in Ohio and the world.

The walls of the Toni Morrison Reading Room are covered in this gratitude. Morrison's face smiles out from covers on *Time* and *Newsweek.* Letters she wrote are kept safe in picture frames, around an enormous painted quilt square depicting Morrison at work. Her friends and family appear in a picture album of the writer's 70th birthday at the New York Public Library. And at the heart of the room is an original portrait of Morrison by Ohio artist John Sokol. From a distance, the portrait looks jagged, almost like a dot matrix. But up close, one can see that Morrison's face is rendered not in lines but in letters, specifically the opening lines of *Song of Solomon*. (Imbler)

As this description suggests, the room is not a facility for scholarly study in the way that, say, Jackson State University's Margaret Walker Center in Jackson, Mississippi, is; it pays homage to the writer's accomplishments rather than enables research. Nevertheless, the space fulfills the basic functions that naming a building or room after a historically significant figure—what Maoz Azaryahu calls "onymic commemoration"—is designed to achieve. As Azaryahu explains, "Remembrance of the name is premised on the principle of a threefold public recognition: recognizing the historical significance of the person(s) [commemorated by the act of naming], leading to recognizing the importance of the person's biographical ties with the location and consequently recognizing the historical significance of the location" (31). If the first function seems obvious enough, the second derives its significance from Morrison's personal connection to the institution as both a patron and employee who frequently in interviews and essays credited her love of literature to the many hours spent perusing its stacks before she left Lorain to attend Howard University in Washington, DC in the late 1940s.

The third aim of recognizing the location's historical significance, however, is more complicated. The physical building that houses the room was built in 1957, roughly a decade after Morrison's departure from Ohio; the actual site she frequented, one of the famous Carnegie Foundation–funded libraries built around the turn into the twentieth century, sits roughly half a mile away. The library system attempts to mitigate this inconvenient reality by dramatizing the room's potential catalytic effect on visitors: its intent is not solely to celebrate but to inspire a similar passion for reading in guests that might just launch the next great American literary career. The library's website makes this point explicit in describing the room's most arresting element, a glass wall upon which is etched a passage from Morrison's December 10, 1993, Nobel Prize banquet speech: "I will leave this hall with a new and much more delightful haunting than the one I felt upon entering: that is the company of the laureates yet to come. Those who, even as I speak, are mining, sifting and polishing languages for illuminations none of us has dreamed of" ("Banquet Speech"). As the website goes on to declare:

> Those words take on an enormous significance when one considers the humble beginnings—and tremendous progress—of the Lorain Public Library System. Which laureates are yet to come? What accomplishments and advances will take place, both within the walls of the library, and/or because of its influences? Because, to paraphrase Morrison, even as we speak, as we think, and as we read, illuminations are being birthed, "illuminations none of us has dreamed of." (Sagert)

The reference to "humble beginnings" suggests another angle on this third function of recognizing the location. The phrase refers not just to the library's ability to spark that creative "mining, sifting and polishing" of "languages" by offering free access to the raw materials of literacy and literary invention. It also refers to the city of Lorain itself, that "small, industrial town" still "largely dependent upon the steel industry" that "in 1931, the year of Morrison's birth ... was heavily populated with migrants from Europe, Mexico, and the American South," where she "grew up among working families of all colors" who "valued hard work and integrity" (Li 1).

In other words, the room calls attention to the unlikelihood that such a blue-collar world might supply even a basic seedbed for the eventual flowering of Morrison's magnitude of "accomplishments and advances." One might argue that in crediting itself for helping ignite the author's passion for books in this otherwise modestly privileged environment, the library depicts her rise to fame as a simple assertion of will, underplaying the significant cultural barriers she and other people of color had to transcend to gain a toehold in the publishing industry. Yet the more pertinent point is that the formative influence that Morrison insisted the library bore on her literary imagination allows the reading room to compensate not only for existing in a different building than she knew, but also for the lack of other, more intimate sites in Lorain that shaped her. The Eudora Welty branch of the Jackson/Hinds Public Library System in Mississippi hosts a comparable space, the Mississippi Writers Room, celebrating the achievements of a range of its state authors, including, of course, Welty. Yet Jackson is also home to the Eudora Welty House and Museum, which serves as the de facto center of Welty tourism in that capital city. In Lorain, however, only one residence in which Morrison grew up remains standing, the home at 2245 Elyria Avenue in which her birth certificate says she was born.[3] Although it attracts literary pilgrims who testify eloquently to the value of visiting the property (Conley), it is not open to the public. For a writer for whom "love and disaster and all other forms of human incident accumulate in [her] fictional houses" (Als 64)—whether the Breedlove home in *The Bluest Eye*, the boarding house in *Sula*, or *Beloved*'s 124 Bluestone Road— the lack of a Morrison domicile that literary pilgrims might visit feels acutely ironic.

In many ways, the Toni Morrison Reading Room's display of newspaper clippings, tribute art, and memorabilia (such as state and municipal proclamations in her honor) exudes the inauspicious haphazardness of many author home museums run by smaller community organizations: there is no unifying narrative to guide the visitor from item to item, information on display cards tends to credit sources rather than provide context, and the arrangement of items seems random. Yet the room also cannot fulfill what Nicola J. Watson calls, in a clever turn of phrase, the main prerogative of writers' houses, which are "primarily designed to 'effect' a figure of the author ... through the preservation and display of his or her belongings, or 'effects'" (4). In the absence of the "quasi-domestic" intimacy that these "effects" engender in any number of the roughly sixty such sites open to the public across the United States (Trubek 4)—whether the Paul Laurence Dunbar House in Dayton, Ohio, the Sinclair Lewis Boyhood Home in Sauke Centre, Minnesota, or the Harriet Beecher Stowe House in Hartford, Connecticut, to name three random examples—the reading room does not project much of an authorial personality or presence. Although Morrison's face stares down from various photos, paintings, and illustrations, and even a fan-sewn quilt that the writer gifted to the library, the dominant feature of the space are the words "Toni Morrison," which are painted in large white letters on one of the glass panes that partition it from the rest of the facility. The net effect is to remind the visitor that the room is dedicated to Morrison and little else. Although Atlas Obscura claims the space "has also become a meaningful destination for Morrison devotees," exactly what deeper knowledge of her work they might gain from a visit

---

[3]Although Morrison's birth certificate cites this address as her birth home, local Lorain historians insist that the Wofford family moved to a different address as early as 1928.

remains unclear. "Lots of times we just stand there and have a conversation about Toni," reports one librarian of his interaction with out-of-towners. "It's always very reverent" (Imbler).

The intent here is neither to criticize the displays nor the curatorial professionalism of the library, especially since all evidence suggests Morrison was perfectly pleased with the space (Li 6). The point, rather, is to suggest that the room reflects the prospects for Morrison tourism in her hometown, which seem limited at best. In August 2021, a coalition of local and state organizations installed a historical marker at the actual site of the library when Morrison worked there, 329 W. 10th Street, which now houses the Lorain Historical Society (formerly the Black River Historical Society). As part of the Ohio History Connection's Historical Marker Program, the Morrison installation joins nearly 1,800 markers erected throughout Ohio since 1957 to "tell the state's history as written by its communities" (Ohio Historical Marker Program). Other writers commemorated range from the famous (Langston Hughes) to authors primarily known to academicians (Hart Crane) to the forgotten (Lois Lenski). The text of the Morrison marker rehearses basic biographical information and highlights the library's role in her creative genesis but offers few specifics other than the truism that her "literature has inspired millions around the world" ("Toni Morrison, Lorain Native"). In this regard, the marker's function is strictly commemorative. It recognizes the site of the former Carnegie library, but within the building itself, the Historical Society offers only a smattering of original artefacts related to the author, such as a copy of her senior high-school yearbook. What few display materials it exhibits tend to be on loan from the library itself, which created them for the 2020 rededication (Payerchin; "Preview of Toni Morrison Photo Exhibit"). The society does cosponsor essay contests for younger residents, occasionally hosts Morrison trivia nights, and offers curriculum guides on its website, but a nonresident seeking material contact with the sources of Morrison's fiction will likely be underwhelmed; most of the organization's energies go to maintaining its Moore House Museum, the one-time home of a local banker and former mayor that spotlights Lorain's 1920s history.[4]

Not every city that ever gave birth to a famous writer can go to the extremes that Red Cloud, Nebraska, has, where the entire economic development plan now centers upon Willa Cather tourism ("Heritage Tourism"). Yet even municipalities with far smaller populations than Lorain's 62,000 residents devote significant resources to appealing to literary tourists. In 2004, Fort Pierce, Florida—population 45,000—unveiled its Zora Neale Hurston Dust Tracks Heritage Trail, a tour comprising "three large kiosks, eight trail markers and a recently-added exhibit and visitor information center" designed to "capture Zora memories in Fort Pierce and chronicle her travels through Florida and the Caribbean" ("Zora Neale Hurston Dust Tracks Heritage Trail"). The markers commemorate significant sites in the writer's final years in the "Sunrise City," from the library now named after her to the gravesite in the Garden of Heavenly Rest that Alice Walker rediscovered in 1973 and where she installed a headstone, an act that symbolically ignited Hurston's posthumous recovery after Walker described the experience in her 1975 essay "Looking for Zora" (*In Search of Our Mothers' Gardens* 93–116). The text and illustrations on these installations go into far more detail than most historical markers. In addition to reminiscences from contemporaries, they provide

---

[4]In fall 2000, Lorain was home to the second biennial Toni Morrison Society Conference, titled "Toni Morrison and the Meanings of Home," which included participation from local residents who had known the Wofford family. See https://www.tonimorrisonsociety.org/conference.html.

narrative context that increases visitors' appreciation beyond general proclamations of the "her-work-inspires-millions-around-the-world" variety.

At present, the Ohio Library Council, of which the Lorain Public Library System is a member, does offer a link on its website to an interactive map created by Professor Jewon Woo and her students at Lorain County Community College that could easily form the basis of a Morrison heritage trail comparable to Fort Pierce's ("Toni Morrison's Lorain"). The handsomely illustrated virtual tour includes various sites referenced in *The Bluest Eye*, including Isaly's Ice Cream and Dairy Products parlor, Dreamland Theater, and Lakeview Park (53, 81–2), along with the public schools the author attended and the two library sites. Although the setting of *Sula*—Medallion, Ohio, and its outlying Black neighborhood, "the Bottom"—"are not figurations of Lorain," as John N. Duvall writes (48), some basic detective work could identify the historical pool halls and boarding houses Morrison may have had in mind when creating her second novel. At the very least, a marker could examine the historical Hannah Peace of Lorain whom Morrison recalled her mother speaking about in hushed tones to provide insight into the "mixture of awe and approbation" with which the Black community regarded its more eccentric members, one of *Sula*'s main themes (*Conversations* 79–80). Either way, the potential effect that linking fictional sites to real-life places in Lorain has is evident in testimonials of Morrison readers who have toured the stops themselves. In a quote to *Cincinnati Magazine* in 2017, the late Cheryl Wall recalled the thrill of visiting Lorain and recognizing locations in *The Bluest Eye*: "Riding around … I was like, 'Oh my gosh, that's the ice cream shop, and that's the storefront where the Breedlove family lived.' I felt like I already knew Lorain" (qtd. in Fehrman).

If the burden of moving beyond "onymic commemoration" even to a basic type of Morrison tourism such as a heritage trail falls squarely upon the shoulders of her hometown, it is because possibilities elsewhere appear fairly slim. As is well known, for much of her writing career, Morrison lived in Rockland County, New York, including post–*Song of Solomon* (1977) the converted boathouse in the village of Grand View-on-Hudson that features prominently in nearly every major personality profile of hers.[5] The December 1993 fire there that destroyed a portion of her personal papers remains a significant moment in her biography (Li 95); the centrality of the rebuilt structure in her life is perhaps most evident in Timothy Greenfield-Sanders's documentary, *Toni Morrison: The Pieces I Am* (2019), where the patio and private dock are put on lavish display. As of this writing, Morrison's surviving son, Ford, retains ownership of the property but has no plans to convert it to an author museum or even to acknowledge its importance with a plaque. Instead, Morrison-related events are held in nearby Nyack, including a 2021 retrospective that kicked off the community historical society's new exhibit space (Brum). Outside of Rockland County, rare attempts at Morrison-adjacent tourism have enjoyed only middling success. In 1998, authorities with the Fair Hill Natural Resource Management Area in Cecil County, Maryland, announced their intent to maintain the set built for Jonathan Demme's film version of *Beloved* as a local attraction, inspired by the *Field of Dreams* baseball diamond erected in the cornfields of Dyersville, Iowa, hoping both Morrison and star Oprah Winfrey's fan base would visit (Shapiro). Although state architectural surveys still document the site's location, preservation plans promoted by then administrator Edward Walls never came to fruition, and the farm house, corncrib, and

---

[5] See Als (64–75) and Kachka, both of whom describe Morrison's house in detail.

barn constructed to represent 124 Bluestone Road were long ago demolished. Although the site is accessible to hikers, no signage documents its importance—the movie's box-office failure rendered potential interest moot.

Meanwhile, controversies over the historical representation of slavery have nearly derailed other tourist opportunities involving *Beloved* along its actual Ohio/Kentucky setting. In 2005, when the Cincinnati Opera staged *Margaret Garner*, Morrison and composer Richard Danielpour's opera about the escaped slave who inspired the novel, cast members and organizers of a concurrent Toni Morrison Society conference confronted a local amateur historian for "whitewashing" the trauma of slavery. At the time, the historian, Ruth Wade Cox Brunings, had positioned herself as the gatekeeper to Maplewood Farm, the plantation in Richwood, Kentucky, from which Garner and her family briefly escaped slavery and the novel's inspiration for Sweet Home. In various publications and public talks, Brunings promoted the theory that Garner had participated in a consensual adulterous affair with her owner, the guilt from which supposedly compelled her to flee the plantation more so than the brutality of slavery. (As is now well remembered thanks to *Beloved*, when her owner recaptured her family in Cincinnati, Garner slit the throat of her two-year-old daughter, Mary, rather than allow her to be returned to bondage). The conflict over Brunings's hypothesis led to a showdown over access to the plantation, with the historian demanding that the Morrison Society bar two scholars whose treatment of Boone County slaveholders (including some of her own ancestors) she judged historically inaccurate. Society members, meanwhile, objected to the docent's repeated use of the phrase "benevolent slavery" both in print and in her tours (Yohe 93–115). While the property's owner ultimately overruled Brunings's demands, the conflict exemplifies the resistance Morrison scholars often face during cultural engagement events to employing her fiction as documentary proof of the traumas Black people have suffered in America.

Not all instances of "onymic commemoration" have the potential to encourage readers to travel to Morrison-specific sites. In some cases, the naming of buildings is at once an honor and a corrective, an acknowledgment of the need throughout American culture for racial parity by recognizing Black contributions. Both Cornell University, where Morrison earned her master's degree in 1955, and Princeton, where she served as the Robert F. Goheen Professor of the Humanities from 1989 until 2006, recently christened buildings in her honor, the latter while she was still alive, the former posthumously. "Building names tell a story," begins a promotional video from Cornell featuring the alumnus chairing the naming committee for its North Campus Residential Expansion program, which in 2021 added approximately 2,000 new beds within five newly constructed dormitories. As the video admits, Toni Morrison Hall is the first campus building named for a woman of color ("North Campus Building Names"), a remarkably overdue honor but one that nevertheless reflects the university's ongoing commitment to inclusivity. Although not specifically timed to the dormitory's grand opening, Cornell's College of Arts and Sciences also sponsored a year-long series of programs celebrating the fiftieth anniversary of *The Bluest Eye* that included exhibits, readings, and a colloquium (all conducted online due to the coronavirus pandemic). Most intriguingly, the college collaborated with a local organization called the Community Quilting Resource Center on a project designed to bridge town and gown by inviting fiber artists from surrounding Tompkins County to create either entire quilts or individual squares celebrating Morrison's life and works for display (Beduyah). The concurrence of the building's dedication and the programming offers a model for extending commemoration into public outreach.

Four years earlier, Morrison attended the ceremony at Princeton where the administration building formerly known as West College, home to the College of Arts and Sciences, was rechristened Toni Morrison Hall. In this case, the dedication was tied to the keynote Morrison delivered at the November 16–19, 2017, Princeton and Slavery Symposium, a "scholarly investigation of the University's historical involvement with the institution of slavery" (Saxon). As university president Stephen L. Eisgruber declared in comments delivered after Morrison's lecture, "Today Princeton revises itself—revises its plaques of stone and its maps both paper and electronic—so that Toni Morrison's name becomes part of the lexicon through which students, faculty, staff and alumni navigate this campus, and thereby part of the evolving tapestry through which our community defines itself" (Dienst). As his remarks suggest, this "revis[ing] of plaques" was part of a painful public self-examination process by which many universities across the country began acknowledging their complicity in historical and ongoing institutional racism. In Princeton's case that meant posting often lost history on a special website featuring "hundreds of primary source documents and more than 80 articles exploring topics like early slavery-related university funding, student demographics and the sometimes shocking history of racial violence on a campus long known as the most culturally 'Southern' in the Ivy League" (Schuessler). By the summer after Morrison's death, the initiative even led to the removal of Woodrow Wilson's name from the University's School of Public and International Affairs and Wilson College.

Yet not all acts of Morrisonian commemoration occur at institutions she attended or taught at or engage such monumental topics as slavery and racial violence. In February 2020, Grinnell College launched its "Inscriptions for the Future" program by unveiling Morrison's name as the first of twelve to be carved into stone in the bricks of its Humanities and Social Studies Center's atrium, a centrally located public space on campus that was formerly a Carnegie Library (not unlike the original Lorain County Library where Morrison worked as a teenager). When the building opened in 1905, a frieze below the roofline was adorned with the names of Shakespeare, Dante, Homer, and other white male eminences. As the program's website notes, Morrison and the other eleven names were selected to "represent who [Grinnell is] today and who we aspire to be—names of people who embody our institution's commitment to social responsibility, building inclusive and sustainable community, and pursuing knowledge in the service of these ends." The project's name specifically grew from an inaugural lecture by Shanna Benjamin, called "Inscriptions for the Future: Toni Morrison and Black Feminist Beginnings," exploring Morrison's legacy of creating "a space for Black women scholars to engage in literature and intellectual conversations about history through their experiences and those that came before them" ("Inscriptions"). As Grinnell's president, Raynard Kington, noted, Morrison was one obvious "thoughtleader" whose intellectual influence on the later twentieth century was undeniable. Thanks to her example, subsequent names would "continue to open a discourse among students and faculty about who is read, taught and heard in academic spaces" (qtd. in Gupta).

But perhaps the most creative act of Morrison christening occurs under the aegis of the author society devoted to studying her. On the writer's seventy-fifth birthday in 2006, the Toni Morrison Society inaugurated its Bench by the Road Project, "a memorial history and community outreach initiative" that installs "benches and plaques at sites commemorating significant moments, individuals, and locations within the history of the African Diaspora," including "Sullivan's Island, South Carolina; Walden Woods in Lincoln, Massachusetts; The 20th Arrondissement in Paris, France; Fort-de-France, Martinique; and, most recently, the Schomburg Center in Harlem,

New York" ("Bench by the Road Project"). The name of the initiative comes from a 1989 interview in which Morrison insisted that she intended *Beloved* to be read as more than a mere literary experience. She created it as a surrogate site for memorializing Black lives lost to slavery precisely because at the time such memorials did not exist:

> There is no place you or I can go, [Morrison says] to think about or not think about, to summon the presences of, or recollect the absences of slaves … There is no suitable memorial, or plaque, or wreath, or wall, or park, or skyscraper lobby. There's no 300-foot tower, there's no small bench by the road. There is not even a tree scored, an initial that I can visit or you can visit in Charleston or Savannah or New York or Providence or better still on the banks of the Mississippi. And because such a place doesn't exist … the book had to. ("Melcher Book Award Acceptance")

Morrison spoke at bench unveiling ceremonies in South Carolina, Oberlin, Ohio, Paris, and New York City in 2008, 2009, 2010, and 2016, respectively. "It's never too late to honor the dead," she told the Sullivan's Island audience as, in the words of the *New York Times*, "she sat down on the six-foot-long, twenty-six-inch-deep black steel bench facing the Intracoastal Waterway. 'It's never too late to applaud the living who do them honor … This is extremely moving to me.'" She also noted the symbolic significance of a bench: "The bench is welcoming, open … You can be illiterate and sit on the bench, you can be a wanderer or you can be on a search" (qtd. in Lee). Each $5,000 installation includes a naming and descriptive plaque, the first attached to the bench itself and the second "mounted in a cement foundation on the ground next to the bench and [to] include a general description of the Project and a more specific statement of not more than thirty-five words describing the Bench's significance" ("Bench by the Road Project").

Since it began, the Morrison Society's unique project has become a subject of frequent analysis in the scholarship of commemoration and memorialization, the symbolism of both its utility as a public amenity and as a platform for contemplating the recovery of Black history frequently explicated. In the words of a recent study of the Sullivan's Island installation, "Transformed from artifact to slave memorial by the Society, the bench … represents something far more valuable than land or waterfront property; it reprises those abstract and concrete mechanisms such as human dignity, pride, and possessions that were confiscated through historical theft. The Bench by the Road ultimately symbolizes ownership of self, as well as ownership of one's own stories" (Woodard 134). In this way, the Morrison Society's project establishes a stage for "public memory practices" that in turn help foster in individuals the critical reflection skills that ideally empower the self-articulation that larger institutional forces of oppression cannot steal. As such, "onymic commemoration" is not a simple act of naming but of empowering audiences *to* name.

GATHERING HER WISDOM

As important as Morrison's name is, excerpts from her work shape public thought far more, circulating within a range of traditional media (television, books, film) and across social-media platforms (memes, Twitter). Thanks to their availability in these forms, her choicest quotes continue to influence the discourse of race, literature, community, and even universal abstractions like love. Yet there remains a danger to the quick-and-easy, bite-sized consumption of these citations: by removing context, these formats risk simplifying the complexity of her thought, turning passages into simple sayings, palliative aphorisms, or worse, outright platitudes.

In effect, the danger represents one that Morrison deftly navigated during her three appearances on *The Oprah Winfrey Show* between 1996 and 2000, when the popular daytime television talk-show host selected a series of her novels (*Song of Solomon*, *Paradise*, and *The Bluest Eye*) for discussion by her mass-audience book club, prompting a tsunami of sales that far outstripped the wider audience she earned after winning the Nobel Prize in 1993. (Morrison did not appear on the 2002 episode discussing *Sula*.) As John Young has written, commentators' fears that Winfrey would analyze the novels "entirely within the rubric of talk-show topics" initially seemed warranted, for the club's discussion of *Solomon* "ignore[d] the critique of American racial history," focusing instead on characters' likability and what the plot could teach viewers about their own personal experience (182). Yet as Young demonstrates, especially in the *Paradise* episode that aired in March 1998, the author denied

> the terms on which the dichotomy [between "serious" literature and "popular" entertainment] is grounded, finding no principled incongruence among Oprah viewers … and readers of "demanding and sophisticated" fiction. Previewing her book club dinner, Winfrey recalls: "I called up Toni Morrison and I said, 'Do people tell you they have to keep going over the words sometimes?' and she said, 'That, my dear, is called reading.'" Morrison's response encourages a serious readerly reaction to her writing within a popular discourse. (187)

As Young argues, the author, abetted by the host (who was entirely aware of readers' tendency to want to escape interpretive challenges by resorting to personal response) reminded the audience of the rigors of critical thinking and of questioning initial reactions—including confusion—to art: "In the end, Winfrey and Morrison both emphasize[d] the experience of reading these books, not simply consuming them" (183).[6]

Morrison's public persona may offer a handy safeguard against this decontextualizing. As Young notes, one of the remarkable aspects of the *Oprah* appearances is the way her imposing professorial demeanor refutes the Barthesian/Foucauldian notion of the "death of the author," the post-structuralist concept that complexity proliferates if the writer's presence is rendered null and void. Quoting Nancy Miller, Young points out how "this move 'prematurely forecloses the question of agency for'" women," who, unlike male writers, cannot performatively reject the "cultural authority" of authorship precisely because they do not a priori presume they possess it.[7] The most popular film clip of Morrison online testifies to the importance of this agency for minority writers. In the weeks surrounding her final birthday in 2019, footage of a 1998 interview with journalist Jana Wendt for an Australian television program called *Toni Morrison: Uncensored* resurfaced thanks to a tweet from cultural studies theorist Robert Randolph, Jr. (known online by his handle "Stony Morrison,

---

[6]Aubry offers a similar analysis of the episode, focusing on how *Paradise* frustrates readers' ability to identify the race of its characters, and how that frustration in turn exposes the arbitrary construction of racial meanings:

> All of the obvious markers of race [in the novel] prove unreliable, Morrison never offers conclusive evidence, and thus readers must acknowledge that the meaning of whiteness or blackness defies full and final comprehension. Race, then, ceases to be an easily comprehensible entity; it does not disappear, but rather emerges as a serious epistemological problem, far more elusive than most people suspect in their ordinary apprehension of racial cues. In a sense, Morrison's claim that when you know the race of another person you know nothing, is true—given the superficial and perfunctory form that most people's knowledge of race ordinarily assumes. (363)

[7]The quote comes from Miller's *Subject to Change* (106).

PhD"). The tweet was shared 16,000 times and "liked" by more than 44,000 (@rrandolphjr). As journalist Kimberly Yam noted, the interview was already notorious among Morrison scholars but discovered an entirely new audience thanks to its "going viral":

> WENDT: You don't think you'll ever change and incorporate books with white lives in them substantially?
> MORRISON: You can't understand how powerfully racist that question is can you? Because you can never ask a white author, "When are you going to write about black people?" Even the inquiry comes from a place of being in the center.
> WENDT (*nodding apologetically*): And being used to being in the center.
> MORRISON: It's inconceivable that where I already am is the mainstream.
>
> (*Toni Morrison: Uncensored*; see also Yam)

Thanks to Randolph/Morrison's tweet, #IAmtheMainstream became a popular hashtag for the remainder of Black History Month 2019 and then again that August as Morrison's death prompted users, including celebrities such as director Ava DuVernay, to reshare the clip several thousand more times. Several obituaries cited the exchange with Wendt as edifying and inspirational, with Morrison's demeanor in particular indicative of Black America's impatience with the presumption of "white" as the baseline measure of any standard of accomplishment. Describing the clip in *The Guardian*, novelist Maxine Beneba Clarke remembered watching the original interview as an aspiring author: "Morrison holds her gaze steady: posture regal, long silver-grey dreadlocks pulled elegantly back from composed face … Watching the sure, gentle-angry way Morrison held her truth all those years ago as a young Australian would-be writer of Afro-Caribbean heritage is etched lesson-deep into my memory" (Clarke). By the first anniversary of Morrison's death, "I Am the Mainstream" became a rallying cry as a collective of Black creatives called Strivers' Row launched a promotional campaign both online and in print borrowing the phrase to highlight Black professionals' central contributions to New York City culture (wearestriversrow).

Clarke's description of Morrison's "sure, gentle-angry way" thus captures why her authorial persona is so integral to shaping the reception of her work. Memes that celebrate her most famous quotes, by contrast, suggest why narrative context is essential to retaining the intricacies of her meanings. At its simplest, a meme is a digital image usually formatted as a .JPEG file that features either a photo of the author or an eye-catching landscape with a quote superimposed over it, or else it simply presents the text itself in an artful typeface across a colorful backdrop. The function of memes is to be "shared" across social-media platforms, whether Facebook or narrower user-demographics sites such as GoodReads.com. They also appear on a bevy of quotation sites with names like brainyquote.com or inspiringquotes.us. The very term "meme" comes from evolutionary biologist Richard Dawkins, who in 1976 abbreviated the Greek word *mimeme* or "imitation" to suggest how an idea, as "a unit of cultural transmission," replicates like a gene: "Just as genes propagate themselves in the gene pool by leaping from body to body via sperm or eggs, so memes propagate themselves in the meme pool by leaping from brain to brain in a process that, in the broad sense, can be called imitation" (192). The Morrison quotes that appear to have replicated most frequently online tend to be those most readily interpreted as maxims or aphorisms: "You wanna fly, you got to give up the shit that weighs you down." "If you are free, you need to free somebody else" (a phrase widely sold on T-shirts online). "You [are] your best thing." "If you surrendered to the air, you could ride it."⁸ As memorials proliferated in August 2019, the quotes also appeared in "listicles" or short articles of bulleted factoids on outlets like the *New York Times*, *Buzzfeed*, and—of course—Oprah.com. Many quotes were retweeted by political figures, rappers and actors, and fellow poets and writers.

Most of these social-media posts drew little criticism. In the *Washington Post*, however, Sandra Newman warned against the oversimplification that may occur when trading memes featuring Morrison quotes:

> If you didn't already know who Morrison was, you might have imagined the world was mourning a celebrity self-help writer, rather than a Nobel Prize-winning novelist known for the idiosyncratic, Gothic richness of her prose, and whose preoccupations were the most gruesome and traumatic episodes of American racism. You would certainly never have guessed that Morrison was famed for writing unflinchingly and graphically about torture, infanticide, incest and child abuse, or that her books are full of uncensored rage at the monumental crimes of white people. The Toni Morrison mourned in August was a comforting, folksy, wise-woman figure who was only concerned that everyone believe in themselves and chase their dreams. (Newman)

As Newman points out, some quotes frequently exchanged through memes are not even actual Morrison passages: the prolifically traded "Something that is loved is never lost"—which no less than then Senator (and future vice president) Kamala Harris retweeted—appears nowhere in *Beloved*, even though Morrison's fifth novel is often credited as its source.⁹

The danger of decontextualizing Morrison brings us full circle back to the passage from Baby Suggs's sermon that strategically adorns the Lynching Memorial in Montgomery. What message are visitors meant to take from reading this excerpt in this space? Scouring the internet, one discovers a profusion of blogs, posts, and tweets that state the inscription teaches "the power of love" (Ater)—a frustratingly abstract phrase that feels more reassuring than reflective. When I initially challenge my students to respond to these words, few if any of them have read *Beloved*. Their reactions invariably grow more complex and even confused after they do. As we discuss Baby Suggs's role in the drama, we focus on the sermon's pronouns, trying to decide who "my people" designates and who "they do not love your neck unnoosed" refers to. Almost unwillingly, classes recognize that if the oration is a message of love, it preaches Black self-love, not agape in general, and that by "they" Morrison means a healthy percentage of "us"—white people, that is. The realization is often dispiriting. Aren't acts of commemoration meant to unify rather than divide? To heal wounds rather than salt them? To clarify rather than cloud?

---

⁸These quotes are drawn, respectively, from *Song of Solomon* (179), her 2003 interview with Pam Houston for *Oprah* magazine (Houston), *Beloved* (389), and *Solomon* again (179).

⁹The proliferation of this imaginary quote is not limited to social media. It also appears in scholarly efforts such as *The Toni Morrison Book Club* (2020), an otherwise excellent collection of collaborative essays by public intellectuals Juda Bennet, Winnifred Brown-Glaude, Cassandra Jackson, and Piper Kendrix Williams that explores how Morrison's words can "illuminate the problems of everyday racism and guide us toward healthy responses and greater clarity" (2). Unfortunately, the book's afterword, a heartfelt letter to the recently deceased author, climaxes with the misattribution:

> All [readers] had of you were the places in ourselves where your words lived, the times when your wisdom called to us, making our experiences into language and thus making us real to ourselves and the world. Surely that was reason enough to love you. We hope so because we still believe in the truth of your words: "Something that is loved is never lost." (208)

Perhaps, I say, before reminding them that literature's job is to confront complexities without resorting to cliché or resolving them with obligatory good cheer. It used to be when undergraduates stared back unconvinced I would stumble and stammer to defend textual ambiguity. Since Morrison's death I am more apt to play them the clip from *Toni Morrison: Uncensored* that has helped popularize the hashtag #IAmtheMainstream. In commemorating Toni Morrison, I suggest, perhaps the best tribute we can pay as we put her to our public uses is to commit to making literary difficulty mainstream.

WORKS CITED

Als, Hilton. "Toni Morrison and the Ghosts in the House." *New Yorker*, Oct. 19, 2003, pp. 64–75.

Associated Press. "Author Dedicates Room." *Montgomery Advertiser*, Jan. 24, 1995, https://www.newspapers.com/image/260121081/. Accessed Sept. 15, 2021.

Ater, Renée. "The National Memorial for Peace and Justice." Khan Academy, n.d., https://www.khanacademy.org/humanities/art-history-for-teachers/xeaa3470a:teaching-with-images/xeaa3470a:go-deeper-oppression-and-resistance/a/the-national-memorial-for-peace-and-justice. Accessed Sept. 15, 2021.

Aubry, Timothy. "Beware the Furrow of the Middlebrow: Searching for *Paradise* on *The Oprah Winfrey Show*." *Modern Fiction Studies*, vol. 52, no. 2, Summer 2006, pp. 350–73.

Azaryahu, Maoz. *An Everlasting Name: Cultural Remembrance and Traditions of Onymic Commemoration*. De Gruyter, 2021.

Beduyah, Jose. "Toni Morrison Quilting Project, to Weave Communities Together, Launches Feb. 22." *Cornell Chronicle*, Feb. 15, 2021, https://news.cornell.edu/stories/2021/02/toni-morrison-quilting-project-weave-communities-together-launches-feb-22. Accessed Sept. 15, 2021.

"Bench by the Road Project." The Toni Morrison Society, n.d., https://www.tonimorrisonsociety.org/bench.html. Accessed Sept. 15, 2021.

Bennet, Juda, et al. *The Toni Morrison Book Club*. U of Wisconsin P, 2020.

Brum, Robert. "Nyack Retrospective: Toni Morrison, in Her Own Words." *Hudson Valley News and Events*, July 6, 2021, https://hudsonvalley.town.news/g/nanuet-ny/n/34270/nyack-retrospective-toni-morrison-her-own-words. Accessed Sept. 15, 2021.

Clarke, Maxine Beneba. "Her Stories Can Crumble a Reader into a Thousand Pieces," in "Toni Morrison: Melissa Lucashenko and Maxine Beneba Clarke Reflect on Late Author's Legacy." *The Guardian*, Aug. 8, 2019, https://www.theguardian.com/books/2019/aug/08/toni-morrison-melissa-lucashenko-and-maxine-beneba-clarke-reflect-on-late-authors-legacy. Accessed Sept. 15, 2021.

Conley, Tara L. "In Toni Morrison's Hometown, the Familiar Has Become Foreign." Bloomberg.com, Aug. 14, 2019, https://www.bloomberg.com/news/articles/2019-08-14/my-pilgrimage-to-toni-morrison-s-ohio-hometown. Accessed Sept. 15, 2021.

Dawkins, Richard. *The Selfish Gene*. Oxford UP, 1976.

Deans, Gary, director. *Toni Morrison: Uncensored*. Beyond Productions, 1998.

Demme, Jonathan, director. *Beloved*. Touchstone Pictures, 1998.

Dienst, Karin. "Princeton Dedicates Morrison Hall in Honor of Nobel Laureate and Emeritus Faculty Member Toni Morrison." Princeton University, Nov. 20, 2017, https://www.princeton.edu/news/2017/11/20/princeton-dedicates-morrison-hall-honor-nobel-laureate-and-emeritus-faculty-member. Accessed Sept. 15, 2021.

Duvall, John N. *The Identifying Fictions of Toni Morrison: Modernist Authenticity and Postmodern Blackness*. Palgrave Macmillan, 2000.

Fehrman, Craig. "How Ohio Has Shaped Toni Morrison's Fiction." *Cincinnati Magazine*, Oct. 31, 2017, https://www.cincinnatimagazine.com/artsmindsblog/how-ohio-shaped-toni-morrison-fiction/. Accessed Sept. 15, 2021.

Greenfield-Sanders, Timothy, director. *Toni Morrison: The Pieces I Am*. Magnolia Pictures, 2019.

Gupta, Shabana. "Toni Morrison to be Honored with HSSC Atrium Inscription." *The Scarlet and Black*, Feb. 21, 2020, https://www.thesandb.com/article/toni-morrison-to-be-honored-with-hssc-atrium-inscription.html. Accessed Sept. 15, 2021.

"Heritage Tourism." *Red Cloud (Nebraska) Tourism and & Commerce*, 2021, https://www.visitredcloud.com/visit/heritage-tourism. Accessed Sept. 15, 2021.

Houston, Pam. "Truest Eye." *Oprah.com*, 2003, https://www.oprah.com/omagazine/toni-morrison-talks-love/all. Accessed Sept. 15, 2021.

Imbler, Sabrira. "In a Special Room in an Ohio Library, Toni Morrison's Legacy Lives On." *Atlas Obscura*, Aug. 8, 2019, https://www.atlasobscura.com/articles/ohio-toni-morrison-reading-room. Accessed Sept. 15, 2021.

"Inscriptions for the Future." *Grinnell College*, 2020, https://www.grinnell.edu/academics/centers-programs/humanities/funding-opportunities/inscriptions-future. Accessed Sept. 15, 2021.

Kachka, Boris. "Who is the Author of Toni Morrison?" *New York*, Apr. 27, 2012, https://nymag.com/news/features/toni-morrison-2012-5/. Accessed Sept. 15, 2021.

Lee, Felicia R. "Bench of Memory at Slavery's Gateway." *New York Times*, Jul. 28, 2008, https://www.nytimes.com/2008/07/28/arts/design/28benc.html. Accessed Sept. 15, 2021.

Li, Stephanie. *Toni Morrison: A Biography*. Greenwood P/ABC-CLIO, 2010.

Margaret Garner. Music by Richard Danielpour, libretto by Toni Morrison, Michigan Opera Theatre, Cincinnati Opera, and Opera Company of Philadelphia, 2005.

Miller, Nancy. *Subject to Change: Reading Feminist Writing*. Columbia UP, 1988.

Morrison, Toni. *Beloved*. Knopf, 1987.

Morrison, Toni. *The Bluest Eye*. Holt, Rinehart and Winston, 1970.

Morrison, Toni. *Conversations with Toni Morrison*, edited by Danille Taylor-Guthrie, UP of Mississippi, 1994.

Morrison, Toni. "Melcher Book Award Acceptance." *UUWorld*, Jan./Feb. 1989, https://www.uuworld.org/articles/a-bench-by-road. Accessed Sept. 15, 2021.

Morrison, Toni. *Paradise*. Knopf, 1998.

Morrison, Toni. *Song of Solomon*. Knopf, 1977.

Morrison, Toni. "Toni Morrison Banquet Speech." Nobelprize.org. https://www.nobelprize.org/prizes/literature/1993/morrison/speech/. Accessed Sept. 15, 2021.

Newman, Sandra. "How Not to Mourn a Beloved Author." *Washington Post*, Sept. 9, 2019, https://www.washingtonpost.com/outlook/2019/09/09/how-not-mourn-beloved-author/. Accessed Sept. 15, 2021.

Nierenberg, Amelia. "Virginia's Fight Over *Beloved*: Glenn Youngkin Leveraged 'Parents' Rights' to Win the Governor's Race." *New York Times*, Nov. 3, 2021, https://www.nytimes.com/2021/11/03/us/virginias-fight-over-beloved.html. Accessed Sept. 15, 2021.

"North Campus Building Names Reflect Inclusive Philosophy." *YouTube*, uploaded by Cornell University, Mar. 23, 2021, https://www.youtube.com/watch?v=I72KplVoHLc&t=7s. Accessed Sept. 15, 2021.

The Ohio Historical Marker Program. *RemarkableOhio.org*, n.d. https://remarkableohio.org/. Accessed Sept. 15, 2021.

Payerchin, Thomas. "Lorain Public Library Creates Toni Morrison Archive." *Morning Journal*, Aug. 6, 2019, https://www.morningjournal.com/2019/08/06/lorain-public-library-creates-toni-morrison-archive/. Accessed Sept. 15, 2021.

"Preview of Toni Morrison Photo Exhibit." *YouTube*, uploaded by the Lorain Historical Society, Feb. 14, 2021, https://www.youtube.com/watch?v=jl4CiatZVd8. Accessed Sept. 15, 2021.

[@rrandolphjr]. "Toni Morrison's Knife Is So Sharp, You Don't Even Realize that She's Slit Your Throat." *Twitter*, Feb. 11, 2019, 11:13 a.m., https://twitter.com/rrandolphjr/status/1095007929898545153.

Robinson, Phil Alden, director. *Field of Dreams*. Universal Pictures, 1989.

Sagert, Kelly Boyer. "Birth of Illumination: First Hundred Years of the Lorain Public Library System." *Lorain Public Library System*, 2001, https://www.lorainpubliclibrary.org/about-lpls/history-of-lpls/birth-of-illumination. Accessed Sept. 15, 2021.

Saxon, Jamie. "Princeton and Slavery Symposium Explores U.S. History 'Writ Small,' Reveals 'Powerful and Fruitful' Research." Princeton University, Nov. 20, 2017, https://www.princeton.edu/news/2017/11/20/princeton-and-slavery-symposium-explores-us-history-writ-small-reveals-powerful-and. Accessed Sept. 15, 2021.

Schuessler, Jennifer. "Princeton Digs Deep into Its Fraught Racial History." *New York Times*, Nov. 6, 2017, https://www.nytimes.com/2017/11/06/arts/princeton-digs-deep-into-its-fraught-racial-history.html. Accessed Sept. 15, 2021.

Serpell, Namwali. "On Black Difficulty: Toni Morrison and the Thrill of Imperiousness." *Slate*, 26 Mar. 2019, https://slate.com/culture/2019/03/toni-morrison-difficulty-black-women.html. Accessed Sept. 15, 2021.

Shapiro, Stephanie. "Fair Hill Has Hope Set for *Beloved* Tourism." *Baltimore Sun*, Aug. 10, 1998, https://www.baltimoresun.com/news/bs-xpm-1998-08-10-1998222106-story.html. Accessed Sept. 15, 2021.

Stevenson, Bryan. *Just Mercy: A Story of Justice and Redemption*. Spiegel & Grau, 2014.

"Toni Morrison, Lorain Native/Toni Morrison, Prize Winning Author." *RemarkableOhio.org*, n.d., https://remarkableohio.org/index.php?/category/1859. Accessed Sept. 15, 2021.

"Toni Morrison's Lorain." StoryMapsJS, 2020. https://uploads.knightlab.com/storymapjs/3bde773f6fea3d4e97bc8a9373de6b0e/toni-morrisons-lorain/index.html. Accessed Sept. 15, 2021.

Trubek, Anne. *A Skeptic's Guide to Writers' Houses*. U of Pennsylvania P, 2010.

Walker, Alice. *In Search of Our Mothers' Gardens: Womanist Prose*. Harcourt, 1983.

Watson, Nicola J. *The Author's Effects: On Writer's House Museums*. Oxford UP, 2020.

Wearestriversrow, "I Am the Mainstream." *Instagram*, Feb. 5–27, 2020, https://www.instagram.com/wearestriversrow/?hl=en.

Woodard, Helena. *Slave Sites on Display: Reflecting Slavery's Legacy Through Contemporary "Flash" Moments*. UP of Mississippi, 2019.

Yam, Kimberly. "Video of Toni Morrison Calling Out Interviewer For 'Powerfully Racist' Question Goes Viral." *Huffington Post*, Aug. 6, 2019, https://www.huffpost.com/entry/toni-morrison-interviewer-racist-question_n_5d49baabe4b0d291ed07bc45. Accessed Sept. 15, 2021.

Yohe, Kristine. "Confronting Margaret Garner in Cincinnati: The Opera, the Toni Morrison Society Conference, and the Public Debate." *Margaret Garner: The Premiere Performances of Toni Morrison's Libretto*, edited by La Vinia Delois Jennings, U of Virginia P, 2016, pp. 93–115.

Young, John. "Toni Morrison, Oprah Winfrey, and Postmodern Popular Audiences." *African American Review*, vol. 35, no. 2, Summer 2001, pp. 181–204.

"Zora Neale Hurston Dust Tracks Heritage Trail." *Welcome to Fort Pierce, the Sunshine City*, n.d., https://www.cityoffortpierce.com/386/Zora-Neale-Hurston-Dust-Tracks-Heritage. Accessed Sept. 15, 2021.

CHAPTER SEVENTEEN

Going to Ground in *Home*: Morrison's Mid-Century Political Modernism

THADIOUS M. DAVIS

In *Home* (2012), Toni Morrison functions as an architect, a mid-century modernist builder of narrativity that heralds a set of strategies designed for living Black in a time of transition. She builds the spare novel around elongated historical and political structures that meld into a narrative operating both within and against the grain of American individualism so much a part of the 1950s, the era in which she locates her action line. In the process, she places her own authorial perspective as a basic force in a grounding charge to expose without nostalgia the time of her own young womanhood when the United States was on the cusp of change for African Americans. The result is a text focused on claiming time and space for reconsidering the seminal moments of a private life through the public lens of defining facets in a cultural moment, and a narrative centered on utilizing the temporal and spatial in representing a nascent but transfiguring moment of a people.

Morrison's narrative revolves around Frank and his younger sister Ycidra ("Cee"), who are conjoined as narrative subjects and racial interlocutors for a particular time and place. Their surname, Money, affirms the political in its temporal and spatial link to Emmett Till, the Black boy mutilated and murdered in Money, Mississippi, in 1955. Morrison's epic-like yet minimalist charting is masculinist in reiterating the necessity of returning whole from warring factions without and within. Frank returns stateside after serving in Korea and, belatedly, makes his way home to Georgia where Cee's life is imperiled. Frank literally goes to ground as a self-described "barefoot escapee from the nut house," whose hiding while traveling evokes the Underground Railroad (Morrison, *Home* 11). His outward but covert journey from the Northwest to the Midwest to the South not only maps his determined quest to reach home and provide safety for Cee, but also fosters his inner journey to make peace with his past, including the formative trauma of being displaced as a child from his home, and his present, particularly his own culpability in a limited existence. Frank travels into that less-visible landscape with self-deceptive excuses and unreliable cartography.

Cee experiences the world differently from Frank. Hers is the more subdued feminist return plotting. As a Black woman confined largely to the domestic sphere in the segregated South, Cee's options for gaining experience and balance seem tied to the will and protection of men. She self-describes as one "so ignorant living in a no-count, not-even-a-town place with only chores, church-school, and nothing else" (*Home* 47). Her vulnerability, especially her meek acquiescence to authority figures, lands her in a near-death circumstance from which she must return home in order to heal and survive. Her physical extrication depends upon Frank and others, but her emotional and psychological freeing comes from her going to ground back in Lotus to discover her own inner resources and strength. Cee travels the shorter physical distance in returning home from Atlanta but a greater distance in inward growth and development into a self-aware, mature womanhood, emotionally and potentially economically free.

Frank and Cee's combined narratives emerge as a political text in which Morrison reconstructs "the narrative of the country" that she believed had been hidden in insistent, romanticized images of a happy, prosperous, wonderful time.[1] Refusing to be seduced by the "fluff" seen in, what she calls, "this Doris Day or *Mad Men*-type of haze," she derails the deceptive work of popular culture in representing a mainstream White world of happiness and prosperity.[2] She does so by restructuring the everyday political and historical contexts of working-class people who happen to be Black. Morrison describes her work in *Home* as "trying to take the scales off the 50s, the general idea of it as very comfortable, happy, nostalgic" (Brockes). With this work, she goes to ground engaging one of the dominant motifs of the 1950s, the house or home as the site of comfort and prosperity that so often cropped up in TV shows, such as *Ossie and Harriet* or *Father Knows Best*. She burrows into the often hidden or overlooked fabric of 1950s life, and she exposes the structures of a segregated society impacting the lived experiences of ordinary Black people before the advancing Civil Rights movement could provoke change. In this sociopolitical endeavor, Morrison attends to the network of power relations holding Frank, Cee, and Black individuals generally in truncated patterns of structural inequality limiting their decision-making capacities and access to satisfying lives, and she does so by utilizing the stylistic traits of mid-century modernism.

The spatial aesthetics of mid-century modernism encapsulate the 1950s and Morrison's compact text. Typically eschewing embellishments and decorative flourishes, mid-century modern design concentrated on organic materials, clean lines, and simple structural elements. Usefulness and function were as significant as form. Minimalist in style and construction, mid-century modernism used sculptured lines in wood furniture and expansive glass windows in constructing houses. The architectural features, such as flat planes, picture windows, and open spaces, highlighted simplicity and synergy with nature. Interior atriums and water features aimed to integrate the indoors with the outdoors by bringing landscaping inside. Architects and builders early on accepted the period's signature building and conceptual designs (Greenberg).

Morrison had begun to use the language of building and construction to designate her work in creative writing well before *Home* appeared. "If I had to live in a racial house," she stated in 1994, "it was, at the least, to *rebuild* it so that it was not a windowless prison into which I was forced, a thick-walled, impenetrable container from which no cry could be heard, but rather an *open house, grounded, yet generous in its supply of windows and doors*. Or, at the most, it became imperative for me to transform this house completely" (Morrison, "Home" 4; emphases added). She speculated how she might deconstruct the racial house. In contemplating rebuilding, she raised questions in the language of architectural building and design: "Could I *redecorate, redesign*, even reconceive the racial house without forfeiting a home of my own? Would life in this

---

[1] Toni Morrison in Conversation with Christopher Bollen, *Interview Magazine*, May 1, 2012.
[2] Toni Morrison in Conversation with Christopher Bollen, *Interview Magazine* May 1, 2012.

renovated house mean eternal homelessness? Would it condemn me to intense bouts of nostalgia for the race-free home I have never had and would never know? Or would it require intolerable circumspection, a self-censoring bond to the locus of racial *architecture*?" ("Home" 4; emphases added). Morrison's 1994 lecture "Home" laid bare not only her approach to "racial construction" but also "a radical distinction between the metaphor of house and the metaphor home" ("Home" 3).[3] Critics, particularly Evelyn Jaffe Schreiber, Linda Wagner-Martin, and Herman Beavers, have grasped the seminal nature of that lecture and its relationship to racial representation in her fiction. Noticeably, Morrison herself places an emphasis on the generative concepts of construction and building in "Home." Her terminology conjoins the art of writing to the act of building, which she subsequently made manifest in her novel *Home*.

There Morrison pursues the spatial aesthetics connected to mid-century modernism while interlocking that aesthetics with political concerns revolving around specific racial issues encumbering Blacks in the 1950s. She takes heed of that period's attention to home construction and built environments and translates it into the longing for a space of physical and psychic safety. After having earlier connected the 1920s "Jazz Age" and its music to the structure of her novel *Jazz*, Morrison turns to the dominant, conceptual 1950s formation of house/home for the construction of *Home*. She chooses the stylistic and structural elements defining the mid-century modern period and links them with the cultural and political phenomena that would accentuate the economic divide between Blacks and Whites in the 1950s and accelerate the modern civil rights movement.

In *Home*, Morrison deploys an unpretentious structure that adheres to the recognizable simplicity of the classical journey-quest narrative with its movement through the natural world, but in her dual attention to a masculine and a feminine version of that narrative, Morrison introduces innovations that have to do with her split focus on a specific temporal and spatial design that has at its center the built structure of domesticity. *Home*, then, set temporally in a period of expanded investment in home building, is spatially located within "a racial house," which is, as Morrison suggests, not a physical structure but an encompassing construction, "a site clear of racist detritus; a place where race both matters and is rendered impotent" ("Home" 7). It is the location that Frank and Cee seek in going to ground, but as raced subjects, they inherit early on the difficulty of finding such a site. Rendered homeless by a racist act of clearing Blacks from their Texas homes and set adrift as vulnerable nomads on the road, Frank understands racial politics: "Better than most, he knew that being outside wasn't necessary for legal or illegal disruption. You could be inside, living in your own house for years, and still, men with or without badges but always with guns could force you, your family, your neighbors to pack up and move—with or without shoes" (*Home* 9). Together with Cee in the quest narrative, he demonstrates what Morrison identifies as the desire for "safety and freedom outside the race house" and the need for "contemporary searches and yearnings for social space that is psychically and physically safe" ("Home" 7).

The construction and style of *Home* references mid-century modernism in the novel's structural dependence on fusing form and function. With no wasted space, an insistent unveiling of the "raced house" functions in the 1950s lives of her two central figures and their immediate associates. Morrison uses identifiable common modernist narrative techniques that are also related to the characteristic properties of mid-century modernism, such as first-person monologue, italicized

---

[3] A reprint of "Home" appears under the title "Race Matters" in Morrison, *The Sources of Self-Regard*, 131–9.

segments for distinguishing narrative shifts, speech out of organic situations, and lack of extensive explanatory segments or restraint from poetic embellishments to language. Morrison's structural emphasis on aligning form and function balances her narrative line with the usefulness of the formal aspects of the journey-quest motif. The darker aspects of the novel evoke the mid-century design aesthetic of darker interiors with low lights, even though large windows open up a view from the interior home to the exterior landscape in which the house was to fit cleanly and naturally into its surroundings.

The larger landscape of Korea, for instance, appears obliquely through the dark lens of the American house. Morrison deploys the contemporary 1950s backdrop of the Korean Conflict and the Korean War (June 25, 1950, to July 27, 1953) in her portrayal of Frank's suffering from posttraumatic stress disorder, from depression, or as he comes to understand his condition, from shame and anger—both intricately related to issues of manhood and expressions of masculinity against the backdrop of war abroad on the global scale in Asia on the Korean peninsula, and at home on the racial front in the Northwest, Midwest, and South. In Korea and its battlefields during the "police action," Frank witnessed the deaths of his childhood friends and his combat victims, including a Korean girl scavenging for food whom he shoots but suppresses the memory by reconfiguring it as the work of another of the soldiers guarding their compound. Here the work of guarding the inside space and keeping the outliers at bay reflects the segregationist housing model that developed in the United States in the 1950s. Morrison expands the sources of Frank's disorder back into his four-year-old self when he fled with his family from Bandera County, Texas, after being given twenty-four hours to get out; his focus is on shoes with flapping soles in that childhood move, which echoes his shoeless escape from the mental hospital after leaving the Army. Morrison relates the dangerous and unsafe outdoors to internality, the interior state of a human being traumatized from childhood. Along with this trauma, the dehumanizing aspect of killing combatants and civilians looms over Frank as "free-floating rage, the self-loathing disguised as somebody else's fault," and he cannot undo the scenes of his childhood friends dying in battle (*Home* 15). His sanity is imperiled by "the memories that had ripened at Fort Lawton," not merely those of the ravishes of war but also those of his terror-scared childhood. Morrison's connection of the two emphasizes the kinship between war in a foreign land on foreigners and war in a homeplace on Blacks, who become foreigners in their own land having to flee persecution and death only to arrive at another destination in which they cannot be absorbed into a wholistic community but are segregated into one that can at any moment scapegoat their difference into a target for racial violence.

In portraying Frank's suffering, Morrison explores the treatment of young soldiers, whether deployed in Korea, Vietnam, Iraq, or Afghanistan, as fodder in war and forgotten at home (Cline). While building on the emotional and physical landscape of mid-twentieth-century America and collapsing into it the narrative of a soldier's struggles at home, she forecasts the extraterritorial international investments that would transform American political infrastructure in significant ways. She interweaves into her narrative an awareness of broad-on-the-ground issues related to war-torn Korea, the North and the South: families reduced in their humanity because of war, and Mongolians sacrificing all in the hope of having allies against China. Morrison sees the emerging terrain of multilaterally linked industrial, military, capital, and intellectual complexes forming the modern world in a foundational period. She recognizes the later shifting of allies and allegiances and the ensuing mobility of large populations worldwide in search of safety, security, and protection from persecution, war, genocide, or famine.

In balancing form and function, Morrison concentrates on the indoors in relationship to the outdoors at home. The correspondence between the outside of the natural world and the inside of constructed edifices is part of Morrison's effort to expose the workings of "the racial house." Indoors and its varied built structures reverberate with the interiority of the self, while outdoors signifies the searches for spaces of safety and environmental protection presumed to be afforded by the natural world. Frank's travel across country allows Morrison to bring in interrelated racial issues from the outside in and the inside out. Using the modern visuality of a picture window enables views both into Frank's mental state and internality and outward into the landscape. Frank looks out from the Greyhound bus: "From the windows, through the fur of snow, the landscape became more melancholy when the sun successfully brightened the quiet trees, unable to speak without their leaves … Against the black and white of that winter landscape, blood red took center stage. They never went away these pictures" (*Home* 19–20). Frank sees the recurring pictures of the bloody deaths of his friends: "a boy pushing his entrails back in, holding them in his palms … or … a boy with only the bottom half of his face intact, the lips calling mama. And he was stepping over them … to keep his own face from dissolving, his own colorful guts under that oh-so-thin sheet of flesh" (*Home* 20).

In a linear opening out to wider society, the picture window aesthetic allows for an emblematic, panoramic projection from the inside out. It enables the natural world, the outdoors to come into view from the inside. That outdoors is the exterior outside of nature and the nature of the 1950s raced world, which is as treacherous and rife with racism as are interior spaces. The symbolic view from the metaphorical window devolves into traumatic scenes: a Black man being beaten outside a train, a Black boy playing with a toy gun shot by police, "dogfights" to death of actual Black men, or a lynching and burial of Black bodies. The racially motivated beating of a Black man for simply trying to buy refreshments at a train stop is visible through the train's window. It is the impetus for an interior reflection of shame—the man's for being beaten and for his wife's trying to protect him, as well as for Frank's as a vulnerable Black man who can only internalize the incident with scenes of his own inability to protect his sister at home or his homeboy friends in battle. Rather than focusing on the Whites who administer the beating, Morrison hones in on the repercussions for the Black participants and observers. Frank projects onto the couple a volatile scenario in which the man will take out his helplessness and humiliation later in beating his wife. The incident recalls Frank approaching a Chevron station, but after seeing the sign on the door, turning away to relieve himself in the bushes outside. The wording that Frank reads is not included, but the context makes it clear that it was some form of "Whites Only," prohibiting Blacks, like Frank, from entering.

Home opens and concludes in the outdoors with home as referent, but the text moves in dual directions toward the interior mind/body and toward home as a physical structure of the body itself. The opening chapter depicts the children Frank and Cee's arrival home, late but unnoticed by their parents. In the last chapter, only the anticipatory announcement of their grown-up movement toward home occurs in Cee's italicized final words: "*Come on, brother. Let's go home*" (*Home* 147). The beginning and ending encode the narrative focus on responses to the outside and its relation to the inside. Graves and burials link the opening and closure, but death and terror do not deter the siblings from desiring a life free from the debilitating incursion of racism, as Frank does in the poetic final segment: "*I stood there a long while, staring at that tree./It looked so strong/So beautiful./Hurt right down the middle/But alive and well*" (*Home* 147; emphases in original).

Structured like the mid-century modern split-level house, which incorporated a few steps leading either up or down to separate rooms or sections of the house, Morrison's narrative divides not only between attention to Frank and Cee, but also between Frank's telling and remembering directed at the reader and his conversing with an unidentified figure who is charged with telling and writing Frank's story. The beginning italicized chapter opens in the outdoors with Frank (the narrator) and Cee crawling on their bellies through high grass when they witness two horses fighting for dominance and "*the winner lop[ing] off in an arc, nudging the mares before him*" (*Home* 4; emphases in original). The children are initially represented as hiding on grounds where they are not safe. They witness the harrowing sight of a Black man struggling to live but being "*whacked*" into a grave by men whose faces they cannot see. The men forcing an alive Black body into a grave are only visible as trousers, as less than a whole, as faceless, identity-less pieces. Morrison evokes the raced house but refuses the master's hand and the White gaze by reducing Whiteness to bodily parts, so that the presumed White men become equivalent to the visible extremities of the Black man they are burying. In objectifying the trousers like the shovel used to beat the Black legs and feet into the grave, Morrison diminishes the power and potential of supposedly strong, whole White men and reduces their faceless humanity to the thingness of the shovel, which nevertheless still performs its deadly purpose.

The lurking threat in the outdoors goes undiminished, and it filters into the indoors space of home. After witnessing the violence, Frank and Cee reach home late and avoid a whipping by being unnoticed by the terrorized grown-ups: "*Some disturbance had their attention*" (*Home* 5, emphasis in original). Although occurring outside, racial violence impacts the inside workings of the home.

The chapter ends in the doubly interior, the family's house and Frank's mind. Frank shifts his first-person account to a narrative voice directed toward someone specific: "*Since you're set on telling my story, whatever you think and whatever you write down, know this: I really forgot about the burial. I only remembered the horses. They were so beautiful, So brutal. And they stood like men*" (*Home* 5; emphases in original). Frank speaks to one telling and writing his story. He speaks as "memory's voice," which Kevin Everod Quashie identifies as follows: "Achieved through the invention and reclamation of stories and bodies, memory's voice always points attention to the self … It is an intricate voice, one that becomes a subject's voice as well as the subject of voice" (Quashie 113). Frank's memory's voice and to a less noticeable extent Cee's operate on two levels of the inside and outside, balancing form and function expected in the structural and technical designs of mid-century modernism. Frank's conversations may also be read as Morrison's construction of a dialogic novel with the talking taking place between parts of Frank's self that would be inaccessible in a realistic novel. But, in representing interiority and exteriority, Morrison does more than fabricate a dialogic; she also disassembles and dismantles so that the components that have contributed to the making of Frank's or Cee's pain-filled memory's voice and the racial house cannot withstand the oral or textual illumination of their past and present mechanizations.

Morrison's layered split-level opening with attention to the exterior and outdoors and interiors and indoors establishes the larger patterning of the text. Her narrative technique of having Frank talk to someone who is writing his story serves two purposes: reflection and projection. By means of reflection, sociopolitical history that is personal, individual, and subjective can enter the text. It associates the fictional form with oral history, memoir, and autobiography, as well as with testimonial. As refection, it embodies the rupture of time and space within the mental state of one human being who becomes a modern racial everyman in his body and mind implosion and his inner search. It displays Frank's seeking of wholeness as he disintegrates incrementally all the while trying to travel back physically and return in memory to the site of the trauma that enfolds his present in tortured visions of the past. Reflection is also a way of accessing that past and making relevant the political references of which Frank is not fully aware.

Frank's journey across country, for example, takes him metaphorically through passage on the Underground Railroad and its conductors. The inferences encompass nineteenth-century African American history and escape from enslavement, but they also overtly reference the twentieth-century phenomenon of facilitating travel for Blacks during the age of segregation. Given shelter, food, clothes, and money at the onset of his escape, Frank receives the protection of racial insider information when church ministers acting as conductors give him the secrets of how to manage his transport away from the dangers of the mental hospital or the local jail. In the A. M. E. Zion church, Reverend John Locke and his wife Jean attend to Frank's freezing and starving body and relay the means to continue his escape: enough money for a Greyhound bus ticket to Portland, and the name and address of Reverend Jessie Maynard at a large Baptist church where he would be aided further. Locke, aptly named for the Enlightenment philosopher who believed that human beings were endowed with natural rights to life, liberty, and property, treats Frank with respect in his home. Maynard, however, repulsed by Frank's appearance, does not allow him inside. An underground conductor, nevertheless, "Reverend Maynard gave [Frank] helpful information for his journey. From Green's travelers' book he copied out some addresses and names of rooming houses, hotels where he would not be turned away" (*Home* 22–3). *The Green Book*, a guide to places where Black people could stay while traveling and where they might eat, was officially *The Negro Motorist Green Book*, published in 1936 by Victor Green, a postal worker. It became better known by scholars after the publication of Cotton Seiler's essay, "'So That We as a Race Might Have Something Authentic to Travel By': African American Automobility and Cold-War Liberalism" (2008), with its African American *Travelguide* illustrations and by majority audiences following the 2018 appearance of the popular film *The Green Book*.[4] More recently, Gretchen Sorin (*Driving While Black*) and Mia Bay (*Traveling Black*) have recounted the history of traveling while Black.

In addition to reflection, projection enables a wider audience with present and future awareness to enter into an exchange with the text. Projection provides Frank with implications in the longer lens of "telling" his story with comparable other lives cohering in framing a pattern. This double-voiced narrative technique accentuates the dialogic structure of the exchanges between Frank's narration and that of an omniscient narrator whom Herman Beavers identifies as possibly the author Morrison herself addressing the nature of writing (Beavers 210). It also functions to underscore the suggestions of magical realism projected into seemingly ordinary situations. The primary example is the elusive apparition of a small man in a wide-brimmed hat and distinctively dressed: "His pale blue suit sported a long jacket and balloon trousers. His shoes were white with unnaturally pointed toes" (*Home* 27). Morrison clearly identifies him as a Zoot-suiter, a substantive 1940s figure, whose unmistakable racialized style flaunted authority, dehumanization, and invisibility, and whose physical presence was a tangible signifier of Black hyper-visibility and potential activism,

---

[4]Cotton Seiler attends to driving as a symbol of freedom and agency fraught with racist restrictions for Blacks in "So That We Might Have Something Authentic to Travel By," 1091–117; and in *A Republic of Drivers*.

especially in a politically charged time (Mazón and Alvarez).[5] However, she also renders him an unreal phantasm appearing magically out of nowhere and disappearing without a trace in three separate moments: inside the train Frank takes on his journey home; inside the Chicago apartment where Frank breaks his trip; and in the outdoors after Frank and Cee bury the bones of the lynched man whose murder they had witnessed as children. It is Cee, and not Frank, who sees the Zoot-suiter in his third and final appearance grinning and swinging his watch chain. Symbolically, his spectral presence conjoins the inside and outside, the interiority and exteriority of the text, and acknowledges the politically transitional and personally freeing moment of the concluding chapter.

Projection is, as well, a way of enabling readers to catapult into the future and associate Frank's and Cee's stories with what is to come. Cee, for example, observes in her time and place the difference between Lotus and Jeffrey, the White town, and she recognizes that had she been allowed to attend the White school in Jeffrey, since Lotus had no school, her life would have been quite different:

> Jeffrey had sidewalks, running water, stores, a post office, a bank and a school. Lotus was separate, with no sidewalks or indoor plumbing, just fifty or so houses and two churches, one of which churchwomen use for teaching reading and arithmetic. Cee thought it would have been better if there were more books to read—not just *Aesop's Fables* and a book of Bible passages for young people—and much much better if she had been permitted to attend the school in Jeffrey. (46–7)

Morrison authorizes readers not only to agree with Cee that with schooling "she would have known better" than to run off with a rat (47), but also to project beyond her immediate condition to the impending change—*Brown v. Board of Education* (1954) and the Supreme Court's unanimous decision declaring unconstitutional racial segregation in the public schools, and *Brown v. Board II* (1955) that followed up the initial decision by the Warren Court with the now infamous "all deliberate speed" that gave rise to all manner of foot-dragging by Southern States and White Citizen Councils. With Cee's commentary, Morrison challenges "separate but equal" by utilizing the difference in facilities and opportunity and subsequent delays in amelioration to project the long-term, whole-life impact of the workings of racial segregation and discrimination.

More directly than with 1950s educational disparities, Morrison taps into the motif of houses and homes and the politics of building and creating new livable communities in the 1950s that changed the way individuals lived or dreamed of living. She locates her text within the exaggerated possibility and paradox of a transformative period that was a critical turning point in American culture, with contradictory aspects of conformity and rebellion, opportunity and stasis operating together (Johns).[6] She registers the disparities in housing conditions for poor, working-class Blacks in urban and rural settings. The diners at Booker's in Chicago laugh knowingly about their housing deprivations: "Me and my brother slept in a freight car for a month … You ever sleep in a coop the chickens wouldn't enter? Aw, man shut up. We lived in an ice house … I slept on so many floors

---

[5]The Zoot Suiter is a political reminder of the 1940s and the Second World War period when White sailors in California awaiting shipping out for combat duty attacked Mexican-American men mainly but also Filipinos and African Americans wearing the distinctive suits and initiated their labeling as un-American, pro-Nazi, and Communist.

[6]Johns brings together period photographs, songs, and newspaper and magazine articles along with interviews and novels to examine major cities, their downtowns, neighborhoods, and suburbs during this transformative period.

first time I saw a bed I thought it was a coffin" (*Home* 28–9). The speakers, all tenacious survivors, manifest suppressed desires for a better life with adequate housing. In Lotus, Lenore, the Moneys' grandfather's wife, resented having her small house invaded by "Pap, Mama, Uncle Frank, and two children ... Over the years the discomfort of the crowded house increased," with worsened sleeping conditions: "Cee slept with her parents on the floor, on a thin pallet hardly better than the pine slats underneath Uncle Frank used two chairs together; young Frank slept on the back porch, on the slanty wooden swing, even when it rained" (*Home* 44–5). In contrast, the Atlanta home of Dr. and Mrs. Beauregard Scott in a "beautiful quiet neighborhood" was "a large two-story house rising above a church-neat lawn" with "a living room that seemed to [Cee] more beautiful than a movie theater. Cool air, plum-colored velvet furniture, filtered light through heavy lace curtains" (*Home* 58–9).

Morrison strips the beautiful veneer from the Scott house by presenting the horrific medical abuse Cee suffered there. She assails the history of medical experimentation on Black bodies and debunks notions of the ethical and humane in that science. Cee undergoes life-threatening gynecological experiments at the hands of Dr. Beauregard Scott, who got "so interested in wombs in general, constructing instruments to see farther and farther into them. Improving the speculum" (*Home* 113). Medical experimentation on Black bodies began during slavery, continued through emancipation, and flourished with the rise of the medical profession in the last half of the nineteenth century as Harriet Washington chronicles (*Medical Apartheid*). Morrison channels the nineteenth-century physician James Marion Sims, the "father of modern gynecology," who developed the modern speculum by experimenting between 1845 and 1849 on enslaved Black women in order to find a cure for vesicovaginal fistula (Cooper Owens). Sims did not use anesthesia, even though it was available (Kapsalis 263–300). He became the leading authority on gynecological surgery and founded the New York Women's Hospital where he performed his operations on White women and headed the American Medical Association from 1876 to 1877 (Kuhn McGregor). Not until the 1990s did medical professionals and scholars begin to interrogate his experiments on enslaved women and raise ethical questions about his being honored with statues in major cities. Only in 2018 did New York remove his fourteen-foot marble statue from Central Park.

In delineating the unethical experimentation that nearly killed Cee, Morrison also infers more recent accounts of the appropriation of a Black woman's body for medical research, such as the highly publicized 2010 book *The Immortal Life of Henrietta Lacks* by Rebecca Skloot. Born in 1920, Henrietta Lacks died of cervical cancer in 1951 at the Johns Hopkins Hospital where during a biopsy her cells were collected without her knowledge. Those cells, known as the HeLa cell line, formed the first immortalized cell line that could be reproduced indefinitely under specific conditions and became one of the most important tools in medical research and instrumental in developing the polio vaccine, cloning, gene mapping, in vitro fertilization, and more (Skloot). Like Lacks, Cee is unknowingly a victim of medical exploitation in which the Black woman's body is not her own. The Lotus women, trying to heal Cee, show their scorn for what they term "the medical industry": "You ain't a mule to be pulling some evil doctor's wagon." (*Home* 122). These women, in contrast to Dr. Scott and his house of horrors, take Cee into a house that becomes a place of physical healing and emotional nurturance.

While Morrison does not elaborate on the economic causes of such stark differences between the houses occupied by Blacks and Whites, she chooses the temporal frame that would entail those causes. She draws upon the signal moment after the Second World War, when political, economic, and social changes characterized the United States as cities expanded and suburbs grew. A major aspect of the expansion involved newly built houses being purchased by Second World War veterans under the Servicemen's Readjustment Act. Known as the GI Bill, that act provided benefits to some sixteen million returning veterans, and gave 6.4 million demobilized soldiers the opportunity to further their education, to borrow money for businesses or farms, and to take out low-cost, zero-down home mortgages (Boucher). Road and highway building projects propelled and encouraged the movement into previously difficult to reach areas outside of urban centers. Increased manufacture of automobiles also facilitated the expansion of homes and businesses into once rural spaces. New loan types and federal home-buying assistance programs whetted appetites for home ownership and made the dream of ownership possible. The extended market for houses fueled new manufacturing processes and technologies to meet the building demand. With faster production times and abundant man-made materials, such as fiberglass, aluminum, and plywood, the housing industry flourished alongside furniture making and home décor in this boom period.

Home ownership became a reality with the development of affordable suburbs along with new ways of living within the home, especially the new Ranch house style and the new convenient appliances, gadgets, and décor, all designed for living the good life. Suburbs grew by 47% in the 1950s, with some twenty million people moving to suburbia. Carefully designed, planned communities modeled on Levittown, Pennsylvania (1947), with its manufactured houses, manicured gardens, and meticulous rules, developed nationwide (Sobel). The United States was changing rapidly and progressively elevating the quality of American life, but not for Americans of color. The problematical underside of the booming postwar economy and housing market was that non-white Americans were mainly excluded from the accessibility of the America Dream. Levittown, for example, with 70,000 residents was mandated as all White and continued, despite legal challenges, to practice racial exclusion. With the growth of similar constructions and new loan mechanisms, the discriminatory exclusion of Black people surged as aggressively fast as the marketplace (Glotzer).

Blacks nonetheless dreamed of homeownership as Lorraine Hansberry depicted in her play *A Raisin in the Sun* (1959). For many Blacks, like Hansberry's Younger family, existing largely outside the bubble of prosperity and success, it was an era of a "dream deferred," as Langston Hughes wrote in *Montage of a Dream Deferred* (1951) and its celebrated poem "Harlem," better known by its first line "What Happens to a Dream Deferred?" Frank understands that deferral all too well in summarizing his spatial reality: "*Nothing to do but mindless work in fields you didn't own, couldn't own, and wouldn't own if you had any other choice*":

> *Lotus, Georgia, is the worst place in the world, worse than any battlefield. At least on the field there is a goal, excitement, daring, and some chance of winning along with many chances of losing ...*
> *In Lotus you did know in advance since there was no future, just long stretches of killing time. There was no goal other than breathing, nothing to win and, save for somebody else's quiet death, nothing to survive or worth surviving for.* (*Home* 83; emphases in original)

Morrison provides a sample of discrimination in housing, real estate, and mortgages that helped to secure a segregated America from the 1950s onward in a Black woman's attempt to purchase a house in Seattle. Lily, with whom Frank had found love after his release from the Army, finds "an advertisement for a lovely [house] for five thousand dollars" and decides "she would happily commute from so nice a neighborhood" to her job at a dry cleaner's: "The stares she had gotten as she strolled the neighborhood didn't trouble her, since she knew how neatly dressed she was and how perfect her straightened hair" (*Home* 73). Lily confronts a restrictive covenant with unequivocal wording that specifically excluded Blacks and other named groups from buying or even renting property in particular neighborhoods: "No part of said property hereby conveyed shall ever be used or occupied by any Hebrew or by any person of the Ethiopian, Malay or Asiatic race excepting only employees in domestic service." (*Home* 73; emphases in original). Morrison takes a page directly from local housing history as the Boeing Company insisted on such exclusionary covenants in all of its properties in Seattle at the time. She implies the longer history of segregated housing and the political struggle against legal segregation and discrimination in housing for which the US Supreme Court set the stage in 1922 by declaring restrictive covenants legal. Persistent challenges to "redlining," the efforts by mortgage lenders and property owners to retain all-white areas, continued in the courts for decades. Morrison uses the backdrop of 1940s legal cases to sketch Lily's thwarted effort to purchase a home.

The Supreme Court, for example, ruled in *Hansberry v. Lee*, a 1940 Chicago case, that since 95% of the residents had not signed a restrictive covenant, it was not effective. The decision meant that the plaintiff Lorraine Hansberry's father Carl could not win a ruling on whether such covenants were legal. In 1948, the Supreme Court in *Shelley v. Kraemer*, a St. Louis case, determined that under the Equal Protection Clause of the Fourteenth Amendment, racially restrictive covenants are prohibited and are unenforceable in court; however, the justices found that racially based restrictive housing covenants are not themselves unconstitutional. Their decision led to the practice continuing by custom through the 1960s, especially within the Federal Housing Administration, which maintained covenants that supposedly were to "provide the surest protection against undesirable encroachments and inharmonious use" (see Federal Housing Authority).

In focusing her narrative lens on Lily's experience with housing, Morrison incorporates the tense politics of the period. She recalls playwright Albert Maltz, one of the Hollywood 10 who refused to testify at Senator Joseph McCarthy's congressional hearings on their involvement with the American Communist Party and as a result were jailed in 1950. Morrison uses the inability of the Skylight Studio, where Lily worked, to get permission to perform the play in rehearsal, Maltz's *The Morrison Case* (1952), as a way of threading in McCarthy-era repressiveness. Picketing and visiting government agents closed down Skylight's previous play and led to the director's arrest and the theater's shutting. Those events highlight the everyday repercussions in ordinary non-activist, apolitical lives as Lily loses her job and resorts to employment for less pay at Wang's Heavenly Palace, a dry cleaning establishment.

Morrison underscores the collaboration of repressive politics and housing discrimination with inclusions of tangential references to Levittown and its influence in maintaining white-only communities. In 1955, when federal agencies denied six Black veterans mortgages to purchase Levittown homes while approving white veterans to finance purchases there, the NAACP, with Thurgood Marshall representing the plaintiffs, sued. The Philadelphia court dismissed the case, ruling that federal agencies were not responsible for preventing discrimination in housing. In 1957, a Black family succeeded in buying a Levittown house from an individual owner, a situation the Levitt family could not control. Because the seller was both Jewish and a Communist, the Levitts and Senator McCarthy labeled all housing activists seeking to end racial discrimination in Levittown or nationwide as Communists, Socialists, and anti-American or un-American (Kushner).

The Levitts also joined McCarthy in branding all-white communities as American and any public housing project not maintaining segregation as Communist.

Compressing the long history of restrictive covenants into the brief depiction of Lily's effort to become a home owner, Morrison illustrates her argument that "dreams of home are frequently as raced themselves as the originating racial house that has defined them. When they are not raced, they are ... landscape, never inscape; utopia, never home" ("Home" 10). Lily equates home ownership with individual identity and success. When she finds a purse of money, she takes it as a sign to renew her faith in purchasing a home, the American dream that had been sidetracked by Frank's presence in relieving her loneliness. She finds "a sliver of freedom, of earned solitude, of choosing the wall she wanted to break through, minus the burden of shouldering a tilted man. Unobstructed and undistracted, she could get serious and develop a plan to match her ambition and succeed" (*Home* 80). Lily embodies the yearning for spatial freedom and safety that she had learned to associate with the security of home ownership.

In her structural design and thematic messages with the attention to the politics of race, however, Morrison underscores that home ownership in itself is not the answer to bodily integrity. She shows how Black people during the 1950s survived as fully human beings within the everyday of racial structures, including physical encroachments that can result in mental trauma. The Lotus residents face their harsh reality with resilience and determination:

> Cee remembered that one of Ethel Fordham's sons had been murdered up North in Detroit. Maylene Stone had one working eye, the other having been pierced at the sawmill by a wood chip. No doctor was available or summoned. Both Hanna Rayburn and Clover Reid, lame from polio, had joined their brothers and husbands hauling lumber to their storm-damaged church. Some evil, they believed, was incorrigible, so its demise was best left to the Lord. Other kinds could be mitigated. The point was to know the difference. (*Home* 123–4)

While making clear that there is no guaranteed refuge from suffering in the North, and that neither illness nor injury rendered the individual exempt from the ravages of racism, the description turns on the collective wisdom of knowing how to live mitigating harmful forces when they can and relying on faith to overcome the rest.

The Lotus characters do not survive in superhuman ways or by means of extraordinary powers, and they are not projected into speculative futures. As in other characters of Morrison's novels, their reliance is on self and community, especially the community of women, though Morison does not paint that community as politically progressive. She instead portrays it as just trying to get by, to live another day. The Lotus women

> took responsibility for their lives and for whatever, whoever else needed them. The absence of common sense irritated but did not surprise them. Laziness was more than intolerable to them; it was inhuman. Whether you were in the field, the house, your own backyard, you had to be busy. Sleep was not for dreaming; it was for gathering strength for the coming day. (*Home* 123)

That commitment to doing meant that "they did not want to meet their Maker and have to explain a wasteful life. They knew He would ask each one of them one question: 'What have you done?'" (123). Their communal work motion, undergirded by a belief in God, makes apparent the bodily integrity in everyday resistance to structures of power in the lives of Black people whose practical traits enable them to figure out how to live and not die in their often debilitating circumstances.

Their pragmatic philosophy of hands-on "doing" also permeates Cee's and Frank's healing in the final pages of the novel. The narrative ends just as it begins in the outdoors, the externality to either the domicile of the body or of the mind. There the subject of manhood raised in the opening with horses that *"rose up like men ... Like men they stood"* (*Home* 3; emphases in original) and in Frank's questions about what constitutes manhood resonate ultimately with Cee's coming to terms with womanhood and not in the traditional narrative of birth and motherhood, but in coming to accept responsibility for herself, her actions, and her being. Frank accepts responsibility for his own dehumanizing desires in killing the Korean girl child scavenging for food. No longer eschewing blame, he understands what it is to grieve without shame or anger. With Cee, he buries the lynched Black man's bones and, in acknowledgment and kinship, nails up a wooden marker that reads, "Here Stands A Man" (145). Placing the violated Black body into the ground in Cee's handmade quilt is the act that telescopes how far Frank and Cee have come from crawling surreptitiously through the grass. They have gone to ground and emerged standing as mature human beings. These parallel acceptances of feelings, of recognizing absence, basically of affective presence, resonate with the larger claiming of space that acknowledges racial identity and affinity, but rejects the encumbering racial house and its debilitations. The figurative and literal burial of a haunting aspect from the past is a way forward to assessing what it means to live with no illusions about the nature of living Black in a segregated world. Their alive, sensate bodies hold out after assaults and stand determined to do, to act, to keep going and functioning. Cee, rendered infertile, is "not beaten. She could know the truth, accept it, and keep on quilting" (*Home* 131). Frank's despair lifts as he understands

> how he had covered his guilt and shame with big-time mourning for his dead buddies. Day and night he had held on to that suffering because it let him off the hook, kept the Korean child hidden. Now the hook was deep inside his chest and nothing would dislodge it. The best he could hope for was time to work it loose. Meantime there were worthwhile things that needed doing. (*Home* 135)

In the end, Morrison theorizes the body itself as home—host to and domicile of emotions, spaces, feelings, the affective reality that causes dislocations because of its very multiplicity of remembering and experiencing on levels simultaneously occurring at once and not integrated with the emotional nexus of the current state of being. Yet, with creativity, resilience, and integrity, Frank and Cee, like the Lotus community, embody the traits that enable them to keep moving in their regular routines and working against self-destructive elements, those outside and within. Morrison's words, "the interiority of the 'othered,' the personal that is always embedded in the public," are ultimately significant in making clear that "the inwardness of the outside" references those raced individuals who are "othered" yet possess "interiority," and are not therefore empty shells ("Home" 12). Morrison recognizes the necessity of representing the rich interiority of Black individuals and of creating a narrative space in which "racial constructs ... reveal their struts and bolts; their technology and their carapace, so that political action, intellectual thought, and cultural production can be generated" ("Home" 12).

As such, *Home* is radical narrative under the guise of showing while telling the everyday of certain Black lives in the 1950s. It imagines the political contexts shaping the sociocultural aspects of specific lives and reveals how these impinge upon not merely individual contours but also upon understanding "the personal that is always embedded in the public." A novel of radical thought,

Home is a felt response to human experience similar to Morrison's description of "word-work" as a way to make "meaning that secures our difference, our human difference—the way in which we are like no other life" (Morrison, "The Nobel Lecture in Literature").[7] For undertaking this work, she had early on posed conceptual questions: "How to be both free and situated; how to convert a racist house into a race-specific yet nonracist home? How to enunciate race while depriving it of its lethal cling?" (Morrison, "Home" 4). In answer to these questions, her political novel is a trajectory of what it means to be human in a particular time and place and under specific circumstances. It is built on aesthetic and political resolve: an intentional and generative construct to feel empathy, to know mercy, and to seek justice out of a cauldron of emotion, belief, and vision.

WORKS CITED

Alvarez, Luis. *The Power of the Zoot: Youth Culture and Resistance during World War II*. U of California P, 2009.

Bay, Mia. *Traveling Black: A Story of Race and Resistance*. Belknap P, 2021.

Beavers, Herman. *Geography and the Political Imaginary in the Novels of Toni Morrison*. Palgrave Macmillan, 2018.

Boucher, Diane. *The 1950s American Home*. Shire Library Publications, 2013.

Brockes, Emma. "Toni Morrison: 'I Want to Feel What I Feel. Even if It's Not Happiness.'" *The Guardian*, Friday, Apr. 13, 2012.

Cline, David P. *Twice Forgotten: African Americans and the Korean War, an Oral History*. U of North Carolina P, 2022.

Cooper Owens, Deidre. *Medical Bondage: Race, Gender, and the Origins of American Gynecology*. U of Georgia P, 2017.

Everod Quashie, Kevin. *Black Women, Identity, and Cultural Theory: (Un)becoming the Subject*. Rutgers UP, 2004.

Federal Housing Authority. *Underwriting Manual: Underwriting Valuation Procedure under Title II of the National Housing Act*, rev. 1938. U.S. Government Printing Office, 1938.

Glotzer, Paige. *How the Suburbs Were Segregated: Developers and the Business of Exclusionary Housing, 1890–1960*. Columbia UP, 2020.

Greenberg, Cara. *Mid-Century Modernism: Furniture of the 1950s*. 1984, rev. ed. Harmony Books/Crown Publishers, 1995.

Hansberry, Lorraine. *A Raisin in the Sun*. 1958. Vintage, 2004.

Hughes, Langston. *Montage of a Dream Deferred*. Henry Holt, 1951; annotated repr. *The Collected Poems of Langston Hughes*, edited by Arnold Rampersad, Alfred A. Knopf/Vintage Classics, 1995.

Jaffe Schreiber, Evelyn. *Race, Trauma, and Home in the Novels of Toni Morrison*. Louisiana State UP, 2010.

Johns, Michael. *Moment of Grace: The American City in the 1950s*. U of California P, 2003.

Kapsalis, Terri. "Mastering the Female Pelvis: Race and the Tools of Reproduction." *Skin Deep, Spirit Strong: The Black Female Body in American Culture*, edited by Kimberly Wallace-Sanders, U of Michigan P, 2002, pp. 263–300.

Kuhn McGregor, Deborah. *Sexual Surgery and the Origins of Gynecology: J. Marion Sims, His Hospital, and His Patients*. Garland, 1990.

Kushner, David. *Levittown: Two Families One Tycoon, and the Fight for Civil Rights in America's Legendary Suburb*. Walker and Company, 2009.

---

[7] The Nobel Lecture is reprinted in Morrison, *The Source of Self-Regard*, 102–9.

Mazón, Mauricio. *The Zoot-Suit Riots: The Psychology of Symbolic Annihilation*. U of Texas P, 1984.

Morrison, Toni. *Home*. Alfred A. Knopf, 2012.

Morrison, Toni. "Home." *The House That Race Built*, edited by Wahneema Lubiano, Vintage, 1998, p. 4.

Morrison, Toni. "The Nobel Lecture in Literature." *The Source of Self-Regard: Selected Essays, Speeches, and Meditations*. Alfred A. Knopf, 2019, pp. 102–9.

Morrison, Toni. *The Source of Self-Regard: Selected Essays, Speeches, and Meditations*. Alfred A. Knopf, 2019.

Seiler, Cotton. *A Republic of Drivers: A Cultural History of Automobility in America*. U of Chicago P, 2008.

Seiler, Cotton. "'So That We Might Have Something Authentic to Travel By': African American Automobility and Cold-War Liberalism." *American Quarterly*, vol. 58, no. 4, Dec. 2006, pp. 1091–117.

Skloot, Rebecca. *The Immortal Life of Henrietta Lacks*. Crown Publishers, 2010.

Sobel, Robert. *The Great Boom, 1950–2000: How a Generation of Americans Created the World's Most Prosperous Society*. St. Martin's P, 2000.

Sorin, Gretchen. *Driving While Black: African American Travel and the Road to Civil Rights*. Liveright Publishing, 2020.

Wagner-Martin, Linda. "Morrison and the Definitions of *Home*." *Toni Morrison: A Literary Life*. Palgrave Macmillan, 2015, pp. 162–77.

Washington, Harriet A. *Medical Apartheid: The Dark History of Medical Experimentation on Black Americans from Colonial Times to the Present*. Doubleday, 2006.

CHAPTER EIGHTEEN

"Only White Folks Got the Freedom to Hate Home": Strategic Empathy and Expanded Intersectionality since Morrison's *Home*

MARIJANA MIKIĆ AND DEREK C. MAUS

In her 1997 essay "Home," Toni Morrison poses several fundamental questions that guide her literary work: "How to be both free and situated; how to convert a racist house into a race-specific yet nonracist home. How to enunciate race while depriving it of its lethal cling?" (5). These questions are integral to Morrison's own work, but she also entreats other authors to respond to them; a substantial number, including Brit Bennett, Bryan Washington, Kaitlyn Greenidge, and Akwaeke Emezi,[1] have done so. Like Morrison, these younger authors construct storyworlds that both depict and challenge the use of such social emotions as guilt and shame in constituting and perpetuating the arbitrary in- and out-group divisions that are fundamental to racial and spatial forms of constraint.[2] In doing so, they show how resisting oppression provides Black characters, especially Black women, with important possibilities for community-building/home-creation. They also write from an intersectional perspective that more explicitly addresses concurrent issues of sexuality and gender identity, thereby opening further rooms in the "racial house [that] ... troubled [Morrison's] work" (5)

The numerous issues this younger generation raises nevertheless remain "aesthetically and politically unresolved" ("Home" 5) because, as Morrison points out, "narration requires the active

---

[1] This list is in no way intended to be taken as exhaustive, but rather as representative of a set of young Black authors whose published works of fiction have enjoyed significant exposure since 2010. Kacen Callender, P. Djèlí Clark, James Hannaham, N. K. Jemisin, Andrea Hairston, Rivers Solomon, Nisi Shawl, Brandon Taylor, and Jacqueline Woodson are just some of the other twenty-first-century authors whose work could be readily discussed within the context we are using here.
[2] Hogan defines the "fundamental organizing principle of social emotions—that is their partial contingency on group divisions" in the following way: "Part of what it means to characterize someone as an in- or out-group member is that one sets a default value for one's emotional response to that person's emotional expressions—parallel for an in-group member, complementary for an out-group member" (*What* 177).

complicity of a reader willing to step outside established boundaries of the racial imaginary" (8–9). As cocreators of the text, readers imaginatively recreate boundaries based simultaneously on physical space and identity traits in their encounters with these authors' narratives, even as they are compelled to respond empathically and critically to the emotional pain produced by such divisions. Morrison and her successors employ Suzanne Keen's concept of authorial strategic empathy "to direct an emotional transaction through a fictive work" (224). Keen distinguishes further between bounded strategic empathy and ambassadorial strategic empathy; the former "occurs within an in-group, stemming from experiences of mutuality, and leading to feeling with familiar others," while the latter "addresses chosen others with the aim of cultivating their empathy for the in-group, often to a specific end" (224). When authors address *both* in- and out-group readers, Keen contends that the result is an intersectional form of empathizing termed "broadcast strategic empathy" that "calls upon every reader to feel with members of a group, by emphasizing common vulnerabilities and hopes" (215).

The authors considered here all use broadcast strategic empathy to encourage the widest possible audience to critique white geographies of domination and to communicate an alternative geographic imagination that fully values Blackness. Moreover, the younger generation of authors builds on Morrison's class- and gender-conscious intersectional understanding of Black identity by also unequivocally foregrounding queer sexualities and/or transgender identities in ways that resonate with how earlier "black queer texts speak at once *against* the larger culture and—most importantly—*within* the black community … [to] suggest that blackness is not undermined by queerness" (Dunning 7, emphases in original). These younger Black writers follow in Morrison's footsteps, while also seeking to widen their readers' "empathetic circle" (Keen 224).

Not only do Morrison's fictional characters transform the meaning of space and place through individual and communal counter-geographies, but her novels also carve out a literary homeplace in which other writers could imagine and practice both individual and communal forms of freedom. According to E. Frances White, though, that homeplace is severely lacking in its acknowledgment of both the history and the potential of queer Black identities. White praises Morrison for "help[ing] those interested in race turn their attention away from an exclusive and isolated focus on blackness toward the simultaneous construction of whiteness and the interaction between the two" (243). However, White also insists that Morrison "fail[ed] to explore homosexuality more fully" even though "it seems inevitable that the rise of homosexuality as an important category and of homophobia as a central preoccupation is also bound to the history of blackness" (250). White charges Morrison with "limit[ing] our understanding of the complex ways sexuality is used" and laments that "Morrison's heterosexist project leaves a heavy veil in place over this history" (250–1) as a result.

Although White's claims contain substantial merit, we do not draw quite so harsh a conclusion from them. As numerous scholars, including Kathryn Bond Stockton, Juda Bennett, Rebecca Balon, and even White herself have noted, Morrison's work *does* support queer readings in several ways, even if it features comparatively few characters explicitly identified as queer, nonbinary, and transgender. With the tacit influence of the generationally liminal Octavia E. Butler—among others—the twenty-first-century authors considered here have not so much lifted a veil on possible connections between Blackness and LGBTQ+ identities that Morrison "chose … not to pursue" (White 239), but have instead magnified and riffed on the queer implications, complications, and opportunities within the sorts of improvised Black home-spaces that Morrison so regularly depicted in her work.[3]

As an exemplar of Brian Norman's category of "neo-segregation narratives," Morrison's novel *Home* (2012) transports readers to the Jim Crow South of the 1950s in part "to expose systems of exclusion and disenfranchisement today" (Norman 3). Like many of her contemporaries, Morrison returns to the literal and figurative "terrain of compulsory race segregation" (Norman 3), both to remember the racial oppression of the past and to interrogate Jim Crow's lingering legacies. *Home* invites readers to map the racially segregated landscapes of the 1950s in tandem with a protagonist who struggles to locate his "home" cognitively and spatially after returning from the Korean War. Frank Money suffers from posttraumatic stress disorder (PTSD), which causes him to relive past trauma through "abrupt, unregulated memories" (Morrison, *Home* 99). By narrating how racialized landscapes both evoke and intensify Frank's feelings of shame and guilt, Morrison lays bare the destructive psychic consequences of what George Lipsitz calls a "white spatial imaginary" (13) on the psyche of an African American war veteran, while subsequently pointing to the ways in which an alternative Black spatial imaginary liberates him and other characters from otherwise constricting negative emotions. *Home*'s interrogation of race, space, and emotion thus requires readers to simulate the affective repercussions of racialized and spatialized binaries. Simultaneously, however, it invites a worlding of the story and a storying of the world that "is radically open to additional otherness, to a continuing expansion of spatial knowledge" (Soja 61), a characteristic that recurs as later authors push the envelope of this radical open[ness] still further.[4]

Home initially focuses on the guilt that arises from Frank's inability to save his "homeboys" during the war. Psychologist Martin L. Hoffman explains that "survivor guilt" occurs when "one cannot justify and therefore does not deserve the advantage one has over the victim; that one's advantage ... violates the principle of fairness, justice, or reciprocity" (190). Frank's avoidance of his hometown of Lotus, Georgia, because "his easy breath and unscathed self would be an insult" (*Home* 15) to his dead friends' parents suggests another prevailing emotion, though; his behavior corresponds to typical phenomenological responses to shame, including the desire to "hide, disappear, or die" (Lewis 748). The "uglier" emotion of shame overrides his guilt, likely in no small measure because of Frank's knowledge of a heinous act—his murder of a Korean girl— that remains withheld from readers at this point.

Morrison depicts how the emotions that Frank brings home from the war affect his struggle to find belonging in a racially segregated space. Through Frank, she negotiates what Patrick Colm Hogan calls "the boundaries that bear on experiential aspects of bodily and peripersonal space, particularly the boundaries or borders that define self and other" ("Affective" 65). When asked where he is from, Frank answers, "Aw, man. Korea, Kentucky, San Diego, Seattle, Georgia. Name it I'm from it" (*Home* 28). He feels no attachment to any of those places, least of all Lotus, which Frank describes as "the worst place in the world, worse than any battlefield" (83). Growing up

---

[3]It is worth noting that Emezi thanked Morrison for writing novels that provided "me a spell that I am using to become free" (https://www.them.us/story/toni-morrison), and Greenidge and Bennett have likewise cited Morrison as a major influence. Although these writers are undoubtedly moving beyond Morrison's work, they are also clearly not doing so from a corrective or hostile perspective.

[4]David Herman describes narrative engagement as a dynamic two-way process, distinguishing between "worlding the story" as the process by which readers imagine and understand a storyworld and "storying the world" as the process by which readers use a fictional narrative to better understand their own world (15).

with abusive and neglectful grandparents and parents who "were so beat by the time they came home from work, any affection they showed was like a razor—sharp, short, and thin" (53), Frank's negative attachment to his hometown is closely linked to his estranged familial relationships, which is why enlisting in the army becomes his means of escape. Ultimately, though, this choice only substitutes one battlefield for another; whether the battles fought there are literal or metaphorical, such a space is nearly impossible to transform into a stable home.

Frank's only remaining attachment to Lotus is his sister, Cee. He always protected her growing up "as they navigated the silence and tried to imagine a future" (*Home* 53). Therefore, Frank returns to Lotus only after receiving an anonymous letter stating that Cee's life is threatened by an unscrupulous gynecologist for whom she works. As Frank considers how to escape from the mental institution in which he has been confined since returning from Korea, he thinks that "maybe that was the reason no Russian-made bullet had blown his head off while everybody else he was close to died over there. Maybe his life had been preserved for Cee, which was only fair since she had been his original caring-for, a selflessness without gain or emotional profit" (34–5). Although his trip home is motivated by saving his beloved sister, it is not entirely selfless; he also hopes to save the picture of himself—"a strong good me" (104)—that lives on inside Cee's mind. Alexa Weik von Mossner asserts that even though "part of our motivations for caring and indeed helping others in distress is ... egoistic," such a recognition "should not devalue the response in any way" (95). Accordingly, rescuing Cee and transferring her into the care of the Black women of Lotus ultimately enables both siblings to envision new ways of addressing their personal and communal traumas.

Before showcasing the restorative potential of a Black spatial imaginary, though, Morrison portrays the negative emotional consequences of an exclusionary white spatial imaginary. As Frank makes his way from Seattle to Georgia, readers join him in using the "Green Book" to "tour" the segregated geographies of the United States of the 1950s. By doing so, readers are invited to simulate his affective experiences of race and space. As she stated in an interview, Morrison "is trying to take the scab off the 50s" (Brockes) partly by revealing the shame that the public displacement of Black bodies evokes in Frank as he "dutifully sat in the last seat [of the Greyhound bus], trying to shrink his six-foot-three-inch body" (*Home* 19). Frank's desire to hide or disappear corresponds closely to the behavioral tendencies associated with shame, and the narrative demonstrates how his shame intensifies as Frank is denigrated by the same country for which he fought.[5] Morrison not only portrays the impact of shame on Black subjects who are routinely forced to view themselves as out of place within essentialist white geographies, but also calls upon her readers to engage empathically with Frank by going "through the shame and disruption of remembering in order to begin to forge relationships that can become communities that can make a difference" (Byerman 10).

As the narrative gradually reveals the roots of Frank's prevailing emotions, readers are repeatedly confronted with unreliable and conflicting information, a process amplified by Frank's frequent first-person intrusions into the generally third-person narration. When Frank initially recalls the

---

[5]Frank's affect in this regard is reminiscent of Tayo, the protagonist of Leslie Marmon Silko's *Ceremony* (1977), who has returned from the Second World War to the Laguna Pueblo reservation of New Mexico. Tayo's readjustment to being "home" again is, of course, further complicated by his mixed racial status, which has marginalized him within both white and Indigenous communities.

death of a Korean girl who is scavenging for food, he tells readers that his relief guard shoots her: "She smiles, reaches for the soldier's crotch, touches it. It surprises him ... he blows her away ... I think the guard felt more than disgust. I think he felt tempted and that is what he had to kill" (*Home* 95–6). Only later does Frank confess that he himself "shot the Korean girl in her face" and that he was "the one she aroused," asking "how could I let her live after she took me down to a place I didn't know was in me?" (134). Frank has previously been relatively easy to empathize with as he struggles to forgive himself, but this new revelation complicates matters by inviting—possibly even demanding—moral disgust. Alongside survivor guilt, Frank has been experiencing what Hoffman calls "transgression guilt," which is caused by "the awareness of harming others" (175). His confession is undoubtedly troubling, but for Frank it signifies an honest reckoning of "how he had covered his guilt and shame with big-time mourning for his dead buddies" (135). Acknowledging the bad in himself—his "bad self" (shame) and his "bad behavior" (guilt)—opens a difficult pathway toward meaningful contrition and, eventually, healing.

Even though Morrison complicates empathic engagement by forcing readers to witness Frank not only as a victim but also as a victimizer, she does so to prevent readers from ignoring the connections between his personal struggles and the broader cultural context. Employing an especially challenging form of Keen's notion of broadcast strategic empathy, Morrison's neo-segregation narrative insists that readers recall the violence of Jim Crow in worlding Frank's and Cee's stories, and thereby acknowledge the legacies of racialized histories and geographies in the storying of their own twenty-first-century worlds. Additionally, Morrison emphasizes the relationship between individual and collective self- and space-making by paralleling Frank's literal and metaphorical journeys toward recovery and release with his sister's process of healing and transformation.

After Frank rescues her from the eugenicist Beauregard Scott (aka, "Dr. Beau"), Cee is nursed back to health by a group of Black women in Lotus whose self- and space-making embodies the inclusive nature of Black geographies; *their* Lotus is something beyond the destructive realm exemplified by Dr. Beau's sadistic experiments on his Black employees. These women not only heal the physical damage inflicted upon Cee, but they also psychologically restore her by attending to lifelong feelings of shame and self-doubt. Being "branded early as an unlovable, barely tolerated 'gutter child' ... [Cee] had agreed with the label and believed herself worthless" (*Home* 128–9). Initially, Cee blames her own putative worthlessness on Lotus's utterly hopeless and confining geographies: "If she hadn't been so ignorant living in a no-count, not-even-a-town place with only chores, church-school, and nothing else to do, she would have known better" (47). Until late in the novel, Lotus represents to Cee what Herman Beavers describes as "tight space" in Morrison's novels: "[It] signals a character's spiritual and emotional estrangement from community and the way it inhibits their ability to sustain a meaningful relationship to place" (6).

Although Cee habitually "blamed being dumb on her lack of schooling," the narration notes "that excuse fell apart the second she thought about the skilled women who had cared for her, healed her" (*Home* 128). Some of them were illiterate and "had to have Bible verses read to them ... [a]nd yet they knew how to repair what an educated bandit doctor had plundered," because their "devotion to Jesus and one another centered them and placed them high above their lot in life" (128). Although their lives are still situated within the segregated landscapes of Jim Crow, they transcend the violence of essentialist space-making by caring for themselves and one another. Correspondingly, self-worth is the first lesson that they teach Cee:

> Look to yourself. You free. Nothing and nobody is obliged to save you but you. Seed your own land. You young and a woman and there's serious limitation in both, but you a person too. Don't let Lenore or some trifling boyfriend and certainly no devil doctor decide who you are. That's slavery. Somewhere inside you is that free person I'm talking about. Locate her and let her do some good in the world. (126)

The women's actions and words profoundly affect Cee, who is no longer willing to allow a "tight space" to define her literal or figurative place in the world. By exemplifying how individual and communal counter-geographies can transform the meaning of space, they teach Cee how to map both freedom *for* herself and freedom *from* shame and self-doubt.

The novel's poetic conclusion is decidedly hopeful as Frank and Cee look at a tree that is "hurt right down the middle" yet still beautiful and strong (*Home* 147). By functioning as a site for Black agency, struggle, and resistance, the novel envisions a productive—if also tenuous—linkage of race, space, and emotion. Morrison emphasizes the value of Black women's liberatory psychology, but their self- and community-making must at the same time be understood as inextricably linked to the ways in which they (locally) transcend rather than overthrow Jim Crow geographies to form more democratic spaces to inhabit.[6] By calling upon her audience to recognize the radical potential of the Black geographic imagination, Morrison highlights that space is never natural or fixed, but that both home and freedom are perpetually in the making.

Octavia E. Butler's fiction is likewise concerned with "questions of concept, of language, of trajectory, of habitation, of occupation" (Morrison, "Home"). Butler famously beseeched Morrison, then an editor at Random House, to help her "escape the science fiction [label]" by publishing her novel *Clay's Ark* (1984). Phoenix Alexander asserts that Butler sought Morrison's assistance in order "to find and build a community of black writers within a genre that would not be as harmful … [to] the concerns (financial, emotional, artistic) that informed her life and work" (Alexander 342). The "archive" of writings that Butler subsequently created before her death in 2006 became "a structure that acts as both shelter and authority, but also as a theoretical space for black women's literature that … emerges as a space in which the prescriptive boundaries of *genre*—both literary genres and genres of the *human*—can be pushed to their theoretical limits and merged to create new and more hospitable forms" (Alexander 343, emphases in original).

Jess S. Bennett deftly theorized the intersectional implication of these "new and more hospitable" forms:

> Across eleven novels and nine short stories, Butler posits that people suffer from the adherence to permanence, such as the heteronormative imperative to maintain fixed gender roles and the marginalization LGBT people experience. The same can be said of racism, as Butler's racist characters resist change through keeping rigid boundaries between themselves and people of other races … When we bring Butler's declarations of curiosity about and literary explorations of identity together with emphasis on the central role of change and necessary adaptability, the

---

[6]*Home* exemplifies what Mitchell calls "making-oneself-at-home," a process that "must be defined and pursued in ways that call upon an authority beyond the nation-state. Its value does not derive from civic inclusion. Many African Americans understand that black people often better embody American ideals than do the straight white men who are the country's archetypal citizens" (23).

result is queerness. Over the span of her work, Butler uses her unique SF aesthetic to explore this queerness as it intersects with discussions of race. (2)

She identifies a concept called "the Butler family ... [that] contests traditional family structures and creates kinship structures that encourage the acceptance of racial difference and queerness" (J. Bennett 23) This idea helps connect the improvisational woman-centered Black communities that Gloria T. Randle and others delineate in Morrison's work with the more radically intersectional social structures found in more recent fiction by Brit Bennett, Bryan Washington, Kaitlyn Greenidge, and Akwaeke Emezi. These authors fuse the "multicultural queerness" of the "Butler family" with the gynocentric Black geographies found in Morrison's fiction. They explore how race intersects with a wide range of identity positionings to express the concerns of diverse Black characters within white supremacist, heteronormative and gender-normative environments. By inviting empathy with queer and trans characters, these novelists challenge normative practices of social exclusion and encourage readers to imagine Black geographies simultaneously as queer and trans geographies.

Brit Bennett's neo-passing novel *The Vanishing Half* (2020) is perhaps the most thoroughly Morrison-esque of the four contemporary novels we have chosen to discuss here. Even though it begins—like *Home*—during the period of legalized segregation, the bulk of its narrative is set in the post–civil rights decades of the twentieth century. Through its initial setting of Mallard, Louisiana—a fictional town established exclusively for light-skinned Black people—*The Vanishing Half* negotiates the dangers of in- and out-group divisions that are pertinent not only to forced legal segregation but also to self-segregation. Mallard's origins are related in the novel's opening pages:

> A town that, like any other, was more idea than place. The idea arrived to Alphonse Decuir in 1848, as he stood in the sugarcane fields he'd inherited from the father who'd once owned him. The father now dead, the now-freed son wished to build something on those acres of land that would last for centuries to come. A town for men like him, who would never be accepted as white but refused to be treated like Negroes. A third place. (5)

This passage's opening sentence evokes Cheryl A. Wall's assertion that home is "a place in the spirit, a place that is necessarily symbolic rather than real" (64). However misguided his attempt may seem to contemporary readers, Mallard's founder aims to give light-skinned Black Americans a rightful sense of place they are denied by the strict, if also superficial, racial divisions of segregated American geographies. In outlining the foundational idea behind Mallard, Bennett reveals how systematic intermarriages between light-skinned Black Americans not only render dark bodies placeless, but how they also make "segregation seem desirable, natural, necessary, and inevitable" (Lipsitz 15).

Amid these geographies of colorism, readers are introduced to the founder's great-great-great-granddaughters, a pair of identical twins named Stella and Desiree Vignes. Growing up in Mallard in the 1950s, the twins feel "trapped by [Mallard's] smallness" (B. Bennett 8) and escape as teenagers to New Orleans, where they work and live together until Stella abruptly disappears from her sister's life. The remainder of the novel recounts how the twins' separate lives—and their daughters' lives—unfold. Having abandoned her abusive husband, Desiree returns to Mallard after fourteen years accompanied by her dark-skinned daughter Jude. Ironically, the husband she escapes from captures the sentiment that accompanies Desiree's return to the home she once could not wait to leave behind: "Negroes always love our hometowns ... [e]ven though we're always from the worst places. Only white folks got the freedom to hate home" (21). Stella, though, is passing for white and living a life of comfort in a gated and wealthy white community in Los Angeles with her boss-turned-husband, Blake Sanders, and their daughter Kennedy. Even though Bennett implicates Stella in the reproduction of white geographies, she avoids turning her into a "tragic mulatta" and punishing her act of passing for what the country's racial logic insists she is not. Instead, Bennett uses Stella's position to negotiate the affective violence of racial and spatial boundaries and entreats all her readers, as cocreators of the text, to reject parochial boundaries in favor of empathic solidarity and inclusion.

Alongside her reimagination of racial passing, Bennett also explores intersections among race, gender, and queer sexualities. Whereas the lightness of Stella's skin enables her to fit in at the cost of largely reinforcing the segregated spatial logic that previously excluded her, the story line revolving around Desiree's daughter, Jude, suggests that solidarity across difference can fashion new ways of belonging. This latter plotline not only refutes the shame imposed on Jude as a dark-skinned Black person in Mallard, but it also demonstrates how inclusive practices of communal space-making pave the way to Jude's emotional well-being after going away to college. The emotional wisdom of the Black women in Lotus is central to Frank and Cee's healing process in Morrison's *Home*, and Jude similarly begins to heal as she shows solidarity with, and finds belonging in, a trans and drag community in Los Angeles, far from Mallard's color-struck parochialism.

Upon leaving Mallard for Los Angeles, Jude soon meets a "golden brown and handsome" (B. Bennett 100) man named Reese Carter at a party and finds herself fascinated with him. Immediately after their first encounter, the novel's omniscient narrator dips into Reese's consciousness to disclose how he, formerly known as Therese Anne Carter, left his old life in El Dorado, Arkansas, behind and adopted a transgender identity as a man. When Reese asks himself "How real was a person if you could shed her in a thousand miles?" (103), it not only reinforces the sense that identity and space are interwoven in terms of both race and gender, but also that the ability to change may necessitate leaving behind a space in which identity is presumed to be fixed by what is externally observable.

When Reese first reveals his transgender identity to Jude and asks her what she thinks about it, she answers, "I don't know … I've never heard anything like it" (B. Bennett 105). The narrator reveals what she does not speak aloud: "She'd always known that it was possible to be two different people in one lifetime" (105). Jude readily empathizes with Reese by drawing parallels to transitional experiences of racial identity with which she is familiar, albeit indirectly. Bennett's narrative invites Black, non-Black, cisgender, and transgender readers alike to empathize with her characters across and beyond familiar in- and out-group divisions. In doing so, she asks readers to appreciate both the painful impact of spaces of exclusion on affective experience and the power of empathy and emotion to transform spaces of exclusion into spaces of belonging.

Both Reese and Jude experience strong self-doubt and shame about their bodies as a result of their struggle to feel at home in the southern spaces they once occupied. At the beginning of their relationship, their respective forms of shame make them want to hide from one another even in the privacy of their shared home. The negative effects of their body-shame begin to unravel, though, as their loving relationship develops and, more importantly, as they become part of a broader community of caring people.

Like the women of Lotus, the community that Jude and Reese discover in Los Angeles is based on a spatial imaginary that, while not exclusively Black or even of color, seeks empowerment by envisioning "identity as the product of interpersonal connections rather than individual differences" (Lipsitz 52):

> The girls had come over. The girls, Barry always said, when he meant the other men who performed alongside him at his drag nights. By spring, Jude had been to enough of Barry's parties to know what everyone looked like without makeup: Luis, who sang Celia Cruz in pink fur, was an accountant; Jamie, who wore a Supremes wig and go-go boots, worked for the power company; Harley transformed himself into Bette Midler—he was a costume designer for a minor theater company and helped the others find their wigs. The girls took Jude in until she felt, almost, like one of them. She'd never belonged to a group of friends before. And they'd only accepted her because of Reese. (B. Bennett 111)

The fact that all of the members of this community accept each other's differences seems to contradict this final thought, itself a vestige of Jude's self-doubt. Reese, after all, is not performing in drag, but is instead a transgender man, and neither Jude's heterosexuality nor her (cis)gender identity seems to be in question. Rather than casting difference as "strangeness," the members of this community collectively reimagine how difference takes place. In so doing, they put forth a counter-geographic imaginary that enables a new kind of affective space free from any shame brought on by double consciousness regarding race, gender, and/or sexuality.

By the end of the novel, Reese has undergone his top surgery and Jude is in medical school in Minnesota. Having broken up and gotten together on numerous occasions previously, they have found stability and trust in their relationship, symbolized by the fact that Reese's aversion to Jude's touch is now directly related to her medical studies rather than to shame: "He always squirmed away when she came home smelling like formaldehyde. He made her shower before kissing him. He never wanted to be touched after the dead people" (328). Although their improvised community has been ravaged by the AIDS crisis, its sense of solidarity remains intact: "There were exes or enemies like Ricardo, known as Yessica, a queen who'd beaten Barry at more balls than he would ever admit. He'd asked to be cremated and Barry had stood along the shore at Manhattan Beach while he was scattered into the ocean" (329).

The explicit association of West Hollywood with a "graveyard" in this context foreshadows the novel's conclusion, as Jude returns with Reese to Mallard for her grandmother's funeral. Jude first recalls the absurd lengths to which Mallard's citizens went to maintain segregation even in death:

> Adele Vignes was buried on the colored side of St. Paul's Cemetery. Nobody expected any different. This was the way it had always been, the white folks in the north side, the colored folks in the south. Nobody complained until the year the eucharistic ministers at the white church that owned the cemetery cleaned tombstones for All Souls Day but only on the north side. When Mallard protested, the deacon did not want a fight, so he dispatched two grumbling altar boys with sloshing buckets to scrub the headstones on the colored side too. Jude almost laughed when her mother had told her—that was the solution, not desegregating the graveyard, just cleaning the headstones on both sides. (342)

As the townspeople gossip at Adele's wake about the "lost daughter" they never accepted, Jude and Reese simultaneously reject Mallard's judgments and reaffirm their togetherness:

> She had slipped out the back door with her boyfriend, holding his hand as they ran through the woods toward the river. The sun was beginning to set, and under the tangerine sky, Reese tugged his undershirt over his head. The sun warmed his chest, still paler than the rest of him. In time, his scars would fade, his skin darkening. She would look at him and forget that there had ever been a time he'd hidden from her. (343)

Whereas *The Vanishing Half* ends with the affirmation of a loving queer bond, Bryan Washington's *Memorial* (2020) begins with an endangered one. The novel is divided into sections set in Houston and Osaka; these are respectively focalized in their narration on Mike and Benson, a long-standing, but troubled gay couple. Benson is an African American who has lived his entire life in greater Houston while Mike is Japanese, though he has lived in the United States since early childhood and has largely assimilated into Houston's ethnically diverse culture. After a brief exposition of the imperiled relationship from Benson's perspective, the novel moves to a peculiar crisis as Mike prepares to depart for Osaka to care for his estranged and dying father just as his mother Mitsuko arrives in Houston from Japan for a visit. Even as Benson and Mike are on the verge of breaking up, Mitsuko and Benson are uncomfortably compelled by circumstance to live together in the couple's apartment in Houston's historically Black Third Ward neighborhood during Mike's indefinite absence. The ensuing bifurcated narrative depicts a series of associations among people of various ages, sexualities, genders, nationalities, races, and ethnicities that challenge a range of assumptions about what constitutes a healthy and loving relationship.

Starting from both an increasingly dysfunctional gay dyad as well as a pair of father-son relationships made toxic by homophobia (among other things), the novel explores unconventional forms of loving connections within a contemporary society that Ben sardonically notes "isn't a best-case country" (Washington 149) for people of color, especially queer ones. Washington hinted at the metaphorical geography of this exploration by noting that he was

> trying to play with the question of what home could be and whether it's possible for any of these characters to settle on an idea of home, and if they don't, whether that dynamism is even a bad thing—if it is a bad thing not to have a home, or to be able to have a home among many different places, or to feel comfortable wherever you are. (Landsbaum)

During their months of physical separation, both Benson and Mike form new attachments that expand their relationship's interracial context. In addition to achieving a food-centered *détente* with Mike's mother that gradually develops into a more accepting intergenerational relationship than the one he has with his own parents, Benson also becomes emotionally and sexually involved with Omar, the older brother of one of the children who attends the aftercare center where Benson works. While trying to navigate the various challenges of caring for his cantankerously bigoted dying father in Osaka, Mike also strikes up a flirtatious, but ultimately nonsexual, friendship with Tan, a Singaporean photographer. A conversation from early in their acquaintance reinforces the novel's recurrent focus on how places, people, and a sense of belonging intertwine. When Mike flatly asserts that "you shouldn't make a home out of other people," Tan challenges him:

> Maybe you've met the wrong people, said Tan. Or you've met the wrong people for you.
> Maybe, I said. But people change. And then you're stuck in whatever your idea of home was.
> There's nothing wrong with that though, said Tan. We all change. We'll all have plenty of homes in this life. It's when you don't that there's an issue. That's settling.

And what's the difference between that and settling into one person?
That's not for me to say. We all live our own lives.
Well, I said. Thanks for nothing. (180)

Mike's cynicism is perhaps understandable given that both his parents have abandoned places he (and they) called home, but this exchange also reveals how it has affected his ability to stay emotionally connected with Benson after four years.

Tan offers him an amended definition of a loving relationship as an emotional home that Mike seems to carry back to Houston after his father's death: "Loving a person means letting them change when they need to. And letting them go when they need to. And that doesn't make them any less of a home. Just maybe not one for you. Or only for a season or two. But that doesn't diminish the love. It just changes forms" (181). Tan and Mike have only a single night's physically erotic (and vague) interaction—"We were two horny men lying on top of each other, not having sex. But we were definitely doing *something*" (210, emphasis in original)—before Mike returns to Houston, but they also quietly leave their relationship unresolved, suggesting that Mike has accepted Tan's mutable definition of love as a home.

Upon returning to Houston, Mike is surprised at the degree Benson and Mitsuko have learned to coexist; he soon thereafter asks to meet Omar during an uncomfortable and long-overdue dinner at which Benson's family and Mitsuko also meet and openly acknowledge their sons' relationship (and, thus, their homosexuality) for the first time. When Mike, Benson, and Omar ultimately meet over hamburgers, their initial interaction is understandably awkward; however, when Omar responds to Mike's self-conscious comment about having gained weight in Japan by stating simply "You're beautiful," his "completely earnest" expression opens up a sense of communal opportunity rather than simply marking a transfer of Benson's affection from one lover to another. Omar's exclamation, "I mean look at us … Isn't this amazing? How we ended up here?" (287) explicitly spatializes this sense of opportunity among these three young queer men of color. Even though *Memorial* leaves the status of all these relationships somewhat up in the air, both of these communal meals evoke a non-speculative-fiction version of a "Butler family" that accepts all its members regardless of their race, nationality, ethnicity, sexuality, or commitment to monogamy.

Beavers claims that Morrison's fiction aims "not to say something different about what it means to be black in the twenty-first century, but to say a different thing altogether about what it means to be human" (20), and this assertion is perhaps ultimately even more true of Kaitlyn Greenidge's debut novel *We Love You, Charlie Freeman* (2016). The novel extends the intertwined exploration of race, gender, sexuality, and even species further, in the process satirically exploding a number of both in-group and out-group discourses that marginalize various types of individuals. It centers on a Black family—the Freemans—that has accepted an invitation to live together with a chimpanzee to whom they will teach sign language as part of an experiment being conducted at the fictional Toneybee Institute for Ape Research in western Massachusetts. The majority of the book's chapters are told through the first-person perspective of the perspicacious elder daughter, Charlotte, who is already going through the "awkward misfortune" (8) of adolescence as her family relocates from Boston to rural—and overwhelmingly white—Courtland County. Other chapters sporadically provide third-person insights about the rest of the Freeman family; still others move backward in time to 1929 to recount the Institute's founding through the first-person perspective of a "thirty-six-year-old orphan" (41) named Nymphadora of Spring City, the insular "colored hamlet" (27) within Courtland County that is nearly as color struck as Mallard.

Nymphadora is marginalized within her own community, which is dominated by a pair of bourgie secret societies—the Saturnites and the Stars of the Morning. These groups' respectability politics both empower and stifle their members, as an oration delivered by Nymphadora's mother shows:

> What makes a Star of the Morning shine, what makes an Infant Star shine among all the other pieces of dust and dirt and rock that are our Lord's creations, is self-control. Denial. Denial builds up inside little Infant Stars like you, makes your moral fiber strong like flint, so that when the world tests you, when the world rubs up against you all vicious and sharp and everything within you, everything is telling you to give in, all you desire is to give in, do you know what happens? You don't give in. You don't become soft. You ignore your desires. The world's trials stir up a light in you so strong, so pure, so true, no man on earth can put it out. (33)

These assertions of indomitability are almost immediately undercut by the revelation that Nymphadora's parents jointly committed suicide out of despair at the financial hardships arising from their desperate attempts to "make [Nymphadora] a presentable bride for a man who never came" (37). Unsurprisingly, Nymphadora's already tenuous connection to the Stars of the Morning frays even further after her parents' self-destruction. Seemingly compensating for this lack of communal connection, Nymphadora soon becomes entangled with the nascent Toneybee Institute through the attentions of its chief scientist, a British anthropologist named Gardner. He takes a personal interest in Nymphadora that masks a much darker professional curiosity rooted in the quasi-scientific racism that underlies the Institute's research into chimpanzees.

The exposure of that deeply racist past gradually validates Charlotte's skepticism about the Institute's ostensible philanthropy, and the ham-fisted "Apology to the African American People" (222) that its founder, Julia Toneybee-Leroy, pens sixty years after its founding only shows how little has changed over that time frame. Charlotte's mother Laurel—whose own obsession with social status and colorist assimilation rivals that of Nymphadora's mother—increasingly turns away from her own children in favor of the needy chimp who has partially usurped her family's identities:

> "They're going to start calling him Charlie," [Laurel] said.
> "They gave him my *name*?" I was disgusted.
> "Only part of your name." My mother was excited. "It's so that he feels comfortable, you know. 'Charlie' fits with Callie and Charlotte." (6, emphasis in original)

The fact that Laurel entirely omits reference to her husband Charles's name here suggests the degree to which she has already begun serving the institute's ethically bankrupt goals rather than her family's well-being. Once Laurel begins surreptitiously breast-feeding Charlie midway through the novel (and simultaneously ignoring the eating disorder that Callie manifests), her seemingly bottomless personal ambition precipitates the Freemans' dissolution as a family unit.

Given that neither the literal space she inhabits as a home (i.e., the Toneybee) nor the figurative home of her nuclear family provide much help to Charlotte in her maturation process, she initially finds a sense of belonging and community in the form of her only Black classmate, toward whom she is initially ambivalent:

> I studied the back of Adia Breitling's head and I prayed that none of these white people would compare her to me ... The whole class, I read the length of Adia Breitling, from the curling ankh to the flop of that heavy skirt, and I thought that I knew her ... To be that beautiful and also that willfully strange did not make sense. It was certainly unfair, almost an insult, I thought. Either way, it meant I could never be friends with her. I was determined to leave strangeness behind at the Toneybee. (115)

Despite this first impression, Charlotte eventually finds herself drawn to Adia and her Afrocentric art-professor mother Marie as the antithesis of her own family, whose overriding concern for conforming to racialized geographies is made explicit through their "rules of what you weren't supposed to do in public, what you weren't supposed to do around white people ... [to] [f]it perfectly—without strain—into space" (139). Charlotte is intrigued by Marie's willingness to take "on the burden of talking about race for Courtland County" in exchange for "one scrap of land where she could dictate all the rules" (140–1). Charlotte also raises a red flag, however, in mentioning the "troubling" fact that Marie's activism echoes the exclusionary mentality of the Stars of the Morning in ignoring "the black people in Spring City ... [except] when decrying the segregation that caused that town's existence" (141).

Adia's attractiveness to Charlotte eventually culminates in a fleeting physical intimacy between the two girls, but the warning signs about Adia and Marie as a sustaining alternate community emerge as Charlotte ponders whether or not to "open my mouth and speak and name what passed between us for what it was—love" (145). Not only does Adia almost entirely refuse to speak about their homosexual experience, the one time she does, she bluntly asserts that "Black people don't know how to love" (145), having been separated from their august past for too long: "In Africa, it was the man's job to offer love and the woman's job to accept it. But that's all ruined now. Marie told me ... We'll have to find kings ... We don't want to go queer like white girls do" (146). Adia's quintessentially "hotep" interpretation of her mother's teachings leaves no space for anything other than an ephemeral queerness, and Charlotte's attempts to restore their homoerotic connection and thereby keep Adia from "talk[ing] us back into history" (146) ultimately fails.

The novel's epilogue suggests that, like Jude and Reese, Charlotte eventually does find acceptance and, in doing so, liberation from the various essentialist geographies of race, gender, and sexuality that she has previously encountered. Although her family's experiences at the Toneybee have become internet clickbait—"I find our family in posts with titles like 'Top Ten Wackiest Sacrifices for Science' and 'Fifty-Three Weirdest Childhood Pets'" (310)—her own married life has become peacefully ordinary and satisfying: "I have Darla. Darla, who is not black but Indian; not from New England, but California ... We met in college, and her complete otherness from me, what made me fall in love with her, has dulled, turned warm, and now I love her for what we share" (315). Although she still thinks about Adia, Charlotte describes Adia's fate of having become "a graphic designer in San Diego, married to a Polish man and mother of three sons" as "entirely disappointing and pedestrian" (317) compared to the idealized image of her as "beautiful and merciless and ready again to devour hearts and history" (318) that Charlotte once cherished unrequitedly. While Adia's choices ultimately reproduce her mother's idealization of heterosexuality, Charlotte echoes Morrison's Lotus women in not allowing "tight space"—produced here through heteronormative constrictions—to determine how she can exist in the world.

Finally, Akwaeke Emezi's *Freshwater* (2018) strategically challenges readers' empathy regarding queerness even further by almost entirely estranging the human body as a home-space. Although Jude, Reese, Benson, and Charlotte all have moments of discomfort with their bodies for various reasons, Emezi's protagonist Ada outdoes them all in transcending conventional conceptions of the body as a vessel for a singular and definitively human entity. Ada's body contains a complex consciousness that describes itself (itselves?) as follows:

> We came from somewhere—everything does … By the time she (our body) struggled out into the world, slick and louder than a village of storms, the gates were left open. We should have been anchored in her by then, asleep inside her membranes and synched with her mind. That would have been the safest way. But since the gates were open, not closed against remembrance, we became confused … We were not conscious but we were alive—in fact, the main problem was that we were a distinct *we* instead of being fully and just *her*. (5, emphases in original)

Emezi has insisted on numerous occasions that this compound identity is not a metaphor for a dissociative disorder or a Westernized *gestalt* consciousness, but rather what is known in the Igbo culture of West Africa as *ọgbanje*, as which Emezi themself identifies: "The possibility that I was an *ọgbanje* occurred to me around the same time I realized I was trans, but it took me a while to collide the two worlds." *Freshwater* demands readers' empathy with a protagonist who "inhabit[s] simultaneous realities that are usually considered mutually exclusive" (Emezi, "Transition").

The novel is alternately narrated through plural consciousness, indicated simply as "We," and through various temporarily isolated personae, including Ada and the uninhibited and vengeful Asụghara, who moves into the foreground after Ada is sexually assaulted by her college boyfriend:

> Ada wasn't there anymore. At all, at all. She wasn't even a small thing curled up in the corner of her marble. There was only me. I expanded against the walls, filling it up and blocking her out completely. She was gone. She might as well have been dead. I was powerful and I was mad, he could not touch me no matter how hard he pushed into her body, he could definitely never touch her. I was here. I was everything. I was everywhere. (64)

Although the language of Asụghara's initial manifestation might suggest Ada's supplantation or eradication, Asụghara later describes their relationship more symbiotically:

> Ada loved me, sha … She loved me because I was strong and I held her together … I loved her because in the moment of her devastation, the moment she lost her mind, that girl reached for me so hard that she went completely mad, and I loved her because when I flooded through, she spread herself open and took me in without hesitation, bawling and broken, she absorbed me fiercely, all the way; she denied me nothing. (70–1)

Ada herself reinforces this symbiosis, suggesting that the myriad spirits "anchored" within her body and mind generally tell the "truest version" of their collective story because "they are the truest version of me" (93). Moreover, Ada accepts the madness that Asụghara claims to have stimulated in her: "I am not entirely opposed to madness, not when it comes with this kind of clarity. The world in my head has been far more real than the one outside … I didn't want to be alone, so I chose them. In many ways, you see, I am not even real" (93).

Having migrated—like Emezi—from her birthplace in Nigeria through numerous locations in the United States and struggled everywhere to find community and human companionship, Ada nearly accepts Asụghara's suggestion to set the spirits within her body free by committing suicide. She chooses instead to alter it surgically, though, a decision that literally and figuratively incarnates a radically inclusive spatial imaginary that creates a home for the totality of the *ọgbanje*:

> Before then, we used to think of the body as belonging truly to the Ada, as something that we were only guests in, something that the beastself [i.e., Asụghara] could borrow. But now that we had been spurned from the gates, now that we were sentenced to meat, it was time to accept that this body was ours too ... We were a fine balance, bigger than whatever the namings had made, and we wanted to reflect that, to change the Ada into us. Removing her breasts was only the first step ... Before Asụghara put us in the emergency room, we had been searching for doctors to alter the Ada, to carve our body into something that we could truly call a home. (187–8)

Emezi's somewhat idiosyncratic construction of *ọgbanje* identity allows them to illustrate that queerness is not a simply a matter of exploding binary notions of gender and sexuality, but rather the radical overlap and transcendence thereof. As the novel ends, Ada has fused Asụghara's protective female power with that of another spirit named Saint Vincent, who represents her desire to be more masculine and her sexual attraction to women; the complex intersection of these spirits (and several others) with Ada's personhood creates the communal queer identity[7] asserted joyously in the novel's final passages:

> Ọgbanje are as liminal as is possible—spirit and human, both and neither. I am here and not here, real and not real, energy pushed into skin and bone. I am my others; we are one and we are many ... The river is full of my scales. With each step, I am less afraid. I am the brothersister who remained. I am a village full of faces and a compound full of bones, translucent thousands. Why should I be afraid? I am the source of the spring. (226)

The ethics of care practiced by Morrison's Black female characters in *Home*, and throughout her literary oeuvre, provide opportunities for a counter-geographic practice that is invested in Black communal place-making. Reading Morrison alongside the fiction of such authors as Bennett, Washington, Greenidge, and Emezi shows not only the continued importance of community as home, but it also emphasizes these writers' investments in further expanding and intersectionalizing communal space in ways that echo Butler's nontraditional "family" units. Although *The Vanishing Half*; *Memorial*; *We Love You, Charlie Freeman*; and *Freshwater* each imagine and interrogate the meaning of home in divergent ways, they all explore acts of home-creation through the experiences of queer Black characters. Additionally, they use broadcast strategic empathy in creating their intersectional storyworlds in an effort to encourage diverse audiences to challenge normative conceptualizations of space and identity across lines of race, gender, and sexuality.

WORKS CITED

Alexander, Phoenix. "Octavia E. Butler and Black Women's Archives at the End of the World." *Science Fiction Studies*, vol. 46, no. 2, July 2019, pp. 342–57.

Beavers, Herman. *Geography and the Political Imaginary in the Novels of Toni Morrison*. Palgrave Macmillan, 2018.

---

[7]Derek Maus is deeply grateful to Aubrey Slaterpryce, a student in my LITR 451 course during the Spring 2021 semester at SUNY Potsdam, for making these astute observations during our class discussions.

Bennett, Brit. *The Vanishing Half*. Riverhead, 2020.

Bennett, Jess S. *Queer Families in Octavia Butler's Science Fiction*. 2019. Middle Tennessee State University, unpublished MA thesis. https://jewlscholar.mtsu.edu/handle/mtsu/6137. Accessed July 11, 2022.

Brockes, Emma. "Toni Morrison: 'I Want to Feel What I Feel. Even if It's not Happiness.'" *The Guardian* Apr. 13, 2012. https://www.theguardian.com/books/2012/apr/13/toni-morrison-home-son-love. Accessed July 11, 2022.

Byerman, Keith. *Remembering the Past in Contemporary African American Fiction*. U of North Carolina P, 2005.

Dunning, Stefanie K. *Queer in Black and White: Interraciality, Same Sex Desire, and Contemporary African American Culture*. Indiana UP, 2009.

Emezi, Akwaeke. *Freshwater*. Grove, 2018.

Emezi, Akwaeke. "Transition: My Surgeries Were a Bridge Across Realities, a Spirit Customizing Its Vessel to Reflect Its Nature." *The Cut*, Jan. 19, 2018. https://www.thecut.com/2018/01/writer-and-artist-akwaeke-emezi-gender-transition-and-ogbanje.html. Accessed July 11, 2022.

Greenidge, Kaitlyn. *We Love You, Charlie Freeman*. Algonquin, 2016.

Herman, David. *Storytelling and the Sciences of Mind*. MIT Press, 2013.

Hoffman, Martin L. *Empathy and Moral Development. Implications for Caring and Justice*. Cambridge UP, 2000.

Hogan, Patrick Colm. *What Literature Teaches Us About Emotion*. Cambridge UP, 2011.

Hogan, Patrick Colm. "Affective Space and Emotional Time: Learning from Lǐ Bái (李白) and Lǐ Qīngzhào (李清照)." *Narrative and the Biocultural Turn*, vol. 5, 2018, pp. 51–80.

Keen, Suzanne. "A Theory of Narrative Empathy." *Narrative*, vol. 14, no. 3, 2006, pp. 207–36.

Landsbaum, Claire. "Bryan Washington Is Writing the Next Generation of Queer Love Story." *Vanity Fair*, Oct. 27, 2020. https://www.vanityfair.com/style/2020/10/bryan-washington-is-writing-the-next-generation-of-queer-love-story. Accessed July 11, 2022.

Lewis, Michael. "Self-Conscious Emotions: Embarrassment, Pride, Shame, and Guilt." *Handbook of Emotions*, 3rd ed., edited by Michael Lewis, et al. Guilford Press, 2008, pp. 742–56.

Lipsitz, George. *How Racism Takes Place*. Temple UP, 2011.

Mitchell, Koritha. *From Slave Cabins to the White House: Homemade Citizenship in African American Culture*. U of Illinois P, 2020.

Morrison, Toni. *Home*. Knopf, 2012.

Morrison, Toni. "Home." *The House that Race Built: Black Americans, U.S. Terrain*, edited by Wahneema Lubiano, Pantheon Books, 1997, pp. 4–12.

Norman, Brian. *Neo-Segregation Narratives: Jim Crow in Post-Civil Rights American Literature*. U of Georgia P, 2010.

Soja, Edward. *Thirdspace: Journeys to Los Angeles and Other Real-and Imagined Places*. Blackwell, 1996.

Wall, Cheryl A. "Trying to Get Home: Place and Memory in Toni Morrison's Fiction." *Toni Morrison: Memory and Meaning*, edited by Adrienne Lanier Seward and Justine Tally, UP of Mississippi, 2014, pp. 53–65.

Washington, Bryan. *Memorial*. Riverhead, 2020.

Weik von Mossner, Alexa. *Cosmopolitan Minds: Literature, Emotion, and the Transnational Imagination*. U of Texas P, 2014.

White, E. Frances. "The Evidence of Things Not Seen: The Alchemy of Race and Sexuality." *James Baldwin and Toni Morrison: Comparative Critical and Theoretical Essays*, edited by Lovalerie King and Lynn Orilla Scott, Palgrave Macmillan, 2006, pp. 239–60.

PART THREE

Morrison Teaching, Teaching Morrison

CHAPTER NINETEEN

Toni Morrison and the Politics of Literary Generosity

MICHAEL NOWLIN

"DISABLING THE ART VERSUS POLITICS ARGUMENT"

In her 2001 lecture "Goodbye to All That," delivered at Harvard's Radcliffe Institute, Toni Morrison stated that "disabling the art versus politics argument" is a fundamental goal of her work (*Source of Self-Regard* 337). I want to argue that this is a far less contentious project than is supposed by some of Morrison's champions and detractors and that it accords rather with her fundamentally liberal position on the question of aesthetic freedom. Morrison's position comes across consistently in her critical writings, meditations, and many interviews given over the years.

I want first to undermine what I see as a dubious critical tendency to pit Morrison's "political" fiction, inasmuch as it can be made to epitomize the necessarily political art of authors from historically subaltern groups, against a supposedly aesthetically purer canonical literature by mainly white male authors, a tendency that far from disabling the art versus politics argument simplistically reinforces it. Morrison occasionally encouraged such approaches, probably most influentially in the oft-quoted penultimate paragraph of her 1984 essay "Rootedness: The Ancestor as Foundation":

> If anything I do, in the way of writing novels (or whatever I write) isn't about the village or the community or about you, then it is not about anything. I am not interested in indulging myself in some private, closed exercise of my imagination that fulfills only the obligation of my personal dreams—which is to say yes, the work must be political. That's a pejorative term in critical circles now; if a work has any political influence in it, somehow it's tainted. My feeling is just the opposite: if it has none, it is tainted. (*What Moves at the Margin* 64)

Judylyn Ryan is fairly typical in underscoring the supposed boldness of this statement, blithely assuming that Morrison made it "at a time when the dictum of art for art's sake had not yet been stripped of its disguise" (151). But leaving aside the fact that the dictum of art for art's sake has been routinely criticized since its emergence in the latter half of the nineteenth century, I would ask which narcissistic, hermetic writers Ryan thinks Morrison was defining herself against here. Morrison cannot have been seriously thinking of Gustave Flaubert, Stéphane Mallarmé, Henry James, W. B. Yeats, James Joyce, T. S. Eliot, Marianne Moore, Marcel Proust, Virginia Woolf, Wallace Stevens, William Faulkner, Samuel Beckett, or Vladimir Nabokov, all boldly experimental authors with varying but qualified aestheticist inclinations. She certainly couldn't have had in mind Oscar Wilde, who made popular, subversive cultural currency of his commitment to art for art's sake. As her criticism of classic American literature attests, she certainly did not have novelists like Nathaniel Hawthorne, Herman Melville, Mark Twain, Gertrude Stein, Willa Cather, or Ernest Hemingway in mind. Was she casting aspersion on any of her major American precursors and contemporaries? It's hard to see how her characterization could seriously describe Flannery O'Connor, Norman Mailer, Ralph Ellison, Joyce Carol Oates, Saul Bellow, Philip Roth, or John Updike. Indeed, a more critical view of the statement suggests that Morrison's writerly antithesis is a straw man and that the claims made for "political" literature are at the expense not of apolitical literature but of writing that virtually nobody cares about.

Morrison also occasionally sounds the kind of censorious note that we also readily associate with politicizing literature in an anti-liberal way. Her 1993 Nobel Lecture, for example, condemns "oppressive language," including sexist, racist, and theistic language, for not merely representing violence but *being* "violence"—a point of dogma now in some quarters—and as such "it must be rejected, altered, and exposed" (*Source of Self-Regard* 104). Marc Conner finds "this call for the policing of language ... troubling," and wonders "which writers Morrison would silence, for which writers she would feel 'shame'" (Conner xxi). But Morrison's public statements mainly suggest she would not silence any writer: "No one should tell any writer what to write, at all, ever," she declared, for example, in a 1987 interview (Taylor-Guthrie 237). Asked once about the outcry against William Styron for presuming to write a novel about Nat Turner, her response was reflexively liberal: "He has a right to write about whatever he wants. To suggest otherwise is outrageous" (Denard 74). With reference to the likes of Ezra Pound, T. S. Eliot, and Louis-Ferdinand Céline, she has stated, "I take no position, nor do I encourage one, on the quality of a work based on the attitudes of an author or whatever representations are made of some groups" (*Playing in the Dark* 90). She almost never draws invidious distinctions between writers. On the rare occasion when she does, she does so in vaguely general terms, without naming names.

Conner nonetheless characterizes as "anathema" to her "the Joycean ideal of the artist—indifferent, invisible, paring his fingernails above the art work with no concern for its reception or its effect" (Conner xxiv). Anathema? Nowhere can Morrison be found speaking negatively of Joyce. Undoubtedly her "authorial" relation to her fictional worlds is more human than godlike, but that makes more for a variation on than a hostile refutation of the Joycean aesthetic—or at least his character Stephen Dedalus's aesthetic, derived from Flaubert ("L'artiste doit être dans son oeuvre comme Dieu dans la création, invisible et tout-puissant; qu'on le sente partout, mais qu'on ne le voie pas"[1]; Flaubert 324). This impersonal, invisible "authorial" presence is one of the hallmarks of literary modernism and especially notable for the onus it puts upon the reader to be more self-reliant. Morrison is thus hardly original in demanding and fostering her readers' participation in the story, and in fact she's rather more traditional than Joyce in this respect. Here she is after writing *Beloved*:

> I like the feeling of a told story, where you hear a voice but can't identify it, and you think it's your own voice. It's a comfortable voice, and it's a guiding voice, and it's alarmed by the same

---

[1] "The artist should be in his work like God in his creation, invisible and omnipotent, so that one feels him everywhere but one can never see him."

things that the reader is alarmed by, and it doesn't know what's going to happen next either. So you have this sort of guide. But that guide can't have a personality; it can only have a sound, and you have to feel comfortable with this voice, and then this voice can easily abandon itself and reveal the interior dialogue of a character. So it's a combination of using the point of view of various characters but still retaining the power to slide in and out, provided that when I'm "out" the reader doesn't see the little fingers pointing to what's in the text. (*Source of Self-Regard* 244)

My point here is not to argue about influences or underscore Morrison's relative typicality in some respects, but to ask rhetorically why academic critics seem compelled to position Morrison against canonical writers in divisive terms of their own making. The motive, I think, lies in the stakes of academically defined literary canons, with their ramifications for academic careers, course offerings, and classroom syllabi: underlying the so-called academic canon wars over the past forty years or so is, ironically, a shared professional belief that "literature" can be authoritatively transmitted in schools, accompanied by a shared sense that even students pursuing higher degrees in literature can't or won't read everything. Morrison versus Joyce is predicated on the either/or, zero-sum logic felt most forcibly when putting together required reading lists: x instead of y, because x is better (or better for you) than y. Choices inevitably have to be made, but they could make for surprising combinations: "I don't mind being taught with Alice Walker, William Shakespeare, Milton, Marguerite Duras, or anybody," Morrison has said—with her eye on the (now more diversely) consecrated (Denard 88). But the voracious, extra-scholastic reader in Morrison naturally seeks more and more, and she famously used her position as a commercial editor and her remarkable bestseller stature to add to the world's literary store. "There is an advantage to having a wide readership, both black and white," she told an interviewer, "which is that it makes it possible for lots of other writers to get published" (36). Her power to expand the range of contemporary authors hardly entailed "anathematizing" what world literature already had to offer, including Joyce, whose most outrageously difficult work brought her mainly pleasure: "I read *Finnegans Wake* after graduate school, and I had the great good fortune of reading it without any help. I don't know if I read it right, but it was hilarious! I laughed constantly!" (88).

Conner is more helpful in particularizing the "art versus politics" argument that as an African American writer Morrison committed herself to disabling, tracing it back, as Morrison herself has, to the Harlem Renaissance and beyond (Conner xiii–xvii). What's really at issue is the way the long-standing art versus propaganda dichotomy was deployed throughout the Jim Crow era to negatively measure African American literature for failing to treat with "universal" disinterestedness the particularities of Black American experience. The extent to which this culturally imposed critical opposition was internalized by African American writers might be gauged by the fact that when W. E. B. Du Bois ostentatiously defied it by proclaiming "All Art is propaganda and ever must be, despite the wailing of the purists" (Du Bois 1000), he was, in the context of Harlem Renaissance debates, pretty much alone. Most of the century's major African American writers—not just Zora Neale Hurston and Ralph Ellison, but also Langston Hughes and Richard Wright—condemned propaganda (Nowlin 105–10, 156–8).[2] Most resented critical apologies for their work on the

---

[2]Unfortunately, Conner follows received wisdom and reproduces the "art versus politics" dichotomy by categorizing the classic African American authors according to one term or the other, Du Bois, Hughes, and Wright all being aligned with the narrowly "political" on the basis of reductive quotations from polemical essays that a more careful reading can show to

grounds of its sociological value. Morrison is very much in line with them in being disturbed "by the sociological evaluations white people make of Black literature" without subordinating these to aesthetics, while in the less-quoted final paragraph of "Rootedness," she acknowledges the "problem" of "harangue passing off as art," and thus distinguishes "harangue" from "art" because harangue is not, like "the best art," "irrevocably beautiful at the same time" as it is "unquestionably political" (Taylor-Guthrie 67; Morrison, *What Moves at the Margin* 64). Because their subject matter broaches more often than not the experience of living under racism, modern African American writers have been uniquely burdened by reductive misrepresentations of their art as "harangue" or "propaganda." This compels the Black American writer "to shout endlessly to white criticism," as Morrison puts it, "These are not my racial politics—they are yours" (*Source of Self-Regard* 337).

Without those particular racial politics and the critical tendencies emanating from them, there would be nothing supposedly radical about Morrison saying, "I don't believe any real artists have even been non-political" (Taylor-Guthrie 4), especially when we consider carefully what she means by this. She distinguishes not between political and nonpolitical artists but between "real artists" and those who aren't, and "real artists" for Morrison seem to be virtually any who have been published and recognized as such, with the greats being inevitable touchstones. All of which should suggest that by real artists' politics Morrison means *a politics peculiar to the nature of art* and inherent in their commitment to their art, which has inescapably moral implications. She does not mean their commitment to any ideological or party line. (Asked if she agreed with *Paradise* being called a "feminist novel," she responded "Not at all. I would never write any 'ist.' I don't write 'ist' novels" [Denard 140].) As a novelist, Morrison believes overtly in what other novelists might only be more tacit about: namely, that the writing and reading of fiction are vital to the health of any *polis*. Furthermore, given Morrison's increasing sense over the years of the disorienting, dehumanizing effects of global capitalism and its new media, she sees them as vital to the preservation of the inner human life. "Fictional literature may be (and I believe it is)," she proclaimed in 1998,

> the last and only route to remembrance, the only staunch in the wasteful draining away of conscience and memory. Fictional literature can be an alternative language that can contradict and elude and analyze the regime, the authority of the electronically visual, the seduction of the "virtual." The study of fiction may also be the mechanism of repair in the disconnect between public and private. (*Source of Self-Regard*, 100)

This is the political pronouncement of a prophet, concerned with redeeming the spiritual and affective lives of individuals so as to empower them to reach out to one another and (re)build genuine communities. She once facetiously called the artist "a politician" when what she meant was that "[he] bears witness"—like "literature" itself, which, "sensitive as a tuning fork, is an unblinking witness to the light and shade of the world we live in" (Taylor-Guthrie 4; Morrison, *Source of Self-Regard*, 126). Morrison is politically first and foremost, then, on the side of *all* (real) writers *qua* writers; for as humanity's witnesses to a human history that regularly dehumanizes and oppresses, they are vital political registers: registering freedom, resistance, and (even negatively

---

be aesthetically oriented as well. For some attention to revealing contradictions within Du Bois's "Criteria of Negro Art," Hughes's "The Negro Artist and the Racial Mountain," and Wright's "Blueprint for Negro Writing," see Nowlin.

and ironically) the standpoint of its better angels. This is what makes all writers—and not just her, presumably—"*sublimely* didactic," as she once called herself (Taylor-Guthrie 74, emphasis added).

Writers are not, however, transcendentally positioned, or historically unsocialized by categories like race, gender, class, or nationality: if they were, there would be little urge to do the arduous work of imaginative writing and thereby stake their claims as witnesses. Morrison's politics are too readily assumed to inhere in her self-identification as "an African American woman writer" working within, as she puts it, a "genderized, sexualized, wholly racialized world" (*Playing in the Dark* 4). And no doubt her proud insistence on her racial and gendered particularity as a writer helped expose the white masculine hegemony underlying the "universality" routinely attributed to great white male authors. But if the qualifying descriptors didn't make her any less of a writer, did they contribute to making her exceptional? They no doubt led her to her particular window in Henry James's capacious house of fiction. Or to put it very differently, they offered her material from which to make cultural capital at an opportune historical moment: "My project became to make the historically raced world inextricable from the artistic view that beholds it, and in so doing encourage readings that dissect both. Which is to say that I claimed the right and range of authorship" (*Source of Self-Regard* 337). It's not clear, though, how claiming an entitlement like "the right and range of authorship" is the same as staking out so particular a project—the first is rather a precondition of the second. In passages like this Morrison's exceptional stature as a living canonical author (let alone Nobel Prize winner) pardonably led her, it seems, to make herself the measure of literary witnessing in general.

She elaborates on what "claiming the right and range of authorship" empowers her to do: "To interrupt journalistic history with a metaphorical one; to impose on a rhetorical history an imagistic one; to read the world, misread it; write and unwrite it. To enact silence and free speech. In short to do what *all writers* aspire to do" (*Source of Self-Regard* 337, emphasis added). It's here she states that she "wanted [her] work to be the work of disabling the art versus politics argument; to perform the union of aesthetics and ethics" (*Source of Self-Regard* 337). If this is what *all writers* aspire to do—Black female, white male, European, African, American, the consecrated, and the unsung—then readers can find the emancipatory, humanizing, deconstructive virtues of literature in countless authors other than Morrison (again, James's "house of fiction" has over a million windows). If this is what *all writers* aspire to do, then judgmentally dividing writers according to political or aesthetic proclivities is a critical or scholastic, that is extra-literary, imposition. What I am calling Morrison's politics of literary generosity here is precisely her steadfast willingness to measure and value the work of her fellow authors past and present by the light of her own risky, solitary, playful, creative-destructive experience of writing as a Black woman, born of an earlier, self-saving initiation into the pleasures of literary reading. Having become an exceptional writer, she increasingly and rightfully identified with other exceptional writers—not least the canonical Americans, however prickly she could sometimes be about comparisons. ("I am typical, I think, of all writers who are convinced that they are wholly original and that if they recognized an influence they would abandon it as quickly as possible," she once said in response to a question about Faulkner [*Source of Self-Regard* 297].) She expressed that identification most brilliantly, subversively, and above all *generously* in her re-apprehension as *a Black female writer-reader* of her classic American precursors' "right and range of authorship" within a "historically raced world inextricable from the artistic view that beholds it."

"AS A WRITER READING": ENHANCING CLASSIC AMERICAN LITERATURE

In the course of praising several American writers—Eudora Welty, Hemingway, O'Connor, F. Scott Fitzgerald—for having written stories with so "truly unique" a "slant" that no one else could have written them, Morrison was asked by her interviewer Elissa Schappell, "Haven't you been critical of the way these authors depicted blacks?" "No!" responded Morrison: "Me, critical? I have been revealing how white writers imagine black people, and some of them are brilliant at it. Faulkner was brilliant at it. Hemingway did it poorly in places and brilliantly elsewhere" (Denard 73).

The interview coincided roughly with the appearance of *Playing in the Dark: Whiteness and the Literary Imagination* (1992), Morrison's signature contribution to academic literary criticism. *Playing in the Dark* was also an early and influential contribution to what is broadly and these days divisively known as "Critical Race Theory," offering an astute critique of the ostensibly race-free, universal themes of classic American literature. Its key ideas had been sketched out in earlier essays, notably the 1988 essay "Unspeakable Things Unspoken: The Afro-American Presence in American Literature," which she had initially planned to call "Canon Fodder" to signal her intervention in the so-called canon wars of the 1980s. But Morrison's intervention was not meant to be ultimately divisive. Morrison came to make a canon she clearly loved more interesting and more pertinent to contemporary discussions about race—to save it not only from those too superficially acquainted with it (if at all) but from its misguided, ostensibly color-blind defenders. She intervened in part because the cause of great literature was at stake: "And I, at least, do not intend to live without Aeschylus or William Shakespeare, or James or Twain or Hawthorne, or Melville, etc., etc., etc. There must be some way to enhance canon readings without enshrining them" (*Source of Self-Regard* 166).

I will forgo any commentary here on Morrison's much discussed and applied concept of "American Africanism" so as to emphasize her commitment to *enhancing without enshrining* classic American literature and the way she grounds her key critical insights in her experience as a fellow writer. An "enshrined" canon connotes the sometimes moribund sacredness of museums and schools when an unthinking reverence inhibits the kind of critical touching and cultural-political exploration that "enhances" a book or artwork and elevates piety to wonder. Morrison uses a more provocative metaphor for the cost of this inhibition: "A criticism that needs to insist that literature is not only 'universal' but also 'race-free' risks lobotomizing that literature, and diminishes both the art and the artist" (*Playing in the Dark* 12). Against the common assumption that political criticism diminishes art and artists by tying them too inextricably to the time and place that they are supposed to transcend, Morrison insists that it does the opposite. But again, this all depends on what political criticism entails: for Morrison, it does not entail measuring a work by its service or disservice to a partisan cause, denouncing a book as "racist" by contemporary standards, or repudiating authors for attitudes and beliefs or presumptions they may have had; for Morrison, these kinds of criticism also diminish art and artists. Indeed, Morrison's critical demonstration may be hard to emulate for most academic critics and student readers because, unlike her, they are generally not literary artists, let alone great ones. For it's *as a writer* that she "politically" illuminates and thus enhances the American classics she explores: "Reading these texts as a writer allowed me deeper access to them" (*Source of Self-Regard* 144).

Those who are not "writers" in the common sense Morrison means here—*creative* writers, *literary* authors—may bristle at the extent to which she grounds her critical knowledge, her "deeper access," in certain mysteries of authorship that bind her to other writers past and present as fellow initiates and masters in a kind of trans-temporal, transnational guild.

> As a reader (before becoming a writer) I read as I had been taught to do. But books revealed themselves differently to me as a writer. In that capacity I have to place enormous trust in my ability to imagine others and my willingness to project consciously into the danger zones all others may represent for me. I am drawn to the ways all writers do this: the way Homer renders a heart-eating cyclops so that our hearts are wrenched with pity; the way Dostoevsky compels intimacy with Svidrigailov and Prince Myshkin. I am in awe of the authority of Faulkner's Benjy, James's Maisie, Flaubert's Emma, Melville's Pip, Mary Shelley's Frankenstein—each of us can extend the list.
>
> I am interested in what prompts and makes possible this process of entering what one is estranged from—and in what disables the foray, for the purposes of fiction, into corners of consciousness held off and away from the reach of the writer's imagination (Morrison, *Playing in the Dark* 3–4).

Fundamental to the mystery of writing fiction is not just the capacity to sympathetically imagine others but to sympathetically inhabit them—*enter* "what one is estranged from." Morrison discovered this in herself *qua* writer, but more particularly *as an African American woman writer* opportunely positioned by her difference, by her experience of otherness or marginality, to critically but sympathetically inhabit the standpoint of her more hegemonically positioned peers:

> To think about (and wrestle with) the full implications of my situation leads me to consider what happens when other writers work in a highly and historically racialized society. For them, as for me, imagining is not merely looking or looking at; nor is it taking oneself intact into the other. It is, for the purposes of the work, *becoming*. (*Playing in the Dark* 4, emphasis in original)

Morrison flags both her difference and her sameness here to authorize the sweeping argument about American literature she goes on to make: not that classic American literature is irredeemably racist, but, given that "writers are among the most sensitive, the most intellectually anarchic, most representative, most probing of artists" (*Playing in the Dark* 15), it is inescapably about the racial divide foundational to the nation's sense of itself. "My project," she continues just before announcing her thesis of the "Africanist presence," "rises *from what I know about the ways writers* transform aspects of their social grounding into aspects of language, and the ways they tell their stories, fight secret wars, limn out all sorts of debates blanketed in their text. And rises *from my certainty that writers always know*, at some level, that they do this" (*Playing in the Dark* 4, emphasis added).

What she applies herself to sympathetically exploring in the actual texts of her American precursors are the *aesthetic* effects—artistic compromises or solutions or aporia—of their imaginative engagement with the inescapable Black stranger in their midst, made metaphorically available to them in "Africanist personae, narrative, and idiom" (*Playing in the Dark* 16). "As a writer reading, I came to realize the obvious: the subject of the dream is the dreamer. The fabrication of an Africanist persona is reflexive; an extraordinary meditation on the self; a powerful exploration of the fears and desires that reside in the writerly conscious. It is an astonishing revelation of longing, of terror, of perplexity, of shame, of magnanimity" (17). Morrison seems to accept here the psychoanalytic axiom that literary works are like dreams, enabling the playful work of imaginative self-estrangement, and engagement not merely with the other but with the self's own otherness. Novels and romances may be like dreams, but they are also forms of witnessing that arise from historical, social, legal, and cultural pressures, impositions if you will—like the "architecture of a *new white man*," for example, at the heart of the American imaginary (15, emphasis in original). And unlike dreams, of course, they're subject to authorial choices and maneuvers, authorial blocks and inspirations, subject, that is, *to the actual discipline, however playful, of writing*—which no one can appreciate better than fellow writers, especially a fellow writer who has won from an outsider's position her own claim to literary mastery. Far from identifying with "the Africanist persona" that undergirds and permeates, indeed haunts white American fiction, Morrison claims to have never been able to see it until becoming not merely a writer, but a successful writer of American fiction, because only then could she recognize it as the master trope for developing and conveying classic American literature's most compelling and inevitable theme: the "new white man's" failure to find freedom and redemption in the new world. She suddenly saw the trope holding everything together when she "began to rely," in her words, "on my knowledge of how books get written, how language arrives; my sense of how and why writers abandon or take on certain aspects of their project. I began to rely on my understanding of what the linguistic struggle requires of writers and what they make of the surprise that is the inevitable concomitant of the act of creation" (17).

Morrison's critique of the racial subtext, even racial pre-text of canonical American literature, in effect, stems from her work of adding to that literature from a standpoint that cannot but see African American experience at its center. This is what enabled her in turn to identify with the self-alienated authors of "white" America who had all glimpsed something of the same while "playing in the dark," and did what they could with this unsettling insight before (or while) falling back upon the all-too-serviceable resource of a figurative Africanism to contain it. On top of the extraordinary novels with which she enriched the national literature her precursors were making, Morrison the critic gave them the attention their writings begged for (*Source of Self-Regard* 181) by showcasing the underappreciated and surprising, subversive and disappointing ways they bear witness to the social and psychic costs of living in a "new" kind of experimental democracy half slave and half free.

Morrison's actual readings—of *Moby Dick*, of *Three Lives*, of *Huckleberry Finn*, among many others—aim to "give the texts a deeper, richer, more complex life than the sanitized one commonly presented to us" (*Source of Self-Regard* 160). "Politicizing" them, in effect, entails *complicating* them, restoring their social content without forsaking those old "new critical" virtues of ambiguity, paradox, and irony: "I would not like to be understood to argue that Melville was engaged in some simple and simpleminded black/white didacticism, or that he was satanizing white people," she clarifies (178). But that *Moby Dick* was inimitable in engaging the contemporary battle over slavery and notions of whiteness mobilized in its defense is harder to deny after her suggestive remarks, followed by the ultimate compliment: "To this day no novelist has so wrestled with his subject" (180). Stein, too, is given her due as a trailblazer, despite racist assumptions she still harbored: "Stein's signal contribution to literature in her encounter with an Africanistic presence is to give this encounter the complexity and the modernity it had otherwise been denied by the mainstream writers of the time" (215). And Morrison repeatedly acknowledged the greatness of Twain's novel in its very failure to free Jim, in good part because no American novel so grappled with "the interdependence of slavery and freedom": "The novel addresses at every point in its structural edifice, and lingers over in every fissure, the slave's body and personality; the way it speaks, what passion legal or illicit it is prey to, what pain it can endure, what limits, if any, there are to its suffering, what possibilities there are for forgiveness, compassion, love" (*Playing in the Dark* 55, 56).

There is nothing reductively "political" about Morrison's race-based critique in these instances; for her, such works "double their fascination and power when scoured for this presence and the writerly strategies taken to address or deny it" (*Source of Self-Regard* 180). The deeper politics of Morrison's criticism lurk in her repeated evocation of literature's "fascination and power." For literature is, finally, one of Morrison's main political values. For Morrison literature is quasi-sacred even in its political function. Literature is political, paradoxically, because it is our best witness to politics, which for Morrison seem more often than not, and especially in their hegemonic forms, poisoned by an all-too-common human flaw: "a deplorable inability to project, to become the 'other,' to imagine her or him. It is an intellectual flaw, a shortening of the imagination, and reveals an ignorance of gothic proportions as well as a truly laughable lack of curiosity" (43). This is why humanity so badly needs writers—because they have that "capacity" she claims for herself "to imagine others" and willingly "project consciously into the danger zones all others may represent for me." Literature is politically necessary—for salvaging and strengthening selves, for making communion and hence communities more possible. That's why it is also dangerous to political tyrannies or would-be tyrannies in their manifold guises.

THE DANCING MIND IN PERIL

When it comes to defending literature and its writers, finally, Morrison is classically liberal. This comes across most unequivocally in *The Dancing Mind*, her acceptance speech for her 1996 National Book Foundation Medal, as well as her anti-censorship work with PEN International that led her to edit the 2012 essay collection *Burn This Book: Notes on Literature and Engagement*—with contributions from fellow writers, including John Updike, Orhan Pamuk, Nadine Gordimer, and Salman Rushdie.

The urgency conveyed by the title of her brief introductory essay "Peril" also inhabits the earlier, more cheeringly titled acceptance speech, and their arguments are essentially the same. That of *The Dancing Mind* mainly differs in being built around a striking juxtaposition that exhibits Morrison's power to imagine others and suggest conventionally unthinkable relations. Both pieces insist on the existence of a powerful form of reprieve from, which is also a form of resistance to, what in context we can safely call "politics." In the earlier essay, she describes a "peace" that "is not at the mercy of history's rule, nor is it a passive surrender to the status quo," and in the later, a "stillness" that is an alternative, superior response to "chaos" than the more habitual ones of "naming and violence" (*The Dancing Mind* 7; *Source of Self-Regard* viii). The former "is the dance of an open mind when it engages another equally open one—an activity that occurs most naturally, most often in the reading/writing world we live in"; the latter a "stillness" that when actively and creatively channeled issues in "art" (*The Dancing Mind* 7; *Source of Self-Regard* viii). Both essays implicitly describe this saving state of suspension from war and chaos and noise—or politics imagined as a perpetual state of siege—as *aesthetic* rather than religious, a state of play, free communion, deeper inquiry, disinterestedness in the sense of genuine curiosity stimulated by and productive of the beautiful.

The existence of this emancipating state is precarious, though, and depends more than anything, for Morrison, on the freedom granted to writers. Not some writers, but all writers. And the responsibility falls on those who have it to speak out on behalf of those who don't:

> Those writers plying their craft near to or far from the throne of raw power, of military power, of empire building and countinghouses, writers who construct meaning in the face of chaos must be nurtured, protected. And it is right that such protection be initiated by other writers. And it is imperative not only to save the besieged writers but to save ourselves. (*Source of Self-Regard* viii)

Is the "ourselves" here only the more fortunate writers? Or all of us as socially organized human beings? The distinction collapses if "a writer's life and work are not a gift to mankind; they are its necessity" (*Source of Self-Regard* ix). Morrison's politics are remarkably author-centric, which aligns with the prophetic strain in her social and cultural criticism but also derives more banally from the fact that her international public identity and sociocultural power are inextricable from her success as a writer in a Western, liberal, and dare one say capitalistic society. In *The Dancing Mind*, she alludes to a fundamental privilege she enjoys vis-à-vis the persecuted, desperate woman writer she met at a Parliament of Writers Congress in Strasbourg: her freedom "as a woman to write and publish unpoliced narrative"; her good fortune not to be living "in countries where the practice of modern art is illegal and subject to official vigilantism and murder" (*The Dancing Mind* 13).

What stands out most about *The Dancing Mind*, though, is the surprising relation she draws between two very different people, and two very differently situated people, by merely juxtaposing their "stories," as she calls them. The second of these is the erudite woman writer she met, doing what she can and must under a murderous authoritarian regime. The first person she only heard about, a privileged, male American graduate student who not until his mid-twenties discovered "his disability": that with all the economic and social benefits in his corner, "he had never learned to sit in a room by himself and read for four hours and have those four hours followed by another four without any companionship but his own mind"—a "skill," Morrison insists, "that was once part of any young literate person's life" (10). His case suggests to her a more benign but still deadening form of "terror" affecting affluent young Americans—a superficial "surfeit and bounty and excess" that alienates them from their own company and by extension makes them unknowable to one another (13, 12).

Fused by Morrison's probing yet sympathetic imagination, the two stories make for a kind of double-faced parable of literature's necessity, a necessity thankfully met by the publishing industry she goes on to praise. "It is a business," she acknowledges, but "the book world" has a deeper, if not exactly spiritual, bottom line:

> Its real life is about creating and producing and distributing knowledge; about making it possible for the entitled as well as the dispossessed to experience one's own mind dancing with another's; about making sure that the environment in which this work is done is welcoming, supportive. It is making sure that no encroachment of private wealth, government control, or cultural expediency can interfere with what gets written or published. That no conglomerate or political wing uses its force to still inquiry or to reaffirm rule. (*The Dancing Mind* 16–17)

This is quite the political statement—*against* any political control of literature, *on behalf of* "the peace of the dancing mind" or the "stillness" conducive to "art." One is tempted to call it a statement on behalf of art for art's sake—except that insofar as art is necessarily a form of communication for Morrison, it is always for other people's sake. Art answers a vital human need and serves indirectly to make us better political animals. In "Peril" Morrison goes so far as to declare life "bleak, unlivable, [and] insufferable" without it, evoking the totalitarian landscapes wrought by the despots and dictators who have always persecuted writers (*Source of Self-Regard* vii). She self-consciously does so from safer, more plentiful shores, those to which "writers facing peril" tend to flee. And liberal states must respond generously, she insists, just as their liberal subjects must: "The rescue we extend to them is a generosity to ourselves" (vii).

WORKS CITED

Conner, Marc C. "Introduction." *The Aesthetics of Toni Morrison: Speaking the Unspeakable*, edited by Marc C. Conner, UP of Mississippi, 2000, pp. ix–xxviii.

Denard, Carolyn C., editor. *Toni Morrison: Conversations*. UP of Mississippi, 2008.

Du Bois, W. E. B. "Criteria of Negro Art." *Writings*, edited by Nathan Huggins, Library of America, 1986, pp. 993–1002.

Flaubert, Gustave. *Correspondance*, edited by Bernard Masson, Gallimard, 1998.

Morrison, Toni. *The Dancing Mind*. Knopf, 1997.

Morrison, Toni. *Playing in the Dark: Whiteness and the Literary Imagination*. Vintage, 1993.

Morrison, Toni. *The Source of Self-Regard: Selected Essays, Speeches, and Meditations*. Random House, 2019.

Morrison, Toni. *What Moves at the Margin: Selected Nonfiction*, edited by Carolyn C. Denard, UP of Mississippi, 2008.

Nowlin, Michael. *Literary Ambition and the African American Novel*. Cambridge UP, 2019.

Ryan, Judylyn S. "Language and Narrative Technique in Toni Morrison's Novels." *The Cambridge Companion to Toni Morrison*, edited by Justine Tally, Cambridge UP, 2007, pp. 151–61.

Taylor-Guthrie, Danille, editor. *Conversations with Toni Morrison*. UP of Mississippi, 1994.

CHAPTER TWENTY

Soldiers, Identity, and Trauma: Teaching *Home* in a War Literature Course

JENNIFER HAYTOCK

War literature by and about Black Americans comprises relatively few texts, if one reads only for combat; far greater is the number of literary works that represent postwar Black experiences. Such texts convey the deep and abiding contradictions and violence at the heart of US values, structures, and culture. Toni Morrison's *Home* sparks discussions of what war entails, who it affects and in what ways, and how the particular experience of being Black in America shapes postwar trauma. With its twined gendered narratives, variety of voices and perspectives, multitude of traumatic experiences, and intricate imagery, *Home* lends itself to a range of conversations, including about trauma on the home front. As Viet Thanh Nguyen insists, "A true war story must not be only about what happens to combat soldiers and their guts but also about the nation and its guts, about running one's refrigerator, which might use a refrigerant made by Dow Chemical, the company that manufactured Agent Orange" (230). The United States' guts also include its long history of racial violence and oppression, constitutive of its structure and power dynamics and resulting in racial trauma, which can create a traumatic response to war specific to Black service members.

The course I teach, titled "Soldiers, Identity, and Trauma in American Literature," fills two roles: as an upper-division English class and as a course that meets the institution's Contemporary Issues requirement. The latter category, the capstone in the General Education program, engages students in interdisciplinary study and significant writing and research. While most students in the course major in English, quite a few students come with different academic backgrounds and take the course because of their interest in the subject. Reading consists of fiction and poetry about soldiers in American wars from the Civil War to the present, with an emphasis on literature of the recent wars (see Appendix) and theoretical essays from the interdisciplinary field of trauma studies. While some of these theoretical readings focus on war-related trauma, most address trauma more broadly. The course transitions from units on "War, war literature, and American war culture," "Trauma, trauma studies, and literary representations of war trauma," "Recent representations of soldier's trauma," "Possibilities for healing and war trauma beyond soldiers"—which is where I include *Home*—to "Art and healing." In addition to a short, close-reading essay and a longer research project, students submit summaries of the theoretical readings and written answers to study questions about the literary texts; I divide the class in half, and they alternate days to hand in written responses to these questions. I usually pose five or six questions per class period, and students choose two of those questions about which to write. The study questions encourage students to keep up with the reading, think about it ahead of time, direct their own learning through their choice of questions to answer, and have a planned contribution to the day's discussion. The questions can also be used as guides for small group work; overall, they provide students with an agenda for each class session.

On the first day of the course, I explain my expertise and scholarly interest: I'm not a military historian, a veteran, or a psychologist. I emphasize that I'm a literary scholar, and I bring to the study of war literature an awareness of how stories and poetry work, what they can share, and how readers can reflect on them. When we get to *Home*, if it is the first text by a writer of color that we read, I explicitly state that I'm white. My institution's student body is also primarily white, and rarely are there more than three or four students of color in this class. My syllabus includes a policy outlining how we talk about a text that contains racial slurs, based on the Class Covenant suggested by Karitha Mitchell.[1] I remind students of this policy at the beginning of our discussion of *Home*.

Before we read *Home*, we cover a variety of theoretical concepts related to war trauma alongside other literary texts. The introduction and chapter 5 of Cathy Caruth's *Unclaimed Experience* explain the origins of trauma theory in the work of Freud and Lacan and provide a definition of trauma as "an event that … is experienced too soon, too unexpectedly, to be fully known and is therefore not available to consciousness until it imposes itself again, repeatedly, in the nightmares and repetitive actions of the survivor." Trauma, she continues, "is always the story of a wound that cries out, that addresses us in the attempt to tell us of a reality or truth that is not otherwise available" (4). While many trauma studies scholars challenge Caruth's concept of trauma as frozen and unchangeable and hence unable to be healed, her explanation of Freudian recursiveness allows students to connect psychological trauma to literary strategies such as repetition, broken or divided timelines, unreliable narrators, and narrative fragmentation. Her metaphor of the "wound that cries out" encourages students to think about the form of a story or poem and how that form connects to meaning, who is talking, and what they are, or aren't, able to convey. Michelle Balaev's "Trends in Literary Trauma Theory" ties the experience and representation of trauma ("a person's emotional response to an overwhelming event that disrupts previous ideas of an individual's sense of self and the standards by which one evaluates society") specifically to the representative possibilities of the novel as well as the importance of culture, or what she calls "place," which she defines as "not only a location of experience, but, significantly, a facet of perception that organizes memories, feelings, and meaning at the level of the physical environment," in a character's experience of trauma (n.p.). Her work helps students understand that personal and cultural experiences and values may influence whether and how a character experiences trauma as well as affects the individual's path to recovery. Balaev's essay also contains overviews of previous scholarship about trauma, including intergenerational and collective trauma. Although I rely on her essay primarily to illuminate issues of culture, healing,

---

[1] I have found Mitchell's podcast "The N-Word in the Classroom: Just Say No" particularly useful for thinking about how I teach, as a white woman with primarily white students. Deanna Blackwell's "Sidelines and Separate Spaces" has helped me think about the experience of Black students in my courses and my responsibility to make sure they have an equal chance to experience "the classroom as a space of inquiry."

and representation in relation to individual trauma, her section on intergenerational trauma starts students thinking along lines necessary for consideration of *Home*.

Once we collectively have an understanding of what trauma is and how it appears in literature, we read "Remembrance and Mourning" from Judith Herman's foundational *Trauma and Healing* to understand strategies for treatment and recovery. I draw students' attention particularly to her description of "reconstructing the story" with the goal of creating a self unified in its past, present, and, eventually, future (176). Telling the story, Herman explains, does not get rid of the trauma or provide "closure" (a term students often default to and which I push them to abandon) but rather helps the story lose its power and its centrality in the survivor's life (195). We also discuss the role of the therapist in providing safety and helping the patient understand her story in a way that "affirms the dignity and value of the survivor" (178–9). This material encourages students to think about characters who may function in the therapist's role and about the reader's own work in critically reading the text.

Early in the semester, I present a history of understanding war trauma, outlining its theoretical evolution from nineteenth-century concepts of "railroad spine" and "soldier's heart" through shell shock, battle fatigue, posttraumatic stress disorder (PTSD), and moral injury. Understanding moral injury helps students make connections to Balaev's concept of place as central to identity and consider that trauma may result not only from what happens to a soldier but also from the soldier's own actions, from performing as an agent rather than suffering as a passive victim.[2] Moral injury, defined as "the lasting psychological, biological, spiritual, behavioral, and social impact of perpetrating, failing to prevent, or bearing witness to acts that transgress deeply held moral beliefs and expectations," conceptualizes the trauma undergone by soldiers fighting among civilian populations under a code of family cultivated by the US military after the war in Viet Nam (Litz 697). Chapter 4, "Recovering Lost Goodness," in Nancy Sherman's *Afterwar* reinforces Herman's and Litz's therapeutic reliance on a benevolent listener, real or imagined, who can hear about the veteran's experiences and hold them accountable for their actions. Sherman refers to this process as cultivating "self-empathy," kindness though not necessarily forgiveness. Students have all this grounding in trauma studies before they encounter Morrison's novel.

Home is the first, and usually only, text about the Korean War covered in the course, so I provide some historical context for this novel. With military history beyond the course's scope, I focus particularly on the experiences of Black service members; Kimberley L. Phillips's *War! What is it Good For?* provides a useful overview. For this course, I emphasize that after the Second World War, the integration of the military was closely bound to other integration struggles in the United States. During earlier wars, Black Americans hoped their military service would lead to greater access to the privileges of citizenship; Frederick Douglass urged young Black men to serve the Union cause to prove their equality, and W. E. B. Du Bois rallied Black Americans to enlist and support the United States during the Great War to secure their rights. The aftermath of both wars saw violent and legal backlash against Black people, a pattern that held true after the Second World War as well.[3] As Phillips explains, "as they pressed for the right to vote, for access to jobs,

---

[2] These ideas also help students see trauma itself as a construct, that, for example, the belief that the First World War shell-shock victim suffered from cowardice, the passivity and hence emasculating experience of the trenches, and fear differs from the Vietnam War veteran's sense of himself as suffering from guilt over criminal behavior.

[3] Texts that can supplement this history include W. E. B. Du Bois's post–First World War essay "Returning Soldiers" and Gwendolyn Brooks's poem "Negro Hero."

and for the right to travel free from terror and segregation, these men and women encountered unprecedented violence, from assaults and beatings to mutilations and murder" (65). The hope for change as a result of military service was even more pronounced during the Korean War: President Harry Truman's Executive Order 9981 in 1948 seemed to promise desegregation and advancement in the armed forces. Further, many Black men saw economic opportunity in the military when they saw none elsewhere.

Once again, however, hopes for greater equality in exchange for military service were thwarted. Truman's Executive Order did not have the effect that many hoped; it states,

> It is hereby declared to be the policy of the President that there shall be equality of treatment and opportunity for all persons in the armed services without regard to race, color, religion or national origin. This policy shall be put into effect *as rapidly as possible, having due regard to the time required* to effectuate any necessary changes *without impairing efficiency or morale*. (emphasis added)

The second sentence allowed branches of the armed forces to resist integration. Furthermore, the order could not effectively enforce "equality of treatment and opportunity," and the consequences of second-class treatment on the front lines were severe:

> Even as they fought in segregated units, black soldiers understood that their participation in combat signaled progress to many [newspaper] readers. But these men also considered the conditions they faced on the battlefield as consequences of their segregation. Unlike white units, the men did not rotate out of combat, and the entire regiment fought without relief for 126 days, beginning in late July [of 1950] and continuing through the start of the bitter winter. They were poorly supplied. Their shoes disintegrated, and they bound their feet with rags and ropes until new ones arrived weeks later. When the temperatures dropped, the men fought without jackets and gloves. (Phillips 114–15)

After the war, Black veterans returned to a nation largely indifferent to their service (and to the Korean War in general) and bent on policing the privileges of whiteness. Yet this was also the beginning of the Civil Rights Movement, with Martin Luther King, Jr. leading the Montgomery bus boycott in 1955. Resistance to Jim Crow was becoming widely organized but not yet successful during the setting of *Home*.

In a course like this one that relies on so many texts by and about white soldiers, students' tendency to see white lives as normal or typical can easily be exacerbated. Thus when I ask students to compare Frank Money's experiences with those of white soldier characters, I risk students coming away with the sense that white trauma is normal or the baseline and that of Black characters (and people) is different, or other, a tendency in white thinking that itself causes trauma to nonwhite Americans.[4] Christina Sharpe's *In the Wake: On Blackness and Being* can be valuable in talking through this issue and helping white students think about the typical, or normal, experience of Black Americans:

---

[4] See Roger Luckhurst, "War and Whiteness," for a discussion of how whiteness embeds itself as normal in American art and literature about war.

> Living in the wake means living the history and present of terror, from slavery to the present, as the ground of our everyday Black existence; living the historically and geographically dis/continuous but always present and endlessly reinvigorated brutality in, and on, our bodies while even as that terror is visited on our bodies the realities of that terror are erased. Put another way, living in the wake means living in and with terror in that much of what passes for public discourse *about* terror we, Black people, become the *carriers* of terror, terror's embodiment, and not the primary objects of terror's multiple enactments; the ground of terror's possibility globally. (15, emphasis in original)

From a clinical perspective, Lillian Comas-Días, Gordon Nagayama Hall, and Helen A. Neville's introduction to a special issue of *American Psychology* differentiates between PTSD and racial trauma in that the latter "involves ongoing injuries due to the exposure (direct and or vicarious) and reexposure to race-based stress," often intergenerational, as trauma affects an individual's ability to parent and as populations experience "historical trauma or soul wounds—the cumulative psychological wounds that result from historical traumatic experiences, such as colonization, genocide, slavery, dislocation, and other related trauma" (2).

Because *Home* is so intricately and carefully constructed, with alternating narrators, key structural events, hidden memories, and lost pasts that present a complex view of trauma and the possibilities of healing, I work methodically through the early sections. I ask students to discuss the epigraph, the mood it sets, and the issues it raises that may frame the novel. By this point in the semester, students are well aware of literary strategies that represent self-alienation, and they often note the contrast between the lightness of the dream and the darkness and shadows of the speaker's house. Some students recognize Freud's uncanny in the speaker's lack of recognition of the house that his key fits: "The 'uncanny' is that class of the terrifying which leads back to something long known to us, once very familiar" (Freud 220). I make sure students know Freud's original term, "unheimlich," or not belonging to the home. Other students might notice that while the novel is titled *Home*, the epigraph refers rather to a "house," opening up discussions of structures, belonging, and emotional connection. Students may note the number of questions in the poem and how they draw attention to the fact that the epigraph's speaker is engaged with an unknown listener.

I give students time to write for a few minutes about the first chapter, focusing on key elements of the memory it presents that might be important later. They bring up the horses and their violent behavior, the dangerous landscape of the field and fence, imagined snakes, silence, getting lost, a body with "that black foot" (*Home* 4), and the act of burial. We close read the language; the horses "stood like men," but they are not men, raising the equation between Black individuals and beasts that justified slavery and its abuses, including the selling of family members away from each other and the infliction of violence on Black bodies. The closing lines of this chapter also generate discussion: To whom is the narrator speaking? What, if anything, is the difference between the narrator's story and what we are reading?

I turn discussion to subjects that students have, by this point in the semester, learned to spot readily, beginning with Frank Money's experiences as a war veteran. Heinemann's *Paco's Story*, for example, portrays the ambivalence of American civilians toward the returning soldier and the struggles male veterans may have in their relationships with women. If we have read Silko's *Ceremony*, students are familiar with the representation of loss of self in a white-dominated psychiatric ward. Once we establish these commonalities, we turn our attention to how Frank's experience is different from that of white characters: he's hassled by police simply for being Black, for example, and aided by a network of Black churches and individuals that assist Black veterans (*Home* 18). Students identify signs of Frank's trauma, such as his anxiety, rage, drinking as self-medication, self-loathing, survivor's guilt, dreams and nightmares, and loss of memory; Lily's experience of living with Frank provides an external view of the traumatized veteran (75–81). Sometimes the class needs prompting to recognize that Morrison's strategy of narrating some sections about Frank in the third person and others in the first person conveys a sense of a split self (students who have encountered the different narrative timelines in Powers' *The Yellow Birds* may recognize this more quickly). In my experience, students are often slow to realize that the zoot-suited man Frank encounters at several points is a ghost or hallucination, perhaps because they don't connect him with war trauma.

Home, of course, opens the way for discussing trauma beyond that of war, including Cee's sexual trauma and the collective and intergenerational trauma of Black Americans. Thus, when we talk about Balaev's concept of place in relation to *Home*, we discuss Lotus but, first, the United States in the 1950s more broadly, a place and culture profoundly hostile to Frank and Cee. Students bring up the racial violence that drove the Money family from their home years earlier; how the law is used against Frank when he is not told the charges against him and is frisked by white police officers for no reason; Frank's sitting in the back of the bus; the Black man kicked out of a coffee shop; the community of Black people who help each other navigate new spaces as they travel; and Cee's limited employment opportunities in restaurants and as a private domestic worker. Many students are struck by the Black characters' acceptance of this oppression, such as the father who believes his child is better off for having been shot and so will now focus on school (31) and the Black man who may take out his shame by beating his wife. Sharpe's concept of the wake of slavery can help students connect the violence and oppression portrayed in the novel to the long scope of American history. Many students, of course, will connect Frank's experiences to the state's ongoing commitment of violence against Black people in the form of police shootings, Tasering, tear-gassing, and strangulation as well as mass incarceration.

Students may be less aware of the context for the abuse Cee receives at the hands of Dr. Beauregard Scott. The titles on his bookshelf—Hermann Joseph Muller's *Out of the Night* (1935), Madison Grant's *Passing of the Great Race* (1916), and L. C. Dunn and Theodosius Dobzhansky's *Heredity, Race, and Society* (1946)—reveal his interest in eugenics, a term Cee does not understand (65). Muller's *Out of the Night* in particular focuses on creating an improved human race by artificially inseminating women, suggesting that Dr. Beau's treatment of the poor women he sees is a massive science experiment on subjects who lack the power and knowledge to object. Students may be familiar with the story of Henrietta Lacks, given the relatively recent bestselling biography of her, or with the "Tuskegee Study of Untreated Syphilis in the Negro Male," which started in 1932 and continued without the informed consent of its participants long after the discovery of penicillin, in 1947, as a treatment for the disease. Students are often surprised to learn of the United States' long history of forced sterilizations of Black women and other women (and men) of color. This abuse, too, is part of the wake of slavery, and students can come to see that war trauma, sexual trauma, and racial trauma are linked.

In this unit of the course, we examine possibilities of healing offered by literary representations of war trauma. *Home* renders several routes to healing, each related to a particular kind of trauma, each demonstrating the possibilities and limits of the theories we've encountered. Recovering buried memories, developing self-compassion, connecting or reconnecting with loved ones and community, telling a story to a benevolent listener: all appear in the novel. At this point in the semester, students recognize the substitution of a palatable memory (the horses) for the burial of the Black man, similar to Nick Adams's replacement of his memory of the man who shot him with the image of a yellow house in Hemingway's "A Way You'll Never Be." Students notice that Frank's memories also cycle back to another moment: the Korean girl and the sexual shame she evokes. Discussing each mention of this girl in order allows them to see how her significance for Frank is revealed more fully with each mention and as he approaches Lotus. In chapter 14, Frank admits that the memory is a lie, to the author (the "you") and to himself: he ("I") takes responsibility for the memory, that he shot the girl, that he was tempted by her offer, and that temptation threatened to destroy him (133–4). Here students often raise moral injury, that Frank's deep sense of shame has shattered him and his moral code, and that to heal he must help Cee.

Yet here we often run into problems, as does Frank. Although Frank rescues Cee physically from the doctor, he must leave her in the care of Lotus's women. These women, who "loved mean," help Cee understand her value and her responsibility for herself as well as for others (*Home* 121); she must be "the one who rescued her own self" (129). Her independence from Frank's chivalric protection, however lovingly meant, leaves Frank without the role he believed would save him, a discovery that leads to his recognition of his own culpability for the fate of the Korean girl. From Cee, Frank learns that being useful is his best strategy, and like Cee, he discovers a community in Lotus, one of male veterans, that can at least provide an answer to his questions about the town's history and the man he and Cee saw buried as children.

Ghosts appear in other texts we read, such as the ghost narrators of *Paco's Story*, but students in this course may be less familiar with the function of ghosts as memories of a traumatized people, as manifestations of soul wounds passed down to Frank and Cee from their parents and community. (Morrison's use of ghosts prepares students for Nguyen's story "Black-Eyed Women" about Vietnamese-American cultural trauma.) To help understand this ghost and his place in the novel's exploration of racial trauma, we turn to Lotus, a place hated by Frank and Cee, the place where they were damaged by an unloving grandmother and absent parents, where they witness the aftermath of racial violence, a place too small for their dreams, "*the worst place in the world*" (*Home* 83, emphasis in original). The need for excitement and opportunity drives Frank and his friends out of Lotus and into the army, and then his survivor's guilt prevents him from returning until he receives the letter about Cee. Balaev's concept of place as "a facet of perception that organizes memories, feelings, and meaning at the level of the physical environment" helps us work through both Frank's and Cee's need to return to Lotus as a way to understand what has happened to them. On their return, they discover communities in Lotus that they previously had not seen or valued; the adults who ignored their long absence as children, who were preoccupied by "*some disturbance*" (5, emphasis in original), are recast as suffering their own trauma at the news that white people forced a Black son to kill his father for their entertainment and to ensure their sense of superior identity. The grandmother who destroyed their sense of worth is reframed as useless and loveless by the women who help Cee. When Frank unerringly leads Cee back to the spot where they saw the Black man disposed of like trash, they rebury him as a "man." Lotus has not changed, but Frank and Cee both come to understand themselves and their trauma by reexperiencing Lotus as a source of strength, resilience, and emotional sustenance.

As we come to the end of the novel, I ask students to look back at the first chapter and consider how the memory plays out in the rest of the novel. Students recognize that the dead man, buried in that first chapter, resurfaces; he must be unburied and reburied, his life and humanity acknowledged. While students are prepared to see this surfacing and recognition as part of the healing of individual psychic trauma, I often have to probe their ideas: after all, Frank and Cee have done little if anything to this man. They may feel guilt for having been unable to save him or preventing his undignified burial, but the larger traumatic context is historical and racial. While both characters have found ways to live with their individual traumatic memories—Frank's "abrupt, unregulated memories" connected to the deaths of his friends that now "did not crush him anymore or throw him into paralyzing despair" (*Home* 99–100); Cee's discovery that she can look "at the slaughter that went on in the world" (143)—they still live in a country that defines itself through its violence toward them. I encourage students to think critically about what Frank and Cee discover about living with individual and intergenerational trauma. Students start to see that the characters' traumatic journeys connect them more tightly to the community that supports them and provides strategies for living in their place; further, they have become equipped to help other Black Americans who no doubt will find their way to Lotus in states of trauma. These characters have also begun to separate the shame that their own actions and moral codes create and the shame that they have internalized from white Americans.[5]

Students who have read other Morrison novels will be familiar with her experimentation with form, with shifting narrators and use of fragmentation. For other students, these techniques may be new. I ask them to pay particular attention to pieces of Frank's story told in the third person and those, in italics, that are spoken by Frank himself. Given their reading in trauma studies, students fairly easily recognize the strategy as one that represents Frank as a divided, traumatized self, one version possibly even unknown to the other, as prefigured in the uncanny elements of the epigraph. I've found my students less prepared to conceptualize the "you" that appears in Frank's first-person sections. Near the end of our discussion, we revisit these "yous," from the first one: "*So you're set on telling my story, whatever you think and whatever you write down, know this: I really forgot about the burial*" (*Home* 5, emphasis in original). Students recognize her as a listener with thoughts of her own, who intends, with Frank's knowledge, to tell, or retell Frank's story, and to write it down. Some students see this "you" clearly as Morrison herself; others argue for an imagined author. I ask the students to take time in class as a writing or group exercise to examine the "you" and Frank's attitude toward her throughout the novel—the hostility in chapter 3 ("*Write about that, why don't you?*" [40]), his need for her to understand him in chapter 5 and his revision of what she wrote earlier that requires the reader to see the text as a collaboration between character and writer (69), the rejection of her omnipotent knowledge in chapters 7 ("*You never lived there so you don't know what it was like*" [84]) and 8, his direction to the author in chapter 11 ("*When you write this down, know this*" [103]), his confession of his lie and insistence on truth in chapter 14, and the

---

[5]As Bouson puts it, "a race-cognizant application of shame and trauma theory ... shows that African Americans have been forced to deal not only with individual and/or family shame and trauma but also with cultural shame and racial trauma as they are designated as the racially inferior and stigmatized Other and thus become the targets of white discrimination and violence" (6).

complete absence of the "you" in chapter 17. Students connect this "you" to Herman's description of the therapist as guide and witness; Litz's listener "who [the patients] have great respect for and who can weigh in as a relevant and generous moral authority" (704); and Sherman's concept of self-empathy.[6] I push them to think of the implications: Herman's theory of healing leads to integration of the trauma victim's memories and creation of a unified story of their life; Litz's work aims for forgiveness; and Sherman's not necessarily for forgiveness but rather for kindness to one's self. I also introduce students to Morrison's own theory of writing that requires readers' emotional participation in the characters' experiences while she provides a place of safety; Morrison, like a Black preacher, demands that her readers "behave in a certain way, to stand up and to weep and to cry and to accede or to change and to modify—to expand on the sermon that is being delivered" (Morrison qtd. in Bouson 19). In this way, students complicate their previous understanding of trauma and healing to understand their own necessary participation in the aftermath.

We usually move into the final unit of the course, "Art and healing," soon after completing *Home*. We have, of course, discussed this subject throughout the course, but we're ready to focus more fully on literature and other forms of art as providing relief from trauma (we sometimes watch documentaries like *Poster Girl* or *We Are Not Done Yet*). More broadly, these art forms, like *Home*, require such response from the reader or viewer that students have to think about war trauma in American society. Phil Klay's work about the recent wars speaks to this issue: his essay "After War, a Failure of the Imagination" argues that veterans have the responsibility to tell their stories and civilians, to hear them. His short story "War Stories" collected in *Redeployment*, describes an encounter between three veterans and a woman looking to produce a play; one veteran resents her proprietary approach to his buddy's story, while the third points out that even maggots provide a useful purpose in eating dead flesh. We're able to think about the role of listeners and readers, receptive if untrained ones, as citizens during the Forever Wars.

Students in this course tend to come away from *Home* with greater sense of the ability of literature to portray trauma in its many forms. White students in particular often express surprise that war trauma may not be the greatest test of human psychological experience. Many students choose this text for their research essays, building impressive connections among the readings of the course and beyond in their arguments. While I rotate a variety of texts through different iterations of this course, Morrison's *Home* remains constant for engaging and electrifying student learning.

APPENDIX: POSSIBILITIES FOR LITERARY READINGS

Benedict, Helen, *Sand Queen*

Crane, Stephen, *The Red Badge of Courage*

Fallon, Siobhan, "You Survived the War, Now Survive the Homecoming" in *You Know When the Men Are Gone*

Fountain, Ben, *Billy Lynn's Long Halftime Walk*

---

[6]The work of Dori Laub on the listener who creates a "holding space" for the trauma victim is also useful here (48). See Evelyn Jaffe Schreiber "Repressed Memory, Testimony, and Agency in Toni Morrison's *Home*" for a reading of the novel that builds on Laub's work.

Heinemann, Larry, *Paco's Story*

Hemingway, Ernest, "A Way You'll Never Be"

Klay, Phil, "War Stories" in *Redeployment*

Mason, Bobbie Ann, *In Country*

Nguyen, Viet Thanh, "Black-Eyed Women" in *The Refugees*

O'Brien, Tim, "How to Tell a True War Story," "Speaking of Courage," *The Things They Carried*, *In the Lake of the Woods*

Powers, Kevin, *The Yellow Birds*

Scranton, Roy, *War Porn*

Silko, Leslie, Marmon *Ceremony*

Turner, Brian, *Phantom Noise*

WORKS CITED

Balaev, Michelle. "Trends in Literary Trauma Theory." *Mosaic*, vol. 41, no. 2, 2008, pp. 149–66.

Blackwell, Deanna M. "Sidelines and Separate Spaces: Making Education Anti-Racist for Students of Color." *Race, Ethnicity, and Education*, vol. 13, no. 4, 2010, 473–94.

Bouson, J. Brooks. *Quiet as It's Kept: Shame, Trauma, and Race in the Novels of Toni Morrison*. SUNY UP, 2000.

Caruth, Cathy. *Unclaimed Experience: Trauma, Narrative, and History*. Johns Hopkins UP, 1996.

Comas-Díaz, Lillian, et al. "Racial Trauma: Theory, Research, and Healing: Introduction to the Special Issue." *American Psychologist*, vol. 74, no. 1, 2019, pp. 1–5. http://dx.doi.org/10.1037/amp0000442. Accessed Dec. 11, 2021.

Freud, Sigmund. "The 'Uncanny.'" 1919. *The Standard Edition of the Complete Psychological Works of Sigmund Freud: An Infantile Neurosis and Other Works*, vol. 17, Hogarth P, 1981, pp. 217–56.

Herman, Judith. *Trauma and Healing*. Basic Books, 1992.

Klay, Phil. "After War, a Failure of the Imagination." *New York Times*, Feb. 9, 2014. https://www.nytimes.com/2014/02/09/opinion/sunday/after-war-a-failure-of-the-imagination.html. Accessed Dec. 11, 2021.

Klay, Phil. "War Stories." *Redeployment*. Penguin, 2014, pp. 213–36.

Laub, Dori. "A Record That Has Yet to Be Made: An Interview with Dori Laub." *Listening to Trauma: Conversations with Leaders in the Theory and Treatment of Catastrophic Experience*, edited by Cathy Caruth, Johns Hopkins UP, 2014, pp. 47–78.

Litz, Brett T., et al. "Moral Injury and Moral Repair in War Veterans: A Preliminary Model and Intervention Strategy." *Clinical Psychology Review*, vol. 29, 2009, pp. 695–706.

Luckhurst, Roger. "War and Whiteness." *War and American Literature*, edited by Jennifer Haytock, Cambridge UP, 2021, pp. 315–29.

Mitchell, Karitha. "The N-Word in the Classroom: Just Say No." *C19 Podcast*, season 2, episode 6, https://soundcloud.com/c19podcast/nword/s-IK96I.

Morrison, Toni. *Home*. Alfred A. Knopf, 2012.

Nguyen, Viet Thanh. *Nothing Ever Dies: Vietnam and the Memory of War*. Harvard UP, 2016.

Phillips, Kimberley L. *War! What Is It Good For?: Black Freedom Struggles and the U.S. Military*. U of North Carolina P, 2012.

Schreiber, Evelyn Jaffe. "Repressed Memory, Testimony, and Agency in Toni Morrison's *Home*." *MFS Modern Fiction Studies*, vol. 66, no. 4, 2020, pp. 724–54.

Sharpe, Christina. *In the Wake: On Blackness and Being*. Duke UP, 2016.

Sherman, Nancy. *Afterwar: Healing the Moral Wounds of Our Soldiers*. Oxford UP, 2015.

Truman, Harry S. Executive Order 9981. Harry S. Truman Library and Museum. https://www.trumanlibrary.gov/library/executive-orders/9981/executive-order-9981. Accessed July 11, 2022.

FURTHER READING ON *HOME* AND TRAUMA

Cucarella-Ramon, Vincent. "'Any Man's Blues': Exposing the Crisis of African-American Masculinity in the Delusion of a Post-Racial United States in Toni Morrison's *Home*." *Studies in the Literary Imagination*, vol. 50, no. 2, 2017, pp. 91–108.

Montgomery, Maxine. "Bearing Witness to Forgotten Wounds: Toni Morrison's *Home* and the Spectral Presence." *South Carolina Review*, vol. 47, no. 2, 2015, pp. 14–24.

Montgomery, Maxine. "Re-Membering the Forgotten War: Memory, History, and the Body in Toni Morrison's *Home*." *CLA Journal*, vol. 55, no. 4, 2012, pp. 320–34.

Pipes, Candice L. "The Impossibility of *Home*." *War, Literature, and the Arts*, vol. 26, 2014.

Visser, Irene. "Fairy Tale and Trauma in Toni Morrison's *Home*." *MELUS*, vol. 41, no. 1, 2016, pp. 148–64.

CHAPTER TWENTY-ONE

Cotton Mather's Witches and Toni Morrison's *Paradise*

JANIE HINDS

Teaching Morrison's *Paradise* in both American Gothic and the Literature of Witchcraft in America courses, I assign the novel side by side with Cotton Mather's *Wonders of the Invisible World* to highlight the status of the "Convent women" as representative witches and to explore the limits of a gothic reading. My position is that *Paradise* uses the seventeenth-century Puritan founding of Massachusetts Bay colony, its isolationist policies and practices, its utopian goals, and especially its exclusionary principles to critique the replication of this historical founding in the US post–civil rights era. In exploring the production and function of witches and other outsiders in American culture from the 1690s onward, these courses challenge students to grapple with the intersections of race, class, and gender. While students are usually prepared to isolate race or gender in literary analysis, they are less prepared to apprehend intersectional nuances in a novel that, among other things, demonstrates the creation of outsiders through the oppressions of intra-racial hierarchies, dramatizes class hierarchies complicated by race and gender, and complicates the boundaries of gothic fiction. Grounding these courses in a reading of at least one Puritan writer contributes to several goals I pursue in teaching American literature: increased understanding of the continuities of power differentials across American history; increased understanding of American historical periods *and* the centrality of historiography; and stronger close-reading abilities, as both Mather and Morrison demand sustained attention to limited and shifting points of view.

Witchcraft in America and American Gothic, both advanced undergraduate courses, have the obviously overlapping tropes and conventions of the supernatural, victimized women, and the foregrounding of sexuality, among others. With its focus on the representation of witches in American literature, the Witchcraft course examines the naturalizing of witches in the American imaginary. That is, the witches that appear from Mather to Morrison are represented as simply a fact of nature: they exist; they are seen to have certain characteristics and to follow certain "laws" of behavior. They may hail from what Mather calls "the invisible world," but that world is no less real or rule bound than our ordinary, natural world. These witches exercise more power than other kinds of characters, but that power is explained: they gain their ability to influence the natural world by association with the devil or, in more nuanced texts, by access to occult knowledge unknown to regular folk. Fundamentally, these witches are not actually supernatural, since their surrounding communities—Mather's community and readers, or the fictional characters in Ruby of *Paradise*—accept their reality; the points of view from which witches are experienced in these texts do not see them as especially supernatural. They are, however, framed as malevolent and too powerful by the ruling-class patriarchy, who view themselves as legitimate, righteous leaders.

From the point of view of gothic fiction, on the other hand, the potential for supernatural, non-naturalized activity continually hovers over the same texts by virtue of their unexplained phenomena. When we read about the women and girls on trial for witchcraft in *Wonders*, for instance, we are told that several of them spit up pins—some a few, some a lot of pins. We as modern readers cannot explain this phenomenon (outside of those who insist on it being faked), just as we cannot explain, inside of the standard laws of nature, how the Convent women in *Paradise* seem to come back from the dead in the end—or magically disappear so they're not shot, or are hallucinated by others in a semblance of return from the dead. The American Gothic course seeks to position *Paradise* in a spectrum of gothicized genres, a spectrum that runs from the outright supernatural of, for example, the English *Castle of Otranto*, to "the fantastic" as described by Tzvetan Todorov, to the magical realism of *Paradise*. In teasing out the distinctions among these subgenres, study of Morrison's novel challenges students to recognize the American gothic practice of naturalizing some elements while refusing to naturalize others. This chapter will devote most space to the Witchcraft course, as it is the more demanding and more complex of the two, and will end with a shorter description of the American Gothic course's treatment of the same material.

WITCHES AT THE CONVENT

Whatever the interpretive frame, the key parallel between Mather's and Morrison's texts has to do with Morrison's Convent women as witches, which is the undeniable truth according to Ruby's patriarchs, if not all of the nine men who invade the Convent in the first and near-last chapter of this circular novel. After they "shoot the white girl first," the men split up to find the remaining three women who, to their mind, need to be dealt with because they "threatened the town's view of itself" (3, 8). They believe they might find "witch tracks" out back of the building (4). Like historical witches, these women "sleep not in a bed, like normal people, but in a hammock"; the men find "a satanic message" written in blood (which we later learn is actually a long-ago note written in lipstick from a mother to her daughter upon abandoning her); and they find, to their horror, infant things like a crib and shoes (7). One of the men moves closer to the baby shoes, "looking for what? More evidence? He isn't sure. Blood? A little toe, maybe, left in a white calfskin shoe?" (8). The women are thought to be part of a cult. The men are sure that terrible things in their town, Ruby, have been somehow caused by these women who live seventeen miles outside of town:

> Outrages that had been accumulating all along took shape as evidence. A mother was knocked down the stairs by her cold-eyed daughter. Four damaged infants were born in one family. Daughters refused to get out of bed. Brides disappeared on their honeymoons. Two brothers shot each other on New Year's Day. Trips to Demby for VD shots common … the one thing that connected all these catastrophes was in the Convent. (11)

Mather's and other historical witches are thought to perform their malice from a distance, so the fact that there is no concrete connection between the Convent women and these events in Ruby only supports, rather than weakens, the men's view of the women. From these textual parallels, the Witchcraft course opens up into Puritan ideology in general and Mather's text in particular, with close attention to race and gender in the construction of witches.

Marni Gauthier and Katrine Dalsgard each examine the theme of American exceptionalism in *Paradise*, with specific attention to the Puritan roots of that exceptionalism. The Puritan story of exceptional America solidified around the escape from persecution in Europe to create an exemplary "city upon a hill," as John Winthrop termed it, built in New England, a space of moral superiority, even of God's chosen people. The Puritan master narrative, in keeping with their typological historiography that read current events and people as "types" of Biblical antetypes, layered the Puritan exodus over the New Testament narrative of Exodus, the "errand into the wilderness" made into a successful (white) civilization by the first-generation male leaders. This Puritan master narrative amounted to a hagiography—a biography of the saints—that, developed by the second and third generations, turned quickly to a jeremiad, a complaint about the moral decay of the community since the time of the saintly first founders. It is easy enough to point out to students the parallels in *Paradise:* the oral history of the creation of Haven-as-paradise and, after it, of Ruby, out of persecution by both whites and Blacks, along with the deeply patriarchal positions of both narratives. Dalsgard and Gauthier successfully argue that this master narrative extends, in *Paradise*, beyond those outlines to specific Biblical parallels favored in Puritan writings, for example, the story of Zechariah ("Old Papa") being led through the wilderness by a spirit (by "the signs that God gave to guide them" [14]) to the place where Haven was to be built, as a latter-day Moses being led through and out of the wilderness by God.[1]

Looking at the ideology that underwrites this master narrative, Gauthier maintains that *Paradise* reconstructs and deconstructs the nation-building consolidation of Americanness in opposition to those considered outsiders, outsiders who may be "among us" but who are unacceptable because of difference in looks and/or behavior. In the Witchcraft course, I point out that Cotton Mather repeatedly defines "the nation," New England, specifically chosen by God, as the envy of Satan, who seeks to recover what was his own dominion from the righteous Puritans.[2] Mather serves as more than just a representative nation-building Puritan, however, and once we cover the master narrative in Puritan mythology and that of *Paradise*, a closer examination of *Wonders of the Invisible World* offers an uncanny array of parallels at both the granular and historiographical levels. Though it was a common enough Puritan trope, the idea of "building a hedge" around God's people to keep Satan's minions out takes on a nearly literal meaning in the context of the witchcraft trials Mather records. "When ungodly people," Mather writes, "give their Consents in witchcrafts diabolically performed, for the Divel [sic] to annoy their Neighbours, he finds a Breach made in the Hedge about us, whereat he Rushes in upon us, with grievous molestations" (11). In light of the literal and figurative troping of the hedge, the history of Ruby, and Haven before it, takes on more significant nuances.

Haven, begun in 1890 by the Old Fathers of *Paradise*, flourished until a railroad was built nearby—close enough to "contaminate" the pure eight-rock (very dark-skinned) founders with impure outsiders. Haven's decline cannot be attributed to the Depression, since the town thrived

---

[1]Linda J. Krumholz examines several Biblical underpinnings of *Paradise*, with specific attention to the concept of paradise itself and its loss in Genesis, along with the centrality of "grace" in the novel. See "Reading and Insight in Toni Morrison's *Paradise*."

[2]There is a subtext here regarding Native Americans as "the devil's people," not unique to Mather. Space does not allow a thorough exploration of the exceptionalist trope of evil Indians in early narratives of discovery and settlement. *Paradise*, however, does explore this trope to a degree in the history of the Convent as a school where Cheyenne-Arapaho girls "once sat and learned to forget" (4) and who secretly "whisper[ed] to each other in a language the sisters had forbidden them to use" (232).

during those years, yet the town failed during the nationwide postwar boom (Gauthier 401). The railroad brought "grovel contaminating the town their grandfathers had made" (*Paradise* 16). Having been thus contaminated by a breach in the hedge, the New Fathers—Deacon (Deek) and Steward Morgan—pack up the failing town to begin again, to build a new hedge around a patriarchal community whose unspoken rules insist that to be protected, women must be pure of race and pure of "virtue," and to be included, young people must not differ from their elders. The "satisfactory" town, in Deek's mind, has "quiet white and yellow houses full of industry; and in them were elegant black women at useful tasks; orderly cupboards minus surfeit or miserliness; linen laundered and ironed to perfection; good meat seasoned and ready for roasting. It was a view he would be damned if K.D. (his nephew) or the idleness of the young would disturb" (111). The industry of Ruby's acceptable women is allegorized by the flower gardens, grown in the 1950s and 1960s when women had leisure to grow something that couldn't be eaten, instead of the useful vegetables of the previous generations. Ironically, these flowers, like the neat houses, signify stagnation rather than growing life.

Rather than actually hedging the town to keep outsiders out, these plantings threaten to breach the hedge as they draw connections among the women from inside and outside the town, and it is from this point in its history that Ruby becomes subject to, in Steward Morgan's mind, "a Convent [that] would beat out the snakes, the Depression, the tax man and the railroad for sheer destructive power" (17). The hedge of righteousness, built on the restricted freedoms of its residents much like the creation of the United States around the limitations on people of color and women on the grounds of security, remains a fiction for all of its being the official history—a fiction because some of the disenfranchised, like Billie Delia Cato and Lone DuPres, step outside of Ruby's protections to interact and form deep bonds with the women of the Convent.

The draw of the Convent, for these women, is its freedom and nurturance. Connie's hot peppers and pepper relish are well-known; even men occasionally drop by for these items. But it is rumored that Connie, witch like, cooks up other, less innocuous concoctions. There is the trip to the Convent Soane made in 1954 to end a pregnancy, and in the present, Connie makes a "tonic" for Soane, who finds the air to be too "thin" after both her sons are killed in Vietnam. Like the witches prosecuted at Salem and elsewhere, Connie, and by extension the other Convent women, more closely represent the "cunning women" of seventeenth- and eighteenth-century England and America, women whose knowledge of plants makes them both useful to and feared by the community—useful until they are feared. The cunning woman's healing powers were sought out, but often seen as magic by those ignorant of medicinal plants; this woman has long been an easy target when the unexplainable occurs. And in fact, Connie has learned—from Lone, Ruby's midwife who spends a lot of time collecting plants—how to "step inside" another person to keep them from dying, at the expense of her own well-being. The association of these women with magical abilities and with plant knowledge supports the characterization of them as witches as their gifts seem to overpower the patriarchal hedge designed to keep "good" women safe and un-free.

One of these good women, Sweetie Fleetwood, the mother of the four "damaged infants" who has not left her house for years taking care of the children, finds herself at the Convent after walking away during a snowstorm in what appears to be a mental health episode. As one of the women who take shelter at the Convent for longer or shorter periods, Sweetie's experience, even as focalized from her point of view, demonstrates care on the part of the Convent women, beginning with Seneca, who finds Sweetie freezing in the road and wraps her in a serape. Sweetie's interpretation, however, is that this care is the ruse of a "demon" and that the women at the Convent, when she and Seneca arrive there, "seemed like birds, hawks ... Pecking at her, flapping ... she prayed for deliverance" (129). When her husband, Jeff, and Anna Flood find her, she reports that "they made me, snatched me" (130), though they had in fact treated her fever with appropriate remedies and understanding. According to Mather and his sources, one type of solid evidence to be used in a witchcraft trial is "Testimony of the Party *Bewitched*," and the "evidence" being sought against the Convent women certainly includes Sweetie's testimony on her return to Ruby.

Additional "testimony" of the bewitched includes that of K.D., who helps incite the nine men to raid the Convent to rid the community of the Convent women, by "talking about how strange one of those Convent girls was and how he knew it right away soon as he saw her get off the bus" (278); what K.D.'s testimony omits is his yearslong affair with said woman, Gigi, until she eventually refuses to see him again. *Wonders of the Invisible World* codifies several "Rules" for the "Discovery of Witches," which, in addition to "testimony," includes "Cursing and Banning (condemning)" and "living a lewd and naughty kind of Life" (xxvii). Indeed, some of the Convent women do swear, and even fight among themselves. That they are sexually promiscuous confirms the official view of them in Ruby as "lewd," living a "naughty kind of Life," even while the promiscuous men of Ruby are not condemned for fornication or even adultery, though both are widely known to take place. To the patriarchal mind in Ruby, which includes some of the women, women's so-called purity is the price of their protection within the hedge of acceptance. These gender distinctions and the stranglehold of patriarchy in *Paradise* are made more transparent to student-readers after exposure to the more obvious gender double standard in Mather's text.

While a few of Ruby's women seek out the Convent women for shelter and nurturance, the Convent women themselves breach the invisible hedge around Ruby. With rare exception, their appearance in town causes some kind of scandal. For example, the Convent women come to Arnette and K.D.'s (forced) wedding, at the invitation of Soane, in a rare mixing of the populations inside and outside the town. Dressed and behaving in ways not acceptable to the conservative strictures of the town, the women threaten the ruling social order by violating the rules for women established by Ruby's "idea of itself." To make matters worse, some young men of Ruby openly fraternize with the Convent women with barely disguised sexual attraction. The women laugh loudly and dance to radio music: dressed in miniskirts, asking for something alcoholic to drink, and "dancing nasty," as Rev. Pulliam's wife puts it (158), these women are seen as Mather's witches were, in their "Exstacies" or unhidden emotional displays (*Wonders* xxix). Mather "recommend(s) ... the Vigorous Prosecution of such, as have rendred (*sic*) themselves Obnoxious according to the best Directions given in the Laws of God, and the wholesome Statutes of the English Nation, for the Detection of Witchcraft" (xxi–xxii). The Convent women are expelled from the wedding. In short, they have made themselves obnoxious by their perceived low-class behavior.

The events at the wedding merely confirm what the ruling Ruby men have already concluded: that the Convent women are the root of the degeneration of the Old Fathers' vision for this exceptional group. The Convent women, to begin with, violate the strict racial hierarchy of the town, since they welcome white as well as Black women. Strict racial hierarchies have underwritten the hegemonic power of Ruby since before it was founded, since Haven. The light-skinned, like Pat Best and her family, are denied full citizenship and representation in town events such as the annual Christmas pageant. Yet racial mixing alone does not mark the Convent women as witches—their different class behavior does. They are "slack" because they haven't industriously gotten their canning jars ready for harvest yet, for example, when the men raid the Convent. They live without obvious means of support—husbands or jobs. They "dance nasty." In Lone's chapter, near the novel's end, the nine men meet to psych themselves up for their raid on the Convent, guns in hand. Lone, something of a seer, hears both what is said and what is thought during this scene. Several men speak, linking the behavior of the Convent women to the town's degeneration:

> Remember how they scandalized the wedding? ... it was that very same day I caught them kissing on each other in the back of that ratty Cadillac (one was actually holding another, trying to warm her). Very same day, and if that wasn't enough to please the devil, two more was fighting over them in the dirt ... Lord, I hate a nasty woman. Sweetie said they tried their best to poison her ... Whatever it is, it ain't natural ... You think they got powers? I *know* they got powers ... No men. Kissing on themselves. Babies hid away ... Bitches. More like witches ... Before those heifers came to town this was a peaceable kingdom. (275–6, emphasis in original)

Steward, characteristically silent at this meeting, has thoughts even more acrimonious than what gets spoken aloud. This twin specifically links the Convent with the breaching of race and family boundaries, while the other men speak of class behavior. Having known all along about his twin's affair with Connie, Steward marshals most of his hatred toward Connie:

> It was a floating blister in his bloodstream ... how close his brother came to breaking up his marriage to Soane. How off the course Deek slid when he was looking in those poison and poisoning eyes ... and just suppose the hussy had gotten pregnant? Had a mixed-up child? Steward seethed at the thought of that barely averted betrayal of all they owed and promised the Old Fathers. (279)

He is angry at his brother, but the cause of the problem, as Steward sees it, is "this new and obscene breed of female," with their "streetwalkers' clothes and whores' appetites" (279). The greatest "betrayal" of Ruby's "idea of itself" would be the production of a mixed-race child. The novel combines race, class, and gender as intersecting platforms at this gathering designed to both create and exclude the outsider witches.[3]

Close reading of point of view is central to a study of this gathering. By this point in the course, the central issues of witchcraft, race, class, and gender have been exposed by reading and discussing the Mather and Morrison texts, and from this point, students can have the perspective to study *how* we know what we know about both texts. The next step is an introduction to historiography as a scaffold for the close reading, since no reading, close or otherwise, is done without a position or ideology of its own. We discuss some approaches historians might take to understand what Morrison would call the "truth": as Morrison explained, history is always informed by imagination,

---

[3]Morrison, well-schooled in the history of witch trials in America, includes at this gathering of the nine Ruby men one, Sargeant, who joins in the witch hunt because he wants the land the Convent sits on:

> He would be thinking how much less his outlay would be if he owned the Convent land, and how, if the women are gone from there, he would be in a better position to own it. Everyone knew he had already visited the Convent—to "warn" them, which is to say he offered to buy the place, and when the response was an incomprehensible stare, he told the old woman (Connie) to "think carefully" and that "other things could happen to lower the price." (277)

In the history of people condemned to death for witchcraft, for several centuries—including the seventeenth-century Salem trials—the condemned's property was forfeited to the state or township (see David C. Brown, "The Forfeitures at Salem, 1692").

but imagination is also always informed by memory, "no matter how 'fictional' the account"; "the crucial distinction for me is not the difference between fact and fiction, but the distinction between fact and truth" ("The Site of Memory," 113). Clearly, the facts within a fiction—the history of these fictional characters—bear a kind of truth, according to Morrison. In the Witchcraft course, we consider types of evidence we might accept as "truthful." Do we trust oral histories more than written ones? Do we trust primary or secondary sources more? When looking for the "truth" of a community, what would be primary and what would be secondary? Once we establish three or four historiographical methods, the class then works in small groups, each assigned a different methodology, for a close reading of, first, the scene of the gathering of men in Lone's chapter and, second, the novel's first chapter, which in the novel's timeline actually follows the men's gathering. The goal is for each group to do a timeline of events discussed in these two chapters, focusing only on the "evidence" their methodology allows them to accept. This is painstaking work and should involve them making charts or diagrams to keep track of their findings. (There are timelines available online, but they do not specify which characters know what, and when they know it.)

On sharing these timelines with the full class, we learn, of course, that they tell different stories, which leads us ultimately to have to decide which is the most "truthful" story—that is, what kinds of evidence Morrison seems to privilege, and why. This exercise is designed to allow students to unearth, individually and collectively, their own proclivities and biases in producing their truths. Gauthier submits that the novel's Pat Best serves as a good example of a legitimate historian: "The methods of a lone genealogist among the citizens of Ruby serve as a model for reading *Paradise*, and as a metaphor for the novel's sense of historiography: 'Any footnotes, crevices, or questions to be put took keen imagination and the persistence of a mind uncomfortable with oral histories'" (Gauthier 399, *Paradise* 188). I ask students in the Witchcraft class to think carefully about this assertion and decide whether or not Pat's historiography is best, and why. A close reading of Pat's history of Haven and Ruby, drawn from studying family Bibles, listening to gossip, and reading her own students' genealogy homework, recognizes the practice of Puritan typology, particularly as she records her thoughts on the annual Christmas pageant. The nativity play, put on since the founding of Ruby, features not one holy family but seven; Pat puzzles over the fact that it used to have nine, then eight families, but has dwindled to seven, guessing that the families who violate the pure-blood law of Ruby stop being allowed representation in the play—her own family included. Whatever the reason, it's clear that the play layers the story of Christ's nativity with the Disallowing: as the holy family was turned away from the inn, so were the dark-skinned families turned away from Fairly, Oklahoma, where they had traveled to settle. This turning away prompted the founding of Haven and the beginning of their official history. Deeply imprinted on the psyche of Ruby's citizens is not the founding itself, nor the actual birth of Christ, but rather the unbearable hurt of being rejected. Telling their story typologically, they glorify their founding and their people; they see themselves as God's elect. Pat Best recognizes the typology in the nativity play, and it is important for my students to recognize, in their study of Pat's own historiography, that she sees Ruby's historiography critically. She sees it as part of the ideology that builds a hedge around the town. It is the methodology of the New Fathers, in particular the Morgan twins.

In this reading exercise, one group is assigned to closely read the novel's oral histories, those produced by Deek and Steward Morgan, who "remember everything that ever happened—things they witnessed and things they have not" (*Paradise* 16). A discussion of memory, individual and collective, is useful here, as is a reminder that Cotton Mather, for all his "recording" of the Salem trials, was not in fact present at the trials; his record is a compilation of his theory of witches combined with what has been reported to him orally and in writing about the trials. It is a secondary source masquerading as a primary source. Just as importantly, students are asked to consider whose point of view in Ruby's history and historiography most closely resembles that of Mather. It should be clear by now that Ruby's patriarchs sound most like Cotton Mather. It follows that the other histories of *Paradise* are counter-histories to the patriarchal, American exceptionalist vision. The official history comes under severe questioning by events as seen from others' points of view—particularly the points of view of women both in Ruby and at the Convent—and even by the close reading of the twins' interior monologues themselves. To seal our understanding that the Morgans have more in common with Cotton Mather than they do with many of the women of Ruby and the Convent, I remind students that Mather's position as a church patriarch was precisely that of the 1970s Morgan twins: third-generation "fathers" whose adulation of the first founders' ideology is put under pressure by the changing times and new ideas of the young people. Both Mather and the Morgans speak and write jeremiads about these changing times; not only the Morgans, but also the Baptist and Pentecostal ministers of Ruby, Pulliam and Cary, preach about "Evil Times" and "Last Days" after the discovery of a Black Power fist painted on the town's central icon, the Oven (102). These men represent the Old Fathers in hagiographic terms, saint like compared to the present generation. Compare Mather: "The first Planters of these Colonies were a *Chosen Generation* of men, who were first so *Pure* as to disrelish many things which they thought wanted *Reformation* else where; and yet withal so *Peaceable*, that they Embraced a Voluntary Exile in a Squalid, horrid, *American* Desart" (*Wonders* x, emphases in original), whereas "Those Interests of the *Gospel*, which were the Errand of our Fathers into these Ends of the Earth, have been too much Neglected ... especially of our Young ones, when they have got abroad from under the *Restraints* here laid upon them" (xi).

It is possible to view the course's reading of *Paradise* along with Mather's *Wonders* as a kind of typological exercise in itself, a layering of a recent "history" over a long-ago "history" in a demonstration of the circularity of history. If seen this way, an unfortunate outcome might be an inability to see change over time, or to simply and finally label the patriarchs of Ruby as witch-hunting Puritans, and leave it at that. It is important that the class does not end these readings on that note. That Morrison, through the characters of Pat Best and other women critical of the town's restrictive, patriarchal hedge, provides a view above and beyond the Puritan view is the point: we do currently repeat the American exceptionalist position that (white) Americans are a kind of chosen people, righteous in restricting outsiders; however, we can *also* contest that history, and try to overcome it. David Schell points out that, in fact, *Paradise* does not end with history prevailing, or the death of the Convent women; it ends with the women's resurrection into a new kind of life, a future created by "taking up the fluid and 'endless work' of narrating the past to each other [to lead] from that past to a possible future" (Schell 91, *Paradise* 318).

THE SUPERNATURAL IN THE GOTHIC

The American Gothic course ends with a pairing of *Wonders* and *Paradise*, as does the Witchcraft course, though in American Gothic we read only select passages from Mather so as to establish the defining characteristics of witches over time, with less attention to the Puritan master narrative. This American Gothic is more an old-fashioned genre course, designed to encourage close-reading skills, with the goal of increased ability to establish subtle differences among texts. A key concept throughout the course is the relative presence or absence of the supernatural, and the interplay of text and reader in the creation of the supernatural. American Gothic is generally considered to be less overtly supernatural than its parent, the English gothic, and thus the course challenges students to find "the gothic" where there are fewer or no supernatural elements.

This course requires clear understanding of several genre-defining concepts, and in fact is organized not chronologically but topically, around these concepts and common tropes of the gothic. Thus, we spend time on the common tropes of the "haunted" house, doubling, and "the female victim," each of which will be immediately recognized when we read *Paradise*. Beyond the tropes, the course works with a spectrum of gothicized genre definitions, using Tzvetan Todorov's concept of "the fantastic" as the middle term of our spectrum. In the history of the gothic, the earliest examples—mostly English—include the unequivocally supernatural. Horace Walpole's *Castle of Otranto* (1764), widely considered the first gothic novel in English, involves such outright supernatural events as an ancient curse coming to pass with a giant helmet falling on a bridegroom on the day of his wedding, and eventually a ghost that destroys the castle. The truly supernatural, which needs careful definition in this course, amounts to things that cannot happen under the regular laws of nature: the dead do not come back and giants and their helmets do not actually exist. The relationship of reader to text in encountering the unquestionably supernatural is suspension of disbelief. We accept the reality as presented, but we accept it as fictional. Cotton Mather, on the other hand, would say events like these—for example, a curse that has physical consequences—are not fictional, but rather that they come from "the Invisible World" or "the Unseen Regions." The supernatural is naturalized by the fundamentalist faith of Puritan believers; the existence of both God and Satan demand that the supernatural be naturalized. Witches, and their ability to deploy forces from the invisible world, are naturalistically explained.

However, for the modern reader, there is a hard and fast line between the supernatural and the natural. Here is where Todorov's analysis of the fantastic becomes useful. He defines the fantastic as the moment of hesitation between belief and disbelief in the supernatural. "The fantastic occupies the duration of this uncertainty. Once we choose one answer or the other, we leave the fantastic for a neighboring genre, the uncanny or the marvelous. The fantastic is that hesitation experienced by a person who knows only the laws of nature, confronting an apparently supernatural event" (25). For the purposes of American Gothic, we can adopt "the uncanny" and/or "the marvelous" as genres in themselves, or we can simply use that moment of hesitation to define a middle ground, the fantastic, between a supernatural and an "explained," non-supernatural text. An important aspect of this study is to reinforce that it is the reader—and sometimes the characters—who creates the genre: it is our hesitation as readers that creates the fantastic.

By the time the class comes to *Paradise* and *Wonders*, all of this ground has been laid. Reading Mather through these lenses is straightforward: Mather believes, but we do not. We may hesitate at the point where the women and girls being tried for witchcraft begin to spit up pins, since we cannot explain this activity other than to attribute it to trickery or misunderstanding on the part of the trial audience. But most readers don't hesitate for long before making a decision, as Todorov explains, about the ontological status of this event. *Paradise* calls for a more robust reading, much of which involves study of the "witchcraft" analyzed in the first part of this chapter. As with the Witchcraft class, the Gothic class generally decides that the Convent women either are not witches, but are only seen as such by the patriarchs of Ruby, or they do have special powers, but those are explained by their knowledge and training. Lone DuPres can hear the thoughts of others, and both Connie and Lone can "step in" to save a dying person, but since *Paradise* reveals that Lone has taught Connie, and that both Connie and Lone have extensive knowledge of healing plants, their "cunning woman" work is part of the natural, not the supernatural, world. Importantly, a gothic treatment produces fear of the unexplainable, whereas *Paradise* does not invite fear of the Convent women since we know their individual stories from their own points of view. They are, in effect, explained, whereas fear comes from the unexplained.

On the other hand, there are unexplainable events in this novel, including the butterflies and especially the mysterious "friend" of Dovey Morgan, who appears out of and disappears into nowhere, whom no one else encounters, and who seems to exist only to provide a sympathetic ear to this lonely woman. More troubling to readers, since the stakes are higher, are the circumstances surrounding the "deaths" of the Convent women. The nine men from Ruby shoot them; we closely witness the death of Connie. And yet the subsequent chapter shows an afterlife for all five of these women, as they encounter those people most important to their early lives—one might say they encounter those whom they love the most. They appear strong and independent, and all but Connie are on their way to new adventures. There is no explaining these events. Unlike the naturalizing of the "witches" of the Convent, these afterlives are supernatural. That *Paradise* includes both treatments of the supernatural can frustrate readers, and it sends us back to our spectrum of gothicized genres.

Only at this point in the course do we begin to study magical realism, which occupies the other end of the spectrum from the outright supernatural. Magical realism generally presents a realistic, recognizable, often even mundane reality, into which appears unexplainable, supernatural elements. Crucially, the supernatural elements are not treated as fear-inducing or extraordinary; they simply appear as if they are natural, more magic than supernatural. The character Jésus Arrabal, in Thomas Pynchon's *The Crying of Lot 49*, describes such "magic" as "another world's intrusion into this one" (88). Magical realism involves neither the fully supernatural of *Otranto* nor the hesitating between ontological realities of Todorov's fantastic: there is no hesitation between the natural and the supernatural and thus no choice finally made by the reader between the two. As readers, we must accept both.

When *Paradise* was published in 1997, I asked a colleague who had read it whether I should read it. With something of a sniff, he replied: "It's gothic." What he meant as a condemnation actually sent me to the book store immediately, and I began teaching it shortly thereafter. Over many readings with several classes, including the American Gothic class that literally frames this novel as gothic, I have come to a clearer sense of why that comment, "It's gothic," irritated me so much. It was an obviously classist sort of comment that relegates the gothic to the less-than-literary status, not worthy of serious study. Since that time, however, I have learned much from my students, from their serious study and close understanding of both the genre and *Paradise*. As one student aptly put it: "It's not gothic. It's just sad."

WORKS CITED

Brown, David C. "The Forfeitures at Salem, 1692." *William and Mary Quarterly*, vol. 50, no. 1, Jan., 1993, pp. 85–111.

Dalsgard, Katrine. "The One All-Black Town Worth the Pain: (African) American Exceptionalism, Historical Narration, and the Critique of Nationhood in Toni Morrison's *Paradise*." *African American Review*, vol. 35, no. 2, Summer, 2001, pp. 233–48.

Gauthier, Marni. "The Other Side of 'Paradise': Toni Morrison's (Un)making of Mythic History." *African American Review*, vol. 39, no. 3, Fall, 2005, pp. 395–414.

Krumholz, Linda J. "Reading and Insight in Toni Morrison's *Paradise*." *African American Review*, vol. 36, no. 1, Spring, 2002, pp. 21–34.

Mather, Cotton. *Wonders of the Invisible World: Observations as Well Historical as Theological, upon the Nature, the Number, and the Operations of the Devils*. 1693, edited by Reiner Smolinski. Electronic Texts in American Studies 19. University of Nebraska at Lincoln.

Morrison, Toni. *Paradise*. Alfred A. Knopf, 1997.

Morrison, Toni. "The Site of Memory." *Inventing the Truth: The Art and Craft of Memoir*, edited by William Zinsser. Houghton Mifflin, 1987, pp. 101–24.

Pynchon, Thomas. *The Crying of Lot 49*. J. B. Lippincott. 1966.

Schell, David. "Engaging Foundational Narratives in Morrison's *Paradise* and Pynchon's *Mason & Dixon*." *College Literature*, vol. 41, no. 3, Summer, 2014, pp. 69–94.

Todorov, Tzvetan. *The Fantastic: A Structural Approach to a Literary Genre*. Translated by Richard Howard. Cornell UP, 1975.

CHAPTER TWENTY-TWO

"What Are You without Racism?": Toni Morrison on Perfectionism and White Supremacy

CHRISTOPHER S. LEWIS

In *The Bluest Eye*, narrator Claudia shares that, in her earliest days, she "had only one desire: to dismember it. To see of what it was made" (20). Unimpressed by "it"—a blonde baby doll, a Shirley Temple teacup, and the overall concept of white girl innocence and beauty that subsumes many of those around her—Claudia instead yearns to investigate what "it"—whiteness—is, "to see of what it was made" (20) and where its cultural associations with beauty, goodness, purity, and perfection originated. This investigation, launched within the first pages of Toni Morrison's first novel, is one of the most enduring elements of Morrison's work overall. "My project," she writes in *Playing in the Dark: Whiteness and the Literary Imagination*, "is an effort to avert the critical gaze from the racial object to the racial subject; from the described and imagined to the describers and imaginers; from the serving to the served" (90). This ongoing disruption of the white gaze—or the point of view that prioritizes, assumes, and esteems whiteness as central, normal, and ultimately superior to blackness—makes Morrison's work one of the most, if not *the* most, important sources of information, knowledge, and wisdom about whiteness and white supremacy in our world today (and this is but one of its accomplishments). "I have spent my entire writing life trying to make sure that the white gaze was not the dominant one in any of my books," Morrison said in a 1998 interview with Charlie Rose that was later shared in Timothy Greenfield-Sanders's 2019 documentary *Toni Morrison: The Pieces I Am*. The deliberation and care with which she undertook this work provides a trustworthy resource today for examining, among other phenomena, whiteness without a white gaze.

Claudia's investigation early on in *The Bluest Eye* contributes to a centuries-long project among African American writers to unveil not only the lives of Black people, but whiteness as well. The writing and storytelling of Phillis Wheatley, Olaudah Equiano, Mary Prince, Frederick Douglass, Harriet Jacobs, and Harriet Wilson, among others, contributed foundational understandings to this project. For example, in his 1845 autobiography *Narrative of the Life of Frederick Douglass*, Douglass writes of a white Northern woman named Mrs. Auld who marries a Southern man and becomes the co-owner of the people he enslaves. She is initially kind to Douglass and begins to teach him to read, but eventually experiences a swift transformation:

> Slavery proved as injurious to her as it was to me ... Under its influence, the tender heart became stone ... The first step in her downward course was in her ceasing to instruct me. She now commenced to practice her husband's precepts. She finally became *even more violent* in her opposition *than her husband himself*. She was *not satisfied with simply doing* as *well* as he had commanded; she seemed *anxious to do better*. (37, emphasis added)

Here, Douglass documents the compromised morality and humanity of white slaveholders. In describing Auld as increasingly vindictive, anxious, and unsatisfied, Douglass describes traits of whiteness that Morrison and other writers continued to explore decades later. Douglass's bold claim that "slavery proved as injurious to her as it was to" him may initially seem puzzling, given that his experience of slavery and Auld's experience of slavery seem incommensurable, but Douglass points to the outwardly and inwardly damaging habits of mind, including perfectionism and social hierarchization, that ultimately lead to the corrosion—what Douglass calls "bec[oming] stone"—of racist psyches.

In *The Bluest Eye*, Claudia shares that her early investigation into whiteness, a phenomenon exemplified for her by Shirley Temple, later became complicated by the education she received: "I learned much later to worship her, just as I learned to delight in cleanliness, knowing, even as I learned, that the change was adjustment without improvement" (23). While she learns to rejoice in the cleanliness and perfection associated with whiteness, Claudia knows this shift remains "repulsive" (23). She models a critical reevaluation, rooted in her own desires and knowledge, of what she is taught via the media, at school, and through American English itself, which Morrison has explained involves "false comfort and fake innocence and evasion and hypocrisy" (*Source* 230). The language and association of whiteness with purity, cleanliness, and perfection is indeed part of this fake innocence and evasion. As Richard Dyer explains in his 1988 essay "White," "It is said (even in liberal textbooks) that there are inevitable associations of white with light and therefore safety, and black with dark and therefore danger, and that this explains racism (whereas one might well argue about the safety of the cover of darkness, and the danger of exposure to light)" (45). These supposedly inevitable associations constitute both the false comfort and the evasion of American English as it has been used for generations. In a 1993 interview with Charlie Rose, Morrison refers to the angry and fevered entitlement among many white people (including Auld in Douglass's writing) and simultaneous belief in white innocence as a "profound neurosis" with severe consequences for white people. She explains,

> The people who do this thing, who practice racism, are bereft. There is something distorted about the psyche ... It's like it's a profound neurosis that nobody examines for what it is ... And it has just as much of a deleterious effect—and possibly equal—on white people as it does black people. I always knew that I had the moral high ground, all my life. I always thought those people who said I couldn't come into the drug store ... or couldn't go in the park—I thought they knew that I knew that they were inferior to me morally. ("Toni Morrison, HBCU Grad" 0:11–1:05)

Referring to racism as a profound and anxious obsession, Morrison anticipates the work of present-day psychologists who are finding similar connections between racist thinking, anxiety, obsession, perfectionism, and vindictiveness toward the self and others. The compulsion to pursue and meet white supremacist standards, and to assess others via those same standards, leads to a dangerous disconnect from the realities, richness, diversity, and possibilities of dirt, imperfection, and a mode of existence not predicated on a false hierarchy of human value. In the same interview, Morrison goes on to say,

> The racist white person ... doesn't understand that he or she is also a race [that is] also constructed ... also made, and [that] also has some kind of serviceability. But ... if I take your race away, and there you are all strung out and all you've got is your little self ... what is that? What are you without racism? Are you any good? Are you still strong? Still smart? Do you still like yourself? ... If you can only be tall because somebody's on their knees, then you have a serious problem. And my feeling is white people have a very, very serious problem. And they should start thinking about what they can do about it. Take me out of it. ("Toni Morrison, HBCU Grad" 1:17–2:35)

Morrison's directive to white people in particular here involves self-reflection and a reevaluation of one's self-esteem, accomplishments, and purported goodness in light of the cultural tendency to define white worthiness against an imagined valuelessness projected onto Black people.

Today, reevaluating the white standards of beauty, perfection, success, cleanliness, and lovability we are taught remains urgent work for all of us, including those of us who are white, people of color, educators, and/or students. According to Tema Okun, the number one trait of white supremacist thinking that manifests across institutions, companies, schools, and other sites of work and power is perfectionism. In her 2001 piece "White Supremacy Culture" from *Dismantling Racism: A Workbook for Social Change Groups*, she names perfectionism directly as a trait of white supremacist culture and lists several tendencies that characterize it: "Making a mistake is confused with being a mistake," "little appreciation [is] expressed among people for the work that others are doing," and perfectionism is "internally felt, [with] the perfectionist failing to appreciate her own good work" (1). In pointing out this connection between perfectionism and white supremacy, Okun prompts us to think about the standards of success and promise we use to assess ourselves and others and to consider the ways in which those standards may be informed by a belief in the hierarchy of human value. (Indeed, part of my interest in perfectionism is my awareness of my own perfectionistic tendencies and the need to challenge them for my own health and for the peace of the people with whom I work, learn, and interact.) This essay explores the interrelated habits of mind and perception—including perfectionism, a belief in the hierarchy of human value, and the white gaze—that can be understood as damaging practices of whiteness. Looking at Morrison's writing and interviews, as well as writing in the field of psychology, I aim to name and analyze these practices while also exploring antidotes for them.

According to a recent study, perfectionism is on the rise. In 2019, psychologists Thomas Curran and Andrew P. Hill found that perfectionism—"defined as a combination of excessively high personal standards and overly critical self-evaluations" and the avoidance of failure (410–11)—among British, Canadian, and US college students has increased over the past twenty-seven years. They explain that "self-oriented perfectionism," or the tendency to assess oneself and one's performance based on the idea of a singular, perfect standard, is positively associated with clinical depression, anorexia nervosa, elevated blood pressure, and suicidal ideation (411). They also explain that "other-oriented perfectionism," or assessing other people based on the idea of a singular, perfect standard, leads to "higher vindictiveness, hostility, and the tendency to blame others, in addition to lower altruism ... and trust" (411). While this study did not compare rates of perfectionism among students from different racial groups, it did find that rates of perfectionism remained consistent across gender. Similarly, in a 2014 study published in the *Journal of Diversity in Higher Education*, K. T. Wang, A. J. Castro, and Y. L. Cunningham found that, among prospective white teachers in the United States, "perfectionistic discrepancy, vertical individualism, and racial color-blindness all predicted lower levels of cultural diversity awareness" (211). Perfectionism is also associated with dichotomous, either/or thinking, according to the study (214). In the world of education especially, we may see perfectionism in a student or in ourselves as a sign of promise, dedication, and discipline. In practice, though, perfectionism is often a sign of anxiety, hostility toward oneself and others, and a culturally biased and limited worldview. And it is damaging for both white students and students of color.

In *The Bluest Eye*, Morrison writes of Black women like the character Geraldine who imbibe the standards and perfectionism of white supremacy at school, leading to a frequent policing of oneself and others:

> They go to land-grant colleges, normal schools, and learn how to do the white man's work with refinement: home economics to prepare his food; teacher education to instruct black children in obedience ... [T]here they learn ... how to behave. The careful development of thrift, patience, high morals, and good manners. In short, how to get rid of the funkiness. The dreadful funkiness of passion, the funkiness of nature, the funkiness of a wide range of human emotions. (83)

The narrator contrasts funk and funkiness with white notions of cleanliness, purity, excellence, and perfection. The history of Black domestic workers creating the very image of spotlessness and reservation in white-owned homes that is supposedly a characteristic of whiteness contradicts the supposed correlation between whiteness and cleanliness, as do "particular stereotypes about white people that are commonly cited in black communities," according to bell hooks, that see white people as dirty, "especially white women—who never seem to do their own cleaning" (qtd. in hooks 341). The white gaze that Morrison's work displaces, though, and that Geraldine learns to see herself through, presupposes that whiteness is clean and mannered. One antidote or challenge to white supremacist and perfectionistic thinking, then, may be found in reevaluating funk and dirt as quite literal grounds for new growth. In a more recent account of how the politics of respectability and perfectionism described by Morrison damaged his sense of self and possibility growing up, Ibram X. Kendi writes in *How to Be an Antiracist* (2019), "I felt the burden my whole Black life to be perfect before both White people and the Black people judging whether I am representing the race well. The judges never let me just be, be myself, be my imperfect self" (203). Here, the "imperfect self" might be understood as someone who is free to explore various paths, emotions, and expressions without being judged or assessed by a singular and narrow cultural standard of success—a standard that is most often set by white people with the institutional, social, and economic power to do so.

In Morrison's fiction, characters like Schoolteacher from *Beloved* (who records pieces of information about the people he enslaves and asks questions of them that Sethe believes "tore Sixo up" [37]) and the doctor in *The Bluest Eye* (who tells his medical students that Pauline and other Black women "deliver [babies] right away and with no pain" [124–5]) represent what Morrison has called "scholarly" racism, given that they are educators who pass racist misinformation on to their students as objective reality. The consequences of such racism for Black students, teachers, patients, and subjects are, of course, profound, limiting opportunity, justifying violence and disenfranchisement, and cultivating self-doubt and self-hatred. The negative consequences of white supremacy and perfectionism for white students, teachers, patients, and subjects are also profound, according to Morrison, warping as they do a given white person's sense of self, the world, and place within it. In her 1988 commencement address to Sarah Lawrence College, Morrison writes,

> Racism is a scholarly pursuit and it always has been. It is not gravity or ocean tides. It is the invention of our minor thinkers, our minor leaders, minor scholars, and our major entrepreneurs. It can be uninvented, deconstructed, and its annihilation begins with visualizing its absence, losing it, and if it can't be lost at once or by saying so, then by behaving as if, in fact, our free life depended on it, because it does. (*Source* 72)

Using the collective word "our" to refer to herself and her racially diverse audience at the commencement, Morrison insists that the freedom, health, and sanity of people of color and white people depend upon the eradication of racism and the standards associated with it. In the same speech, Morrison explains how all-consuming racism is for many white people, whose standards of excellence and other modes of being are often shaped by a passionate hatred and obsession with, or even a less overt but nevertheless ever-present comparison to, Black people. She writes,

> If I spend my life despising you because of your race, or class, or religion, I become your slave. If you spend yours hating me for similar reasons, it is because you are my slave. I own your energy, your fear, your intellect. I determine where you live, how you live, what your work is, your definition of excellence, and I set limits to your ability to love. I will have shaped your life. That is the gift of your hatred; you are mine. (*Source* 72)

Here Morrison is explicit about the psychological impacts white supremacist ideology may have on white people, finding that a preoccupation with purity, hierarchy, being on top, and perfection ends up compromising white people's perceptions of reality, as well as their freedom of movement, thought, and emotion.

Mark Smith makes a similar point in his book *How Race Is Made* (2006), writing that

> Even as segregationists claimed black difference and sensory offensiveness, even as they publicly reviled black scent, mocked the sound (more often [heard as] noise) of blackness, and proclaimed the terrible dangers of coming into contact with black skin, they also experienced blackness with rude appetite and appalling eagerness. White tongues tasted food prepared by black hands; white noses smelled black maids who washed white clothes and tidied white houses; white bodies inhaled, touched, and tasted black wet nurses; white men experienced the intimacy of black women while publicly proclaiming the utter necessity of protecting white womanhood from the touch and taste of black men. (5–6)

This racist obsession and preoccupation, even while it proclaims to distinguish white from Black people, nevertheless reveals a terrifying intimacy needed for a white identity—and one that ultimately compromises the humanity of white people. As Morrison writes of the Ku Klux Klan in *Beloved*, "Desperately thirsty for black blood, without which it could not live, the dragon swam the Ohio [River] at will" (66). Internalizing white supremacist standards, then, provides white people with a sense of identity and authority that is both dragon like and monstrous.

Thus, while one of the privileges of racism, presumably, for the fledgling white person is that, even in his weakest of moments, he has an entire group/class of people to look down upon and to dehumanize in order to fortify his own sense of self, because this standing is unearned, it is always simultaneously shaky, rooted as it is in a warped fantasy. James Baldwin clarifies this point in his 1963 essay "My Dungeon Shook," writing that white people are

> still trapped in a history which they do not understand; and until they understand it, they cannot be released from it. They have had to believe for many years, and for innumerable reasons, that black men are inferior to white men. Many of them, indeed, know better, but, as you will discover, people find it very difficult to act on what they know. To act is to be committed. And to be committed is to be in danger. In this case, the danger, in the minds of most white Americans, is the loss of their identity. (*Collected* 294)

Baldwin similarly writes of white people being trapped by history and by commitment to a white identity that is predicated on the expectation that Black people come last. This look down upon, this white gaze, is a delusion, of course, but a powerful one. In *The Origin of Others*, Morrison discusses one part of this gaze as "the European fixation on the meaning of nakedness" among various African people, explaining that it can be found "in H. Rider Haggard's novels, or in Joseph Conrad's fiction, or in virtually all Western travel writing" (105). In those texts, Morrison says, "An unclothed or sparsely clothed body could signify only childish innocence or undisciplined eroticism—never the voyeurism of the observer" (105). This white gaze involves, then, a lack of self-reflection and cultural humility that projects one's own standards—along with the desires, fears, and proclivities that led to those cultural standards—onto another. In this case, the white observer's sexual curiosities and interests become evidence not of their own desires; rather, they are warped into assessments of the character and/or sexual proclivities of people of color.

Recent work by Zadie Smith further clarifies this point. Writing about racism as a virus that infects white people, she explains in *Intimations* (2020),

> Patient zero of this particular virus stood on a slave ship four hundred years ago, looked down at the sweating, bleeding, moaning mass below deck and reverse-engineered an emotion—contempt—from a situation that he, the patient himself, created. He looked at the human beings he had chained up and noted that they seemed to be the type of people who wore chains. (77)

Forgetting the effort, labor, and gruesome violence—his own included—that led to the enchained, enslaved people below deck, patient zero sees the result as natural order. And he, of course, is among the top of this order, even if not at the very top, as would be the (now also white) landed gentry and royals whose superiority was indicated by their possession of literal property and wealth. Perhaps this newly white patient zero faced limited and controlled professional, educational, economic, and other self-defining options on both land and sea due to a classist and economic hierarchy of human value in Europe that predates the concepts of race and racism as we currently understand them. Indeed, believing in this hierarchy as natural in the first place, rather than assessing it for the social construction it is, suggests that patient zero's sense of self is already compromised, as he might believe himself to be naturally inferior to the landed gentry and aristocratic classes he cannot enter. But, finding a possible kinship with them through this new white racial identity, patient zero is willing to delude himself that the people he is enslaving are somehow naturally inferior to him.

As James Baldwin writes, "The [white] American delusion is not only that their brothers are all white but that the whites are all their brothers" ("Open" 12).

Psychologists today have found that the conditions in which patient zero lived and worked have a tendency to lead to the vindictiveness and violence associated with racism and the belief in white supremacy, as "there is a significant relation between feeling controlled or thwarted and propensities to objectify, dehumanize, or sit in harsh judgment of others" (Neff and Sepällä 189). Having been controlled and thwarted by those with greater social power and material wealth, patient zero is likely to lash out at those with less power than he has, rather than cultivate respectful human bonds with them. In *The World and Africa* (1947), W. E. B. Du Bois finds the results of these conditions to be damaging for both white people and people of color. He writes, "It was bad enough to have the consequences of [white racist] thought fall upon colored people the world over; but in the end it was even worse when one considers what this attitude did to the European worker. His aim and ideal was distorted ... He began to want not comfort for all men, but power over men" (222). In lieu of strong, and therefore equitable and just, human relationships and community, racism infected the European worker's sight, according to Du Bois, ultimately leading to weaker communities and social structures that do not actually serve the European worker as well as they could, both materially and psychologically. In *Intimations*, Smith similarly explains, "The DNA of this virus is *economic at base*. Therefore, it is most effectively attacked when many different members of the plague class—that is, all economically exploited people, whatever their race—act in solidarity with each other" (81–2, emphasis in original). This solidarity exists and has been lived, but all too fleetingly. More often, racism propels white people to identify with other white people, regardless of the drastic economic differences that may exist between them. Meanwhile, the landed gentry and royals benefit from the system of racism that divides economically disadvantaged people and, more often than not, protect their wealth (and their sense of superiority tied to that wealth) savagely.

Today's psychologists have also found that what they call "hyper egoic states," or states that often involve seeing oneself as superior to others,

> can breed a sense of entitlement. People with an elevated sense of entitlement believe that they deserve preferential treatment. Inevitably, other people (or life circumstances, or the universe, or God) will fail to treat entitled people as well as they believe they deserve. The entitled person is likely to frame this disappointment as an injustice—and perhaps a humiliation as well—and is likely to take offense. Along these lines, studies show that entitlement is associated with being easily offended ... and promotes aggressive responses to ego threat. (Exline 260)

We might think of white people who believe that whiteness makes them superior to people of color—or "the people who believe they are white" (2), according to Ta-Nahesi Coates—as living in this hyper egoic state. Such a state is also associated with zero-sum beliefs about the world, according to psychologists Jennifer Crocker and Amy Canevello:

> People with zero-sum beliefs assume that what is good for one person is bad for the other ... They assume that when a conflict occurs, one person will emerge the winner and the other the loser. They indicate agreement with items such as, "In most relationships, when one person gets what he or she wants, the other person usually suffers," and "What is good for one person is often bad for another." ... Egosystem motivation is typically associated with viewing relationships and situations as zero-sum in nature. (275)

In a world of increasing wealth gaps, and where perfectionistic students and teachers adopt this habit of mind in part as a response to their awareness of the intense competition for resources that exists in this world, the development of this zero-sum vision of life is understandable, especially as a knee-jerk reaction to these conditions. But thoughtful self-reflection and reflection on our world in general can lead to different, more productive, more equitable, and ultimately more generative visions. In "White Supremacy Culture," Tema Okun also identifies "power hoarding" as a trait of white supremacy that manifests across various organizations and identifies "power sharing" (5) as an important antidote for it. In practice, she says, this can mean "develop[ing] the power and skills of others and to do so consciously and deliberatively" (5).

Morrison's fiction explores the domino effect that power hoarding can have when it comes to people with various levels of power, with Black women often bearing the brunt of everyone else's anxieties regarding their social statuses. For example, in *Sula*, the character of Jude has high hopes he will be hired for a construction job—a job for which he was greatly qualified—so he "stood in lines for six days running [but] saw the gang boss pick out thin-armed white boys from the Virginia hills and … bull-necked Greeks and Italians, [hearing] over and over, 'Nothing else today. Come back tomorrow.' … [H]e got the message" (82). This inequity sparks a "rage" (82) in Jude, which leads him to pursue other social markers of manhood like marriage to a woman. In turn, he looks to Nel to support and buttress the sense of manhood denied to him by the racist white employment structure:

> So it was rage, rage and a determination to take on a man's role anyhow that made him press Nel about settling down. He needed some of his appetites filled, some posture of adulthood recognized, but mostly he wanted someone to care about his hurt, to care very deeply. … Without that someone he was a waiter hanging around a kitchen like a woman. With her he was head of a household pinned to an unsatisfactory job out of necessity. The two of them together would make one Jude. (82–3)

Thus, the power hoarding of the white men ends up having drastic consequences in the intimate lives of Jude and Nel. And Nel's desires in particular—her pursuit of agency and power—remain relatively unthought and unconsidered in both Jude's vision of the world and the vision of the white men who deny him employment.

We might also ask what this inequity sparks in the white boys and men who do receive the coveted construction opportunity. Likely a sense of manhood, standing, comfort, and relief. But, as Morrison, Baldwin, Smith, Douglass, Du Bois, and others have written, this feeling of manhood and of standing is determined by racist patterns, not by the white men's actual skills relative to Black workers, and so this newfound sense of accomplishment and self depends upon a racist fantasy of Black inferiority. If someone is always behind you in line, your sense of self might be buttressed, regardless of your actual abilities and competencies in relation to the people waiting behind you. One antidote, then, is waking up from this fantasy.

According to psychologists today, "hypo egoic phenomena," or a state of mind that envisions interconnectedness among people as opposed to strict, ego-driven separations, can serve as counterpoints to the habits of mind like perfectionism and power hoarding that characterize hyper egoic phenomena and white racism. Humility—both personal and cultural—has been identified as an important example of these hypo egoic phenomena. According to a 2019 article by Daryl R. Van Tongeren, Don E. Davis, Joshua N. Hook, and Charlotte vanOyen Witliet, humility involves "an ability to acknowledge and own one's limitations ... recognize the fallibility of one's beliefs, and have a clearer sense of one's strengths and weaknesses. Interpersonally, humility involves the degree to which one has an orientation toward the needs and well-being of others" (463). They also write that "humility has been shown to positively correlate with life satisfaction ... as well as [to] buffer the negative effects of stress on well-being" (465). The personal health benefits associated with humility also become communal health benefits, as the anxiety over status and standing that so often leads to interpersonal and intergroup violence, discrimination, and destruction are not leading motivators for the humble person. According to Mark Leary, coeditor of *The Oxford Handbook of Hypo-Egoic Phenomena* (2017),

> In our view, humility is not about underestimating or downplaying your accomplishments or positive characteristics. Everyone who has studied humility agrees that humble people probably see themselves more accurately than the average person, so they know that they're good at whatever it is they're good at ... The central feature that characterizes humble people, in my view, is "hypo-egoic nonentitlement"—they do not think that they are entitled to be treated special as a person because of their accomplishments or positive characteristics (qtd. in Dolan).

Thus, humility and the sobering self-assessment that accompanies it can be strong forces for community building, personal satisfaction, and justice, especially when done with a critical consciousness of the realities of racism and discrimination in mind: "The emerging consensus appears to be that the conceptual core of humility includes, at a minimum, the willingness to view oneself accurately and an other-oriented rather than self-focused interpersonal stance that appreciates others' strengths and contributions, which leads to openness to learn from others" (Hill and Laney 244).

As such, cultural humility can be understood as one antidote to the traits of white supremacy associated with perfectionism in the United States. According to psychologists Lisa Asbill and Amanda Waters, cultural humility is best understood as "a lifelong commitment to self-evaluation and self-critique," "a desire to fix power imbalances," and the development of "partnerships with people and groups who advocate for others" (3–5). While self-critique may seem like a troubling habit of perfectionism, here Asbill and Waters endorse a practice of self-critique that pursues excellence, not perfection, through lifelong learning about oneself, one's culture, and the culture of other people, and that understands failure and mistakes as valuable opportunities for growth. Indeed, Tema Okun writes about this shifted relationship to both success and failure as critical for eliminating white supremacy from our organizations. She endorses a culture "where it is expected that everyone will make mistakes and those mistakes offer opportunities for learning; when offering feedback, always speak to the things that went well before offering criticism; ... [when offering criticism,] offer specific suggestions for how to do things differently" ("White Supremacy Culture" 2).

Humility and the process of humbling oneself is especially and foundationally important for those of us who have the capacity to exercise authority over others in our lives and for those of us who have occupied privileged social positions relative to others. In *A Mercy*, the character Rebekka reflects upon this reality while pondering the story of Job in the Bible: "What shocked Job into humility and renewed fidelity was the message a female Job would have known and heard every minute of her life" (107). That is, for many, an honest and clear assessment of one's own strengths and weaknesses has been necessary knowledge for surviving in and navigating a world that offers routine discrimination and insult. This same humility, though, can also be understood as a clearer understanding of our individual roles in history's longer ecosystem of anti-racist resistance and community building. I'll conclude by sharing some words from Morrison's essay "The Slavebody and the Blackbody," wherein she reflects on one means of helping white people realize identity without and in opposition to racism. Writing before spaces like the National Underground Railroad Freedom Center, the National Memorial for Peace and Justice, the National Museum of African American History of Culture, and many other significant anti-racist memorials and museums existed, Morrison lamented the lack of memorials recognizing African American history, the injustices of racism, and resistance to racism in our country. She wrote,

> I can't explain to you why I think [such recognition is] important, but I really do. I think it would refresh. Not only that, not only for black people. It could suggest the moral clarity among white people when they were at their best, when they risked something, when they didn't have to risk and could have chosen to be silent; there's no monument for that either. (*Source* 75)

The risk that Morrison refers to here echoes Baldwin's idea that, when white people confront racism, we are "in danger" of losing a convenient, serviceable identity. The risk, then, is potentially an act of remaking the self and reimagining the self unbuttressed by racist fantasy. One actionable way of risking may be to release ourselves and others from the perfectionistic standards and power hoarding many of us have imbibed as a means of assessing promise and success. Challenging those same standards on institutional levels can then further amplify and expand this work.

In the past, Morrison's own work has been read and dismissed through the very lenses she endeavored to critique and displace throughout her career. A now infamous 1973 review of her novel *Sula* by Sara Blackburn in the *New York Times*, which is also quoted in *The Pieces I Am*, praised Morrison in racist terms by saying she was "far too talented to remain only a marvelous recorder of the black side of provincial American life" (3). Framing Black lives as small in relation to Morrison's tremendous talent, and missing completely the many insights into whiteness and white supremacy found in *Sula*, Blackburn displays racially biased white standards of artistic excellence, academic rigor, and beauty that have long misjudged, marginalized, and shamed Black art and lives. This method of assessing an artist's work may also be understood as perfectionistic, given that it assesses all work through a rubric that epitomizes the exploration of white people, concerns, and lives. Thankfully, Morrison's work offers antidotes to this way of thinking, including a consistent point of view that never centers, prioritizes, or normalizes whiteness.

WORKS CITED

Asbill, Lisa, and Amanda Waters. "Reflections on Cultural Humility." *CYF News*. Aug. 2013. https://www.apa.org/pi/families/resources/newsletter/2013/08/cultural-humility. Accessed July 18, 2022.

Baldwin, James. *Collected Essays*. Penguin, 1998.

Baldwin, James. "An Open Letter to My Sister, Miss Angela Davis." *The New York Review*, Jan. 7, 1971, https://www.nybooks.com/articles/1971/01/07/an-open-letter-to-my-sister-miss-angela-davis/. Accessed July 18, 2022.

Coates, Ta-Nehisi. "Letter to My Son." *The Atlantic*. July 4, 2015.

Crocker, Jennifer, and Amy Canevello, "Egosystem and Ecosystem: Motivational Orientations of the Self in Relation to Others." *The Oxford Handbook of Hypo-egoic Phenomena*, edited by Kirk Warren Brown and Mark R. Leary, Oxford UP, 2017, pp. 271–83.

Curran, Thomas, and Andrew P. Hill. "Perfectionism Is Increasing Over Time." *Psychological Bulletin*, vol. 145, no. 4, 2019, pp. 410–29.

Dolan, Eric W. "New Psychology Study Identifies 'Hypo-Egoic Nonentitlement' as a Central Feature of Humility." *PsyPost*. Oct. 13, 2019. https://www.psypost.org/2019/10/new-psychology-study-identifies-hypo-egoic-nonentitlement-as-a-central-feature-of-humility-54657. Accessed July 18, 2022.

Douglass, Frederick. *Narrative of the Life of Frederick Douglass, an American Slave, Written by Himself*. Dover, 1995.

Du Bois, W. E. B. *The World and Africa: An Inquiry into the Part which Africa Has Played in World History*. International P, 1965.

Dyer, Richard. "White." *Screen*, vol. 29, no. 4, 1988, pp. 44–65.

Exline, Julie J. "Forgiveness and the Ego: Why Hypo-Egoic States Foster Forgiveness and Prosocial Responses." *The Oxford Handbook of Hypo-Egoic Phenomena*, edited by Kirk Warren Brown and Mark R. Leary, Oxford UP, 2017, pp. 257–69.

Greenfield-Sanders, Timothy, director. *Toni Morrison: The Pieces I Am*. PBS American Masters, 2019.

Hill, Peter C., and Elizabeth K. Laney, "Beyond Self-Interest: Humility and the Quieted Self." *The Oxford Handbook of Hypo-egoic Phenomena*, edited by Kirk Warren Brown and Mark R. Leary, Oxford UP, 2017, pp. 243–55.

hooks, bell. "Representing Whiteness in the Black Imagination." *Displacing Whiteness: Essays in Social and Cultural Criticism*, edited by Ruth Frankenburg, Duke UP, 1997, pp. 338–46.

Kendi, Ibram X. *How to Be an Antiracist*. One World, 2019.

Morrison, Toni. *Beloved*. Plume, 1998.

Morrison, Toni. *The Bluest Eye*. Knopf, 2003.

Morrison, Toni. *A Mercy*. Vintage, 2009.

Morrison, Toni. *The Origin of Others*. Harvard UP, 2017.

Morrison, Toni. *Playing in the Dark: Whiteness and the Literary Imagination*. Vintage, 1993.

Morrison, Toni. *The Source of Self-Regard: Selected Essays, Speeches, and Meditations*. Knopf, 2019.

Morrison, Toni. *Sula*. Plume, 1982.

Morrison, Toni. "Toni Morrison, HBCU Grad, Takes White Supremacy To Task." *YouTube*, uploaded by TheAncestorsGift, Mar. 25, 2012, https://www.youtube.com/watch?v=6S7zGgL6Suw&t=3s. Accessed July 18, 2022.

Neff, Kristin D., and Emma Seppälä, "Compassion, Well-Being, and the Hypo-Egoic Self." *The Oxford Handbook of Hypo-Egoic Phenomena*, edited by Kirk Warren Brown and Mark R. Leary. Oxford UP, 2017, pp. 189–203.

Okun, Tema. "White Supremacy Culture." 2001. https://www.dismantlingracism.org/uploads/4/3/5/7/43579015/okun_-_white_sup_culture.pdf. Accessed July 18, 2022.

Smith, Mark. *How Race Is Made: Slavery, Segregation, and the Senses*. U of North Carolina P, 2006.

Smith, Zadie. *Intimations*. Penguin, 2020.

Van Tongeren, Daryl, et al. "Humility." *Current Directions in Psychological Science*, vol. 28, no. 5, 2019, pp. 463–8.

Wang, K. T., et al. "Are Perfectionism, Individualism, and Racial Color-Blindness Associated with Less Cultural Sensitivity? Exploring Diversity Awareness in White Prospective Teachers." *Journal of Diversity in Higher Education*, vol. 7, no. 3, 2014, pp. 211–25.

CHAPTER TWENTY-THREE

Teaching Toni Morrison's *Sula* in a "Post-Racial" Moment

MARC K. DUDLEY

William Faulkner famously declared in 1951, "The past is never dead. It's not even past."[1] This phrase reverberates in each of the novels of Toni Morrison, herself a student of the Faulkner aesthetic. Barack Obama would borrow Faulkner's phraseology in his famous "A More Perfect Union" speech as he addressed that most egregious of stains upon the Americas sociohistorical record: the "peculiar institution" of slavery.[2] President Obama's election was the milestone for which so many had waited for so long. However, Morrison, knowing better, spent a career chasing that elusive "post-racial" moment and demonstrating to us a need for a real racial reckoning before it would or could ever be had. Just as important though, at every step along the way, Morrison shows us that Black lives matter; and *Sula* demonstrates that point from the first. It is a novel best taught to those old enough to appreciate, even embrace, its ambiguity, because its author revels in that ambiguity. And for that reason, I typically save this book for my senior-level classes and/or graduate courses.

Toni Morrison has been a curricular mainstay and a perennial favorite among students for decades now. That reading list usually includes *The Bluest Eye*, *Song of Solomon*, and even *Beloved*. Students are often introduced to those works in high school, or early in their college careers. First, I'd argue that *Sula* deserves to be on that list; but it almost never is. Second, I'd argue that students are often not ready for several of those aforementioned texts; but *Sula*, in all its pithy complexity, is perhaps the most digestible of the set.

I typically pair novel readings with one or two of Morrison's better-known critical works; excerpts from "Unspeakable Things Unspoken: The Afro-American Presence in American Literature" work well to define an important part of Morrison's aesthetic. In it, she argues, among other things, for a reevaluation of canonical standards, and an embrace of African American Vernacular traditions. My initial lesson begins with a little bit of biography. Facts and factoids about Toni Morrison abound; her story is everywhere, but some items are well worth repeating here. Morrison, in her first novels and in particular in *Sula*, became the living embodiment of that Black Arts prescriptive for Black artists and critics alike writing in that post-1960s revolutionary moment: to question establishment

---

[1] For these oft-quoted lines, see Faulkner's novel *Requiem for a Nun*.
[2] "A More Perfect Union." Then Senator Barack Obama gave what has come to be known as his "race speech" in March of 2008, almost a year before he would assume the title of President of the United States (Dionne and Reid).

(read "white") narratives and to break new communal ground in telling a markedly Black story, to make Black lives matter. In much of her work—and this novel is no exception—she actively gives voice to what she long believed to be a forgotten if not often ignored contingent in both American literature in general and in African American literature specifically: the Black woman.

As my students begin reading *Sula*, I expressly ask them to bear in mind a few things that prove helpful in reading the novel. First, I underscore Morrison's love for language. As was the charge of the Black Arts, she places an emphasis on the African American Vernacular writ large. She privileges dialect and folklore and the like, and features it prominently in the narrative. I note that Morrison's style is, in some ways, like Gwendolyn Brooks's before her, as much poetry as it is prose. That said, her prose style can be just as complex as that of the poet. Like Brooks, Morrison, too, has her Black Arts moment.

Unpacking Morrison's Black Arts moment begins with class discussion of the curious prefatory segment that precedes the novel proper. At barely four pages, that opening sequence featuring what Morrison calls the "nigger joke" sets the tone for the rest of the text. Our classroom conversation begins with a question: Why does Morrison begin here, in this space, with what amounts to a prelude?[3] Often students suggest that that tone is ominous, and forecasts some of the doom and death we encounter just pages into the novel. It is in fact an origin story. More particularly, though, I insist to them, it is an effective authorial tool used to set the stage, thematically, for everything that follows. First and foremost, it acts as a literary easement of sorts for those looking in from the outside (particularly those looking in from outside the Black community) as readers engage with the thorniest of issues. What are these issues? And, based on the preface, just what is this novel about? This set of questions makes for a great entry point for even the shyest or most reluctant of students to engage the text. Most often students will begin to craft a thematic list that includes place, pain, and sorrow (related to being Black, and social inequity. I remind them of Black Arts star Amiri Baraka's fiery declaration in his poem "Black Art": "Poems are bullshit unless they are / teeth or trees or lemons piled / On a step." But Morrison mutes this urgency and gives us a political text that celebrates Blackness at times almost quietly. That "nigger joke" undergirding the preface, I tell them, is Morrison rendering manageable broken promise(s) and Black pain. Moreover, Medallion's communal pain is the same pain felt by Black communities everywhere; and their choice of coping mechanisms is a repurposing of that "joke." Theirs is a blues-like engagement with an Ellisonian, tragi-comic treatment. Medallion's beginning is a "joke" (a lie, actually), and its end an absurd tragedy as community gives way to gentrification. In each instance, white action comes at the expense of Black action. Racism becomes then that phantom presence in the text, moving about quietly, but powerfully all the same. That story, Morrison insists, needs to be told.

The import of story to Morrison explains her decision to begin the novel, not with Sula, the story's namesake, but with Shadrack. So much of my questioning has to do with the *why* of it all; so much of our collective conversation is about authorial choice. Having been an editor, Morrison understands the reader's position. Slowly easing into the story of Sula (and Nel) is organic, some students suggest. It even adds to the mystery and power of her story, suggest still others. Additionally, though, beginning with Shadrack allows Morrison to engage with two primary themes at once: *name* and *myth*, as a brand of *story*.

---

[3]Morrison in fact suggests in the novel's ancillary material that she ultimately decided to include the preface at her editor's suggestion, as a literary easement of sorts for the outside (read "white') reader.

In her engagement with name, Morrison's affinity with the Bible becomes clear (I tell students to note how she refashions scripture to tell markedly Black stories). Moreover, naming has a long, storied history in the African American Vernacular tradition. I underscore for students the long legacy of (re)naming as an act of agency and self-ownership, especially in the African American community—from the story of Frederick Douglass, to that of Malcolm X, to Muhammad Ali. I use this portion of our discussion to return to our beginning point; we see myth, too, I remind them, explored already with that prefatory "joke" (Medallion's origin story), and soon after explored in the character of Shadrack and his celebration of National Suicide Day:

> Then Nebuchadnezzar spake, and said, Blessed be the God of Shadrach, Meshach, and Abednego, who hath sent his angel, and delivered his servants that trusted in him. (Daniel 3:28, King James Bible)

Shadrach, Meshach, and Abednego are soothsayers whose faith helps them survive Babylonian King Nebuchadnezzar's charges of heresy and his fiery furnace. In an apt analog, Morrison's Shadrack, as a military recruit, places his faith in country and returns from war psychically burned, broken. His story begins in 1919, the year after the armistice and the year of Morrison's first chapter. Shadrack's faith fails to save him. As such, he becomes a stand-in for every Black man similarly shattered by war and spurned by nation. Many volunteered, even in the face of great bigotry, hoping to earn respect, inclusion, and true freedom through national service. Shadrack, like that of so many others like him, is met, not with fanfare and parade, but with suspicion and jail time. Some were beaten, a few even lynched, for their seeming presumptuousness.[4] Staring into a jail's toilet, Shadrack is desperate for evidence of his being. His American return brings with it an existential crisis. The smile that returns his own then becomes Morrison's celebratory moment for a community. I tether this analysis to previous discussions of W. E. B. Du Bois, using *Souls* and discussions of "double consciousness" as a framing device for Shadrack's existential moment. Further, I remind students that Morrison wants us to remember and appreciate the fact that were it not for this narrative (after the nightshades were "torn from their roots"), we would not know Shadrack or *his* America.

Once more, I steer students back to our starting point and suggest ways in which Morrison adheres to the Black Arts charge of rejecting Anglo (Western) myths, telling a decidedly Black story. We then extrapolate Shadrack's myth, and examine other characters through a similar lens. Morrison goes to the Bible again in crafting Eva Peace (whose missing leg is itself the stuff of legend) and recreating biblical myth. She is a namer of things ("the deweys" are one example), and a mother to many (she adopts and tends to several in the community in that boarding house of hers). *Sula's* Eva is arguably both Adam and Eve of Genesis; and she is Black.

This is very much a Black, communal story. Shadrack's and Eva's narratives are only part of that story. Sula comes to us, about midway through the novel, all grown up with calcified personality. Like the plague of robins marking her return to Medallion, Sula is a force of nature; and the indicators abound early on as we witness her cutting off part of her finger in defense of her friend Nel when boys bully them as girls. However, Sula is not just an object of interest; she is an object of ire. That said, just why is this woman, our story's central character, so reviled by her own

---

[4]For a wonderful examination of America's racial dynamics in the year of that grand return, see Krugler.

community? Her nonconformity is the most common answer by students. To that reply, I add further complications. Sula, like a broken Shadrack, is also a reflection of the society rejecting her; as such, she serves as a constant and stark reminder of their own failings. Her outcast sensibility also conveniently provides another suggested connection to the aforementioned Black Arts prescriptive.

Refusing to abide by societal rules, mores, and expectations, Sula is an outright renegade; Morrison would call her "an outlaw." To help make Morrison's case, I place Sula in proper sociohistorical context. She is a poor, Black woman coming of age and negotiating issues of race, class, and gender in a country whose own negotiation of said spaces has hardly been a negotiation at all. When we happen upon Sula midway through the novel, we find her to be poor and Black, but also college educated, well traveled, and openly flouting societal norms every step of the way. She is independent, spirited, and free, and unapologetically so. She is also sexually liberated at a time when women were comparatively bound (by social stricture). Moreover, she is all of these things to the detriment of her relationships with family, friend(s), and lovers. Further, she willingly and wantonly crosses that unspoken color line and has sex with white men. In these ways, Sula is indeed that outlaw Morrison suggests she is.

That said, I remind students of a Vernacular concept we would have explored earlier in the semester. I have them assess Sula through the lens of the "bad woman." After a prolonged absence, she returns to her hometown with all of the notoriety of a Stagger Lee, legendary criminal and folk and blues icon, a plague of robins announcing that return, her reputation preceding her.[5] Some students indict her, calling her spirited and independent nature, indeed her self-interest, "selfish." Others quickly defend her. Perhaps, I offer, therein lies the genius of Morrison's characterization: in its very grayness.

In this light, I ask students to (re)consider Sula's relationships, especially with Nel Wright, her best friend from childhood. Do they see it as one where love is reciprocated? How do we know? Further, can we compare Sula's sexual encounters with her mother's? Hannah is sexually promiscuous simply because she loves sex; indeed, she revels in the company of men. Sula's reasons appear to be altogether different; and I ask students to think about the *how* and the *why* of that declaration. This is especially true in light of Sula's sexual dalliance with Nel's husband, Jude. Is Sula's tryst a betrayal? To this point, late in the novel, as adults, Sula and Nel discuss many things, including the nature of good and evil, and Sula pointedly asks Nel, "How you know it was you [who was good]?" This is a loaded question to be sure, and one that prompts a healthy reevaluation of prominent characters. That reevaluation comes, too, through the prism of another prominent theme: love. And that's where our discussion goes next.

Morrison revisits this theme again and again in so many of her texts, and it is useful in decoding the novel. *Sula* introduces us to "Womanism," something I label a particular brand of love. I use this as an opportunity to introduce Alice Walker and her concept to the class. "Womanism," as she conceived it, was a feminist tradition especially tailored to African American women and their particular experiences(s). Often bereft of strong male figures in their lives (slavery early on, and more recently, mass incarceration, having ripped families apart), African American women have often relied on strong Black feminist networks for survival. Morrison, following Black Arts directives, exalts that network in *Sula*. The "womanist" text becomes then not a denigration of

---

[5] See Davis for a particularly thorough treatment of Black women and blues music as feminist political activism.

men (read "man-hating"), but an express celebration of women of color. I have students note that *Sula* privileges the constancy and stability of women over the inconsistency of men (a lamentable fact of life for many of the featured women in this novel). Moreover, "Womanism," in the feminist tradition, privileges the strong, independent, sometimes precocious, woman. Additionally, it privileges the love that a woman shows herself, other women, and her community at large.

I use this opportunity to enumerate a few associative elements linked to love, elements that get explored to some degree in the novel, many of which become a part of a classroom list. Morrison engages with that list, exploring each of the major forms of love in her novel: *agape love* (unconditional love), *erotic love* (passionate, sexual love demonstrated to some degree by both Hannah and Sula), and *philial love* ("brotherly" or "sisterly" love, that shared by Sula and Nel). Each of the chapters in Morrison's novel asks us to (re)consider, to some degree, our various definitions and conceptions. This portion of the conversation often proves valuable in drawing into the classroom conversation even the most reticent of personalities. Whether it's the myriad examples of "tough love" that Eva demonstrates repeatedly in the narrative ("wasn't no playin' in 18 and 95," she reminds her daughter, when Hannah laments a tenderness absent in her relationship with her mother), or Hannah's hyper-affection for so many of the town's men (strangely appreciated by their wives), or the unquestioned sisterly bond shared by Nel and Sula, Morrison shows us repeatedly that complications abound when trying to pin down a workable definition (and understanding) of love. However, one unifying truism for us as we work to define the concept is that most beautiful of mantras articulated by Nikki Giovanni in her poem "Nikki Rosa": "Black Love is Black Wealth."

Once my students have had a chance to consider prominent themes like "love," I force a brief return of sorts and usually toss out additional questions about our text's titular character, Morrison's "bad woman." Does Sula love Nel? Is Sula's dalliance with Jude a betrayal? Moreover, is Sula Peace capable of truly loving another in the conventional sense of the word? Arguably, Sula seeks out rather insignificant sexual relations, not necessarily out of a deep-seated need for communion with another human being; rather, she does so out of a deep-seated need for communion with (her)self. To this point, we note as a group Sula's interior monologue when she reflects on past lovemaking episodes as an experience not of communion, but of heartrending solitude. That said, when read through this lens, I insist, Sula's seemingly selfish moments become the grandest examples of Womanist independence and self-love. She is arguably her own best friend, her very own soul mate, and perhaps therein lies part of the key to a community's survival (and maybe, I suggest, this becomes part of a greater lesson for Nel and for us on the virtues of Womanism).[6]

At this juncture, in a reprise of sorts, I bring the class back to its original launching conversational point. I usually ask early on in the course for students to consider the likes of Richard Wright's Bigger Thomas in *Native Son* through the various lenses of conventional hero, antihero, tragic hero, monster, and/or "simple" bad man. We could make a compelling case for any one of these "easy" categories, I suggest. From a modern perspective, many of us can even point to Sula's admirable qualities and suggest that she is indeed heroic. A classic hero follows a traditional arc, making his/her fall all the more tragic. Arguably, though, few of us would, I insist, call her narrative movement an ascension, and certainly none of the community's members would deem it so. What most will

---

[6]There is a communion of souls here between kindred feminist spirits as bell hooks explores similar sacred ground in her criticism. See hooks's brilliant treatise on love and community.

concede is that she is defiant to the end and abides by her own (a)moral code ("What is bad or evil," Morrison asks? "How you know it was you [who was good]?" Sula asks Nel). Thus, the antihero moniker would seem to be arguably the better label. The antihero, taking the less-traditional path, engages the world from the outside, and yet we identify with them and their engagements from our position in the audience. Sula clearly abides by a code of her own making, and even those who judge her must respect her for that fact. But still, what does any of it mean?

For at least a partial answer to this question, I again point to that Vernacular tradition so intrinsic to the Black Arts aesthetic. I remind my class about the virtues of that "bad (wo)man" tradition heralding the social deviant pushing back (sometimes at the expense of others) against societal restrictions. Here that oppressor is a phantom white patriarchy, unseen but felt. And while she seems to divide readers looking in from the outside, Sula is the glue that keeps Morrison's constructed community intact; and for that we are to admire her.

Medallion's tunnel construction project also binds the community, as a source of perpetual hope and disappointment for its unemployed ranks. In the end, that project regains prominence in the narrative and proves worthy of a second look as I seek to close out our classroom conversation. That tunnel project, like the war effort raging in Europe as the novel opens, is indicative of all of the broken promises made by whites, historically, to this nation's Black citizens. In it, Medallion's men, particular those of color, see opportunity (to work, to provide for themselves and their families, to craft something with their hands, to realize their manhood). In this same project, the white men who do the building and the hiring also see opportunity: to control, to exploit, to deny and denigrate. They openly deny men like Jude employment and perpetuate the community's brokenness.

Curiously though, that tunnel-as-symbol is just one of a handful of textual instances wherein Morrison invests herself in an active, overt engagement with the color line. Race relations frame this story from its inception (with the retelling of the so-called "nigger joke"), but Morrison seemingly goes out of her way to make whiteness a kind of phantom subtext. This is first and foremost an expressly Black story. That said, the imprint of whiteness is there, often written between the lines. The "nigger joke" and the tunnel make a classroom conversation about that phantom presence all the easier to have. We see it, too, in Helene Wright's acts of cultural denial (her insistence that Nel pull her nose to "ameliorate" her "negro" features, for example). Such examples also serve then as a convenient entry point into conversations about intra-racism or "colorism" within a community seemingly free of white influence.

While the novel ends with literal gloom and doom (and chaos), as the aforementioned tunnel collapses upon itself, the tragedy also arguably brings with it bittersweet, but important lessons for us. Sula takes ill and dies, and her death brings revelation to Nel and to the reader. The community realizes (much as Sula prognosticates it) their loss and its meaning in light of her sudden absence. And Nel, perhaps only too late, realizes her own loss with her friend's passing. Read through a pronounced Womanist lens, Nel learns a most difficult lesson here: It was Sula (her strength and love) she missed most all those years following the betrayal and Jude's unceremonious exit from Nel's life. Morrison points here to the real truth undergirding all of it in the end: that (woman's) love, that Black love, in all its terrifying iterations, is the important thing to divine here and to appreciate. Like those circles of sorrow that envelop Nel at the end of the narrative, this truth is profound and perpetual.

Finally, as a way to punctuate our series of classroom discussions, I return to where we began: to the notion of authorial intent and aesthetic methodology. Moreover, I underscore the importance of Morrison's timeline for her novel's chapters; her narrative arc follows the years between 1919 and 1965. This novel begins with Black American investment in the First World War (as seen through the lens of the aforementioned "nigger joke") and ends with its implied immersion in and push for civil rights. Within this basic framework, and with the likes of Shadrack, Jude, Nel, and Sula as metonymical communal representatives, Morrison seems to encapsulate in this pithy novel all of modern Black America in its march toward freedom. In *Sula*, Morrison shows us that not only do Black lives matter, but theirs is *the* story to pass on. Collectively realizing this powerful truth, we close Morrison's confounding little book wiser and all the more satisfied.

WORKS CITED

Baraka, Amiri. "Black Art." *Anthology of Modern American Poetry*, edited by Cary Nelson, Oxford UP, 2000, pp. 898–9.

Davis, Angela Y. *Blues Legacies and Black Feminism*. Vintage P, 1998.

Dionne, E. J. Jr, and Joy-Ann Reid, editors. *We Are the Change We Seek: The Speeches of Barack Obama*. Bloomsbury Publishing, 2017.

Faulkner, William. *Requiem for a Nun*. Random House, 1951.

hooks, bell. *Salvation: Black People and Love*. William Morrow, 2001.

Krugler, David F. *The Year of Racial Violence*, 1919. Cambridge UP, 2015.

CHAPTER TWENTY-FOUR

"Understand[ing] All Too Well What Is Meant": Teaching Toni Morrison's "Recitatif"

CATHERINE SELTZER

While ideally Toni Morrison's "Recitatif" would be read within the context of Morrison's oeuvre—the story lends itself to being considered alongside the depictions of girlhood in *The Bluest Eye*, *Sula*, and *Beloved*, for instance—most of us find ourselves teaching it as detached from Morrison's canon. Its relative brevity and its frequent anthologization make "Recitatif" the most obvious way to include Morrison's voice in introductory literature courses or surveys of American literature. As an introduction to Morrison, though, "Recitatif" can be problematic. Formally, "Recitatif" is an outlier in Morrison's oeuvre, the only short story among a rich canon of novels and essays. As significantly, the story strays from the exploration of an explicitly Black consciousness that dictates most of Morrison's work. Instead, "Recitatif" balances its attention neatly between two protagonists, one Black and the other white, and the narrative steadfastly refuses to assign race to either character.

The challenge of teaching "Recitatif," then, is often two-fold. On the one hand, we want to ensure that students—particularly those who have not yet encountered Morrison's novels—are directed to the themes that commonly define her work. Certainly, these are evident in "Recitatif": the notions of female friendship, communal trauma, and cultural memory-making become sites of meditation throughout the narrative. The second (often more difficult) challenge, though, is to focus on what makes the story exceptional in her canon—in short, to work with students to tease out the implications of Morrison's treatment of race in the story. Black identity is a theme that defines all of Morrison's work, of course, but in "Recitatif," in which the racial identification of each character has been obscured if not fully erased, Morrison plays with race as a construct in ways that are more complex than they may first appear to students.

Arguably, it is the instinct of almost all readers when first approaching a text to rapidly categorize characters by gender, class, and race, creating a shorthand for their identification moving forward. As Robyn Warhol and Amy Shuman have noted, this is almost automatic in the case of race: "In American fiction race is usually specified and always coded: this character is black, that one is white, and once the narration has established those conditions, the authorial audience attaches to each character all the connotations and stereotypes those racial terms signify in U.S. culture" (1012). In refusing to specify race in "Recitatif," Morrison ultimately challenges us to rethink those "connotations and stereotypes." What often happens first, though, is that the readers fall into what have been reliable patterns of reading in the past and begin sifting through the text for the racialized codes that seem critical for interpretation. After a bit of class discussion, they come to realize that "obvious" racial signifiers Morrison has planted throughout the story—references to food preferences, religion, or the regularity with which a character washes her hair—are not so obvious after all. It is a powerful exercise; Morrison's self-labeled "lark" of a story never fails to "provoke and enlighten," as she had intended ("Art of Fiction" 102). Yet its unpacking is not an easy process. Even after I had been teaching "Recitatif" for years, I would often find myself sending up a small prayer before teaching it again, hoping that my students would be generous with one another as they stumbled through the brambles of cultural bias that the story presents to its readers.

In the preface to *Playing in the Dark*, Morrison observes that

> the kind of work I have always wanted to do requires me to learn how to maneuver ways to free up the language from its sometimes sinister, frequently lazy, almost always predictable employment of racially informed and determined chains. (The only short story I have ever written, "Recitatif," was an experiment in the removal of all racial codes from a narrative about two characters of different races for whom racial identity is crucial.) (21)

When I began teaching "Recitatif," years ago now, much of the point of the discussion was to allow the students to catch themselves in reassigning the codes that Morrison had removed or, in some cases, scrambled. The takeaway of the class session—and presumably, by extension, the story itself—was that each of us is complicit in thinking that is "lazy," "predictable," and even, distressingly, "sinister." As satisfyingly tidy as that lesson might be, it was one that often left scars along the way. Students who had raised their hands to declare they had the answer to the story's unvoiced question of Twyla's and Roberta's respective races could feel exposed, regardless which race they had assigned to the characters. And emphasizing students' imposed readings of the racial identities of the characters also had the effect of distracting us from a consideration of the ways in which the characters (mis)read one another. The result was that I often walked away from the classroom with the sinking feeling that I had not effectively captured the real richness of the story.

I've found that I've been more satisfied with the way the story has worked in my classes in recent years, not simply because I teach it a little differently than I used to, but because my students—and, indeed, the world in which we live—are a little different. "Recitatif" has taken on a new resonance in classrooms that have been deeply and irrevocably shaped by the murders of Michael Brown (2014), Eric Garner (2014), Breonna Taylor (2020), and George Floyd (2020), among others, and by the subsequent growth of the Black Lives Matter movement. The larger cultural discussion has ensured that most students now accept the idea that our backgrounds and experiences have ingrained us with cultural and racial biases, many of which we may not recognize consciously. As a result, the more straightforward "lesson" of "Recitatif"—that we make assumptions about race even in the absence of fact—can be addressed at the beginning of a discussion now, rather than serving as a dramatic dénouement. This gives us space to explore the consequences of Morrison's invitation to engage in misreadings throughout "Recitatif," only to catch ourselves in our "laziness," and, as significantly, to think about the reasons that Twyla and Roberta misread one another.

****

I've taken to entering class discussions of "Recitatif" by introducing an excerpt from the poet Claudia Rankine's *Citizen* (2015), a book that has been identified as "part documentary, part lyric procedural" in its capturing of racism in America (Chiasson 73).[1] Early in the book, Rankine suggests the essential volatility that inherently underlies relationships between Black and white friends:

> A friend argues that Americans battle between the "historical self" and the "self self." By this she means you mostly interact as friends with mutual interest and, for the most part, compatible personalities; however, sometimes your historical selves, her white self and your black self, or your white self and her black self, arrive with the full force of your American positioning. Then you are standing face-to-face in seconds that wipe the affable smiles right from your mouths. What did you say? Instantaneously your attachment seems fragile, tenuous, subject to any transgression of your historical self. And though your joined personal histories are supposed to save you from misunderstandings, they usually cause you to understand all too well what is meant. (14)

Here, Rankine highlights the ways in which even the most intimate and generous relationships can be clouded by a fraught knowledge of the larger contexts in which they exist. *Citizen* also introduces terminology that is particularly helpful in considering Twyla and Roberta's relationship in class discussions—the "self self" and the "historical self." Our initial challenge in approaching each of Twyla and Roberta's encounters is to map the way the girls/women make their "self selves" available to one another and to identify where we catch glimpses of their "historical selves." Our second task in reading "Recitatif" is also grounded in *Citizen*. Like "Recitatif," Rankine's piece implicates the reader: there is the contention that we, too, approach a conversation (or text) with the unshakable "full force of [our] American positioning." In reading "Recitatif," then, we must be attentive to our "historical selves," considering how our identities shape us as readers. If we understand that Morrison is placing racial signifiers ripe for misinterpretation throughout the story, how might we catch ourselves in the act of assigning them meaning? Alternately, how might we read against our own potential misreadings? (I often share with my students that a number of scholars have disclosed their own racial identities in their readings of the work, including Elizabeth Abel, in her now-canonical essay "Black Writing, White Reading: Race and the Politics of Feminist Interpretation," and Ann Rayson, in "Decoding for Race: Toni Morrison's 'Recitatif' and Being White, Teaching Black." In doing so, these scholars indicate their awareness of their "historical selves," rejecting the projection of distanced subjectivity often associated with academic authority.)

We get a sense of Twyla's "historical self" early in the story. In speaking of her first day at "St. Bonny's," the orphanage to which she has been sent, she explains,

> It was one thing to be taken out of your own bed early in the morning—it was something else to be stuck in a strange place with a girl from a whole other race. And Mary, that's my mother, she was right. Every now and then she would stop dancing long enough to tell me something important and one of the things she said was that they never washed their hair and they smelled funny. Roberta sure did. Smell funny, I mean. So when the Big Bozo (nobody ever called her Mrs. Itkin, just like nobody ever said St. Bonaventure)—when she said, "Twyla, this is Roberta.

I am grateful to my colleagues Howard Rambsy and Liz Cali for their generous conversations about teaching Morrison's work in their own classrooms.

[1] Rankine has observed that her work is in conversation with Morrison's. In 2020, she explained in an interview that "I feel like *Citizen* was just the next book that looked at the same dynamic that Toni Morrison was looking at or Frederick Douglass was looking at or James Baldwin, obviously" (interview by Jeffrey Brown).

Roberta, this is Twyla. Make each other welcome." I said, "My mother won't like you putting me in here." ("Recitatif" 607)

Twyla makes no effort to mask her inherited racism here, and while we may be inclined to judge it, in fact the reader's tendency is to similarly retreat into the historical-self, relying on a racialized shorthand to assign identities to both Twyla and Roberta. The primary "clues" here—Twyla's mother's belief that those of Roberta's race "smell funny" and the characters' names—point both ways, though. The uncleanliness of the otherized body is a stereotype that exists among all races, and the names "Twyla" and "Roberta" become more racially ambiguous when one bears down on them.[2] In class, then, we read through this first encounter twice, once with the assumption that Twyla is white and Roberta is Black, and then again, with Twyla as Black and Roberta as white. The exercise reveals to students the ways in which they may have responded to potentially racialized codes based on their own historical-selves.[3] Stopping at this early point in the text to offer alternate racial identities of each character also has the added benefit of loosening the commitment students may feel to their initial readings of the characters; by identifying each reading as legitimate (and thus simultaneously problematic), students are challenged to think more broadly about the way the characters approach one another as the discussion moves forward.

Pausing at this point also allows us to think about the complexity of the transmission of the historical-self. Twyla's knowledge of other races comes from her mother, Mary, and after repeating Mary's contention that people of another race "smell funny," Twyla announces with some satisfaction, "she was right." From the story's first line, though, we know that Mary is a *not* dependable source of insight: Twyla has been sent to the orphanage because of Mary's neglect, which Twyla views in literal terms, pointing to Mary's habit of "dancing all night" (607). Later, when Mary visits St. Bonny's a month into Twyla and Roberta's stay, we are able to fully comprehend her inability to support Twyla. Most obviously, Mary is incapable of providing nourishment for Twyla even in the most literal sense: unlike Roberta's mother, who brings a full lunch for her daughter, Mary neglects to bring any food for the visit. Mary is "unsuitable" in other ways as well: the outfit she wears to St. Bonny's—tight green pants and a "fur jacket so ripped she had to pull to get her hands out of them"—embarrasses Twyla (609). And in spite of her sexualized appearance, Mary is depicted as no more mature than Twyla. Twyla tells us that when her mother spots her outside the orphanage's chapel, Mary "smiled and waved like she was the little girl looking for her mother—not me" (609). The self-centeredness and immaturity that Mary displays early in the visit are made manifest when she is snubbed by Roberta's mother, though. Seemingly unconcerned by her daughter's feelings or

---

[2]Each semester, a number of my white students insist that there is no stereotype of white uncleanliness, and thus, Twyla must be white and Roberta Black. In fact, evidence of this stereotype is plentiful. The comedian Dave Chapelle's now-famous 2003 skit "Trading Spouses" traded on often profane racial stereotypes, and one scene mocked whites' suspect hygiene practices specifically. More recently, there have been public debates about the necessity of "leg washing" in which a number of high-profile white women, including the singer Taylor Swift, have questioned its necessity, and another, started by the designer Stella McCartney, advocates for washing clothes less often, further fueling stereotypes of whites' attitudes toward hygiene. See Nicole Froio. As for names, Elizabeth Abel points out, "If Twyla's name is more characteristically black than white, it is perhaps best known as the name of a white dancer, Twyla Tharp, whereas Roberta shares her last name, Fisk, with a celebrated black (now integrated) university" (476).
[3]In his essay, "Race and Response: Toni Morrison's 'Recitatif'," David Goldstein-Shirley provides a fairly comprehensive list of all of the markers of racialized identity that are commonly (mis)read by the story's readers.

the fact that, as one of only a few visitors, she is on display—and in St. Bonny's chapel, no less—Mary sputters and sulks when she realizes the slight:

> This light bulb goes off in her head and she says "That bitch!" really loud and us almost in the chapel now. Organ music whining; the Bonny Angels singing sweetly. Everybody in the world turned around to look. And Mary would have kept it up—kept calling names if I hadn't squeezed her hand as hard as I could. That helped a little, but she still twitched and crossed and uncrossed her legs all through service. Even groaned a couple of times. Why did I think she would come there and act right? Slacks. No hat like the grandmothers and viewers, and groaning all the while. When we stood for hymns she kept her mouth shut. Wouldn't even look at the words on the page. She actually reached in her purse for a mirror to check her lipstick. All I could think of was that she really needed to be killed. The sermon lasted a year, and I knew the real orphans were looking smug again. (610)

Mary's behavior is so horrifying to Twyla that she momentarily wishes her mother dead, a circumstance that would have aligned her with the "real orphans" at St. Bonny's, girls whose hardness stands in stark contrast to Twyla's immediate vulnerability (609).

Mary's record of maternal failure—her inability to "act right" in any of the scenarios in which her daughter depends upon her—provides some insight into Twyla's inclination to claim Mary's racism as her own. Physically and emotionally abandoned by her mother, Twyla must create an imagined maternal presence that is both powerful and protective. Twyla's assertion to "Big Bozo" upon being matched with Roberta that "my mother won't like you putting me in here" is as much an articulation of domestic fantasy as it is an expression of racial prejudice, then. As much as Twyla may think her mother "needed to be killed" during Mary's tantrum in the chapel, Twyla is also desperate for a mother who might serve as an anchor for her own identity. Accordingly, Twyla is inclined to cling to whatever thin history is offered her, especially if it suggests superiority in some way. In the world of St. Bonny's—ruled over by the indifferent "Big Bozo" and, more immediately, by the often-cruel "gar girls"—and in the absence of a strong mother, Twyla has little power other than that suggested in the inherited "historical self" Mary offers in her casual prejudice.

The evident irony of Twyla's "historical" (racist) posturing is that Roberta quickly becomes the one person who is able to appreciate Twyla's "self-self." The girls have been thrown together when they are assigned to be roommates, but their real link is in their curious status at St. Bonny's: both Roberta and Twyla have living mothers and thus are not "real orphans." Their status belies a sense of real loss: both girls understand themselves to have been "dumped" (607). It is something neither can speak about, but Roberta is able to express her understanding of their shared positioning through a series of sympathetic silences. Most notably, when Bozo responds to Twyla's announcement that Mary will not approve of her living with someone of another race by suggesting that Mary ought to take Twyla home, a cruel recognition of the scenario's unlikeness, Roberta says nothing. Twyla is deeply shamed by Bozo's comment, and she notes that "if Roberta had laughed I would have killed her, but she didn't" (607). Roberta is ostensibly stung by Twyla's racist indignation, but she also understands Twyla's abandonment. This fact is confirmed a few minutes later when Twyla must confess to Roberta that her mother is not "sick," as Roberta's is, but rather, "She just likes to dance all night" (607). Roberta offers only a knowing, "Oh," and Twyla observes that "I liked the ways she understood things so fast" (607). Almost certainly, Roberta does not actually understand why Mary is incapable of caring for Twyla, but what she does understand is Twyla's shame. Later, Twyla would observe that she and Roberta had been "two little girls who knew what nobody else in the world knew—how not to ask questions. How to believe what had to be believed. There was politeness in that reluctance and generosity as well" (614). It is in their sympathetic silence that they are able to recognize their "self-selves," forming a friendship that suggests sisterhood. As Warhol and Shuman have noted in their analysis of the story, it is soon after Roberta offers Twyla her silent acceptance of Twyla's situation that "the narrator's 'I' morphs into a 'we' that speaks for the two girls' mutual understanding and their unspoken agreement to elide the racial differences between them, even though others won't let them forget it" (1014). We are given a linguistic illustration of the depth of their knowledge of one another.

The anxiety of racial difference is still present in the story's earliest pages, though, and is primarily rendered visible through the character of Maggie. In first introducing Maggie in the narrative, Twyla describes her as "the kitchen woman with legs like parentheses," a reference to Maggie's physical disability, but also a suggestion of the ways in which her presence interrupts the text, reminding us of the potential for racial ambiguity to trouble both the story's characters and readers ("Recitatif" 608). If Twyla and Roberta have set aside the question of race in the service of their friendship, Maggie becomes an unrecognized site for their anxiety. Recalling the St. Bonny's orchard, a space Maggie sometimes crossed on her way to the bus stop, Twyla insists that "nothing really happened there. Nothing all that important I mean … Maggie fell down there once" (608). Even on a first reading, Twyla's story is recognizably suspect; the repeated dismissal of the importance of the scene in the orchard calls attention to it rather than diminishing it, and the reference to Maggie's "falling" seems conspicuously incomplete.

When reading the scene in which Maggie is first referenced with students, we begin by focusing on the framework into which she is introduced, a space that is notable for its blurring of boundaries and insistent contradictions. In almost every way, the orchard resists clear definition. The staff tries to keep the younger girls out, for example, but they find their way into the older girls' territory nevertheless, a suggestion of the porous borders that define the space. Beyond this, the orchard is filled with trees whose progress seems to defy time, beginning as crones—"empty and crooked like beggar women"—and then becoming fertile, "fat with flowers" (608). More compellingly, Twyla reveals that the gar girls are not all orphans, as the younger girls are. Instead, they are "put-out girls, scared runaways most of them. Poor little girls who fought their uncles off but looked tough to us, and mean" (608). The difference between "poor little girls" who have been "dumped," as Roberta and Twyla have, and those who have been "put out" may be seen as slight. It is possible to see the gar girls' meanness as a desperate posture, simply another way of "not asking questions" through the adoption of anonymizing, "gargoyle-esque" masks (609, 613). The orchard, it seems, is a space where binaries of all sorts are rendered problematic and, consequently, where memory is blurred.

It is in this context that we are introduced to Maggie, who also defies the easy boxes used to assign identity. The only reference to Maggie's race is Twyla's identification of her as "sandy-colored," but she notes a similar ambiguity in Maggie's age: while Maggie is an adult, she dresses like a child, a decision that invites the girls' contempt. Twyla notes, "She wore this really stupid little hat—a kid's hat with earflaps—and she wasn't much taller than we were. A really awful little hat. Even for a mute, it was dumb—dressing like a kid, and never saying anything at all" (608). Twyla's anger seems misplaced, at best, another hint of her unreliability. Here, she seems to suggest that Maggie's absolute vulnerability may be Maggie's own fault, a testament to her "dumbness" (an unkind, if perhaps unconscious, play on her muteness). In this first account, Twyla confesses that she and Roberta called Maggie names and that when Maggie "falls" they do not help her up.

It is at the end of the passage that we learn that it is the day before the "fall" that the girls have been told their mothers will be visiting. This information, delivered as if it is a bit of conversational filler, actually becomes one of the story's important, if ultimately indefinite, "clues." As Roberta and Twyla experience anxiety about the impending visit from their mothers, Maggie must serve as a sharp reminder of the ways in which the adults in their lives have failed them, as Maggie herself seems to have failed to become fully adult. At the same time, Maggie simultaneously mirrors the ways in which the girls remain painfully vulnerable. If Twyla and Roberta call Maggie names and refuse to help her up, as Twyla recalls in the narrative, then almost surely it is because Maggie has become an outlet for the anger the girls cannot express otherwise. Their treatment of her gives them a sense of power that they are denied by both their mothers and by St. Bonny's.

The account of the girls' treatment of Maggie shifts throughout the story, becoming more troubling as the context in which it is recounted becomes more loaded. Even in this first—most mild—account of "what happened to Maggie," though, Twyla expresses shame for the part she and Roberta have played. She explains that while she and Roberta had concluded that Maggie was deaf, as an adult she comes to "think we were wrong. I think she could hear and didn't let on. And it shames me even now to think there was somebody in there after all who heard us call her those names and couldn't tell on us" (608). If Maggie can hear, then she suffers from the girls' insults in a way that feels deeply recognizable to Twyla. Her muteness may be the consequence of physical disability, but regardless, Maggie shares Twyla and Roberta's knowledge of "how not to ask questions. How to believe what had to be believed." Twyla's shame, then, suggests her recognition that Maggie possesses a "self self," an identity apart from the role of victim that the girls have projected upon her. Even as the story of what has happened to Maggie shifts, and the girls potentially become more implicated in the violence against her, it is the recognition of Maggie as "somebody in there" that haunts them.

****

When Roberta and Twyla encounter one another years later, it is outside of the bubble that has compelled them to connect as "self-selves" as children. In their first meeting outside of St. Bonny's, Twyla is waiting tables in a Howard Johnson's, which she understands on some level to be repair work. Recalling Mary's failure to bring a real lunch to her visit to St. Bonny's, Twyla observes, "The wrong food is always with the wrong people. Maybe that's why I got into waitress work later—to match up the right people with the right food" (610). If Twyla still defines herself in terms of the personal, though, Roberta has chosen to recast herself in terms of the historical moment. She appears as the physical embodiment of the cultural shift in 1960s America: her "hair was so big and wild I could hardly see her face," Twyla observes, somewhat disapprovingly. "She had on a powder blue halter and shorts outfit and earrings the size of bracelets. Talk about lipstick and eyebrow pencil. She made the big girls look like nuns" (611). (In fact, the two men who accompany Roberta, both with counterculture-inspired looks of their own, seem more like additional accessories than people. While they laugh when Roberta laughs and roll their eyes in sympathy with Roberta's disgust, they add nothing of their own to the conversation.)[4]

---

[4] As Elizabeth Abel has noted, this is in keeping with Morrison's strategy of ensuring that Roberta and Twyla's relationship is "unmediated by the sexual triangulations (the predations of white men on black women, the susceptibility of black men to white women) that have dominated black women's narrative representations of women's fraught connections across racial lines" (471).

The meeting between the young women is short and painful. Twyla is out of touch in a way that seems not only impossible to Roberta, but offensive. When Twyla responds to Roberta's announcement that she is joining to see "Hendrix," by enthusiastically asking, "What's she doing now?" for example, Roberta sharply corrects Twyla, and reflexively calls her "asshole" (612). Twyla's naiveté is not confined to music. In their subsequent meeting, Roberta casually explains her behavior at the Howard Johnson's as a consequence of "how it was in those days: black—white" and suggests, "You know how everything was" (615). It is an explanation that leaves Twyla genuinely stymied. In Twyla's sense of the world, Howard Johnson's is a melting pot: "Busloads of blacks and whites came into Howard Johnson's together. They roamed together then: students, musicians, lovers, protesters. You got to see everything at Howard Johnson's and blacks were very friendly with whites in those days" (615). In Twyla's construction of it, the restaurant functions as a stand-in for St. Bonny's: not only is it accessible to a variety of people, but it offers a kind of fundamental care. It is here that Twyla "gets the right food to the right people"—providing basic nurturance—and while Twyla recognizes that the Howard Johnson's is run down, in the starkness of the predawn hours, she also believes it looks "like shelter," an echo of St. Bonny's (611). As a result, while Twyla is self-aware enough to worry when she first approaches Roberta in the restaurant that "maybe [Roberta] didn't want to be to be reminded of St. Bonny's or to have anybody know she was ever there," Twyla is not concerned that their essential connection has changed (615). In Twyla's thinking, the women inhabit a space that is similar to the one in which they first knew each other.

Roberta has a different understanding of the world she occupies, however, and it is clear while she is in the Howard Johnson's that she is attempting to position her voice within the context of a larger historical-self. Consequently, Roberta creates distance between the intimacy of the selves that she and Twyla shared as girls by dismissing Twyla, both through the repetition of the contemptuous utterance "Wow," and the sharper "asshole." (Interestingly, it is the "stingy 'wow'" that Twyla carries forward in memory, clearly recognizing the disgust that underlies it [613].) Twyla may not fully comprehend the dynamic in which she and Roberta are engaged, but instinctively she seeks to wound Roberta in return by using the tools of the personal: in response to Roberta's scorn, she asks, "How's your mother?" a question she understands to be loaded (612). Roberta's reply, "Fine," treats the question as innocuous, but she returns fire by politely, devastatingly, inquiring, "How's yours?" With this exchange, the lines between historical-selves and self-selves are blurred in ways that presumably leave both Twyla and Roberta destabilized. Certainly, after their exchange, Twyla's sense of the Howard Johnson's as a protective space is shattered. As she replies to Roberta's question, assuring her with palpable guardedness that Mary is "pretty as a picture," she thinks to herself, "Howard Johnson's really was a dump in the sunlight" (612).

Roberta and Twyla's next encounter, years later when both are married and rooted in families of their own making, is fraught in different ways. In this case, the women run into one another in the new, upscale grocery store in the community. When Twyla does not recognize Roberta at first, she bristles at being called out to as "Twyla" by an unknown speaker, and she curtly offers her married name, "Mrs. Benson," as a corrective. The title suggests that marriage has changed Twyla, protecting her in some substantial way, but the characteristics that had defined Twyla in her youth are still visible: as a working-class woman, she is tentative about her place in the fancy grocery store and only relaxes when she finds the brand of ice cream favored by her son and father-in-law, reassurance that she is able to provide "the right food to the right people." Roberta has more obviously reaped the benefits of an identity altered by marriage. As "Mrs. Kenneth Norton," she is wealthy. Her husband is an IBM executive, a man who does something with "computers and stuff," as she explains to Twyla disinterestedly, and she now has a chauffeur—who is neither Black nor white, but Asian—and two servants (614). Twyla cannot help but view Roberta with some resentment when she first sees her, thinking, "Everything is so easy for them. They think they own the world" (613). It is a claim loaded with implications about Roberta's class status, but that also contains suggestions of racism, although, in keeping with the story's larger project, it is not clear if the accusations may be levied against privileged whites or the Black beneficiaries of corporate diversity efforts.

The women never address this tension directly; in fact, Twyla delights in the fact that in their initial conversation, they act "like sisters separated for much too long" (614). A lingering anxiety is ultimately revealed, however, when it becomes clear that the women hold competing recollections of what has happened to Maggie in the orchard. Twyla's story about Maggie falling down is challenged by Roberta's insistence that the gar girls "knocked her down and tore her clothes," a memory that she contends Twyla has "blocked" (614–15). Roberta's account is deeply troubling to Twyla: Maggie's victimization may be painful to her, but what seems to be more upsetting is the suggestion that Twyla has misremembered her childhood. Roberta's account is a challenge to Twyla's construction of self. Twyla expresses her anger and confusion in a burst of resentment toward Roberta: she thinks angrily, "Couldn't [Roberta] just comb her hair, wash her face, and pretend everything was hunky-dory [?]" (615). In its intimation of the value in Roberta's clean face and brushed hair, we may read Twyla's suggestion as an expression of her desire for Roberta to exist more easily within a traditional construction of (white or Black) identity. Roberta's memories, like her "wild hair" and dramatic makeup in the Howard Johnson's, challenge Twyla to consider the historical-self in ways that are deeply uncomfortable for her.

Ultimately, the women move toward repair of sorts when they again inquire about one another's mothers. In this reprised conversation, both are more candid: Mary has never stopped dancing, Twyla acknowledges, and Roberta's mother never "got well," she confesses. The brief exchange is poignant, an adult acknowledgment of grief and loss, but, significantly, one that does not "ask too many questions," and so recognizes an essential sympathy of selves. It is a thin attempt to plaster over a larger rupture, though. Twyla is resentful that "Roberta had messed up my past somehow with that business about Maggie"; in short, Roberta has inserted the historical into the more comfortable world defined by the intimacy of "self-selves" (615).

****

It is in the women's next encounter when their historical-selves and self-selves fully clash, and they find themselves "standing face-to-face in seconds that wipe the affable smiles right from [their] mouths," to borrow again from Rankine. The racial identifications that the two have largely ignored in childhood and have addressed only tangentially in subsequent meetings are called out more directly when they are drawn into the "strife" that surrounds the bussing debate in the New York suburbs (615). Twyla becomes involved when she sees Roberta at a protest holding a sign that says, "MOTHERS HAVE RIGHTS TOO." Up until this point, she had few feelings about bussing:

> Joseph [Twyla's son] was on the list of kids to be transferred from the junior high school to another one at some far-out-of-the-way place and I thought it was a good thing until I heard it was a bad thing. I mean I didn't know. All the schools seemed dumps to me, and the fact that one was nicer looking didn't hold much weight. But the papers were full of it and then the kids

began to get jumpy ... I thought Joseph might be frightened to go over there, but he didn't seem scared so I forgot about it. (616)

It is only when she sees Roberta's sign that Twyla becomes determined to take the other side. For many students, it is this scene that crystallizes Twyla's and Roberta's racial identities: Roberta, who is opposed to bussing, must be white, while Twyla, who has suddenly determined she is in support of it, must be Black. Bussing was a proposal that found pushback among all who were involved, however, and while the narrative of white protest, led by those threated by the diversification of schools, may be more persistent, there is an ample historical record of Black protest of bussing as well. As studies demonstrate, Black communities tended to pay the greater price for bussing, both in the distance their children were compelled to travel to attend school and the subsequent neglect of schools located in historically Black neighborhoods.

If Morrison has used bussing as something of a red herring (at least in her invitation to racialize the story's characters), it is also less central to Twyla and Roberta's dispute than it might seem. Certainly, for Roberta, bussing is a signifier of injustice, either as it symbolizes impingement on her white privilege or, alternately, as it represents a burden placed on the Black community. Twyla is less concerned with the historical discussion that Roberta sees herself as engaging in: arguably, it is Roberta's sign that compels her to join the protests. Roberta's suggestion that mothers play a distinctive role in shaping laws and norms violates Twyla's sense of the world. She may be a mother herself, but we see her as largely passive in this role. More significantly, Twyla will always understand herself as an abandoned child, and she had believed the same was true of Roberta, who had been her "sister" in the experience at St. Bonny's. (Tellingly, Twyla tries to reify this connection on the picket line when she tells Roberta that anyone who "think[s] they can decide where my child goes to school" is akin to Bozo [616].) Roberta's sign functions as a direct rebuke to Twyla, an erasure of their shared "self-selves" in an attempt to assert the historical, racialized self.

It is notable, though, that Roberta's sign is something of a paradox. When Twyla first approaches Roberta, telling her, "My boy's being bussed too, and I don't mind," Roberta chastises her, explaining, "It's not about us, Twyla. Me and you. It's about our kids" (616). Roberta's remark seems a direct contradiction of the sign she hoists at the protest, which highlights mother's rights and makes no mention of "our kids." Indeed, at some level, Roberta seems to want it both ways until she is confronted by Twyla. Twyla's insistence that the issue is solely personal pushes Roberta to embrace the historical. These are the "seconds that wipe the affable smiles right from [their] mouths," and when Twyla's car is rocked by anti-bussing protesters, Roberta looks on impassively. Twyla had believed that Roberta would help her, the adult manifestation of their pattern of coming to the other's aid when they were being chased by the gar girls at St. Bonny's, and accordingly, we understand the moment in which Twyla's "arm shot out of the car window, but no receiving hand was there" as one of conscious abandonment (617). Roberta does not fully sever the connections of "self-selves," though, until she once again revises Twyla's memory of Maggie. Amid the chaos of the protest, she tells Twyla, "Maybe I am different now, Twyla. But you're not. You're the same little state kid who kicked a poor old black lady when she was down on the ground. You kicked a black lady and you have the nerve to call me a bigot" (617). It does not matter that Roberta immediately confesses to kicking Maggie along with Twyla: Roberta has effectively overwritten Twyla's understanding of her essential self with one shaped by the brutality of her racial history, be it one located in racial prejudice (if Twyla is white) or self-loathing (if she is Black).

Twyla responds by joining the other side of the protest the next day, creating signs that will be meaningful only to Roberta. (For instance, she creates a poster that says "How Would You Know?" in response to Roberta's "Mothers Have Rights Too," an ambiguous, if not actually nonsensical, yin to Roberta's yang [618].) By making the protest a personal matter, Twyla attempts to rewrite the narrative Roberta has introduced, reasserting the primacy of the intimate self. She continues to be troubled by the memory of Maggie, however, which she now understands is a mechanism for understanding her relationship to race and to power (and powerlessness). Twyla is certain she did not kick Maggie ("I didn't do that, I couldn't do that"), but she is distressed by the fact that she can't identify Maggie's race (618). Ultimately, she determines

> that the truth was already there, and Roberta knew it. I didn't kick her; I didn't join in with the gar girls and kick that lady, but I sure did want to. We watched and never tried to help her and never called for help. Maggie was my dancing mother. Deaf, I thought, and dumb. Nobody inside. Nobody who would hear you if you cried in the night. Nobody who could tell you anything important that you could use. Rocking, dancing, swaying as she walked. And when the gar girls pushed her down, and started roughhousing, I knew she wouldn't scream, couldn't— just like me and I was glad about that. (618)

It is an ugly truth, and it does little to resolve the mystery of Twyla's and Roberta's respective racial identities. Twyla's epiphany—confirmed by Roberta when the two women meet a final time on Christmas Eve years later—is valuable in many ways, though. It insistently reiterates the blurring of lines that we associate with Maggie from her first appearance in the text. Here, Twyla decides there is "nobody inside," a contradiction of her earliest claim that there "was somebody in there after all," a move that links Maggie equally to Mary and to Twyla. Tellingly, Roberta also sees Maggie as a representation both of her mother and of herself. She muses, "I thought she was crazy. She'd been brought up in an institution like my mother was and like I thought I would be too. And you were right. We didn't kick her. It was the gar girls. Only them. But, well, I wanted to. I really wanted them to hurt her." She concludes, "wanting to is doing it" (620).

Roberta believes—and Twyla fears—that there is a racial component in their desire for violence, but their inability to confidently distinguish Maggie's race makes it impossible for the characters (or the reader) to fully identify the dynamic at work. The women do not know whether Maggie was Black—"I really thought so," Roberta explains, "But now I can't be sure"—and so they cannot interpret their rage toward Maggie in relation to their historical-selves (619). Ultimately, they must settle for an account of their pasts in which Maggie represents their own helplessness, a story that is valid but that is rooted squarely in the "self-self." It allows the women to reaffirm their connection to one another, which they do by repeating their confessions about their abandonment as children. "Did I tell you? My mother, she never did stop dancing," Twyla tells Roberta. "Yes. You told me. And mine, she never got well," Roberta replies. Offered without any awkward inquiry, these acknowledgments operate as small gifts, a recognition of what Rankine has identified as the "joined personal histories are supposed to save you from misunderstandings" (620).

And yet, the last line lines of the story, uttered by Roberta, suggest that while the characters' historical-selves may remain an unresolvable mystery, they are not forgotten and, in fact, are critical even in their elision: "Shit, shit, shit. What the hell happened to Maggie?" (620). The lines function as a *cri de coeur*, and arguably, they operate as the "recitatif" of the title—a vocalization somewhere between song and the spoken word, used to introduce narrative into an interlude. If we think of

Roberta's question this way, we understand that the story's ending is simply a pause, an invitation from Morrison to reread the text through multiple interpretations of Maggie's experience, and thus to reinterpret Roberta and Twyla, tracing their shifting contexts in ways that are often reflective of our own.

WORKS CITED

Abel, Elizabeth. "White Reading: Race and the Politics of Feminist Interpretation." *Critical Inquiry*, vol. 19, no. 3, 1993, pp. 470–98.

Chiasson, Dan. "Color Codes." *The New Yorker*, vol. 90, no. 33, 2014, pp. 73.

Froio, Nicole. "The Hygiene Culture Wars that Started on Social Media." *Zora*, Aug. 1, 2019, https://zora.medium.com/the-hygiene-culture-wars-that-started-on-social-media-3e5c0ac8be55. Accessed Oct. 12, 2021.

Goldstein-Shirley, David. "Race and Response: Toni Morrison's 'Recitatif'." *Short Story*, vol. 5, no. 1, 1997, pp. 117–86.

Morrison, Toni. "The Art of Fiction No 134." Interview with Elissa Schappell and Claudia Brodsky Lacour, vol. 128, Fall 1993, pp. 82–125.

Morrison, Toni. *Playing in the Dark: Whiteness and the Literary Imagination*. Vintage, 1993.

Morrison, Toni. "Recitatif." *The Norton Anthology of American Literature*. 9th ed., vol. E, edited by Nina Bayn, et al., Norton, 2017, pp. 607–20.

Rankine, Claudia. *Citizen: An American Lyric*. Penguin, 2015.

Rankine, Claudia. Interview by Jeffrey Brown, *PBS NewsHour*, July 29, 2020.

Rayson, Ann. "Decoding for Race: Toni Morrison's 'Recitatif' and Being White, Teaching Black." *Changing Representations of Minorities East and West*, edited by Smith, Larry E., U Hawai'i P, 1996, pp. 41–6.

Warhol, Robyn, and Amy Shuman. "The Unspeakable, the Unnarratable, and the Repudiation of Epiphany in 'Recitatif': A Collaboration between Linguistic and Literary Feminist Narratologies." *Textual Practice*, vol. 32, no. 6, 2018, pp. 1007–25.

CHAPTER TWENTY-FIVE

Toni Morrison's *Home*: One Scene, Four Takes

TRUDIER HARRIS

Toni Morrison's *Home* (2012) is about trauma and violence, especially the trauma that leads to violence. The novel suggests that the most productive way out of trauma is through the power of narrative, narrative that has multiple authors and that binds communities together in mutual sharing of the story. For the discussion here, I focus on one of the most compelling scenes in the novel, which is a tale of narrated trauma that sparks recovery. It is the scene in which Black men playing checkers on a porch in Lotus, Georgia, relate the tale of how white men in the 1940s have pitted a Black man and his son against each other in a fight to the death (Morrison, *Home* 137–40). Those controlling the madness insist that the Black men use knives in the fight, and the white men make it clear that only one of the Black fighters will leave the isolated barn alive. In what they consider a game, the white men make bets. The Black men on the porch recount what Jerome, the son, has related to them about being forced to kill his father:

> "He told us they [the white males who sponsored the 'game'] brought him and his daddy from Alabama. Roped up. Made them fight each other. With knives."
> "No, sir. Switchblades. Yep, switchblades … Said they had to fight each other to the death … One of them had to die or they both would. They took bets on which one." … "Boy said they slashed each other a bit—just enough to draw a line of blood. The game was set up so only the one left alive could leave. So one of them had to kill the other." … "They graduated from dogfights. Turned men into dogs."
> "Can you beat that? Pitting father against son?"
> "Said he told his daddy, 'No, Pa. No.'"
> "His daddy told him, 'You got to.'"
> "That's a devil's decision-making. Any way you decide is a sure trip to his hell."
> "Then, when he kept on saying no, his daddy told him, 'Obey me, son, this one last time. Do it.' Said he told his daddy, 'I can't take your life.' And his daddy told him, 'This ain't life.' Meantime the crowd, drunk and all fired up, was going crazier and crazier, shouting, 'Stop yapping. Fight! God damn it! Fight!'" (*Home* 138–9)

Echoing the Battle Royal scene in Ralph Ellison's *Invisible Man* (1952), but with far more lethal consequences, this scene makes clear that there is no question as to who "they" are that roped the father and son and brought them from Alabama to Georgia (17–29). *They* represent the ubiquitous and controlling forces under the umbrella of white supremacy generally responsible for causing violence and death for African Americans in the Jim Crow South. What the white men do showcases power and control, total agency in the face of the absence of agency in the people whom they capture, humiliate, and kill.

During the telling of the narrative, primary character Frank "Smart" Money is viscerally shocked by the story. His reaction is in part recognition, for he realizes that the place at which that atrocity occurred is the same space that he and his younger sister Ycidra ("Cee") had come upon when they were children. Comparable to Alice Walker's Myop in "The Flowers," young Frank internalizes what he witnesses, but he does not have the astuteness of Myop to register fully what he has seen (or perhaps he registers it much too fully, which leads to its total repression). Myop drops the flowers she has been collecting when she comes upon the skeleton of a man who has been lynched (Walker 119–20). Frank responds to seeing a Black man buried by "taming his anger down," as Gwendolyn Brooks would say, which means that the incident haunts him from the moment of its occurrence until he sits on the porch with the old men almost a decade and a half later.[1] Like Sethe, who chooses to remember the natural beauty of Sweet Home, especially the trees, instead of the Black men hanging from those trees, Frank has preferred to remember the beautiful horses that pranced and fought, who *rose up like men* (emphases in original) in the pasture near the barn where the Black man has died (Morrison, *Beloved*; *Home* 3). The memory of the horses stays with him and overshadows the fact that he and his sister had inadvertently witnessed the final act in that horrific son-killing-father drama. They had seen men burying a body, during which a foot protruded from the grave almost in resistance to the demise of the body attached to it. It is only at the point of inescapably recalling trauma and not being able to tame it down again that Frank can begin to confront many of the violent episodes and moral lapses in his life. This porch-gathering, storytelling scene, then, serves multiple functions in the novel, including inspiring Frank's emotional confrontation with and acceptance of his tragic past.

BLOOD ON THE ROCKS: A CASUAL COCKTAIL

With a very few words, Toni Morrison evokes a history of violent attacks against Black bodies on US soil. As noted, the ubiquitous *they* in the tale do not have to be named, for everyone within hearing on the porch knows the reference. They are the ones who justified slavery by supporting theories that argued for the dehumanization of Blacks. They are the ones who participated in and/ or supported the Ku Klux Klan in its rampages against Blacks. They are the ones responsible for, as Douglas Blackmon refers to the condition, "slavery by another name," which included the convict lease system, Jim Crow, sharecropping, and every other form of repression that white people could bring to bear against and upon Black people (Blackmon). In this specific case, Morrison references a well-documented practice: forcing men of African descent to fight against one another for the entertainment of whites, which probably began on plantations when white owners forced Black

---

[1] Gwendolyn Brooks uses the phrase in her novel, *Maud Martha* (1953), which appears in *Blacks* (141–322), in reference to her title character, who, as a strikingly dark-skinned woman, must suffer a host of indignities from whites as well as Blacks. Frank thus shares with Maud Martha a racially inspired anger that must be controlled.

men to fight one another. The practice has been portrayed in movies such as *Mandingo* (1975) and *Django Unchained* (2012), as well as in autobiographical and literary narratives.[2]

One way of documenting the practice was through interviews with formerly enslaved persons; many of these were recorded during the 1930s through the Works Progress Administration. Memories of slavery included accounts of Black men fighting each other for the entertainment and financial gain of their masters. In one Texas narrative, a formerly enslaved Black man, John Finnely, recalls the fights as well as the reputation of one of the Black men in whose prowess his master placed quite a bit of faith. "De nigger fights am more for de white folks' joyment but de slaves am 'lowed to see it. De massas of plantations match dere niggers 'cording to size and bet on dem. Massa Finnely have one nigger what weighs 'bout 150 pounds and him powerful good fighter and he like to fight. None lasts long with him" ("Texas Genealogy Trails, Slave Narratives"). The good fighter is Tom, who, in one contest, almost meets his match. Although he and his opponent "both am bleedin' and am awful sight," Tom finally gets the upper hand by repeatedly kicking his opponent in the stomach until he is a quivering mass, at which point his master declares "Dat 'nough." The bloody cocktail of entertainment is brought to a halt only when the prospect of financial loss outweighs enjoyment. Given the fact that so many enslaved persons were whipped severely (remember Frederick Douglass's aunt as well as Harriet Jacobs's accounts of beatings on the plantation where she resided) and sometimes to their death, it is certainly not the sight of blood that evokes termination of the contest, for no such squeamishness defined punishments for those enslaved (Douglass; Jacobs).

Growing up only a few years removed from the most damaging and lasting effects of slavery in the South, Richard Wright recounts in his autobiography, *Black Boy* (256–66), how he found himself in the untenable position of having white males forcing him to fight Harrison, another young Black man. Though neither youngster wants to fight, the campaign waged against them is so strong that they finally begin to distrust each other. White men on the job where they work prime the pump, so to speak, by bringing tales to each of the young men about the other. They try to talk each other out of believing what the white men are saying, but their distrust of each other continues to grow, despite Wright's assertions to Harrison that "I suppose it's fun for white men to see niggers fight" and "I don't want to fight for white men. I'm no dog or rooster" (260, 263).

Finally, the pressure is so great that Wright and Harrison give in to it. While they do not succumb to stabbing each other surreptitiously (the primary instigator even offers Wright a knife), they believe they can end the weeks-long agitation from the white men by agreeing to fight with gloves for four rounds for five dollars each. They agree initially to fake fighting just enough to get the white men to leave them alone. Once engaged in combat, however, they are unable to resist inflicting as much pain upon each other as they can. Here is Wright's account of what happens:

Now shame filled me. The white men were smoking and yelling obscenities at us.

---

[2]In discussing "Mandingo fighting," that is, contests between enslaved men that ended in death, Aisha Harris comments that such events probably did not happen because it would have been against the economic interests of slaveholders. She does record, however, that less lethal staged fights did indeed occur among enslaved men. See Harris, "Was There Really 'Mandingo Fighting.'" Sergio Lussana also argues that it would not have been in the best financial interests of slaveholders to allow those enslaved to fight to the death or even to the point of becoming maimed. Lussana argues in addition that the enslaved often staged fights among themselves, which was a way of validating masculinity and solidifying community. His comments appear in "To See Who Was Best on the Plantation."

> "Crush that nigger's nuts, nigger!"
> "Hit that nigger!"
> "Aw, fight, you goddamn niggers!"
> "Sock 'im in his fu—k—g piece!"
> "Make 'im bleed!" …
>
> The fight was on, was on against our will. I felt trapped and ashamed. I lashed out even harder, and the harder I fought the harder Harrison fought. Our plans and promises now meant nothing. We fought four hard rounds, stabbing, slugging, grunting, spitting, cursing, crying, bleeding. The shame and anger we felt for having allowed ourselves to be duped crept into our blows and blood ran into our eyes, half blinding us. The hate we felt for the men whom we had tried to cheat went into the blows we threw at each other. (265)

After the fight, Wright observes: "I could not look at Harrison. I hated him and I hated myself. I clutched my five dollars in my fist and walked home" (265–66). The two young men avoid each other from that point on, and Wright believes that he has done "something unclean, something for which [he] could never properly atone" (Wright 266). Having been forced, like Jerome and his father, to act like dogs, perhaps Wright is a bit harsh in judging his response. However, with the chorus of perverted satiation surrounding them—a chorus that anticipates both Ellison's and Morrison's novels—there can be no restoration of self-esteem concerning the incident. Fortunately for Wright and Harrison, the fight does not end in the death that the white men had initially planned for one of them.

Perhaps we can understand Wright's and Harrison's actions in the context of humiliation and response. Both young men are ashamed that the white men have manipulated them, and both know that they have no power to force the white men to stop treating them like dogs. They therefore take out their frustrations on each other by becoming more aggressive and violent as the sparring goes on. In a world in which they cannot define the terms of their humanity, they slip easily into the dehumanization that the white men have assigned to them. Their boxing does not end in death, but it does end in even more thorough humiliation, for these young men have had their innermost fears and insecurities exposed and manipulated for the entertainment of the white men who have ensured that the fight will indeed occur. Inherent in Wright's protests is his desire that he and other young Black men should have more agency, more control over the circumstances of their lives. Yet, the racial and economic circumstances of their existences are what drive Harrison to give in to the pressure and, eventually, for Wright to follow him. Wright and Harrison may exist in a post-slavery world, but both young men are still controlled by white men who believe that Black labor is to be expended for their financial gain and their enjoyment. Social, cultural, and racial manipulation in this instance shares traits with the purely physical manipulation that Jerome and his father experience in *Home*.

Following Wright and antedating Morrison, Ralph Ellison depicts similar forced violence and humiliation in that Battle Royal scene of *Invisible Man*. Young Black men are routinely propositioned by local white males of the upper classes to provide entertainment for them through boxing each other and scrambling for coins on an electrified rug. The unnamed narrator inadvertently joins the group when the local elite white citizenry invites him to deliver an oration. One of the other young Black men, angry that the narrator's participation in the Battle Royal has meant the elimination of compensation for one of their number, especially targets the narrator. In this instance, economics and a perverse pride drive what the young men do. They may humiliate themselves before the white men, but they are paid for doing so. Functional economics push true pride into the background. There is no space in their world to dwell on humiliation; they do as asked and earn their pay while egged on by drunken white men. Readers are not allowed a glimpse into the interiority of the majority of the youngsters who are forced to fight, so they can only glean meaning from the narrator's own exterior reactions.

Comparable to what Wright experienced—as well as to the account that the men on the porch relate in *Home*—the narrator and his companions must endure insults such as "black bastard," "coon," "Slug him, black boy! Knock his guts out!," and "Uppercut him! Kill him! Kill that big boy!" (Ellison, *Invisible Man* 22, 23). The drunken white men, one of whom threatens to enter the boxing ring and kill one of the young Black men, continue to shout insults at the blindfolded and bleeding youngsters, all of whom pound away at each other. When only the narrator and the angry young Black man, Tatlock, are left to slug it out for the promised five dollar grand prize, the narrator, like Wright, attempts to bring about a truce by suggesting that they fake a knockout and Tatlock can have the money, to which Tatlock advises him to "Go to hell!" (25). The narrator attempts to raise the prize money for Tatlock from five to seven dollars if Tatlock will end the madness, to which Tatlock replies, "Give it to your ma" (25). Resorting to playing the dozens and then fighting as viciously as he can, Tatlock joins Wright and Harrison in allowing anger at an impossible situation to intensify the dehumanization that he already feels as a result of being a part of this spectacle. Lack of control of his emotions parallels the lack of control that he, the narrator, and the other young Black men feel in having their humanity measured in a few paltry dollars that equate them to dogs or roosters—that is, entertainment value only.

What Morrison therefore evokes by referencing a history of forced violence layers fiction and reality into a cauldron that is a witches' brew of unadorned, unabashed power. The power has no control or limits because the very highest echelon of the society wields it. Thus, there are no checks and balances among the people who could create them. If the most powerful of the powerful do not believe in any way that they are doing anything wrong, then no sanction can be placed on what they do—at least not by anyone who matters. Certainly Wright can feel shame and guilt for what he has done, and he can recognize the manipulative proclivities of those white men he encounters in that factory, but his heightened awareness has no impact upon their behavior. The white men can toy with Wright and Harrison, and other young Black men like them, as long and as frequently as they wish. Similarly, the narrator in *Invisible Man* might understand the dynamics of the madness in which he participates, but it is knowledge without power, for he has absolutely no control over anything that happens during that evening. Of course he does give the speech that he has written, slipping up and saying "social equality" instead of "social responsibility," but he backpedals when the men challenge him (Ellison, *Invisible Man* 31).[3] By joining Ellison and Wright in echoing history

---

[3] Of note with Ellison's novel, in contrast to Wright's memoir and Morrison's narrative, is that the fight between the young Black men has an element of white female sexuality introduced into it. As the young men are fighting, the drunken men bring a nude white woman into the room and toss her into the air among them. The young men who witness the scene are all affected by it, and one of them even has an erection. Of course much has been written about this "you can see but you can't touch" flaunting of white female sexuality before Black males, and of course one of the major reasons white men gave for the lynching of Black males in the South was for presumed inappropriate attention to or alleged rape of white women. It could easily be imagined that Jerome and his father in *Home* could just as well have been accused of such. An accusation is unnecessary, however, for the men simply embrace the pleasure of seeing one Black man kill another, an intent that is implicit in what Wright and Harrison encounter as well as what the young men encounter in *Invisible Man*. After all, one

and literature, Morrison shares a kinship in community just as her characters share a kinship in proximity to each other in Lotus.[4]

OF DOGS AND MEN/WOMEN: MUTUAL DEHUMANIZATION, MUTUAL EXPENDABILITY

Combatants during slavery, Richard Wright, the young Black men in Ellison's Battle Royal, and Jerome and his father are all dehumanized and expendable. Either they themselves, as with Wright, or the narrators recounting their circumstances, as with the men on the porch in Lotus, emphasize their dehumanization and expendability by analogies to animals, specifically dogs. The front porch narrators note that the white men who have forced Jerome to kill his father graduated from staging dog fights to staging fights between humans, in this case, Black male human beings. In contrast to Jerome and his father, fighters during slavery—and Wright and the Invisible Man afterward—acquiesce to their dehumanization. Driven by economics or personal gains with master or employer, some voluntarily gave what controllers required, while others had no choice. For example, one enslaved man was so good at fighting and earning money that his master not only paid him for his successes but finally granted freedom to him.[5] Wright and Harrison similarly acquiesce not only for monetary gain but also to get the white men to cease psychologically assaulting them. Ellison's narrator, like Wright, understands the connection between exploitation and financial gain; still, neither he nor Wright has the agency to resist.

One text echoes another as references to dogs become the dominant image to evaluate the routine dehumanization that Black men suffer when forced to fight each other. The metaphor is fitting, though, not only in its reference to Black men fighting Black men, but because it highlights the dehumanization that saturates and is at the crux of *Home*. The dehumanization inherent in such categorization reflects the precarious conditions of existence under which most of the characters live. Consider, for example, the point at which Frank's parents, along with other Blacks in their community, are driven from their home in Texas. Just as Morrison references a history of Black men fighting Black men, she also references the history of Black dispossession from land and property when whites wanted to occupy it. One need think no farther than Ida B. Wells-Barnett's grocery-store-owning friends in Memphis who are lynched because whites consider their store competition or Wright's uncle being lynched in Arkansas because his saloon business is deemed to be too profitable (Wells-Barnett, "Southern Horrors" 34–37; Wright). When Black people become

---

of the white men there has to be restrained when he avows that he is going to jump into the ring and kill one of the young Black men: "'Let me at that big nigger!' ... 'Let me at those black sonsabitches!' ... 'I want to get at that ginger-colored nigger. Tear him limb from limb'" (Ellison, *Invisible Man* 21). For more on white women as the impetus to lynching, see Harris, *Selected Works of Ida B. Wells-Barnett*, particularly "Southern Horrors: Lynch Law and All Its Phases" (14–45) and Wells-Barnett, "A Red Record: Tabulated Statistics and Alleged Causes of Lynchings in the United States, 1892–1893–1894" (138–252); Harris, *Exorcising Blackness*.

[4]The pattern that Wright and Ellison showcase is duplicated in contemporary society, some cultural observers maintain, in the payment that African American males receive to bash each other for predominantly white entertainment, with that entertainment ranging from brutal boxing to slightly less brutal football to almost tolerable basketball. See Rhoden.

[5]Aisha Harris comments, "Tom Molineaux was a Virginia slave who won his freedom—and, for his owner, $100,000—after winning a match against another slave. He went on to become the first Black American to compete for the heavyweight championship when he fought the white champion Tom Cribb in England in 1810. (He lost.)" Sergio Lussana also mentions Molineaux (911).

obstacles to white acquisitiveness, they are displaced without any remote consideration for their humanity. Frank's parents were such obstacles. Though his mother is pregnant with Cee, and though few of the displaced Black folks have transportation out of Texas, they are simply ordered to leave. They are told that, if they value their lives, they will go; they do. The scene that Frank recounts is one that was acted out many times in African American history:

> *Mama was pregnant when we walked out of Bandera County, Texas. Three or maybe four families had trucks or cars and loaded all they could. But remember, nobody could load their land, their crops, their stock ... Talk about tired. Talk about hungry ... You don't know what heat is until you cross the border from Texas to Louisiana in the summer. You can't come up with words that catch it.* (Morrison, *Home* 39, 40, 41; emphases in original)

Historical displacement of Black people from their homes and property is so well known that Morrison does not have to dwell on it with complex details or descriptions. Black folks are on the road in the early twentieth century with all their worldly goods. They did not move voluntarily. They were moved. It is likewise unnecessary for Morrison to itemize in detail what they have been forced to leave; history tells us that it was something whites desired and took, just as they desired entertainment and took the lives of Jerome and his father (Jerome also essentially "dies" as a result of being forced to knife his father to death). There is no concern for a pregnant mother, for poor people trudging along with wheelbarrows full of the only possessions they could carry, for the faint and elderly or for the too-young-to-walk. All that matters is that white men view them only as obstacles to their desire, and those white men demanded that they move. There is no mention of anyone having died along the trail, but the hardships Frank, his family, and the others suffer are excruciating. The white power structure that sets these hardships in motion obviously has no concern for the mass of Black humanity that treads its way from Texas through several states and finally into Georgia.

Arguably, the metaphor of dehumanization and expendability could also be extended to Frank's tour of duty in Korea. Which young American men are most likely for the powers that be to send off to war? They are certainly not primarily the upper and middle classes. Those most susceptible to being drafted—or to electing the military as a way out of their economic circumstances—are usually working-class youth who see enlisting in the military as one way out of poverty and other limiting circumstances. Escaping poverty and the social limitations of a small town are certainly what appeal to Frank and his friends Stuff and Mike. Frank notes,

> *Lotus, Georgia, is the worst place in the world, worse than any battlefield ... there was no future, just long stretches of killing time. There was no goal other than breathing, nothing to win and, save for somebody else's quiet death, nothing to survive or worth surviving for. If not for my two friends I would have suffocated by the time I was twelve ... Maybe a hundred or so people living in some fifty spread-out rickety houses. Nothing to do but mindless work in fields you didn't own, couldn't own, and wouldn't own if you had any other choice ...*
> *Mike, Stuff, and me couldn't wait to get out and away, far away.*
> *Thank the Lord for the army.*[6] (Morrison, *Home* 83–4; emphases in original)

---

[6]The sense of hopelessness that Frank articulates echoes that of many characters in Jesmyn Ward's novels. I think especially of *Where the Line Bleeds*, in which two brothers graduate from high school in a small southern town but have such limited prospects for employment that their primary option is dealing drugs.

In the absence of opportunity for financial advancement in Lotus, Frank and his friends, like Wright and Ellison's narrator, take the money that the military offers to them, with that impersonal bureaucracy having no consideration for whether or not the young men could possibly survive their tour in Korea. Frank, Stuff, and Mike are, like the enslaved, expendable bodies of muscle and bone in service to the desires of their superiors.

Expendability in war is sometimes color-blind, but it is made even more so with these young Black men because of the stifling circumstances out of which they seek escape. While war is a longer-lasting alternative than the immediacy of a staged fight, it nonetheless illustrates that the value of Black lives is minimal. By going to war, these young Black men still imitate those who acquiesce to staged fights because they embrace their expendability. And expendable they are, for, in bloody detail comparable to that she employs in *Sula* in recounting Shadrack's memories of the First World War, Morrison depicts the horrible deaths of Stuff and Mike as well as the trauma that leaves Frank suffering from posttraumatic stress disorder (Morrison, *Sula* 7–8; *Home* 97–9). The only places the dead soldiers matter is in Frank's mind and the memories of loved ones. Not having lived to reap the benefits of embracing their own expendability, Stuff and Mike have no more value on the racist-driven landscape of America than Jerome and his father. Whether under the guise of federal institutions or in the casual arrangements of fights for entertainment, Black men do not fare well on American soil or representing it on foreign soil. Indeed, upon Frank's return to the United States, the only reward he receives for his service is institutionalization and inhuman designation, as Reverend Locke notes: "An integrated army is integrated misery. You all go fight, come back, they treat you like dogs. Change that. They treat dogs better" (Morrison, *Home* 18).

Dehumanization and expendability are the two forces that guide what happens to Frank's sister Cee as well. Cee thus provides another connecting line from slavery to her present in what happens to her as Dr. Beauregard Scott experiments upon her with medications and examinations that are designed to accomplish who knows what in his misguided quest for more knowledge about how the female body operates.[7] His physical location also enables Dr. Scott's practice, for Dr. Scott is isolated in his suburban Atlanta home, with an uncaring wife and a housekeeper who knows that it is in her best interest not to inspect too closely what Dr. Scott is doing. Dr. Scott can thus prescribe self-concocted medicines for poor afflicted Black women. Sick Black women come into his home office for his examinations and medications without realizing that they are giving up their health—and possibly their lives—to his eugenics experimentation. Gullible Cee is initially so enamored of the doctor that she sees no need to distrust him. By the time Sarah, the housekeeper, realizes that something is wrong and informs Frank, the damage has already been done. Although readers do not get details of precise medications or procedures Dr. Scott has inflicted on Cee, they do know that, by the time Frank rescues her, the damage is major. Not only does it take the healing women in Lotus *months* to heal Cee, but, once they have done so, they tell her that she can no longer bear children. Deliberately experimenting on a healthy young woman (Dr. Scott has been especially curious about her sex life and whether or not Cee has ever been pregnant) whom he concludes is perfect for his experiments, Dr. Scott epitomizes a medical profession dominated by whites who exert total control over Black bodies. He may just as well have ordered Cee into a boxing ring or

---

[7]Such experimentations upon enslaved women are well documented. See, for example, Owens and Washington.

into a war zone and watched her return battered, bloody, and beaten. She does not matter to him beyond his experiments, and, conscienceless, he sees her as totally expendable.

Again, there is the fact of acquiescence in one's own demise for, if Cee had not been so trusting of the doctor, if she had not needed a job so desperately, then she would not have ended up in his clutches. Economic necessity drives her tragic consequences just it drives those of most of the Black men who are forced to fight each other or who go off to fight in wars. It is no wonder, then, that, though she might feel sorrow and shed drenching tears as a result of this exploitation, she has no recourse against Dr. Scott. Even if she were daring enough to report him to some authority, she would probably not be heard; even if she were heard, Dr. Scott could easily defend himself by asserting the truth—that Cee agreed to participate in everything he did to her. Though Morrison does not dwell on the details, the overall sense of expendability at the hands of white power is nonetheless prominent. Cee, like the Venus Hottentot, is a body that excites curiosity, and that curiosity dehumanizes her in no less effective ways than all the fighting Black men are dehumanized. Miss Ethel and the other women recognize what Cee has suffered, and Miss Ethel focuses specifically upon the dehumanization when she tells Cee: "You ain't a mule to be pulling some evil doctor's wagon" (Morrison, *Home* 122). Ethel advises Cee not to let "no devil doctor decide" who she is; instead, Cee needs to escape the "slavery" implicit in her dehumanization and find the "free person" that Ethel knows lurks within Cee (126).[8]

The loser in the contest between Jerome and his father presents an additional depth of dehumanization in that he is reduced to a foot, and he lacks a name. The townspeople remember Jerome's name only because one of them has a relative with the same name. Still, Jerome has no last name. From this perspective, he joins his father in being one of the countless unnamed Black men whose identities get erased for white pleasure encased in white exploitation, domination, financial gain, psychological violence, and murder. Jerome and especially his father are metonyms for thousands of lynched or otherwise violently dispatched Black men. Erasure ensures that there is no memorial for most of them; thus Frank's final act in the novel becomes even more significant. By reburying the killed Black man, Frank creates a memorial that indicates the culmination of the restoration of his own memories about that fateful night. While Frank cannot shape the features of the man who has been killed, he can, fighting against that white desire to erase Black life, remember that he existed. That memory is a crucial part of the healing that Frank undergoes to become a truly functional and emotionally secure human being.

Just as the absence of a name marks Jerome's father as generically subject to white violence in the United States and substitutable for any Black man in the country, so does the reduction of his body to a foot. Metonymically, that conspicuously visible foot, *"that black foot with its creamy pink and mud-streaked sole being whacked into the grave"* (emphases in original), epitomizes the devaluing of Black life and Black humanity that underscores the fight into which the two Black men have been coerced and the racist dynamics that brought it about (Morrison, *Home* 4). Jerome's father might well be a stray dog hit by a passing car whose rotten corpse was simply tossed into a hole to be rid of the abomination. A Black foot with its pink sole visible to two children almost frightened out of their minds is the legacy bequeathed to Frank and Cee on that mind-numbing evening. Both

---

[8]Irene Visser, in her analysis of how the fairy tale "Hansel and Greta" operates in the novel, asserts that "Dr. Scott's residence is a sham protection covering a malicious intent, and the doctor parallels the witch, determined to entrap homeless young women in order to cannibalize them." See "Fairy Tale and Trauma in Toni Morrison's *Home*" (153).

will have to claw their way out of what they have witnessed (though Frank's wrestling—or lack thereof—with the incident is more the focus of the novel than Cee's). Still, with what happens to Cee, for Black men *and* Black women in Morrison's novel, dehumanization and expendability are applied in equal conscienceless doses.

A DOWNWARD GLANCE AT THE ROOT OF TRAUMA

Frank Money is a sometimes violent alcoholic who suffers from posttraumatic stress disorder as a result of having served in the Korean War, watching two of his friends die horribly, and having been involved in the death of a civilian. Certainly his Korean experience is significant in inducing trauma in Frank, but his original trauma lies elsewhere. Witnessing whites bury a Black man has been so intense and Frank has buried it so deeply in his psyche that it takes most of the novel for him to come to grips with it. The root of Frank's trauma results from what happens in the barn with Jerome and his father as he and Cee witness the father's being buried.[9] In the very first section of the novel, Frank recalls how he and Cee, who *"shouldn't have been anywhere near that place"* (emphases in original) happen upon and witness a man's being buried in a very unceremonious and uncaring way (Morrison, *Home* 3):

> *We saw them pull a body from a wheelbarrow and throw it into a hole already waiting. One foot stuck up over the edge and quivered, as though it could get out, as though with a little effort it could break through the dirt being shoveled in … When she* [Cee] *saw that black foot with its creamy pink and mud-streaked sole being whacked into the grave, her whole body began to shake. I hugged her shoulders tight and tried to pull her trembling into my own bones because, as a brother four years older, I thought I could handle it.* (Morrison, *Home* 4; emphases in original)

That incident solidifies Frank as protector of Cee even though it is traumatic. *Them* in this instance is just as significant as *they* will be when he hears the story related later. Any Black person living in the South in the first half of the twentieth century would have known immediately to whom that reference pointed. Contrary to Frank's assertion, Frank is *not* able to "handle it" (Harack).[10] He feels tremendously vulnerable and emasculated. Indeed, he suppresses the helplessness and powerlessness so deeply that it will be almost two decades before he confronts fully what he and Cee have witnessed. Echoing Sethe, his memory is selective, and he recalls the beautiful horses in the pasture instead of the barn in which the fight has occurred or the burying of the loser of that fight.

Suppressing his trauma means that Frank goes off to Korea with hidden frustration and repressed anger. He is able to unleash the anger after Mike is killed. "Now, with Mike gone, he was brave, whatever that meant. There were not enough dead gooks or Chinks in the world to satisfy him. The copper smell of blood no longer sickened him; it gave him appetite" (Morrison, *Home* 98).

---

[9]Maxine Montgomery also points to this scene as the site of Frank's original trauma. However, she posits that the killed Black man has been lynched instead of sliced to death by his own knife-wielding son. See Montgomery, "Re-Membering the Forgotten War."

[10]Some scholars tie Frank's actions in this scene and throughout the novel to misguided notions of masculinity. For a representative example, see Harack, "Shifting Masculinities and Evolving Feminine Power."

Unleashing one kind of anger, however, only creates space into which more anger can creep. On his trip from the Midwest to Georgia, for example, Frank gets off the train when it pauses for repairs. He walks into a small town and encounters two women fighting behind a store—even as a disengaged but interested man looks on. It is clear that the man is pimp to the two women. For some reason—or specifically because he has assigned himself the role of protector of women—Frank feels unbridled anger at what he witnesses, and, when the man questions his presence and pushes him, Frank attacks the pimp.

> Frank dropped his Dr Pepper and swung hard at the man, who, lacking agility like so many really big men, fell immediately. Frank leaped on the prone body and began to punch his face, eager to ram that toothpick into his throat. The thrill that came with each blow was wonderfully familiar. Unable to stop and unwilling to, Frank kept on going even though the big man was unconscious. (Morrison, *Home* 101)

Back on the train, Frank wonders "at the excitement, the wild joy the fight had given him. It was unlike the rage that had accompanied killing in Korea. Those sprees were fierce but mindless, anonymous. This violence was personal in its delight" (Morrison, *Home* 102). Trapped in a rage at racial circumstances that he is unable to resolve, Frank mirrors some of the young Black men coerced into fighting each other. His original trauma of being out of place and witnessing a burial has been triggered in Korea and is triggered again here. Just as Tatlock asserted that he would enjoy beating up the Invisible Man, so Frank enjoys beating the pimp. There is something primal about it, so primal that he reduces himself to a state of inhumanity, a reduction that will not be restored for some time.

The original trauma of having witnessed the burial of Jerome's father, compounded by Korea, is also arguably the source of Frank's interactions with Lily, the woman with whom he is living when the letter comes about Cee's condition. It is noteworthy that Lily tolerates him for as long as she does, because he loses every job he gets, mopes around the house, and sits for hours at a time staring at the floor, often in a state of partial dress/undress, such as having one shoe on, one shoe off, and a sock in hand. That original trauma has taught Frank how truly helpless he is in the world. He could place his hand over Cee's mouth to prevent her from speaking or screaming, but there is nothing else he could do. No matter that he is a mere youngster, Frank has felt the touch of southern white racism in the walk from Texas and in the story he hears later of the one Black man who refused to move in the twenty-four-hour period allotted: "Just after dawn at the twenty-fourth hour he was beaten to death with pipes and rifle butts and tied to the oldest magnolia tree in the county—the one that grew in his own yard" (Morrison, *Home* 10). Thorough acquaintance with the South thus spurs Frank to grab Cee quickly, hide, and remain quiet. By repressing his anger/frustration/fear, and by being unable to release it in any healthy way later, Frank resorts to unhealthy romantic relationships, to making the women with whom he partners complicit in his own degradation. The trauma has made him a walking time bomb; while Korea certainly allows him to explode a portion of it, much remains within him.

His movement toward recovery begins when Frank realizes that Cee no longer needs him to be her big brother and masculine protector. Cee's acceptance of her barrenness sparks Frank to confront the truth that he has failed in another protector role, that he was the one who killed the little girl in Korea. The child had come scraping through the garbage at the fence near his encampment, touched his crotch when he came near, and had aroused sexual desires in Frank that made him feel monstrous. The fact that she reminds him of Cee burdens his conscience with a hint of incest and is, finally, too much for him to bear. He admits his guilt:

> *I shot the Korean girl in her face.*
> *I am the one she touched.*
> *I am the one who saw her smile.*
> *I am the one she said "Yum-yum" to.*
> *I am the one she aroused.*
> *A child. A wee little girl.*
> *I didn't think. I didn't have to.*
> *Better she should die.*
> *How could I let her live after she took me down to a place I didn't know was in me?* (Morrison, *Home* 94; emphases in original)

By shooting her, Frank again tamed down the anger he experienced for having learned a deeply hidden truth about himself even as he suppressed the casual thought of the girl's having reminded him of Cee. Cee's acceptance of barrenness thus encourages Frank to move forward in overcoming his own traumas, accepting the brutal ugliness of his own alcohol-sated life, and admitting that he is as guilty, in some ways, as are the men who ordered Jerome to kill his father. In both instances, power—sheer, raw power—has been put into effect against the powerless. There is nothing that a Black father and son could do against whites who kidnapped them and forced one to kill the other. Equally striking, there is no way that a ragged, begging young Korean girl could stand up against the might of the US military. She is a pawn in their desires just as Jerome and his father are pawns to the whites who treat them like dogs. In this perverted instance of equality, Frank has stood for the very might of the country and institutions that had consistently oppressed him. Frank forces the Korean girl into the role that many enslaved people had to play; by ingratiating themselves to the master, they hoped for some boon, just as the little Korean girl hopes to win a favor from Frank. It is worthy of note that, when Frank first hears the girl near the fence, he thinks, "*A dog, maybe?*" (emphases in original), which fascinatingly overlays the scene with the same dehumanizing imagery that informs what happens in that unforgettable barn (Morrison, *Home* 94).

The extent to which it is necessary for Frank to admit and accept his original trauma as well as his violent and troubled past is clear from the couple of encounters with and reactions to young girls he has after his return from Korea. Each incident reveals the extent to which Frank is mentally wounded and thoroughly incapable of moving forward healthily. When he sees a little girl injured in an accident and bleeding from her nose, he remarks that "a sadness hit [him] like pile-driver," his stomach feels as if he is about to regurgitate, and he rushes off "feeling shaky," after which he spends several nights in a park before policemen force him out (Morrison, *Home* 69). At a church convention with Lily, "a little girl with slanty eyes reached up over the opposite edge of the table to grab a cupcake. Frank leaned over to push the platter closer to her. When she gave him a broad smile of thanks, he dropped his food and ran through the crowd," for he is floored by the memory of "Yum-Yum" (Morrison, *Home* 76–7). Not only does his action lead Lily closer to dissolving their relationship, but it shows that Frank is mired in traumatic memories and that he has no healthy pathway forward. He recalls the Korean child on yet another occasion as he journeys toward Lotus (99–100). Upon hearing Cee's revelation that she is barren, he wonders, "Who would do that to a young girl? And a doctor? What the hell for?" (132). As protector and provider, the doctor has failed, just as Frank has failed as protector and provider to the Korean civilian who perhaps thought that the American presence was something in her favor. Referring to Cee as "young girl" is hardly indistinguishable from his references to the Korea girl, for he is the "who" who has indeed "done that" to a "young girl." Frank has tried to erase the girl from his memory just as he has tried to erase Jerome's father from his memory. He cannot bring the Korean girl back to life, but he can alleviate the taint to her reputation that has been implicit in his earlier narrative about her—giving the impression that she was the perverse one, that she was somehow complicit in her own demise. It is only as a result of Cee's growth and by listening to the men on the porch tell the full story of Jerome and his father that Frank can truly begin the process of healing.

THE TRADITION OF ORALITY

Throughout her novels, Toni Morrison has made clear the power of the human voice in the telling of stories relevant to her various fictional communities. Consider the gossiping women in *The Bluest Eye* (1994), for example; they inform readers of everything from where Mr. Henry rents a room to tales of Cholly's sexual violation of Pecola to comments about the inadequacy of the insurance money Aunt Jimmy has allotted for her burial. Similar gossipy voices cascade through stories of what Sula's powers are reputed to be in *Sula* (1974), to Pilate's lack of a navel in *Song of Solomon* (1977), to what the women reputedly do at the Convent in *Paradise* (1998; see Morrison, *The Bluest Eye*; *Sula*; *Song of Solomon*; *Paradise*). Morrison peoples her novels with communities and community voices, and, through the reach of her narratives, teaches her readers to believe those voices when they present themselves as trustworthy. Readers might not believe that Sula can make someone choke on a chicken bone, but they are more inclined to believe the hatred that spews forth upon the women in *Paradise*. For Morrison, the validity of Black oral tradition was manifest in her own family and the stories that circulated there as well as in what she learned and studied of African American culture. Stories, Morrison's narratives tell us, can recount the truth of history, can shape human behavior in the present, and can present pathways to the future. With the story of Jerome's being forced to kill his father, Morrison allows the passing down of stories to reinforce the truth of racial terror.

The men who relate the narrative, including the less-than-likable Salem, who is Frank's grandfather, are not rich, do not hold esteemed positions in their community, and are not highly educated. They are, nonetheless, central to the community in that they participate in its rituals, inherit and pass on its tales, and initiate those, like Frank, who need initiation into the true goings-on in the world. The space that they occupy is ages old in its connection to venues in which old-timers relate folk truths. The men are gathered on a "cluttered porch" where they play checkers almost every evening. Space and time lead to the recounting that is so crucial to folk narratives (Morrison, *Home* 137). These men, who are probably not valued overly much beyond their own community, fall into the tradition of elders who play a central role in the folk life and oral transmission that enable younger generations to understand more fully their places in the world. In this space and in the realm of their imaginations, they exhibit what it has been impossible for history or white evil to kill—the ability to share, to warn, and to make clear the nature of the world that surrounds them.

Indeed, there is a wonderful transcendence about what they relate. They can laugh at racism; for example, they find it humorous—in the sense of it is amazing what he does not know—when Frank asserts that white men staged dogfights at the now infamous barn on the isolated property that he and Cee visited. "More like men-treated-like-dog fights," one of them avows just after another "covered his mouth to funnel the laugh coming out" (138). This blues-informed laughing to keep from crying has the same "tell the tale in order to survive the implications of its danger and violence" that undergirds other African American expressions. Humor that is not really funny is one response to the situation. The men can also be philosophical about it. In a world in which they have little power, the power of the tongue is crucial. No matter, they conclude, if the son killed the father or the father killed the son, "Any way you decide is a sure trip to his hell" (139). They recognize that there can never be any recovery from the psychological damage of that forced violence and violation. The strikingly perverse way in which it occurs might leave a body alive, but it will not leave a living soul. No one, no matter how strong, can remain whole after having endured such a traumatic experience. The men on the porch see clearly the physical and psychological damage that has been done; by keeping it alive in their aching consciousnesses, as Ralph Ellison would say, they epitomize the significance of the blues narrative.[11]

What the men on the porch pass on to Frank as a result of reciting the narrative—though they themselves might not be aware of this effect—is the pathway to overcome his own blues, his own trauma as a result of having witnessed the burial of the killed father. Frank's response to the narrative of Jerome and his father thus illustrates how oral tradition can inform present circumstances and aid in healing the past (Visser 148–64).[12] The narrative leads Frank to reinstate a Black man's body in the place where he has preferred to see beautiful horses. He can therefore lead Cee back to that traumatic space of their childhood, unbury the Black man's bones, wrap them in Cee's newly constructed quilt (the healing women teach Cee to quilt during her recovery), and rebury them in a place that brims with light and life—beside a stream at the base of a huge "sweet bay tree" (Morrison, *Home* 144). By burying the bones as upright as he can and by appending a wooden headstone that reads "Here Stands A Man," Frank reasserts the humanity of the man who has been so brutally used and turned into a dog (145). Thus the power of voices and the story they contain have afforded Frank the self-determination to do the best he can to provide a corrective note to history. By reburying Jerome's father, Frank is able to re-center the Black history and hurt that he has tried to escape. Horses may matter, but human beings matter more. By having elided the existence of the Black man, Frank has denied history and kinship with Jerome's father, just as he denied—in the way he initially told the narrative—that he had anything to do with the young Korean girl's death. Orality thus becomes therapy in enabling him to recall and correct, as best he can, the things that he has denied.

Perhaps even more significant than Frank's corrective actions in response to the narrative is what it suggests about community and community survival. The old men recall that Jerome has come into town crying, traumatized, and bloodied from what he has been forced to do. Quickly realizing that they cannot allow the local sheriff to see Jerome in his condition because he would have imprisoned him immediately, the citizens of Lotus immediately go into action: "Rose Ellen and Ethel Fordham collected some change for him so he could go on off somewhere. Maylene too. We all pulled together some clothes for him. He was soaked in blood ... We led him out on a mule" (Morrison, *Home* 139). The community achieves group solidarity in the face of racist attack. The dynamic that

---

[11]Ellison's comments on the blues can be found in "Richard Wright's Blues."
[12]Irene Visser also argues that narrative is crucial to healing from trauma in *Home*. She asserts, however, that the *entire* novel, which Frank relates to his "scribe," is the "trauma narrative" that leads to healing.

was operative fifteen years prior to Frank's return to Lotus is still extant, for it is this same Ethel Fordham to whose home Frank takes the experimented-upon Cee, and Ethel and other women of Lotus heal Cee. What Dr. Beauregard Scott does in experimenting upon Cee echoes the absolute power over Black lives that the white men who kidnapped Jerome and his father and brought them to Georgia exhibited. And while Cee might have gone willingly into Dr. Scott's home and even initially accepted the so-called medicines that he administered to her, she is woefully unaware of the consequences of her acquiescence. Only Dr. Scott knows what the possible consequences are, and he, like the white men in the barn, does not care. Indeed, when Frank rescues Cee from his house, "Dr. Beau cast him a look of anger-shaded relief. No theft. No violence. No harm. Just the kidnapping of an employee he could easily replace" (112).

Group solidarity is also apparent in the scene with Dr. Scott as well as in several previous encounters that Frank has had. Frank learns of Cee's situation through Sarah, Dr. Scott's housekeeper, who has befriended Cee and learned that Frank is the only relative of whom she makes mention. It is Sarah who writes to Frank and thus initiates his return to Georgia, for only his love for and concern about Cee could force Frank out of the inertia into which he has lapsed during his relationship with Lily. Sarah simply refuses to allow Cee to die in Dr. Scott's home. Noteworthy as well is the fact that Sarah stands between Dr. Scott and Frank when Frank is carrying Cee from Dr. Scott's home. Sarah is aggressive in preventing Dr. Scott from calling the police, because she knows that Dr. Scott's wife will intercede if Dr. Scott attempts to object to what she has done. So, Sarah as community member initiates the journey, and other Black people along the way from Seattle to Lotus, Georgia, assist Frank in achieving his objective. After he breaks out of the institution to which he has been confined, he seeks aid from Reverend Locke. Reverend Locke and his wife Jean not only feed Frank and provide him with clothing, but the Reverend points him to another minister who can help him in Portland after he purchases the bus ticket that Frank will need to get that far on his journey. That minister in Portland, Jessie Maynard, might be judgmental about Frank, but he nonetheless provides assistance. A man Frank meets on the train to Chicago offers him a drink and recommends places to eat and sleep in Chicago. Once arrived in that city, Frank receives even more assistance from a man he meets in a restaurant; Billy Watson not only allows Frank to spend the night in his home, but he takes him shopping the next morning so that Frank can purchase clothes at a Goodwill store. None of these helpers has an obligation to assist Frank, but they all do as part of the masses of Black people who understand the racial dynamics in America. Even the young thugs who rob Frank in Atlanta serve a role in moving Frank along his journey, for a kindly man discovers him, gives him a few dollars, and directs him along his way (107). Misfortune is thus met with benevolence, just as Cee's misfortune with Dr. Scott meets with Sarah's benevolence and eventually Frank's rescue. All of these characters are a part of the larger community referenced in the actions relayed in the story of Jerome and his father.

Through storytelling, the townspeople share history, and, as with Jerome, Cee, and Frank, they also share resources and knowledge. Their knowledge of what happened in the barn and their sharing of that knowledge with Frank is the catalyst for emotional transformation and putting past ghosts to rest. It is also the catalyst for Frank's seeing clearly what he has tried to deny. And it is the catalyst for building a future that incorporates the past even as it realizes the need for moving forward from that past. The story of the death of Jerome's father, therefore, is a microcosm of the history of Black folks on US soil. No matter the traumas, bloodshed, and violence they experienced, the only way they can go is forward. They move into the future hammered with the pain of the past but understanding that that pain has honed them, as Claude McKay would say, into stronger souls and finer frames.[13] It is one of the few recourses to surviving and possibly thriving in a world where the cancer of racism has so eroded democratic promise that healthy Black lives and futures are never a priority.

WORKS CITED

Blackmon, Douglas. *Slavery by Another Name: The Re-Enslavement of Black Americans from the Civil War to World War II*. Random House, 2008.

Brooks, Gwendolyn. *Maud Martha*. *Blacks*. The David Company, 1987, pp. 141–322.

Douglass, Frederick. *Narrative of the Life of Frederick Douglass, an American Slave, Written by Himself*. Belknap, 1960.

Ellison, Ralph, *Invisible Man*. 1952. Vintage, 1980.

Ellison, Ralph. "Richard Wright's Blues." *Shadow and Act*. Signet, 1964, pp. 89–104.

Finnely, John. "Texas Genealogy Trails, Slave Narratives." http://genealogytrails.com/tex/state/slavenarra2.htm. Accessed Nov. 2, 2022.

Harack, Katrina. "Shifting Masculinities and Evolving Feminine Power: Progressive Gender Roles in Toni Morrison's *Home*." *Mississippi Quarterly*, vol. 69, no. 3, Summer 2016, pp. 371–96.

Harris, Aisha. "Was There Really 'Mandingo Fighting,' Like in *Django Unchained*?" https://slate.com/culture/2012/12/django-unchained-mandingo-fighting-were-any-slaves-really-forced-to-fight-each-other-to-the-death.html. Accessed Aug. 14, 2022.

Harris, Trudier. *Exorcising Blackness: Historical and Literary Lynching and Burning Rituals*. Indiana UP, 1984.

Harris, Trudier, editor. *Selected Works of Ida B. Wells-Barnett*. Oxford UP, 1991.

Jacobs, Harriet. *Incidents in the Life of a Slave Girl*. Harvard UP, 1987.

Lussana, Sergio. "To See Who Was Best on the Plantation: Enslaved Fighting Contests and Masculinity in the Antebellum Plantation South." *Journal of Southern History*, vol. 76, no. 4, Nov. 2010, pp. 901–22.

McKay, Claude. *Selected Poems of Claude McKay*. Harcourt, 1953.

Montgomery, Maxine. "Re-Membering the Forgotten War: Memory, History, and the Body in Toni Morrison's *Home*." *CLA Journal*, vol. 55, no. 4, June 2012, pp. 320–34.

Morrison, Toni. *Beloved*. Knopf, 1987.

Morrison, Toni. *The Bluest Eye*. Plume, 1994.

Morrison, Toni. *Home*. Knopf, 2012.

Morrison, Toni. *Paradise*. Knopf, 1998.

Morrison, Toni. *Song of Solomon*. Knopf, 1977.

Morrison, Toni. *Sula*. Knopf, 1973.

Owens, Deidre Cooper. *Medical Bondage: Race, Gender, and the Origins of American Gynecology*. UGA P, 2017.

Rhoden, William C. *Forty Million Dollar Slaves: The Rise, Fall, and Redemption of the Black Athlete*. Three Rivers P, 2007.

Visser, Irene. "Fairy Tale and Trauma in Toni Morrison's *Home*." *Melus*, vol. 40, no.1, Spring 2016, pp. 148–64.

Walker, Alice. "The Flowers." *In Love and Trouble: Stories of Black Women*. Harcourt Brace Jovanovich, 1973, pp. 119–20.

---

[13] Here, I echo Claude McKay's poem, "Baptism," in which he describes how a narrator immersed in the hatred that white America spews upon him becomes "A stronger soul within a finer frame." See *Selected Poems of Claude McKay* (35, 14).

Ward, Jesmyn. *Where the Line Bleeds*. Simon & Schuster, 2008.

Washington, Harriet. *Medical Apartheid: The Dark History of Medical Experimentation on Black Americans from Colonial Times to the Present*. Doubleday, 2006.

Wells-Barnett, Ida B. "A Red Record: Tabulated Statistics and Alleged Causes of Lynchings in the United States, 1892–1893–1894." *Selected Works of Ida B. Wells-Barnett*, edited by Trudier Harris, Oxford UP, 1991, pp. 138–322.

Wells-Barnett, Ida B. "Southern Horrors: Lynch Law in All Its Phases." *Selected Works of Ida B. Wells-Barnett*, edited by Trudier Harris, Oxford UP, 1991, pp. 14–45.

Wright, Richard. *Black Boy*. Perennial, 1966.

FURTHER READING

Dokosi, Michael Eli. "How Enslaved Blacks Beating Each Other to Near-Death Was a Great Source of Entertainment and Cash for White Plantation Owners." https://face2faceafrica.com/article/how-enslaved-blacks-beating-each-other-to-near-death-was-a-great-source-of-entertainment-and-cash-for-white-plantation-owners.

Ramirez, Manuela Lopez. "The Shell-Shocked Veteran in Toni Morrison's *Sula* and *Home*." *Atlantis: Journal of the Spanish Association of Anglo-American Studies*, vol. 38, no. 1, June 2016, pp. 129–47.

Wagner-Martin, Linda. "Frank Money, Cee, and the Maternal in *Home*." *Toni Morrison and the Maternal: From* The Bluest Eye *to* Home. Peter Lang, 2014, pp. 151–66.

BIBLIOGRAPHY

PRIMARY

Novels

Morrison, Toni. *Beloved*. Knopf, 1987.
Morrison, Toni. *The Bluest Eye*. Holt, Rinehart, & Winston, 1970.
Morrison, Toni. *God Help the Child*. Knopf, 2015.
Morrison, Toni. *Home*. Knopf, 2012.
Morrison, Toni. *Jazz*. Knopf, 1992.
Morrison, Toni. *Love*. Knopf, 2003.
Morrison, Toni. *A Mercy*. Knopf, 2008.
Morrison, Toni. *Paradise*. Knopf, 1998.
Morrison, Toni. *Song of Solomon*. Knopf, 1977.
Morrison, Toni. *Sula*. Knopf, 1973.
Morrison, Toni. *Tar Baby*. Knopf, 1981.

BOOKS FOR CHILDREN

Morrison, Toni. *Remember: The Journey to School Integration*. Houghton Mifflin, 2004.
Morrison, Toni, with Slade Morrison. *The Big Box*. Jump at the Sun, 1999.
Morrison, Toni, with Slade Morrison. *The Book of Mean People*. Hyperion, 2002.
Morrison, Toni, with Slade Morrison. *Little Cloud and Lady Wind*. Simon and Schuster, 2010.
Morrison, Toni, with Slade Morrison. *Peeny Butter Fudge*. Simon and Schuster, 2009.
Morrison, Toni, with Slade Morrison. *Who's Got Game? The Ant or the Grasshopper?* Scribner, 2003.
Morrison, Toni, with Slade Morrison. *Who's Got Game? The Lion or the Mouse?* Scribner, 2003.
Morrison, Toni, with Slade Morrison. *Who's Got Game? The Mirror or the Glass?* Scribner, 2004.
Morrison, Toni, with Slade Morrison. *Who's Got Game? Poppy or the Snake?* Scribner, 2004.
Morrison, Toni, with Slade Morrison. *Who's Got Game? Three Fables*. Scribner, 2007.

EDITED COLLECTIONS

Morrison, Toni, ed. Preface. *The Black Book*, edited by Middleton Harris, et al., Random House, 1974, n.p.
Morrison, Toni, ed. Foreword. *The Black Book*, edited by Middleton Harris, et al., Random House, 2009, n.p.
Morrison, Toni, editor. "Peril: Introductory Essay." *Burn This Book: PEN Writers Speak Out on the Power of the Word*. Harper, 2009, pp. 1–4.
Morrison, Toni, editor. "Introduction: Friday on the Potomac." *Race-ing Justice, En-gendering Power: Essays on Anita Hill, Clarence Thomas and the Construction of Social Reality*. Pantheon, 1992, pp. vii–xxx.

Morrison, Toni, and Claudia Brodsky Lacour, editors. "Introduction: The Official Story: Dead Man Golfing." *Birth of a Nation'hood: Gaze, Script, and Spectacle in the O. J. Simpson Case*. Pantheon, 1997, pp. vii–xxviii.

NON-FICTION BOOKS

Morrison, Toni. *Five Poems* (illustrated by Kara E. Walker). Rainmaker, 2002.
Morrison, Toni. *Conversations with Toni Morrison*, edited by Danielle Taylor-Guthrie. UP of Mississippi, 1994.
Morrison, Toni. *Toni Morrison: The Last Interview and Other Conversations*. Melville House, 2020.
Morrison, Toni. *The Origin of Others*. Harvard UP, 2011.
Morrison, Toni. *Playing in the Dark: Whiteness and the Literary Imagination*. Harvard UP, 1992.
Morrison, Toni. *The Source of Self-Regard, Selected Essays, Speeches, and Meditations*. Knopf, 2019.
Morrison, Toni. *Toni Morrison: Conversations*, edited by Carolyn C. Denard. UP of Mississippi, 2008.
Morrison, Toni. *Virginia Woolf's and William Faulkner's Treatment of the Alienated*. 1955. English Department, Cornell University, MA Thesis.
Morrison, Toni. *What Moves at the Margin: Selected Nonfiction*, edited by Carolyn C. Denard, UP of Mississippi, 2008.

OTHER WRITINGS

Morrison, Toni. Afterword. *The Bluest Eye*. Plume, 1994, pp. 209–16.
Morrison, Toni. "Back Talk: Toni Morrison." Morrison with Christine Smallwood. *Nation*, Dec. 8, 2008.
Morrison, Toni. "A Bench by the Road." *The World*, vol. 311, 1989, pp. 4–5, 37–41.
Morrison, Toni. "Black Matters." *Grand Street*, vol. 10, no. 4, 1991, pp. 205–25.
Morrison, Toni. "City Limits, Village Values: Concepts of the Neighborhood in Black Fiction." *Literature and the American Urban Experience: Essays on the City and Literature*, edited by Michael C. Jaye and Ann Chalmers Watts. Manchester UP, 1981, pp. 35–44.
Morrison, Toni. "Clinton as the First Black President." *New Yorker*, Oct. 5, 1998.
Morrison, Toni. "Cooking Out." *New York Times Book Review*, June 10, 1973, pp. 4.
Morrison, Toni. "'The Foreigner's Home': Introduction." Louvre Museum Auditorium Exhibit, Paris, Nov. 6, 2006.
Morrison, Toni. Foreword. *Black Photographer's Annual*, edited by Joe Crawford. Another View, 1972, pp. i–ix.
Morrison, Toni. Foreword. *Jazz*. 1999. Vintage, 2004, pp. xv–xix.
Morrison, Toni. Foreword. *Love*. Vintage, 2005, pp. ix–xii.
Morrison, Toni. Foreword. *August Wilson's The Piano Lesson*. Theatre Communications Group, 2007, pp. vii–xiii.
Morrison, Toni. Foreword. *Song of Solomon*. Vintage, 2004, pp. xi–xiv.
Morrison, Toni. Foreword. *Sula*. Vintage, 2004, pp. xi–xvii.
Morrison, Toni. "Good, Bad, Neutral Black." *New York Times Book Review*, May 2, 1971, pp. 3+
Morrison, Toni. "'Harlem on My Mind': Contesting Memory—Meditations on Museums, Culture and Integration." Louvre Museum Auditorium, Paris, Nov. 15, 2006.
Morrison, Toni. "Home." *The House That Race Built: Black Americans, U.S. Terrain*, edited by Wahneema Lubiano. Pantheon, 1997, pp. 3–12.
Morrison, Toni. "Honey and Rue." Lyrics, musical score by Andre Previn. 1992.
Morrison, Toni. "'I Start with an Image,' interview with Pam Houston." *AARP Magazine*, July 2009, pp. 122–4.

Morrison, Toni. "Interview with Melvyn Bragg." *The South Bank Show*. Weekend Television, Channel ITV, 1987.

"Interview with Maya Joggi." *Brick*, vol. 76, 2005, pp. 97–103.

Morrison, Toni. "Interview with Monice Mitchell, Toni Morrison Chafes at Being Labeled 'Role Model,'" *Charlotte Observer*, Sept. 2, 1990, p. 6c.

Morrison, Toni. "Interview with Florence Noiville." *Literary Miniatures*. Seagull, pp. 112–17.

Morrison, Toni. "Interview with Francois Noudelmann." *Black Renaissance*, vol. 12, no. 1, Oct. 2012, pp. 36–51.

Morrison, Toni. "Interview with Ntozaka Shange." *American Rag*, Nov. 1978, pp. 48–52.

Morrison, Toni. "Interview with Jean Strouse, 'Toni Morrison's Black Magic'" *Newsweek*, Mar. 30, 1981, pp. 53–5.

Morrison, Toni. Introduction. *Adventures of Huckleberry Finn by Mark Twain, The Oxford Mark Twain*, edited by Shelley Fisher Fishkin. Oxford UP, 1996, pp. xxxii–xli.

Morrison, Toni. "Jean Toomer's Art of Darkness: Review of Toomer's *The Wayward and the Seeking*." *Washington Post Book World*, July 13, 1980, p. 1.

Morrison, Toni. *Margaret Garner: An Opera in Two Acts*. Rev. ed. Associated Music, 2004.

Morrison, Toni. "Maya Angelou." New York Memorial, Sept. 12, 2014.

Morrison, Toni. "Memory, Creation, and Writing." *Thought: A Review of Culture and Idea*, vol. 59, 1984, pp. 385–90.

Morrison, Toni. "Presentation for 'Roundtable on the Future of the Humanities in a Fragmented World,'" *PMLA*, vol. 120, no. 3, 2005, pp. 715–17.

Morrison, Toni. Presentation of National Medal in Literature to Eudora Welty. Public Broadcasting System, July 6, 1980 [phonotape, Michigan State University Voice Library, cat. No. M3395, band 11]. Audio.

Morrison, Toni. "Reading." *Mademoiselle*, vol. 81, May 1975, p. 14.

Morrison, Toni. *Recitatif A Story*. Knopf, 2022.

Morrison, Toni. "Recitatif." *Confirmation: An Anthology of African American Women*, edited by Amiri Baraka and Amina Baraka, Morrow, 1983, pp. 243–66.

Morrison, Toni. "Review of *Amistad 2*, edited by John A. Williams and Charles Harris; *The Black Aesthetic*, edited by Addison Gayle; *New African Literature and the Arts, 2*, edited by Joseph Okpaku." *New York Times Book Review*, Feb. 28, 1971, p. 5.

Morrison, Toni. "Review of *The Black Man in America, 1791–1861*, by Florence Jackson; *Black Politicians*, by Richard Bruner; *Black Troubadour*, by Charlamae Rollins; *Forward March to Freedom: The Biography of A. Philip Randolph*, by Barbara Kaye; *Gordon Parks*, by Midge Turk; *Jackie Robinson*, by Kenneth Ruddeen; *James Weldon Johnson*, by Harold W. Felton; *Jim Beckwourth*, by Lawrence Cortest; *The Magic Mirrors*, by Judith Berry Griffin; *The Making of an Afro-American: Martin Robinson Delany*, by Dorothy Sterling; *Men of Masaba*, edited by Humphrey Harmon; *The Orisha: Gods of Yorubaland*, by Judith Gleason; *The Picture Life of Thurgood Marshall*, by Margaret B. Young; *The Rich Man and the Singer: Folktales from Ethiopia*, by Mesfin Habre-Mariam; *Sidewalk Story*, by Sharon Bell Mathis; *Soldiers in the Civil War*, by Janet Stevenson; *Songs and Stories of Afro-Americans*, by Paul Glass; *Tales and Stories for Black Folks*, by Toni Cade Bambara; *Unsung Black Americans*, by Edith Stull." *New York Times Book Review*, May 2, 1971, Pt. 11, p. 43.

Morrison, Toni. "Review of *Con*, by M. E. White." *New York Times Book Review*, Sept. 3, 1972, p. 6.

Morrison, Toni. "Review of *Hero in the Tower*, by Hans Hellmut Kirst; *Love Songs*, by Lawrence Sanders." *New York Times Book Review*, Oct. 1, 1972, p. 41.

Morrison, Toni. "Review of *Who Is Angela Davis: The Biography of a Revolutionary*, by Regina Nadelson." *New York Times Book Review*, Oct. 29, 1972, p. 48.

Morrison, Toni. "Start the Week: Toni Morrison Special." BBC Radio 4. Dec. 8, 2003. Audio.

Morrison, Toni. "Strangers." *New Yorker*, vol. 74, Oct. 12, 1998, pp. 69–70.

Morrison, Toni. "Toni Morrison." *I Dream a World: Portraits of Black Women Who Changed America*. Rev. ed., edited by Brian Lanker, Tabori Stewart, and Chang, 1999, p. 36.

Morrison, Toni. "Toni Morrison Discusses *A Mercy*." *Book Tour, National Public Radio*. Interview by Lynn Neary. Oct. 27, 2008. Print, Audio.

Morrison, Toni. "Toni Morrison: More Than Words Can Say." *Rolling Out*, vol. 3, no. 43, Apr. 29, 2004, pp. 16–17.

Morrison, Toni. "Toni Morrison on Cinderella's Stepsisters" [adapted from commencement address given at Barnard College, May 1979], *Ms*, vol. 8, Sept. 1979, pp. 41–2.

Morrison, Toni. "Toni Morrison on Theater." *Lincoln Center Theater Review*, vol. 40, Winter/Spring 2005, pp. 20–2.

Morrison, Toni. "Unspeakable Things Unspoken: The Afro-American Presence in American Literature, The Tanner Lecture in Human Values." *Michigan Quarterly Review*, vol. 28, no. 1, Winter 1989, pp. 1–34.

Morrison, Toni. "Why Did the Women Get Shot?" *The Straits Times Interactive*, Jan. 17, 1998, p. 2.

Morrison, Toni. "Writing Lyrics." Louvre Museum Auditorium, Paris, Nov. 26, 2006.

PAPERS

Firestone Library, Princeton University, Princeton, New Jersey holds the Toni Morrison papers and manuscripts archive.

SECONDARY, SELECTED

Abel, Elizabeth. "Black Writing, White Reading: Race and the Politics of Feminist Interpretation." *Critical Inquiry*, vol. 19, Spring 1993, pp. 470–98.

Adell, Sandra. *Double-Consciousness/Double Bind: Theoretical Issues in Twentieth- Century Black Literature*. U of Illinois P, 1994.

Aguir, Sarah Appleton. "'Passing On' Death: Stealing Life in Toni Morrison's *Paradise*." *African American Review*, vol. 38, no. 3, 2004, pp. 513–19.

Als, Hilton. "Ghosts in the Attic." *New Yorker*, Oct. 27, 2003, pp. 62–73.

Anderson, Melanie R. *Spectrality in the Novels of Toni Morrison*. U of Tennessee P, 2013.

Andrews, Jennifer. "Reading Toni Morrison's *Jazz*: Rewriting the Tall Tale and Playing with the Trickster in the White American and African-American Humor Traditions." *Canadian Review of American Studies*, vol. 19, no. 1, 1999, pp. 87–107.

Andrews, William L., et al., eds. *The Oxford Companion to African American Literature*. Oxford UP, 1997.

Askeland, Lori. "Remodeling the Model Home in *Uncle Tom's Cabin* and *Beloved*." *American Literature*, vol. 64, no. 4, 1992, pp. 785–805.

Atlas, Marilyn Judith. "The Darker Side of Toni Morrison's *Song of Solomon*." *Society for the Study of Midwestern Literature Newsletter*, vol. 10, 1980, pp. 1–13.

Atlas, Marilyn Judith. "Toni Morrison's *Beloved* and the Reviewers." *Midwestern Miscellany*, vol. 18, 1990, pp. 45–57.

Atlas, Marilyn Judith. "A Woman Both Shiny and Brown." *Society for the Study of Midwestern Literature Newsletter*, vol. 9, 1979, pp. 8–12.

Atwood, Margaret. "Haunted by their Nightmares: *Beloved*." *New York Times Book Review*, vol. 1, Sept. 13, 1987, pp. 49–50.

Aubry, Timothy. "Beware the Furrow of the Middlebrow: Searching for *Paradise* on *The Oprah Winfrey Show*." *The Oprah Affect: Critical Essays on Oprah's Book Club*, edited by Cecilia Konchar Farr and Jaime Harker. State U of New York P, 2008, pp. 163–88. Print

Awkward, Michael. *Inspiriting Influence: Tradition, Revision and Afro-American Women's Novels*. Columbia UP, 1989.

Babb, Valerie. "*E Pluribus Unum?* The American Origins Narrative in Toni Morrison's *A Mercy*." *MELUS*, vol. 36, no. 2, 2011, pp. 147–64.

Babbitt, Susan E. "Identity, Knowledge and Toni Morrison's *Beloved*: Questions about Understanding Racism." *Hypatia: A Journal of Feminist Philosophy*, vol. 9, no. 3, 1994, pp. 1–18.

Badt, Karin Luisa. "The Roots of the Body in Toni Morrison: A *Mater* of 'Ancient Properties,'" *African American Review*, vol. 29, Winter 1995, pp. 567–77.

Baillie, Justine Jenny. *Toni Morrison and Literary Tradition: The Invention of an Aesthetic*. Bloomsbury, 2013.

Baker, Houston A., Jr. *Workings of the Spirit: The Poetics of Afro-American Women's Writing*. U of Chicago P, 1991.

Bakerman, Jane S. "Failures of Love: Female Initiation in the Novels of Toni Morrison." *American Literature*, vol. 52, no. 4, 1981, pp. 542–63.

Bambara, Toni Cade. *The Salt Eaters*. Random, 1980.

Barnett, Pamela. "Figurations of Rape and the Supernatural in *Beloved*." *PMLA*, vol. 112, 1997, pp. 418–27.

Barrett, Eileen. "'For Books Continue Each Other …': Toni Morrison and Virginia Woolf." *Virginia Woolf: Emerging Perspectives: Selected Papers from the Third Annual Conference on Virginia Woolf*, edited by Mary Hussey and Vara Neverow. Pace UP, 1994, pp. 26–32.

Bassett, Reverend P. S. "Interview with Margaret Garner." *Toni Morrison: Beloved*, edited by Carl Plasa. Columbia UP, 1998, pp. 39–41.

Beaulieu, Elizabeth Ann, ed. *Toni Morrison Encyclopedia*. Greenwood, 2003.

Beavers, Herman. *Geography and the Political Imaginary in the Novels of Toni Morrison*. Palgrave Macmillan, 2018.

Bell, Bernard W. *Bearing Witness to African American Literature*. Wayne State UP, 2012.

Bell, Bernard W. *The Contemporary Afro-American Novel: Its Folk Traditions and Modern Literary Branches*. U of Massachusetts P, 2004.

Bell, Pearl K. "Self Seekers." Commentary, vol. 72, Aug. 1981, pp. 56–60.

Benedrix, Beth. "Intimate Fatality: *Song of Solomon* and the Journey Home." *Toni Morrison and the Bible*, edited by Shirley A. Stave. Peter Lang, 2006, pp. 94–115.

Bennett, Barbara. *Scheherazade's Daughters, The Power of Storytelling in Ecofeminist Change*. Peter Lang, 2012.

Benston, Kimberly. "I Yam What I Yam: Naming and Unnaming in Afro-American Literature." *Black American Literature Forum*, vol. 16, Spring 1992, pp. 3–11.

Benston, Kimberly. "Re-weaving the 'Ulysses Scene': Enchantment, Post-Oedipal Identity and the Buried Text of Blackness in *Song of Solomon*." *Comparative American Identities: Race, Sex and Nationality in the Modern Text*, edited by Hortense Spillers. Routledge, 1991, pp. 87–109.

Bent, Geoffrey. "Less Than Divine: Toni Morrison's *Paradise*." *Southern Review*, vol. 35, no. 1, Winter 1999, pp. 145–9.

Berger, James. "Ghosts of Liberalism: Morrison's *Beloved* and the Moynihan Report." *PMLA*, vol. 111, no. 3, 1996, pp. 408–20.

Bergner, Gwen. *Taboo Subjects: Race, Sex, and Psychoanalysis*. U of Minnesota P, 2005.
Bernard, Emily. "The Seer in Our Midst." *Oprah Magazine*, Apr. 2019, pp. 87–8.
Berret, Anthony J. "Toni Morrison's Literary Jazz." *CLA Journal*, vol. 32, Mar. 1989, pp. 267–83.
Bigsby, Christopher. "Jazz Queen (interview with Toni Morrison)." *The Independent*, Apr. 26, 1992, pp. 28–9.
Billingslea-Brown, Alma Jean. *Crossing Borders through Folklore: African American Women's Fiction and Art*. U of Missouri P, 1999.
Birat, Kathie. "Stories to Pass On: Closure and Community in Toni Morrison's *Beloved*." *The Insular Dream: Obsession and Resistance*, edited by Kristiaan Versluys. V U UP, 1995, pp. 324–34.
Bjork, Patrick. *The Novels of Toni Morrison: The Search for Self and Place Within the Community*. Peter Lang, 1992.
Blackburn, Sara. "You Still Can't Go Home Again." *New York Times Book Review*, Dec. 30, 1973, p. 3.
"Black Writers in Praise of Toni Morrison." *New York Times Book Review*, Jan. 24, 1988, p. 36.
Blair, Sara. *Harlem Crossroads: Black Writers and the Photograph in the Twentieth Century*. Princeton UP, 2007.
Blake, Susan L. "Folklore and Community in *Song of Solomon*." *MELUS*, vol. 7, no. 3, Fall 1980, pp. 77–82.
Bluestein, Gene. *The Voice of the Folk: Folklore and American Literary Theory*. U of Massachusetts P, 1972.
Bononno, George A. *The Other Side of Sadness: What the New Science of Bereavement Tells Us about Life After Loss*. Basic, 2009.
Bouson, J. Brooks. *Quiet As It's Kept: Shame, Trauma, and Race in the Novels of Toni Morrison*. State U of New York P, 2000.
Bow, Leslie. "*Playing in the Dark* and the Ghosts in the Machine." *American Literary History*, vol. 20, no. 3, Fall 2008, pp. 556–65.
Boyce Davies, Carole. *Black Women, Writing and Identity: Migrations of the Subject*. Routledge, 1994.
Bracks, Lean'tin L. *Writings on Black Women of the Diaspora*. Garland, 1998.
Branch, Eleanor. "Through the Maze of the Oedipal: Milkman's Search for Self in *Song of Solomon*." *Literature and Psychology*, vol. 41, no. 1–2, 1995, pp. 52–84.
Brivac, Sheldon. *Tears of Rage: The Racial Interface of Modern American Fiction: Faulkner, Wright, Pynchon, Morrison*. Louisiana State UP, 2008.
Broeck, Sabina. *White Amnesia—Black Memory? American Women's Writing and History*. Peter Lang, 1999.
Brogan, Kathleen. *Cultural Haunting, Ghosts and Ethnicity in Recent American Literature*. U of Virginia P, 1998.
Brophy-Warren, Jamin. "A Writer's Vote: Toni Morrison on Her New Novel, Reading Her Critics and What Barack Obama's Win Means to Her." *Wall Street Journal Weekend*, Nov. 7, 2008, pp. W5.
Brundage, W. Fitzhugh. *The Southern Past: A Clash of Race and Memory*. Harvard UP, 2005.
Burr, Benjamin. "Mythopoetic Syncretism in *Paradise* and the Deconstruction of Hospitality in *Love*." *Toni Morrison and the Bible: Contested Intertextualities*, edited by Shirley A. Stave, Peter Lang, 2006, pp. 159–74.
Burrows, Victoria. *Whiteness and Trauma: The Mother-Daughter Knot in the Fiction of Jean Rhys, Jamaica Kincaid, and Toni Morrison*. Palgrave Macmillan, 2004.
Busia, Abena P. A. "The Artistic Impulse of Toni Morrison's Shorter Works." *Cambridge Companion to Toni Morrison*, edited by Justine Tally, Cambridge UP, 2007, pp. 101–11.
Butler, Robert. *Contemporary African American Fiction: The Open Journey*. Fairleigh Dickinson UP, 1998.
Butler, Robert James. "Open Movement and Selfhood in Toni Morrison's *Song of Solomon*." *Centennial Review*, vol. 28–9, Fall-Winter 1984–85, pp. 58–75.
Butler-Evans, Elliott. *Race, Gender and Desire: Narrative Strategies in the Fiction of Toni Cade Bambara, Toni Morrison and Alice Walker*. Temple UP, 1989.
Byatt, A. S. *Imagining Characters: Conversations About Women Writers: Jane Austen, Charlotte Bronte, George Eliot, Willa Cather, Iris Murdoch, and Toni Morrison*. Vintage, 1997.

Byerman, Keith. "African American Fiction." *American Fiction after 1945*, edited by John N. Duvall, Cambridge UP, 2012, pp. 85–98.

Byerman, Keith. *Remembering the Past in Contemporary African American Fiction*. U of North Carolina P, 2005.

Caldwell, Gail. "West of Eden: Toni Morrison's Shimmering Story of an Oklahoma Paradise That's Asking for Trouble." *Boston Globe*, Jan. 11, 1998, pp. F1.

Callahan, John F. *In the African-American Grain, The Pursuit of Voice in Twentieth- Century Black Fiction*. U of Illinois P, 1988.

Campbell, Jane. *Mythic Black Fiction: The Transformation of History*. U of Tennessee P, 1986.

Cantiello, Jessica Wells. "From Pre-Racial to Post-Racial? Reading and Reviewing *A Mercy* in the Age of Obama." *MELUS*, vol. 36, no. 2, 2011, pp. 165–83.

Carby, Hazel V. *Reconstructing Womanhood: The Emergence of the Afro-American Woman Novelist*. Oxford UP, 1987.

Carlacio, Jami L., ed. *The Fiction of Toni Morrison: Reading and Writing on Race, Culture, and Identity*. NCTE, 2007.

Carmean, Karen. *Toni Morrison's World of Fiction*. Whitston, 1993.

Century Douglas. *Toni Morrison (Black Americans of Achievement Series)*. Chelsea House, 1994.

Charles, Julia S. *That Middle World: Race, Performance, and the Politics of Passing*. University of North Carolina Press, 2020.

Charles, Ron. "Toni Morrison's Feminist Portrayal of Racism." *Christian Science Monitor*, Jan. 29, 1998, p. B1.

Childs, Dennis. "'You Ain't Seen Nothin' Yet': *Beloved*, the American Chain Gang, and the Middle Passage Remix." *American Quarterly*, vol. 61, June 2009, pp. 271–97.

Chinweizu, Onwuchekwa Jemie, and Ihechukwu Maduibuika. *Toward the Decolonization of African Literature*. Howard UP, 1983.

Christian, Barbara. "Beloved, She's Ours." *Narrative*, vol. 5, 1997, pp. 36–49.

Christian, Barbara. *Black Women Novelists: The Development of a Tradition 1892–1976*. Greenwood, 1980.

Christian, Barbara. "Layered Rhythms: Virginia Woolf and Toni Morrison." *Modern Fiction Studies*, vol. 39, Fall/Winter 1993, pp. 483–500.

Christian, Barbara. "'The Past Is Infinite': History and Myth in Toni Morrison's Trilogy." *Social Identities*, vol. 6, no. 4, 2000, pp. 411–23.

Christianse, Yvette. *Toni Morrison: An Ethical Poetics*. Fordham UP, 2013.

Christol, Helene. "The African American Concept of the Fantastic as Middle Passage." *Black Imagination and the Middle Passage*, edited by MariaDiedrich, et al., Oxford UP, 1999, pp. 164–73.

Christopher, Lindsay M. "The Geographical Imagination in Toni Morrison's *Paradise*." *Rocky Mountain Review*, vol. 63, no. 1, 2009, pp. 89–95.

Churchwell, Sarah. "History as a Warehouse of Horrors." *The Guardian*, Apr. 28, 2012, p. 6.

Cliff, Michelle. "Review of Toni Morrison's *Paradise*." *Village Voice*, Jan. 27, 1998, pp. 85–6.

Clifford, James. *Routes: Travel and Translation in the Late Twentieth Century*. Harvard UP, 1997.

Cohen, Leah Hager, "Point of Return." *New York Times Book Review*, May 20, 2012, pp. 1, 18.

Coleman, James W. "Beyond the Reach of Love and Caring: Black Life in Toni Morrison's *Song of Solomon*." *Obsidian*, vol. 2, no. 1.3, Winter 1986, pp. 151–61.

Collins, Patricia Hill. "The Meaning of Motherhood in Black Culture and Black Mother/Daughter Relationships." *Sage*, vol. 4, no. 2, 1987, pp. 3–10.

Collins, Patricia Hill. "Shifting the Center: Race, Class, and Feminist Theorizing about Motherhood." *Representations of Motherhood*, edited by Donna Bassin, et al., Yale UP, 1994, pp. 56–74.

Colter, Cyrus. "Review of *Tar Baby*." *New Letters*, vol. 49, Fall 1982, pp. 112–14.

Conner, Marc C. "Wild Women and Graceful Girls: Toni Morrison's *Winter's Tale*." *Nature, Woman, and the Art of Politic*, edited by Eduardo A. Velasquez, Rowman & Littlefield, 2000, pp. 341–69.

Coonradt, Nicole M. "To Be Loved: Amy Denver and Human Need—Bridges to Understanding in Toni Morrison's *Beloved*." *College Literature*, vol. 32, no. 4, 2005, pp. 168–83.

Cooper-Clark, Diana. *Interviews with Contemporary Novelists*. St. Martins, 1986.

Coser, Stelamaris. *Bridging the Americas: The Literature of Paule Marshall, Toni Morrison, and Gayl Jones*. Temple UP, 1995.

Cowart, David. "Faulkner and Joyce in Morrison's *Song of Solomon*." *Toni Morrison's Fiction: Contemporary Criticism*, edited by David Middleton, Garland, 1997, pp. 95–108.

Crouch, Stanley. "Aunt Medea." *New Republic*, Oct. 19, 1987, pp. 38–43.

Croyden, Margaret. "Toni Morrison Tries Her Hand at Playwriting." *New York Times*, Dec. 29, 1985, p. H6.

Cummings, Kate. "Reclaiming the Mother('s) Tongue: *Beloved, Ceremony, Mothers and Shadows*." *College English*, vol. 52, no. 5, 1990, pp. 552–69.

Curti, Lidia. *Female Stories, Female Bodies: Narrative, Identity and Representation*. New York UP, 1998.

Cutter, Martha J. "The Story Must Go On and On: The Fantastic, Narration, and Intertextuality in Toni Morrison's *Beloved* and *Jazz*." *African American Review*, vol. 34, no. 1, 2000, pp. 61–75.

Daily, Gary W. "Toni Morrison's *Beloved*: Rememory, History, and the Fantastic." *The Celebration of the Fantastic: Selected Papers from the Tenth Anniversary International Conference on the Fantastic in the Arts*, edited by Donald E. Morse et al., Greenwood, 1992, pp. 142–50.

Dalsgard, Katrine. "The One All-Black Town Worth the Pain: (African) American Exceptionalism, Historical Narration, and the Critique of Nationhood in Toni Morrison's *Paradise*." *African American Review*, vol. 35, no. 2, 2001, pp. 233–48.

Daly, Brenda O., and Maureen T. Reddy, eds. *Narrating Mothers: Theorizing Maternal Subjectivities*. U of Tennessee P, 1991.

Daniels, Steven V. "Putting 'His Story Next to Hers': Choice, Agency, and the Structure of *Beloved*." *Texas Studies in Literature and Language*, vol. 44, no. 4, 2002, pp. 349–67.

David, Ron. *Toni Morrison Explained*. Random House, 2000.

Davidson, Rob. "Racial Stock and 8-Rocks: Communal Historiography in Toni Morrison's *Paradise*." *Twentieth Century Literature*, vol. 47, no. 3, 2001, pp. 355–73.

Davis, Cynthia A. "Self, Society and Myth in Toni Morrison's Fiction." *Contemporary Literature*, vol. 23, no. 3, 1982, pp. 323–42.

Davis, Kimberly Chabot. "'Postmodern Blackness': Toni Morrison's *Beloved* and the End of History." *Twentieth Century Literature*, vol. 44, no. 2, 1998, pp. 242–60.

Davis, Thadious M. *Southscapes*. U of North Carolina P, 2011.

DeLancey, Dayle B. "Motherlove Is a Killer: *Sula, Beloved*, and the Deadly Trinity of Motherly Love." *Sage*, vol. 7, no. 2, Fall 1990, pp. 15–18.

Denard, Carolyn C., ed. *Toni Morrison: Conversations*. UP of Mississippi, 2008.

Denard, Carolyn C., ed. *Toni Morrison: What Moves at the Margin, Selected Nonfiction*. UP of Mississippi, 2008.

de Weever, Jacqueline. *Mythmaking and Metaphor in Black Women's Fiction*. St. Martin's P, 1991.

Diu, Nisha Lilia. "*Home* by Toni Morrison: Review." *The Telegraph*, May 10, 2012.

Dixon, Melvin. *Ride Out the Wilderness: Geography and Identity in Afro-American Literature*. U of Illinois P, 1987.

Donahue, Deirdre. "Morrison Presents a Profound *Paradise*." *USA Today*, Jan. 8, 1998, p. 1D.

Donaldson, Susan V. "Telling Forgotten Stories of Slavery in the Postmodern South." *Southern Literary Journal*, vol. 40, no. 1, 2008, pp. 267–83.

Douglas, Christopher. "What *The Bluest Eye* Knows about Them: Culture, Race, Identity." *American Literature*, vol. 78, no. 1, 2006, pp. 141–68.

Doyle, Laura. "Bodies Inside/Out: Violation and Resistance from the Prison Cell to *The Bluest Eye*." *Feminist Interpretations of Maurice Merleau-Ponty*, edited by Dorothea Olkowski and Gail Weiss, Pennsylvania State UP, 2006, pp. 183–208.

Dreifus, Claudia. "Chloe Wofford Talks about Toni Morrison." *New York Times Magazine*, Sept. 11, 1994, Sec. 6, pp. 72–5.

Dubey, Madhu. *Black Women Novelists and the Nationalistic Aesthetic*. Indiana UP, 1994.

Dubey, Madhu. "The Politics of Genre in *Beloved*." *Novel: A Forum on Fiction*, vol. 32, no. 2, 1999, pp. 187–206.

Durrant, Sam. *Postcolonial Narrative and the Work of Mourning*. State U of New York P, 2004.

Dussere, Erik. *Balancing the Books: Faulkner, Morrison, and the Economics of Slavery*. Routledge, 2003.

Duvall, John N. "Doe Hunting and Masculinity: *Song of Solomon* and *Go Down, Moses*" *Arizona Quarterly*, vol. 47, no. 1, 1991, pp. 95–115.

Duvall, John N. *The Identifying Fictions of Toni Morrison: Modernist Authenticity and Postmodern Blackness*. Palgrave, 2010.

Duvall, John N. "Morrison and the (Faulknerian Dark) House of Fiction." *Faulkner and Morrison*, edited by Rieger, Christopher and Robert W. Hamblin, Southeast Missouri State UP, 2013, pp. 19035.

Edelberg, Cynthia Dubin. "Morrison's Voices: Formal Education, the Work Ethic, and the Bible." *American Literature*, vol. 58, May 1986, pp. 217–37.

English, James F. *The Economy of Prestige: Prizes, Awards and the Circulation of Cultural Value*. Harvard UP, 2005.

Evans, Mari, editor. *Black Women Writers (1950–1980): A Critical Evaluation*. Doubleday Anchor, 1984.

Eyerman, Ron. *Cultural Trauma: Slavery and the Formation of African American Identity*. Cambridge UP, 2001.

Espinola, Judith. "Woolf, Virginia, Influence of." *The Toni Morrison Encyclopedia*, edited by Elizabeth Ann Beaulieu, Greenwood P, 2003, pp. 380–2.

Fabre, Genevieve. "Genealogical Archeology or the Quest for Legacy in Toni Morrison's *Song of Solomon*." *Critical Essays on Toni Morrison*, edited by Nellie McKay, G. K. Hall, 1988, pp. 105–14.

Fahy, Thomas. *Freak Shows in Modern American Imagination: Constructing the Damaged Body from Willa Cather to Truman Capote*. Palgrave, 2007.

Fallon, Robert. "Music and the Allegory of Memory in *Margaret Garner*." *Modern Fiction Studies*, vol. 52, no. 2, Summer 2006, pp. 524–41.

Faulkner, William. *Absalom, Absalom!* Vintage, 1936.

Faulkner, William. *Sound and the Fury*. Vintage, 1929.

Faulkner, William. *The Wild Palms*. Vintage, 1939.

Felman, Shoshana, and Dori Laub. *Testimony: Crises of Witnessing in Literature, Psychoanalysis, and History*. Routledge, 1992.

Feng, Pin-Cha. " 'We Was Girls Together': The Double Female Bildungsroman in Toni Morrison's *Love*." *Feminist Studies in English Literature*, vol. 15, no. 2, Winter 2007, pp. 37–63.

Ferguson, Ann. *Blood at the Root, Motherhood, Sexuality, and Male Dominance*. Pandora, 1989.

Ferguson, Rebecca Hope. *Rewriting Black Identities; Transition and Exchange in the Novels of Toni Morrison*. Peter Lang, 2007.

Fitzgerald, Jennifer. "Selfhood and Community: Psychoanalysis and Discourse in *Beloved*." *Modern Fiction Studies*, vol. 39, no. 3–4, 1993, pp. 669–87.

Fitzgerald, Judith. "Woes Aplenty in this *Paradise*." *Toronto Star*, Jan. 31, 1998, p. M15.

Fleischner, Jennifer. *Mastering Slavery: Memory, Family, and Identity in Women's Slave Narratives*. New York UP, 1996.

Flint, Holly. "Toni Morrison's *Paradise*: Black Cultural Citizenship in the American Empire." *American Literature*, vol. 78, no. 3, 2008, pp. 585–612.

Fraile-Marcos, Ana Maria. "Hybridizing the 'City upon a Hill' in Toni Morrison's *Paradise*." *MELUS*, vol. 28, no. 4, 2003, pp. 3–33.

Franco, Dean. "What We Talk About When We Talk About *Beloved*." *Modern Fiction Studies*, vol. 52, no. 2, 2006, pp. 415–39.

Frank, Arthur W. *The Wounded Storyteller: Body, Illness, and Ethics*. U of Chicago P, 1995.

Freyd, Jennifer. *Betrayal Trauma: The Logic of Forgetting Childhood Abuse*. Harvard UP, 1996.

Frye, Marilyn. "On Being White: Thinking Toward a Feminist Understanding of Race and Race Supremacy." *The Politics of Reality: Essays in Feminist Theory*. Crossing, 1983, pp. 110–27.

Fulmer, Jacqueline. *Folk Women and Indirection in Morrison, Ní Dhuibhne, Hurston, and Lavin*. Ashgate, 2007.

Fultz, Lucille P. "Images of Motherhood in Toni Morrison's *Beloved*." *Double Stitch: Black Women Write about Mothers and Daughters*, edited by Patricia Bell-Scott, Beacon, 1991, pp. 32–41.

Fultz, Lucille P. *Toni Morrison: Playing with Difference*. U of Illinois P, 2003.

Fultz, Lucille P. editor. "Introduction: The Grace and Gravity of Toni Morrison." *Toni Morrison: Paradise, Love, A Mercy*. Continuum Bloomsbury, 2013, pp. 1–19.

Furman, Jan. *Toni Morrison's Fiction*. U of South Carolina P, 1993, 2014.

Gallego, Mar. "*Love* and the Survival of the Black Community." *Cambridge Companion to Toni Morrison*, edited by Justine Tally, Cambridge UP, 2007, pp. 92–100.

Garland-Thomson, Rosemarie. "Disability." *The Toni Morrison Encyclopedia*, edited by Elizabeth Ann Beaulieu, Greenwood, 2003, pp. 99–101.

Garland-Thomson, Rosemarie. *Extraordinary Bodies: Figuring Physical Disability in American Culture and Literature*. Columbia UP, 1997.

Gascuena Gahete, Javier. "Narrative Defusion and Aesthetic Pleasure in Toni Morrison's *Love*." *Figures of Belatedness: Postmodern Fictions in English*, edited by Javier Gascuena Gahete and Paule Martin Salvan, Servicio de Publicaciones, Universidad de Cordoba, 2006, pp. 259–73.

Gates, Henry Louis, Jr. *Figures in Black: Words, Signs, and the "Racial" Self*. Oxford UP, 1987.

Gates, Henry Louis, Jr. *The Signifying Monkey: A Theory of African-American Literary Criticism*. Oxford UP, 1988.

Gates, Henry Louis, Jr., and K. A. Appiah, eds. *Toni Morrison: Critical Perspectives Past and Present*. Amistad, 1993.

Gauthier, Marni. *Amnesia and Redress in Contemporary American Fiction*. Palgrave, 2011.

Gibson, Donald B. "Text and Countertext in The *Bluest Eye*." *Toni Morrison: Critical Perspectives, Past and Present*, edited by Henry Louis Gates, Jr. and K. A. Appiah, Amistad, 1993, pp. 159–74.

Gillespie, Carmen R., editor. *Toni Morrison, Forty Years in the Clearing*. Bucknell UP, 2012.

Gilman, Sander L. "Black Bodies, White Bodies: Toward an Iconography of Female Sexuality in Late Nineteenth-Century Art, Medicine, and Literature." *"Race," Writing, and Difference*, edited by Henry Louis Gates, Jr., U of Chicago P, 1986, pp. 223–61.

Gilroy, Paul. "Living Memory: An Interview with Toni Morrison." *Small Acts: Thoughts on the Politics of Black Cultures*. Serpent's Tail, 1993, pp. 175–82.

Goldman, Anne E. "'I Made the Ink': (Literary) Production and Reproduction in *Dessa Rose* and *Beloved*." *Feminist Studies*, vol. 16, 1990, pp. 313–30.

Goulimari, Pelagia. *Toni Morrison*. Routledge, 2011.

Gray, Paul. "Paradise Found." *Time*, Jan. 19, 1998, pp. 62–8.

Greene, Gayle. "Feminist Fiction and the Uses of Memory." *The Second Signs Reader: Feminist Scholarship, 1983–1996*, edited by Ruth-Ellen B. Jones and Barbara Laslett, U of Chicago P, 1996, pp. 184–215.

Grewal, Gurleen. *Circles of Sorrow, Lines of Struggle: The Novels of Toni Morrison*. Louisiana State UP, 1998.

Griffin, Farah Jasmine. "Wrestling Till Dawn: On Becoming an Intellectual in the Age of Morrison." *Toni Morrison, Forty Years in the Clearing*, edited by Carmen R. Gillespie, Bucknell UP, 2012, pp. 116–27.

Groover, Kristina K. *The Wilderness Within: American Women Writers and Spiritual Quest*. U of Arkansas P, 1999.

Guth, Deborah. "A Blessing and a Burden: The Relation to the Past in *Sula, Song of Solomon* and *Beloved*." *Modern Fiction Studies*, vol. 39, no. 3&4, Fall/Winter 1993, pp. 575–96.

Gutmann, Katharina. *Celebrating the Senses: An Analysis of the Sensual in Toni Morrison's Fiction*. Francke Verlag, 2000.

Gwin, Minrose C. *Black and White Women of the Old South: The Peculiar Sisterhood in American Literature*. U of Tennessee P, 1985.

Gysin, Fritz. "The Enigma of the Return." *Black Imagination and the Middle Passage*, edited by Maria Diedrich, et al., Oxford UP, 1999, pp. 183–90.

Haaken, Janice. "The Recovery of Memory, Fantasy, and Desire: Feminist Approaches to Sexual Abuse and Psychic Trauma." *Signs: Journal of Women in Culture and Society*, vol. 21, no. 4, 1996, pp. 1069–94.

Halberstam, Judith. *Female Masculinity*. Duke UP, 1998.

Hall, Alice. *Disability and Modern Fiction: Faulkner, Morrison, Coetzee and the Nobel Prize for Literature*. Palgrave, 2012.

Hamilton, Cynthia S. "Revisions, Rememories and Exorcisms: Toni Morrison and the Slave Narrative." *Journal of American Studies*, vol. 30, no. 3, 1996, pp. 429–45.

Handley, William R. "The House a Ghost Built: Allegory, Nommo, and the Ethics of Reading in Toni Morrison's *Beloved*." *Contemporary Literature*, vol. 36, no. 4, 1995, pp. 676–701.

Harding, Wendy, and Jacky Martin. *A World of Difference: An Inter-Cultural Study of Toni Morrison's Novels*. Greenwood, 1994.

Harris, Trudier. *Exorcising Blackness: Historical and Literary Lynching and Burning Rituals*. Indiana UP, 1984.

Harris, Trudier. *Fiction and Folklore: The Novels of Toni Morrison*. U of Tennessee P, 1991.

Harris, Trudier. *Saints, Sinners, Saviors: Strong Black Women in African American Literature*. Palgrave, 2001.

Harris, Trudier. "Religion and Community in the Writings of Contemporary Black Women." *Women's Writing in Exile*, edited by Mary Lynn Broe and Angela Ingram, U of North Carolina P, 1989, pp. 151–69.

Harris, Trudier. "Toni Morrison." *Oxford Companion to Women's Writing in the United States*, edited by Cathy N. Davidson and Linda Wagner-Martin, Oxford UP, 1995, pp. 578–80.

Haskins, Jim. *Toni Morrison: Telling a Tale Untold*. Twenty-First Century Books, 2003.

Hassan, Ihab. *The Postmodern Turn: Essays in Postmodern Theory and Culture*. Ohio State UP, 1987.

Hawthorne, Evelyn. "On Gaining the Double-Vision: *Tar Baby* as Diasporean Novel." *Black American Literature Forum*, vol. 22, no. 1, 1988, pp. 97–107.

Hedin, Raymond. "The Structure of Emotion in Black American Fiction." *Novel*, vol. 16, no. 1, Fall 1982, pp. 35–54.

Heinert, Jennifer Lee Jordan. *Narrative Conventions and Race in the Novels of Toni Morrison*. Routledge, 2009.

Heinze, Denise. *The Dilemma of "Double Consciousness": Toni Morrison's Novels*. U of Georgia P, 1993.

Heise-von der Lippe, Anya. "Others, Monsters, Ghosts: Representations of the Female Gothic Body in Toni Morrison's *Beloved* and *Love*." *The Female Gothic: New Directions*, edited by Diana Wallace, Andrew Smith, Palgrave Macmillan, 2009, pp. 166–79.

Henderson, Carol E. *Scarring the Black Body: Race and Representation in African American Literature*. U of Missouri P, 2002.

Henderson, Mae G. "Toni Morrison's *Beloved*: Re-Membering the Body as Historical Text." *Comparative American Identities: Race, Sex, and Nationality in the Modern Text*, edited by Hortense J. Spillers. Routledge, 1991, pp. 62–86.

Herman, Judith. *Trauma and Recovery*. HarperCollins, 1992.

Herman, Judith. *Trauma and Recovery: The Aftermath of Violence—from Domestic Abuse to Political Terror*. Basic, 1997.

Higgins, Therese E. *Religiosity, Cosmology, and Folklore: The African Influences in the Novels of Toni Morrison*. Routledge, 2001.

Hilfer, Anthony C. "Critical Indeterminacies in Toni Morrison's Fiction: An Introduction." *Texas Studies in Literature and Language*, vol. 33, no. 1, Spring 1991, pp. 91–5.

Hilfrich, Carola. "Anti-Exodus: Countermemory, Gender, Race, and Everyday Life in Toni Morrison's *Paradise*." *Modern Fiction Studies*, vol. 52, no. 2, 2006, pp. 322–49.

Hill, Michael D. *The Ethics of Swagger: Prizewinning African American Novels, 1977- 1993*. Ohio State UP, 2013.

Hill, Michael. "Toni Morrison and the Post-Civil Rights American Novel." *Cambridge Companion to the American Novel*, edited by Leonard Cassuto, Cambridge UP, 2011, pp. 1064–83.

Hirsch, Marianne. *The Mother/Daughter Plot: Narrative, Psychoanalysis, Feminism*. U of Indiana P, 1989.

Hirsch, Marianne. "Maternity and Rememory: Toni Morrison's *Beloved*." *Representations of Motherhood*, edited by Donna Bassin, et al., Yale UP, 1997, pp. 92–110.

Hirsch, Marianne, and Ivy Schweitzer, "Mothers and Daughters." *The Oxford Companion to Women's Writing in the U. S.*, edited by Cathy N. Davidson and Linda Wagner-Martin. Oxford UP, 1995, pp. 583–5.

Hogan, Michael. "Built on the Ashes: The Fall of the House of Sutpen and the Rise of the House of Sethe." *Critical Insights: Toni Morrison*, edited by Solomon O. Iyasere and Marla W. Iyasere. Salem P, 2010, pp. 127–46.

Hogue, W. Lawrence. "Postmodernism, Traditional Cultural Forms, and the African American Narrative: Major's *Reflex*, Morrison's *Jazz*, and Reed's *Mumbo Jumbo*." *Novel*, vol. 35, no. 2–3, Spring–Summer 2002, pp. 169–92.

Holloway, Karla F. C. *Moorings and Metaphors: Figures of Culture and Gender in Black Women's Literature*. Rutgers UP, 1992.

Holloway, Karla F. C. "Narrative Time/Spiritual Text: *Beloved* and *As I Lay Dying*." *Unflinching Gaze: Faulkner and Morrison Re-envisioned*, edited by Carol A. Kolmerten, et al., UP of Mississippi, 1997, pp. 91–8.

Holloway, Karla F. C., and Stephanie Demetrakopoulos. *New Dimensions of Spirituality: A Biracial and Bicultural Reading of the Novels of Toni Morrison*. Greenwood, 1987.

Hoofard, Jennifer. "Thinking about a Story." *Writing on the Edge*, vol. 17, no. 2, 2007, pp. 87–99.

Horvitz, Deborah M. *Literary Trauma: Sadism, Memory, and Sexual Violence in American Women's Fiction*. State U of New York P, 2000.

House, Elizabeth B. "Artists and the Art of Living: Order and Disorder in Toni Morrison's Fiction." *Modern Fiction Studies*, vol. 34, Spring 1988, pp. 27–44.

House, Elizabeth B. "The 'Sweet Life' in Toni Morrison's Fiction." *American Literature*, vol. 56, 1984, pp. 181–202.

House, Elizabeth B. "Toni Morrison's Ghost: The Beloved Who is Not Beloved." *Studies in American Fiction*, vol. 18, no. 1, 1990, pp. 17–26.

Hubbard, Dolan. "In Quest of Authority: Toni Morrison's *Song of Solomon* and the Rhetoric of the Black Preacher." *CLA Journal*, vol. 35, 1992, pp. 288–302.

Hull, Gloria T., et al., editors. *All the Women Are White, All the Blacks Are Men, but Some of Us Are Brave: Black Women's Studies*. Feminist P, 1982.

Iannone, Carol. "Toni Morrison's Career." *Commentary*, vol. 84, Dec. 1987, pp. 59–63.

Inoue, Kazuko. "'I Got a Tree on My Back': A Study of Toni Morrison's Latest Novel, *Beloved*." *Language and Culture*, 1988, pp. 69–82.

Irving, John. "Morrison's Black Fable." *New York Times Book Review*, vol. 1, Mar. 29, 1981, pp. 30–1.

Iyasere, Solomon O., and Marla W. Iyasere, eds. *Understanding Toni Morrison's Beloved and Sula*. Whitston, 2000.

Jablon, Madelyn. "Rememory, Dream Memory, and Revision in Toni Morrison's *Beloved* and Alice Walker's *The Temple of My Familiar*." *CLA Journal*, vol. 37, 1993, pp. 136–44.

Jackson, Chuck. "A 'Headless Display': *Sula*, Soldiers, and Lynching." *Modern Fiction Studies*, vol. 52, no. 2, 2006, pp. 374–92.

Jenkins, Candice M. "Pure Black: Class, Color and Intraracial Politics in Toni Morrison's *Paradise*." *Modern Fiction Studies*, vol. 52, no. 2, 2006, pp. 270–96.

Jennings, LaVinia Delois. *Toni Morrison and the Idea of Africa*. Cambridge UP, 2008.

Jessee, Sharon. "The Contrapuntal Historiography of Toni Morrison's *Paradise*: Unpacking the Legacies of the Kansas and Oklahoma All-Black Towns." *American Studies*, vol. 46, no. 1, 2006, pp. 81–112.

Jesser, Nancy. "Violence, Home, and Community in Toni Morrison's *Beloved*." *African American Review*, vol. 33, no. 2, 1999, pp. 325–45.

Jimoh, A. Yemisi. *Spiritual, Blues, and Jazz People in African American Fiction*. U of Tennessee P, 2002.

Johnson, Barbara, "'Aesthetic' and 'Rapport' in Toni Morrison's *Sula*." *Textual Practice*, vol. 7, no. 2, 1993, pp. 165–72.

Johnson, Charles. *Being and Race: Black Writing since 1970*. Indiana UP, 1988.

Johnson, Diane. "The Oppressor in the Next Room." *New York Review of Books*, Nov. 10, 1977.

Jones, Bessie, and Audrey Vinson. *The World of Toni Morrison*. Kendall/Hunt, 1985.

Jones, Gayl. *Liberating Voices: Oral Traditions in African American Literature*. Harvard UP, 1991.

Jones, Tayari. "*Home* by Toni Morrison: Review." *San Francisco Gate*, May 6, 2012.

Jordan, Elaine. "'Not My People': Toni Morrison and Identity." *Black Women's Writing*, edited by Gina Wisker, Macmillan 1993, pp. 111–26.

Joyce, Joyce Ann. "Structural and Thematic Unity in Toni Morrison's *Song of Solomon*." *CEA Critic*, vol. 49, Winter/Summer 1986-1987, pp. 185–98.

Juncker, Clara. "Unnatural Lives: Toni Morrison's Historical Universe." *Xavier Review*, vol. 32, no. 1&2, 2012, pp. 57–74.

June, Pamela B. *The Fragmented Female Body and Identity*. Peter Lang, 2010.

Junker, Carstan. *Frames of Friction: Black Genealogies, White Hegemony, and the Essay as Critical Intervention*. Campus Verlag, 2010.

Kachka, Boris. "Toni Morrison's History Lesson." *New York Magazine*, Sept. 1-8, 2008, pp. 90–1.

Kakutani, Michiko. "Books of the Times: *Love* by Toni Morrison. Family Secrets, Feuding Women." *New York Times*, Oct. 31, 2003, p. 37.

Kakutani, Michiko. "Soldier Is Defeated by War Abroad, Then Welcomed Back by Racism." *New York Times*, May 7, 2012, p. C1.

Kakutani, Michiko. "Worthy Women, Unredeemable Men." *New York Times*, Jan. 6, 1998, p. 8.

Kang, Nancy. "To Love and Be Loved: Considering Black Masculinity and the Misandric Impulse in Toni Morrison's *Beloved*." *Callaloo*, vol. 26, no. 3, 2003, pp. 836–54.

Kastor, Elizabeth. "'Beloved' and the Protest: Why Black Writers Decried Book Award 'Oversight,'" *The Washington Post*, Jan. 21, 1988. Final ed., p. B1.

Keenan, Sally. "'Four Hundred Years of Silence': Myth, History, and Motherhood in Toni Morrison's *Beloved*." *Recasting the World: Writing after Colonialism*, edited by Jonathan White, Johns Hopkins UP, 1993, pp. 45–81.

Khayati, Abdellatif. "Representation, Race, and the 'Language' of the Ineffable in Toni Morrison's Narrative." *African American Review*, vol. 33, no. 2, Summer 1999, pp. 313–24.

King, Debra Walker. *Deep Talk, Reading African-American Literary Names*. UP of Virginia, 1998.

King, Lovalerie. *Race, Theft, and Ethics: Property Matters in African American Literature*. Louisiana State UP, 2007.

King, Lovalerie, and Lynn Orilla Scott, eds. *James Baldwin and Toni Morrison: Comparative Critical and Theoretical Essays*. Palgrave, 2006.

Klotman, Phyllis Rauch. *Another Man Gone: The Black Runner in Contemporary Afro-American Fiction*. Kennikat, 1977.

Konen, Anne. "Toni Morrison's *Beloved* and the Ghost of Slavery." *Beloved, She's Mine*," edited by Genevieve Fabre and Claudine Raynaud. CETLNA, 1993, pp. 53–67.

Koolish, Lynda. "'To Be Loved and Cry Shame': A Psychological Reading of Toni Morrison's *Beloved*." MELUS, vol. 26, no. 4, 2001, pp. 169–95.

Krumholz, Linda. "Blackness and Art in Toni Morrison's *Tar Baby*." *Contemporary Literature*, vol. 49, no. 2, 2008, pp. 263–92.

Krumholz, Linda. "The Ghosts of Slavery: Historical Recovery in Toni Morrison's *Beloved*." *African American Review*, vol. 26, no. 3, Autumn 1992, pp. 395–408.

Krumholz, Linda. "Reading and Insight in Toni Morrison's *Paradise*." *African American Review*, vol. 36, no. 1, 2002, pp. 21–34.

Kubitschek, Missy Dehn. *Toni Morrison: A Critical Companion*. Greenwood, 1998.

LaCapra, Dominick. *Writing History, Writing Trauma*. Johns Hopkins UP, 2001.

Lawrence, David. "Fleshly Ghosts and Ghostly Flesh: The Word and the Body in *Beloved*." *Studies in American Fiction*, vol. 19, no. 2, 1991, pp. 189–201.

Lawson, Erica. "Black Women's Mothering in a Historical and Contemporary Perspective: Understanding the Past, Forging the Future." *Mother Outlaws: Theories and Practices of Empowered Mothering*, edited by Andrea O'Reilly, Women's P, 2004, pp. 193–201.

Lee, Catherine Carr. "The South in Toni Morrison's *Song of Solomon*: Initiation, Healing, and Home." *Studies in Literary Imagination*, vol. 31, no. 2, 1998, pp. 109–23.

Lee, Dorothy H. "The Quest for Self: Triumph and Failure in the Works of Toni Morrison." *Black Women Writers (1950–1980)*, edited by Mari Evans, Doubleday, 1984, pp. 346–60.

Lee, Sue-Im. *A Body of Individuals: The Paradox of Community in Contemporary Fiction*. Ohio State UP, 2009.

Leonard, John. "Travels with Toni." *The Nation*, Jan. 17, 1994, p. 62.

Lepow, Lauren. "Paradise Lost and Found: Dualism and Edenic Myth in Toni Morrison's *Tar Baby*." *Contemporary Literature*, vol. 28, no. 3, 1987, pp. 363–77.

Le Seur, Geta. "Moving beyond the Boundaries of Self, Community, and the Other in Toni Morrison's *Sula* and *Paradise*." *CLA Journal*, vol. 46, no. 1, 2002, pp. 1–20.

Levy, Andrew. "Telling *Beloved*." *Texas Studies in Literature and Languages*, vol. 331, no. 1, 1991, pp. 115–23.

Li, Stephanie. *Toni Morrison: A Biography*. Greenwood Biographies, 2010.

Lillvis, K. "Becoming Self and Mother: Posthuman Liminality in Toni Morrison's *Beloved*." *Critique*, vol. 54, no. 4, Oct. 2013, pp. 452–64.

Liscio, Lorraine. "*Beloved*'s Narrative: Writing Mother's Milk." *Tulsa Studies in Women's Literature*, vol. 11, no. 1, 1992, pp. 31–46.

Loichot, Valerie. *Orphan Narratives*. U of Virginia P, 2007.

Lubiano, Wahneema. "The Postmodernist Rag: Political Identity and the Vernacular in *Song of Solomon*." *New Essays on Song of Solomon*, edited by Valerie Smith, Cambridge UP, 1995, pp. 93–116.

Luszczynska, Ana M. *The Ethics of Community: Nancy, Derrida, Morrison and Menendez*. Continuum, 2012.

Lydon, Susan. "What's an Intelligent Woman To Do?" *Village Voice*, July 1–7, 1981, p. 41.

MacKinnon, Catherine A. *Toward a Feminist Theory of the State*. Harvard UP, 1989.

Macpherson, Heidi Stettedahl. *Courting Failure: Women and the Law in Twentieth Century Literature*. U of Akron P, 2007.

Madsen, Deborah L. *Allegory in America: From Puritanism to Postmodernism*. Macmillan, 1996.

Makward, Edris, and Leslie Lacy, eds. *Contemporary African Literature*. Random House, 1972.

Malmgren, Carl D. "Mixed Genres and the Logic of Slavery in Toni Morrison's *Beloved*." *Critique*, vol. 36, no. 2, 1995, pp. 96–106.

Mandel, Naomi. "'I Made the Ink': Identity, Complicity, 60 Million and More." *Modern Fiction Studies*, vol. 48, no. 3, 2002, pp. 581–612.

Marks, Kathleen. *Toni Morrison's "Beloved" and the Apotropaic Imagination*. U of Missouri P, 2002.

Marshall, Brenda. "The Gospel According to Pilate." *American Literature*, vol. 57, 1985, pp. 486–9.

Martin, Curtis. "Bibliography." *Narrative Technique in the Writing of Contemporary American Women*, edited by Catherine Rainwater and William J. Scheick. UP of Kentucky, 1985, pp. 205–7.

Mathieson, Barbara Offutt. "Memory and Mother Love in Toni Morrison's *Beloved*." *American Imago: Studies in Psychoanalysis and Culture*, vol. 47, no. 1, 1990, pp. 1–21.

Matus, Jill. *Toni Morrison*. Manchester UP, 1998.

Mayberry, Susan Neal. *Can't I Love What I Criticize? The Masculine and Morrison*. U of Georgia P, 2007.

Mayberry, Susan Neal. Visions and Revisions of American Masculinity in *A Mercy*." *Toni Morrison: Paradise, Love, A Mercy*, edited by Lucille P. Fultz, Continuum Bloomsbury, 2013, pp. 166–84.

Mbalia, Dorothea Drummond. *Toni Morrison's Developing Class Consciousness*. 1991, Rev. ed. Susquehanna UP, 2004.

McAlpin, Heller. "'Home': Toni Morrison's Taut, Triumphant New Novel." *NPR*, May 15, 2012. Audio.

McBride, James. "Jazzed." *New York Times Book Review*, Mar. 3, 2019, p. 10.

McCuskey, Brian. "Not at Home: Servants, Scholars, and the Uncanny." *PMLA*, vol. 121, no. 2, 2006, pp. 421–36.

McDowell, Deborah E. "Harlem Nocturne." *Women's Review of Books*, vol. 9, no. 9, 1992, pp. 1–5.

McDowell, Linda. *Gender, Identity and Place: Understanding Feminist Geographies*. U of Minnesota P, 1999.

McHaney, Pearl Amelia. "Southern Women Writers and Their Influence." *Cambridge Companion to the Literature of the American South*, edited by Sharon Monteith, Cambridge UP, 2013, pp. 132–4.

McKee, Patricia. "Geographies of *Paradise*." *New Centennial Review*, vol. 3, no. 1, 2003, pp. 197–223.

Medora, Dana. "Justice and Citizenship in Toni Morrison's *Song of Solomon*." *Canadian Review of American Studies*, vol. 32, no. 1, 2002, pp. 1–13.

Mellard, James M. "'Families Make the Best Enemies': Paradox of Narcissistic Identification in Toni Morrison's *Love*." *African American Review*, vol. 43, no. 4, Winter 2009, pp. 699–712.

Menand, Louis. "The War Between Men and Women." *New Yorker*, Jan. 12, 1998, pp. 78–82.

Metress, Christopher. "Dreaming Emmett." *The Toni Morrison Encyclopedia*, edited by Elizabeth Ann Beaulieu, Greenwood, 2003, pp. 105–7.

Michael, Magali Cornier. *New Visions of Community in Contemporary American Fiction: Tan, Kingsolver, Castillo, Morrison*. U of Iowa P, 2006.

Middleton, Joyce Irene. "Imagining Paradise." *Word-Work: The Newsletter of the Toni Morrison Society*, vol. 23, no. 3, Autumn 1991, pp. 27–42.

Mihan, Anne. *Undoing Difference*. Universitatverlag Winter, 2012.

Miller, Alice. *Breaking Down the Wall of Silence: The Liberating Experience of Facing Painful Truth*. Translated by Simon Worrell. Dutton, 1991.

Miller Budick, Emily. "Absence, Loss, and the Space of History in Toni Morrison's *Beloved*." *Arizona Quarterly*, vol. 48, no. 2, 1992, pp. 117–38.

Mishkin, Tracy. "Theorizing Literary Influence and African-American Writers." *Literary Influence and African-American Writers*, edited by Tracy Mishkin, Garland, 1996, pp. 3–20.

Mix, Debbie. "Toni Morrison: A Selected Bibliography." *Modern Fiction Studies*, vol. 39, no. 3&4, 1994, pp. 795–817.

Mobley, Marilyn Sanders. "Call and Response: Voice, Community, and Dialogic Structures in Toni Morrison's *Song of Solomon*." *New Essays on Song of Solomon*, edited by Valerie Smith, Cambridge UP, 1995, pp. 41–68.

Moglen, Helen. "Redeeming History: Toni Morrison's *Beloved*." *Cultural Critique*, vol. 24, 1993, pp. 17–40.

Mohanty, Satya. "The Epistemic Status of Cultural Identity: On *Beloved* and the Postcolonial Condition." *Cultural Critique*, vol. 24, 1993, pp. 41–80.

Monteith, Sharon. *Advancing Sisterhood? Interracial Friendships in Contemporary Southern Fiction*. U of Georgia P, 2000.

Montgomery, Maxine, ed. *Contested Boundaries: New Critical Essays on the Fiction of Toni Morrison*. Cambridge Scholars, 2013.

Moore, Geneva Cobb. "A Demonic Parody: Toni Morrison's *A Mercy*." *Southern Literary Journal*, vol. 44, 2011, pp. 1–18.

Moreland, Richard C. *Learning from Difference: Teaching Morrison, Twain, Ellison, and Eliot*. Ohio State UP, 1999.

Morgenstern, Naomi. "Mother's Milk and Sister's Blood: Trauma and the Neo-Slave Narrative." *differences: A Journal of Feminist Cultural Studies*, vol. 8, no. 2, 1996, pp. 101–26.

Mori, Aoi. *Toni Morrison and Womanist Discourse*. Peter Lang, 1999.

Mueller, Stefanie. *The Presence of the Past in the Novels of Toni Morrison*. Winter, 2013.

Murray, Rolland. "The Long Strut: *Song of Solomon* and the Emancipatory Limits of the Black Patriarchy." Callaloo, vol. 22, no. 1, 1999, pp. 121–33.

Nicol, Kathryn. "Visible Differences: Viewing Racial Identity in Toni Morrison's *Paradise* and "Recitatif." *Literature and Racial Ambiguity*, edited by Teresa Hubel and Neil Brooks. Rodolpi, 2002, pp. 209–31.

Nnaemeka, Obioma. *Sisterhood: Feminists and Power from Africa to the Diaspora*. Africa World P, 1989.

Novak, Phillip. "'Circles and Circles of Sorrow': In the Wake of Morrison's *Sula*." *PMLA*, vol. 114, no. 2, 1999, pp. 184–93.

Nowlin, Michael. "Toni Morrison's *Jazz* and the Racial Dreams of the American Writer." *American Literature*, vol. 71, 1999, pp. 151–74.

Ochoa, Peggy. "Morrison's *Beloved:* Allegorically Othering 'White' Christianity." *MELUS*, vol. 24, no. 2, 1999, pp. 107–23.

O'Reilly, Andrea. "In Search of My Mother's Garden, I Found My Own: Mother-Love, Healing, and Identity in Toni Morrison's *Jazz.*" *African American Review*, vol. 30, Fall, 1996, pp. 367–79.

O'Reilly, Andrea. *Toni Morrison and Motherhood: A Politics of the Heart*. State U of New York P, 2004.

Otten, Terry. *The Crime of Innocence in Toni Morrison's Fiction*. U of Missouri P, 1989.

Otten, Terry. "Horrific Love in Toni Morrison's Fiction." *Modern Fiction Studies*, vol. 39, no. 3, 1993, Apr. 1995, pp. 651–7.

Otten, Terry. "'To Be One or to Have One': 'Motherlove'" in the Fiction of Toni Morrison." *Contested Boundaries: New Critical Essays on the Fiction of Toni Morrison*, edited by Montgomery, Maxine, Cambridge Scholars, 2013, pp. 82–95.

Owens, Louis. "As if an Indian Were Really an Indian: Native American Voices and Postcolonial Theory." *Native American Representations: First Encounters, Distorted Images and Literary Appropriations*, edited by Gretchen Bataille, U of Nebraska P, 2001, pp. 11–25.

Page, Philip. *Dangerous Freedom: Fusion and Fragmentation in Toni Morrison's Novels*. UP of Mississippi, 1995.

Page, Philip. "Furrowing All the Brows: Interpretation and the Transcendent in Toni Morrison's *Paradise.*" *African American Review*, vol. 35, Winter 2001, pp. 639–51.

Paquet, Sandra Pouchet. "The Ancestor as Foundation in *Their Eyes Were Watching God* and *Tar Baby.*" *Callaloo*, vol. 13, no. 3, 1990, pp. 499–515.

Paquet-Deyris, Anne-Marie. "Toni Morrison's *Jazz* and the City." *African American Review*, vol. 35, no. 2, 2001, pp. 219–31.

Parker, Emma. "'Apple Pie' Ideology and the Politics of Appetite in the Novels of Toni Morrison." *Contemporary Literature*, vol. 39, no. 4, 1998, pp. 614–43.

Parker, Emma. "A New Hystery: History and Hysteria in Toni Morrison's *Beloved.*" *Twentieth Century Literature*, vol. 47, no. 1, 2001, pp. 1–19.

Parrish, Timothy. "Introduction." *The Cambridge Companion to American Novelists*, edited by Timothy Parrish, Cambridge UP, 2013, pp. xvii–xxxii.

Patell, Cyrus R. K. *Negative Liberties: Morrison, Pynchon, and the Problem of Liberal Ideology*. Duke UP, 2001.

Peach, Linden. *Toni Morrison*. St. Martin's, 2000.

Peach, Linden. "Toni Morrison." *American Fiction after 1945*, edited by John N. Duvall, Cambridge UP, 2012, pp. 233–43.

Peterson, Christopher. "Beloved's Claim." *Modern Fiction Studies*, vol. 52, no. 3, 2006, pp. 548–69.

Peterson, Nancy J. *Against Amnesia: Women Writers and the Crises of Historical Memory*. U of Pennsylvania P, 2001.

Phelan, James. "Sethe's Choice: *Beloved* and the Ethics of Reading." *Ethics, Literature, and Theory: An Introductory Reader*, edited by Stephen K. George, Rowman and Littlefield, 2005, pp. 299–314.

Podnicks, Elizabeth, and Andrea O'Reilly, eds. *Textual Mothers/Maternal Texts: Motherhood in Contemporary Women's Literatures*. Wilfrid Laurier UP, 2010.

Portales, Marco. "Toni Morrison's *The Bluest Eye*: Shirley Temple and Cholly." *Centennial Review*, vol. 30, 1986, pp. 496–506.

Price, Reynolds. "Review of *Song of Solomon.*" *New York Times Book Review*, Sept. 11, 1977, p. 1.

Pullin, Faith. "Landscapes of Reality: The Fiction of Contemporary Afro-American Women." *Black Fiction: New Studies in the Afro-American Novel Since 1945*, edited by A. Robert Lee, Vision, 1980, pp. 173–203.

Rabinowitz, Paula. "Naming, Magic and Documentary: The Subversion of the Narrative in *Song of Solomon*, *Ceremony*, and *China Men*." *Feminist Re-Visions*: *What Has Been and Might Be*, edited by Vivian Patraka and Louise Tilly, U of Michigan P, 1983, pp. 26–42.

Rainwater, Catherine. "Worthy Messengers: Narrative Voices in Toni Morrison's Novels." *Texas Studies in Literature and Language*, vol. 33, no. 1, 1991, pp. 96–113.

Ramadanovic, Petar. *Forgetting Futures: On Memory, Trauma, and Identity*. Lexington Books, 2001.

Rampersad, Arnold. *Ralph Ellison: A Biography*. Knopf, 2007.

Raynaud, Claudine. "The Poetics of Abjection in *Beloved*." *Black Imagination and the Middle Passage*, edited by Maria Diedrich, et al., Oxford UP, 1999, pp. 70–85.

Reames, Kelly. *Toni Morrison's Paradise*. Continuum, 2001.

Reames, Kelly Lynch. *Women and Race in Contemporary U.S. Writing, From Faulkner to Morrison*. Palgrave, 2007.

Reed, Andrew. "'As if word magic had anything to do with the courage it took to be a man': Black Masculinity in Toni Morrison's *Paradise*." *African American Review*, vol. 39, no. 4, 2005, pp. 527–40.

Reed, Harry. "Toni Morrison: *Song of Solomon* and Black Cultural Nationalism." *Centennial Review*, vol. 32, no. 1, Winter 1988, pp. 50–64.

Reyes, Angelita. "Ancient Properties in the New World: The Paradox of the 'Other' in Toni Morrison's *Tar Baby*." *Black Scholar*, vol. 17, Mar.–Apr. 1986, pp. 19–25.

Rice, Alan J. *Radical Narratives of the Black Atlantic*. Continuum, 2003.

Rice, Herbert William. *Toni Morrison and the American Tradition: A Rhetorical Reading*. Peter Lang, 1996.

Richards, Phillip M. "*Sula* and the Discourse of the Folk in African American Literature." *Cultural Studies: Toni Morrison and the Curriculum*, edited by Warren Crichlaw and Cameron McCarthy, Routledge, 1995, pp. 270–92.

Rieger, Christopher, and Robert W. Hamblin, eds. *Faulkner and Morrison*. Southeast Missouri State UP, 2013.

Rigney, Barbara Hill. *Lilith's Daughters, Women and Religion in Contemporary Fiction*. U of Wisconsin P, 1982.

Rigney, Barbara Hill. "'A Story to Pass On': Ghosts and the Significance of History in Toni Morrison's *Beloved*." *Haunting the House of Fiction: Feminist Perspectives on Ghost Stories by American Women*, edited by Lynette Carpenter and Wendy K. Kolmar, U of Tennessee P, 1991, pp. 229–35.

Rigney, Barbara Hill. *The Voices of Toni Morrison*. Ohio State UP, 1991.

Rimmon-Kenan, Shlomith. "Narration, Doubt, Retrieval: Toni Morrison's *Beloved*." *Narrative*, vol. 4, 1996, pp. 109–23.

Roberson, Gloria Grant. *The World of Toni Morrison*. Greenwood, 2003.

Roberts. John W. *From Trickster to Badman, The Black Folk Hero in Slavery and Freedom*. U of Pennsylvania P, 1989.

Rodrigues, Eusebio L. "Experiencing *Jazz*." *Modern Fiction Studies*, vol. 39, Fall/Winter 1993, pp. 748–52.

Rody, Caroline. *The Daughter's Return: African-American and Caribbean Women's Fictions of History*. Oxford UP, 2001.

Rody, Caroline. "Toni Morrison's *Beloved*: History, 'Rememory,' and a 'Clamor for a Kiss'." *American Literary History*, vol. 7, no. 1, 1995, pp. 92–119.

Rokotnitz, Naomi. "Constructing Cognitive Scaffolding through Embodied Receptiveness: Toni Morrison's *The Bluest Eye*." *Style*, vol. 41, no. 4, 2007, pp. 385–408.

Romero, Channette. "Creating the Beloved Community: Religion, Race and Nation in Toni Morrison's *Paradise*." *African American Review*, vol. 39, 2005, pp. 415–30.

Rosen, Lois C. "Motherhood." *Toni Morrison Encyclopedia*, edited by Elizabeth Ann Beaulieu, Greenwood, 2003, pp. 218–25.

Rosenblatt, Paul C., and Beverly R. Wallace. *African American Grief*. Routledge, 2005.

Roynon, Tessa. *The Cambridge Introduction to Toni Morrison*. Cambridge, UP, 2013.

Rubenstein, Roberta. *Home Matters: Longing and Belonging, Nostalgia and Mourning in Women's Fiction*. Palgrave, 2001.

Ruddick, Sara. *Maternal Thinking: Toward a Politics of Peace*. Ballantine, 1989.

Rushdy, Ashraf H. A. "Daughters Signifyin(g) History: The Example of Toni Morrison's *Beloved*." *American Literature*, vol. 64, 1992, pp. 567–97.

Rushdy, Ashraf H. A. "'Rememory': Primal Scenes and Constructions in Toni Morrison's Novels." *Contemporary Literature*, vol. 31, no. 3, 1990, pp. 300–23.

Samuels, Wilfred D., and Clenora Hudson-Weems. *Toni Morrison*. Twayne, 1990.

Sanna, Ellyn. "Biography of Toni Morrison." *Toni Morrison*, edited by Harold Bloom, Chelsea, 2002, pp. 3–37.

Schapiro, Barbara. "The Bonds of Love and the Boundaries of Self in Toni Morrison's *Beloved*." *Contemporary Literature*, vol. 32, no. 2, 1991, pp. 194–210.

Scheiber, Andrew. "Blues Narratology and the African American Novel." *New Essays on the African American Novel*, edited by Lovalerie King and Linda F. Seltzer, Palgrave, 2008, pp. 33–49.

Schmudde, Carol E. "The Haunting of 124." *African American Review*, vol. 26, no. 3, 1992, pp. 409–16.

Schreiber, Evelyn Jaffe. *Race, Trauma, and Home in the Novels of Toni Morrison*. Louisiana State UP, 2010.

Schur, Richard L. "Locating *Paradise* in the Post-Civil Rights Era: Toni Morrison and Critical Race Theory." *Contemporary Literature*, vol. 45, no. 2, 2004, pp. 276–99.

Scruggs, Charles. *Sweet Home: Invisible Cities in the Afro-American Novel*. Johns Hopkins UP, 1993.

Segal, Lynne. *Slow-Motion: Changing Masculinities*. Virago, 1997.

Seward, Adrienne Lanier, and Justine Tally, editors. *Toni Morrison: Memory and Meaning*. U of Mississippi P, 2014.

Sharpe, Christina. *Monstrous Intimacies: Making Post-Slavery Subjects*. Duke UP, 2010.

Shea, Lisa. "Georgia on Her Mind." *Elle*, May 7, 2012, p. 236.

Sherman, Sarah Way. "Religion, The Body, and Consumer Culture in Toni Morrison's *The Bluest Eye*." *Religion in America*, edited by Hans Krabbendam and Derek Rubin, VU UP, 2004, pp. 143–56.

Showalter, Elaine. *A Jury of Her Peers: American Women Writers from Anne Bradstreet to Annie Proulx*. Knopf, 2009.

Sielke, Sabine. *Reading Rape*. Princeton UP, 2002.

Simpson, Ritashona. *Black Looks and Black Acts: The Language of Toni Morrison in The Bluest Eye and Beloved*. Peter Lang, 2007.

Skerrett, Joseph T., Jr. "Recitation to the Griot: Storytelling and Learning in Toni Morrison's *Song of Solomon*." *Conjuring: Black Women, Fiction, and Literary Tradition*. edited by Marjorie Pryse and Hortense J. Spillers. Indiana UP, 1985, pp. 192–202.

Sklar, Howard. "'What the Hell Happened to Maggie?': Stereotype, Sympathy, and Disability in Toni Morrison's 'Recitatif.'" *Journal of Literary and Cultural Disability Studies*, vol. 5, no. 2, 2011, pp. 137–54.

Slattery, Patrick. *The Wounded Body: Remembering the Markings of Flesh*. State U of New York P, 2000.

Smith, David Lionet. "What Is Black Culture?" *The House that Race Built*, edited by Wahneema Lubiano, Pantheon, 1997, pp. 178–94.

Smith, Denitia. "Toni Morrison's Mix of Tragedy, Domesticity and Folklore." *New York Times*, Jan. 8, 1998, pp. E1, E3.

Smith, Valerie. *Self-Discovery and Authority in Afro-American Narrative*. Harvard UP, 1987.

Smith, Valerie. *Toni Morrison: Writing the Moral Imagination*. Wiley-Blackwell, 2012.

Spallino, Chiara. "*Song of Solomon*: An Adventure in Structure." *Callaloo*, vol. 8, Fall 1985, pp. 510–24.

Spargo, Clifford R. "Trauma and the Specters of Enslavement in Morrison's *Beloved*." *Mosaic*, vol. 35, Mar. 2002, pp. 113–31.

Spaulding, A. Timothy. *Re-forming the Past: History, The Fantastic, and the Postmodern Slave Narrative*. Ohio State UP, 2005.

Spillers, Hortense J. "A Hateful Passion, A Lost Love." *Feminist Issues in Literary Scholarship*, edited by Shari Benstock, Indiana UP, 1987, pp. 181–207.

Spillers, Hortense J. "Mama's Baby, Papa's Maybe: An American Grammar Book." *African American Literary Theory: A Reader*, edited by Winston Napier, New York UP, 2000, pp. 257–79.

Stanley, Sondra Kumamoto. "Maggie in Toni Morrison's 'Recitatif,'" *MELUS*, vol. 36, no. 2, 2011, pp. 71–88.

Story, Ralph. "An Excursion into the Black World: The 'Seven Days' in Toni Morrison's *Song of Solomon*." *Black American Literature Forum*, vol. 23, no. 1, Spring 1989, pp. 149–58.

Steiner, Wendy. "The Clearest Eye: *Playing in the Dark*." *New York Times Book Review*, Apr. 5, 1992, p. 17.

Sudarkasa, Niara. *The Strength of Our Mothers: African and African American Women and Families*. Africa World P, 1996.

Sweeney, Megan. "'Something Rogue': Commensurability, Commodification, Crime, and Justice in Toni Morrison's Later Fiction." *Modern Fiction Studies*, vol. 52, no. 2, 2006, pp. 440–69.

Tal, Kali. *Worlds of Hurt: Reading the Literatures of Trauma*. Cambridge UP, 1996.

Tally, Justine. *Paradise Reconsidered: Toni Morrison's (Hi)stories and Truths*. LIT Verlag, 1999.

Tally, Justine. *The Story of Jazz: Toni Morrison's Dialogic Imagination*. LIT, 2001.

Tally, Justine. ed. *The Cambridge Companion to Toni Morrison*. Cambridge UP, 2007.

Taylor-Guthrie, Danille, ed. *Conversations with Toni Morrison*. UP of Mississippi, 1994.

Terry, Jennifer. "A New World Religion? Creolisation and Condomble in Toni Morrison's *Paradise*." *Complexions of Race: The African Atlantic*, edited by Fritz Gysin and Cynthia S. Hamilton. Lit Verlag, 2005, pp. 61–82.

Thompson, Lisa. *Beyond the Black Lady: Sexuality and the New African American Middle Class*. U of Illinois P, 2009.

Thurman, Judith. "A House Divided." *New Yorker*, Nov. 2, 1987, pp. 175–80.

Treherne, Matthew. "Figuring In, Figuring Out: Narration and Negotiation in Toni Morrison's *Jazz*." *Narrative*, vol. 11, no. 2, May 2003, pp. 199–212.

Troupe, Quincy, and Rainer Schulte, ed. *Giant Talk: An Anthology of Third World Writings*. Random House, 1975.

Turner, Darwin T. "Theme, Characterization, and Style in the Works of Toni Morrison." *Black Women Writers (1950–1980)*, edited by Mari Evans. Doubleday, 1984, pp. 361–9.

Updike, John. "Dreamy Wilderness." *New Yorker*, Nov. 3, 2008, pp. 112–13.

Van Sertina, Ivan. *They Came Before Columbus*. Random House, 1976.

Verdelle, A. J. *Miss Chloe: A Literary Friendship with Toni Morrison*. Harper, 2022.

Vickroy, Laurie. "The Politics of Abuse: The Traumatized Child in Toni Morrison and Marguerite Duras." *Mosaic: A Journal for the Interdisciplinary Study of Literature*, vol. 29, no. 2, 1996, pp. 91–109.

Vickroy, Laurie. *Trauma and Survival in Contemporary Fiction*. U of Virginia P, 2002.

Vrettos, Athena. "Curative Domains: Women, Healing and History in Black Women's Narratives." *Women's Studies*, vol. 16, Oct. 1989, pp. 455–74.

Wade-Gayles, Gloria. "The Truths of Our Mothers' Lives: Mother-Daughter Relationships in Black Women's Fiction." *Sage*, vol. 1, Fall 1984, pp. 8–12.

Waegner, Cathy Covell. "Ruthless Epic Footsteps: Shoes, Migrants, and the Settlement of the Americas in Toni Morrison's *A Mercy*." *Post-National Enquiries: Essays on Ethnic and Racial Border Crossings*, edited by Jopi Nyman. Cambridge Scholars P, 2009, pp. 91–112.

Wagner-Martin, Linda. "'Closer to the Edge': Toni Morrison's *Song of Solomon*." *Teaching American Ethnic Literatures: Nineteen Essays*, edited by John Maitino and David Peck. U of New Mexico P, 1996, pp. 147–57.

Wagner-Martin, Linda. *A History of American Literature from 1950 to the Present*. Wiley-Blackwell, 2013.

Wagner-Martin, Linda. *The Routledge Introduction to American Postmodernism*. Routledge, 2019.

Wagner-Martin, Linda. "Teaching *The Bluest Eye*." *ADE Bulletin* (MLA), vol. 83, Spring 1986, pp. 28–31.

Wagner-Martin, Linda. *Telling Women's Lives, The New Biography*. Rutgers UP, 1994.

Wagner-Martin, Linda. *Toni Morrison and the Maternal, From The Bluest Eye to Home*. Peter Lang, 2014.

Wagner-Martin, Linda. *Toni Morrison and the Maternal, From The Bluest Eye to God Help the Child*. 2nd ed. Peter Lang, 2019.

Wagner-Martin, Linda. *Toni Morrison, A Literary Life*. Palgrave Macmillan, 2015.

Wagner-Martin, Linda. "Toni Morrison's Mastery." *Narrative Technique in the Writing of Contemporary American Women*, edited by Catherine Rainwater and William J. Scheick. UP of Kentucky, 1985, pp. 191–205.

Walker, Alice. *In Search of Our Mothers' Gardens*. Harcourt Brace Jovanovich, 1983.

Walker, Melissa. *Down from the Mountaintop: Black Women's Novels in the Wake of the Civil Rights Movement, 1966–1989*. Yale UP, 1991.

Wall, Cheryl A. "Toni Morrison: Editor and Teacher." *The Cambridge Companion to Toni Morrison*, edited by Justine Tally. Cambridge UP, 2007, pp. 139–50.

Wall, Cheryl A. "Trying to Get Home: Place and Memory in Toni Morrison's Fiction." *Toni Morrison: Memory and Meaning*. edited by Adrienne Lanier Seward and Justine Tally. UP of Mississippi, 2014, pp. 53–65.

Wall, Cheryl A. *Worrying the Line: Black Women Writers, Lineage, and Literary Tradition*. U of North Carolina P, 2005.

Wallace, Kathleen R., and Karla Armbruster. "The Novels of Toni Morrison: Wild Wilderness Where There was None." *Beyond Nature Writing: Expanding the Boundaries of Ecocriticism*, edited by Kathleen R. Wallace and Karla Armbruster, U of Virginia P, 1997, pp. 211–30.

Wallace, Maurice. "Print, Prosthesis, Impersonation: Toni Morrison's *Jazz* and the Limits of American Literary History." *American Literary History*, vol. 20, no. 4, Winter 2008, pp. 794–806.

Wallace, Michelle. *Black Macho and the Myth of the Superwoman*. John Calder, 1978.

Wanzo, Rebecca. *The Suffering Will Not Be Televised: African American Women and Sentimental Political Storytelling*. State U of New York P, 2009.

Wardi, Anissa Janine. "A Laying On of Hands: Toni Morrison and the Materiality of Love." *MELUS*, vol. 30, no. 3, 2005, pp. 201–18.

Wardi, Anissa Janine. *Water and African American Memory*. U of Florida P, 2011.

Warner, Anne Bradford. "New Myths and Ancient Properties: The Fiction of Toni Morrison." *Hollins Critic*, June 1988, pp. 1–11.

Warrren, Kenneth W. *What Was African American Literature?* Harvard UP, 2011.

Washington, Teresa N. *Our Mothers, Our Powers, Our Texts: Manifestations of Aje in Africana Literature*. Indiana UP, 2005.

Wegs, Joyce. "Toni Morrison's *Song of Solomon*: A Blues Song." *Essays in Literature*, vol. 9, 1982, pp. 211–23.

Weinstein, Arnold. *Nobody's Home: Speech, Self, and Place in American Fiction from Hawthorne to De Lillo*. Oxford UP, 1993.

Wen-Ching, Ho. "'I'll Tell'—The Function and Meaning of L in Toni Morrison's *Love*." *EurAmerica*, vol. 36, no. 4, 2006, pp. 651–75.

Werner, Craig Hansen. *Playing the Changes: From Afro-Modernism to the Jazz Impulse*. U of Illinois P, 1994.

Wester, Maisha L. *African American Gothic, Screams from Shadowed Places*. Palgrave, 2012.

White, E. Frances. "The Evidence of things Not Seen: The Alchemy of Race and Sexuality." *James Baldwin and Toni Morrison: Comparative Critical and Theoretical Essays*, edited by Lovalerie King and Lynn Orilla Scott, Palgrave Macmillan, 2006, pp. 239–60.

Widdowson, Peter. "The American Dream Refashioned: History, Politics and Gender in Toni Morrison's *Paradise*." *Journal of American Studies*, vol. 35, no. 2, 2001, pp. 313–35.

Wilentz, Gay. "An African-Based Reading of *Sula*." *Approaches to Teaching the Novels of Toni Morrison*, edited by Nellie McKay and Kathryn Earle. MLA, 1997, pp. 127–34.

Wilentz, Gay. "Civilizations Underneath: African Heritage as Cultural Discourse in Toni Morrison's *Song of Solomon*." *Toni Morrison's Fiction, Contemporary Criticism*, edited by David L. Middleton, Garland, 2000, pp. 109–33.

Wilentz, Gay. *Healing Narratives, Women Writers Curing Cultural Dis-Ease*. Rutgers UP, 2000.

Williams, Dana A. "Dancing Minds and Plays in the Dark: Intersections of Fiction and Critical Texts in Gayle Jones's *Corregidora*, Toni Cade Bambara's *The Salt Eaters*, and Toni Morrison's *Paradise*." *New Essays in the African American Novel*, edited by Lovalerie King and Linda F. Seltzer, Palgrave, 2008, pp. 93–106.

Williams, Dana A. *In the Light of Likeness—Transformed: The Literary Art of Leon Forrest*. Ohio State UP, 2005.

Williams, Lisa. *The Artist as Outsider in the Novels of Toni Morrison and Virginia Woolf*. Greenwood, 2000.

Williams-Forson, Psyche. *Building Houses out of Chicken Legs: Black Women, Food, and Power*. U of North Carolina P, 2006.

Williamson, Jennifer. *Twentieth-Century Sentimentalism: Narrative Appropriation in American Literature*. Rutgers UP, 2013.

Willis, Susan. "Eruptions of Funk: Historicizing Toni Morrison." *Black American Literature Forum*, vol. 16, no. 1, 1982, pp. 34–42.

Willis, Susan. *Specifying: Black Women Writing the American Experience*. U of Wisconsin P, 1986.

Wisker, Gina. "Remembering and Disremembering *Beloved*: Lacunae and Hauntings." *Reassessing the Twentieth-Century Canon*, edited by Nicola Allen and David Simmons. Palgrave Macmillan, 2014, pp. 266–80.

Wisker, Gina. *Toni Morrison: A Beginner's Guide*. Hodder, 2002.

Wolfe, Joanna. "'Ten Minutes for Seven Letters': Song as Key to Narrative Revision in Toni Morrison's *Beloved*." *Narrative*, vol. 12, no. 3, 2004, pp. 263–80.

Wolff, Cynthia Griffin. "'Margaret Garner': A Cincinnati Story." *Massachusetts Review*, vol. 32, 1991, pp. 417–40.

Wood, Michael. "Sensations of Loss." *Aesthetics of Toni Morrison*, edited by Marc C. Conner, UP of Mississippi, 2000, pp. 113–24.

Woodward, Kathleen. "Traumatic Shame: Toni Morrison, Televisual Culture, and the Cultural Politics of the Emotions." *Cultural Critique*, vol. 46, 2000, pp. 210–40.

Woolf, Virginia. *Mrs. Dalloway*. Chatto, 1925.

Worden, Daniel. *Masculine Style: The American West and Literary Modernism*. Palgrave, 2011.

Wyatt, Jean. "Giving Body to the Word: The Maternal Symbolic in Toni Morrison's *Beloved*." *PMLA*, vol. 108, 1993, pp. 474–88.

Wyatt, Jean. "*Love*'s Time and the Reader: Ethical Effects of Nachtraglichkeit in Toni Morrison's *Love*." *Narrative*, vol. 16, no. 2, May 2008, pp. 193–221.

Wyatt, Jean. *Risking Difference: Identification, Race, and Community in Contemporary Fiction and Feminism*. State U of New York P, 2004.
Yalom, Marilyn. *Maternity, Mortality, and the Literature of Madness*. Pennsylvania State UP, 1985.
Yardley, Jonathan. "Toni Morrison and the Prize Fight." *The Washington Post*. Jan. 25, 1988. Final ed., p. C2.
Yeager, Patricia. *Dirt and Desire: Reconstructing Southern Women's Writing, 1930–1990*. U of Chicago P, 2000.
Yohe, Kristine. "Enslaved Women's Resistance and Survival Strategies in Frances Ellen Watkins Harper's 'The Slave Mother: A Tale of Ohio' and Toni Morrison's Beloved and Margaret Garner." *Gendered Resistance: Women, Slavery, and the Legacy of Margaret Garner*, edited by Mary E. Frederickson and Delores M. Walters, U of Illinois P, 2013, pp. 99–114.
Young, John K. *Black Writers, White Publishers: Marketplace Politics in Twentieth-Century African American Literature*. UP of Mississippi, 2006.
Yukins, Elizabeth. "Bastard Daughters and the Possession of History in *Corregidora* and *Paradise*." *Signs*, vol. 28, no. 1, 2002, pp. 221–47.
Zauditu-Selasse, Kokahvah. *African Spiritual Traditions in the Novels of Toni Morrison*. UP of Florida, 2009.

ONLINE SOURCES

The Toni Morrison Society online news and bibliography: www.tonimorrisonsociety.org

CONTRIBUTORS

Justine Baillie specializes in contemporary and postcolonial theory, women's writing, the international novel, and African American literature. She is the author of *Toni Morrison and Literary Tradition*. She has published on Faulkner's *Go Down, Moses*, Kazuo Isheguro's *A Pale View of Hills*, and Caryl Phillips's *Crossing the River* and *Three English Lives*. In 2020, Baillie edited *Global Morrison*, a special issue of *Contemporary Women's Writing*. In 2015, Baillie took up a visiting professorship in women's writing at Université Paris 8, Vincennes-Saint-Denis; she has subsequently been writing a monograph, *Transnational Paris*.

Corinne Bancroft is Visiting Assistant Professor of English at the University of Victoria. Trained at Hamilton University and the University of California at San Diego, she has published in various academic journals, *Narrative* among them.

Janine Bradbury is senior lecturer in literature at the University of York, UK. She specializes in representations of passing for white in modern and contemporary African American women's writing. In 2022, Palgrave will publish her book *Contemporary African American Women Writers and Passing*.

Keith Clark is professor of English and African American Literature at George Mason University. Among his recent books are *The Radical Fiction of Ann Petry, Black Manhood in James Baldwin, Ernest J. Gaines, and August Wilson*, and *Navigating the Fiction of Ernest J. Gaines: A Roadmap for Readers*.

James A. Crank, Associate Professor of Literature at University of Alabama, is a Bogliasco and National Humanities Center fellow. He cohosts the podcast *The Sound and the Furious*. Among his books are *Understanding Sam Shepard*, *Race and New Modernisms*, and an essay collection, *New Approaches to Gone with the Wind*. Forthcoming are *Understanding Randall Kenan* and *The Dirty South: Region, Refuse, Representation, 1970–2020*.

Kirk Curnutt is professor of English and Chair of the Department of English at Troy University. Most recently, he coedited *The New Hemingway Studies* with Suzanne del Gizzo and edited *All of the Belles: The Montgomery Stories of F. Scott Fitzgerald*. He also recently edited *American Literature in Transition: 1970–1980*.

Jameela F. Dallis is an independent scholar, poet, arts writer, and content strategist. Her publications include poetry, interviews, and scholarly book chapters. She received her PhD in English from the University of North Carolina, Chapel Hill.

Thadious M. Davis is Geraldine R. Segal Professor of American Social Thought, Emerita and Professor of English at the University of Pennsylvania. She is the author or editor of thirteen books, including *Southscapes: Geographies of Race, Region, and Literature*; *Nella Larsen: Novelist of the Harlem Renaissance*; *Understanding Alice Walker*; and *Faulkner's "Negro": Art and the Southern Context*.

Marc K. Dudley is professor of English at North Carolina State University. His recent books include *Bloodlines and the Color Line: Hemingway, Race, and Art*; *Understanding James Baldwin*; and the edited collection, *Teaching Hemingway and Film*.

Thomas Fahy, professor of English and director of graduate studies at Long Island University Post, has published numerous books, among them *Dining with Madmen: Fat, Food, and the Environment in 1980s Horror*; monographs on both Truman Capote and Tracy Letts; and a number of edited collections such as *The Philosophy of Horror* and *Peering Behind the Curtain: Disability, Illness, and the Extraordinary Body in Contemporary Theatre*. He has also published three novels.

Leslie Elaine Frost is Teaching Associate Professor in English at the University of North Carolina, Chapel Hill. She is the author of *Dreaming America: Popular Front Ideas and Aesthetics of Children's Plays of the Federal Theatre Project*. She is currently studying a range of New Deal graphic arts projects.

Gurleen Grewal is Associate Professor of Literature at the University of South Florida, Tampa. Her fields of specialization are Global Contemporary Women Writers, and her current research is in contemplative poetics and philosophical themes in literature. Her postcolonial feminist book *Circles of Sorrow/Lines of Struggle: The Novels of Toni Morrison* won the Toni Morrison Society Book Award.

Kristina K. Groover is professor of English at Appalachian State University. She has published *The Wilderness Within: American Women Writers and Spiritual Quest* as well as *Religion, Secularism, and the Spiritual Paths of Virginia Woolf*. She has also edited *Things of the Spirit: Women Writers Constructing Spirituality*.

Trudier Harris is University Distinguished Research Professor at University of Alabama. She has lectured throughout the world. Among her twenty-six book publications are *The Scary Mason-Dixon Line: African American Writers and the South* (2009) and *Martin Luther King, Jr., Heroism, and African American Literature* (2014).

Jennifer Haytock is professor of English at the State University of New York, Brockport. Among her books are *At Home, At War: Domesticity and World War I in American Literature*, *The Routledge Introduction to American War Literature*, and *Edith Wharton and the Conversations of Literary Modernism*. Her most recent edited collection is *War and American Literature*.

Janie Hinds is professor of English and Director of Liberal Studies at the State University of New York, Brockport. She is the author of *Private Property: Charles Brockden Brown's Gendered Economics of Virtue* and *The Multiple Worlds of Pynchon's "Mason & Dixon": Eighteenth Century*

Contexts, Postmodern Observations as well as articles on Olaudah Equiano, Charles Willson Peale, Benjamin Rush, and Edgar Allan Poe.

David H. Krause, Professor Emeritus of English at Dominican University, holds a PhD from Yale. Among his publications are a trilogy of essays about reading Faulkner's *Absalom, Absalom!*

Jennifer Larson teaches film, literature, and composition at the University of North Carolina, Chapel Hill. She is the author of *Understanding Walter Mosley* (2016) and *Understanding Suzan-Lori Parks* (2012). She has published as well in such academic quarterlies as *Women's Studies* and *South Carolina Review*.

Christopher S. Lewis is Director of the Office of Nationally Competitive Awards at Ohio University. With a PhD from the Ohio State University, he has taught at Western Kentucky University and Franklin and Marshall College, specializing in African American literature and queer studies. He has published in *Arizona Quarterly*, *College Literature*, *MELUS*, and other quarterlies.

Derek C. Maus, professor of English at the State University of New York, Potsdam, writes widely on recent African American literature. He is the author of *Understanding Colson Whitehead* (and its expanded edition) as well as a monograph on Percival Everett. He has edited *Conversations with Colson Whitehead* and *Post-Soul Satire*. He also publishes widely on twentieth-century Russian and US satire.

Deborah E. McDowell is Alice Griffin Professor of Literary Studies and former director of the Carter G. Woodson Institute at the University of Virginia, Charlottesville. Her publications include *"The Changing Game": Studies in Fiction by African-American Women* and *Leaving Pipe Shop: Memories of Kin* as well as numerous essays, book chapters, and scholarly editions. She is coeditor (with Claudrena Harold and Juan Battle) of *The Punitive Turn: Race, Inequality, and Mass Incarceration*. Extensively immersed in the study of African American literature, she founded the African American Women Writers Series for Beacon Press and served as its editor from 1985 to 1993. This project oversaw the publication of many works from both the nineteenth and twentieth centuries. She served as project editor for the *Norton Anthology of African-American Literature*, now in its third edition. Currently the principal investigator for the Julian Bond Papers Project, she has been the recipient of such grants as the Mary Ingraham Bunting Fellowship, the National Research Council Fellowship of the Ford Center, and others.

Marijana Mikić is completing her doctorate at the University of Klagenfurt, Austria. She is coeditor of *Ethnic American Literatures and Critical Race Narratology*, forthcoming from Routledge. She focuses on Brit Bennett, N. K. Jemisin, Bryan Washington, Kaitlyn Greenidge, and others.

Michael Nowlin is professor of English at the University of Victoria. Among his recent books are *Literary Ambition and the African American Novel* (2019), *Richard Wright in Context* (2021), and *The Cambridge Companion to F. Scott Fitzgerald*, second edition (2021).

Kelly L. Reames is professor of English at Western Kentucky University. Among her publications are *Women and Race in Contemporary U.S. Writing: From Faulkner to Morrison* and a monograph in the Continuum Books series on *Paradise*. She is coeditor of both the Palgrave *Navigating Women's Friendships in American Literature and Culture* and this collection.

Catherine Seltzer is professor of English at Southern Illinois University, Edwardsville. She is the author of *Elizabeth Spencer's Complicated Cartographies: Reimagining Home, the South, and Southern Literary Production* and *Understanding Pat Conroy*. She is completing a biography of Conroy presently.

Andrew Scheiber is professor of English and Chair of the Department at the University of St. Thomas in St. Paul, Minnesota, where he teaches American literature, theory, and writing. He has published widely on Henry James, Nathaniel Hawthorne, Roland Barthes, Walter Mosley, August Wilson, and Toni Morrison: his areas are nineteenth- and twentieth-century literature. His current research focuses on the relationships between jazz and blues to literary and pedagogical practice.

Linda Wagner-Martin is Frank Borden Hanes Professor of English and Comparative Literature Emerita, the University of North Carolina, Chapel Hill. She has received the Hubbell Medal for service to American literature. Among her recent books are *Hemingway's Wars: The Public and Private Battles*, *The Routledge Introduction to American Postmodernism*, *Walt Whitman, A Literary Life*, and *The Life of the Author: Maya Angelou*.

Kristine Yohe is associate professor of English at Northern Kentucky University where she specializes in African American literature and culture, specifically on Toni Morrison, Frank X. Walker, and Affrilachian poetry. She directed the Toni Morrison Society's biennial conference, which premiered the opera *Margaret Garner*. She publishes regularly on history, Morrison, and Walker.

INDEX

Abednego 345
Abel, Elizabeth 353, 354 n.1, 337 n.4
abolitionists 167, 214–15
Adams, Elizabeth 235 n.8
Adler, J. S. 200
Aeschylus 300
Aesop's Fables 268
African American culture xv, 16, 47–58, 59–67, 169, 178, 206–10, 267–8, 331
    family 21, 23–5, 82, 169, 172–3
    history of 59–71, 80–2, 92–3
    language (Orality) 84, 92–3, 101–3, 331, 343–4, 375–8
    religious belief 24–5, 55–7, 169–74
African American literature 32 n.1, 33 n.2, 75 n.1, 101–3, 125–6, 144, 175, 297, 343
African philosophy and culture 79–83, 168–9, 174, 207–9, 290, 336
    oral narratives 375–6
    witchcraft (*see also* ghosts) 174, 319–20
Afro-Pessimism 101–21
Afrophobia 108
Alabama Memorial Preservation Act 187
Alexander, Allen 36 n.7
Alexander, Phoenix 282
Ali, Muhammad 217, 345
Allais, Lucy 208 n.10, 208 n.11
Allen, James 186 n.6
Als, Hilton xiii, 249, 251 n.5
American Beach 128–9
American individualism 261–75
American literature 86, 236–7, 296, 301–4, 319–20
ancestors xi, 75 n.1, 78–9, 87, 126–7, 155–66, 173–4
ancient properties 76, 80, 173–4
Anderson, Sherwood 227–8
Andres, Emmanuelle 148
Andrews, William 31 n.1
Anglocentrism 25, 37, 108
anti-hero 347–8
Anzaldua, Gloria 16–18, 27
Apel, Dora 192–3
Asbill, Lisa 339

Ashcroft, Bill 82–3
Aubry, Timothy 255 n.6
Austen, Jane 134
Avery, Faith 76
Awkward, Michael 27 n.9
Azaryahu, Maoz 24

Bacon, Jaqueline 192 n.18
Bahktin, Mikhail 98
Bailey's Café 144
Baker, Gregg 223–4
Baker, Houston A., Jr. 162–3
Balaev, Michelle 309
Baldwin, James xv, 108, 108 n.4, 144, 153, 155–6, 173, 178, 230–6, 336–8, 340, 353 n.1
Balon, Rebecca 279
Bambara, Toni Cade xii, 17 n.3, 155, 217
Baraka, Amiri 344
Bassard, Katherine 185 n.4
Bast, Florian 185 n.5
Bay, Mia 267
Beaulieu, Elizabeth Ann 34 n.3
Beavers, Herman 263, 267, 281, 287
Beckett, Samuel 295
Beiles, Sinclair 151
Bellow, Saul 296
Beloved (film) 91–9, 239 n.12, 251–2
Bench-by-the-Road Project 167, 224, 253–4
Benjamin, Shanna 253
Benjamin, Walter 81
Bennett, Brit 158 n.4, 277–92
Bennett, Juda 160, 163–4, 278
Benson, Alan 191, 223
Bhabha, Homi K. 77–8
Bhagavad Gita 168
Bible 145 n.6, 169, 175–7, 191, 268, 281, 321, 339, 345
Biles, Simone 57–8
Black Arts Movement 343–8
Blackburn, Sara 340
*BlackGirlMagic 47–8
Black Lives Matter 102, 197, 343–4, 349, 352

Black Madonna 171, 178
Blackmon, Douglas 364
Blackwell, Deanne 308 n.1
Blascoer, Frances 200
blues narrative 17, 26 n.8, 178
body 83, 93–4, 98, 102–5, 157, 171, 173, 185–6, 190, 266, 269–70, 273, 284–5, 290, 311, 371
Borges, Jorge Luis 167
Botting, Fred 125
Bouson, J. Brooks 75 n.1, 314
Braddock, Jeremy 79
Brady, Matthew 216
braided narratives 16, 21–2, 24–5, 29
Braithwaite, John 201, 203, 207 n.9
Brenkman, John 160
broadcast strategic empathy 277–9
Brockes, Emma 142, 262, 280
Brodsky, Claudia 142, 246–7
Brogan, Kathleen 164
Bronte, Emily 132 n.10
Brooks, Gwendolyn 31, 39–40, 309 n.3, 344, 364 n.1
Brown v. Board of Education 64, 143, 268
Brown, Angela 223–4
Brown, David C. 324 n.3
Brown, Michael, Jr. 352
Brown, William Wells 116 n.10, 158
Budig, George 224
Buinines, Ruth Wade Cox 223–4, 252
Bump, Jerone 27 n.9
bussing 360
Butler, Judith 185–6, 188, 193
Butler, Octavia E. 278, 282, 291
Butler-Evans, Elliott 75 n.1
Byerman, Keith 75 n.1, 280

Callendar, Kacen 277 n.1
Candomble 171, 172
Canevello, Amy 337
Canon wars 297, 300
Caribbean in Morrison's fiction 76–7, 125
Carroll, Charles 116 n.10
Carter, Angela 117
Caruth, Cathy 308–9, 131 n.1
Castro, A. J. 334
Cather, Willa 60, 250, 296
Cavell, Stanley xiii
Celine, Louis-Ferdinand 296
Cesaire, Aime 113
Chapelle, Dave 354 n.2
Charles, Pam 142
Chase, Larry 129
Chauvin, Derek 208

Chavers, Linda 47–8
Chesnutt, Charles 33 n.2, 116 n.10, 158
Chopin, Kate 156
Christie, Angela 99
Christian, Barbara 228 n.1, 233 n.6
Christianity 85, 167–80, 185, 272
Churchwell, Sarah 142
cisgender 284
civil rights 59–63, 70, 79, 84, 125, 143, 187 n.9, 230, 262, 310, 349
Civil Rights Act 60, 64–5, 72, 129
Civil War 70, 116, 188, 191, 217, 221, 223, 240, 307
Clarke, Maxine Beneba 256
Clark, P. Djeli 277 n.1
class 18, 31, 53, 84, 174, 278, 323, 359
Cleage, Pearl 31, 33 n.2
Clough, Patricia Ticimeto 55
Coates, Ta-Nehisi 181, 188, 190 n.17, 190, 337
Coleman, James 185
collaboration 314
Collins, Addie Mae 104 n.1
colorism 101–21, 155–6, 159, 283
Comas-Dias, Lillian 311
Combahee River Collective 16–17
community 16, 21, 27, 29, 43, 56, 70, 105, 146, 149, 155, 160, 164, 185, 198, 202, 209, 222, 228, 272–3, 280, 285, 313–14, 344, 351, 375–6
communism 65, 144, 151, 271–2
Confederacy 187, 187 n.9
Conner, Marc 296
Connerton, Paul 188
Conrad, Joseph 336
Cornell University xi, xii, 178, 231, 233–4, 252
Coronavirus pandemic 252
Coverley, Merlin 159, 163
Crane, Hart 250
Crenshaw, Kimberle Williams 15–19, 27
criminal justice 197–211
critical race theory xv, 15–17, 23, 245 n.2, 300
Crocker, Jennifer 337
Cruz, Celia 285
cults 320
Cummings, Pip 174–5
Cunningham, Y. L. 334
Curran, Thomas 333–4
Czaykowska-Higgins, Ewa 19 n.4

Dalsgard, Katrine 321
Danielpour, Richard 220–1, 252
Dante Alighieri 228, 253
Davis, Angela 217
Davis, Christine 48

Davis, Jefferson 187
Dawkins, Richard 256
Day, Doris 262
Demeter 168–9, 171, 173
Demme, Jonathan 98–9, 239 n.12, 251
Desdemona 117 n.11, 174–5, 228
diaspora 75–89, 171, 178
Dickens, Charles 192
Dimock, Wai Chee 201–2
disallowing 325
Django Unchained 365
Dobzhansky, Theodosius 312
Dostoyevsky, Feodor 228, 301
Douglass, Frederick 25–6, 103, 110–11, 152–3, 309, 331–2, 338, 345, 353 n.1, 365, 337–8, 345
dreams 161, 301–2
Dred Scott Decision 103, 189
Du Bois, W. E. B. 67–8, 153, 173, 246, 297, 309 n.3, 337–8, 345
Dumas, Henry 217
Dunbar, Paul Lawrence 249
Dunn, L. C. 312
Duras, Marguerite 297
Duvall, John N. 230 n.4
DuVerney, Ava 256
Dyer, Richard 332

eating disorders 288
Eburne, Jonathan P. 79
Eisgruber, Stephen L. 253
Elam, Michele 158
Elechi, Oko O. 208
Eleusinian Mysteries 172–3
Eleusis 168
Eliot, T. S. 295–6
Elliott, Kamilla 134, 136
Ellison, Ralph 41–2, 106 n.2, 144, 148, 153, 155, 296–7, 344, 363–4, 363, 366–8, 370, 373, 376
Emezi, Akwaeke 277–92
epistemology 75–89
Equal Justice Initiatives 183–96, 246
Equiano, Olaudel 331
eros 171–2
eugenics 312, 370–2
eve 171

Fabre, Michel 145–6
Facebook 47, 256
Fanon, Franz 101–2, 113
Father Knows Best 262
Faulkner, William 128, 134, 173, 227–43, 246, 295, 299–300

feminism 17–18, 75–89, 170–1, 174, 179, 261–3, 351
Ferguson, Rebecca 92, 97
Field of Dreams 251
Flaubert, Gustav 295–6, 301
Flint, Holly 108 n.3
Floyd, George 152, 197, 209, 352
foregrounding 91–9
Forrest, Leon 217
Foucault, Michel 199, 202, 255
Fowler, Roger 91–9
Franchot, Jenny 110 n.5
fratricide 84
Freud, Sigmund 311
Friedman, Edward 27 n.9
Froio, Nicole 354 n.2
Fry, Gladys-Marie 125
Fugitive Slave Law 189, 214, 216–17
Furman, Jan 36 n.7

Gaines, Ernest 33 n.2
gar girls 355, 361
Garner, Eric 352
Garner, Margaret 105, 167, 213–26, 239, 252
Gass, William 118
Gates, Henry Louis, Jr. 156 n.3
Gauthier, Marni 321, 325
Gelfand, Janelle 220
gender identity 15, 83, 277–8
Gerieault, Theodore 82, 87
ghosts 54–7, 92, 124, 37, 148–9, 164, 178, 193, 313–14
GI Bill 270
Gilroy, Paul 80–2
Giovanni, Nikki 347
Glidden, George 116 n.10
Goddu, Teresa A. 125–6
Goldstein-Shirley, David 354 n.3
Gordimer, Nadine 303
Gorra, Michael 241 n.11
gospel 17, 25–6, 170
Gothic 123–40, 319–29
Goulimari, Pelagia 75 n.1
Goyal, Yogita 76, 83
Grant, Madison 116 n.10, 312
Grant, Robert 61
Gras, Delphine 159, 161, 164
Grattan, Sean 118
Graves, Denyce 224
Green, Misha 158 n.4
Green, Victor 267
The Green Book 141, 267, 280
Greene, J. Lee 116 n.10

Greenfield-Sanders, Timothy 245, 251, 331
Greenidge, Kaitlyn 277–92
Grewal, Gurleen 25
Griffin, Farah Jasmine 157
Grinnell College 253
Gulf of Tonkin Resolution 64
Gussow, Adam 206 n.8

Haggard, H. Rider 336
Haggerty, George 131
Hairston, Andrea 277 n.1
Hakemuler, Jemelian 98
Haley, Alex 162
Hall, Gordon Nagayama 311
Hall, Rebecca 158 n.4
Hamlet 228
Hannaham, James 277 n.1
Hansberry v. Lee 271
Hansberry, Lorraine 270–1
Harack, Katrine 372 n.10
Harlem 108 n.4, 197, 200
"Harlem" 270
Harlem Renaissance 62, 115, 297
Harlow, Jean 178
Harper, Frances Ellen Watkins 216
Harris, Kamala 257
Harris, Middleton 214, 217
Harris, Trudier 34 n.3, 76 n.2
Hartman, Saidiya 78, 110, 112, 160, 213
Hasian, Marouf 189 n.14
Hawthorne, Nathaniel 40, 296, 300
Heffernan, Teresa 92–3, 99
Heise-von der Lippe, Anya 126, 133
Hemingway, Ernest 246, 296, 300, 313
Herman, David 279 n.4
Herman, Judith 309, 315
Hesera, Cynthia 167–8
Hill, Andrew P. 333–4
Hoffman, Martin L. 279, 281
Hogan, Patrick Colm 277 n.2, 279
home 83–8
Homer 253
homophobia 279
Hooks, Bell 334, 347 n.6
Hoover, J. Edgar 65
Horan, Katy 174
horses 147, 266, 273, 311, 313, 364, 376
Howard University xii, 178, 234, 248
Hudson, Pam 123, 138
Hughes, Langston 246, 250, 270, 297
Hull, Gloria T. 17
humor 227, 375–6

Hurston, Zora Neale 109–10, 118, 155 n.1, 250, 297
Hyman, Ramone 44 n.11

"I am the mainstream" 256
IBM 359
imagination 160–1, 167–80, 218, 227
incest 22, 28, 133, 139 n.15
infanticide 104
Instagram 47
intersectionality 15–22, 25–7, 277–93
Irwin, Alexander 171

Jackson, Andrew 227
Jackson, Chuck 61
Jacobs, Harriett 365
James, Henry 295, 103–4, 301, 331
James, Joy 155 n.1, 164
Jazz 206–9, 263
Jefferson, Thomas 102–3, 109–10, 116–17
Jemisin, N. K. 277 n.1
Jenkins, Candice 114 n.9
Jennings, La Vinia 223
Jesser, Nancy 146
Jewett, Chad 206 n.8
Jim Crow 59–61, 63, 66–7, 102, 107–8, 114, 142, 184, 197, 279, 281, 297, 364
Johns, Michael 248
Johnson, James Weldon (poet) 153, 158, 246
Johnson, James Weldon (Journalist) 62
Johnson, President Lyndon Baines 64–7, 71
Jones, Edward P. 145
Jones, Gayl xii, 217
Jones, Kimberly 152
Jordan, June 217
Joyce, James 295–7
justice 197–208

Kachka, Boris 245–6, 251 n.5
Kali 177–8
Kang, K. T. 334
Keen, Susan 278, 281
Keene, Jennifer D. 63
"Keep the Homefires Burning" 141
Kenan, Randall 128 n.6
Kendi, Ibram X. 334
Khayati, Abdellatif 97
King, Martin Luther, Jr. 17 n.3, 64, 71, 85, 187 n.9, 310
King, Rodney 197
King, Shannon 199
Kington, Raynard 253
Kinsey, David 177

Kitaiskaia, Taisia 174
Klay, Phil 315
Knadler, Stepherd 203
Knauer, Christine 63–4
Korean War 141–54, 213, 261–75, 279, 309, 369–74
Krumholz, Linda J. 321 n.1
Ku Klux Klan 126, 335, 364

Laborly, Claire 224
Lacks, Henrietta 269, 312
Larkin, Ernest E. 176–7
Larsen, Nella 156–7, 158 n.4
Leary, Mark 339
Leder, Drew 186
Ledoux, Ellen Malenas 130
Lee, Rachel 93, 97–8
Lee, Spike xii
Lee, Stagger 346
Legacy Museum 183–96
Lenski, Lois 250
Leonard, John 142
Lepore, Jill 197 n.1
lesbianism 17–18, 61
Levittown, Pennsylvania 270–2
Lewis, Sinclair 249
Li, Stephanie 151, 249, 251
life-forms 170–1
Lin, Maya 184
Lipsitz, George 279, 283, 285
listicles 257
literary generosity 295–305
Litz, Brett 309, 315
Locke, Jean 267
Locke, John 267
Loraine, Ohio 37, 42, 49, 178, 213, 247–9
Luckhurst, Roger 310 n.4
Lucks, Daniel S. 63–4, 71
Lucy, Autherine 231
lynching 32, 61, 66–8, 184–6, 234, 372
The Lynching Museum. *See* The National Memorial for Peace and Justice

Mad Men 142, 262
madness. *See* trauma
magic 47–8, 125
magical realism 48, 267, 328
Mailer, Norman 296
Malcolm X 345
Mallarme, Stephane 295
Malgren, Carl D. 22 n.6
Maltz, Albert 271
Mandel, Naomi 91–2, 97

Mandingo 365
Mark Twain 229, 296, 300, 302
Marshall, Brenda K. 159
Marshall, Thurgood 271
Martin, Trayvon 152
masculinity 67, 84, 133, 144–5, 147–8, 173–4, 263, 273, 372
M*A*S*H 144, 149 n.8
Mather, Cotton 319–29
Mayberry, Susan Neal 133
Maynard, Jessie 267
McAuliffe, Terry 245 n.2
McCarthy, Joseph 142, 271
McCartney, Stella 354 n.2
McDowell, Deborah 71–2
McKay, Claude 62, 376
McKee, Jessica 203 n.7
McNair, Denise 104
Melville, Herman 296, 300, 302
meme 256–7
memoir 266–7
memory 82, 146, 184–6, 266–7, 279, 311, 313, 325–6, 351, 371–2
memorialization 183–96, 208, 246, 254, 257, 371
Meredith, James 232
Meshach 356
Middle Passage 17 n.3, 81–2, 87, 92, 94
Midler, Bette 285
Miller, Nancy 255
Milton, John 297
Mitchell, Karitha 308
Mobley, Marilyn Sanders 75 n.1
modernism 82, 86, 261–75, 296
Money, Mississippi 261
Montgomery, Alabama 183–96
Montgomery, Maxine Lavon 161–3, 372 n.9
Moore, Marianne 295
Moraga, Cherrie 16–18, 27
Morgan, Piers 58
Morrison, Chloe 169, 172, 178
Morrison, Harold (son) 251
Morrison, Kevin Slade (son) 168
Morrison, Toni
    aesthetics xiii, xv, 16–18, 21, 31–2, 91–8, 123–4, 156, 175, 198–200, 227–43, 261–75, 375–8
    as African American woman writer 178, 299, 301
    birth of xi, 169
    as Catholic 169
    childhood 169
    as daughter 261, 375
    death of xi, 174–5, 245, 256–7
    divorce 169

as mother 169–70
as Nobel Prize winner 247–8, 257, 299
as Princeton chaired professor 247, 252–3
prizes, awards, and honors 174, 247–9
as public intellectual 15, 17, 75–89, 252
as Random House editor 217, 219, 282, 344
as reader 227–43, 299
EDITED BOOKS
Birth of a Nation'hood: Gaze, Script and Spectacle in the O. J. Simpson Case 16 n.2
Black Book, The 105, 214, 217, 239
Burn This Book 15, 303
Race-ing Justice, En-gendering Power: Essays on Anita Hill, Clarence Thomas and the Construction of Social Reality 16 n.2
NON-FICTION BOOKS
The Origin of Others 336
Playing in the Dark: Whiteness and the Literary Imagination 85, 236–7, 296, 299–301, 331, 352
The Source of Self-Regard listed by individual titles of essays under "Shorter Writings" (British edition, *Mouth Full of Blood,* 75–89)
NOVELS
Beloved xiii, 32, 34, 47–58, 80–1, 91–9, 104–5, 110, 125–7, 142, 144, 146, 155, 159, 173–4, 176–7, 183–96, 199, 205, 213–26, 232–5, 237–8, 245–6, 249, 251–2, 254, 257, 334–5, 343, 364, 372
The Bluest Eye xv, 15–29, 31–45, 47–58, 105–6, 127, 133, 144, 163, 168, 173, 178, 213, 228–9, 249, 251–2, 255, 331–2, 334, 343–75
God Help the Child 32, 87 n.6, 155–66
Home 32–3, 141–54, 173, 177, 213, 261–75, 277–93, 307–17, 363–79
Jazz 42, 115, 127, 170, 173, 197–211, 219, 263
Love 82, 123–40
A Mercy 82, 170, 173, 176–7, 213, 339
Paradise 15, 75–89, 101–21, 127, 170–1, 173, 175, 177, 255, 298, 319–29, 375
Song of Solomon 32–3, 42, 119, 127, 155, 160, 170, 173–4, 176, 213, 229, 248, 255, 257, 343, 375
Sula xi, xiii–xiv, 32, 42, 59–73, 82, 162, 170, 174–6, 249, 251, 255, 338, 340, 343–9, 370, 375
Tar Baby 75 n.1, 75–89, 155 n.1
SHORTER WRITINGS
"Afterword," *The Bluest Eye* 19–20
"Art of Fiction," 352
"Black Matter(s)" 300, 302
"Cinderella's Stepsisters," 79, 84
"The Dancing Mind" 303–4
"The Dead of September" 87
Desdemona 173–5

"Dreaming Emmett" 234–5
"Eulogy" 230, 332
"Eve Remembering" 171–2
"Faulkner's Women" 231, 299
"The Foreigner's Home" 82, 113, 298
"Foreword" to *Beloved* 219–20
"Foreword" to *Jazz* 126
"Foreword" to *Love* 124
"Foreword" to *Paradise* 105
"The Future of Time" 82, 86–7
"Gertrude Stein and the Difference She Makes" 82, 302
"God's Language" xv
"Goodbye to All That" 295
"Home" 277–8
"Invisible Ink: Reading the Writing and Writing the Reading" 234
"Literature and Public Life" 84–7
Margaret Garner xii, 217, 220–3, 252
"Memory, Creation and Fiction," 193, 298–9
"Moral Inhabitants" 303
"Mourning for Whiteness" 230–1
"Nobel Prize Banquet Speech" 248
"Nobel Prize Lecture" xv, 84, 86, 274, 296
"On *Beloved*" 218, 296
"Peril" 230, 303–5
"Race Matters" 84–5, 263
"Racism and Fascism" 83
"Recitatif" 163, 351–62
"Rememory" 159
"Rootedness: The Ancestor as Foundation" 75 n.1, 111 n.6, 118, 126–7, 155, 159, 295
"Sarah Lawrence" 335
"The Site of Memory" 110, 160, 213, 325
"The Slavebody and the Blackbody" 102–3, 340
"The Source of Self-Regard" 208, 218–19, 222, 224
"Unspeakable Things Unspoken: The Afro-American Presence in American Literature" 61, 77 n.3, 79, 91–3, 173, 237, 300–2, 343
"The War on Error" xi, 86
"Wartalk" 84, 87
"The Writer Before the Page" 76, 81
"Women, Race, and Memory" 84
Moses 321
Moses, Cat 26–7
mother-daughter relationships 23–4, 34, 78, 168–72
movies 50–2
Moyers, Bill xiii
Mowesko, Marg 169
Muller, Hermann Joseph 312
muteness 356–7

NAACP (National Association for the Advancement of Colored People) 62–3, 271–2
Nabokov, Vladimir 295
Nag Hammadi, The (Thunder, Perfect Mind) 170
nationalism/nationhood 75–89
National Museum of African American History and Culture 340
The National Memorial for Peace and Justice (Montgomery, Alabama) 183–96, 246, 340
National Underground Railroad Freedom Center 224, 340
Native American 105–6, 167, 321 n.2
nature 151, 170–2, 175, 262
Naylor, Gloria xv, 144, 217
Nebuchadnezzar 345
Neiman, Susan 186 n.7, 188 n.11
neo-segregation 281
neo-slave narrative 97
Neville, Helen A. 311
Newman, Sandra 257
Newsweek 247
Newton, Zachary 22–3
Ngom, Ousmane 55
Nguyen, Viet Thanh 307, 313
"nigger joke" 344, 348
Noah, Trevor 152 n.11
Noble, Thomas Satterwhite 216
Nott, Josiah 116 n.10
Nyack-on-the-Hudson 167–8

Oates, Joyce Carol 296
Obama, President Barack 142, 343, 343 n.2
Obama, Michelle 47
obituaries 256
O'Brien, Tim 60
O'Connor, Flannery 296, 300
O'Donnell, Patrick 229
The Odyssey 144
Ogbanje 290
Ogunyemi, Chikwenye Okonjo 27 n.9
Okri, Ben 86, 86 n.5
Okun, Tema 333, 338–9
Omale, Don Juan O. 208
The Oprah Winfrey Show 255
Orishas 171
Osaka, Naomi 57–8
Ossie and Harriet 262
Othello 117 n.11, 174, 228
"Outlaw women" 138, 345–6

"Paco's Story" 313
Pagels, Elaine 170, 172, 176

Paliewicz, Nicholas 189 n.14
Pamuk, Orhan 303
Paquet, Sandra Pouchet 155 n.1
Paris 76–89
passing 155–66, 283–4
Patterson, Orlando 101–2
pedophilia 38–9, 133, 139 n.15
Penner, Erin 142
perfectionism 331–41
Persephone 168, 171, 173
Petry, Ann 33 n.2
Phelan, James 22–3
Phelts, Marsha Dean 129
Phillips, Delores 33 n.2
Phillips, Kimberly L. 309–10
Piedade 171
Pierce-Baker, Charlotte 162–3
Plath, Sylvia 246
Polanyi, Michael 203
policing practices 197–211
political writing 59–63, 83, 185, 261–75, 295–8
postcolonialism 75–89, 113, 168
post-racial 343–9
post traumatic stress disorder (PTSD). *See* trauma
Pound, Ezra 296
poverty 18, 49–50, 53, 65, 67, 102, 200, 209
Powers, Kevin 312
Prince, Mary 331
Prison industrial complex 83–4, 102
prohibition 200
Proust, Marcel 295
public uses of 245 n.2, 245–60
Puckett, Newbell Niles 43 n.19
Pynchon, Thomas 328

Quarles, Benjamin 143
Quashie, Kevin Everod 266
queer sexualities 278, 282–7, 291
quest 263
quilting 150, 161–3, 252, 273

race riots 65–8, 199–200
racism 17–18, 47–9, 59–73, 83–6, 103–8, 141–69, 197–203, 261–75, 331–41, 344, 351–62
Ramirez, Manuela Lopez 61
Randle, Gloria T. 283
Randolph, Robert, Jr. ("Story Morrison, PHD") 255–6
Rankine, Claudia 352–3, 353 n.1, 359
rape 19–21, 24, 28, 52–3, 157, 163, 170, 221
Read, Andrew 112
red-lining 271
Reinhardt, Mark 216

rememory 159, 163, 190
Reyes, Angelita 220
Rhee, Jeong-eun 159
Rice, Tamir 104
Robertson, Carole 104 n.1
Robinson, Randall 192 n.18
Roof, Dylann 104 n.1
Roosevelt, President Franklin Delano 63
Rose, Charlie 150, 331–3
Rosenberg, Jonathan 62
Roth, Philip 158 n.4, 296
Roye, Susmita 36 n.7, 44 n.12, 53
Ruas, Charles 236
Rubenstein, Roberta 201 n.8
Rushdie, Salman 86, 115, 302
Rushdy, Ashraf 159
Ryan, Judylyn 75 n.1, 295–6

Sacks, Marcy 199–200
Sanchez, Sonia 247
Santos, Sherrod 247
Savage, Kirk 184 n.3, 186 n.8
Savage, William 172
Schappell, Elissa 300
Scheiber, Andrew 206 n.8
Schell, David 326
Schreiber, Evelyn Jaffe 185 n.5, 263
Schult, Tanja 184 n.2, 186 n.7, 189
Schur, Richard 16 n.2
Scott, Patricia Bell 17
Scott, Sir Walter 227–9
Scruggs, Charles 199, 205
segregation 59–66, 72, 124, 262, 267, 271, 279, 285
Seiler, Cotton 267
Selective Service Act of 1940 62–3
Senna, Danzy 158 n.4
Serpell, Namwali 246
Servicemen's Readjustment Bill 270
Settlement Fee 189
sewing 205–6
Sexton, Jared 101–3
Shadrach 345
Shange, Ntozake xii
sharecropping 364
Sharpe, Christina 310–12
Shakespeare, William 117 n.11, 174, 234, 253, 297, 300
Shaw-Thornburg, Angela 80 n.4
Shawl, Nisi 23 n.1
Shelley v. Kraemer 241
Shelley, Mary 301

Sherman, Nancy 309
Sherry, Andrew J. 235 n.8
Shine, Ted 31
Showalter, Elaine 132 n.10
Shuman, Amy 351
Silko, Leslie Marmon 280 n.5, 311–12
Sims, Dr. James Marion 269
Sixteenth Street Baptist Church 64, 104 n.1
Skloot, Rebecca 269
slavebodies 93, 102–3
slave mother 216
slave narrative 96–7, 110
slavery 17 n.3, 34, 54–7, 79–80, 84, 92–3, 101–21, 126, 143, 155–6, 159, 183–96, 213, 216, 269, 311–12, 364, 371
Smith, Barbara 17, 61
Smith, James K. A. 178
Smith, Mamie 206 n.8
Smith, Mark 335
Smith, Zadie 336–8
Snitow, Ann 142
Soja, Edward 279
Sokol, John 248
Solomon, Rivers 277 n.1
"The Song of Songs" 176–7
Sorin, Gretchen 267
sororicide 84
Spargo, R. Clifton 185 n.5
Spillers, Hortense xii, 101, 115
spirituality 55–7, 144, 169, 176
St. Anthony 169
St. John of the Cross 176–8
St. Teresa of Avila 177
Stave, Shirley 157
Stein, Gertrude 82, 296, 302
Stepto, Robert 36
Stevens, Wallace 295
Stevenson, Bryan 183–4, 187, 190–1, 246
Steverson, Delia 35 n.4, 35 n.5
Stinney, George 104
Stockton, Kathryn Bond 278
Stone, Lucy 215
Stovall, Tyler 80
Stowe, Harriet Beecher 249
Student Nonviolent Coordinating Committee (SNCC) 64–5
Students for Democratic Society (SDS) 65
Styron, William 296
survivor guilt 279, 312–13
Sweeney, Megan 201, 208
Swift, Taylor 354 n.2

Tabone, Mark 107 n.3
Tally, Justine 128 n.7
Taney, Roger B. 103–4
Tar baby myth 75–89
Tate, Claudia 145
Taylor, Brandon 277 n.1
Taylor, Breonna 104, 352
Taylor, Charles 178
Taylor, Nikki M. 215
Taylor, Thomas 172
Temple, Shirley 27, 44, 51–2, 178, 332
Testimonial 266–7
Thompson Carlyle V. 61
Thompson, CaShawn 47–9, 58
Thoreau, Henry David 168
Till, Emmett 144 n.4, 234–6, 261
Tillich, Paul 171
Time 247
Todorov, Tzvetan 320, 327
Toni Morrison Day (Ohio), February 18 247
Toni Morrison Hall 252
Toni Morrison: The Pieces I Am (film) 234 n.7, 245, 251, 331, 340
Toni Morrison Reading Room (Loraine, Ohio Library) 247
Toni Morrison Society 167, 245, 252–4
Toni Morison: Uncensored 255, 258
Toomer, Jean 62
transgender 284
transnationality 80, 82, 85–6
Traore, Rokia 174
trauma 49–51, 54–6, 60, 61–9, 79, 133, 142, 149, 155, 159, 162–3, 185, 190, 215, 261–75, 279, 307–17, 351, 363–79
Traylor, Eleanor xii
Truman, President Harry (Executive Order 9981) 63, 310
Truth, Sojourner 17 n.3, 189
Tubman, Harriet 17 n.3
"Tuskegee Study of Untreated Syphilis in the Negro Male" 312
Tutu, Desmond 207 n.9, 208 n.10
Twitter 47, 254

Underground Railroad 141, 168, 214, 265, 267
Updike, John 296, 303

Van Tongeren, Daryl R. 338
Vega-Gonzalez, Susana 124 n.2, 130, 161–3
Vendrame, Alessandra 233 n.6
Venus Hottentot 371
Vietnam 59–63, 73, 264
Vietnam Veterans Memorial 184
Vine, Steve 185 n.5
violence 59–73, 115, 186, 203, 266, 363–79
Visser, Irene 371 n.8, 376 n.12
Von Holderstein Holtermann, Jakob 208
Voting Rights Act of 1966 60, 64–5, 70, 72
Votrube, James 224

Wagner-Martin, Linda 23, 263
Walker, Alice xii, 33 n.2, 125, 156, 161, 250, 297, 346–7, 364
Walker, Margaret 248
Wall, Cheryl 251, 283
Wallace, Maurice O. 147 n.7
Wallace, Michelle xii
Walpole, Horace 124, 128 n.6, 131, 134, 320, 327
Walters, Delores 215, 224
war 32–4, 59–73, 107, 141–54, 307–17, 345–7 (*see* Korean War, Vietnam)
Ward, Jessmyn 369 n.6
Warhol, Robyn 351
Washington, Bryan 277–92
Washington, Harriet A. 269
Washington, Mary Helen xii
Waters, Amanda 339
Watkins, Mel xiii
Watson, Nicole J. 249
Weik von Mossner, Alexa 280
Weinstein, Philip 229 n.4, 233
Weisenberger, Steven 215
Wells-Barnett, Ida B. 246, 368–9
Welty, Eudora 249, 300
Wendt, Jana 255
Werner, Craig H. 76 n.2
Werrlein, Delra T. 22
Wesley, Cynthia 104 n.1
Wester, Maisha L. 126–7
Wheatley, Phillis 331
White, E. Francis 278–9
The White Gaze xv, 35 n.5, 150, 266, 331, 334, 336
White supremacy 331–41 (and *see* Racism)
Whitehead, Colson 158 n.4
Whitman, Walt 168
Wilde, Oscar 296
Wilderson, Frank 101–3, 115, 119
Williams, Carolyn Randell 157
Williams, Dana 113, 114 n.8
Williams, Patricia J. 16 n.2
Wilson, Harriet 331
Wilson, Olly 206
Wilson, President Woodrow 62, 66, 253
Winfrey, Oprah 98, 255–6

Winthrop, John 321
Witchcraft 319–21
witnessing 169
Wofford, Chloe Ardelia, 245 (*see* Morrison, Toni)
Wofford, George (father) 217
Wofford, Rama Willis (mother) 217
womanism 346–8
Woo, Jewon 251
Woodard, Helena 254
Woodman, Marion 170–1, 173, 178
Woodson, Jacqueline 277 n.1
Woolf, Virginia 233, 246, 295
work 84, 152, 174, 178, 198, 206, 274, 352
Wright, Richard xi, 31 n.2, 33 n.2, 35 n.5, 36 n.6, 111 n.7, 141–56, 297, 347, 365–8, 370
Wyatt, Jean xiv

Yam, Kimberly 256
Yanuck, Julius 216
Yeats, W. B. 295
Yemanja 171
Yohe, Kristina 252
Yoruba 171
Young, James 184, 188, 192
Young, John 255–6
Youngkin, Glenn xv, 224, 245 n.2

Zauditu-Selassie, Kokahvah 169 n.1
Zehr, Howard 201
Zheng, John 151
Zoot-suiter 267, 268 n.5, 312

www.ingramcontent.com/pod-product-compliance
Lightning Source LLC
Chambersburg PA
CBHW080933300426
44115CB00017B/2803